FAMILIES WITH FUTURES

Families With Futures
A Survey of Family Studies
for the 21st Century

Meg Wilkes Karraker & Janet R. Grochowski
University of St. Thomas

LEA
2006

LAWRENCE ERLBAUM ASSOCIATES, PUBLISHERS
Mahwah, New Jersey   London

Acquisitions Editor:	Cathleen Petree
Editorial Assistant:	Victoria Forsythe
Cover Design:	Kathryn Houghtaling Lacey
Full-Service Compositor:	TechBooks
Text and Cover Printer:	Hamilton Printing Company

This book was typeset in 10.5/12 pt. Times, Italic, Bold, and Bold Italic.
The heads were typeset in Engravers Gothic, Zapf Humanst and Revival.

Lawrence Erlbaum Associates, Inc., Publishers
10 Industrial Avenue
Mahwah, New Jersey 07430
www.erlbaum.com

Library of Congress Cataloging-in-Publication Data

Families with futures : a survey of family studies for the 21st century /
edited by Meg Wilkes Karraker & Janet R. Grochowski.
    p. cm.
  Includes bibliographical references and index.
  ISBN 0-8058-5469-X (case : alk. paper)
  1. Family—Study and teaching. I. Karraker, Meg Wilkes. II. Grochowski, Janet R.
  HQ10.F3385 2006
  306.85—dc22

                                        2005025918

Printed in the United States of America
10 9 8 7 6 5 4 3 2 1

Contents in Brief

Contents

Epilogue

Appendices

ACKNOWLEDGMENTS AND DEDICATIONS

In the early stages of this project, we had the great pleasure exchanging ideas with four fine undergraduate family studies scholars: Jillian Berg, Annie Metcalf, Samantha Mills, and Georgia Rice. Their participation was supported by *Partnership-in-Learning* grants from Faculty Development at the University of St. Thomas.

Our great thanks also go to a battalion of family studies scholars who substantially enriched this work by contributing original writings based on their personal, professional and research areas of expertise. Their names and biographies accompany their contributions throughout this book.

During the writing process, we had the great advantage of an assembly of colleagues who read and re-read pages, sections, and chapters, offering useful commentary. Thanks to Jillian Berg, Kathy Brothen, Valerie Clark, J. Kenneth Davidson Jr., Katie Ettel, Sue Hammons, Katherine Justak, Amanda Kaiser, Karen Kaphingst, Hamilton McCubbin, Phyllis Goudy Myers, Erin Phillips, and Sue Ann Schramm. Ellen Uhrich provided valuable assistance in managing the many versions of the manuscript.

Families with Futures also benefited from timely, critical suggestions from two family studies scholars of high repute, Katherine Allen and Roma Stovall Hanks. We thank them both for their generous insights and kind suggestions to improve the final manuscript.

Finally, Herbert W Wilkes Jr. patiently read every page, multiple times. Still, any errors that remain are purely our responsibility.

Our collaboration with Lawrence Erlbaum Associates, Inc. has been truly auspicious. Both Bill Webber and later Cathleen Petree remained enthusiastic to the end, while the Lawrence Erlbaum staff guided us through final production with Joanne Bowser and the fine staff at TechBooks. We appreciate both the support they accorded our project and the respect they extended to us as authors and scholars. Every author should be so fortunate.

Please note the order of authorship in this work is purely arbitrary.

ABOUT THE AUTHORS

Janet R. Grochowski, Ph.D. After completing my Bachelor of Science at the University of Wisconsin-Madison, I earned two Doctor of Philosophy degrees at the University of Minnesota. The first was a dual major in Family Social Science and Health Studies Education and the second was in Social and Philosophical Foundations of Learning with an emphasis on resilience. My research reflects an interdisciplinary preparation and boundless curiosity in the areas of family studies and health studies with special interest in youth and family resiliency. This professional interest extends into the undergraduate courses I teach including family studies, human sexuality, nutrition, aging, substance use and abuse, stress management, and professional preparation courses. Currently I hold the position of Professor and Director of Family Studies and of Health Studies plus serve as Chair of Health and Human Performance Department at the University of St. Thomas.

This writing adventure not only deepened my appreciation for the efforts of family studies scholars and professionals but also the support from my own family. Although my parents, Gladys and Edward Kortens, died long before I reached adulthood, their love and encouragement served as beacons in my professional journey. Growing up in a stepfamily, where I was the second youngest of 10 children, broadened my understanding of how family members need interdependence in order to negotiate the changes and challenges of family life.

My partner of over 30 years, Richard Grochowski, is my best friend, love, husband, and father of our children. His wise counsel, patience, and sense of humor are precious to me. Our children, Eric Alan Grochowski and Emily Rose Grochowski, have taught me the beauty and reward of loving and caring for others. I dedicate my part of this book to you, Emily and Eric, as you begin your professional adventures and continue your world travels.

Finally, I am fortunate to have an intelligent and insightful co-author who also is my dear and steadfast friend. Meg, you have made this writing experience enriching and exciting. I joyfully anticipate our next research and writing adventures. Thank you.

Meg Wilkes Karraker, Ph.D. I earned my Bachelor of Arts at Clemson University, my Master of Science at North Carolina State University, and my Doctor of Philosophy at the University of Minnesota, all in sociology with supporting course work in anthropology, psychology, and women's studies. In complement to my research and teaching interests in family, I am interested in the impacts of social structure on quality of life. I teach undergraduate courses in sociological theory, gender, adolescence, and, of course, families. My present position is that of Professor and Chair of Sociology and Criminal Justice at the University of St. Thomas.

A book like this offers me an opportunity to extend appreciation to four teacher/scholars who nurtured and supported my early development. I gratefully acknowledge the role of the following sociology professors, all now deceased, who encouraged my interests on the intersections of social forces and social life: William Capel of Clemson University, Glen McCann of North Carolina State University, Reuben Hill of the University of Minnesota, and Roberta Simmons, also of the University of Minnesota.

As with all my professional work, I owe the greatest debt to my own family. I grew up in a military family, moving every three years to a different community in the United States and Germany. At each new location, my mother settled my sister Jean and me into a new school and made the necessary connections for Girls Scouts, music lessons, and our beagle, while my father went about the business of a career in the United States Army. Building this family together, and observing their relationship with each other and with my sister and me and now our own families, my parents Mary and Herbert Wilkes have inspired me to examine the values and norms that contribute to family resilience over their own half-century of marriage.

Mark Karraker, my husband of a quarter century, models the best a person can be in the roles of friend, spouse, and parent (only grumbling a little when I ask him to wait for "just another page"). Amelia Wilkes Karraker and Miriam Wilkes Karraker, lovely daughters and citizens of the world, are constant reminders that building supportive, respectful, dependable family relationships are worth every effort.

Finally, to have found such an intelligent and creative colleague and affectionate and constant friend as I have found in you, dear Janet, has made the journey of writing this book a consummate pleasure for me. I eagerly anticipate the next tapestry we will weave together!

PROLOGUE

FROM "WHAT WAS" THROUGH "WHAT IS" TO "WHAT COULD BE"

Perhaps you share our concern that the mass media often portray family members as ineffectual and even ridiculous, as badly intentioned and even evil. Perhaps, like us, you are concerned that public discourse (often with thinly veiled political intent) tends to root a myriad of social problems in the presumed failure of the family as a social institution. You may be aware that, probably because "good news" is "no news," the large body of scientific research on families most often focuses on what *was* and *is wrong* in families. Like us, you may be moved to ask:

> *Where is the appreciation of the possibilities for what every family could be?*

The book you have before you grew in part out of our frustration with popular, political, and academic paradigms of families. In *Families With Futures* we:

Focus on the inter-disciplinary field of family studies

Apply family studies to everyday family life

Study changes in concepts and processes of families

Tempt learners to more critically examine family relationships

In doing so, we draw on three touchstones that guide our personal and professional perspectives on families:

- Families are dynamic, evolving organisms.
- Families are in constant interplay with environments.
- Families and their members are creative and resilient.

This Prologue sets forth our distinctive approach to the scientific discipline of family studies. The next 13 chapters are framed around five units that correspond to the core topics in family studies. The 14th, concluding chapter of the book draws the text to a conclusion around family studies as a strategic discipline. The Ethical Principles and Guidelines of the *National Council on Family Relations* and a comprehensive *Family Studies Resources* complete the book.

Each chapter opens with a concise Chapter Preview that surveys the chapter content. Each chapter finishes with a glossary and a set of provocative questions to enable the reader to both reflect and move forward in thinking about families. Finally, in addition to References for Cited Works, each chapter offers electronic, organizational, and print resources to carry the learner deeper into the material.

Families With Futures offers a genuinely fresh approach for understanding families. Based on earlier work,[1] we present undergraduate learners with a unique opportunity to explore not only "what was" and "what is" in family studies but also "what could be" for families today. We charge you, dear reader, to set out on a mission to engage clergy, educators, employers, politicians, and others in meaningful understanding and appreciation of the institution of family in all its rich, messy complexity. Not the least of all, we hope you will engage your own families in this journey from "what was" through "what is" to "what could be."

---

[1]Grochowski, Janet R. 2000. "Families as 'Strategic Living Communities.'" Paper presented at the annual meetings of the American Academy of Health Behavior, September, Santa Fe, NM.

PART

I

THE ART AND SCIENCE OF FAMILY STUDIES

CHAPTER

1

THE CHANGING WORLD OF "FAMILIES"

CHAPTER PREVIEW

What is a *family*? Questions of the form and function of family continue to challenge family study scholars in the 21st century. We extend the definition of family well beyond individuals related by blood or marriage and sharing the same *household* to include *fictive kin* and others who play a significant role in the life of family members. Gerson (1991: 57) points to a "growing social and ideological cleavage between traditional family forms and the emerging alternatives."

The *demography* of families in the United States is shifting. Likewise, conceptualizations of class, ethnicity, and race, as well as the meaning of *gender*, *sex*, and *sexual* (including *transgender*) *orientation* are being reconstructed and scholars are increasingly aware of how intersections among these boundaries form a *matrix of domination*. Examination of social and cultural changes in the 21st century propels us toward greater inclusiveness in terms of accepting the many portraits of "families" while confronting illusions about "the way we never were."

The experience of "family" profoundly impacts us on individual, community, and global levels. Although the picture each of us would draw of our family differs, we would all likely agree our families have had powerful emotional and social influences on our lives. Who we choose to exclude is as important as who we choose to include in our definitions of "family." The concept *strategic living communities* (© Grochowski 2000) reflects the complex, dynamic, evolving, fluid nature of these critical social systems. This approach acknowledges, however, a *competent*, resilient family is not an invincible family. Every family has areas of limitation and periods of vulnerability.

The shift from *deficit-centered* to *strength-centered* focus in the latter part of the 20th century is reflected in the emphasis on family *resiliency* and families as complex adaptive systems with the potential not only to survive but also even to thrive on challenge and change. The scholarly study of families continues to emerge from singular disciplines toward an exciting interdiscipline. This is the art and science of *family studies*.

SHIFTING CONCEPTS OF "FAMILY"

Family: As Much an Idea as a Thing

What is this entity that possesses such significance for the happiness of individuals, the well-being of communities and nations, and the very survival of humanity? Each reader of these words has her or his own perception of what a *family* is or should be. Most of us live within a family—or more correctly a series of families—over our lifetimes. We derive our understanding of family through experience, as well as through contact with other kin, friends, and coworkers.

Social institutions shape our images of family. Television offers impressions of functional (and some argue more often than not dysfunctional) families. Some schools persist in holding events like "donuts for Dads" or "muffins for Moms" when some or even many students may not live with a father or may in fact live with two mothers. Medical facilities insist unless we can document a narrow legal definition of "next-of-kin" we have no say in the care of loved ones. These all construct images of what constitutes a "normal" family.

The United States Bureau of the Census defines a *family* as two or more people who are related by blood, marriage, or adoption and who live together. The Bureau of the Census defines *household* as one or more people who share a residential unit, excluding barracks, dormitories, prisons, or other group quarters.

The *Vanier Institute of the Family* (2004) defines family in a way consistent with traditional anthropological and sociological definitions of family. Family is

... any combination of two or more persons who are bound together over time by ties of mutual consent, birth and/or adoption or placement and who, together, assume responsibilities for variant combinations of some of the following:

- Physical maintenance and care of member
- Addition of new members through procreation or adoption
- Socialization of children
- Social control of members
- Production, consumption, distribution of goods and services, and
- Affective nurturance—love.

Although the majority of American households today are families, the percentage of households that are families has been declining. In 1960, 85% of households were families, but by 2000 only 69% of households were families (United States Bureau of the Census 2000).

Declining fertility, later marriage, and frequent divorce mean fewer Americans are living in units composed of a husband, a wife, and their dependent children. In fact, the percentage of such two-parent households decreased from 44% in 1960 to 24% in 2000. The most dramatic changes in household composition occurred in the 1970s. However, the rate of these changes in family composition has slowed considerably, with no appreciable change since the mid-1990s.

We might prefer to describe "family" in deeply personal ways, imbued with the ebb and flow of experiences throughout a lifetime. Clearly, however, "family" is a social construct. Defining "family" remains challenging. Early efforts include Murdock's view of family as "a social group characterized by common residence, economic cooperation, and reproduction" (Murdock 1949 quoted in Morgan 1975: 20). However, such definitions reveal assumptions that fail to represent the diverse nature of family structure and arrangement.

For example, family members may not share the same residence. Such is the case when a couple with children separate or divorce, leaving the children residing with a custodial parent. Some couples choose or find themselves in a "commuter marriage," pursuing employment in one city for the longest portion of a week or month, while commuting to spend time with spouses in another city on weekends or during holidays. Families that launch daughters and sons to higher education or employment may cease to share a domicile. Yet these living arrangements do not preclude strong emotional, legal, and other social ties.

Likewise, the frequency child support is contested and uncollected, the rise in pre- and postnuptial agreements, and the extent to which some husbands and wives maintain individual autonomy over day-to-day finances challenge the assumption of economic cooperation. Finally, the many families formed through adoption or foster parenting, the quality of special relationships with *fictive kin*—Stack's (1974) concept referring to individuals to whom we are not related by blood or marriage, as well as the implications of the new birth technologies—negate Murdock's assumption about the reproductive foundation of "family."

These assumptions about families as residential, economic, and reproductive units promote bias and misunderstanding of the depth and potential of "family." In later chapters we discuss the place of fictive kin, as well as families formed by gay men and lesbians, as authentic families. We explore families in a way that encourages society to stretch the canvas to allow more room for the vast colorful array of family pictures and arrangements.

Is it possible to agree on a definition of "family"? Perhaps "family" is the kind of thing we "know it when we see it." Some find it easier to say what a family is "not," as we see in Clark's discussion of Thomas Jefferson's family (Box 1.1). We challenge you to embrace a more inclusive approach to defining families based on three premises.

- Families are dynamic, evolving organisms.
- Families are in constant interplay with internal and external environments.
- Families and their members are creative and resilient.

BOX 1.1 "Thomas Jefferson's Family"
Christy M. Clark

In October 1998 The Jefferson Foundation (2000) released a report in which DNA evidence conclusively linked the families of the third president of the United States, Thomas Jefferson, and his slave, Sally Hemings. Jefferson, 30 years older than Hemings, acquired ownership of Sally when he married. Jefferson's wife Martha, who died in 1782, was rumored to be Sally's half-sister (Graham 1961). Some had long speculated that the Jefferson and Hemings families were related. Newspapers of the time like the *Pike County Republican* published an autobiographical narrative of a former slave Madison Hemings, son of Sally Hemings. Madison Hemings' story supported the allegation first circulated among Jefferson's political enemies and later by many abolitionists that Jefferson had kept a mulatto mistress and fathered her children (Malone and Hochman 1975; Neiman 2000). This official report and analysis of Jefferson's visits to Monticello when Hemings was in residence confirmed that the revered founding father Thomas Jefferson had in fact fathered five and perhaps all six of Sally Hemings's children (Ellis 2000).

For all the questions the DNA analysis answered, it leaves many more unanswered. Most importantly, are the Hemings and Jeffersons part of the same family? The answer bears on such practical matters as entitlement to burial in the Jefferson family plot and decision making concerning Monticello and the Jefferson Foundation as well as the social status attached to the family name. The answer depends on the definition of family.

Genetically, the Hemings and Jeffersons are linked by common blood. Legally things are more complicated. Today a DNA test would conclusively reveal biological paternity and make explicit certain economic and social obligations. However, at that time, even if legally acknowledged by the father, such children had no claim to the family name, let alone property.

More intimate connections of family are even more difficult to assess. Did the Hemings and Jeffersons consider themselves "family" at an emotional level? Oral history in the Hemings family indicates there was great affection and loyalty between Sally and Thomas (Ellis 2000). Further, Jefferson's actions indicated preferential treatment for Hemings and her children, who were top household servants, receiving the best food and clothing and the lightest work duties. Most significantly, in his will Jefferson freed all of Sally's sons, along with her brother. His will did not free Sally or her daughter Harriet, but Graham (1961) speculated that this was done in their best interest, due to Sally's age and Harriet's position within the household.

> Jefferson had every reason to suppose that his mistress and his daughter would be better assured of personal happiness and material welfare as slaves, rather than as indigent freedwomen. (Graham 1961: 98)

Could Thomas Jefferson have loved a woman who he considered inferior by essence of her race (Graham 1961)? Could Sally Hemings have freely loved a man who had absolute control of her life? What indeed makes a family? What are the meaning and significance of biological roots, financial support, public acknowledgment, and conjugal love?

REFERENCES

Ellis, Joseph J. 2000. "Jefferson: Post-DNA." *William and Mary Quarterly*, Third Series, 57, 1 (January): 125–38.

Graham, Pearl. 1961. "Thomas Jefferson and Sally Hemings." *Journal of Negro History* 46, 2 (April): 89–103.

Neiman, Fraser D. 2000. "Coincidence or Casual Connection? The Relationship Between Thomas Jefferson's Visits to Monticello and Sally Hemings Conceptions." *William and Mary Quarterly*, Third Series, 57, 1 (January): 198–210.

The Jefferson Foundation. 2000. "Monticello Jefferson-Hemings Report." (http:www.Monticello.org/plantation/dnareport1.html) Retrieved 5/30/02.

Malone, Dumas, and Steven H. Hochman 1975. "Note on Evidence: The Personal History of Madison Hemings" *The Journal of Southern History* 31, 4 (November): 524–28.

Christy M. Clark is a graduate student in American history at the University of Iowa. She studies African-American women and work in the United States during the 19th and 20th centuries and Latin America social and political history.

Demography, Change, and Diversity

Many of the brush strokes in the changing portrait of American families can be traced to large-scale changes in the population characteristics, the *demography*, of American society.

For example, Americans are living longer. Life expectancy at birth climbed from 70.8 years in 1970 to 77.0 years in 1999 and is projected to reach 78.5 by 2010. Couples who marry in their late 20s may face another 5 decades "'til death us do part." Also, on the average, the life expectancy for females is more than 5 years longer than the life expectancy for males (United States Bureau of the Census 2001). What are the financial hazards for a woman who reaches advanced age without a husband in a society in which women continue to earn less than do men?

A journalist, writing on the state of the American family during the last decade of the 20th century argued:

> The American family does not exist. Rather, we are creating many American families, of diverse styles and shapes . . . We have fathers working while mothers keep house; fathers and

mothers both working away from home; single parents; second marriages bringing together
people from unrelated backgrounds; childless couples; unmarried couples; with and without
children; gay and lesbian parents. We are living through a period of historic change in
American family life. (Footlick 1990: 14)

In 2000 the American Psychological Association devoted an entire issue to examination
of cultural variations—both similarities and differences—in families. In his published
remarks to that group, Parke (2000) focused on the strengths of families from different
cultural, ethnic, and racial groups. In doing so, Parke broke from earlier weakness or deficit
models of the family and focused attention on the strengths of diverse families. He noted the
existence of differences not only between groups but also within groups as families adapt to
the demands of ecological niches. In addition to testing the generalizability of assumptions
about family processes, studies of the diversity of families serve as a basis for providing
culturally sensitive programs and services and formulating socially responsible policies.

Class, Ethnicity, and Race

Ethnocentric images of the *normal American family* (Pyke 2000) are pervasive in American
culture. Such images prescribe the structure of families and embody values and norms
that direct family relationships. At the same time, such images exclude many families
(including non-White, childless, single, and same sex) as *other* and deviant.

Dalmadge, a White woman married to a Black man with whom she has biracial children,
has written poignantly of the experiences of a biracial family in a racial society. Based
on her own experiences and those of others living in Black–White unions, she describes
a racialized society in which educational, religious, and residential systems remain segregated and in which institutions have low tolerance for racial ambiguity, yet also provide no
language to describe biracial identity. Dalmadge argues the meaning of being "biracial"
is evolving, but the United States has yet to recognize itself as a society where multiracial
individuals and families are a part of the norm (Dalmadge 2000).

Pyke (2000) found images of the *normal American family* were powerful in shaping
how adult children of Korean and Vietnamese immigrants living in the United States
viewed relations with parents. The adult children in Pyke's study viewed their parents as
"unloving, deficient, and not normal" (251). At the same time, however, the same adult
children were critical of the high individualism in American families, especially with
regard to care of elderly parents.

As the 2000 census reveals, changes in ethnic and racial composition in society are
escalating. Increasingly scholars (Baca Zinn 2001; Gerson 1991) argue in favor of aban-
doning the bias of one family type as being "normal" and all others as "variations" or
"deviants." Such bias prevents us from gaining rich understandings and lessons of what it
means to be a member of a family and how to best support families in our communities.

Scholars are no longer insensitive to the relative neglect of families of color in family
research. However, as Murry, Smith, and Hill (2001: 911) summarized in the lead article
in a special section on race, ethnicity, culture, and family processes in the *Journal of
Marriage and the Family:*

> . . . race and ethnicity are often confounded with socioeconomic indicators and community
> of residence. This makes it difficult to identify the true effects of ethnicity and culture. In
> addition, race and ethnicity may interact with chronic poverty in such a way as to further
> interfere with and reduce life opportunities.

Murry, Smith, and Hill conclude by challenging family studies scholars to adapt "culturally grounded perspectives," which take into account the complicated associations among race and ethnicity, socioeconomic status, culture, and other factors.

Gender

Serious scholarly debate regarding the use (or misuse) of the terms *gender* and *sex* in sociology, psychology, health studies, and other disciplines dates at least to the last quarter of the 20th century (see Gould and Kern-Daniels 1977). These terms have been used inconsistently in marriage and family textbooks, as well as in journals such as the *American Journal of Sociology, American Sociological Review, Journal of Social and Personal Relationships, Sociological Perspectives*, and even the *Journal of Marriage and the Family* and *Sex Roles* (Laner 2000).

Laner (2000) pleads with social scientists to use these terms correctly and consistently. Laner (471) defines *sex* as the biological term, often referring to female or male. She defines *gender* as the social term, referring to characteristics assigned by social groups to one sex or the other, with usual forms feminine and masculine. However, such differentiation still does not address the situation of individuals who may be born with ambiguous genitalia ("hermaphroditic" [sic]) or genotype (e.g., XXY) or individuals who are *transgender*. The last are individuals who may elect to undergo hormonal or surgical intervention in order to achieve greater consonance between physiology and internal perceptions of gender.

Regardless of the terminology, attitudes toward gender and gender roles do frame family life in powerful ways. In her analysis of data from the *National Survey of Families and Households*, Kaufman (2000) found egalitarian attitudes are associated with decreased fertility intentions among women, but increased fertility intentions and marital stability among men. Single men with egalitarian attitudes were more likely to cohabit. However, they were also more likely to intend to have a child and less likely to divorce than men with traditional attitudes. Women with egalitarian attitudes were both less likely to intend to have a child and to actually have a child than women holding traditional attitudes.

Other research likewise demonstrates the significance of attitudes toward gender in determining family outcomes. For example, a study of Iranian immigrants to the United States found men were significantly more traditional than women on attitudes toward premarital sex, marriage, and the family, even after adjusting for respondent's age (Hojat et al. 2000). This discrepancy may explain the high rate of marriage dissolution among Iranian immigrants and may contribute to understanding interpersonal tension among immigrants. Such findings have implications for family and marital therapy, as well as assimilation of new members of society.

Sexual Orientations

Perhaps nothing reveals the rigidity of definitions of family more than attitudes toward unions formed by gays and lesbians. Unlike marriages, which require civil licenses, cohabiting couples—regardless of *sexual orientation*—are not systematically recorded in any official way. The best available estimates of this population are from the Current Population Reports (CPR), based on annual data collected by the Census Bureau from a representative sample of the population.

According to the 2000 Census, same-sex couples headed 594,391 homes in the United States (Armas 2001: 1). Contrary to stereotypes, gay and lesbian coupled households are not limited to large urban areas. Gay or lesbian couples have formed households in nearly every county in every state and the District of Columbia. Gay (two male) couples slightly outnumber lesbian (two female) couples. A large number of the same-sex couples are raising children. In the 1998 Census, 167,000 gay or lesbian couples reported they had children 15 or younger living with them (United States Bureau of the Census 2000).

In the majority of the United States, the legal system does not recognize same-sex partners as married or same-sex parents and their children as families. The discrimination and prejudice against same-sex families is based on ignorance and fear same-sex parents are not fit or are even dangerous parents because of their sexual orientation. A concept of "family" that excludes gay men and lesbians contributes to harsh and false images, such as:

> the belief that gay men and lesbians do not have children or establish lasting relationships and the belief that they invariably alienate adoptive and blood kin once their sexual identities become known. (Weston 2001: 27)

As a relatively new area of family study, research on gay and lesbian relationships is subject to criticism that samples are limited by race, ethnicity, culture, and class, and by the paucity of observational or longitudinal studies. However, emerging research indicates the family relationships of gays and lesbians are more similar than different from the family relationships of heterosexual couples. For example, Patterson (2000: 1064) found:

- Relationships of lesbian and gay couples are just as supportive as those of heterosexual couples.
- Home environments created by lesbian and gay couples are just as conducive to positive psychosocial growth of family members as those created by heterosexual couples.

In this century, stereotypes and stigma of same-sex families may serve to advance certain ideological agenda, but will do little to enhance the well-being of spouses and partners, parents, and children. Future studies of same-sex and all families need to evolve from what is "wrong" to what are the "strengths" in families.

Finally, a growing body of scholarship illuminates the extent to which the boundaries we have examined here—class, ethnicity, race, gender, sexual orientation—constitute a complex web that shapes roles and statuses in family and other social institutions. Collins (1990) characterizes this *matrix of domination* as interlocking systems of oppression. Collins frames a new paradigm, Black feminist thought, which rejects a separate or even an additive model of oppression. Instead, she sees oppression in terms of interlocking systems of race, class, gender, and sexual identity. We cannot understand the impact of any of these issues without understanding the associations among them.

THE SIGNIFICANCE OF FAMILIES

The Importance of Families for Individuals

Individuals and their families adapt a multitude of structures to meet the emotional, financial, and other needs of family members. Wald (2001: 1) summarizes the significance of marriage and family for individuals in the following statement.

> Being able to marry can contribute significantly to the emotional and economic well being of couples. Living with married parents provides a number of benefits and protections to children. Society benefits when people choose to marry. . . . promoting the emotional and economic well being of adults; enhancing the capacity of parents to promote the well being of children; and promoting stable relationships.

Although we might take issue with Wald's (2001) emphasis on marriage, rather than a broader conceptualization of long-term commitment between intimates, data from the *General Social Surveys* reveal the quality of family and other interpersonal relationships is important for personal happiness (Aldous and Ganey 1999). (This appears to be especially true for women.) As Moffett writes, families are with us, even when the unit is fractured.

BOX 1.2 "Children of Suffering Families"
Patrick Sean Moffett, C.F.C., Ph.D.

Children travel with their families, even when they travel alone. So do adults. There are regions of the life space of the individual in which family members constitute a very real and salient force that extends beyond time, geography, and even death. Emotions, imperatives, cautions, fears, blessings, curses, approbations, and corrections echo even from a distant past taking an invasive role in present thoughts, feelings, and action tendencies. I hear my mother's voice, see my father's smile, recall my brother's challenge, and resonate with my sisters' concern. Faced with a decision, I have little doubt about what they would approve, what they would not want to accept.

Separation is part of life; it is often a gradient for growth. Life is full of those moments when frighteningly, or delightedly, we are on our own. The remarkable experience is the discovery of our unique capacity to pull from seemingly nowhere the resources to do what needs to be done.

For a growing number of the world's children, separation from their families of origin is an event they will face in early adolescence. Television images projected by satellite into the most remote and depressed areas of the globe reveal another world of possibilities. Young adventurers, some legally, most clandestinely, find their way onto foreign shores in a search for refuge from wars, political pressures, or economic oppression, or simply in the hope of finding a chance in life.

Excursions into the Balkans to re-trace the journeys of such youngsters revealed conditions that have promoted modern-day versions of indentured servitude and even slavery. Loving parents were thrilled to know that their son or daughter was still alive. When asked if they would welcome home the prodigal child, they became intensely uneasy. How does a mother acknowledge her deepest hurt, the belief that it would be best that her son, her daughter, not return? As one mother tearfully expressed: "Those people want him to be bad. They are still around. They will take him away again."

We found that the contact with the family, as brief as it had been, became a most significant factor in our relationships with the youngsters. Openings to new depths of sharing, of confidence, of identification and transference became increasingly evident in case conferences and staff supervision sessions.

Many of the youngsters had perceived themselves as responsible for the family of origin: Find a job, earn the money to send home to take care of younger sisters and brothers. Only word from home could release these boys and girls from unrealistic goals. The *do*s and *don't*s, the hopes and expectancies emerging from earlier images of significant others had become obstacles to discernment and growth.

Court mandates, the conditions of foster or adopting parents, even the expressed wishes of the individual will not cancel the resilient psychological presence of the family of origin. Projects aimed at self-awareness or the accompanying of a child or an adult call for interventions expansive enough to accommodate all who insist on being part of the journey.

Patrick Sean Moffett, CFC, Ph.D., psychologist, is President Emeritus of Boys' Towns of Italy, Inc. and the former Chief Executive Officer of the Girls' Town and the Boys' Towns of Rome. He is currently Director of Mission Education for the Congregation of Christian Brothers.

The Consequences of Families for Communities

Family

... is a cohesive system of customs and rituals that regulates the relationship between partners and relationships between the couple, the extended family, and the community. (Miller and Browning 1999: 596)

Although definitions of family structures and functions vary widely (Freymeyer and Johnson note in Box 1.3 some of the particularities of the Southern family) the significance of family runs through all societies, providing an institutional framework that ensures parenting and caring necessary for the persistence of communities and whole societies.

In essence, for communities and nations, the concept of family holds the promise of stability in a rapidly changing world. This complex structure must adapt to negotiate the challenges of change on macrosocietal levels (e.g., cultural shifts, economic changes, environmental events, political demands) as well as on microsocietal levels (e.g., life-span changes, health issues, addition, loss of members).

BOX 1.3 "Southern Families"
Robert H. Freymeyer, Ph.D. and Barbara E. Johnson, Ph.D.

One of our Northern-born friends met her Southern husband while attending Ole Miss. Her southern-born and bred in-laws always considered her as the Yankee "outcast" until she gave birth to their first child and son on Confederate Memorial Day! Then, she became part of their *Southern* family.

This story illustrates how distinctiveness characterizes the culture of the American South. The South's heritage and traditions, coupled with its political and geographical separation, have led to the development of unique social patterns and institutions, including the family. Although the South has changed in recent years, our research shows that Southerners still hold norms and values about marriage and family and form family units distinct from those found in other regions of the United States.

Southern states, notably Mississippi, Alabama, Tennessee, and Kentucky, have the highest marriage rates. Southerners value marriage and family as social institutions. For example, our studies found that Southerners, as compared to non-Southerners, express more disapproval of cohabitation before marriage and more frequently view homosexual, premarital, teenaged, and extramarital sexual relations as always wrong. Furthermore, although average household size does not differ by region, Southerners report fewer unrelated persons living in their households. Kin networks also provide social support. A majority of Southerners report spending a social evening with relatives at least several times a month.

Southern families exhibit traditional gender role expectations in continuity with their patriarchal heritage. Southern men, historically, served in the role of strong, respected family provider and disciplinarian in a culture that stressed masculine attitudes toward violence and emphasized defending the family's (especially the woman's) honor. More Southerners continue to see women's primary roles as child-bearing and rearing, not labor force participation. Southerners believe it is better for everyone if the man achieves outside the home, earns the family income, and runs the country. Also, Southerners express more concern than non-Southerners about a working woman's ability to develop a close maternal relationship with her children. A Southern woman's place continues to be the socioemotional leader in the home.

We discovered Southerners socialize their children differently from non-Southerners. Although both Southerners and non-Southerners want children to learn to think for themselves, Southerners are most likely to list obedience as the most desired characteristic for children to learn. Additionally, almost three fourths of Southerners believe a good, hard spanking is sometimes necessary for discipline as compared to approximately half of non-Southerners. This reflects an authoritarian view on child rearing, also demonstrated by a desire to protect and set rules for their children. Southerners, for example, hold more conservative views on distributing birth control information to teenagers and about permitting sex education in the schools.

In recent years, the South's economic and social structure has become more similar to that found in other regions of the United States. The South also has experienced considerable inmigration. Yet, Southerners maintain many distinctive attitudes and behaviors, and southern families continue to differ in structure and function from those found elsewhere in the United States. Since, the family is one of the most important socializing agents in our culture, the uniqueness of Southern families should persist for generations, as suggested by our friend's experience.

Robert H. Freymeyer, Ph.D., is Professor of Sociology at Presbyterian College. *Barbara E. Johnson*, Ph.D., is Professor of Sociology at the University of South Carolina Aiken. This husband–wife team has conducted several studies on the southern family and the effects of recent migration on the family.

The Gravity of Families for Humanity

In the 1970s, a soft-drink company popularized a song that began, "I'd like to teach the world to sing in perfect harmony. . . . " The jingle, widely promoted on radio and television—the latter complete with a large circle of people of apparently diverse nationalities holding hands—evoked a sense the world is one place, we are one family, and we are in this together. If only the leap from this image to reality were as simple as a song.

We need to consider family not only on a multicultural level but also on a global level. Yet, when asked to define a global community, the talk most easily turns to networking of an economic sort. Reflecting on the potential effects of terrorism and mass destruction on children and families, as Larney does on the effects of World War II on families, this may be a significant challenge for this century. An inclusive concept of family could serve us well as a species for we all must negotiate global challenges and changes.

BOX 1.4 "Family Effects of Being a Child during War"
Barbara Elden Larney, Ph.D.

The experience of being a young child during war has significant impact on families of origin and families formed when the child reaches adulthood. My study involved in-depth interviews of a snowball sample of 55 volunteers from the 1934 to 1939 German birth cohort. A comparison of biographical information about the participants with national representative data showed the participants to be very similar to the general population (Larney 1994).

Living in Germany during World War II brought a child face-to-face with direct, immediate, personal experience with bombings, destruction of homes and loss of possessions, and death of parents and other loved ones. Almost all the individuals in my study had vivid memories of air raids and bombings, some recalled the experience of becoming refugees, and others recounted searching for dead family members. Still others found themselves living in combat areas and remembered dodging shells and enemy fire.

In my study, most (80%) fathers (as well as some of the mothers) were temporarily or permanently absent because of the war. Obviously, the economic situation of the family was strongly influenced by the presence or absence of the father during and after the war, with families where the father did not return being much more likely to report financial problems. The basic hardships of war also changed the productive role of the children in the family, as they learned early to participate in the tasks of providing and contributing to the family welfare.

The presence or absence of fathers appears to have been a determining factor in the educational pattern of sons. Of the 25 male participants of this study only 6 continued education after the mandatory age 14; the others chose to work and learn trades. Sons in families where the fathers remained at home during the war were three times more likely to follow the patterns of their father's education.

The quality of relationships in the family was also significantly altered by war. The family of soldiers who returned after the war was twice disrupted, once when the father left and again when he returned, affecting not just the long-term relationship with the fathers but also with the mothers. During the fathers' absence, mothers often developed very close relationships with their children. When the fathers returned, the children frequently had to yield this dominant place. This forced the children to deal with new issues of loyalty, leadership, abandonment, and, in some cases, jealousy.

For some, these feelings appear to have affected their lifelong relationship with each parent. Although three fourths of the participants in my study described their present and past relationships with their parents in positive terms, participants whose fathers were temporarily absent during the war but returned later were more likely to describe relationships with their mothers in negative terms.

War affected the pattern of communication within the family. My research documents that the "legacy of silence" exists not only in families where the parents had been perpetrators or victims of Nazi crimes but also in families where the parents were not involved in the Nazi regime. Two-thirds of the participants never or very seldom talked with their fathers about the war. Even fewer of the participants ever or occasionally talked with their parents about their parents' role during the Third Reich, even though most of these participants suspected their parent's role had been benign. Furthermore, most (over 80%) indicated they had never or very seldom talked with their siblings about the Nazi era, and over half of them indicated they had never or very seldom discussed World War II or the Third Reich with their own children.

Elder's (1974) research has suggested a shift toward the increased value of the family to those facing severe hardship. In this study, some respondents' values shifted away from the family and altruism to purely personal interests. However, this was found only among those who had the most severe experiences during the war. Perhaps having a limited amount of adversity in early life results in increased reliance on and importance of the family, whereas severe adversities may result in an increasing tendency towards self-centered interests.

REFERENCES

Elder, Glenn H. 1974. *Children of the Great Depression: Social Change in Life Experience.* Chicago: University of Chicago Press.

Larney, Barbara Elden. 1994. *Children of World War II in Germany: A Life Course Analysis.* (Doctoral Dissertation). Phoenix, AZ: Arizona State University.

Barbara Elden Larney, Ph.D., researches the effects of war on children. Her work was partially funded by a Peace Scholar Award of the United States Institute of Peace. She grew up during and after World War II in Germany. She admits to being haunted by those experiences even today and acknowledges their profound impact on her life.

A 21st-CENTURY RECONSTRUCTION OF "FAMILY"

Who Constitutes Your Family?

On a piece of paper, draw a quick sketch of your family. You can be as elaborate or as simple as you like, perhaps even just using stick figures to represent family members. Include individuals who fill the roles of husband and wife, parent and child, brother and sister, as well as any extended relations such as grandparents, aunts and uncles, and cousins who you consider to be part of the group you call "family." Your portrait will share features with portraits others draw.

Your portrait will also differ in appearance in significant ways as well, especially if you enhance your portrait by noting who is excluded, as well as who is included. We invited a sample of single mothers to participate in this exercise. At first, when asked to draw their family, they drew the expected figures: husbands and wives, parents and children, extended kin and in-laws. However, when we asked them to add additional family members who might not fit the conventional definition of family, they often included friends and neighbors. When we asked them to remove family members, we were surprised to find many chose to exclude individuals to whom they or their children were related by blood or marriage (Karraker and Grochowski 1998).

If you specify those to whom you feel close or distant, or if you qualify the warm or chilly relationship (try using red or blue colors to shade these connections) among various family members, even more differences will emerge. Explore the quality of these relationships further, considering relative positions of power and privilege and you gain a sense of appreciation for the challenge of negotiating the definition of "family" in an authentic and meaningful way for individuals, communities, and humanity.

So, what does "family" mean? Our conception of family includes gays or lesbians who have formed civil or other committed unions, step- or noncustodial parents, and adoptive and foster children. We also include fictive kin, that is, those significant individuals to whom we have no relationship by blood or marriage but who nonetheless occupy important roles in our family constellations.

Families as Strategic Living Communities ©

As we have demonstrated, families come in a myriad of configurations, any one of which can effectively organize intimate life according to norms and roles, while providing ways of communicating, problem solving, and sustaining their members (Goldenberg and Goldenberg 1985: 3). Grochowski's (2000) concept of *strategic living communities* (SLC) © expands the conventional definition of family to all members who offer intimacy and commitment. Much like creative artists, families need to define themselves in terms of who they are, how they feel, and what they want. Such a highly proactive organism needs support and encouragement in all its rich variety, rather than rigid definitions and stereotypes.

Families in Decline or Families in Transition?

Ignorance of differences can translate into fear of the unknown. Likewise, cultural, demographic, economic, social, technological, and other changes affecting families are sources of personal uncertainty and social concern, regardless of the culture, history, or society. The 20th century was no exception. During the 1900s, American society witnessed dramatic shifts in children's and women's employment, compacts among corporations and workers, the role of government in mandating and enforcing civil rights, opportunities for sexual expression, and technological advances that touched virtually every aspect of social life.

Compared to previous generations, Americans are more likely to delay marriage—or never marry at all—and to cohabit before marriage. Young adults are more likely to return to living with parents or be in a gay or lesbian relationship. For a time we also witnessed an increase in births to unmarried women as well as an increase in the divorce rate. We have seen increases in the proportion of children living in a single-parent household (usually mother-headed, but occasionally father-headed) and of children growing up in situations with multiple family composition (Bianchi and Casper 2001; Teachman, Tedrow, and Crowder 2000).

The editors of the comprehensive *Handbook of Marriage and the Family* (Sussman, Steinmetz, and Peterson 1999: 2–3) assert:

> ... it no longer makes sense to use nuclear families as the standard against which various forms of the family (e.g., divorced families, single parent families, and stepfamilies) are measured.... families are constantly changing and adapting to meet the current and emerging demands of a dynamic society.... change and diversity are the norm.

These changes assuredly reflect shifts in men's and women's roles in society, particularly in the growing importance of women's employment, and likely the lower importance of marriage as a source of economic stability. At the same time, we have witnessed the growing economic inequality among American families (Teachman, Tedrow, and Crowder 2000).

However, Bianchi and Casper (2001: 1) of the *Population Reference Bureau* observe that recent trends during the last half of the 20th century indicate there has been a "quieting of changes [or at least the pace of change] in the family." They found little change during the 1990s in the proportion of two-parent or single-mother families or in the living arrangements of children, young adults, and the elderly. Furthermore, the rapid growth in unmarried cohabitation has slowed, and the divorce rate has not only slowed but also declined in the last 2 decades.

Skolnick (2001) argues we need to move "beyond nostalgia and moral panic" that often grips discussions on the state of the family. In fact, Coontz (1992) chose *The Way We Never Were* as the title about the false wistfulness that surrounds American views of family. The pessimism emerging from conservative quarters puzzles some who study the trends relating to families.

Skolnick (2001: 45) argues the massive changes facing families today do not spring from

> moral decay or some deep flaw in the American character. Rather these changes spring from the demographic, economic, and social changes that have transformed America and other advanced industrial countries in the twentieth century.

In the face of these changes and life-span demands, family structures and arrangements that worked in earlier centuries or even the first half of the last century bear less relevance to the challenges of today. For example, we have evolved from an information age to a knowledge age, with an accompanying increase in demands for both formal education and self-directed learning. Advances in health and longevity demand families plan further into the future than previous generations. Other technological advances offer both challenges and opportunities for distance learning, mobility, and telecommuting.

Wisdom and experience tell us we cannot go backwards. Those who are pessimistic and cynical when viewing the family in society are trying to frame the present (and perhaps even craft the future) using the lens of the past. We are not advocating a naive view of the family or a reckless approach to family studies. Rather we challenge readers not to take the easy path of using nostalgia or myth to define present and future families. Yes, we can learn from the past, but we must not be limited or confined by its myopic lens.

Toward a Strength-Centered, Resiliency Focus

Why, when faced with adversity or change, some families not only survive but also thrive, whereas others with similar attributes succumb, virtually stuck in their predicament? The value in this question lies in the asking as well as the answers. The last three decades witnessed a shift in the study of families from describing "what is wrong with" to seeking "what works in" families. This shift from a *deficit-centered* to a *strength-centered* focus invites family study professionals to see families inclusive of all their diversity and as *competent*. Even distressed families have strengths and resiliency potential. Such a paradigm shift emphasizes *resiliency* and challenges students of families to move beyond a *deficit* approach.

Resiliency is more than merely "surviving" adversity. Just surviving a flood does not mean one is resilient; the "survivor" may internalize the perspective of victimization, express chronic anger, or be consumed by "survivor's guilt." Such survivors do not grow from the experience (Wolin and Wolin 1993). Resilient individuals and families reap some learning from an ordeal, regain a sense of control, and move on.

Walsh (1998) cautions that to be resilient is not to be *invincible*. Resilient individuals are not impervious to challenge, conflict, or change. In fact, resiliency presumes change, challenge, and conflict are inevitable parts of every family's life. An "invincible super person" myth leads to blaming those who struggle with adversity, while suggesting those who are resilient merely slip through unscathed as lucky souls. Such a dichotomy breeds contempt for those who stumble, yet faint recognition for those who "make it." This cultural attitude blinds us to the reality that resiliency is

> . . . struggling well: experiencing both suffering and courage, effectively working through difficulties both internal and interpersonally. (Higgins 1994, quoted in Walsh 1998: 6)

Resilient families are those who not only meet demands but also learn from the experience, add what they learn to their adaptation and coping repertoire, and move on with life.

This paradigm emphasizes the competence and potential of families (Barnard 1994; Walsh 1993, 1998), which prompts family study professionals to help families explore how they may survive, heal, and thrive even under devastating odds, while recognizing and celebrating their own diversity. As a complex, dynamic process, family resilience ebbs and flows with time and circumstance. When families honor their strengths, they more often engage in creative, resilient behaviors when faced with challenges, conflicts, and change.

Resiliency is at the heart of the concept of viewing families as *strategic living communities* ©. Families are "strategic"; they are capable of resilient change through complex adaptive structures. Families are "living"; they are organic, evolving, and dynamic. Families are "communities"; they are composed of interdependent members interacting with outside systems.

FAMILY STUDIES: AN EMERGING INTERDISCIPLINE

Contributions of the Core Disciplines of Family Studies

Many academic programs in *family studies* are housed in schools of human ecology (some which grew out of old programs in home economics). As Figure 1.1 demonstrates, contemporary family studies is a complicated conglomerate, drawing not only on the traditional social sciences, such as sociology, psychology, and economics, but also on some of the newer academic disciplines which apply social scientific methods to specific areas of family life (e.g., communication). Theology and religious studies have long had a vested interest in consideration of families; political science, especially through the examination of law and public policy, is also an important stakeholder in family studies.

Social workers and gerontologists have always had the family as a primary unit of analysis. Educators, epidemiologists, medical professionals, and public health workers have recently arrived at the realization families play a key role in achievement and maintenance of the individual's well-being and intervention in cases of disease and risk. Some family studies programs have found a place for business scholars in light of the succession and family dynamics involved in family businesses.

In the last half of the 20th century, growing awareness of the accelerating speed and depth of change prompted the emergence of a new discipline, future studies. Future studies does not attempt to predict the future (like fortunetellers and prophets). Rather, future studies can assist individuals and families, organizations and corporations, and communities and societies in visualizing their preferred futures. Futurists invite us to visualize what could be and contemplate what we are willing to do to achieve our preferred futures,

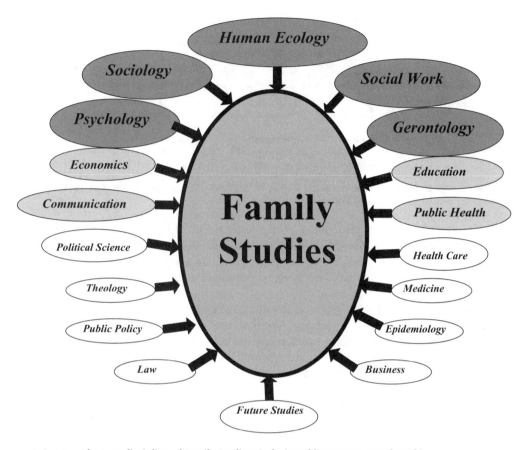

FIG. 1.1. The Interdiscipline of Family Studies © designed by Janet R. Grochowski.

a process demanding proactive engagement. The University of Houston–Clear Lake *Studies of the Future* program (2002: 1) provides a glimpse into the efforts of professionals engaged in future studies.

> Working as facilitators or consultants, futures researchers can help [others] envision their preferred futures and compare those visions with current trends and scenarios of possible futures. This process leads to the kind of practical planning and policy-making that truly brings about change.

The Art and Science of Family Studies

From the discipline's inception in the 1920s, family studies was premised on the belief science could contribute to the understanding of family relations, which could in turn advance the quality of family life and society (Burgess 1926). In his Presidential Address to the *National Council on Family Relations* in 1999, Doherty (2000: 319) of the University of Minnesota called for

> ... a new model for thinking about the relationship between researchers, practitioners, families, and communities.

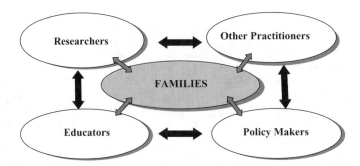

FIG. 1.2. An Integrated Model of Family Studies © 2003 Janet R. Grochowski and Meg Wilkes Karraker with design by Janet Grochowski.

Doherty argues the role of the family professional needs to shift from service provider through whom knowledge about families "trickles down" from family scientists to family citizen. He advocates instead that family professionals need to be collaborators with researchers, practitioners, and families themselves to understand and promote family well-being (see Fig. 1.2).

In "A Conscious and Inclusive Family Studies" Allen (2000) argues the theories, methods, and areas of investigation in family studies should reflect the diversity of families. Furthermore, she believes family scholars should acknowledge, confront, and integrate our own subjective experiences into our research. Allen contends our responsibilities to readers, students, selves, and the families we study require us to consider intersections define family diversity: age, class, gender, race, and sexual orientation.

Family scholars in the 21st century must move beyond often narrow definitions of "family" toward what Daly (2003) calls "theories families live by." As we begin our journey through this book, we invite you to consider what the dynamic, interdisciplinary conceptualizations of "family" we have explored in this chapter mean in terms of your future professional experience and the lives of families with whom you study and work.

BOX 1.5 "Reuben L. Hill"
Paul Mattessich, Ph.D.

Reuben Hill had just begun a visiting professorship in Norway, at age 73, when a heart attack abruptly ended his career as one of the most influential family scholars of the 20th century. Despite "retirement," Reuben expected a busy 1985 to 1986 year, including teaching a course on the links among family research, theory, and therapy, and delivering lectures at several European universities. The activities planned for the coming year exemplified characteristics that Reuben's colleagues, students, and others greatly admired. Foremost among those were his energy, creativity, dedication, his ability to work in different languages and cultures and, above all, his determination to promote high-quality research that would both advance theory about families and produce significant, practical, life-enriching benefits for people.

Hill focused attention on the dynamics of family life that enable families to meet members' needs in the present, yet adjust to new demands in the future. He addressed questions, such as How do individuals whose lives intersect as partners, parents, children, and grandparents manage to support one another, meeting their own needs while contributing to the well-being of other family members? How do families, with typically little training, accomplish tasks that are critical for nurturing newborns, socializing new generations of adults, and sustaining society? How do families cope with crises that occur due to death, divorce, war, and environmental catastrophes? How do families sustain energy and resources to function as well as they do, sometimes defying the odds; and how can families function even better?

These questions led naturally to inquiries about stress and resiliency. Hill sought to identify the "normal, predictable" stressors that confront every family as a result of expectable changes. For example, changes such as formation of a new household through marriage; increased parental responsibilities after childbirth; and emerging individual and dyadic tasks that parents must address as they grow older and children leave home. This led to formulation of the "family development" framework for understanding families and to the testing of theories of family development. Hill searched for the basic patterns of life that all families experience – whether structured along typical lines for the United States (e.g., two-parent or single-parent families) or along other cultural lines. By blending research and theory about expectable developmental processes with research and theory about unpredictable stressors (e.g., severe illness or war separation) Hill influenced generations of students and colleagues to explore family dynamics.

Current students and researchers may not realize the difficulty family sociologists faced at the time Hill and his contemporaries pioneered their work. As recently as the 1930s, some researchers lost faculty positions because they studied courtship and mate selection. Hill led the campaign to uncover the truth about family life through careful scientific examination. In the 1960s, he gave a speech noting that family research had finally become liberated enough to study topics that many people wanted to avoid, such as alternative family forms, family violence, and sexual behavior.

Hill's early work included "Family Planning and Control of Population Size in Puerto Rico." This helped him realize the value of constructing theoretical models to represent family decision-making and other aspects of family dynamics. The Puerto Rican research, along with "Middletown in Transition," a study of different generations of the same families, led him to assert the need for doing longitudinal studies and inter-generational studies, in order to understand the continuities and discontinuities in norms, values, aspirations, and behaviors that different generations of the same extended family exhibit over time. Hill felt strongly that research to understand families requires strong empirical work, such as surveys, along with case studies and observation, to obtain depth and provide insight into family processes. He emphasized mixed method approaches in his own research and in class assignments.

Hill founded the *Minnesota Family Study Center* at the University of Minnesota, where he became a Regents Professor. The *Center* housed many studies related to family problem solving, family stress, family adjustment to social change, family economic behavior, family interaction with kin, and other topics. Formation of the *Center* and its subsequent contributions to family studies furthered Hill's dream to portray with the greatest possible scientific credibility the facts about the dynamic, resilient nature of families. For one example, what enables families to accomplish tasks to meet the changes needs generated by their aging members, while simultaneously adapting to—and dealing with—demands placed on them by external networks of kin and by the community?

Paul Mattessich is Director of *Wilder Research Center* in Minnesota, an institute dedicated to strengthening individuals, families, and communities through research. He worked with Reuben Hill from 1972 to 1985.

GLOSSARY

Competent	Invincible
Deficit-centered	Matrix of domination
Demography	Resiliency
Family	Sex
Family studies	Sexual orientation
Fictive kin	Strategic living communities
Gender	Strength-centered
Household	Transgender

FOR YOUR CONSIDERATION

1. Politicians, religious leaders, and others lay claim to being "pro-family." What does that phrase mean to you, in the context of the significance of family for individuals, communities and nations, and humanity?

2. As a family studies scholar, what is your position on the debate concerning the descendants of Thomas Jefferson?

3. Of the sources of family diversity discussed in this chapter, which one is the easiest for you to reconcile with your own experience and beliefs? Which is the hardest for you to reconcile?

4. Define *family studies* to someone new to the field.

FOR FURTHER STUDY: WEB SITES, ORGANIZATIONS, AND PUBLICATIONS

Web Sites and Organizations

National Council on Family Relations
www.ncfr.org
This is an interdisciplinary organization serving family scholars and practitioners. The site offers a wealth of research, articles, and numerous links.

Population Reference Bureau
www.prb.org
This site "provides timely and objective population information" on both world and American demographic trends. Focal areas include families and households, as well as women's labor force status and children and youth. *Quickfacts* and reports based on data from the *U.S. Bureau of the Census*, the *United Nations*, the *World Health Organization*, and other organizations are available online and in print.

Family Diversity Projects
www.familydiv.org
This Web site is sponsored by Family Diversity Projects, Inc., a nonprofit organization devoted to educating employees, students, parents, teachers, politicians, religious leaders and communities, and the general public about family diversity. This site includes positive images of families which are multiracial, which may include gay, lesbian, bisexual, and transgendered members, and members with physical, mental, and emotional challenges.

Publications

Browning, Don S., Bonnie J. Miller-McLemore, Pamela D. Couture, K. Brynolf Lyon, and Robert M. Franklin. 2000. *From Culture Wars to Common Ground: Religion and the American Family Debate*, 2/e. Louisville, KY: Westminster John Knox.

The authors of this book explicate the different viewpoints in the family debates, explain the assumptions and context of each, and suggest limitations of each perspective.

Demo, D. H., K. R. Allen, and M. A. Fine, eds. 2000. *Handbook of Family Diversity.* New York: Oxford University Press.

Featuring chapters authored by prominent scholars from a variety of fields, this handbook discusses family interaction and processes from a variety of dimensions including age, class, gender, race, sexual orientation, and family structure.

Encyclopedia of Family Life. 1999. Pasadena, CA: Salem Press.

This five-volume reference provides an overview of the family, including cross-references, and bibliographies. The last volume includes a subject index and a list of family support groups.

The History of the Family: An International Quarterly

This interdisciplinary journal "charts new directions in the historical study of the family." In addition to historical anthropology, historical sociology, economic history and psychology, the journal publishes comparative research on families across cultures.

Sussman, Marvin B., Suzanne K. Steinmetz, and Gary W. Peterson, eds. 1999. *Handbook of Marriage and the Family*, 2/e. New York: Plenum.

This reference work is a comprehensive revision of an earlier edition published in 1987. The volume is organized around five sections: family diversity, theory and methods, changing family patterns and roles, family and other institutions, and changing family patterns and roles.

Weeks, Jeffrey, Brian Heaphy, and Catherine Donovan. 2001. *Same Sex Intimacies: Families of Choice and Other Life Experiments.* New York: Routledge.

These authors apply Giddens' term *experiments in living* to explain the societal condition in which families of blood and marriage are being joined by families of choice that challenge the heterosexual assumption.

REFERENCES FOR CITED WORKS

Aldous, Joan, and Rodney F. Ganey. 1999. "Family Life and the Pursuit of Happiness." *Journal of Family Relations* 20, 2 (March): 155–80.

Allen, Katherine R. 2000. "A Conscious and Inclusive Family Studies." *Journal of Marriage and the Family* 62, 1 (February): 4–17.

Armas, Genaro C. 2001. "Gay Homes More Visible." *The Detroit News*, August 22. http://detnews.com/2001/census/0110/04/a05-275269.htm (Retrieved 7/17/02)

Baca Zinn, Maxine. 2001. "Feminist Rethinking from Racial-Ethnic Families." In *Shifting the Center: Understanding Contemporary Families*, 2/e, ed. Susan Ferguson. Mountain View, CA: Mayfield, 18–26.

Barnard, C. P. 1994. "Resiliency: A Shift in Our Perception?" *American Journal of Family Therapy* 22, 2 (Summer): 135–144.

Bianchi, Suzanne M., and Lynne M. Casper. 2001. "American Families." www.prb.org/pubs/population_bulletin/bu55-4/55_4_intro.html (Retrieved 3/4/01).

Burgess, Ernest W. 1926. "The Family as a Unit of Interacting Personalities." *The Family* 7: 3–9.

Collins, Patricia Hill. 1990. *Black Feminist Thought: Knowledge, Consciousness, and the Politics of Empowerment.* Boston, MA: Unwin Hyman.

Coontz, Stephanie. 1992. *The Way We Never Were: American Families and the Nostalgia Trap.* New York, NY: Basic Books.

Dalmadge, Heather M. 2000. *Tripping on the Color Line: Black-White Multiracial Families in a Racially Divided World.* New Brunswick, NJ: Rutgers University Press.

Daly, Kerry. 2003. "Family Theory Versus the Theories Families Live By." *Journal of Marriage and Family* 65, 4 (November): 771–84.

Doherty, William J. 2000. "Family Science and Family Citizenship: Toward a Model of Community Partnership with Families." *Family Relations: Interdisciplinary Journal of Applied Family Studies* 49, 3 (July): 319–26.

Footlick, Jerrold K. 1990. "What Happened to Family? (The 21st Century Family)." *Newsweek* 114: 27, 14–20, 24.

Gerson, Kathleen. 1991. "Coping with Commitment: Dilemmas and Conflicts of Family Life." In *America at Century's End*. ed. Alan Wolfe. Berkeley, CA: University of California Press, 35–57.

Goldenberg, H., and I. Goldenberg. 1985. *Family Therapy: An Overview*, 2/e. Monterey, CA: Brooks/Cole.

Gould, Meredith, and Rochelle Kern-Daniels. 1977. "Toward a Sociological Theory of Gender and Sex." *The American Sociologist* 12, 4 (November): 182–9.

Grochowski, Janet R. 2000. "Families as 'Strategic Living Communities.'" Paper presented at the annual meetings of the American Academy of Health Behavior, September, Santa Fe, NM.

Higgins, Gina O'Connell. 1994. *Resilient Adults: Overcoming a Cruel Past*. San Francisco, CA: Jossey-Bass.

Hojat, Mohammadreza, et al. 2000. "Gender Differences in Traditional Attitudes Toward Marriage and the Family: An Empirical Study of Iranian Immigrants in the United States." *Journal of Family Issues* 21, 4 (May): 419–34.

Karraker, Meg Wilkes, and Janet R. Grochowski. 1998. "Dual Vision Research for a Postmodern Perspective on Single Mothers' Families." Paper presented at the Annual Meetings of *Sociologists of Minnesota*, Minneapolis, MN.

Kaufman, Gayle. 2000. "Do Gender Role Attitudes Matter?" *Journal of Family Relations* 21, 1 (January): 128–44.

Laner, Mary Riege. 2000. "'Sex' versus 'Gender': A Renewed Plea." *Sociological Inquiry* 70, 4 (Fall): 462–74.

Miller, R. Robin, and Sandra Lee Browning. 1999. "The Importance of the Multicultural Approach: An Introduction." *Journal of Family Issues* 20, 5 (September): 596–601.

Morgan, D. H. J. 1975. *Social Theory and the Family*. London: Routledge & Kegan Paul.

Murdock, George Peter. 1949. *Social Structure*. New York, NY: Macmillan.

Murry, Velma McBride, Emilie Phillips Smith, and Nancy E. Hill. 2001. "Race, Ethnicity, and Culture in Studies of Families in Context." *Journal of Marriage and the Family* 63, 1 (November): 911–14.

Parke, Ross D. 2000. "Beyond White and Middle Class: Cultural Variations in Families: Assessments, Processes, and Policies." *Journal of Family Psychology* 14, 3 (September): 331–33.

Patterson, Charlotte. 2000. "Family Relationships of Lesbians and Gay Men." *Journal of Marriage and the Family*, 62, 4 (November): 1052–69.

Pyke, Karen. 2000. "'The Normal American Family' as an Interpretive Structure of Family Life among Grown Children of Korean and Vietnamese Immigrants." *Journal of Marriage and the Family* 62, 1 (February): 240–55.

Skolnick, Arlene. 2001. "The State of the American Family." In *Shifting the Center: Understanding Contemporary Families*, 2/e, ed. Susan Ferguson. Mountain View, CA: Mayfield, 41–53.

Stack, Carol. 1974. *All Our Kin: Strategies for Survival in a Black Community*. New York, NY: Harper & Row.

Sussman, Marvin B., Suzanne K. Steinmetz, and Gary W. Peterson, eds. 1999. *Handbook of Marriage and the Family*, 2/e. New York, NY: Plenum.

Teachman, Jay D., Lucky M. Tedrow, and Kyle D. Crowder. 2000. "The Changing Demography of America's Families." *Journal of Marriage and the Family* 62, 4 (November): 1234–46.

United States Bureau of the Census. 2000. *Current Population Surveys, 1960–2000*. March. Washington, DC: Government Printing Office.

United States Bureau of the Census. 2001. Table No. 96, "Expectation of Life at Birth, 1970 to 1999, and Projections 2000–2010." *Statistical Abstract of the United States: 2001*. Washington, DC: Government Printing Office.

University of Houston-Clear Lake. 2002. "What is Futures Studies?" http://www.cl.uh.edu/futureweb/futdef.html (Retrieved 7/22/02).

Vanier Institute of the Family. 2004. www.vifamily.ca/about/about.html (Retrieved 09/23/04).

Wald, Michael. 2001. "Same Sex Couples: Marriage, Families, and Children." http://lawschool.stanford.edu/faculty/wald/couple.shtm (Retrieved 3/15/01).

Walsh, Froma. 1993. "Conceptualization of Normal Family Processes." In *Normal Family Processes*, 2/e, ed. Froma Walsh. New York, NY: Guilford, 2–72.

Walsh, Froma. 1998. *Strengthening Family Resilience*. New York, NY: Guilford.

Weston, Kath. 2001. "Exiles From Kinship." In *Shifting the Center: Understanding Contemporary Families*, 2/e, ed. Susan Ferguson. Mountain View, CA: Mayfield.

Wolin, Steven, and Sybil Wolin. 1993. *The Resilient Self: How Survivors of Troubled Families Rise Above Adversity*. New York, NY: Villard.

2

FAMILY SCHOLARSHIP IN ACTION: THEORIES, METHODS, AND ETHICS

CHAPTER PREVIEW

Theories and research methods are tools for expanding our understanding of families. *Exchange theory* and *symbolic interaction theory* are two mirrors for understanding family dynamics. *Family development theory*, grounded in understanding of *life cycle*, along with *life-course theory*, and *family systems theory* are three prisms for understanding family changes. *Conflict theory, structural functional theory*, and *family ecology theory* are three keys to understanding family contexts. We argue for the benefits of multiple perspectives and note that *feminist perspectives* and *postmodernism* have broad implications for understanding families across perspectives. For each theory, we discuss the principles and concepts and offer an exemplar drawn from research or practice.

Family scholars have an array of research methods from which to choose, including *experiment, observation, survey, case study*, and *archival* techniques. In practice, each method has its own strengths and weaknesses. However, ultimately, multiple methods may yield the richest results. *Longitudinal* and *comparative* studies are challenging but essential to viewing families across time and space. The pursuit of a deeper understanding of families carries with it concern for *ethics*. We close this chapter with a question: *How will you study families in meaningful, realistic, and ethical ways?*

THEORIES FOR UNDERSTANDING FAMILIES

As in any discipline, family *theory* provides a road map for finding a way to a deeper understanding of families and family dynamics. At its best, family theory goes beyond description of family life to yield explanation of systems and relationships. The most sophisticated theory may even lead us to attempt to predict the course for families. Futurists, however, would argue that we should more properly strive to forecast possible futures than to predict likely outcomes. In this section, we describe seven of these road maps, two "mirrors for understanding family dynamics" (*exchange theory* and *symbolic interaction theory*), two "prisms for understanding family change" (*family development theory* and *family systems theory*), and three "keys to understanding families in context (*conflict theory, structural functional theory*, and *family ecology theory*). Furthermore, we advise family scholars to consider multiple perspectives, especially *feminism* and *postmodernism*. For each theory, we also offer an exemplar of that theory in action.

Two Mirrors for Understanding Family Dynamics

At the very root, families are composed of individuals living in a relationship with other individuals. We begin this section with a discussion of the principles and concepts of two theories that address this *microsocial* aspect of family dynamics.

Exchange, sometimes called *rational choice*, theory begins with the assumption that in families, as in other social situations, individuals choose to enter into and continue in relationships in which they can maximize their *rewards* and minimize their *costs*. Furthermore, exchange theory posits that we seek relationships in which the exchange of goods, services, status, and other resources will be equitable. Exchange theorists may explain the attraction between attractive young women and wealthy older men through a rather cold-hearted calculus in which physical beauty and sex appeal is exchanged for economic security and status. Conversely, exchange theory provides insight into the rationale battered women may apply in deciding to stay in an abusive relationship in which they bear the cost of physical or emotional abuse in "exchange" for physical and social security for themselves and their children.

BOX 2.1 "Commuting: Pragmatic Choice in Dual-Earner Households"
Heather Hofmeister, Ph.D., and Phyllis Moen, Ph.D.

The average worker in the United States spends 40 minutes a day, over 3 hours a week, in transit. Morning commute time is traded for time spent sleeping, jogging, or getting children dressed and fed; evening commute time is exchanged for time spent in dinner preparation, interacting with other family members, and leisure. To arrive at a "livable" solution, individuals and families consider the sacrifices and benefits of long commutes in light of both job and housing availability and desirability.

But some workers commute far more minutes than do others. What accounts for differences in commuting time? One solution is to distribute commute time between working members of the household as part of the broader household division of labor, like paid work, washing the dishes, or preparing dinner. The spouse with the longer commute may "substitute" that commute time for other household responsibilities by doing less around the house. Or a longer commute may reflect a sacrifice on the part of the commuter so that the family can live in a more desirable neighborhood or the other spouse can be closer to his or her workplace.

Time is a scarce and finite resource, especially in dual-earner households. Rational choice theory suggests that couples make tradeoffs with each other, with their time, and with the location of work and home to *maximize benefit* to the household. Extrapolating from Becker (1981), the worker who is earning the most should be "specializing" in the work domain and is best able to "afford" a longer commute. This earner's overall investment in work, even considering the commute time, makes it worthwhile to the household to lose that spouse or parent to the road for those hours a day. In support of this theory, research shows that, with dual-earner couples, spouses with the higher earnings, longer hours, or greater job prestige tend to have the longer commute.

Commutes are not only a demand on individual workers' time but also a time- and resource-commitment borne by workplaces, households, and neighborhoods. A long commute may be part of the price paid for a higher salary at work. In a sense, the higher salary justifies the long drive, and so high earners are willing to go farther, literally, for the money.

Our life-course, role context perspective is more one of *pragmatic* rather than *rational* choice; our data (Hofmeister 2002; Moen 2002) from the *Cornell Couples and Careers Study* (funded by the Alfred P. Sloan Foundation) show that working couples strategize as to where they live, often based on husbands' jobs. These decisions, in turn, tend to limit the job options of wives. Parenthood also is a key context in which working couples make choices about where to live, where to work, and, correspondingly, how long to commute. Given women's traditional caregiving role, working mothers tend to be the ones to pick up and drop off their young preschoolers from childcare, often resulting in a longer commute time for them.

Other key contexts affecting commute times are policies and practices about telecommuting, working flexibility (especially off-peak) hours, carpools, and, importantly, public transportation. Thus, we see individual "choices" as embedded in a web of social relations and social structures related to work, family, gender, and organizational as well as community constraints and supports. Rational choice theory focuses on making optimal decisions. A life-course, role context approach focuses on the limited number of options actually available as people are constrained by prior choices (buying a home, taking one job over another, marrying, and having a child) and the multilayered circumstances that call for pragmatic, rather than optimal, strategic actions.

REFERENCES

Becker, Gary S. 1981. *A Treatise on the Family.* Cambridge, MA: Harvard University Press.

Hofmeister, Heather. 2002. *Couples' Commutes to Work Considering Workplace, Household, and Neighborhood Contexts: The Traffic Triangle.* Ph.D. diss. Cornell University.

Phyllis Moen. 2002. *It's About Time: Couples and Careers.* Ithaca, NY: Cornell University Press.

Heather Hofmeister, Ph.D., received her doctorate from Cornell University in 2002. Her award-winning research views couples' work and family dynamics, including commuting, across the life course.
Phyllis Moen, Ph.D., is McKnight Presidential Chair in Sociology at the University of Minnesota. She also served as founding director of the Bronfenbrenner Life Course Center and director of the Cornell Employment and Family Careers Institute at Cornell University.

Symbolic interaction theory begins with a different set of assumptions. Where exchange theory assumes that people are predictably inclined to pursue their own self-interest even in intimate relationships, symbolic interactionists see human beings as less predictable and capable of constructing complex *meanings* around their own and others' behaviors with some measure of creativity. Symbolic interactionists argue that individuals acquire a sense of self through language, gestures, and other social interaction with significant others.

BOX 2.2 "Decision Making in Adoption"
Nelwyn B. Moore, Ph.D., and J. Kenneth Davidson, Sr., Ph.D.

In 1999, 1.30 million births or 33% of all reported births were to unmarried women in the United States, of which more than 374,000 were to unmarried teenagers. These numbers translate into a birthrate of 42.9% for teens (Ventura and Bachrach 2000). In spite of severe health, educational, psychological, and economic consequences, 99% of unmarried teens who give birth today choose to keep their babies. This pattern is a quantum leap from two generations ago when the vast majority of babies born to unmarried mothers were relinquished for adoption (Chandra, et al. 1999).

The National Council for Adoptions reported that unrelated adoptions rose from 33,800 in 1951 to 89,200 in 1970. However, they fell substantially in the mid-1970s, remaining relatively stable at approximately 50,000 annually from 1974 to present (Placek 1999).

Although adoption as a solution to an unwanted pregnancy may be an ancient practice, the scientific study of adoption is relatively new. The rationale underlying the need for adoption research is based on the premise that the adoption option can solve both personal and societal problems (Davidson and Moore 1996). In order to promote the adoption option, it is important to identify salient variables in the pregnant adolescent's perception of the situation that forms the basis of her decision to place or keep.

The research literature reveals several theoretical frameworks that have been used to study the issues of adoption. These include the familiar psychoanalytic and cognitive development perspectives as well as the expectancy value theory that focuses on the perceived desirability and likelihood of outcomes. A review of the independent variables used in previous research about adoption suggests that reference group theory, which is a component of symbolic interaction theory, is also an appropriate underlying theoretical framework for such investigation. The reference group orientation considers the perspectives of various social groups in evaluating and interpreting the social behavior of an individual. This theoretical perspective assumes that people make fundamental judgments, decisions, and self-assessments based on psychological identifications with social groups of which one is a member or aspires to be a member (Shibutani 1955).

Although several theories have provided useful data concerning the adoption option, reference group theory seemed the most closely related theoretical framework for a study of adoption decision making to be conducted at a large residential facility for pregnant, unmarried persons. Because the goal was to collect data from pregnant teens during their process of decision making about placing for adoption or keeping their babies, an anonymous questionnaire was administered to the volunteer respondents at 8 months of gestation. The resulting sample included 178 pregnant, unmarried teens with no prior pregnancy that, after giving birth, placed their babies for adoption.

A number of factors revealed in this investigation supported the reference group perspective as an important theoretical framework for the study of adoption decision making. Contextual factors such as family, religious values, and peer influence emerged as important variables in the process of adoption decision making. In fact, several reference-group socialization experiences related to unintended pregnancies had occurred in the lives of these Placers. One fourth of them had sisters who had become premaritally pregnant and two thirds had at least one close friend who had been premaritally pregnant, almost two thirds of whom chose to carry to term rather than to abort. The indication that the behavior of the Placers in this study was a phenomenon of psychological identification with their social peer group became even more apparent when it was revealed that one third of their close friends had chosen to place their baby for adoption. This figure is remarkable when compared to only 1% of the general population of unmarried, pregnant teens who place their babies for adoption. And, the fact that so many Placers were themselves adopted or had an immediate family member who was adopted underscores the significance of other contextual factors. It could be argued that because of their earlier socialization experiences with adoption, the teens in this study perceived the adoption option as a positive alternative for their unintended pregnancy.

If indeed society wishes to promote the adoption option, implications from this research suggest the wisdom of exploring educational programs whose models are based on reference group theory. By using reference group theory to explore the decision-making process of teens who choose to place their babies for adoption, family scientists may further discern how behavior is shaped by culture and how culture is shaped by behavior.

REFERENCES

Chandra, A., Abma, J., Maza, P., and Bachrach, C. 1999. "Adoption, Adoption Seeking, and Relinquishment for Adoption in the United States." *Advance Data From Vital Statistics*, No. 306. Hyattsville, MD: National Center for Vital Statistics.

Davidson, J. Kenneth, Sr., and Nelwyn B. Moore. 1996. *Marriage and Family: Change and Continuity*. Boston: Allyn & Bacon.

Placek, P. J. 1999. "National Adoption Data." In *Adoption Factbook III*, eds. C. Marshner and W. L. Pierce. Washington, DC: National Council for Adoption, 24–68.

Shibutani, T. 1955. Reference groups as perspectives. *American Journal of Sociology* 60: 562–9.

Ventura, S. J., and C. A. Bachrach. 2000. "Nonmarital Childbearing in the United States, 1940–99." *National Vital Statistics Reports*, 48, 3. Hyattsville, MD: National Center for Vital Statistics.

J. Kenneth Davidson, Sr., Ph.D., is Professor Emeritus of Sociology at the University of Wisconsin-Eau Claire. *Nelwyn B. Moore, Ph.D.,* is Professor Emerita of Child and Family Studies at Southwest Texas University San Mareos.

Exchange and symbolic interaction theories both have supporters and detractors. Critics of exchange theory argue that human relationships are not really so predictable (and mercenary) as that theory purports. Critics of symbolic interaction theory argue that human interaction is not really so creative (and fluid) as that theory contends. Other family studies scholars focus on the changes experienced by families and their members over time. In the next section, we examine two theories that take as the unit of analysis the family unit itself.

Three Prisms for Understanding Family Changes

Family development theory views families as moving through a series of normative events marked by the addition or subtraction of members, the stages of children's lives in the family, and changes in contacts between the family and other institutions (Ingoldsby, Smith, and Miller 2004). Different theorists offer different numbers of and names for these stages. Duvall's (1957) classic model consists of eight stages, with the salient roles and family tasks for each stage. Aldous (1996) offers a more concise model of four stages:

1. Formation/couples beginning
2. Childbearing/childrearing years
3. Children leaving home/the middle years
4. Elderly couple/the final years

Both of these models are grounded on the assumption that a couple who marry will raise their children together and grow old together. In fact, Laszloffy (2002) has charged that family development theory is flawed by an assumption of universality and an over-emphasis on single generational issues. However, Aldous (1996) has reworked her model of the family life career to be applicable to a wider variety of families, including people who have children and never marry, who have children before they marry, who marry and divorce but do not remarry, or who divorce and remarry.

The linkage between the arrival of children and decline in the quality of marital life is widely reported and found to be more complicated than it appears. For example, a recent study of Chinese couples links the arrival of children with lower marital quality and decreasing domestic inequality, but only for certain types of marriage (Pimentel 2000).

Sands and Goldberg-Glen's (2000) study of grandparents as primary caregivers for their grandchildren and of children and grandchildren as primary caregivers for parents and grandparents also reveal the value of family development theory. Older adults parenting their grandchildren are out of synch with conventional *age norms*. Relevant research (e.g., Dellmann-Jenkins, Blankenmeyer, and Pinkard 2000) shows an increase in social psychological stress and social service needs among members of this population.

Although some family scholars (Ingoldsby, Smith, and Miller 2004; White and Klein 2002) present *life course theory* as a strand of family developmental theory, others (e.g., Allen 1998) argue that life-course theory is a distinct school. Elder (1985, 2002, 2003), a pioneer of this theory, has focused a lifetime of study in which he relates human development to changing environments, especially socialization and educational processes. Beginning with his classic *Children of the Great Depression* (1974/1999), Elder's work has illuminated how the directions of individuals' lives are formed by social and historical context. This theory has inspired research in areas including child development (Hartup and Weinberg 2002), combat experience and emotional health, impairment, and resilience in later life (Elder 1986; Elder and Clipp 1989; Elder, Shanahan, and Clipp 1997), psychological stress (Elder, George, and Shanahan 1996), rural families (Conger and Elder 1994, Elder and Conger 2000), urban adolescents (Furstenberg et al. 1999), work–family dynamics (see Moen's work, represented in Box 2.1), and an impressive array of other longitudinal research studies (Phelps, Furstenberg, and Colby 2002).

BOX 2.3 "The Sacred Life Cycle of Families"
Fr. Craig Albrecht

A primary function of organized religion is ministering to family throughout the life cycle. In the Catholic Church, sacraments mark sacred points in family life, moments of grace that recall before the larger community the individual's relationship to family and others and to God. Ministry around the sacred cycle of families is a part of what has been called "the theology of the hatched, matched, and dispatched." Three of the most critical sacraments for Catholics occur at pivotal stages in the family life cycle: birth (baptism), marriage (matrimony), and death (anointing of the sick and reconciliation). Two more sacraments, holy communion (eucharist) and profession of faith (confirmation) signify the individual's entry into adulthood and connection to the greater human family.

Just as each family is uniquely defined by its history and lived experience, so each of these sacred rites marking transitions in the family life cycle uniquely reflects family development. Since at least the early Christian Church, infant baptism soon after birth has been the norm in the Roman Catholic Church. A child would live, grow, and be catechized in the life of the parish faith community until receiving first communion, and then, in the teen years, confirmation. Some years later the adult would perhaps celebrate marriage, reconciliation, or occasionally anointing of the sick.

Today, these norms are as different as families themselves. Baptism is as likely to occur anytime throughout the life cycle as in infancy. More couples than ever before live together prior to marriage. The Church discourages this practice as being detrimental to both the freedom to enter a sacramental relationship and the future stability of the marriage. Couples are marrying later in life and the incidence of divorce is almost as high for those who enter marriage as a Christian sacrament as for those who enter marriage as a purely civil union. Couples who continue regular family worship do, however, have lower rates of divorce than couples who do not.

Finally, regardless of faith practice, frequent worshipper and occasional practitioner at the time of death individuals and families want clergy present to anoint, for confession, or to celebrate the full funeral rites of the Church. From birth to death, the sacraments define in a most public way Christians' relationship to God and to family as we pass through the stages of family life and experience growth and development, change and transition.

Fr. Craig Albrecht is pastor of Sacred Heart Church and sacramental minister to St. Patrick Church, both in Merrill, Michigan. He also serves as chaplain to Nouvel Catholic Central High School in Saginaw, MI.

Family systems theory looks at the family as a whole unit, that is, a *system* composed of *subsystems* striving to maintain *equilibrium.* Family systems theory has been advanced by *family therapy* as a way to understand why patterns of family life, even negative patterns, persist, even across generations. Family systems theory helps us understand the principle of *boundaries*. This includes boundaries between the family and other families or between the family and other institutions, as well as boundaries between family members. Family systems theory may shed light on how partners' housework domains change following retirement from employment (Szinovacz 2000).

BOX 2.4   "Adoption in the Case of the Older Abused and Neglected Child"
Nan Beman, M.S.W.

A major life change like adoption requires that a social worker understand not only a child's connections with his or her family system, but the child's own understanding of those connections. In the following case, the social worker secured the entire family in order to engage the child in the idea of being adopted into a permanent family.

Eight years old when her birth parents' parental rights to her were legally terminated, Anna's only family consists of a paternal half-sister, Jenny, who lived with her own grandmother, Alice. Alice is the only adult from the extended family to maintain contact with Anna. At the time the social worker responsible for finding an adoptive home for Anna received the case, Anna was living in a temporary shelter waiting for a foster home placement.

Upon reviewing Anna's file, the social worker noted seven reports to child protection authorities, beginning at two months of age when Anna was found to have "failure to thrive." Anna's mother had never bonded to her daughter and, by consistent neglect and some physical abuse, eventually convinced authorities that she should never be Anna's parent again. Unfortunately, by the time this decision was ordered by the court, Anna had suffered years of instability.

Essentially, Anna believed that there would never be anyone who would care for her. Anna craved and at the same time distrusted intimacy. When someone was willing to care for Anna, she would behave in a way that made nurturing this child extremely difficult. She regularly attacked other children, threw tantrums, and broke household items. This behavior escalated as Anna grew older.

Alice was very concerned about Anna, and the social worker felt it was important for Anna to maintain this, the only family contact she had. Eventually, Anna was able to visit Alice and Jenny, but Alice was always very clear that she would never be able to be a full-time parent to Anna. On learning that Alice planned to adopt Jenny, Anna grew very angry and threatened to run away and live with her biological mother.

The social worker located Anna's mother and arranged a meeting between Anna and her mother. Anna's mother was able to help Anna understand that Anna had been given up, not because she was a "really bad kid," rather because the mother had problems and had done a very bad job being a mother. Anna's mother had also grown up in foster homes, and she told Anna that was not the life she wanted for Anna. This meeting was painful but powerful in moving Anna toward accepting an adoptive family.

The story does not end here. Anna was adopted by parents who have no other children. She lives close enough to Jenny and Alice to see them regularly. Although Anna does not see her birth mother, her adoptive parents know how to contact Anna's mother and can do so in the future.

Anna is now in mainstream schooling and has taken a break from therapy. The adoptive parents expect some serious regressions, but understand Anna's situation in terms of her connections to parent-, sibling-, and extended family subsystems. All of the possible support systems around Anna had to be brought together to prepare her to become attached to people that she did not know at all. This adoptive placement succeeded because Anna's family and social systems were incorporated into her future.

Nan Beman, M.S.W., has over 25 years of experience in social work for child welfare. She is State Programs Administrator Coordinator for the Minnesota Department of Human Services.

Both family development and family systems theories address the change (and stability) of families. However, anthropologists and sociologists also focus on the family as a social institution and how individual families are embedded in economic, historical, social, and other contexts. In the next section, we use three *macrosocial* theories as keys to understanding families in context.

Three Keys for Understanding Families in Context

Conflict theory views the family as a replication of social relations in society in general, seeing relations that develop over time to benefit some groups over others. On the societal level, conflict theorists may speak of the "haves" and "have nots," and of the former having a *vested interest* in maintaining the *status quo* or current state of affairs in social relations. As a macrosocial theory, conflict theory focuses less on individuals as the source of *oppression* and more on the power of *ideology* to serve as a justification for sexist, racist, homophobic, or other social structural systems that keep some groups from enjoying the advantages and privileges of other groups. For example, conflict theory illuminates the significance of "protective" labor laws that limited the hours and conditions of women's employment, coincidentally serving as a means of ensuring women's economic dependence on fathers and husbands. Conflict theory may also help understand religious and other sources of opposition to extending family entitlements to gay and lesbian family unions.

BOX 2.5 "On Being a (Lesbian) Family in American Society"
Melissa Sheridan Embser-Herbert, Ph.D.

Compared to many other lesbian families across the country, we are incredibly fortunate in that we live in Minnesota in the early 21st century. Yet, as a lesbian family, there are plenty of hurdles in addition to those faced by the typical heterosexual family.

First, we had to locate a sperm bank that was willing to provide sperm to a "single" woman. This wasn't difficult, as it has been in years past, but we also wanted one that would be affirming of our choice, as a lesbian couple, to begin a family. We were successful there, too, but thank goodness for the Internet and overnight mail!

We were able to work with a lesbian attorney on the reams of paperwork that an unmarried, yet committed, couple needs to ensure that each person has legal protections should something happen to the other. For example, unlike a birth dad, if my partner had died while giving birth, I would have had no legal relationship with a surviving infant. Because we live in a place that allows second-parent adoptions I was able to adopt our son within weeks of his birth. But, had I been the husband of a woman who had become pregnant via donor insemination I would have automatically had parental rights and would not have had to spend the time and money securing status as an adoptive parent. In the interim, I carried a medical power of attorney with me so that I would be able to consent to medical care for our son should the need arise.

During the pregnancy, my partner and I were lucky to work with health care personnel who were very supportive and nonjudgmental. Yet, there were the puzzled observers—"Uh, yes, we're both prospective parents and, yes, I'm an active participant in this process." At the hospital, the staff was as understanding as those at the clinic had been. Well, there was the Personal Care Attendant who thought I must be the grandma...We theorized that she had no other framework for two women so involved in the birth and I *am* a few years older—though not old enough to be my partner's mother!

But, even with all the positive experiences, we face constant challenges to our family and have concerns about the future. My partner and I cannot file taxes together. Only one of us can take the dependent deduction. The implications of having to file taxes separately are far too complex to address here, but know that there are significant financial consequences for not being considered a family, or even a household, in terms of tax law.

Fortunately, our employers include domestic partners in health coverage. If this were not the case, one of us would have to pay for family coverage while the other paid for single coverage. This is the case for many GLBT families. In thinking about our son's day care, we have to be careful that those with whom we entrust his care do not "have issues" about his having two moms. We were alarmed when we heard that a caregiver in another room of our son's day care had attributed one boy's misbehavior to the fact that he has two moms. We have to be on constant alert, especially where our son is concerned. Do we have it better than most lesbian families in this country? Yes. Do we face constant challenges to our status as a family? Yes. But, is it worth it? My answer would be a resounding, "Yes."

Melissa Sheridan Embser-Herbert and her family live in St. Paul, MN, where she is an Associate Professor of Sociology at Hamline University.

Structural functional theory begins with an entirely different set of assumptions about society. Rather than viewing society as a system of oppositional camps, structural functionalists see the persistence of society as rooted in *value consensus*. The family *institution* is organized around patterns of *values* (ideas about what is good and right) and *norms* (expected patterns of behaviors). Such a predictable, agreed-on set of structures ensures that families will meet certain important *functions* necessary for a society to persevere. The family in contemporary American society does not play the dominant part in economic production that it plays in other cultures or that it played in earlier times in American history. Nonetheless, the American family continues to function as the primary institution responsible for *child socialization*, *economic support*, and *emotional security*.

Parsons (Parsons and Bales 1955) foretold dire consequences if the roles traditionally assigned to women and men became blurred. He predicted that as women undertook more *instrumental* roles associated with earning a living for the family (roles he ascribed to their husbands), their performance of their *expressive* roles would suffer. He also predicted this shift would inevitably result in greater marital instability and compromises to the socialization of children. To an extent, his predictions have come true. Employed women do have higher divorce rates than do other women. (After all, employed women have greater economic options to remaining in a dangerous or unsatisfactory marriage.) However, marital stability—or the absence of divorce—cannot be construed to be the equivalent of either successful performance of family roles or conjugal happiness.

The functionalist perspective, although not as influential as in earlier decades, still offers insights into families in society. Onaga, McKinney, and Pfaff (2000) apply the concept of *functions* in their assessment of community-based programs for people with psychiatric conditions. Their research indicates that such programs serve many of the same purposes for people with psychiatric conditions as do families.

BOX 2.6   "The Imperative of Fathers"
Leon C. Intrater, Ph.D.

The strength of paternal relevance is witnessed by the statement "I have a father who loves me," even among children who have not seen or heard from their fathers for many years. I have also witnessed numerous child custody hearings during which fathers' parenting weaknesses are inflated and strengths minimized in the legal battlefield, leaving children and other family members with erroneous, frustrated, and hateful perceptions of men who may be well-meaning and capable fathers.

I recall the case of a 17-year old homeless teen I accompanied to court to establish *no fault dependency status.* These proceedings would allow her to live in an independent living program and to benefit from state-funded educational, social, and other youth services. At a legal hearing regarding the guardianship status of a minor child, the proceedings required the presence of the girl's father. This man had been incarcerated for 13 years for the murder of her sibling. At the hearing to establish the state of Illinois as her legal guardian, the father was brought to court, ankles shackled and accompanied by two correctional officers, each holding a rifle. The father had a swastika tattooed on his forehead and maintained a look of anger during the entire process. However, in the courtroom, this 17-year-old girl (who had not seen her father since she was 4 years old) ran to him crying, "Daddy! Daddy!" with (as she later verbally verified) no thought of personal fear or danger.

In this, and in so many other instances, the child's perception of *father* is so much more complicated than his role as mere breadwinner. Father is not the less important parent who, in time, will not matter to children. Certainly, some fathers abandon or otherwise fail their children, but even absent or seriously flawed fathers will not be "gotten over." Through my work in psychotherapy with "fatherless" children and fathers who have been, for one or more various reasons, blocked from having full or any influence on the development of their children, I am convinced that fathers are not "options" but rather are imperatives in children's and families' development.

Leon C. Intrater, Ph.D., a psychologist, is founder of *Neon Street Center for Homeless Youth,* a national program of the YMCA of Metropolitan Chicago. He has over 20 years of experience in direct service and management in public and private mental health programs.

The final theory in this section, *family ecology theory*, presents the family as embedded in a set of environments—human-built, social–cultural, and natural physical–biological (Bubolz and Sontag 1993). These environments are not entirely deterministic but set constraints and opportunities for families referred to as *social capital.*

Crosnoe's (2004) study is but one that examines the extent to which social capital in families and schools overlap to shape adolescent development. In a nationally representative study, Crosnoe found that adolescents who had more social capital at home in the form of emotional closeness often reaped greater benefit from social capital at school. In other words, emotional closeness between parents and their adolescents appears to be an effective channel for transmitting social capital, for example, in the form of parents' aspirations for their children and parents' involvement at school, which enables those children to take better advantage of social capital at school.

In another study which reviewed 19 programs aimed at promoting healthy choices by adolescents in the area of sexuality, Meschke, Bartholomae, and Zentall (2000) found parenting to be related to adolescent sexual behavior through communication, values, monitoring, and a sense of connection with the teen. Their findings led them to support incorporating ecological models in the design and evaluation of programs designed to foster healthy choices about sexuality among teens.

An ecological approach suggests that social policymakers should consider developing a *family impact statement*, much like an environmental impact statement, when contemplating legislation or social action that might compromise or expand the potential for families to succeed. This concept is discussed further in chapter 14.

BOX 2.7 "Grace Under Pressure"
Laura Charles

My husband and I were excited to go to have our first ultrasound to see our child. We had a miscarriage the year before and we were hoping this would ease our minds. All of my appointments had showed progress and each time we heard a strong heartbeat. During the first 20 weeks, we read classic children's books and wrote letters to our unborn child. We scoured every child-care book and I was meticulous about what I ate. Mostly, we dreamed about what our child would be like.

As I lay down with the cold metal equipment being swished across my belly, my husband and I giggled nervously. The technician then told us she was having a hard time seeing any details because the amniotic fluid was so low. The doctor came in and asked if I had been leaking. "No," I replied, "definitely not." He said we would have to see a specialist. We asked, "But everything will be okay, right?" He said, "Potentially."

The specialist told us our baby had no kidneys and that his condition was "incompatible with life." The doctor asked did we want to "terminate the pregnancy now or carry it to term?" I couldn't even look at her. We just kept crying together as we held sweaty hands.

Later we decided to carry the baby as long as possible. We had more memories to make. For 4 months we waited to hold him, knowing in the end he would die. We found a support group online which helped the most because the other participants were going through exactly the same thing we were. We read books about preparing for birth and death at the same time. How could we bury our child? And yet, planning for that kept us sane. We learned that crying is healthy and talking is therapeutic. We held a small rock with the word "hope" engraved on it. We found friends and family who would let us talk freely, cry with us, and sometimes even get angry with us. We held tightly to our faith and prayed often.

We were blessed with a beautiful baby at 37 weeks gestation. He was alive for 90 minutes. We held him, kissed him, and took many pictures. Six months later, we continue to meet both online and in person with two support groups. We see him in the sunsets, the bunnies that hop across our yard, and in the new growth in the garden we planted for him.

Laura Charles is an elementary school art teacher. She and her husband Kevin live in Minneapolis and now have a son, Noah.

Multiple Perspectives

In the preceding section, we organized seven theories for understanding families according to their unit of analysis. In exchange and symbolic interaction theories, we have two mirrors for understanding families as face-to-face interactions. In family developmental and family systems theories, we have two prisms for understanding families as greater than the sum of their parts. In conflict, structural functional, and family ecology theories we have three keys to understanding families in the contexts of the larger society.

Presenting these theories as we have, implying they are mutually exclusive explanations for family life, is both misleading and limiting. No one theory effectively provides a complete in-depth view that encompasses the complicated nature of families. Deeper understanding calls for the use of multiple perspectives. For example, Marsiglio, Hutchinson, and Cohan (2000) draw on both symbolic interaction and life-course (family development) theories to understand fatherhood readiness and fathering visions among young men who have not yet fathered a child. The obvious response to this challenge is to seek to exploit multiple paradigms whenever possible.

Another option is to consider perspectives that offer multiple lenses on families. As described in chapter 1, gender is a critical aspect of family. Walker (1999) reminds us that gender shapes partnerships, parenthood, work, and kinship. *Feminism* argues that gender matters not only to the quality of life of women but also to the internal workings of families and to the place of families in society. From a feminist perspective, male dominance damages not only women but also families, children, and men and men's relationships with women as well as with other men.

In their analysis of scholarship in three key family studies journals (*Family Relations, Journal of Family Issues, Journal of Marriage and the Family*), Thompson and Walker (1995: 847) argued that feminism has found a place in the discipline, albeit "often at the margins of family scholarship rather than at the center." Still, they identified five themes in family studies with strong cores of feminist scholarship:

1. Social construction of gender as a central concept
2. Commitment to gender equality and social change
3. Feminist practice
4. Centrality of women's lives and experiences
5. Questioning "the family"

Baber and Allen (1992: 1) offer one feminist stance on women's experiences in families. From their perspective:

> . . . families, particularly those based on traditional ideologies and practices, are tension-filled arenas, loci of struggle and domination between genders and across generations. . . . women's lives are constrained by even their most intimate and caring relationships. . . . [but] women [find ways to] resist domination and become innovators in the family nexus of caring and struggle.

Baber and Allen (1992) analyze sexualities, reproductive, caregiving, and work, but conclude with a set of basic requirements for feminist families: economic autonomy, relational equality and choice, reproductive freedom, and lifelong education for a critical consciousness.

BOX 2.8 "Designing a Feminist Family"
Nancy Gruver and Joe Kelly

For 21 years, we've managed to create a working feminist family. But it didn't always look like we could.

"Joe, I can't get the babies to stop crying!" Nancy was on the phone, frantic, "I need you to come home."

Working a shift alone at The Shelter, Joe said, "I'm the only one here; I have to answer the phone and we're full tonight. It's my job."

Nancy replied, "But we were going to share this! I need help with the kids."

Pressures on our commitment to peer marriage came from the start, when our first child turned out to be two—unexpected twin girls. We chaotically tried holding together our careful (and naive) plans to balance work, individual pursuits and the first kid singular.

We both kept our jobs (by choice and necessity), but worked part-time on opposite schedules. Usually, only one of us was home with the kids (and colic, allergies, etc.). Joe wore two *Snugglies* on his chest, frustrated that he wasn't a woman, with female-folklore training and X-chromosome instinct to calm a child.

He'd call Nancy at the gallery she managed. "What am I supposed to do? They only eat 2 ounces, then fall asleep. Then the colic kicks in, they wake up and seem hungry. But I can't tell. Help!"

Nancy replied, "A customer just walked in, Honey. I'll be home by six. Try calling my Mom."

Feminists when we married, we vowed to live the partnership and its responsibilities equally. True, Joe spent a tad more time watching baseball than vacuuming. Nancy gardened a tad more often than she tuned up the 1974 Gremlin.

But then came the crucible of parenting twins. Perhaps it was more of a volcano; filled with mystery and warmth, fire and brimstone. In the forge of raising these daughters we'd prove whether or not feminist principles or patriarchal practices would out.

Even at their smallest, our little women were amazing people. Like every child, they were miracles in their own lives and ours. Still, Nancy wanted to be a person first and then a mother, with an outside work life. Even with their extraordinary demands, she wanted other realms—and felt deeply guilty about it. "They're so tiny and needy; am I heartless to put my needs first?" Meanwhile, Joe battled the *Provider Demon*. "Fathers provide. I work part-time at lousy pay. We're on WIC in a rat-hole apartment. How can I be such an inadequate provider for my daughters?" Many times, we felt we were letting our kids down by choosing to meet our very personal needs (time away from the babies for Nancy and more time with them for Joe). Those desires flouted the roles defined for mom and dad by our culture, but ignoring them was wasted effort. In the end, our "selfishness" didn't have a negative effect.

Listening to our hearts' desires, we forged a family where all four of us get support to dream our personal dreams and then try to live them, wacky or inconvenient as they seem. That's our definition of a feminist family.

Nancy Gruver and *Joe Kelly* are parents of twin daughters, Nia Kelly and Mavis Gruver. They founded *New Moon: The Magazine for Girls and Their Dreams* (www.newmoon.org), where Nancy is publisher. Joe is executive director of the national nonprofit organization, *Dads and Daughters* (www.dadsanddaughters.org).

In contrast to the theories presented earlier in this section, advocates of *postmodernism* see preconceived assumptions and principles as biasing studies of family life. Postmodernists contend that the search for unifying principles to understand societal arrangements, including family dynamics, changes, and contexts, is futile. They see all reality as created through interpersonal interaction, yet infinitely subjective (Winton 1995). Furthermore, postmodernists analyze contemporary life through *linguistic narratives*, that is, patterns of language and other forms of communication.

Writing of the postmodern family, Ritzer (2000: 141–2) describes the "kitchen as filling station."

> The [family] meal is probably not what it once was. Following the fast food model, people have even more options to "graze," "refuel," nibble on this, or snack on that rather than sit down at a formal meal. Also, because it may seem inefficient to do nothing but just eat, families are likely to watch television or play computer games while they are eating. The din, to say nothing of the lure, of dinnertime TV programs such as *Wheel of Fortune* and of the "bings" and "whines" associated with computer games is likely to make it difficult for family members to interact with one another. We need to decide if we can afford the loss . . .

The challenge of postmodernism may be to differentiate between a postmodern society and productive efforts to understand families in that kind of society. Some family studies scholars seem to be making that leap. Merkle and Richardson (2000) have examined "digital dating" on the Internet, with an eye toward developing an understanding of how this technology, available on a large, impersonal scale, will impact that most intimate of life choices, mate selection.

BOX 2.9   "Family Reunification for Runaway Youth"
Aaron Hagebak

Trust and confidence are difficult to establish with youth in crisis. Likewise, understanding of the complex structures of families and the subtle layers of their relationships often eludes those working to reestablish connections between youth and their families. Every family's reality is vastly different due to culture and experience. My job is to help families reveal their own resources to mend wounds and to lessen strife at home.

When I encounter youth and their families at the *Bridge*, they are deeply entrenched in their discord. Because there is often little time to work with youth and their families in our short-term residential facility, the work must be focused and to the point. My role is to facilitate families' use of conversation to enable them to discover possibilities and options, strengths and capacities that have been overshadowed by crisis. Such a postmodern approach to family counseling revolves around stories as a means for the storyteller to convey a social context for the crisis. I help youth and their family members develop a line of questioning that is neither invasive nor judgmental, thereby enabling all of us to see a picture painted by the family in their own words.

A 14-year-old girl and her mother and stepfather may come to see us late one night. All three of them have different perceptions of the problem, as well as dissimilar solutions. The girl thinks she has too little freedom and that her mother loves her stepfather more than her mother loves her. The parents think their daughter does not respect them and fear that she may be using drugs. At home no one hears the others because of the constant yelling and fighting. When they come for family counseling, the counselor makes sure everyone's voice is heard and that they communicate their feelings about the issues. A short stay in our shelter may be useful for the girl so everyone can have a break and some time to think about the situation in a new light. When they come back together to talk again, there is more hope in the air, as each person lays out dreams for the future and steps to achieve goals on which all three family members can agree.

These narrative techniques, combined with solution-based therapies, provide families with a means to seek authentic solutions drawn from their own experiences and family contexts. Our goal during therapy is for youth and their families to feel safe and respected, empowered and uplifted, and, whenever possible, reunited. Our success is grounded in our view that, through narrative methods, families can reveal to themselves the very strengths on which they can draw to find their way in the face of crisis.

Aaron Hagebak is currently Program Coordinator at *The Bridge for Runaway Youth*, a short-term residential facility for youth that are estranged from their families, in Minneapolis.

Some family scholars have attempted to synthesize different theories. For example, Baber and Murray (2001: 23) offer a postmodern feminist approach to teaching human sexuality. They begin with the assumption that all theory is socially constructed and that even contradictory or incoherent experiences can lead to personally and professionally useful information. Baber and Murray extend students' thinking about diversity and emphasize a strengths (vs. problem) approach. They aim to provide students with the tools to maximize their own sexual health and minimize sexual exploitation of themselves and others.

In "Family Theory Versus the Theories Families Live By," Daly (2003) offers a criticism of the relevance of family theories. He (771) finds "a significant disjunction between the way families live their lives and the way we theorize about families." Daly argues that many everyday family concerns, for example, emotions, myths, and spirituality, are inadequately addressed by family theories. Clearly, the next generation of family scholars has much work to do.

RESEARCH METHODS: SYSTEMATIC TECHNIQUES FOR GATHERING INFORMATION ABOUT FAMILIES

Family scholars have an array of research methods from which to choose. In this section, we describe five of those techniques, the advantages along with the hazards of each. We conclude by recommending the consideration of multiple methods, as well as longitudinal and comparative studies.

Experiments

Experiments rarely come first to mind when we think of studying families. After all, how do you bring a family into a laboratory? We discuss the problem of validity later in this section, but first offer the experiment as a model against which other methods can be measured. The experimental method also provides an ability to determine *causal* relationships between variables.

Family researchers have applied experimental methods to families with encouraging results. For example, Fagan and Stevenson (2002) conducted an experimental study of a parenting intervention for African-American Head Start fathers. Fathers recruited in a Head Start agency were randomly assigned to either a control group who viewed a videotape series on parenting or to an experimental group who participated in "Men as

Teachers." "Men as Teachers" is a curriculum of six components: the role of fathers, the need to challenge racism in society, reasons why men abuse their children, and three sessions on child rearing.

Among the fathers in the experimental group, Fagan and Stevenson (2002) found significant improvement in attitudes about their ability to teach their pre-school-age children. Fathers in the experimental group also showed significant gains in self-esteem and parenting satisfaction. Fagan and Stevenson's experiment indicates programs with features that empower fathers have the potential to influence in positive ways African-American Head Start fathers' parenting attitudes.

In another study, Jacob and Leonard (1988) brought 49 married male alcoholics and their wives into a laboratory on three separate occasions. First, researchers used couples' responses to develop two topics for behavioral change for each couple. In the next two visits to the laboratory, each couple was videotaped discussing one topic.

The researchers made alcoholic beverages available during one session but not during the other. The experimental treatment of the availability of alcohol was coupled with the researchers randomly designating the second and third nights as "dry" or "wet." Furthermore, Jacob and Leonard (1988) had information on whether the alcoholic husbands' drinking patterns were "steady" or "episodic." For the steady-drinking husbands, Jacob and Leonard observed not only more negativity among the wives but also more problem-solving behavior among the couples during "drink night." Jacob and Leonard concluded that in families with steady-drinking alcoholics, problem solving might reinforce alcohol use because drinking episodes enables marital interaction, which contributes at some level to problem solving.

A classic experiment involves:

- *Randomization*: random assignment of subjects
- *Control group*: observed but not treated during the procedure
- *Experimental group or groups*: observed both before and after a treatment is administered
- *Observations*: data recorded for both the control and the experimental groups both before and after the time a treatment is administered

If observations of the experimental group differ before and after the treatment is administered, then the researcher finds support for the conclusion that the treatment caused the change between the first and second. This conclusion can only be drawn, however, if observations of the control group (which did not receive the treatment but was merely observed) do not change during the experiment. Finally, the strength of conclusion of causality is directly related to researchers' confidence that they have maintained both the control group and the experimental group under comparable conditions.

One problem with experiments is that of *validity*. Is family behavior in a laboratory setting a true picture of family behavior? Do family members interact in artificial ways when they are placed in unfamiliar circumstances and observed, even covertly, by researchers? For this reason and others (e.g., ethical concerns for manipulating intimate relationships), the use of experimental methods is limited and usually of a quasiexperimental nature.

Observation

Observation methods address problems of validity by examining the family in uncontrived settings ostensibly engaging in customary behavior. A researcher may be an *unobtrusive observer*, examining the family unknown to the members. Also, a researcher may be a *participant observer*, engaging in the social action either known or unknown to those being studied.

The use of observation has a long tradition in studies of families. Rosenblatt and Fischer (1993) applaud Thomas and Znaniecki's *The Polish Peasant in Europe and America* (1918–1920) for their record of the family lives of immigrants in Chicago in the first decades of the 20th century. Stack's (1974) *All Our Kin: Strategies for Survival in a Black Community* has long been cited as an exemplar of observational research on poor families coping with everyday situations.

Observational research has advantages and risks. Observers risk ethical compromise if they engage in deception, not revealing the true nature of their presence to those being studied. In doing so, if their true mission is discovered, they risk alienating subjects. Participant observers, on the other hand, risk *going native* to the extent that they become so immersed in the social milieu they are observing that their objectivity is compromised. They may also find themselves witness to unsettling or even illegal situations. Besides the potential for personal compromise, social scientists (unlike attorneys, clergy, or physicians) are not protected by anything like *client privilege* from legal prosecution.

However, beyond the opportunity to examine families in their natural settings, observational research often reveals a level of qualitative richness that is unmatched by other research methods. The path to that rich data is, however, a long and costly one. Gaining the trust of subjects and developing an authentic appreciation for their social worlds is a labor-intensive undertaking. Even then, the best observational research is open to criticisms concerning *reliability*. That is, observers must be concerned that the observations noted cannot be accepted as credible and accurate representations of family life beyond that actually observed.

Surveys

From Blood and Wolf's (1960) interviews with wives in Detroit in the 1950s through the *National Survey of Families and Households* almost a half century later (e.g., Presser 2000), use of the *survey* has a long history in family studies. Surveys are an efficient way to gather information about not only attitudes but also past behaviors and present intentions. Furthermore, the perceived anonymity accorded by a *questionnaire*, either of the familiar "pen-and-paper" variety or a newer electronic variety, may enhance respondents' willingness to provide honest responses.

A skillfully administered *interview*, face to face, by telephone, or by another method, may also yield useful data. However, researchers must be sensitive to the *social desirability effect*, the likelihood that respondents will choose to answer in ways that make a favorable impression on the interviewer.

Pretesting questions, including both *close-ended* and *open-ended*, as well as conducting a *pilot study* using the entire survey protocol, can do much to correct hazards associated with this method. Ultimately, the extent to which survey results can be inferred as applicable to a larger population depends on the degree to which the survey was administered to a *representative sample*. Treas and Giesen (2000) have achieved such a nationally representative sample of married or cohabiting American couples. Their research enables them to conclude that sexual infidelity is most likely "among those with stronger sexual interests, more permissive sexual values, lower subjective satisfaction with their union, weaker network ties to partner, and greater sexual opportunity" (48).

Case Studies

In 1996, Pipher followed publication of *Reviving Ophelia: Saving the Selves of Adolescent Girls* (1994) with another book based on her reflections on stories and *case studies* drawn from counseling families in Lincoln, Nebraska. In *The Shelter of Each Other: Rebuilding Our Families* she wrote of the anguished families she met through her *clinical* practice.

> ... hate-filled, violent families, families with addictions, families in which the parents were not grown ups and the children had no childhoods and families in which the children were starving for moral nourishment. I know how destructive families can be, how stifling and riddled with pain. But I also know that this is not the whole, or even the most interesting part of the story. (Pipher 1996: 3–4)

Both books were "best sellers," offering readers glimpses into the lives of families who were experiencing troubles like their own or like families they knew or imagined.

Pipher's (1996) undergraduate training in anthropology and *ethnography* has served her well. She opens *The Shelter of Each Other* with a story from the case of her own family. She evocatively describes the setting of a conversation during a family camping trip when her son Zeke was 10 and her daughter Sara was 4.

> A moon the shape and color of a pumpkin rose over the lake. Sara snuggled into her father and said a line so beautiful that I can quote it fifteen years later: "I'm melting into richness." (Pipher 1996: 1)

Her son Zeke told his parents about a boy he knew, a boy who reportedly saved his mother from a mugger. Zeke shared that he hoped a robber would break into their house because "Nothing would make me happier than saving our family from bad guys." Such stories, whether offered as personal narrative in research or in case study in clinical practice, reveal much about the quality of a family's everyday experiences.

The case study method was applied to good effect in a study of differences in vocabulary between children born to low-income adolescent mothers (Luster et al. 2000). The children were administered the *Peabody Picture Vocabulary Test-Revised* at the time they were making the transition to kindergarten. The researchers found compelling differences between the children who scored in the top and those who scored in the bottom quartiles, but used case studies to powerfully illustrate how the circumstances and experiences of the most and least successful children differ.

Case studies often offer a "good read," telling as they do stories, especially *personal narratives,* in which individuals are afforded an opportunity to say, in their own words, what their lives mean to them. Our own research on single mothers' families and futures inspired the title of the book you are reading. We examined the demographic, family history, and social psychological cases of over two dozen single mothers. We then invited these women to tell us, in their own words, how they viewed themselves as mothers and what they envisioned in the future for themselves and their children (Grochowski and Karraker 2000, Karraker and Grochowski 2000).

Over and over again these women told us (often in these very words and with this inflection): "I am a *good* mother!" (Karraker and Grochowski 1997) When juxtaposed against findings from the larger body of research conclusions drawn from studies using other methods, this comment was pointedly revealing. In contrast to the survey research that finds these women hopelessly deficient in parenting and life management skills, these women possessed high self-esteem and low alienation. Furthermore, they were emboldened enough to claim a positive identity for themselves and to take active possession of their futures.

Sprey (2000) argues that theorizing, and particularly discovery, in family studies would be enhanced by greater use of imagination and metaphor. We believe this is consistent with an emphasis on narrative in general and storytelling in particular. *Grounded theory*, theory that flows inductively from observations rather than being deduced from abstract theories, holds special promise for revealing the social construction of identity and other family dynamics. Hill and Thomas (2000) have used such techniques in their study of the development of racial identity in interracial partner relationships. Haworth-Hoeppner (2000) has also used a grounded theory approach with open-ended interviews in her efforts to understand the role of culture and family in the production of eating disorders.

The problem of *generalizability*, present to an extent in all research methods, is particularly imperious in case studies. The very reason that Sigmund Freud's (1963) cases are so intriguing is those accounts tell of interpretations of dreams and other interpretations of the subconscious far removed from the day to day experience of most readers. With a critical eye, we must ask the extent to which Freud's conclusions about human psychology and relationships, including family relationships involving incest and parent–child interactions, was severely limited by his practice with upper middle-class Viennese women in the 19th century.

Archival Research

International organizations such as the *Guttmacher Institute* and the *World Health Organization*, federal agencies such as the *United States Bureau of the Census* and the *Department of Education*, as well as state and some county and city bodies, employ large numbers of demographers, economists, and sociologists. These social scientists systematically collect statistics and analyze data on a wide variety of topics germane to family life, including sexuality and population, maternal and infant health, employment and income, and educational achievement and aspirations. Much of this *archival research* is available and accessible to the public.

Beyond those and other official sources of archival data, historians, women's studies scholars, and other researchers turn to such disparate sources of information on families as diaries, letters to the editor, parish records, and other existing data to document the everyday lives of families. A poignant example of family life in the early history of the Minnesota territory is found in the letters between Lizzie Caleff Bowler and her husband James Madison ("Mad") Bowler, an enlisted man and officer in the Third Minnesota Volunteer Infantry Regiment during the Civil War (Fitzharris, 1996: 16). After the birth of their daughter Lizzie wrote that their daughter

> ... was so cross [with colic]. I wish you were here to help me take care of her some of those long nights.

Lizzie also wrote that she would not join Mad in Arkansas as her sister

> Kate [had] one foot in the grave and the other almost there, ... [she] is nothing but a skelaton [sic] she does not attempt to walk any more ... her mind is so weakened it is like that of a child.

Although archival research may represent substantial savings in terms of convenience and cost of data collection (costs offset by the difficulty of locating and gaining access to records in an interpretable form), scholars hoping to exploit archived data are faced with the problem of compounded errors. Even if research collected by others for purposes other than research on families is relevant to the family issues under investigation, that research may be tainted by such errors as selective recording or retention and "corrections" and other changes made by sometimes well-intentioned recorders of the day.

Triangulation and Research Across Time and Space

Social research is costly in terms of direct expenses associated with data collection, as well as the absence of a guarantee that a line of research will yield interesting or significant findings. Some excellent texts on methodology advise those conducting social research to employ multi-method techniques, sometimes called *triangulation*. When their initial efforts to use mail questionnaires yielded very low response rates, McGraw, Zvonkovic, and Walker (2000) added focus groups and "loosely structured" (71) qualitative telephone interviews for a study of work and family processes of commercial fishermen and their wives. While the introduction of multiple methods was apparently initially motivated by a desire to improve data quality, the consequence was to recast the research. McGraw, Zvonkovic, and Walker (72) came to the realization that

> Researchers can intentionally create the potential for participants to affirm their lives and personal relationships or discover discontent within themselves.

In this case, the application of multiple methods resulted not only in enhanced data quality but also in revelation of different agendas between researchers and participants and consequent ethical implications.

Much like approaching a question from multiple theoretical perspectives, the meaningful study of families calls for the use of surveys that can yield highly *quantitative* findings and observational and case studies that can offer *qualitative* richness and depth. In other words, family studies demand consideration of the full range of methodologies available.

Two additional methodological techniques warrant mention here. Just as families are not static but dynamic, evolving organisms, research needs to examine families across time and space. *Longitudinal* research in which the same families are followed over a period of time lends insights into changes across the family life cycle and the life span of family members. For example, although alcohol use is known to increase during adolescence, six waves of interviews with a sample of adolescents indicates that parental support and parental monitoring curb the development of patterns of alcohol misuse among adolescents (Barnes et al. 2000).

Comparative studies allow family studies scholars to examine families relative to different cultures *(cross-cultural)* or *historical* periods. Stenberg's (2000) study of the transmission of welfare dependency across generations is an interesting example of research that attempts to extend our understanding of families and family processes across societies. Using a longitudinal data set and focusing on Sweden, Stenberg found indications that welfare dependency was transmitted across generations, but that children who did not show a combination of other problems related, for example, to poor school adjustment and parental criminality, did not show signs of intergenerational dependency. In conducting this research on an ethnically homogeneous population, Stenberg's research offers insights into the interaction of welfare dependency with race.

Obviously, both longitudinal and comparative studies have special problems, not the least of which is retention of participants for the duration of a long-term study. For over two decades Booth and his colleagues on the *Marital Instability over the Life Course* project have moved beyond a mere description to a deeper explanation of long-time married life (Amato and Booth 1995; Booth and Edwards 1985, 1989; Booth et al. 1986; Myers and Booth 1996, 1999). If we hope to move beyond a myopic view of families as fixed in the culture in which we live at this time, family studies must embrace more comparative research agenda such as those represented by Haas's (1986) cross-national investigation of American and Swedish wives' orientation to bread winning. Special issues such as the September 2000 volume of *Journal of Family Psychology* move to address such concerns by examining not only families in other cultures, but also cultural variations within American society.

Evaluation Research

Evaluation research joins these other research methods and bridges the gap between family scholarship and family practice. For example, mediation services and parent education are increasingly offered to families experiencing divorce. Hughes and Kirby (2000) surveyed mediators, parent educators, judges, and attorneys and found that attorneys perceived mediation services and parent education less useful and effective than did mediators, parent educators, and judges. Mediators, parent educators, and legal professionals most commonly mentioned "less legal involvement, more parental agreements, and better adjustment of family members" as indicators of the success of mediation (58).

Most mediation programs were established in the 1990s, but empirical research on the effectiveness of such programs is not conclusive (Hughes and Kirby 2000). Curiously then, Hughes and Kirby found that although most parent educators in their study reported collecting some evaluation data, less than half of the mediators did so. They call for improving the evaluation of mediation and parent education programs for families experiencing divorce. They recommend focusing on efficacy, effectiveness, and cost effectiveness.

CONCLUSIONS: HOW WILL YOU EXPLORE FAMILIES IN MEANINGFUL, REALISTIC, ETHICAL WAYS?

Social Science Investigation, Professional Practice, and Personal Lived Experience

Sociology and psychology, the social science traditions that have most shaped scholarly traditions in family studies, have a long history of admonishing students of the family to maintain an objective, "value-free" perspective on our subject of investigation. Likewise, clergy, physicians, social workers, and other professionals are required to retain clear boundaries between themselves and the families and individuals under their care. These standards are difficult to achieve and maintain, but are intended to insure research and intervention are conducted in an objective way and research conclusions and care plans are not tainted by personal *bias*.

After all, personal lived experience is always lurking in the background of social scientific research, coloring the issues we choose to investigate, the methods we apply to those issues, and the interpretations and conclusions we draw from our findings. Not only scholars but also professionals serving families meet each professional challenge with their own histories and experiences that are embedded in their own class, ethnicity, gender, race, religion, and other social contexts.

In other words, all of us seeking to understand families—researchers and professionals—must be aware of the extent to which our lived experience can lead us to *ethnocentrism*, assumptions and judgments based on our own experiences. In similar ways, because we each encounter culture and society from the perspective of people with certain class, race, gender, and other identities, as well as sexual orientations or fears, the specters of *classism, racism, sexism, heterosexism,* or *homophobia* threaten to cloud our understanding of families in society.

Writing of "Theory and Human Values," White (2005: 161) observed:

> For many of us, this cry to put values back into our science and research raises thorny problems—such as whose values, and the issue of bias and credibility. . . . I think real [scientific] progress is only achieved when scholars research what they find interesting or fun or of value.

However, even if it were possible, wholesale dismissal of personal lived experience risks missing the opportunity to peer through a crystal window on families. Each of us has personally experienced, in a limited but crystal-clear way, satisfying and positive as well as dissatisfying and negative family relationships. We invite you to be mindful of the crystal window of personal, lived experience which can be a source of bias, but also a source of inspiration.

Ethical Imperatives

Bias has an insidious way of being more than merely a matter of the intrusion of oppositional attitudes into family research and practice. Bias may also be manifest in disregard for the welfare of families, their members, or their communities. In this way, bias may translate not just into poorly executed research or practice, but also into research and practice that places families, their members, and their communities in positions of risk to physical, psychological, or social well-being.

Social scientists studying families should adhere to certain principles. At the outset, researchers have a responsibility to carefully weigh the potential for physical, psychological, or social harm against the potential gains of the research. This can be called a *subject risk/research benefit ratio*. Participants should be instructed on the nature of the research and any attendant hazards so they can extend or withhold their permission to participate, that is, *informed consent*. Participants should be assured of *confidentiality* in circumstances where revelation of their identity, participation, or responses could place them at risk of damaged relationships or reputation. *Human subjects committees* or *institutional review boards* of organizations that fund or sponsor research may enforce these and other ethical obligations.

Researchers may also argue a certain degree of subject risk is justified by the potential benefits that may eventually accrue from the research. For example, asking rape victims to discuss sexual assault may compromise a victim's sense of well being and safety. As a stipulation of funding such a project, the *National Institutes of Mental Health* and other organizations that fund such research may require the researchers to budget for and offer follow-up counseling to participants.

Likewise, researchers may argue complete informed consent might compromise the reliability of participants' responses. For example, if told in advance you will be asked to express your attitudes about sexual behavior and rape, would you agree to participate in an interview? On the other hand, you might welcome the opportunity to express your opinions about relations between men and women. Even in circumstances where most people agree to participate in a study, researchers should be concerned by the sampling bias introduced when some people refuse to participate. The non-participants may share other characteristics such as being more or less conservative than those who agree to participate.

Family practitioners often find themselves in parallel circumstances. The families and members with whom they consult may be required to participate in treatments that are uncomfortable, painful, dangerous, or of uncertain outcome. Not infrequently, those families and family members are not engaging with the family practitioner out of choice, but rather have been ordered to do so by courts, parents, or other authorities. While the ethic of confidentiality is powerful, the challenge is greater in settings involving open courts, small towns, or closed communities.

A final potential ethical consideration involves consideration of the uses to which the knowledge might be applied. Social research is costly and employment can be scarce. Agencies may have a political agenda that must be advanced if the research is to be funded. Would you accept research support, even something like access to a mailing list, from an organization with a creed affirming the oppression of some families? Would you accept a position from an organization standing for "family reunification at all costs"?

Ethical Principles and Guidelines (National Council on Family Relations 1995: 1) were established by the *National Council on Family Relations* to:

- Inspire and encourage family scientists to act ethically
- Provide ethical guidance in areas family scientists may overlook
- Provide guidance in dealing with often complex ethical issues
- Enhance the professional image and status of family scientists by increasing the level of professional consciousness

Those principles hold family scientists to a high standard.

Family scientists are respectful of all individuals, do not unethically discriminate, do not develop intimate personal relationships in their role as family scientists, are sensitive to the complications of multiple role relationships, protect the confidentiality of their students or clients, and do not engage in sexual harassment. (National Council on Family Relations 1995: 1)

Refer to Appendix A for the full text of the *Ethical Principles and Guidelines*. The full code not only outlines principles that apply to all family scientists but also principles for specific professional arenas of teaching, clinical practice, research, employment, and writing. Interestingly, the code includes a section which explicitly exhorts family scientists to serve as "advocates for individuals and families" and to "participate in developing policies and laws that are respectful and empowering to them" (National Council on Family Relations 1995: 4).

Writing on tensions in work and family research, McGraw, Zvonkovic, and Walker (2000) advocate the practice of *reflexivity*, whereby family scholars open their research practices and themselves to scrutiny. White (2005: 166) also argues for trustworthy methods in family science:

. . . so that we can do good acts (ideology and morality). Indeed, good intentions informed by less than credible information and theory are a waste of resources and potentially a contributor to immoral acts.

One point that may be missing in discussions of research ethics is a charge to the individual to critically examine one's own personal standards of integrity. To whom and to what principles are you accountable in your efforts to explore families in meaningful, realistic, and ethical ways?

GLOSSARY

Archival	Feminist perspectives
Case study	Family systems theory
Comparative	Life cycle
Conflict theory	Longitudinal
Ethics	Observation
Exchange theory	Postmodernism
Experiment	Social capital
Family development theory	Structural functional theory
Family ecology theory	Survey
Family life-course theory	Symbolic interaction theory

FOR YOUR CONSIDERATION

1. Discuss how one theoretical perspective offers you the most promise for helping you explain a family issue that concerns you. Identify another theory that would enrich your understanding.

2. Which research methods would you use to investigate this issue? What limitations would those methods involve? Are some methods more compatible with certain theoretical approaches?

3. In what circumstances can you see yourself being placed in an ethically compromising situation as a family studies scholar? To whom would you turn? What is the "line in the sand" that you would not cross?

FOR FURTHER STUDY: WEB SITES, ORGANIZATIONS, AND PUBLICATIONS

Web Sites and Organizations

American Psychological Association
   www.apa.org/ethics/
   This site provides a link to the *American Psychological Association's Code of Ethics.*

American Sociological Association
   *www.asanet.org/*members/ecoderev.html
   This site provides a link to the *American Sociological Association's Code of Ethics.*

National Council on Family Relations
   www.ncfr.org/
   This is the site of the National Council on Family Relations.

Publications

Bengtson, Vern, Alan Acock, Katherine Allen, Peggy Dilworth-Anderson, and David Klein. eds. 2005. *Sourcebook in Family Theories and Methods: A Contextual Approach.* New York: Plenum.
In February 2000 the *National Council on Family Relations'* passed an initiative to fund more projects in family research and theory. Until that initiative bears fruit, this newly edited volume remains one of the strongest compilations of theories and methods in family studies.

Day, Randall, K. Gilbert, Barbara Settles, and Wesley R. Burr. eds. 1995. *Research and Theory in Family Science.* Pacific Grove, CA: Brooks/Cole.
This book introduces family studies students to family studies, with an emphasis on theories and research, and topics such as communication, sexuality, parenting, reproduction, health, violence, divorce, remarriage, and death. The editors include discussion of careers in family science.

Fox, Greer Litton, and Velma McBride Murry. 2000. "Gender and Families: Feminist Perspectives and Family Research." *Journal of Marriage and the Family* 62, 4 (November): 1160–72.
Fox and Murry define feminist scholarship in terms of reflexivity, the centrality of practice, a focus on social processes, and a critical stance. They then describe the impact of feminist perspectives on family research during the 1990s and conclude with a discussion of the feminist backlash.

Price, Sharon J., Patrick C. McKenry, and Megan J. Murphy. 2000. *Families Across Time: A Life Course Perspective.* Los Angeles, CA: Roxbury.
This edited volume applies the life course perspective to a range of parent-child, spousal, and sibling relationships. The 17 essays represent a diversity of families, including cohabiting, divorced, remarried, gay/lesbian, and African American. Essays also address family life education and clinical implications of this perspective.

Sommerville, Jennifer. 2000. *Feminism and the Family: Politics and Society in the U.K. and the U.S.A.* New York: St. Martin's.
This study examines the intersections between gender and the family. The author focuses on the "new feminism" and the "war over the family" in the context of socioeconomic and cultural changes that have changed traditional gender relations and the material and social psychological conditions of the family in the 21st century.

White, James M. 2005. *Advancing Family Theories.* Thousand Oaks, CA: Sage.
A complement to White and Klein's *Family Theories*, this book examines the value of "theories as tools for studying families." The author includes a persuasive chapter on rational choice theory and the family and an engaging chapter on the newer transition theory.

White, James M., and David M. Klein. 2002. *Family Theories: An Introduction, 2/e.* Thousand Oaks, CA: Sage.
This second edition of Klein and White's book presents seven theories (exchange, symbolic interaction, family developmental, systems, conflict, ecological, and feminist) in a manner that is accessible to beginning and intermediate readers, while sufficiently detailed and referenced to serve as a solid resource for family studies scholars.

Winton, Chester A. 1995. *Frameworks for Studying Families.* Guilford, CT: Dushkin.
Winton is a sociologist and a licensed family counselor. His overview of five theories (developmental, structural–functional, conflict, social exchange, and symbolic interaction) includes applications of each theory to two family issues (love and divorce) and his professional experience in Great Britain, Hong Kong, and Israel. He attempts to synthesize theories and offers a postmodern critique.

REFERENCES FOR CITED WORKS

Aldous, Joan. 1996. *Family Careers: Developmental Change in Families.* New York: Wiley.

Allen, Katherine R. 1989. *Single Women/Family Ties: Life Histories of Older Women.* Newbury, CA: Sage.

Amato, Paul, and Alan Booth. 1995. "Changes in Gender Role Attitudes and Marital Quality." *American Sociological Review* 60, 1 (February): 58–66.

Baber, Kristine M., and Katherine R. Allen. 1992. *Women & Families: Feminist Reconstructions.* New York: Guilford.

Baber, Kristine M., and Colleen I. Murray. 2001. "A Postmodern Feminist Approach to Teaching Human Sexuality." *Family Relations* 50, 1 (January): 23–33.

Barnes, Grace M., et al. 2000. "The Effects of Parenting on the Development of Adolescent Alcohol Misuse: A Six-Wave Latent Growth Model." *Journal of Marriage and the Family* 62, 1 (February): 175–86.

Blood, Robert O., Jr., and Donald M. Wolf. 1960. *Husbands and Wives: The Dynamics of Married Living*. New York: Free Press.

Booth, Alan, and John N. Edwards. 1985. "Age at Marriage and Marital Instability." *Journal of Marriage and the Family* 47, 1 (February): 67–75.

Booth, Alan, and John N. Edwards. 1989. "Transmission of Marital and Family Quality over the Generations: The Effect of Parental Divorce and Unhappiness." *Journal of Divorce* 13, 2: 41–58.

Booth, Alan, David R. Johnson, Lynn K. White, and John N. Edwards. 1986. "Divorce and Marital Instability Over the Life Course." *Journal of Marriage and Family Issues* 7: 421–42.

Bubloz, Margaret M., and M. Suzanne Sontag. 1993. "Human Ecology Theory." In *Sourcebook of Family Theories and Methods: A Contextual Approach*, eds. Pauline G. Boss et al. New York: Plenum, 419–48.

Conger, Rand D., and Glen H. Elder, Jr. 1994. *Families in Troubled Times: Adapting to Change in Rural America*. Hawthorne, NY: Aldine.

Crosnoe, Robert. 2004. "Social Capital and the Interplay of Families and Schools." *Journal of Marriage and the Family* 66, 2 (May): 267–80.

Daly, Kerry. 2003. "Family Theory Versus the Theories Families Live By." *Journal of Marriage and the Family* 65, 4 (November): 771–84.

Dellman-Jenkins, Mary, Maureen Blankemeyer, and Odessa Pinkard. 2000. "Young Adult Children and Grand-children in Primary Caregiver Roles to Older Relatives and Their Service Needs." *Family Relations* 49, 2: 177–86.

Duvall, Evelyn M. 1957. *Family Development*. New York: Lippincott.

Elder, Glen H., Jr. 1974/1999. *Children of the Great Depression: Social Change in Life Experience*. Chicago: University of Chicago Press.

Elder, Glen H., Jr. 1985. *Life Course Dynamics: Trajectories and Transitions, 1968–1980*. Ithaca, NY: Cornell University Press.

Elder, Glen H., Jr. 1986. "Military Times and Turning Points in Men's Lives." *Developmental Psychology* 22, 2: 233–45.

Elder, Glen H., Jr., and Elizabeth Colerick Clipp. 1989. "Combat Experience and Emotional Health: Impairment and Resilience in Later Life." *Journal of Personality* 52, 2: 311–41.

Elder, Glen H., Jr., and Rand D. Conger. 2000. *Children of the Land: Adversity and Success in Rural America*. Chicago: University of Chicago Press.

Elder, Glen H., Jr., Linda K. George, and Michael J. Shanahan. 1996. "Psychosocial Stress Over the Lifecourse." In *Psychosocial Stress: Perspectives on Structure, Theory, Life Course, and Methods*, ed. Howard B. Kaplan. Orlando, FL: Academic Press, 247–92.

Elder, Glen H., Jr., Michael J. Shanahan, and Elizabeth Colerick Clipp. 1997. "Linking Combat and Physical Health: The Legacy of World War II in Men's Lives." *American Journal of Psychiatry* 154, 3: 330–36.

Fagan, Jay, and Howard C. Stevenson. 2002. "An Experimental Study of an Empowerment-Based Intervention for African American Head Start Fathers." *Family Relations* 51, 3 (July): 191–98.

Freud, Sigmund. 1963. *Three Essays on the Theory of Sexuality*. New York: Basic Books.

Fitzharris, Joseph C. 1996. "Lizzie Caleff's War of the Rebellion." Paper presented at the Fort Snelling Civil War Symposium. Fort Snelling, MN.

Furstenberg, Frank F., Jr., Thomas D. Cook, Jacquelynne Eccles, Glen H. Elder, Jr., and Arnold Sameroff. 1999. *Managing to Make It: Urban Families and Adolescent Success*. Chicago, IL: University of Chicago Press.

Grochowski, Janet R., and Meg Wilkes Karraker. 2000. "The Use of Storytelling to Enhance Resiliency Among Single Mothers." Presented at a Conference of the *Academy of Health Behavior*, Sante Fe, NM.

Haas, Linda. 1986. "Wives Orientation toward Breadwinning: Sweden and the United States." *Journal of Family Issues* 7: 358–81.

Hartup, Willard W., & Richard A. Weinberg, eds. 2002. *Child Psychology in Retrospect and Prospect: In Celebration of the 75th Anniversary of the Institute of Child Development*. Minnesota Symposia on Child Psychology, Volume 32. Mahwah, NJ: Lawrence Erlbaum Associates.

Haworth-Hoeppner, Susan. 2000. "The Critical Shapes of Body Image: The Role of Culture and Family in the Production of Eating Disorders." *Journal of Marriage and the Family* 62, 1 (February): 212–27.

Hill, Miriam R., and Volker Thomas. 2000. "Strategies for Racial Identity Development: Narratives of Black and White Women in Interracial Partner Relationships." *Family Relations* 49, 2: 193–200.

Hughes, Robert, Jr., and Jacqueline J. Kirby. 2000. "Strengthening Evaluation Strategies for Divorcing Family Support Services: Perspectives of Parent Educators, Mediators, Attorneys, and Judges." *Family Relations* 49, 1: 53–61.

Ingoldsby, Bron B., Suzanne Smith, and J. Elizabeth Miller. 2004. *Exploring Family Theories.* Los Angeles, CA: Roxbury.

Jacob, T., and K. E. Leonard. 1988. "Alcoholic-Spouse Interaction as a Function of Alcoholism Subtype and Alcohol Consumption." *Journal of Abnormal Psychology* 97, 2: 231–37.

Journal of Family Psychology. 2000. Special Issue: "Cultural Variations in Families." 14, 3 (September).

Karraker, Meg Wilkes, and Janet R. Grochowski. 1997. "Single Mothers' Accounts of Resiliency in Parenting: Considerations for a 'Dual Vision' Methodology." Presented at the Third Annual *Qualitative Research Conference*, University of St. Thomas, St. Paul, MN.

Karraker, Meg Wilkes, and Janet R. Grochowski. 2000. "Single Mothers' Lives and Personal Change: Weaving Qualitative Findings into a Qualitative Tapestry." Paper presented at the Conference on *Qualitative Research in Education*, Athens, GA.

Laszloffy, Tracey A. 2002. "Rethinking Family Development Theory: Teaching with the Systematic Family Development (SFD) Model." *Family Relations* 51, 3 (July): 206–14.

Luster, Tom, et al. 2000. "Factors Related to Successful Outcomes Among Preschool Children Born to Low-Income Adolescent Mothers." *Journal of Marriage and the Family* 62, 1 (February): 133–46.

Marsiglio, William, Sally Hutchinson, and Mark Cohan. 2000. "Envisioning Fatherhood: A Social Psychological Perspective on Young Men Without Kids." *Family Relations* 49, 2: 133–42.

McGraw, Lori A., Anisa M. Zvonkovic, and Alexis J. Walker. 2000. "Studying Postmodern Families: A Feminist Analysis of Ethical Tensions in Work and Family Research." *Journal of Marriage and the Family* 62, 1 (February): 68–77.

Merkle, Erich R., and Rhonda A. Richardson. 2000. "Digital Dating and Virtual Relating: Conceptualizing Computer Mediated Romantic Relationships." *Family Relations* 49, 2: 187–92.

Meschke, Laurie L., Suzanne Bartholomae, and Shannon R. Zentall. 2000. "Adolescent Sexuality and Parent-Adolescent Processes: Promoting Healthy Teen Choices." *Family Relations* 49, 2: 143–54.

Myers, Scott M., and Alan Booth. 1996. "Men's Retirement and Marital Quality." *Journal of Family Issues* 17, 3 (May): 336–57.

Myers, Scott M., and Alan Booth. 1999. "Marital Strains and Marital Quality: The Role of High and Low Locus of Control." *Journal of Marriage and the Family* 61, 2 (May): 423–36.

National Council on Family Relations. 1995. *Ethical Principles and Guidelines.* Minneapolis, MN: National Council on Family Relations.

Onaga, Esther E., Kathleen McKinney, and Judy Pfaff. 2000. "Lodge Programs Serving Family Functions for People with Psychiatric Disabilities."*Family Relations* 49, 2: 207–16.

Parsons, Talcott, and Robert Bales. 1955. *Family Socialization and Interaction Process.* Glencoe, IL: Free Press.

Phelps, Erin, Frank F. Furstenberg, Jr., and Anne Colby (eds.). 2002. *Looking at Lives: American Longitudinal Studies of the 20th Century.* New York: Russell Sage Foundation.

Pimentel, Ellen Efron. 2000. "Just How Do I Love Thee?: Marital Relations in Urban China." *Journal of Marriage and the Family* 62, 1 (February): 32–47.

Pipher, Mary Bray. 1994. *Reviving Ophelia: Saving the Selves of Adolescent Girls.* New York: Ballantine.

Pipher, Mary Bray. 1996. *The Shelter of Each Other: Rebuilding Our Families.* New York: Ballantine.

Presser, Harriet B. 2000. "Nonstandard Work Schedules and Marital Instability." *Journal of Marriage and the Family* 62, 1 (February): 93–110.

Ritzer, George. 2000. The McDonaldization of Society (New Century Edition). Thousand Oaks, CA: Pine Forge.

Rosenblatt, Paul C., and Lucy Rose Fischer. 1993. "Qualitative Family Research." Chapter 7, pages 167–177 *Sourcebook of Family Theories and Methods: A Contextual Approach*, eds. Pauline G. Boss et al. New York: Plenum.

Sands, Roberta G., and Robin S. Golberg-Glen. 2000. "Factors Associated with Stress Among Grandparents Raising Their Grandchildren." *Family Relations* 49, 1: 97–105.

Sprey, Jetse. 2000. "Theorizing in Family Studies: Discovering Process." *Journal of Marriage and the Family* 62, 1 (February): 18–31.

Stack, Carol B. 1974. *All Our Kin: Strategies for Survival in a Black Community.* New York: Harper & Row.

Stenberg, Sten-Ake. 2000. "Inheritance of Welfare Recipiency: An Intergenerational Study of Social Assistance Recipiency in Postwar Sweden. *Journal of Marriage and the Family* 62, 1 (February): 228–39.

Szinovacz, Maximiliane E. 2000. "Changes in Housework After Retirement: A Panel Analysis." *Journal of Marriage and the Family* 62, 1 (February): 78–92.

Thomas, W. I., and Florian Znaniecki. 1918–1920. *The Polish Peasant in Europe and America.* Chicago: University of Chicago Press.

Thompson, Linda, and Alexis J. Walker. 1995. "The Place of Feminism in Family Studies." *Journal of Marriage and the Family* 57, 4 (November): 847–65.

Treas, Judith, and Deidre Giesen. 2000. "Sexual Infidelity among Marriage and Cohabitating Americans." *Journal of Marriage and the Family* 62, 1 (February): 48–60.

Walker, Alexis J. 1999. "Gender and Family Relationships." In *Handbook of Marriage and the Family,* 2/e, eds. Marvin Sussman, Suzanne K. Steinmetz, and Gary W. Peterson. New York: Plenum, Chapter 16, 439–74.

White, James M. 2005. *Advancing Family Theories.* Thousand Oaks, CA: Sage.

White, James. M., and David M. Klein. 2002. *Family Theories: An Introduction.* Thousand Oaks, CA: Sage.

Winton, Chester A. 1995. *Frameworks for Studying Families.* Guilford, CT: Dushkin.

FROM RISK TO RESILIENCY

Resiliency: Families "At Their Best"

CHAPTER PREVIEW

Resiliency or resilience is an ability to recover quickly from illness, change, or misfortune; buoyancy (*American Heritage Dictionary of the English Language, Fourth Edition* 2000). Family studies scholars recognize the critical importance of "bouncing back" from change and challenge and the part resiliency plays in our health and relationships. Resiliency is not a static state, rather a series of dynamic contextual processes in which one can struggle well (Higgins 1994) when faced with expected and unexpected life events.

The resiliency paradigm in family studies draws from multiple disciplines. Early *stress theory* emphasized variables (*stressors*) before including the context of meanings (*perceptions* and *appraisals*) and resources, which enabled families under stress to regain *homeostasis*. Today, family studies scholars are more likely to emphasize *salutogenesis* over *pathogenesis* and to include consideration of *sense of coherence*. A sense of coherence reflects interrelated components of *comprehensibility*, *manageability*, and *meaningfulness* that contribute to a proactive approach to living.

This more recent resiliency paradigm first recognizes that individuals facing challenging situations are not just *at risk*, but can be resilient, and that study of *protective processes* can deepen our understanding of strategies that enhance, maintain, and renew family processes. Scholars have identified "inside-out" *protective factors* (i.e., capacities and attributes including a sense of purpose and *compelling futures*) and "outside-in" protective factors (i.e., buffers).

Family scientists using a systems approach examine protective factors and processes in families' *adjustment* and *adaptation*. The *Double ABCX Model,* preceded by the *ABCX model,* reveals not only the dynamic interactions of vulnerabilities (stressors, strains, *pileup*) and strengths (resources, support, and *coping*) but also the impacts of family meanings (beliefs, perceptions, and appraisals), schema, and external community environments on family well-being. The *FAAR Model* depicts family resiliency as a balance between demands and resources as families wrestle to regain equilibrium and harmony. Such models not only enhance our understanding of protective processes but also deepen our understanding of family *recovery factors* in the larger context of family resiliency.

Family scholars are recognizing families' innate *resiliency processes*, while attempting to understand processes that enhance, maintain, and renew those processes. Proactive resiliency, including *participatory partnerships* and a *resilient attitude* can engage individuals, their families, and external communities in a *reflective—immediate—projective orientation*.

RESILIENCY: AN EVOLVING PARADIGM

For most people, *resiliency* means "bouncing back" from adversity. Resiliency is that and more. Resilience is not merely surviving a crisis or breezing through risk unscathed. To the contrary, being resilient means struggling well (Higgins 1994) and working through life's inevitable changes and challenges. Resilient families who experience hardship learn from those experiences, adjust or adapt as necessary, and then move on. In other words, they not only "bounce back," they "spring forward" (Grochowski 2000).

Resiliency is certainly not the same as invulnerability. Walsh (1998) warns of equating vulnerability with weakness and invulnerability with strength. All individuals and families are exposed to risk and stress (although some certainly more than others). Family resiliency is complex, dynamic, and contextual.

What is it about families that allows them to face adversity and challenges over the lifecycle and survive and even thrive in the face of seemingly overwhelming odds? What makes some families fall apart or deteriorate in the face of crises demanding changes, while other families negotiate these troubled times with relative ease by finding new patterns and modifying old patterns of functioning? (McCubbin, Thompson, and McCubbin 1996: xxv)

Family textbooks have traditionally included a section that focuses on crisis and adjustment, with a heavy emphasis on the etiology of family problems. In this chapter we emphasize *salutogenesis*, a health-focused orientation ("what is right") over *pathogenesis*, a disease-focused orientation ("what is wrong") with families.

We begin with the premise that all families are vulnerable to external and internal *stressors*, but that each family is a complex, adaptive system. Such an approach offers family studies professionals a greater opportunity to move beyond diagnosis of family problems and toward enhancement of family futures.

Stressors as Agents of Change

Stress theory offers a starting point in resiliency construct development. Although the term *stress* was used in physical science as early as the 17th century, not until the 19th century was stress recognized as influential in illness (Lazarus and Folkman 1984). Stress means change and "[t]here is nothing permanent except change" (Heraclitus, 1960: 313). Change—and the increasing rate of change—remains a constant in family life in both predictable and unpredictable situations. Perhaps family studies scholars need to move from the analogy of a family tree (slow growing, solidly rooted, and stationary) to a family vine (quickly changing shape in response to conditions, diverse and expansive in terms of family arrangements, and mobility).

Homeostasis is the process of maintaining internal stability when confronted with change and outside challenges (Cannon 1935). Cannon is credited with the inclusion of psychological stress as important stimuli to physiological stress through systematic research on the effects of stress in detailed observations of bodily changes (Dohrenwend and Dohrenwend 1981). Stressors are any agents (physiological, psychological, or emotional; virtual or real) that challenge homeostasis and trigger stress responses (Selye 1956).

These early efforts contributed significantly to the emergence of the concept of stress as well as to the medical science philosophy of the mind–body relationships (Lovallo 1997) and to the view that organisms can be active responders and not merely reactors to change.

Perceptions and Appraisals

Stress is the "personal [family] interpretation and subjective experiencing of risk" (Blum 2002: 3). Lazarus and Folkman (1984) propose that one's *perceptions* (observations and understandings) and *appraisals* (evaluating the significance of a stressor, responses, and resources) have consequential influences on our bodily physiological reactions including emotional and psychological responses. Within their model, belief and commitment help explain some of the variance in how individuals and families respond to stressors. Consider the situation if, while driving to work my car has a flat tire. I might find the situation inconvenient and disruptive, but not disastrous or life changing. On the other hand, if this same situation were perceived as devastating or life altering (e.g., I believe I would be fired for missing work, or my child will miss her chemotherapy session), my different appraisal would result in variance in the meaning I give to a situation and, consequently, to my resulting stress response.

Lazarus and Folkman's (1984) model adds another layer to stress theory with secondary perception and appraisal. Secondary perception and appraisal indicate how individuals and families perceive and assess resources such as coping strategies and social supports in facing the stressor. For example, secondary perception and appraisal of resources might include appraisal of one's overall health plus attitudes ranging from "I'm too busy to get sick now" to "I'm doomed to get sick." An example on a family level is a family perception and appraisal of "We can get through this because we have each other" or "No one cares what happens to us, it's hopeless." The power of an individual's and a family's perception and assessment of resources and control speaks volumes in the story of how well we cope, survive, and thrive when challenged.

Family stress is "pressure or tension [change] in the family system—a disturbance in the steady state of the family (Boss 2002: 16). Boss affirms that the family is not an isolated system, for it constantly deals with balancing dimensions it cannot control (external) and dimensions it can control (internal). In her Contextual Model of Family Stress, Boss illustrates family stress management as an inevitable process within a larger context in which families live. Whether good (eustress), bad (distress), or both, family stress affects family members and the family as a whole. The issue for families is how to effectively navigate through stress.

Salutogenesis: Setting the Stage

Antonovsky's work (1979, 1987) reflects a paradigm shift from an established pathogenic orientation toward an approach he coined as *salutogenesis*. A salutogenic paradigm translates into working from a position of studying the causes of diseases to the causes of

---

BOX 3.1 "Tribute to Aaron Antonovsky 1923–1994"
Luís A. Saboga Nunes, M.P.H.

Aaron Antonovsky was born in the United States in 1923. After serving in the U.S. army in World II, he obtained his Ph.D. in sociology from Yale University. Aaron immigrated to Israel in 1960, settled in Jerusalem, and worked at the Israel Institute for Applied Social Science and in the Department of Social Medicine of the Hebrew University of Jerusalem-Hadassah. By the end of the 1960s, Antonovsky's role as a leading figure in medical sociology was established when he published several articles on social class differences in morbidity and mortality. His first major paper, published in 1967 and reprinted countless times throughout the world, was one of the first efforts to call attention to this risk factor. This paper is still widely cited in the literature, as research on social class remains a primary focus of public health.

In 1972, Aaron became one of the pioneers in the establishment of the medical school of the Ben-Gurion University of the Negev. As incumbent of the Kunen-Lunenfeld Chair in Medical Sociology, he had two central roles in the medical school. Being the first chairman of the committee, he designed the medical school's much copied admissions process. In addition, he established and headed the Unit of the Sociology of Health, which had a leading role in shaping the school's biopsychosocial and community orientation. During his 20 years in Beer Sheva, Antonovsky taught countless physicians and students how to look in a new way at the medical profession, at disease and health, and at society as a whole. During the years that Aaron's work in the medical school was bringing him international recognition in the medical education community he continued to develop as a theoretician and researcher. Already in the 1960s, his contribution to research on the stress process was acknowledged.

In the 1970s, he began to develop the salutogenic model of health and illness which attained worldwide professional attention in his 1979 book, *Health, Stress and Coping*, and its sequel, *Unraveling the Mystery of Health* published in 1987. A breakthrough in research on the relationship between stress and illness, the salutogenic model influenced the thinking of medical and behavioral scientists about the factors that form the basis of human health. His fundamental contribution was to point out the consequences of a pathological orientation toward sickness and disease. He argued persuasively that a far more useful view is obtained when researchers and clinicians instead focus on health and the forces that help people maintain effective functioning even in the presence of hazardous influences. Aaron's extensive writing and lecturing in Israel and throughout the world have inspired many professionals in medicine and nursing, psychology, psychiatry, education, and sociology to include salutogenic thinking in their own clinical work and research.

The concept and measure of the sense of coherence, which is central to the salutogenic model and to the understanding of the relationship between the social system and the individual's well-being, has been used by nearly 150 researchers around the world; the measure has been translated into 20 languages. Antonovsky published over 100 papers and wrote or edited 12 books. In his work, he combined creative conceptual thinking with sophisticated quantitative methodologies, which were expressed in an informal, charming and crystal clear writing ability. Recognition of his talents and achievements was expressed in 1993 when he was awarded an honorary doctorate from the Nordic School of Public Health.

Aaron retired from the medical school in 1992, but remained an active researcher and lecturer at meetings throughout the world. He became ill during a conference in Lisbon in May and passed away on July 7, 1994.

Three years after (in July 1997), also from Lisbon and as a tribute to his contribution to a better understanding of humans beings, the first home page at http://www.angelfire.com/ok/soc was activated by L. A. Saboga Nunes, a participant in his presentation in Lisbon. Following the increasing number of accesses and info-processing demands, a new design and Internet protocol was established at http://www.salutogenesis.net in the beginning of 2002, as a more efficient tool was developed to empower researchers dedicated to the salutogenic paradigm.

Luís A. Saboga Nunes, M.A., M.P.H., is Sociologist of Health and Assistant Professor at the National School of Public Health in Lisbon, at the Department of Health Promotion. The following tribute to Dr. Antonovsky is quoted with permission from a Web site created in his memory www.ensp.unl.pt/saboga/soc.

health. This concept expands beyond the field of health as family studies professionals explore "what is right" and not just "what is wrong" with families. At the core of this philosophical approach is what Antonovsky termed a *sense of coherence*. Sense of coherence reflects an "approach to living" that embodies three interrelated components. *Comprehensibility* is defined as the cognitive ability to understand and put events in perspective, thus giving a sense of control over the situation. *Manageability* reflects the belief that one (family) has the resources to cope successfully with the challenges. The final component, *meaningfulness*, is an ability to find meaning from situations and the demands they create plus the ability to learn from the experience of doing so; problems are reinterpreted as challenges (Antonovsky 1994).

A salutogenic approach to studying stress contributes to our understanding of resiliency. Resiliency research lies primarily in two areas of study: one in child psychology and the other in family studies (Benard 2004; Cowan 1991; Hawley and DeHann 1996). Just as family stress affects family members as well as the family unit, so too family resiliency is revealed at individual and family levels. We begin with an overview of individual resiliency.

RESILIENT INDIVIDUALS

One tradition in research on individual resiliency focuses on identifying resilient children who managed to overcome multiple risk factors and studying *protective factors* present in the lives of these resilient survivors (Rutter 1979). The focus on protective factors extended beyond the fields of health, psychology, and psychiatry to sociology, social work, education, communication, and youth development. This multiple discipline investment in resiliency construct development reflects an evolution of the interdisciplinary field of family studies as well.

Longitudinal and Cross-Cultural Resilience Studies

Early resiliency research included international cross-cultural and life-span longitudinal developmental studies. Those studies followed children living under high-risk conditions, including children who were living with parents who were mentally ill, alcoholic, abusive, or criminal, or in communities that were poverty stricken or violent or war-torn.

One of the most ambitious longitudinal studies on resiliency is Werner and Smith's (1982, 2001) *Kauai Longitudinal Study*. This study followed a cohort of 698 children born in 1955 from birth to adulthood. With the contributions of professionals representing social work, pediatric medicine, public health, education, psychology, and counseling, researchers gathered such information concerning the physical and psychological states, the appearance of stressor events and buffering agents, and the behaviors on this cohort for over four decades.

One third of the cohort was identified as *at risk*, living in challenging socioeconomic and or family conditions. Of these at-risk children, two thirds experienced four to six additional risk factors, including poor school performance, problems learning, mental health concerns, or teen pregnancy. "Against the odds," the study discovered that most of the cohort living in high-risk environments developed into "complete, confident and caring adults" (Werner 1995: 84).

Focus on this resilient group revealed protective factors common to resilient individuals. These factors included an easy temperament, the ability to elicit help from others, autonomy, good communication and problem-solving skills, internal locus of control, positive self-concept, at least moderate cognitive competence, and belief that their life had purpose and future. This study also identified family and community "protective buffers" such as having a relationship with at least one caring adult.

Other research (Garmezy 1981, 1985, 1987; Garmezy and Rutter 1983; Murphy and Moriarty 1976; Rutter 1985, 1987) has examined how children surmounted the challenges of abuse and neglect. These studies emphasize the impact of cognitive and social competence in children who thrive against the odds. Garmezy's (Garmezy 1987, 1991; Garmezy, Masten, and Tellegen 1984) *Project Competence* models use capability, capacity, attribute, proficiency, and other patterns to describe the effects of stress and personal competence on resiliency in school-aged children (Garmezy and Masten 1991; Masten and Coatsworth 1998; Masten 2001; Masten and Reed 2002).

Stress and resilience may actually enhance competence as long as the stress level is not so high as to overwhelm. This is reflective of Selye's (1974) eustress concept, which explains that stress response experiences are beneficial for individuals in that they can learn and grow from successfully meeting challenges.

More recent studies of child resilience in cross-cultural and poverty settings reveal similar findings related to the relationship between competence and resilience. Luthar's (1999) work with inner-city youth and among children of substance abusers (1995) and Dugan and Coles's (1989) cross-cultural studies of street children in Brazil and American inner-city ghettos found many children rising above the severe conditions of their environments. Most (at least 50% and often 70%) of the children in these high-risk environments developed social competence and overcame the odds to lead successful lives. Based on such research, an individual's capacities and attributes (inside-out protective factors) were identified.

Inside-Out Protective Factors (Capacities and Attributes)

[handwritten annotation: protective – anything that prevents or reduces vulnerability]

Garmezy (1985) describes the strengths of a resilient individual as one who works well, plays well, loves well, and expects well. Other scholars include self-efficacy (Benard 1991, 2004; Wolin and Wolin 1993; Werner and Smith 1992; Rutter 1985), spirituality (Dugan and Coles 1989), positive beliefs (Taylor 1989), humor (Cousins 1989; Lefcourt 2001, 2002; McBroom 2002), problem solving (Grotberg 1998, 1999), hardiness (Kobasa 1979; Kobasa, Maddi, and Kahn 1982) and learned optimism (Seligman 1994, 2002) as capacities and related attributes bearing on the strengths of a resilient person. Still other work (Blum 2002; Resnick et al. 1997; Rutter 2000) suggests the powerful impact of wellness on resiliency. In sum, capacities and attributes of resilient individuals include:

- Social competence: responsiveness, cultural flexibility, empathy, communication skills, and a sense of humor

- Problem-solving skills: planning, seeking assistance, thinking critically, creatively, reflectively, hardiness, cognitive competence, acting versus reacting, and resourcefulness

- Autonomy: sense of identity, self-efficacy, self-awareness, self-esteem, self-confidence, task-mastery, internal locus of control, self-efficacy, plus adaptive distancing from negative messages and conditions

- Wellness and Health: interplay of physical, emotional, intellectual, spiritual, interpersonal and social, and environmental dimensions.

- Sense of purpose and belief in bright futures [compelling futures]: goal direction, educational aspirations, achievement motivation, persistence, hopefulness, optimism, spirituality, and sense of coherence.

Benard (1991, 2004) emphasizes that the sense of purpose and belief in a bright future is fundamental to resiliency. Vaillant (2000) notes that anticipation or vision of future is more than mere planning, as it includes a compelling emotional sense of future. This position is supported by a story-based, dual-methodological study of the impacts of belief in compelling futures on resiliency (Grochowski 1998).

BOX 3.2 **"Inside-Out Protective Capacities and Attributes Model"** © 2003
Janet R. Grochowski, Ph.D.

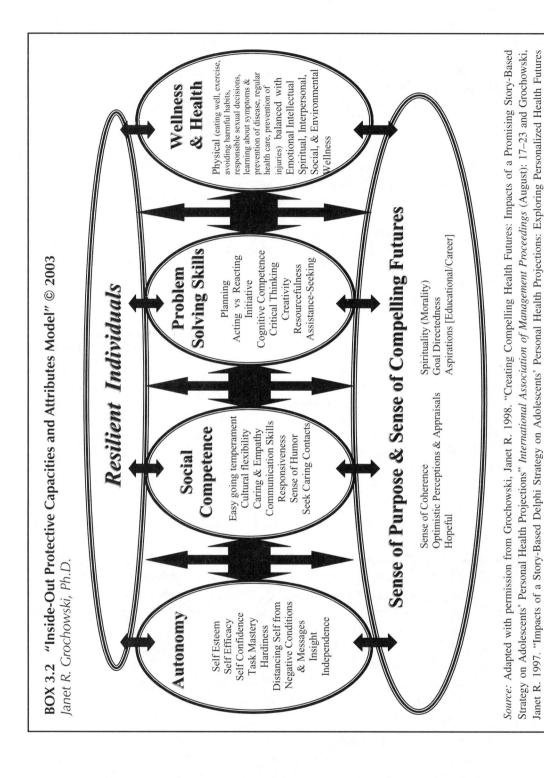

Resilient Individuals

Autonomy

Self Esteem
Self Efficacy
Self Confidence
Task Mastery
Hardiness
Distancing Self from
Negative Conditions
& Messages
Insight
Independence

**Social
Competence**

Easy going temperament
Cultural flexibility
Caring & Empathy
Communication Skills
Responsiveness
Sense of Humor
Seek Caring Contacts

**Problem
Solving Skills**

Planning
Acting vs Reacting
Initiative
Cognitive Competence
Critical Thinking
Creativity
Resourcefulness
Assistance-Seeking

**Wellness
& Health**

Physical (eating well, exercise,
avoiding harmful habits,
responsible sexual decisions,
learning about symptoms &
prevention of disease, regular
health care, prevention of
injuries) balanced with
Emotional Intellectual
Spiritual, Interpersonal,
Social, & Environmental
Wellness

Sense of Purpose & Sense of Compelling Futures

Sense of Coherence
Optimistic Perceptions & Appraisals
Hopeful

Spirituality (Morality)
Goal Directedness
Aspirations [Educational/Career]

Source: Adapted with permission from Grochowski, Janet R. 1998. "Creating Compelling Health Futures: Impacts of a Promising Story-Based Strategy on Adolescents' Personal Health Projections" *International Association of Management Proceedings* (August): 17–23 and Grochowski, Janet R. 1997. "Impacts of a Story-Based Delphi Strategy on Adolescents' Personal Health Projections: Exploring Personalized Health Futures Through a Self-Directed Learning Strategy," *Dissertation Abstracts International.*

Resiliency requires more than protective factors, however. Zubrick and Robson's (2003) research on Australian Aboriginal youth indicates that resilience is an inferential and contextual construct. An individual's family and external community add context to resilience. Luthar and Cicchetti (2000) caution family scientists to avoid the erroneous assumption that children and youth who are resilient become so on their own; thus, when they are not resilient it is their "fault." The assumption that resiliency operates in a vacuum may lead to poor practice and policy. "[R]esilience is not a genetic trait that only a few 'superkids' possess" (Benard 1999: 6). Enduring risk and crisis does not automatically result in resiliency, but doing so does offer opportunity for growth, as noted in the Chinese symbol for crisis representing both "danger" and "opportunity." Resilience is an instinctive network of dynamic and contextual inside-out and outside-in properties.

Outside-In Protective Factors (Buffers)

Inside-out protective factors (capacities and attributes) interact with and can be strengthened by external outside-in protective factors or buffers. Resiliency literature from a variety of disciplines (Benard 2004; Blyth and Roelkepartian 1993; Leffert et al. 1998; Masten, Best, and Garmezy 1990; Masten and Coatsworth 1998; Masten and Reed 2002; Murphy and Moriarty 1976; Rutter 1987; Werner and Smith 1992) has identified protective factors found in family and external community environments which influence individuals' resiliency. Figure 3.1, based on earlier work (Benard 1991, 2004) reveals three major resiliency promoting environment categories. The first encompasses caring relationships that express compassion, caring, respect, and interest grounded in listening, safety, basic trust, and attachment. A second category is holding reasonably high expectations (verbal and nonverbal messages that communicate clear and consistent messages that guide and challenge). The third includes opportunities for meaningful participation and contribution or required helpfulness (Rachman (1979), that is, options to experience age-appropriate responsibilities, decision-making, meaningful dialog, plus giving back, a connectedness.

As often found in complex concepts, researchers use various terms to describe similar phenomena. Masten (2002a, 2002b) uses a similar term, "protective systems", to refer to these outside-in factors. These include:

- Attachment systems
- Human information processing systems
- Self-regulation systems for attention, emotion, arousal, and behavior
- Pleasure-in-mastery motivational system
- Family systems
- Community organizational systems
- Spirituality and religious systems

School serves as an example of non-family community for fostering protective factors that strengthen family resiliency. Schools provide caring and support from relationships between teachers and students that convey respect, trust, safety, and consistent messages of belonging (Brooks 1991; Crosnoe 2004; Felner 2000; Howard and Johnson 2004; Werner and Smith 1992). Resiliency-enhancing schools also hold reasonably high expectations that all students can succeed plus providing the support and encouragement necessary for

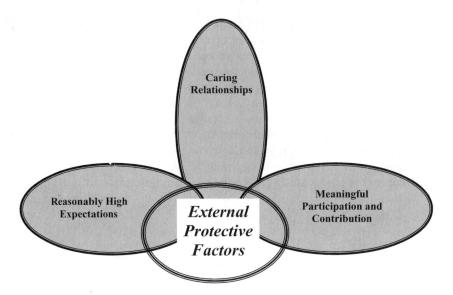

FIG. 3.1.   "Outside-In" Protective Factors (Buffers) Model © 2003 Janet R. Grochowski, Ph.D.
Source: Adapted with permission from Grochowski, Janet R. 1998. "Creating Compelling Health
Futures: Impacts of a Promising Story-Based Strategy on Adolescents' Personal Health Projections"
International Association of Management Proceedings (August): 17–23.

them to do so (Kurth-Schai 1988; Resnick et al. 1997). Finally, schools as a non-family
environment encourage students' participation and involvement, a connectedness (Blyth
and Roehlkepartain 1993) and "required helpfulness" (Rachman 1979) within the school
and in the outside community.

Paradigm Shift to Protective Processes

As the complexity of protective factors became more apparent, scholars (Rutter 1987,
1990) recognized that resiliency involved *protective processes*. Rutter's emphasis on the
dynamic nature of resilience serves as a benchmark in resiliency research.

> [Protective factors] are highly robust predictors of resilience [and] likely to play a key role
> in the processes involved in people's response to risk circumstances. But they are of limited
> value as a means of finding new approaches to prevention. . . . [W]e need to focus on protective
> mechanisms and processes . . . . to ask why and how some individuals manage to maintain high
> self-esteem and self-efficacy in spite of facing the same adversities that lead other people to
> give up and lose hope. (Rutter 1987: 316–18)

Rutter invites professionals to search not for broadly defined protective factors, but for
specific developmental and situational mechanisms involved in those protective processes.
That is, the "search is not for factors that make us feel good, but for processes that protect
us against risk mechanisms" (Rutter 1987: 318). These processes include transactional
relationships among individual, familial, and external communities. Figure 3.2 provides
an interpretation of these protective processes.

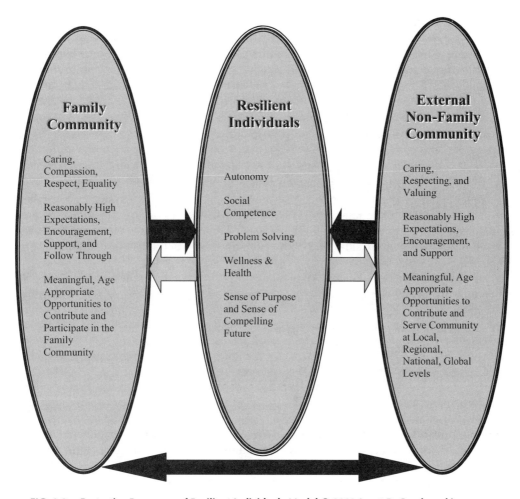

FIG. 3.2.   Protective Processes of Resilient Individuals Model © 2003 Janet R. Grochowski.

FAMILY RESILIENCY: MORE THAN THE SUM OF ITS PARTS

In the last decades of the 20th century, researchers gleaned an increased understanding that individuals (subsystems) influence and are influenced by the systems (families and external communities) they live in. Although the mounting research on resilient individuals hints at the vital role of family (regardless of how that is defined or structured), investigations of what makes a resilient family are less prolific. McCubbin and colleagues (1997: 1) describe a resilient family as having

1. Elasticity: The property of the family system that enables it to maintain its established patterns of functioning after being challenged and confronted by risk factors

2. Buoyancy: The family's ability to recover quickly from a misfortune, trauma, or transitional event causing or calling for changes in the family's patterns of functioning

Emphasizing family strengths and exploring what it is that enables families not only to survive but also to thrive under adversity provides family researchers an expanded focus on the larger population of families who succeed at negotiating expected and unexpected changes and challenges of the life cycle. Walsh (1998, 2002) reminds family professionals not to think of healthy families as problem free or to use a mythical traditional family as a blueprint. To do so is contemptuous and generates shame and blame for families labeled nontraditional. "It is not family 'form,' but rather family 'processes' that matter most in healthy functioning and resilience" (Walsh 1998: 16).

Families as Complex Adaptive Communities

As discussed in chapter 1, families are complex adaptive systems. Many family scholars apply family systems theory to capture the dynamics of families under stressful situations. In chapter 2, family systems theory is described from a position that a system is more than the sum of its individual members (Hall and Fagan 1968). This approach allows family scientists more flexibility in studying families as dynamic, interrelated, "strategic living communities" © (Grochowski 1997, 2000) with diverse structures and relationship sets, impacted by external social systems.

Karraker and Grochowski's (2000) qualitative study of single mother resiliency reveals a dynamic display of women determining their preferred futures in terms of the following:

- Who they want to include as well as exclude from their preferred image of family
- What they want their family to be
- What they were willing to do to reach their compelling future

The participants in this study responded in a positive way when asked to design, create their own strategic living community ©. They also expressed appreciation for being given the opportunity to affirm their role as a "good mother" and for living in an authentic family arrangement. Finally, the participants identify attitudes and behaviors that could assist in reaching their preferred family image. Specifically, we argue for studying the "stories" of families, and their members tell about what was, what is, and what they prefer in terms of family. Such findings hint at a dynamic interplay of individual, familial, and external community systems.

Research Models of Family Adjustment and Adaptation

Generally when facing change and challenge, a family adjusts and, if necessary, adapts. Family *adjustment* and *adaptation* often are measured in terms of a family being in or out of control. Adjustment reflects short-term, temporary family changes, whereas adaptation evokes long-term changes in family behavior patterns, roles, rules, and perceptions (Boss 1988). For example, a family adjusts to a member remaining home for a week due to the flu with temporary shifts in work and home responsibilities. When faced with a long-term challenge such as a child who develops cancer and requires at-home care, a family needs to adapt to more permanent changes in work, household jobs, and family time. McCubbin and her colleagues (2002) identify a family's rapid mobilization and reorganization along with external social support as crucial resiliency factors.

As with individual resiliency studies, family resiliency researchers identified protective factors before recognizing processes of family resiliency. McCubbin and his colleagues (1997) argued that family scientists used a double-lens approach including family protective and *recovery factors*. Table 3.1 displays a protective factor lens and includes where

TABLE 3.1
Family Protective Factors (FPF)

Family Protective Factors (FPF)	Family Stages			
	Couple	Childbearing & School-age	Teenage & Young Adult	Empty Nest & Retirement
• Accord: Balanced interrelationship among family members that allows them to resolve conflicts and reduce chronic strain	X	X		
• Celebration: Acknowledging birthdays, religious occasions, and other special events	X	X	X	X
• Communications: Sharing beliefs and emotions with another. Emphasis is on how family members exchange information and caring with each other.	X	X		X
• Financial management: Sound decision-making skills or money management and satisfaction with economic status	X	X	X	
• Hardiness: Family members' sense of *control* over their lives, *commitment* to the family, *confidence* that the family will survive no matter what	X	X	X	X
• Health: The physical and psychological well-being of family members	X			X
• Leisure activities: Similarities and differences of family member preferences for ways to spend free time	X			
• Personality: Acceptance of a partner's traits, behaviors, general outlook, and dependability	X		X	X
• Support network: Positive aspects of relationships with in-laws, relatives, and friends		X	X	
• Time and routines: Family meals, chores, togetherness, and other ordinary routines contributing to continuity and stability in family life	X	X	X	X
• Traditions: Honoring holidays and important family experiences carried across generations	X	X	X	X

Source: Adapted with permission from McCubbin, Hamilton I., Marilyn McCubbin, Anne Thompson, Sae-Young Han, and Chad Allen. 1997. "Families Under Stress: What Makes Them Resilient." Paper presented at the meetings of the *American Association of Family & Consumer Sciences,* June, Washington, DC. www.cynfernet.extension.umn.edu/research/resilient.html (Retrieved 08/01/02).

TABLE 3.2

Family Recovery Factors (FRF)

FRF—Summary of longitudinal research findings on families faced with chronic childhood illness (McCubbin et al. 1997: 5–6)
- Family integration: Parent(s) efforts to keep the family together and maintain an optimistic outlook
- Family support and esteem building: Parent(s) efforts to get support from the community and friends in developing self-esteem and self-confidence
- Family recreation orientation, control, and organization: Family's emphasis on active recreation toward participation in various recreational and or sporting activities. Emphasis on family control and organization, rules, and procedures
- Family optimism and mastery: Family's efforts to maintain sense of order and optimism

FRF—Summary of longitudinal research findings on families faced with prolonged war-induced separations (McCubbin et al. 1997: 6)
- Self-reliance and equality of members: Deliberate family efforts to change its patterns of functioning plus change in the social, psychosocial, and economic conditions
- Family advocacy: Family is able to adapt to context of crisis, involvement with/support of collective efforts of families in similar situations to effect positive changes in the milieu.
- Family meanings: Family makes necessary accommodations in establishing viable patterns of functioning designed to promote stability, harmony, and balance in face of adversity.
- Family schema: Families over time create an internally regulated sense of shared values, beliefs, expectations, and rules that guide and shape the major domains of family functioning: work-family relationships, disciplining and raising children, the marital relationship, and intergenerational responsibilities, etc. Collectively these serve as the family's schema in promoting family harmony and balance in context of crisis.

Source: Adapted with permission from McCubbin, Hamilton, Marilyn McCubbin, Anne Thompson, Sae-Young Han, and Chad Allen 1997. "Families Under Stress: What Makes Them Resilient." Paper presented at the meetings of the *American Association of Family & Consumer Sciences,* June, Washington, DC. www.cynfernet. extension.umn.edu/research/resilient.html (Retrieved 08/01/02).

they are most influential during the family life cycle. Table 3.2 depicts a "reaching deep inside" aspect of families adapting to challenge in terms of recovery factors.

Family protective factors have been applied in studies of families experiencing varying degrees of change across the life cycle (Jackson et al. 2003; McCubbin et al. 1988; Olson et al. 1983; Stinnett and DeFrain 1985). Family recovery factors have been applied in studies of families experiencing hardship and hard times, such as families challenged by military service (e.g., Drummet, Coleman, and Cable 2003; McCubbin et al. 1976), families faced with childhood chronic illness (Garwick et al. 2002; McCubbin 1989; McCubbin et al. 2002), families facing developmental transitions (Jackson et al. 2003; McCubbin and McCubbin 1988), and families experiencing economic challenges (McCubbin and Thompson 1989; Murry et al. 2002). International studies reveal culture and ethnicity as vital contributors to the understanding of family recovery factors (McCubbin 1998; McCubbin et al. 1998).

Hill's *ABCX model* (1949, 1958) was a starting point for research on families under stress. His model reveals the relationships among A (stressor), B (resources), C (definition of the stressor), and X (crisis). Hill argues that precrisis interactions (ABC) result in the family unit determining a degree of response, which can range from mild stress to crisis (X).

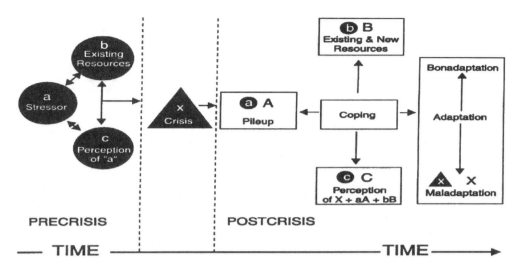

FIG. 3.3. Double ABC-X Model ©
Source: Adapted with permission from McCubbin, Hamilton I., and Joan M. Patterson. 1982.
"Family Stress and Adaptation to Crises." In *FamilyStress, Coping, and Social Support*, eds. H. I.
McCubbin, A. E. Cauble, and J. M. Patterson. Springfield, IL: Charles C. Thomas, 26–47.

Family scientists began to broaden the focus from identifying stressors that increased the risk of adverse adjustments toward exploring the uncharted areas of why some families not only survived but also even flourished in adverse circumstances. Burr's (1973, 1982) work emphasizes the ability of families to recover from stress, that is, a regenerative power in families. This regenerative power of families is a pivotal feature of the *Double ABCX Model* (Figure 3.3; McCubbin and Patterson 1982, 1983a, 1983b). This model expanded on Hill's work with inclusion of postcrisis or poststress adaptation, that is, coping and social supports which influence family adaptation to a crisis.

Family Meanings (Perceptions and Appraisals)

The Double ABCX model expands perception (cC) of the original stressor, but also the perception of the *pileup* of other stressors and strains (aA) and resources (bB). Family precrisis and postcrisis meanings (perceptions and appraisals) is influenced by beliefs, reframing the situation, and bestowing specific meaning on the stress situation and the family's adjustment to it.

The meanings families attach to both predictable and unpredictable stressors in terms of their family sense of coherence lay a foundation for how they will weather changes and challenges. Family meanings are "the interpretations, images, and views that have been collectively constructed by family... They are the family's social constructions, the product of their interactions" (Patterson and Garwick 1994: 80–1). These meanings are influenced by the symbolic interaction within a family that includes the "language, rituals, rules, and roles" the family unit and its members understand and accept (Boss 2002: 37).

Reiss (1981) emphasized that these shared meanings and beliefs play a key role in reducing ambiguity and uncertainty in families. Family worldview and family purpose and preferred futures have far-reaching impacts on whether a family believes it can control and effectively respond to challenges. This worldview also shapes a family's willingness to seek and use new information, skills, and competencies.

BOX 3.3 "Promoting Resilience in Families of Children with Chronic Conditions"
Ann Garwick, Ph.D.

For decades, family practitioners and researchers have wondered why some children and families do well when confronted with the diagnosis of a chronic illness or disability, whereas others have great difficulty adjusting to the demands of a chronic condition. Research to date indicates that most families who have a child with a chronic condition are functioning well. However, family members of children with chronic conditions are at increased risk for experiencing psychosocial problems, such as depression. Meanwhile, research on resilience and associated risk and protective factors, such as social support, is informing intervention strategies that promote healthy family functioning. Two key factors that influence families' resilience or ability to "bounce back" from adverse circumstances include (1) the resources families have to deal with the situation and (2) the meanings that they attribute to the situation.

In our cross-cultural research with families who have children with chronic conditions, we have found that the time of diagnosis is a critical time for families when they often wonder "why" the condition happened and need to find information and additional resources to help them manage the condition. Coming to terms with "why" the condition happened is an important task for families to accomplish so they can move on to deal with other pressing issues, such as learning how to care for their child's condition. Resilient families tend to emphasize positive versus negative reasons for the condition and are able to find an explanation about the cause of the condition that makes sense to them.

Over time, resilient families of children with chronic conditions learn how to balance the demands of the condition with the demands of family life. They are able to incorporate the management of the chronic condition into their routines of daily living in ways that minimize family disruption. The ability to celebrate together as a family, in spite of the chronic condition, is another hallmark of resilient families.

The availability of a broad base of economic, psychosocial, and health care resources enhances the family's ability to manage the challenges of living with a chronic condition. Adequate resources that fit the families' needs are important protective factors that can help families cope effectively.

Ann Garwick, Ph.D., R.N., L.M.F.T., L.P., is an Associate Professor and Director of the Center for Child and Family Health Promotion Research in the School of Nursing, University of Minnesota.

Of course, each family member may have a different interpretation of this view and various family myths (Wamboldt and Wolin 1989). Patterson (1988, 2002) offers the *FAAR Model* in which family meanings play a vital role in how families balance demands and resources. In the FAAR (Family Adjustment and Adaptation Response) transactional model demands are identified as a complex mixture of stressors, strains, and hassles. Often it is the drain of daily strains (e.g., role conflict, role overload, and role strain) and everyday hassles (e.g., the snow storm, a traffic jam, and lost glasses) that can tip the demand scale.

Coping: How Families Adjust and Adapt

Patterson discusses resources as the counterbalance to demands. She categorizes resources as capabilities (including family competence, skills, and traits) and coping strategies. Family balancing (adjusting and adapting) challenges and strengths can be described as family *coping*.

Family coping research draws on sociology (e.g., Burr 1973; Pearlin and Schooler 1978) as well as child development (e.g., Masten and Coatsworth 1998; Masten and Reed 2002), health care (e.g., Antonovsky and Sourani 1988), cognitive psychology (e.g., Lazarus 1966, 1976; Lazarus and Folkman 1984), and multidisciplinary efforts (McKenry and Price 2000). Healthful family coping is "the process of managing a stressful event or situation by the family as a unit with no detrimental effects on any individual in that family" (Boss 2002: 79). When a family copes, it does not just maintain the status quo. Rather, coping can include rebellion and change from established family patterns. For example, Chesla (1999) found healthful coping shifts in her study of couples living with non-insulin-dependent diabetes.

When focusing on resilience in families with a member living with HIV (Human Immunodeficiency Virus), researchers identified the vital role of HIV-positive mothers' perceptions her family's and friends' social support in reducing loneliness and easing some of the emotional distress (Serovich et al. 2001). The *Healthlink Worldwide* organization reports that resilience in African children living in families with HIV/AIDS (Autoimmunodeficiency Syndrome) is enhanced when families engage in open communication, expressing emotions, creating goals (compelling futures), talking about loving relationships, expressing spirituality, a supportive community, and helping others. An opportunity to assist another fosters a sense of resourcefulness and self-esteem (Carnegie 2003).

Although some coping behaviors assist the family in successfully negotiating challenges, other coping strategies can detract from healthful adjustment and adaptation. For example, a mother may work overtime to help with the financial stress placed on the family. This action adds strain in terms of childcare and family time, but may act as a positive learning experience for the family. Other coping behaviors can lead to chronic maladaptation. For example, one family member's use of violence to cope with the frustration of downsizing at work greatly contributes to decreased family sense of coherence and successful adaptation.

Coping can be learned or even inherited. Boss (2002) argues that some unfortunate coping strategies such as violence and aggression may be transmitted within a family and thus need to be interrupted if the family is to survive and thrive in time of change and challenge. All family members, including children and youth, need to be taught healthful coping skills (Rutter 1979, 1985).

Coping also hinges on the rhythm and timeline of the changes and challenges families face. For example, a persistent challenge such as a family member with a chronic illness requires the family to rearrange routines and often lifestyles, whereas a brief event such as parent staying home with acutely ill child demands quick response, but less duration.

A family resiliency model includes not only family meanings, schema, and cultural influences on adaptation but also family boundaries (i.e., who is and is not part of the family). Ambiguity about boundaries (e.g., physically or emotionally absent parents) may cause confusion in coping and moving on in the face of stressors. Likewise, ambivalence may be present in families. Boss (2002: 122) reminds family studies professionals that "the goal is not to eliminate ambiguity and ambivalence in family processes, but to increase tolerance for ambiguity and thus minimize ambivalence and immobilization from guilt and shame."

Researchers warn of over simplification of the dynamic and contextual nature of family processes (Burr and Klein 1994). Family resilience exists in multiple contexts which challenges family studies scholars to embrace the clinical studies of family studies practitioners which often pay greater attention to the contextual nature of family resilience (Ganong and Coleman 2002). Oswald (2002) offers a rich contextual examination of resilience in gay and lesbian families, whereas Seccombe (2002) explores resiliency in families living in poverty. Both are contexts in need of greater attention by family studies scholars.

Family practitioners need to create healthful strategies and environments to engage families, their members and the outside community in the proactive process of enhancement, maintenance, and renewal of processes that enhance family resiliency.

Family Resiliency Processes (Interactions of Strengths and Buffers)

Family *resiliency processes* reflect families balancing strengths and buffers (resources) against challenges and demands. McCubbin and colleagues (1997) offer the following nine interacting family strengths and buffers.

In normative and nonnormative life events and changes, *family problem-solving communication* serves as a crucial tool through which families create shared sense of meaning, develop and orchestrate coping strategies, and maintain harmony and balance. This communication may be affirming (i.e., pattern of family communication conveying support, caring, and exerting a calming influence) or incendiary (i.e., pattern of family communication that tends to exacerbate a stressful situation such as yelling and screaming). All families have both, but in the face of challenges, demands, and crises the incendiary pattern may dominate, causing the resultant imbalance to contribute to family deterioration and undermining the family's ability to adapt.

In addition to *equality* for all family members, *spirituality* appears in resilient families. Families facing crisis often need more than reasoning and logic to explain the reality of their situation. Spirituality may or may not include religious faith, but fundamentally it provides an avenue to help adjust and adapt to that which brings anguish or pain.

During demanding times, families need *flexibility* as they change their patterns of functioning, including roles, rules, meanings, and in some cases lifestyles to achieve harmony, balance, and recovery. Families also require *truthfulness* during these challenging situations. Truthfulness is needed within the family system, but also truthfulness from those social, medical, educational, and political agencies and programs that inform and guide families through difficult circumstances.

Families' "sense of a compelling future" (Grochowski 2000; Grochowski, Harkins, and Stewart 1998), their sense of *hope*, often is cloudy or even absent with adversity. An element of hope can be seen in families' ability to create and maintain images of compelling futures and renewal of this process in the face of adversity.

All family systems work to develop patterns of behavior and functioning with the sole purpose of creating predictability and stability, the milieu for harmony and balance. Families cultivate such practices as having meals together, spending quality time with the children, or just simply "hanging out together," often referred to as *family time and routines*. During a family crisis, family time and routines are often disrupted, set aside, or canceled and replaced by a total devotion to the family problem and all of its accompanying hardships. When faced with adversity, resilient families need to retain some family routines to maintain the family's stability and continuity.

In the face of risks, families draw from a network of relationships, *social support,* to facilitate their durability. In the case of crisis, family systems not only draw from extant sources of support but also oftentimes will seek additional, if not unique, forms of support that will help give meaning to the situation, help develop coping strategies, and, more importantly, foster the family's ability to change. McCubbin and colleagues (1997) argue that social support has five dimensions:

- Emotional support (e.g., sharing information of caring)
- Esteem support (e.g., sharing information affirming the value of family members and what they do)
- Network support (e.g., sharing information that members belong to a larger group to whom they have a responsibility and from which they get something in return)
- Appraisal support (e.g., sharing information of evaluation to give members a sense of boundary)
- Altruistic support (e.g., sharing information indicating the importance of giving of one's self for the benefit of others as a means of enhancing one's self esteem)

Finally, there is little doubt in the minds and reasoning of family scientists that physical and emotional *health* [wellness] of family members are essential protective and recovery factors in promoting resiliency in family systems.

These nine family strengths and buffers while important, are only part of resilience in families. Family resiliency is not a "one size fits all" model. Just as there is diversity in family composition and definition, family resiliency processes are highly variable. Figure 3.4 submits an image of this non-linear interface of family resiliency processes.

DYNAMIC RESILIENCY: KEEPING THE "MAGIC"

The paradigm of family resiliency is based on evidence of the power of protective and preventive factors, and whereas family protective and recovery factors are identifiable and vital, those factors are not complete in themselves. The interactions of the individual family members in the context of their family and the surrounding community provide a more nuanced picture of the dynamic, multifaceted nature of family resiliency.

The family resiliency paradigm reflects an evolution in thinking from problem and deficiency based to one of challenge and strength, a salutogenic philosophy. Family resiliency processes hold center stage for many resiliency researchers and practitioners. Box 3.4 describes some key resilience processes.

Implications for Future Research and Application

Werner (1999: 11) warns that resiliency may be "too popular for its own sake." Heeding this warning, family study professionals strive to avoid simplistic assumptions regarding family resiliency. Table 3.3 poses scholarly questions and paradoxes in the study of resiliency.

Boss (2002) also offers 10 recommendations for future family resiliency research and practice:

- Increase study of diverse families in crises while including community perspectives
- Continue to study family boundary ambiguity—who is in, who is out and how this boundary is influenced by genetics, development, economics, history, culture
- Develop greater awareness of applicability of theoretical models

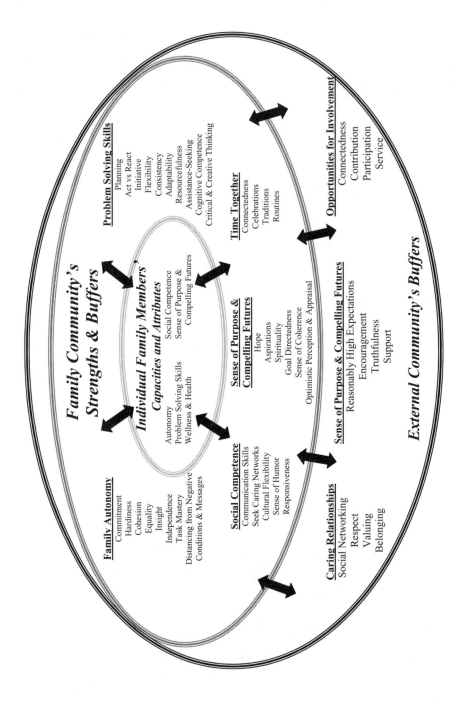

FIG. 3.4. Innate Wisdom Model : Family Resiliency Processes © 2003 Janet R. Grochowski.
Source: Adapted with permission from Grochowski, Janet R. 1997. "Strategic Living Context Communities–Families Who Thrive in the Future." Presented at the International World Future Society Conference, July, San Francisco, CA.

BOX 3.4   "Key Processes In Family Resilience"
Froma Walsh, Ph.D.

Froma Walsh developed a Family Resilience Framework to identify and target key processes that strengthen family capacities to rebound from crises and master stressful life challenges. This framework is informed by two decades of social science and clinical research seeking to understand crucial variables contributing to individual and family resilience. Drawing together findings from the numerous studies, this framework synthesizes key processes for resilience within three domains of family functioning: family belief systems, organization patterns, and communication processes.

FAMILY RESILIENCE FRAMEWORK

Belief Systems

1. Make Meaning of Adversity
   - View resilience as relationally based—versus "rugged individual"
   - Normalize, contextualize adversity and distress
   - Sense of coherence: Crisis as meaningful, comprehensible, manageable challenge
   - Causal/explanatory attributions: How could this happen? What can be done?

2. Positive Outlook
   - Hope, optimistic bias; confidence in overcoming odds
   - Courage and en-*courage*-ment; affirm strengths, focus on potential
   - Active initiative and perseverance (can-do spirit)
   - Master the possible; accept what can't be changed

3. Transcendence and Spirituality
   - Larger values, purpose, meaning in life
   - Spirituality: Faith, congregational support, healing rituals
   - Inspiration: Envision dreams, new possibilities; creative expression; social action
   - Transformation: Learning, change, and growth from adversity

Organizational Patterns

4. Flexibility
   - Open to change: Rebound, reorganize, adapt to fit new challenges
   - Stability through disruption: Continuity, dependability, follow-through
   - Strong authoritative leadership: Nurturance, protection, and guidance
   - Varied family forms: cooperative parenting/caregiving teams
   - Couple/co-parent relationship: equal partners

5. Connectedness
   - Mutual support, collaboration, and commitment
   - Respect individual needs, differences, and boundaries
   - Seek reconnection, reconciliation of wounded relationships

6. Social and Economic Resources
   - Mobilize kin, social & community networks; Seek models, mentors
   - Build financial security; balance work/family strains

Communication/Problem Solving

7. Clarity
   - Clear, consistent messages (words and actions)
   - Clarify ambiguous information; truth seeking/truth speaking

8. Open Emotional Expression
   - Share range of feelings (joy and pain; hopes and fears)
   - Mutual empathy; tolerance for differences
   - Take responsibility for own feelings, behavior; avoid blaming
   - Pleasurable interactions; humor

9. Collaborative Problem-solving
   - Creative brainstorming; resourcefulness
   - Shared decision making; conflict resolution: Negotiation, fairness, reciprocity
   - Focus on goals; take concrete steps; build on success; learn from failure
   - Proactive stance: Prevent problems; avert crises; prepare for future challenges

Froma Walsh, Ph.D., is Professor and Co-Director of the Center for Family Health at the University of Chicago.

- Merge streams of research so as to better understand both family and family member responses to stress and crisis
- Integrate gender differences
- Study biases including the expectation that we demand more resiliency from families with less power or status
- Listen more to subjective data, including families stories about family values and beliefs
- Increase focus on intergenerational family stress and resiliency
- Increase interdisciplinary collaboration
- Increase use of both quantitative and qualitative studies

Family professionals and individuals also need to explore what constitutes effective strategies and environments that foster resiliency processes. Linked to this challenge is the need to study the "learnability" and "transferability" of these processes. Herein lies the "proactive" nature of a resiliency paradigm.

Studies of successful approaches to learning, that is, learnability and transferability of resiliency processes, reveal the importance of building relationships based on caring, respect, and trust (Schorr 1988), as well as the importance of community and family partnerships (Doherty 2000). *Participatory partnerships* translates into "the conditions that allow [individuals and families] innate potential for social competence, problem solving, sense of identity and efficacy, and hope for the future to unfold" (Benard 2002: 8). We recommend a need to change the current paradigms from:

   ...risk to resilience, from control to participation, from problem-[centered] to positive development, from Eurocentrism to multiculturalism, from seeing youth [families] as problems
   to seeing them as resources, from institution-building to community-building, and so on.
   (Benard 1999: 8)

TABLE 3.3
Defining Resiliency: Questions and Paradoxes

Defining Resiliency: Questions
- To what extent are resiliency processes "generic" vs. related to specific risks?
- To what extent can resiliency processes be introduced in a preventive mode before crises or challenges occur?
- To what extent are resiliency processes transferable across situations or contexts?
- To what extent are resiliency processes "learnable" from one individual, family, and community to another?
- To what extent are resiliency processes learned or exercised on a continuum (i.e., with extremes inhibiting them)?
- To what extent are resiliency processes a set of consequences or responses to "high-risk" circumstances, or are they different depending on the level of risk?
- To what extent does the combination of individual strengths or problems result in defining a family system's strengths or liabilities "beyond the sum of the parts?"
- What, exactly, is the relationship among individual, family, and community resiliency in research? (i.e., Does individual "success" imply or ignore family well-being?)
- What is the relationship of resiliency to moral and ethical behavior? (e.g., What are the impacts of expedient behaviors such as giving up on a relationship vs. working at it or ignoring a drug dealer in your neighborhood that can lead to "resilient" outcomes survival, personal success?)

Defining Resiliency: Paradoxes
- Symmetry: The same behavior (e.g., parent support) may result in different outcomes (e.g., dependency or self-confidence) or different behaviors (e.g., neglect and careful mentoring) may result in the same outcomes (e.g., self-reliance).
- Strong individual values (e.g., creativity) may be at odds with strong family values (e.g., cohesion, cooperation) or strong family values (e.g., cohesion, thrift) may conflict with some cultural values (e.g., individualism and consumerism).

Source: Adapted with permission from Silliman, Ben. 1994. "1994 Resiliency Research Review: Conceptual & Research Foundations." *Children, Youth, and Families Education and Research Network.* www.cyfernet.org/ research/resilreview.html (Retrieved 2/24/02).

Optimism and Learned Resourcefulness

Holding an optimistic attitude toward life is vital to family resiliency. Optimism is anticipation, buoyancy, calmness, confidence, hopefulness, and resourcefulness. Optimism is not fantasy, delusion, apparition, fallacy, or helplessness. The concepts of learned resourcefulness (Rosenbaum 1983, 1990) and learned optimism (vs. learned helplessness; Seligman 1994, 2002) have tremendous potential. Likewise, psychological attachment theory (Bretherton 1985) and Noddlings's (1984) work on caring environments remind us that individuals, families, and external communities need a sense of living and working in caring, purposeful, and supportive environments. This does not mean a denial of change or challenge. Instead, it means that within each family system and its family subsystems there needs to be a worldview regarding the ability to meet and thrive in change and challenge.

Bouncing Back and Springing Forward

A resiliency approach requires the development of a *resilient attitude*. This means focusing on strengths and buffers while working through limitations and barriers. A resilient

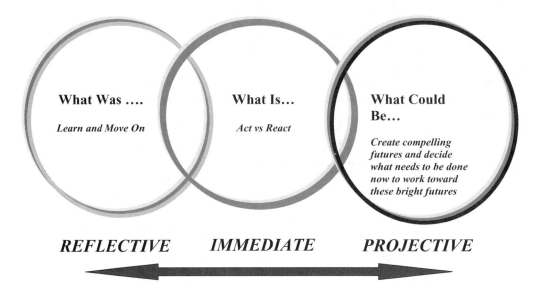

FIG. 3.5. Reflective—Immediate—Projective Orientation Model © 2003 Janet R. Grochowski
Source: Adapted with permission from Grochowski, Janet R. 1998. "Creating Compelling Health
Futures: Impacts of a Promising Story-Based Strategy on Adolescents' Personal Health Projections"
International Association of Management Proceedings (August): 17–23.

attitude also encompasses a realization that life is not a quest to attain perfection, but
rather a journey of adjusting and adapting to living well. Higgins (1994: 319) reminds
professionals that "facilitating resiliency is more a matter of orientation than specific
intervention." Lessons from approaches to foster resiliency in youth (Henderson 1999)
may be expanded to families. Such approaches would communicate a resilient attitude
by focusing on what is working in the family, focusing on the strengths and buffers
with at least the same (or greater) emphasis than the limitations and challenges, building
participatory partnerships—networks of support from within and without family communities, and being reasonably persistent by recognizing that not every family can be equally
resilient.

Few will deny the value of promoting family resiliency, yet the challenge of how to
enhance, maintain, and renew family resiliency processes remains contentious. According
to Benard, "Fostering resiliency is a process and not a program . . . [it is] an emphasis on
process and how we do what we do" (1999: 8). Family resiliency begins with recognition
of family strengths and buffers plus a need for a resiliency—and salutogenic—attitude.

Proactive resiliency is resilience at a heightened level of awareness and intent. Balance is the foundation of successful, healthful adjustment, and adaptation to the changes
and challenges of life. Families need to be encouraged and supported in their efforts to
positively impact their resiliency processes. Such a proactive orientation suggests that
creating compelling futures of what could be for individuals, their families, and external communities in terms of resiliency processes may be an initial stage in proactive
resiliency. This is not passive, wishful thinking, but rather an active, anticipatory approach
to assist individuals, families, and external communities in answering important questions: "What could be?" "What do we want in terms of resiliency processes?" and the
pivotal question, "What are we willing to do now to reach these preferred compelling
futures?"

Grochowski developed an image of such a *reflective-immediate-projective orientation* (Figure 3.5) in which one learns from the past, creates compelling futures as guides, and then decides what one must do today to reach these preferred futures.

In the 21st century, the study of family resiliency continues to evolve from fixed characteristics to dynamic, contextual understandings of the complex nature of being resilient. This means the ability to bounce back from change and adverse circumstances and to spring forward toward compelling futures (Grochowski 2000). A challenge for current family studies professionals is to learn how to effectively empower individuals, their families, and external communities to recognize, enhance, maintain, and renew the "innate wisdom" of family resiliency processes, thereby effectuating families at their best.

GLOSSARY

ABCX model	Participatory partnerships
Adjustment	Perceptions
Adaptation	Pileup
Appraisals	Protective factors
At risk	Protective processes
Comprehensibility	Recovery factors
Compelling futures	Reflective—immediate—projective orientation
Coping	Resiliency (resilience)
Double ABCX model	Resiliency processes
FAAR model	Resilient attitude
Homeostasis	Salutogenesis
Manageability	Sense of coherence
Meaningfulness	Stress theory
Pathogenesis	Stressors

FOR YOUR CONSIDERATION

1. Give an example of how perception and appraisal can positively or negatively impact how a family responds to change or challenge.

2. Consider this scenario: You are a family professional who will be working with a child who is having behavioral problems in school. In your interview with the family you learn that this is an economically disadvantaged, single-parent family. How would you approach this child and the family if you begin with a risk factors approach? If you begin with a protective factors approach?

3. Consider this scenario: You are working on a public policy committee whose charge is to expand services to low-income neighborhoods. How would you explain 'family resiliency processes' to your colleagues as a necessary part of addressing this problem?

4. This chapter argues that resilient families not only "bounce back" but "spring forward." Give an example of a challenging family situation in which the family not only bounces back, but springs forward.

FOR FURTHER STUDY: WEB SITES, ORGANIZATIONS, AND PUBLICATIONS

Web Sites and Organizations

Children, Youth and Families Education and Research Network (CYFERnet)
www.cyfernet.org
CYFERnet offers professionals working with children, youth, and families reliable, practical, research-based information on the Web. The information is timely, well supported, and includes state networking sources.

National Network for Family Resilience (NNFR)
www.nnfr.org
Several functions and resources of the *NNFR* are now incorporated within the Children, Youth, and Families Education and Research Network (CYFERNet) as noted previously.

National Resilience Resource Center (NRRC)
www.cce.umn.edu/nrrc/research.shtml
Spanning more than five decades across a wide variety of disciplines, NRRC works from a strength-based philosophy. The organization strives to engage emerging resilience research agendas and places emphasis on internal as well as external protective factors and processes. This site links to three major resources including: The Carter Center, Promoting Positive and Healthy Behaviors in Children, The U.S. Center for Substance Abuse Prevention, Central CAPT—Resilience Research for Prevention Programs, and The University of Minnesota, CARE—Research and Practice.

Project Resilience
www.projectresilience.com
Project Resilience a private organization with teaching materials, products, and training options. The core of this project is promotion of a strength-based approach to youth and adults as they struggle with change and challenges including family disruption, poverty, violence, substance abuse, and racism.

Resiliency in Action
www.resiliency.com
The Resiliency in Action site shares information on the theory and practice of resiliency. The site offers a reader-friendly format plus materials, products, and training options. Major emphasis is resiliency in youth.

SEARCH Institute
www.search-institute.org
This institute proposes a strength-based approach to healthy youth growth and development and offers information, products, and training options related to the *40 Developmental Assets* program.

Project Competence
Established by Norman Garmezy, this 20-year study of 205 children is currently directed by Professor Ann Masten at the University of Minnesota's Institute of Child Development.

Stress, Coping and Resilience: Individuals and Families Project
The project focuses on family stress, coping, and resiliency with primary emphasis on "families." The Project examines resiliency in family faced with complex challenges such as military separation and loss, chronic illness, poverty, race and ethnicity issues. This research-based project operates out of the University of Hawaii with Professor Marilyn McCubbin, Co-Director and Washington State University with Dr. Laurie McCubbin, Co-Director.

Publications

Brooks, Robert, and Sam Goldstein. 2001. *Raising Resilient Children: Fostering Strength, Hope and Optimism in Your Child.* Chicago: Contemporary Books.

The authors' extensive experience working with children and their families supports the premise that parents play a vital role in enhancing a sense of resiliency in their children. They discuss creating an environment that nurtures this kind of resiliency. This environment includes empathy, optimism, respect, unconditional love, authentic listening, calmness and patience.

McKenry, Patrick, and Sharon Price. eds. 2000. *Families and Change: Coping With Stressful Events and Transitions.* Thousand Oaks, CA: Sage. In this second edition, McKenry and Price present a discussion and examination of literature related to families' responses to various transitions and other unexpected life events. This book includes an interdisciplinary tone while blending research, theory, and application. *Families and Change* is intended to serve as a basic or supplementary text for undergraduate and introductory graduate courses relating to family concerns and challenges.

REFERENCES FOR CITED WORKS

American Heritage Dictionary of the English Language, Fourth Edition. 2000. Boston, MA: Houghton Mifflin http://dictionary.reference.com/search?q=resilience (Retrieved 3/1/05).

Antonovsky, Aaron. 1979. *Health, Stress, and Coping.* San Francisco, CA: Jossey-Bass.

Antonovsky, Aaron. 1987. *Unraveling the Mystery of Health.* San Francisco, CA: Jossey-Bass.

Antonovsky, Aaron. 1994. "The Sense of Coherence: An Historical and Future Perspective." In *Sense of Coherence and Resiliency: Stress, Coping, and Health*, eds. H. I. McCubbin, E. A. Thompson, A. I. Thompson, and J. E. Fromer. Madison, WI: University of Wisconsin Press.

Antonovsky, Aaron, and T. Sourani. 1988. "Family Sense of Coherence and Family Adaptation." *Journal of Marriage and Family* 50, (February): 79–92.

Benard, Bonnie. 1991. *Fostering Resiliency in Kids: Protective Factors in the Family, School, and Community.* Portland, OR: Western Center for Drug-Free Schools and Communities.

Benard, Bonnie. 1999. "From Research to Practice: The Foundations of the Resiliency Paradigm." In *Resiliency in Action: Practical Ideas for Overcoming Risks and Building Strengths in Youth, Families, and Communities*, N. Henderson, B. Bernard, and N. Sharp-Light (eds.). San Diego, CA: Resiliency in Action, Inc., 5–9.

Benard, Bonnie. 2002. "The Foundations of the Resiliency Framework: From Research to Practice." *Resiliency In Action.* www.resiliency.com/htm/research,htm (Retrieved 7/29/02).

Benard, Bonnie. 2004. *Resiliency: What We Have Learned.* San Francisco, CA: WestEd.

Blum, Robert. 2002. "Risk and Resilience: A Model for Public Health Interventions for Adolescents." *Canadian Association of Adolescent Health.* http://www.acsa-caah.ca (Retrieved 8/19/02)

Blyth, Dale A., and Eugene Roehlkepartain. 1993. "Healthy Communities, Healthy Youth." Minneapolis, MN: Search Institute.

Boss, Pauline G. 1988. *Family Stress Management.* Newbury Park, CA: Sage.

Boss, Pauline G. 2002. *Family Stress Management: A Contextual Approach*, 2/e. Thousand Oaks, CA: Sage.

Bretherton, Inge. 1985. "Growing Points of Attachment: Theory and Research." In *Monographs of the Society of Research in Child Development Serial*, No. 209, Vol 50, No 1–2, ed. Everett Waters. Philadelphia, PA: Blackwell

Brooks, Robert. 1991. *The Self Esteem Teacher.* Loveland, OH: Treehause Communications.

Burr, Wesley R. 1973. *Theory Construction and the Sociology of the Family.* New York: Wiley.

Burr, Wesley R. 1982. "Families Under Stress." In *Family Stress, Coping, and Social Support*, eds. H. I. McCubbin, A. E. Cauble, and J. M. Patterson. Springfield, IL: Charles C Thomas, 5–25.

Burr, Wesley R., and Shirley R. Klein. 1994. *Reexamining Family Stress: New Theory and Research.* Thousand Oaks, CA: Sage.

Cannon, W. B. 1935. "Stresses and Strains of Homeostasis" (Mary Scott Newbold Lecture). *American Journal of Medical Sciences* 189: 1–14.

Carnegie, Rachel. 2003. "Listening to Children: Children as Partners in Research." www.healthlink.org.uk/ewa-ccath04.htm (Retrieved 3/6/05).

Chesla, Catherine. 1999. "Becoming Resilient: Skill Development in Couples Living with Non-Insulin Dependent Diabetes." In *The Dynamics of Resilient Families*, eds. H. I. McCubbin, E. A. Thompson, A. I. Thompson, and J. A. Futrell. Thousand Oaks, CA: Sage, 99–133.

Cousins, Norman. 1989. *Head First: The Biology of Hope*. New York, NY: Dutton.

Cowan, P. A. 1991. "Individual and Family Life Transitions: A Proposal for a New Definition." In *Family Transitions*, eds. P. A. Dowan and E. M. Hetherington. Hillsdale, NJ: Lawrence Erlbaum Associates, 3–30.

Crosnoe, Robert. 2004. "Social Capital and the Interplay of Families and Schools." *Journal of Marriage and Family* 66, 2 (May): 267–80.

Doherty, William. 2000. "Family Science and Family Citizenship: Toward a Model of Community Partnership with Families." *Family Relations* 49 (July): 319–25.

Dohrenwend, Barbara, and Bruce Dohrenwend, eds. 1981. *Stressful Life Events and Their Contexts*. New York, NY: Neale Watson Academic Publications.

Drummett, Amy Reinkober, Marilyn Coleman, and Susan Cable. 2003. "Military Families Under Stress: Implications for Family Life Education." *Family Relations* 52, 3 (July): 279–87.

Dugan, Timothy, and Robert Coles, eds. 1989. *The Child in Our Times: Studies in the Development of Resiliency*. New York, NY: Brunner/Mazel.

Felner, Robert. 2000. "Educational Reform as Ecologically Based Prevention and Promotion: The Project on High Performance Learning Communities." In *The Promotion of Wellness in Children and Adolescents* eds. D. Cicchetti, J. Rappaport, I. Sandler, and R. Weissberg. Washington, DC: Child Welfare League Association, 271–307.

Ganong, Lawrence, and Marilyn Coleman. 2002. "Introduction to the Special Section: Family Resilience in Multiple Contexts." *Journal of Marriage and Family* 64 (May): 346–48.

Garmezy, Norman. 1981. "Children Under Stress: Perspectives on Antecedents and Correlates of Vulnerability and Resistance to Psychopathology." In *Further Explorations in Personality*, eds. A. I. Rubin, J. Arnoff, A. M. Barclay, and R. A. Zucker. New York, NY: Wiley, 196–269.

Garmezy, Norman. 1985. "Stress-resistant Children: The Search for Protective Factors." In *Recent Research in Development Psychopathology. Journal of Child Psychology and Psychiatry Book Supplement* No. 4. ed. J. E. Stevenson. Oxford, England: Pergamon, 213–33.

Garmezy, Norman. 1987. "Stress, Competence and Development: Continuities in The Study of Schizophrenic Adults, Children Vulnerable to Psychopathology, and the Search for Stress Resistant Children." *American Journal of Orthopsychiatry* 57, 2: 593–607.

Garmezy, Norman. 1991. "Resilience in Children's Adaptation to Negative Life Events and Stressed Environments." *Pediatric Annals* 20: 459–66.

Garmezy, Norman, and Ann Masten. 1991. "The Protective Role of Competence Indicators in Children at Risk." In *Perspectives on Stress and Coping*, eds. E. M. Cummings, A. L. Greene, and K. H. Karrakei, Hillsdale, NJ: Lawrence Erlbaum, Associates, 151–74.

Garmezy, Norman, Ann Masten, and A. Tellegen. 1984. "The Study of Stress and Competence in Children: A Building Block for Developmental Psychopathology." *Child Development* 55: 97–111.

Garmezy, Norman, and Michael Rutter. 1983. *Stress, Coping and Development in Childhood*. New York, NY: McGraw-Hill.

Garwick, Ann, Joan Patterson, L. Meschke, F. Bennett, and Robert Blum. 2002. "The Uncertainty of Preadolescents' Chronic Health Conditions and Family Distress." *Journal of Family Nursing* 8, 1: 22–31.

Grochowski, Janet R. 1997. "Strategic Living Context Communities: Families Who Thrive in the Future." Paper presented at the *International World Future Society* Conference, July, San Francisco, CA.

Grochowski, Janet R. 1998. "Creating Compelling Health Futures: Impacts of a Promising Story-Based Strategy on Adolescents' Personal Health Projections." *International Association of Management Proceedings* (August): 17–23.

Grochowski, Janet R. 2000. "Families as 'Strategic Living Communities.'" Paper presented at the annual meetings of the *American Academy of Health Behavior*, September, Santa Fe, NM.

Grochowski, Janet R., Arthur Harkins, and Brenda Stewart 1998. "Strategic Living Organizations: Families for the Future." *Futurics: Quarterly Journal of Futures Research* 21, 1 and 2: 24–9.

Grotberg, Edith. 1998. "I Am, I Have, I Can: What Families Worldwide Taught Us About Resilience." *Reaching Today's Youth* (Spring): 36–9.

Grotberg, Edith. 1999. "Countering Depression With the Five Building Blocks of Resilience." *Reaching Today's Youth* 4 (Fall): 66–72.

Hall, A. D., and R. E. Fagan. 1968. "Definition of System." In *Modern Systems Research for the Behavioral Scientist*, ed. W. Buckley. Chicago, IL: Aldine, 81–92.

Hawley, D. R., and L. DeHann. 1996. "Toward a Definition of Family Resilience: Integrating Life-Span and Family Perspectives." *Family Process* 35, 3: 283–98.

Henderson, Nan. 1999. "Fostering Resiliency in Children and Youth: Four Basic Steps for Families, Educators, and Other Caring Adults." In *Resiliency in Action: Practical Ideas for Overcoming Risks and Building Strengths in Youth, Families, and Communities*, eds. N. Henderson, B. Benard, and N. Sharp-Light. San Diego, CA: Resiliency in Action, 161–67.

Heraclitus. 1960. In *Great Quotations*, ed. G. Seldes. New York, NY: Caesar-Stewart.

Higgins, G. 1994. *Resilient Adults: Overcoming a Cruel Past*. San Francisco, CA: Jossey-Bass.

Hill, Rubin. 1949. *Families under Stress*. Westport, CT: Greenwood.

Hill, Rubin. 1958. Generic Features of Families under Stress. *Social Casework* 49: 139–50.

Howard, Sue, and Bruce Johnson. 2004. "What Makes the Difference? Children and Teachers Talk About Resilient Outcomes for Children 'At-Risk.'" University of South Australia. www.aare.edu.au/99pap/how99727.htm. (Retrieved 12/4/04).

Jackson, Yo, Sarah Sifers, Jared Warren, and Dori Velasquez. 2003. "Family Protective Factors and Behavioral Outcome: The Role of Appraisal in Family Life Events." *Journal of Emotional and Behavioral Disorders* 11: 103–11.

Kobasa, Suzane C. 1979. "Stressful Life Events, Personality and Health." *Journal of Personality and Social Psychology* 37, 1: 1–11.

Kobasa, Suzane. C., S. R. Maddi, and S. Kahn. 1982. "Hardiness and Health: A Prospective Study." *Journal of Personality and Social Psychology* 42: 168–77.

Kurth-Schai, R. 1988. "The Roles of Youth in Society: A Reconceptualization." *Educational Forum* 52, 2: 113–32.

Lazarus, R. S. 1966. *Psychological Stress and the Coping Process*. New York, NY: McGraw-Hill.

Lazarus, R. S. 1976. *Patterns of Adjustment*. New York, NY: McGraw-Hill.

Lazarus, R. S., and S. Folkman. 1984. *Stress, Appraisal and Coping*. New York, NY: Springer.

Lefcourt, Herbert. 2001. *Humor: The Psychology of Living Buoyantly*. New York, NY: Plenum.

Lefcourt, Herbert. 2002. "Humor." In *Handbook of Positive Psychology*, eds. C. Snyder and S. Lopez. New York, NY: Oxford University Press, 619–31.

Leffert, N., P. I. Benson, P. C. Scales, A. R. Sharma, D. R. Drake, and Dale A. Blyth. 1998. "Developmental Assets: Measurement and Prediction of Risk Behaviors Among Adolescents." *Applied Developmental Science* 2: 209–30.

Lovallo, William R. 1997. *Stress and Health: Biological and Psychological Interactions*. Thousand Oaks, CA: Sage.

Luthar, Suniya. 1995. "Social Competence in the School Setting: Prospective Cross-Domain Associations Among Inner-City Teens." *Child Development* 66: 416–29.

Luthar, Suniya. 1999. *Poverty and Children's Adjustment*. Thousand Oaks, CA: Sage.

Luthar, Suniya, and D. Cicchetti. 2000. "The Construct of Resilience: Implications for Interventions and Social Policies." *Development and Psychopathology* 12: 857–85.

Masten, Ann., Karin Best, and Norman Garmezy. 1990. "Resilience and Development: Contributions from the Study of Children Who Overcome Adversity."*Development Psychopathology* 2: 425–44.

Masten, Ann, and John Douglas Coatsworth. 1998. "The Development of Competence in Favorable and Unfavorable Environments: Lessons from Research on Successful Children." *American Psychologist* 53, 2: 205–20.

Masten, Ann. 2001. "Ordinary Magic: Resilience Processes in Development." *American Psychologist* 56: 227–38.

Masten, Ann. 2002a. "Competence, Risk, and Resilience in Development."*Institute of Child Development*. http://education.umn.edu/icd/faculty/Masten.htm (Retrieved 7/31/02).

Masten, Ann. 2002b. "Children Who Overcome Adversity to Succeed in Life." *University of Minnesota Extension Service.* www/extemsopm/umn.edu/distribution/familydevelopment/components/7565_06html (Retrieved 7/31/02).

Masten, Ann, and Marie-Gabreille Reed. 2002. "Resilience in Development." In *Handbook of Positive Psychology*, eds. C. Snyder and S. Lopez. New York, NY: Oxford University Press.

McBroom, Patricia. 2002. "Positive Emotions, Including Laughter, are Important Paths Out of Trauma, According to UC Berkeley Psychologist." *Campus News*, September, 1.

McCubbin, Hamilton, Marilyn McCubbin, Anne Thompson, Sae-Young Han, and Chad Allen. 1997. "Families Under Stress: What Makes Them Resilient." Paper presented at the meetings of the *American Association of Family & Consumer Sciences*, June, Washington, DC. www.cynfernet.extension.umn.edu/research/resilient.html (Retrieved 08/01/02).

McCubbin, Hamilton. 1998. "Resiliency in African American Families: Military Families in Foreign Environments." In *Resiliency in Ethnic Minority Families: African-American Families*, eds. H. I. McCubbin, E. A. Thompson, A. I. Thompson, and J. Futrell. Boston, MA: Sage, 67–97.

McCubbin, Hamilton I., B. Dahl, G. Lester, D. Benson, and M. Robertson. 1976. "Coping Repertoires of Families Adapting to Prolonged War-Induced Separations." *Journal of Marriage and the Family* 38: 461–71.

McCubbin, Hamilton I., Ann I Thompson, P. Pirner, and Marilyn McCubbin. 1988. *Family types and Strengths: A Life Cycle and Ecological Perspective*. Edina, MN: Burgess International.

McCubbin, Hamilton, and Marilyn McCubbin. 1988. "Typologies of Resilient Families: Emerging Roles of Social Class and Ethnicity." *Family Relations* 37: 247–54.

McCubbin, Hamilton I., Marilyn McCubbin, Anne Thompson, Sae-Young Han, and Chad Allen. 1997. "Families Under Stress: What Makes Them Resilient." Paper presented at the meetings of the *American Association of Family & Consumer Sciences*, June, Washington, DC. www.cynfernet.extension.umn.edu/research/resilient.html (Retrieved 08/01/02).

McCubbin, Hamilton I., Jo A. Futrell, Elizabeth Thompson, and Anne Thompson. 1998. "Resilient Families in an Ethnic and Cultural Context." In *Resiliency in African-American Families*, eds. H. I. McCubbin, E. A. Thompson, A. I. Thompson, and J. A Futrell. Thousand Oaks, CA: Sage, 329–51.

McCubbin, Hamilton I., and Joan M. Patterson. 1982. "Family Stress and Adaptation to Crises." In *FamilyStress, Coping, and Social Support*, eds. H. I. McCubbin, A. E. Cauble, and J. M. Patterson. Springfield, IL: Charles C Thomas, 26–47.

McCubbin, Hamilton I., and Joan M. Patterson. 1983a. "The Family Stress and Adaptation to Crisis: A Double ABCX Model of Family Behavior." In *Family Studies in Review Yearbook*, eds. D. Olson and B. Miller. Beverly Hills, CA: Sage, 87–107.

McCubbin, Hamilton I., and Joan M. Patterson. 1983b. "The Family Stress Process: The Double ABCX Model of Adjustment and Adaptation." *Marriage and Family Review* 6: 7–37.

McCubbin, Hamilton I., and Anne Thompson. 1989. *Balancing Work and Family Life on Wall Street: Stockbrokers and Families Coping With Economic Instability*. Edina, MN: Burgess.

McCubbin, Marilyn A. 1989. "Family Stress and Family Strengths: A Comparison of Single and Two-Parent Families with Handicapped Children." *Research in Nursing and Health* 12, 2: 101–10.

McCubbin, Marilyn A., Karla Balling, Peggy Possin, Sharon Frierdich, and Barbara Beyne. 2002. "Family Resiliency in Childhood Cancer." *Family Relations* 51, 2 (April): 103–11.

McKenry, Patrick. E., and Price, S. J. eds. 2000. *Families & Change: Coping with Stressful Events and Transitions*. Thousand Oaks, CA: Sage.

Murphy, Lois, and Alice Moriarty. 1976. *Vulnerability, Coping, and Growth: From Infancy to Adolescence*. New Haven, CT: Yale University Press.

Murry, Velma McBride, Gene Brody, Anita Brown, Joseph Wisenbaker, Carolyn Cutrona, and Ronald Simons. 2002. "Linking Employment Status, Marital Psychological Well-Being, Parenting, and Children's Attributions About Poverty in Families Receiving Government Assistance." *Family Relations* 51: 112–20.

Noddlings, Nel. 1984. *Caring: A Feminine Approach to Ethics & Moral Education*. Berkeley, CA: University of California Press.

Olson, David, Hamilton McCubbin, H. Barnes, A. Larsen, A. Muxem, and M. Wilson. 1983. *Families: What Makes Them Work*. Beverly Hills, CA: Sage.

Oswald, Ramona Faith. 2002. "Resilience Within the Family Network of Lesbians and Gay Men: Intentionally and Redefinitions." *Journal of Marriage and Family* 64, (May): 374–83.

Patterson, Joan. M. 1988. "Families Experiencing Stress: The Family Adjustment and Adaptation Response Model." *Family Systems Medicine* 6, 2: 202–37.

Patterson, Joan. 2002. "Integrating Family Resilience and Family Stress Theory." *Journal of Marriage and Family* 64 (May): 349–60.

Patterson, Joan M., and Anne Garwick. 1994. "Theoretical Linkages: Family Meanings and Sense of Coherence." In *Sense of Coherence and Resiliency: Stress, Coping, and Health*, eds. H. I. McCubbin, E. A. Thompson, A. I. Thompson, and J. E. Fromer. Madison, WI: University of Wisconsin Center for Excellence in Family Studies, 71–89.

Pearlin, L., and Carmi Schooler. 1978. "The Structure of Coping." *Journal of Health and Social Behavior* 19: 2–21.

Rachman, S. 1979. "The Concept of Required Helpfulness." *Behavior Research and Theory* 17: 1–6.

Reiss, D. 1981. *A Family's Construction of Reality*. Cambridge, MA: Harvard University Press.

Resnick, Michael, Bearman, P. S., Robert Blum, Bauman, K. E., Harris, K. M., Jones, J., Tabor, J., Behring, T., Sieving, R. E., Shew, M., Ireland, M., Bearinger, L. H., and J. R. Uldry. 1997. "Protecting Adolescents from Harm; Findings from the National Longitudinal Study on Adolescent Health." *Journal of the American Medical Association* 278, 10: 823–32.

Rosenbaum, Max. 1983. "Learned Resourcefulness as a Behavioral Repertoire For Self-Regulation of Internal Events: Issues and Speculations." In *Perspective on Behavior Therapy in the Eighties*, eds. M. Rosenbaum, C. M. Franks, and Y. Jaffe. New York, NY: Springer, 54–73.

Rosenbaum, Max. ed. 1990. *Learned Resourcefulness: On Coping Skills, Self-Control, and Adaptive Behavior*. New York, NY: Springer.

Rutter, Michael. 1979. "Protective Factors in Children's Responses to Stress and Disadvantage." In *Primary Prevention of Psychopathology*, Vol. 3: *Social Competence in Children*, eds. M. W. Kent and J. E. Rolf. Hanover, NH: University Press of New England, 49–74.

Rutter, Michael. 1985. "Resilient Children." *Psychology Today* (March): 57–65.

Rutter, Michael. 1987. "Psychosocial Resilience and Protective Mechanisms." *American Journal of Orthopsychiatry* 57, 3: 316–31.

Rutter, Michael. 1990. "Psychosocial Resilience and Protective Mechanisms." In *Risk and Protective Factors in the Development of Psychopathology*, eds. J. Rolf, A. Masten, D. Cicchetti, K. Nuechterlein, and S. Weintraub. New York, NY: Cambridge University Press, 181–214.

Rutter, Michael. 2000. "Medicine Meets Millennium." Paper presented at the *World Congress on Medicine and Health*, (July). www.mhhannover.de/aktuelles/projekte/mmm/germanversion/d_fs_programme/speech/Rutter_V.html. (Retrieved 07/28/02).

Schorr, L. B. 1988. *Within Our Reach*. New York, NY: Basic Books.

Seccombe, Karen. 2002. "'Beating the Odds' Versus 'Changing the Odds': Poverty, Resilience, and Family Policy." *Journal of Marriage and Family* 64 (May): 384–94.

Seligman, Martin. 1994. *Learned Optimism*. New York, NY: Random House.

Seligman, Martin. 2002. "Positive Psychology, Positive Prevention, and Positive Therapy." In *Handbook of Positive Psychology*, eds. C. Snyder and S. Lopez. New York, NY: Oxford University Press, 3–9.

Selye, Hans. 1956. The *Stress of Life*. New York, NY: McGraw-Hill.

Selye, Hans. 1974. *Stress Without Distress*. Philadelphia, PA: Lippincott.

Serovich, Julianne, Judy Kimberly, Katie Mosack, and T. L. Lewis. 2001. "The Role of Family and Friend Social Support in Reducing Emotional Distress among HIV-Positive Women." *AIDS Care* 13 (June): 335–41.

Stinnett, Nick, and John DeFrain. 1985. *Secrets of Strong Families*. Boston, MA: Little Brown.

Taylor, S. E. 1989. *Positive Illusions: Creative Self-deception and the Healthy Mind*. New York, NY: Basic Books.

Vaillant, George. 2000. "Adaptive Mental Mechanisms: Their Role in a Positive Psychology." *American Psychologist* 55: 89–98.

Walsh, Froma. 1998. Strengthening *Family Resilience*. New York, NY: Guilford.

Walsh, Froma. 2002. "A Family Resilience Framework: Innovative Practice Applications." *Family Relations* 51: 130–37.

Wamboldt, F., and S. Wolin. 1989. "Reality and Myth in Family Life: Changes Across Generations. *Journal of Psychotherapy and the Family* 4: 141–65.

Werner, Emmy. 1995. "Resiliency in Development." *Current Directions in Psychological Science* (June): 81–5.

Werner, Emmy. 1999. "How Children Become Resilient: Observations and Cautions." In *Resiliency in Action: Practical Ideas for Overcoming Risks and Building Strengths in Youth, Families, and Communities*, eds. N. Henderson, B. Benard, and N. Sharp-Light. San Diego, CA: Resiliency in Action.

Werner, Emmy, and Ruth Smith. 1982. *Vulnerable But Invincible: A Longitudinal Study of Resilient Children and Youth*. New York, NY: Adams, Bannister, and Cox.

Werner, Emmy, and Ruth Smith. 1992. *Overcoming the Odds: High Risk Children from Birth to Adulthood*. Ithaca, NY: Cornell University Press.

Werner, Emmy, and Ruth Smith. 2001. *Journeys from Childhood to Midlife: Risk, Resilience, and Recovery*. Ithaca, NY: Cornell University Press.

Wolin, Steven, and Sybil Wolin. 1993. *The Resilient Self: How Survivors of Troubled Families Rise Above Adversity*. New York, NY: Villard.

Zubrick, Stephan, and Anna Robson. 2003. "Resilience to Offending in High-Risk Groups—Focus on Aboriginal Youth." Report to the Criminology Research Council, South Australia. www.aic.gov.au/crc/reports/2003-10-zubrick.pdf (Retrieved 10/20/04)

4

HURRIED FAMILY CULTURE: FAMILY TIME IN A DIGITAL AGE

CHAPTER PREVIEW

Wait a minute! American families spend more time engaged in activities away from home and with non-family members than at any other point in history. Over the centuries Western concepts of time have shifted to meet the demands of being on time and counting minutes. Yet we continue to struggle to establish *lived moments* against the pressure to do more in less time. These lived moments have a relative nature in how they are remembered in terms of duration and pleasantness of the moments. When lived moments become optimal experiences or *flow* families escape the boundaries of schedules and engage in an activity simply for the sheer sake of doing it.

Family time often is more of a "pit stop" as family members retreat from external communities. Yet, family time is often colored by nostalgic myths that leave families feeling guilty and frustrated with the time they do share together. Families with multiple demands often find they experience *time famine* in which *time bind* (increased demands) often results in *multitasking* and *time deepening* (cramming more into the same time frame).

We contrast *time urgent families* with *time relaxed families* who face similar demands but use time more as a tool and less as a dictator. In contrast to juggling family time, we depict balancing family time, that is, choosing how to invest family time rather than cramming more activities into a finite period.

Caregiving reflects a more compassionate expression of family time. This speaks to an issue of *quality time* and being able to distinguish clock time and *care time*. We argue that how families construct their time together must meet that particular family's circumstances and perceptions.

But what of all those marvels of technology and telecommunications that hold promises of buying us more time? In 2000, 51% of households had at least one computer, and of those households, 41.5% were connected to the Internet. What are the benefits and costs to family time with living in a digital age? Technology brings greater motility including *residential mobility*, which can allow for *weekend-families* who live part of their time away from home.

Advances in digital technology impact how families live, work, play, and learn. Harnessing technology to enhance learning experiences, *edutainment*, continues to spread and with its expansion a growing need for families to be wise consumers of it. The Internet offers a virtual world of information. The opportunities and related responsibilities of a digital age fall on *connected families* to choose wisely. Families who choose to shape their time together as lived moments instead of rushed minutes truly turn the hands of family time.

THE CONSTRUCTION OF FAMILY TIME

The late biopsychologist Gibbon wrote that time is our human "primordial context" in which we all live. Thus, time includes the natural rhythms from migrating geese, the feeling of jet lag after crossing time zones, and the rhythms and cycles of aging. Wright (2002) argues that humans have a virtual stopwatch in their brains called an "interval timer" with which they establish a sense of how quickly or slowly events pass. This interval timer is highly flexible, though of variable accuracy, so many of us wear wristwatches.

For families, time is perceptual, dynamic, and contextual. The perceived speed of *lived moments* varies from individual to individual, family to family, and culture to culture. Levine's (1997) notes that cultural definitions of "being on time" vary. For example, "island time" often refers to whenever the individual arrives is the accepted time of arrival which does not conform to Western concepts of punctuality, that is, not too late, but also not too early. Cultural variation in time perceptions is revealed by Sardar in his description of how the "West 'colonized' time by spreading the expectations that life should become better as time passes" (Ezzell 2002: 75).

This is a perception that time as an arrow with direction, precision, and speed producing a different appreciation for time as a determiner of progress. Yet, time is not an absolute measure. According to Einstein, it is relative to the lived experience where our memories (past) and perceptions (future) color our present time. Anticipation of the future is key to understanding present time (Daly 1996). Hence, attempts to increase accuracy in keeping time (counting the minutes or keeping up) need to be balanced with appreciation of the dynamic nature of lived moments (moments remembered rather than measured by minutes).

Keeping Time

Mechanical measures of time are relatively new. For a great expanse of human history, nature's clocks including a circadian clock, which reflects natural cycles of wake and sleep, the rise and fall of blood pressure, and hormonal secretions, determined time (Box 4.1).

BOX 4.1 "A Chronology of Keeping Time"[1]

- Reckoning time—Solar (lightness and darkness cycles), lunar month (phases of the moon), and solar year (seasons) time has been reckoned by humans throughout history.

- Pulse time—The first weight-driven clock appeared in 1283.

- Uniform time—In the early 14th century, a day was divided into 24 equal segments. By the 1580s smaller segments of minutes and seconds were added.

- Portable clocks—In the 15th century the use of clocks in domestic life increased. Tension-spring clocks were being replaced by weighted clocks and the fusee (a cone-shaped mechanism that allowed one to rewind the clock).

- Pendulum clocks—The 1650s and 1660s saw a drive for greater accuracy emerging from an increasing emphasis on science. In response to this demand, the first pendulum clock was developed in 1656.

- Innovative clockworks—The spiral balance spring increased accuracy in the measurement of time.

- Nineteenth century—By this time clocks and pocket watches were being mass produced.

- Standard time—Four time zones across the continental United States were established in 1883. (Additional time zones for Alaska and Hawaii were added later with the most recent time zone, Hawaii-Aleutian Standard Time, started in 1983).

- Quartz movement—The 20th century saw a shift to electronic watches.

- Atomic clocks and beyond—The use of atomic clocks with ultraprecision and micro-sized timekeeping with measurements of attosecond (one billionth of a billionth of a second) increases in the 21st century.

---

[1]*Source:* Adapted with permission from Andrewes, William. "A Chronicle of Time Keeping," *Scientific American* (September 2002): 76–85.

Although some standard measure of time occurred as early as 5,500 BC with early sundials, precise time measure (clocks with minute and second hands) did not appear until the late 16th and early 17th centuries. The concept of being "on time" became meaningful (some would argue demanding) at this point in history. This shift from natural rhythm time (sun rise and set, ocean tides, phases of the moon, seasons, etc.) to clock time reflects changes in the economic, social, and psychological aspects of human culture. Clocks provided means for precise meeting times, transportation schedules, and industrialization's push to market. Time indeed became money.

Contrary to clock time, lived moments can be experienced when zipping through time zones or waiting in the airport, as time seems to crawl when awaiting a delayed flight. While traveling to Australia from the Midwestern United States, one of the authors' family experienced lived moments, not only cutting through 15 time zones but also virtually traveling into the future by crossing the International Date Line. Questions from the children (eight and 10 years of age) on this 14-hour flight, "Mom, what time is it really?" deepened appreciation for the abstract nature of time and how we determine it.

Stretching Time: Experienced Versus Remembered Duration

The concept of time includes tempo, the "changing rhythms and sequences, stresses and calms, cycles and spikes" of living (Levine 1997: 25). Tempo includes the duration and density of time. Density of time implies demands on how time is used. Overcommitment (i.e., more demands than time) is a frequent complaint in families. The pull of numerous commitments often leads to the perception that days, months, and years pass too quickly. Families who are overcommitted and neglect time together may regretfully view the hectic pace as "time lost." Duration of time refers the relative nature of our psychological clock. This means "experienced duration" often varies from "remembered duration" of an event (Block 1990). For example, building on Einstein's theory of relativity, enjoying four hours with friends seems like four minutes, whereas four minutes of waiting for the medical test results of an ill child seems like four hours.

The speed or pace of our lives impacts and colors our perceptions and experiences (Bohannan 1980; Schor 1991). This "distorted psychological clock" accounts for why pleasant events seem to pass quickly and are couched in less time urgency. Older family members often comment on the extent to which the relative speed of time increases as one ages, so that a child's year between kindergarten and first grade feels "forever," whereas a parent's year between the kindergarten and high school graduation feels like a moment.

Levine (1997) describes five factors that influence time duration or a family's ability to "stretch" time. First, family members' impressions of an event as pleasant versus obligatory is vital to stretching time. A pleasant event could be a quiet evening together where the time seems to fly. An example of an obligatory event could be a yearly-required visit with disagreeable relatives where time seems to stand still. Naturally, most families endure some obligatory events; the point here is that time duration is remembered as long or short based on how the event is perceived in terms of pleasantness.

Second, time is stretched by the felt level of urgency toward an event such as feeling urgent-less versus urgent-filled. Urgent-less events could include taking an afternoon walk with no precise destination or timelines. An urgent-filled occurrence is reflected in an event of a parent waiting for the return of a teenager who is overdue and is driving home on a stormy night.

Third, events during which family members perceive themselves as being active instead of just being busy also impact time duration. Being active means engaging in activities that hold some importance or pleasure and are not just to fill in the gaps of the day. This is the opposite of being busy where one believes staying in a constant state of doing is necessary. American culture prizes being busy and "doing" over "being." For example, families sacrifice time and finances to keep their members busy (e.g., lessons, camps, and sports), often emphasizing that because "time is money" members must make every minute count. Providing such opportunities can enrich, but in the rush to stay busy, overcommitted families may neglect teaching their members how to relax or appreciate simple pleasures of life such as family conversation and laughter.

Families' overscheduled children (and adults) are those without any down time or free time just to be. Elkind (1981, 2001) raises the issue of overcommitted children, in what he coined "the hurried child" condition. His recommendations include remembering that children need developmentally sound activities to engage in and that they are not "little adults." In his later work, *Ties That Stress*, Elkind emphasizes the need for parents and family studies professionals to appreciate that as the traditional family structure crumbles, families need to plan for new family structures and time together (1998). Rosenfeld and Wise (2001) warn that overscheduling children and "hyperparenting" are done with the best of intentions, but often leave families gasping for time. According to them, in families with children "[t]he fact is, parenting should not take all one's time, money, and energy" (2001: xxi). This hurriedness negatively impacts family life.

An additional influence on the stretching of time focuses on having experiences that are varied and tap into one's creativity. Engaging in varied activities rather than in hard and fast routines with little flexibility or self-expression positively impacts perceived duration of family events. Rigid family routines and events include the monotony of having every minute accounted for with little or no room for diversion. This often leads to boredom and a sense that time crawls. Contrary to rigid routines, varied and creative events add interest and novelty, which makes time invested seem worthwhile. For example, consider a family who not only allows but also encourages family members to explore sport, art, music, drama, hobbies, and other activities regardless if they excel in them. This means that each family member engages in activities in which she or he does not have to perform, achieve, or count the products of that activity. Naturally, one can overdo it with trying too many things at one time. Although variety adds "spice" to life, as in cooking, too much can be overpowering.

Such time-stretching moments are often described as "optimal experiences" or *flow*, "the state in which people are so involved in an activity that nothing else seems to matter; the experience itself is so enjoyable that people will do it even at great cost, for the sheer sake of doing it" and time seems to disappear (Csikszentmihalyi 1990: 4). Families engaged in flow experiences go beyond pleasure. According to Csikszentmihalyi pleasure is a component of the quality of life, a return to homeostasis. Flow experiences are those moments in which families enjoy events that not only meet prior expectations (e.g., having everyone home for the holiday) or satisfy a need or desire (e.g., being with those you love), but also go beyond what a family had planned on doing or experiencing—something unexpected, perhaps even unimagined (e.g., taking a break from the usual holiday routines, a family engages every member in building a snow fort, or, for those in warmer climates, a sand castle). The result is not planned or scheduled, but evolves.

Play and playful experiences are examples of flow. Ellis (1973) described play as a necessary aspect of human learning and performance that can totally absorb individuals. Play allows families and their members to immerse in an activity and escape the boundaries of time with comments such as, "Where did the time go?" "I could have played this all day." As is discussed in the next chapter, play and humor are also noted as vital to healing.

Families can stretch time together, therefore, by creating experiences that are pleasant over obligatory, relaxed, over hurried, engaging rather than busy, and varied instead of rigid routines. Time together can indeed be stretched so even if limited in minutes, it is long in remembered duration.

EVERYDAY RHYTHM: THE TICK TOCK OF THE FAMILY CLOCK

Family time can be like the pit stop of the racing world, where

> ...depleted energy resources are replenished in the name of "get up and go"..."Family time is more like the coincidental sharing of space and time that arises from the intersection of busy lives. (Daly 1996: 67)

For many families, time together is a pit stop. The question goes beyond why to what to do about it? In an increasingly fast-paced world, families often find themselves struggling to manage members' schedules while desperately trying to fit it all in. "Time has become the dominant currency in families" (Daly 1996: 9).

Daly explains in Box 4.2 that learning about factors that influence how families define and measure their time is vital to understanding family behaviors and choices.

BOX 4.2 "Families and Time"
Kerry Daly, Ph.D.

One of our main challenges for understanding families is to get beneath some of our taken for granted assumptions about time. On the surface, we tend to think of time in quantifiable, standardized units such as hours, weekends, or the 40-hour work week. As a result, we tend to think of time as a measure for how we apportion our energies and activities.

Time diaries are one of the main instruments for assessing time allocations in the study of families. Time diary studies typically look at the distribution of time across paid work, unpaid work activities in the home (including housework and childcare), leisure activities, and personal care activities (e.g., eating and sleeping). Although time diaries reveal how families distribute their time, these studies do not provide much insight into some of the other ways that families experience time. With globalization, the rise of technology, and the movement of women into the paid labor force, families face new challenges in their efforts to deal with time in their everyday lives.

Cultural Changes

Families live in a world of accelerated time demands. In response to forces such as industrialization, information technology, and globalization in the world economy, families must contend with an escalating pace of life. Our language of time is dominated by the cultural values of speed and efficiency. The Internet never sleeps and, as a result, information and products can be moved around the world instantaneously without regard to temporal borders.

With this pervasive speedup, families are increasingly angst-ridden about the shortage of time. Family and work activities are both "time-consuming." With the recent historical shift from single-provider to dual-earner family models, time famine has become a more common aspect of everyday family experience. Stress and role overload arise when time is insufficient to complete required tasks and families frequently lament the shortage of time for being together. As the world puts on pace with respect to the exchange of information and commercial goods, so too has the family put on pace as a way of adapting to these changes.

Organizational Changes Within Families

As the tempo of life has quickened, families face new challenges in managing the everyday organization of their often competing schedules. With parents going to jobs and children going off to daycare or school, the daily schedule begins with a ritual of dispersion with each family member called to their own temporal routine. Increasingly families must devote ever more attention to *managing time* in order to ensure the synchronization of dropoffs and pickups, constant and continuous coverage for dependent children (and sometimes elders), and punctuality in paid work and a growing number of outside activities. Women are typically the chief conductors of the family schedule, sometimes relying on a complex, centralized family calendar that involves careful monitoring and a delicate series of negotiations with spouses, children, coaches, grandparents, and others.

Changes in the Ideology and Reality of Family Time

The debates over family time are colored by the ideological debates about the family itself. In the same way that families of the past have been romanticized and idealized, so too has family time. An idealized construction of family time is based on the principles of togetherness, choice, and mutual engagement. These principles may be more reflective of an ideal than a reality. Some people do retreat into their homes to be with their families. However, many people bring the pace and demands of the competitive world of work home. Given the increases in the amount of time that we give to work and the escalation of the pace of activities in the workplace, the home often becomes the site of a parallel set of tasks and responsibilities. The duties of parenthood, the tasks of household cleanliness, and the incessant demands of a consumer-based culture often leave little sense of engaged, pleasant involvement among family members. However, the ideal persists. People want to spend more time with their families. People are willing to trade work time for family time. People yearn for the sense of calm and togetherness that is deeply embedded in our beliefs about family time.

The Politics of Time—Who Controls and Who Is Being Controlled

The escalating sense of time scarcity brings more conflicts—within families as well as between families and the social order—about time control, allocation, and entitlement. Families live at the intersection of their own internal time needs associated with intimacy and rejuvenation and the unrelenting external forces of a sociotemporal order that demand compliance and punctuality. The temporal politics of the family in society involves constant, day-to-day negotiation of time that is often perceived to be externally based and controlled. Another internal politics of time involves negotiations between parents and children, women and men, and adult children and their aging parents. For example, the gender politics of time point to a set of ongoing disparities between women and men in the way that they spend and control their time. Most men continue to spend more time in paid work than at home, and most women continue to spend more time on household labor in the home than do men. Therefore, family responsibilities for women are more like to "spill-over" into their work time, resulting in more day-to-day tensions in the management of the work–family balance. This has resulted in women having to be more adaptable than men in meeting the care needs of their children and elders. Women are more likely than men to arrange their work schedules in a way that will accommodate the demands of family caregiving.

Kerry Daly, Ph.D., is Professor in the Department of Family Relations and Applied Nutrition at the University of Guelph in Ontario, Canada.

Recent studies reinforce the importance of giving family time a high priority (Crouter, Head, and Jenkins-Tucker 2004; Daly 2003). Families adjust by going faster and being more time efficient, yet often losing a sense of purpose and belonging in the blur of doing it all. They wrestle with what Hochschild (1997: 249) terms the *time bind*. She urges "a national dialogue on the most difficult and frightening aspect of our time bind: the need for 'emotional investment' in family life in an era of familial divestiture and deregulation."

Is this *time famine* just about clock time or is it as much our perception of time demands? Daly (1996: 41) argues that

[F]amilies live at the abrasive meeting point of a progressive but nostalgic tradition and the multiple contingencies of a demanding present that is expressed through television, consumerism, and the constraints of work and the calendar.

The cultural confusion of living a 21st-century lifestyle with fast-paced, diverse opportunities and demands, while confined in a nostalgic mindset of "traditional family time," often leaves families frustrated.

How families define family time is impacted by social, economic, technological, and cultural factors. The definition of family time is also influenced by misconceptions such as nostalgic images of "the way we never were" (Coontz 1992; Clark 2002; Daly 2002, 2004) which cloud families' perceptions of their time together. Prior to the 20th century when more American families worked where they lived, the separation of family time and work time was less distinct.

Family time as a separate time and space is a relatively recent concept, but the nostalgic idea of perfectly joyful family gatherings may leave families feeling disappointed or frustrated because their family gatherings are anything but joyful. According to Coontz (1997: 109) "[m]any of the problems commonly blamed on breakdown of the traditional family exist not because we've changed too much but because we haven't changed enough."

The ideology of family togetherness means different things to different families. Gaps between expectations and actual experiences often leave families feeling guilty or concerned that somehow they do not measure up to the myth of "one big happy family." Shaw (1992) argues that a one-sided, highly idealized view of family time that dominates current culture often leaves families wondering if something is "wrong" with them.

Not only do families need to reconsider time together, they need to redefine how they choose to enjoy their precious family time. As we discuss in chapter 10, family traditions and rituals are critical to family life. However, some family events are significant sources of family stress as members struggle to "do all the ritual things" even if they are not enjoyable. This calls on families to reconsider the value and meaning of traditions and rituals in family life, perhaps creating new traditions and rituals to fit with 21st-century challenges.

Daly (2003, 2004) describes a significant misalignment between how policymakers and researchers theorize about families and how families actually live. The Norman Rockwell mental image of family gatherings is quite removed from the current diverse portraits of today's families. Particularly blended family communities serve as an example of a need to redefine family time. Blended families often have difficulties negotiating former family-time behaviors and may have to strike out in creating their own unique family-time experiences, which are new to both lumped-together family segments.

Women's and men's differing views of work and leisure impact how each gender defines family time (Daly 2002; Shaw 1992). In dual-earner families, in order to save time, women often do more than one task at a time (e.g., entertaining a preschool-aged child, loading the dishwasher, making dinner and trying to watch the evening news; Hochschild 1989). *Multitasking* is attempting to accomplish several tasks at once, a work habit likely more common among women than men. *Time deepening* (Robinson and Godbey 1997), another term for multitasking, is specifically applied to parents working outside of the home who struggle to do more in less time both at work and at home. Myers' (1999) research reveals that while multitasking appears to be more efficient, pursuing several tasks at the same time is actually less efficient. Furthermore, multitasking may increase the risk of accident and often poses health concerns such as mental burnout, anxiety, and depression (Anderson 2004; Woznicki 2001).

Daly (1996, 2002) takes this point further and argues that age also challenges family time. Children's' views of enjoyable family times may vary considerably from that of their parents or guardians (e.g., the obligatory trip to see older second cousins).

The following section explores some classic family times (mealtime and weekends). These family-lived moments are subject to the nostalgic trap of thinking, for instance, "if one family member (usually the woman) would just stay home, these situations would be so much easier." Such thinking neglects to consider the realities of current social arrangements and infers blames to certain family members who appear to fail to live up to nostalgic expectations.

Sharing Meals and Evenings

This daily (or less frequent) gathering can be one of the most important times in the life of a family. During meals, family members may leave the outside world to be together and catch up on events of the day. However, meals could not come at a more hectic point in the day. Mornings often begin with a complex sequence of rushing to be on time for school, work, and other commitments. Breakfast may be less a meal than a series of passages through the kitchen as family members gulp down breakfast while looking over homework and appointment books.

Orchestrating an evening meal becomes even more difficult as each member's life expands into external communities. Racing to gather up members from the endless extracurricular activities including music and dance lessons, athletic and drama practices, youth and adult groups, committees (school, community, civic, and religious), work-related meetings, and exercise routines along with meal preparation demand calmness and patience, both of which may be in short supply at the end of most family members' days. Fatigue and stress carried over from the school day or work day can dull the enjoyment of time together. Couple this with the developmental needs of different family members—most four-year-olds cannot defer the final meal of the day until all family members finally gather at eight o'clock in the evening and family meal time may add to rather than detract from a busy day.

In spite of the difficulties, research (Snow, Tabors and Dickinson 2001) supports the value of families eating at least one meal together each day. One of the first steps is to realize that "good conversation" is a vital ingredient to family mealtime. Baranowski (2002) suggests that, if family mealtime is not already a regular daily event, start by scheduling one family dinner together each week. Make mealtime conversations a setting for building family ties, while avoiding the litany of the work or school headaches or announcing the household chore list. Design developmentally appropriate conversation-starting rituals, such as having each family member share something interesting, a joke, or a question they would like to talk about. Finally, keep the tone positive and supportive, sometimes challenging when discussing subjects on which family members may disagree. Doing so not only gives family members an opportunity to express their opinions but also offers a chance to model civil discourse.

One of the primary stressors of family mealtime is the shortage of time to prepare meals, particularly nutritious, attractive meals. When families learn about how to cook (a survival skill), they also need to learn "time-savvy tips" (Children's Nutrition Research Center 2002). Nutritionists at the Children's Nutrition Research Center recommend ways to reduce the time spent in meal preparation, including making weekly meal plans, making double batches and freezing half, involving family members in a division of labor around cleanup after and next-day meal preparation.

If regular family mealtime is not possible for a family, eating in shifts or "grazing" may define that family's mealtime. It is important to remember that good conversation is not limited to sitting at the same table and sharing food. Sharing of good conversation can occur in other family-time together. The point is that families can create such time recognizing their importance and enjoying these lived moments. As stated by Coontz (1997), there may not have been enough change in how families design their time together. It is up to families, therefore, to create or invent their own ideal family time.

Weekend Family Time

The weekend (or whichever days family members are not at school and work) would seem to be a time when most families have earned a respite from the workweek. However, bringing work home and home offices all contribute to the blurring of the work–home week. Likewise, as family members spend more and more time away from home, weekends often become the two days to catch up with household duties, shopping, and external socializing. The haven of the weekend, therefore, may be breeched from the encroaching workweek and from within by household demands.

Hochschild (1989) expands her earlier work, which examined the hectic lives of women who work outside of the home and their demanding second shift with a portrait of dual-earner families struggles with balancing work and home. Her three-year field study of companies that claimed employee-friendly conditions revealed a surprising finding in that employees did not take advantage of many of the policies due to an overwhelming feeling that "work becomes home and home becomes work," because time at work can be more calm and supportive, whereas time at home often is hectic and demanding (1997: title page). Her ethnographic findings also challenge contemporary assumptions of more positive family work–home juggling. Hochschild states that not only is there a second shift for dual-earner families, but a "third shift," which she defines as the emotional work needed to negotiate the frustration and tension of partners and children anguished over diminished family time. Reexamining our time bind in terms of family time means placing greater emphasis on recognizing the value of, and encouraging an attitude toward, enjoying time together rather than simply doing more in the same time period. Doherty and Carlson (2002) encourage families to avoid the guilt of enjoying down time and actively engage in relaxing the activity schedule to not only make room for but also value family time.

Do families really have less free time? Robinson and Godbey (1997) counter conventional wisdom that American families have less free time and more problems balancing work and home. Using a systematic time-diary longitudinal study, they found that although Americans see themselves as overworked actually, according to time-diaries, they are underestimating their free time (time away from work and household tasks) and overestimating time they work at home doing housework and work brought home from the office. These quantitative measures (time-diaries) tried to measure qualitative aspects (perceived use of time). Although interesting, their findings reflect nationally representative data prior to 1985. Much has changed since 1985 in terms of impacts of family structure, family mobility, diversity, and of course technology. The Economic Policy Institute (2004) argues that positions such as those of Robinson and Godbey fail to recognize the primary factor of many women working part time. This factor artificially lowers the average of weekly hours. A more complete measure of how families are working takes into account another factor that more family members are in the job market.

When families feel rushed and hurried as they try to fit more into the same time slot, this skews their perceptions of time and how busy they are. Perhaps these two points of view are not so different in that both reveal working adults (and children) as hurried and frantic in the unending quest to juggle everything into one day. Having one hour of free time after a day crammed with fast-paced demands and unending schedules seems "shorter" than an hour of free time after a relaxing day of calmly paced events. In order to create more time together, families need to modify nostalgic definitions of family time to better match realities of 21st-century families.

JUGGLING OR BALANCING FAMILY TIME

The perception of feeling chronically rushed has been described as "perceptual activation" (Wright, McCurdy, and Rogoll 1992). Time urgency refers to engaging in activities with intensity and anxiety surrounding failing to keep up. Levine (1997: 19) describes this as "the struggle to achieve as much as possible in the shortest period of time." Examples of time-urgent behaviors are presented in Table 4.1.

Granted, most families are *time-urgent families* at some time. Time-urgent behaviors reflect living under the rule of the clock so much so that families are compelled to rush through living forgetting to (and often regretting they did not) enjoy the moments of family life. *Time-relaxed families* are more flexible in their attitude toward the pressure of the clock. These families respond to time demands more selectively while recognizing the value of "down time" and spontaneity. They have a greater appreciation for lived moments over clock time.

This chapter offers that the distinction between living by the moment as more fulfilling to families than living by the minute. Living by the minute is what Ulmer and Schwartzbard (1996) called "hurried sickness," which means rushing through life with little regard for actually living it fully. Hurried sickness reveals itself in symptoms such as a dulled interest

TABLE 4.1

Time Urgent Families

Time Urgent Families (TUF) covet time more than Time-Relaxed Families (TRF), even though both face busy schedules and multiple demands. A difference is that TUF's attitude toward clock time is rigid and unrelenting. They may have forgotten or, in the case of children, never learned what it means to enjoy unscheduled time as a means to relax and be spontaneous without feeling guilty of "wasting time."

- Concern with clock time: TUF life's events are dictated by the clock even during periods of relaxation, "down time."

- Speech patterns: Sentences are rushed, spoken faster than those around you. Members in TUF often interrupt others who take too long to get to the point.

- Eating habits: Here the concept of "fast food" has less to do with how quickly the food is prepared and more to do with how fast it is consumed.

- Walking speed: Walking with a TUF is indeed a race regardless whether it is to catch a flight or stroll in a park. Others often ask them to slow down.

- Driving: Slow traffic raises TUF members' blood pressures regardless of the purpose of the trip. Easily angered by slow drivers, these members react as if they are the only ones with someplace to go.

- Schedules: Every event and occurrence for the day and night is scheduled with allotted times noted. TUF members are compulsive about schedules and resist spontaneous happenings.

- List making: Many individuals and families make lists. But, TUF's list making is rigorous with every outing having a detailed list.

- Nervous energy: Individuals and their family members easily feel bored and restless.

- Waiting: Few individuals and their families like to wait. Yet for TUF waiting is almost more than they can tolerate.

- Alerts: Others may notice and even suggest that TUF members need to slow down, take it easy, relax, loosen up. TUF may ignore such suggestions as irrelevant.

Source: Adapted with permission from Robert Levine. 1997. *A Geography of Time: The Temporal Misadventures of a Social Psychologist.* New York, NY: Basic Books.

in activities that are not measured, graded, or extrinsically rewarded. This diminished ability to concentrate or focus often accompanies this lackluster interest. Also, the Past–Present–Future Orientation is out of sync in that the family dwells on the past or only looks to the future without taking the time to live in the present. A flowing Past–Present–Future Orientation (as discussed in chapter 3) is vital to a family's resiliency processes.

Compare the impacts of family behaviors and choices of a time-urgent family with that of a time-relaxed family in Box 4.3. The parents' or guardians' names in these stories are gender neutral.

The pace of "hurried families" (Daly 1996) affects the quality of life and colors the health and wellness of family members. Yet, a slower pace of lifestyle is not without its own risks and disadvantages. Cultures with slower paced lifestyles often suffer from depressed economic conditions, which negatively impact health care availability and general health. Living a hurried life appears to hold both risk and opportunity. A question is how to move beyond juggling (cramming more into each minute) to balancing (giving attention to inner and external needs without the guilt of not doing it all).

BOX 4.3 "Minced Minutes or Meaningful Moments"
Janet R. Grochowski, Ph.D.

Typical Week of a Time-Urgent Family

Pat and Chris and their three children have lived together as a family for the past seven years. Juan (age 10) and Julio (age eight) are children from Pat's former relationship and Maria (age five) was adopted five years ago. Pat is a computer programmer and Chris runs a plant nursery. Both work 40-plus-hour workweeks with work seeping into their evenings and weekends. Pat is active in the local school levy drive, whereas Chris chairs the county small business organization. Juan and Julio play soccer, and each takes music lessons outside of school. Maria is in all-day kindergarten with tumbling lessons after school.

This family has a tight schedule, which they guard. Meeting everyone's activity needs requires some organization, but in this family the clock rules, even during weekends and family time. Here is a snapshot of this hurried family's weekdays and weekend.

Monday–Friday

The regular school and workweek are strictly scheduled. Everyone is up at his or her appointed time to reduce a traffic jam in the bathroom. As Chris rushes to get ready for work, gulps down a pop-up breakfast, and makes sure the children's lunch money is on the table next to their backpacks, Pat returns home from the obligatory short walk of the family dog, Cleo, and hurries to shower and change. The split-second timing is amazing as the three children rush into the kitchen 10 minutes apart; sadly everyone ends up eating alone. By 6:45 a.m., the door opens and they all fly out like homing pigeons on a mission as they race off to school and work. Pat is really late; due to walking the dog, so Maria is dropped off in great haste with no hugs. The rest of the school and work day seems to move along with precision and punctuality.

In the late afternoon and evening, minutes are counted even more closely. Pat is running late and drives aggressively to pick up Maria from school. Still steaming over the traffic, Pat grumbles about how early Maria's school day ends while driving to drop her off at the Tumble-Fun center across town.

This week, Chris is scheduled to walk their pet dog, Cleo, another chore added to the list of demands for his after-work time. Chris stops at home to get Cleo and then picks up Juan and Julio at 3:00 p.m. to deliver them to their weekly music lessons. While waiting for the lessons to finish, Chris walks Cleo (grumbling about how dogs need two walks a day) and contacts four members of the small business group by cell phone about their meeting that night. Both approaching 50, Chris and Pat know they need to get some exercise into their lives, but they simply cannot make time for it.

Dinner must be started by 7:00 p.m. and ended with all cleanup completed by 7:30. Dinner talk is limited to who needs to be where, when, and for how long. Family time is organized into homework scheduled from 7:30 to 8:30 while Chris rushes to the small business meeting back at the shop. Pat monitors the homework for the boys while keeping Maria occupied with a series of videos. While doing this, Pat contacts fellow volunteers working on a school bond issue via e-mail.

Everyone is home by 8:45 p.m., and a strict bedtime routine begins. All showers (no time for baths) are organized according to a bathroom use schedule. Wanting to be sure to have some time together, they schedule a five- to 10-minute family talk focusing on schedules for next day, noting who covers the school conferences, grocery shopping, and dropping off and picking up. Chris or Pat dominates these family talks with little input from the children. Nine o'clock means bedtime for the children while Pat and Chris each attack some paperwork. Not to waste time, the children get ready for bed and then simply call out "Good Night" from upstairs. Pat and Chris shout back "Sleep well" as they remain locked into the last few items on their to do list. At last, they both fall into bed after double-checking their respective alarm clocks so they are sure to be on time for the next day's round of schedules.

Saturday–Sunday

Weekends are viewed as time to get done what could not be crammed in during the week. This means sleeping in to 6:30 a.m. and breakfast completed by 7:00. The children are fully scheduled for the day with boys soccer practice from 8:00 to 10:00, music lessons from 10:30 to 11:00, lunch at a fast-food stop because they need to be at scouts by noon, picked up from scouts and off to a cousin's birthday party at 3:00, home and pizza at 6:00 p.m., followed by a video until 9:30, then off to bed.

Maria does not waste a minute either. She is ushered to the 9:00 a.m. story time at the library, followed with grocery shopping with Chris. Once home, it is off to a neighborhood playtime followed by a scheduled nap after lunch. During Maria's nap, Chris multitasks: folds the laundry while talking to a client on his cell phone. Chris is scheduled to return to work at 2:00 p.m., so Pat promptly returns to cover the home front and carry out the scheduled afternoon events. Her tasks include making out a meal plan for the week, picking up a pizza and video for the night, getting the children to help pick up the yard, and, of course, walking Cleo.

Sunday begins with the family rushing off to religious services. The service seems to drag as Pat rechecks her watch and instinctively times the sermon. Chris discretely balances the checkbook while the children squirm in their seats. Finally, the service over, they quickly escape, skipping out a side door, avoiding clergy greetings and socializing with friends in order to beat the rush out of the parking lot. They have work to complete and must get back.

Once home, the day seems to disappear as a pall of "tomorrow is Monday" clings to everyone. Pat and Chris grumble about bills and how they need more time for the "things that really matter." The boys complain that they want some time to be with their friends. Pat and Chris remind them that there are simply too many activities in their day to waste time just "doing nothing." Maria knows that everyone is just too busy to spend time with her, so she turns on the television. So ends—and begins—another week for this hurried family.

Typical Week of a Time-Relaxed Family

Max and Robin and their three children have lived together as a family for the past seven years. Juan (age 10) and Julio (age nine) are children from Max's former relationship and Maria (age five) was adopted five years ago. Max is a computer programmer and Robin runs a plant nursery. Both work 40-plus-hour workweeks with work trying to seep into their evenings and weekends. Max is active in the local school levy drive while Robin chairs the county small business organization. Juan and Julio play soccer and each takes music lessons outside of school. Maria is in all-day kindergarten with tumbling lessons after school.

This family has multiple demands and need to organize activities. In this relaxed family, they remain appreciative of moments together and a need for flexibility. Here is a snapshot of this flow family's weekdays and weekend.

Monday–Friday

The regular school and workweek still means having a schedule as a guide. Max and Robin are up at 6:00 a.m. They take turns doing these first few activities of the day. Today, Robin showers, changes, and then organizes a simple but wholesome breakfast, which was selected the night before. Max takes the family dog, Cleo, out for a 30-minute walk or jog, which means exercise for both. The children get themselves ready for school and stagger bathroom use. Max is back and showers while Robin and the children sit down for breakfast that is simple and brief, but relaxed. Max joins them in the kitchen in time to share in the "Good mornings" as they wish each other a good day followed with "Love you!" as Robin and the boys leave for work and school. Max and Maria are out the door 15 minutes later after a light breakfast and turning on the slow cooker for dinner. Max chats with Maria on the way to her school. The school and work day seems to move along with precision and punctuality, but Max takes a moment to call Robin and asks how things are going with a new client. Robin calls a friend recovering from an illness to offer good wishes and see if the family needs anything.

Late afternoon and evening activities require balance and calmness. Max will be a few minutes late picking up Maria from school so calls ahead on the cell phone to alert the teacher. Max greets Maria warmly and actively listens to her as she explains her day while they drive to the Tumble-Fun center across town.

This week Robin is scheduled for Cleo's afternoon walks (lucky dog gets two walks). This activity is rotated among Max and Robin and the two boys. When Robin picks up Julio at 3:00 p.m. to deliver him to his music lesson, Cleo goes along and Robin walks her in the park. This is a chance for Robin to enjoy being outside, so the walk with Cleo is seen as a welcomed break in the day and not a chore. Besides, it is a way to get that 30-minute speed walk in. After the walk, Robin still has 10 minutes before Julio is done with his lesson, so calls are made to four members of the small business group about the meeting that night. As Robin and Julio drive home, they chat about their day and Cleo. Robin and Max have made it a point to schedule some time for exercise during their busy days as seen in their dog-walking routines. They want to get the children into the habit of exercise, so three days a week the entire family engages in some type of family outing such as an after dinner walk, or a 30-minute game of ultimate frisbee or soccer. Dinner preparation and cleanup are family affairs, with each member contributing. Conversations during the preparation, eating, and cleanup aim to include all members of the family and might include arranging the timing of various activities, but aim to keep the focus on a question, joke, or story that one family member (rotates each day) brings to that day's dinner experience.

Family time is balanced with homework and the meeting Robin needs to attend. Max monitors the homework for the boys and reads a few stories to Maria. Robin returns from the meeting and the five of them take a few moments to talk about their day, plans for the weekend, and so forth. Bedtime is calm with the boys getting themselves ready and some unscheduled time before bed to read, work on a hobby, or just think. Robin enjoys some moments with Maria while Max e-mails fellow school levy workers. During the 10 minutes before bed, Max and Robin go to each child wishing each a "Good night and sweet dreams" plus hugs and kisses.

Once the children are in bed, Max and Robin take a few moments to sit together and talk about their day. They listen to each other, for they realize that it is easy to take each other for granted when balancing multiple responsibilities and activities, multitasking. Some nights they complete needed paperwork or workout, but not until they have at least taken a few moments to talk with each other. They go to bed after checking their respective alarm clocks, but are sure to wish each other a good night.

Saturday–Sunday

Weekends are viewed as time to enjoy and not merely time to get more done. This means sleeping in a little and enjoying a special family-involved Saturday breakfast. This week Max takes the boys to soccer practice from 8:00 to 10:00 and music lessons, which follow, from 11:00 to 11:30. The boys also belong to scouts, but with soccer, they and their parents and guardians agreed to postpone scouting meetings until after the soccer season ends. Lunch turns into a picnic followed by everyone helping in cleaning up the house and yard plus walking Cleo. They find household chores and yard work go faster if everyone helps. The boys are off to a cousin's birthday party at 3:00 and return home about 6:00. With everyone home around 6:30, the five now enjoy a special no-fuss dinner, perhaps pizza with a salad. Convenience meals are a nice treat once in a while. Following dinner, they watch a video together and even talk about it after.

Maria enjoys varied activities as well. She and Robin go to the 9:00 a.m. story time at the library, followed by helping with the grocery shopping. Robin learned long ago that grocery shopping with children depends on attitude and including them in the adventure. Once home, Robin and Maria make a game out of putting the things away. This week, Maria's neighborhood playtime is at the neighbors home, so Robin walks her over. While Maria is at playgroup, it is Robin's turn to do the laundry. After playgroup, Robin picks up Maria for a special family picnic lunch followed by a nap. During Maria's nap, Robin calls a client on the cell phone. Robin is scheduled to return to work at 2:00, so Max covers the home front and carries out the remaining afternoon activities including cleaning up the house and yard, folding the laundry and putting it away, and walking Cleo. While the boys are off at the birthday party, Max and Maria design a meal plan for the week, and pick up a pizza and video for that night.

Sunday begins with the family deciding that this week they will attend religious services. When they do not attend, they enjoy their spirituality in other ways, such as volunteering at the food shelf or walking the homeless dogs at the Humane Society. This week, however, they are at a religious service that seems to go along well enough as Max considers this time to reflect important. For Robin this also means some moments to reflect and consider friends and family. The boys stay for the service and think about how they might use something said as a "dinner conversation" topic—it's Juan's turn tonight. Maria is with children her own age at the services children's center, which today has them outside identifying leaves. When the service is over, the five of them join friends for some light refreshments and conversation and catching up on how neighbors are doing. A half-hour later, they leave and take a scenic route home. On the way home they talked about how they will spend the afternoon. Max and Robin do have some work to do, but they also decide that taking two or three hours to be with the kids and each other is important too. They decide on a trip in the nature center. The boys ask if they can ask some friends to join them. Max and Robin agree and ask Maria if she wants someone too. Not today she says. Instead, she would like Robin to tell her a story about her favorite character, Stuart Little. They try to make each day an adventure—which is what it is like living in a flow family.

The concept of balancing is central to understanding family-time perceptions. Juggling family time is often described as being active in the many areas at once. Obsession with doing it all leaves families, no matter how much they accomplish, feeling exhausted and always behind. Balancing includes the paying attention to needs for calmness while being engaged and not constantly tugged by a schedule. This translates into accepting that families may not be able to do it all. Hunt and Hait (1990) discuss the need to "decelerate." To this add a viewing family time as an adventure that is lived and not a rigid recipe to follow.

The Power of Time and Caregiving

Levine (1997) claims that the taking and giving of time are two sides of a very powerful social tool. A giving side of this power is revealed in a family member who unconditionally (there lies the true meaning) waits for another family member to return home from a late practice or work day, or listens to the telling of a story about how their day went. Such caring reveals the loving side of the power of time. To give one's time unconditionally is indeed a caring gift. Caring for and taking care of may be couched in the term *caregiving*.

Cancian and Oliker (2000: 2) describe caregiving as the "feelings of affection, responsibility combined with actions that provide responsively for an individual's personal needs or well-being, in a face-to-face relationship" which reflect this unconditional giving of one's time. Caring takes time, and time often is considered the most precious gift one can give to another. Yet, ironically a fast-paced society does not value caregiving as it does paid experiences and often deems caring as "women's work." Cancian and Oliker challenge family professionals to move beyond these limited perceptions of caring and who takes the time for caring. Oliker (Cancian and Oliker 2000: 4–5) raises this issue with stating, "I wonder if Americans will accept lives with little time for care or if we will limit the growing demands of workplaces and expand caregiving by bringing both government and men more actively into the labors of love." The current family-paid-leave policy in the United States requires employers of more than 50 workers to provide up to 12 weeks of unpaid leave (typically only provides six weeks) for birth, adoption, a serious illness or to care of a family member. This policy ranks America at the bottom of family-leave policies where over nearly 60 other countries (developed and underdeveloped) offer a minimum of 12 paid weeks of family leave (Noll 2004). Although family professionals and the medical community recognize that 12 weeks of paid leave as desirable for family well-being and caregiving, social policies and employers often fail to deliver on claims of valuing families.

From Managing to Living Family Time

Family Studies professionals such as Daly (2003, 2004) support a position that *quality time* is vital to relationships. Yet, how families define and express quality time varies and often serves as a source of frustration and misunderstanding. Quality time may mean sharing time with loved ones that is relaxed and free of interruptions and conflicts. The challenge lies in finding such respites during family time where some interruptions, tension, and conflict naturally occur. Finding the "right time" for quality time requires that families recognize quality time and create moments for such experiences.

> Quality time doesn't mean devoting all free time exclusively to a child [or other family member] to compensate for the time lost. Children [and family members] shouldn't expect to always be the center of attention. (Ginsberg quoted in Williams 2002: 1)

Quality time, therefore, is time of authentic interacting, and not merely sharing the same room. This interaction might include attentive listening, unhurried moments during family togetherness such as mealtime, and relaxed moments together at bedtime.

Do parents who work outside of the home spend as much quality time with their children as do stay-at-home parents? Research indicates that employed mothers spend almost as much time in direct interaction with their children and related school activities as mothers who were not employed outside the home, plus the quality of childcare provided by employed moms did not differ from that of full-time homemaker moms (Bryant and Zick 1996; Holmes 1998; Lang 1997; Muller 1995). Just being in the home at the same time does not equal quality time. Quality time includes those moments of caring and connectiveness, not merely minutes one "puts in."

Yeung et al.'s (2001) study of children's time with fathers in two-parent families revealed that fathers are spending more time with their children than previously observed. However, the type of interaction occurring during this father–child time remains varied. Watching a football game with an infant resting on his chest does provide some contact time, but watching the game in one room with the children in another appears to be less interactive.

Family time is about privacy, ownership, and sharing (Daly 1996). Daly offers two approaches to recreating family-time expectations and actual experiences. First, find and define time boundaries. This means decisions such as no phone calls or television during dinner or reducing the number of activities for children and parents. Second, he recommends reconstructing what family time means to the family; are family lived moments expanding or "time consuming" (Daly 2001a)? To do this, families need to understand and live the difference between clock time and *care time* (Daly 2001b). Clock time runs on lists, but our "to do lists" often don't include care time (Table 4.2). "Lists and calendars keep us running–sometimes right past or right over the people who need us most" (Daly 2001b: 1).

A shift in cultural philosophy, which values healthful balancing of clock and care time is needed. Recent studies reveal that parents' feelings about time with their children remain unsettled as they struggle to balance home and work lives (Milke et al. 2004).

> Although time management holds out the promise that we can control time in a better way, there is an underlying assumption that we continue at the same speed by simply doing a better job of squeezing it all in. Time management, as a tool for personal and professional

TABLE 4.2

Clock Time Versus Care Time

Clock Time	*Care Time*
Demands attention based on how long it takes	Demands attention based on priorities and values over schedules and deadlines
Is external, requiring struggle to control speed and efficiency	Is internal, giving moments to others often at unscheduled and perhaps inopportune times
Minutes we manage (or try to manage)	Moments to which we surrender
Demands that "quality family" time must fit into the prearranged time slot	Recognizes that quality time cannot be shoehorned into an already crowded day, but requires attention and empathy for the needs of others
Exact "to do lists" that ignore time for caring	Organized but not dominated by schedules so that caring needs are recognized and receive response as they arise
A mono-time-framed orientation in which the primary focus is on the future with faint regard for the present	A multi-time-framed orientation in which the primary focus is on the present with appreciation for the past and perception of preferred futures

Source: Adapted with permission from Kerry Daly. 2001. "Clock Time and Care Time: Clashing Values, Competing Demands." www.uoguelph.ca/cfww/daly_time.html (Retrieved 10/26/2001)

survival, is based on the same values as the world of work: enhancing productivity, increasing efficiency, and avoiding the greatest sin of all, wasting time. . . . The dizzying speed of our lives keeps us in a trancelike state of preoccupation. . . . Time management does little to change the intoxicating effects of a fast-paced culture; it simply serves as a tool for living with the malaise. (Daly 1996: 210)

"Families are seeking support connection, not speed and efficiency" (Rankine 2002: 2). Living family time has more to do with making decisions based on agreed family values. Such decisions include making tradeoffs such as "freedom from versus freedom to" engage in certain experiences. This creates not only a redistribution of time in families but also a reinterpretation of assumptions about time such as the "powerlessness" imposed on families as they struggle to balance the exciting and challenging demands of life together (Daly 1996).

Families at Play

According to Webster (*Webster's II New Riverside Dictionary* 1996: 745), vacation is "a period of time for pleasure, rest, or relaxation, esp. one with pay granted to an employee". Vacations provide opportunities for flow experiences rather than for an over-scheduled event that leaves many family members aching to get back to work or school. Perhaps vacations could indeed be vacations if families dropped the myth that there is some "perfect" getaway if only one spends more time and money to get there. Deciding what it means to relax and enjoy some flow experiences together deserves as much, perhaps more, attention.

Crawford et al. (2002) challenge the assumption that couples who play together are happier and more satisfied with their marriages. This 13-year study followed 73 newly married couples. This research indicates that just being together is not enough to ensure bliss. Likewise, family members need to be candid regarding which desired activities each likes and dislikes. For example, a father may assume the best family vacation is time spent at his parents' home, whereas his mate and children hold entirely opposite views. Unless this family communicates and negotiates what constitutes a family vacation, dissatisfaction may undercut the experience for all members.

Learning to balance and not merely juggle family time begins with recognition of the importance of care time over clock time and a need to create more meaningful moments during everyday family activities.

FAMILY TIME IN A DIGITAL AGE

Managing family time also means assessing how technology acts as servant or master. Technology holds great promise as a means for staying connected, informed, engaged, aware, and entertained. Yet these same attributes can lead to separation, unwanted influences, isolation, or overstimulation.

Transportation: "Are We There Yet?"

The 19th century social critic de Tocqueville (1831) noted that Americans revealed an extraordinary level of mobility due to attitudes and beliefs supporting mobility for economic and social reasons. The automobile embraces the very word "mobile." American culture often equates cars with freedom to go where and when it pleases. However, this freedom is often accompanied by traffic congestion and longer commuting times. Nationally, the average person spent 26 more hours commuting annually in 2000 than in 1990. At the same time, carpooling has decreased, and commuters make less use of public transportation (United States Census Bureau 2000).

Individuals and their families are spending more and more time in automobiles slugging their ways to and from work, school, and home activities. The car also offers some unexpected impacts on family time. Faulkner (2002) notes that American families spend less time around the dinner table together than they do in the family car as they drive or are transported to and from their many activities. Thus, the potential for family time and conversation while driving together is significant. According to Reams, a child psychologist, car talk is "an unstructured kind of in-between time" (Faulkner 2002:162) which often is more comfortable or at least a less formal environment for families. Aside from cell phones, portable CD players, hand-held computers, or the occasional car equipped with a television and VCR/DVD, most families are "trapped" together in a vehicle for regular periods of time. Faulkner suggests that families put this precious family time to good use and turn off the cell phones and CD/DVD players and talk which includes active listening.

Layering technology onto an American culture of mobility increases the potential for *weekend-families* in which members of a family may work and live miles, states, or continents apart during the week and return home for regular periods of time such as weekends. This impacts how distant families work and share family time. Perhaps as important as the development is the availability of these transportation technologies. The ability to visit distant family members may influence individuals to be more mobile.

Innovations in transportation coupled with changes in education, employment, family structure, housing, and retirement impact families (Gober 1993) as they negotiate transportation issues in terms of flexible *residential mobility*. Residential mobility refers to a frequent change of residence, either in the same city or town or between cities, states, or countries. Technological advances in transportation provide the means for carrying more people further and faster than at any time prior, thus significantly contributing to residential mobility.

High residential mobility demands a social cost such as losing contact with friends, family, and community ties. Yet residential mobility can also bring social gains in the forms of better employment, as well as novel adventure, starting over with new friends or community. Hence, the costs and benefits of residential mobility appear to vary and depend on a family's flexibility (economic and social) and adaptability.

Another set of questions revolving around the issue of transportation technology and families focuses on why some families experience higher residential mobility than do other families of equal socioeconomic means. In a longitudinal study of residential mobility experiences of children and their families of origin, Myers (1999) considers this question of who is more mobile. Residential mobility lifestyles appear to be influenced by one's family of origin's mobility experiences. Myers submits "given the high rate of divorce, remarriage, and dual-career households [it] nearly guarantees continuing high rates of [residential] mobility for children, adolescents, and adults" (880). "Picking up and moving," however, can be difficult for families, especially dual-career couples who often find geographic relocation challenging since both partners must find employment.

Household Appliances: Doing More in Less Time

> Dishwashers, washing machines, vacuum cleaners, central heating/air, and freezers have lightened the load of homemakers—but not always reduced their hours of toil (Shapiro 1997–1998: 38).

Although few families that have them would part with any of those time and labor-saving appliances, having them has not shortened the workday as much as would be expected. Although appliances promise to make quick work of household chores, with this "ease" comes increased expectations and standards for households in terms of doing more, better, faster, and in less time.

Women still do the lioness share of such work, but that has less to do with technology and more to do with culture (Hochschild 1989, 1997). The failure of technology to add more free time results from the fact that families continue to squeeze more and more into their shrinking days and run faster to keep up with the clock.

Television: Intrusion or Addition to Family Time?

Researchers have documented many negatives related to television viewing, including ubiquitous views of sex and violence to the numbing impact of much program content. Some critics have even labeled the mass habituation with television as addiction (Kubey and Csikszentmihalyi 2002). Although technological advances in television including enhanced TV, digital television, WebTV, and DirecTV have made this medium rich in imagery, some worry about the "social, structural ownership" of television programming (Bryant and Bryant 2001: xi).

How much television do families watch? Researchers (American Academy of Pediatrics 2004; Kaiser Family Foundation 1998) report an average American watches over four hours of television per day with 40% of households always or often watching television while eating dinner. For American children, the statistics are even more striking. According to Drew Altman, the president of the Kaiser Family Foundation,

[W]atching TV, playing video games, listening to music and surfing the Internet have become a full-time job for the typical American child. (Weitz 1999)

Children aged two to 17 spend on average 19 hours and 40 minutes per week watching television, far exceeding time spent using other media such as listening to music (over 10 hours per week) or using the computer or playing video games (over four hours per week). Almost two thirds (64%) of children aged two to 18 spend more than an hour a day watching television, and 17% spend over five hours per day watching television. Television indeed is "king" of children's (and most adults) media use time. Concerns over the sedentary lifestyle of children focuses on health issues such as Type Two Diabetes as will be discussed in chapter 5 (Kaiser Family Foundation 2004a, 2004b)

Kotler, Wright, and Huston (2001) argue that although the role of television as not only child companion but also family member will continue in the 21st century, families need to take responsibility for wise use. Yet, they also take a position that technological advances and increased variety in television programming can be harnessed for positive uses. However, such constructive use of television will require the cooperative efforts of families, the entertainment industry, and policymakers in expanding educational and supporting prosocial programming.

On an encouraging note, children are reading for pleasure, on the average over five hours per week, even more than playing computer games or surfing the Internet for fun. However, over the course of a year, American school-aged children spend 60% more time watching television than being in school (Kaiser Family Foundation 1999). Sadly, this research indicates that parents spend less than an hour on the average (38.5 minutes) each day engaged in meaningful conversation with their children (Table 4.3).

Yet, television can produce positive impacts. Documentaries such as several produced by the Public Broadcasting Service provide information in an entertaining medium. Such selective television viewing that includes family conversations is called *edutainment*. Edutainment, also referred to as enter-education or infotainment, provides a means to inform the public on a concern or issue (Kaiser Family Foundation 2004a). Cable, Satellite, and WebTV also hold promise of such programming, but families need to actively choose rather than passively submit to what is offered and viewed. Watching television (including cable, VCR, or DVD) together (at least in the same room) may be a source of shared family activity, particularly if the programming elicits conversation and discussion. Again, families have to be selective and proactive in the use of this technology.

Telecommunications: Did You Get My Message?

The transistor, created in 1947, revolutionized telecommunications (Begley 1997–1998). From this innovation, advances in telephones, pagers, cell phones, fax machines, photocopiers, and photocells soared. Consider the impacts on family time in terms of staying connected and sharing information across miles. These technologies also mean that "getting away" includes remembering to turn off your cell phone or pager. Establishing family time today involves some challenging decisions about limiting telecommunication interruptions during dinner or other designated family-lived moments.

The development and interrelationships among digital technologies such as televisions, phones, and computers raise opportunities and cautions as they impact family time. The home computer and its ability to access global information and resources through the Internet changes how families work, learn, communicate, and live.

TABLE 4.3

Children's Work-Week of Media Use

Amount of time children spend using media each day, on average[1]	
All kids 2–18	5:29
2–7-year-olds	3:34
8 and older	6:43
Amount of time kids spend each day, on average[2]	
Watching TV	2:46
Listening to music	1:27
Reading for fun	:44
Watching videos	:39
Using a computer for fun	:21
Playing video games	:20
Online	:08
Percentage of kids who spend more than an hour a day	
Watching TV	64%
Reading for pleasure	20%
Listening to CDs or tapes	19%
Using a computer for fun	9%
Playing video games	8%
Online	3%
Playing computer games	2%
Amount of time kids spend each week, on average[3]	
Watching TV	19:19
Listening to music	10:04
Reading	5:15
Using a computer for fun	2:29
Playing video games	2:17
Percentage of kids who have a TV in their bedroom	
All kids 2–18	53%
2–7-year-olds	32%
8 and older	65%
Percentage of kids who use a computer in a day	
All kids 2–18	42%
2–7-year-olds	26%
8 and older	51%
Percentage of kids who have a computer in the home	
All kids 2–18	69%
2–7-year-olds	62%
8 and older	73%
Lower income[4]	49%
Upper income	81%
Percentage of kids who have a computer in their bedroom	
All kids 2–18	16%
2–7-year-olds	6%
8 and older	21%

(continued)

TABLE 4.3

(continued)

Percentage of school-aged children who use a computer in a typical day, by income[4]	
In school	
Lower income	32%
Upper income	30%
Out of school	
Lower income	23%
Upper income	48%
Parental oversight	
Percentage of kids	
With no rules about TV	49%
In homes where TV is usually on during meals	58%
Percentage of time parents watch TV with their kids[5]	
2–7-year-olds	19%
8–18-year-olds	5%

Key: 1, time is presented in hours:minutes; 2, times cannot be summed due to use of more than one medium at a time; 3, week-long averages based on mean times with each medium, separating out weekday and weekend reports. Times cannot be summed due to use of more than one medium at a time; 4, income categories are based on the median income of the zip code in which the child lives (for 2–7-year-olds) or goes to school (for 8–18-year-olds), and represents the following ranges: "low income" is less than $25,000, and "high income" is $40,000 or more; 5, based on media-use diaries.

Source: Adapted with permission from A Report of the Kaiser Family Foundation, "Kids & Media @ the New Millennium: A Comprehensive National Analysis of Children's Media Use." (November 1999). www.kff.org/content/1999/1535/ChartPack.pdf (Retrieved 10/04/02).

Computers and the Internet: From Wired to Wireless Families

The August 2000 United States census findings report that 54 million households, or 51%, had one or more computers, up from 42% reported in late 1998. This same report notes that more than half of all adults 18 years old and over (55%) live in a household with at least one computer in 2000, up from only 46% in 1998 (Newburger 2001).

The development of the microprocessor in 1971, which dramatically reduced the size and cost of computers, had significant impacts on home computing and thus family time. These innovations of smaller, faster, more affordable computers led the way to the widespread availability of personal computers. More user-friendly software plus the mouse-driven point-and-click innovations followed, allowing computers to surge into offices, homes, and schools altering how we work and learn.

Forty-two percent of American households have Internet access today (Newburger 2001; United States Department of Commerce 2000). Figure 4.1 reveals an increase in computer and Internet access. The Internet offers extensive educational and recreational resources as well as the opportunity to develop and refine technological and research skills. The Internet also can serve as an avenue for unwanted and inappropriate material and as a time-draining isolator of family time. Almost seven out of 10 American children (69%) have a computer at home, and nearly half (45%) have Internet access from home. Yet, even with this relative widespread access to computers and the Internet, children aged two to 18 spend far more time watching television (average almost three hours per day) than surfing

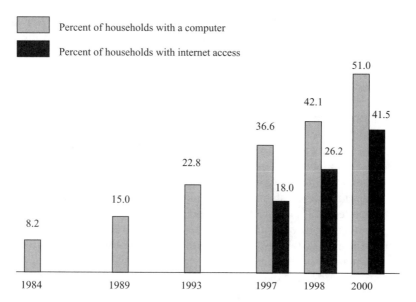

FIG. 4.1.   Computers and Internet Access in the Home: 1984 to 2000.
Source: Adapted from Newburger, Eric. 2001. "Home Computers and Internet Use in the
United States: August 2000." *Current Population Reports, United States Census Bureau*
(September). www.census.gov/rod/2001pubs/p23-207.pdf (Retrieved 09/30/02).
Note: Data on Internet access were not collected before 1997.

the net (less than 30 minutes per day; Kaiser Family Foundation 1999). Thus, contrary to popular assumptions and fears, the study did not find evidence of significant numbers of children spending endless hours playing computer games or surfing the Internet. Jonassen claims that in order to understand a culture there is a need to understand the tools it uses, which is especially true with digital tools such as computers and the Internet as discussed in Box 4.4.

BOX 4.4   "Technology as Social Discourse Tool"
David H. Jonassen, Ph.D.

Tools are an everyday part of most human activity. Tools can assume many different forms when used by people to transform objects in their environment. The use of culture-specific tools shapes the way people act and think. Human activity can be understood only by comprehending the tools and signs that mediate it. In order to understand a culture, you must understand its tools.

Modern computer networks that facilitate immediate access to the world's information and nearly instantaneous communication with anyone anywhere have provided a level of global connectivity that was inconceivable a mere decade ago. This connectivity is redefining culture. Rather than being constrained by simultaneous location, communication is being redefined by need and interest. Computer networks support discourse and learning communities through different forms of computer conferences. In education, networked technologies have fostered the development of knowledge-building communities. In knowledge-building communities, students actively and strategically pursue learning as a goal. They produce their own knowledge databases in their own knowledge-building community of students.

Through networks like KIDLINK, the Global Schoolhouse, Learning Circles, and many other educational telecommunications projects, students are forming global learning communities where participants conduct research (read, study, view, and consult with experts), share information in the pursuit of a meaning, and reflect on the knowledge that they have constructed and the processes used to construct. Telecommunications have created keypals, global classrooms, electronic mentoring, information exchanges, electronic publishing, electronic field trips, pooled data analysis, parallel problem solving, collaborative electronic writing, serial creations, and social action projects. Students are escaping the boundaries of their classroom and community to play on an ever-expanding information field.

Telecommunications are redefining the concept of classroom and the culture of learning. Those advantages also accrue to families who share and pursue common purposes. When technologies are used as social discourse tools representing ideas, generating products, and communicating with others, as well as for accessing information, they can amplify the ways that students think and work. The key to creating meaning is ownership of the ideas that are created. Technology provides the tools for organizing, creating, and expressing.

David Jonassen, Ph.D. is Distinguished Professor of Education at the University of Missouri where he teaches about learning technologies and educational psychology.

Although the "digital divide" between the "haves and have-nots" (or as some would say the "have now and have later") continues to shrink, poor families remain digitally deprived (U.S. Department of Commerce 2000). Digital technology also has not been equally available in American schools. Yet, the National Center for Education Statistics (2001) reports that some progress has occurred in terms of Internet accessibility in public schools. By the beginning of the 2000 school year, almost all public schools (98%) were connected as compared to only 35% in 1994. This report also notes that there were virtually no differences in school access to the Internet by factors of poverty level or metropolitan status in 2000. By fall 2000, 77% of classrooms were connected to the Internet as compared to 3% in 1994. Interestingly, a digital divide reported in public schools existed in terms of how Internet-savvy students use the Internet for school and personal use as compared to how they use it under the teacher's direction, which was viewed as too elementary for them (Levin and Arafeh 2002).

Learning and the Connected Family

A digital divide often exists within families as well where some members soar ahead in their understanding and use of digital technologies whereas other members lag behind or even refuse to engage in it.

Papert, a mathematician and cofounder of the Massachusetts Institute of Technology's artificial-intelligence lab, has studied how children learn with computers since the 1960s. Learning happens best when it is self-directed and in experiences that include learning about how one learns (Papert 1996). Papert responds to a list of concerns often raised about computers and children. A common worry is that the computer separates the family. His response, "That's up to you" (1996: 201). *Connected families* are healthy communities with a keen learning culture where digital technologies serve as tools in pursuit of learning and in being curious about life.

The discussion surrounding the impacts of digital technology on society in general and families in particular suffers from nostalgia. Research suggests that, with any technology after the novelty wanes, most original negative effects on families, such as declines in communication among members disappear (Jordan 2002). However, exposure to inappropriate and even dangerous marketing, solicitation, and unhealthy relationships over the Internet as well as cyber bullying are real concerns calling for public debate. Families need to be proactive regarding the use of these tools through modeling and discussing the benefits and risks. Family educators (Silliman 2002) suggest the following guides for various age groups of Internet users:

- 2–3 years—watching family members or playing with age appropriate software programs
- 4–7 years—this age group learns quickly and enjoys the rich and diverse recreational and educational software available. Learning how to e-mail and playing some interactive games work well.
- 8–11 years—middle-school-aged children are ready to use the Internet for the many online resources and interactive learning sites available. Adults need to provide careful guidance regarding wise use of the medium and staying safe while online.
- 12–14 years—teens with computer experience quickly move onto more sophisticated projects and evaluation of resource sites. Again, guidance is needed to reinforce wise Internet use habits.
- 15–18 years—Building on the previous computer experience, this age group can use the net to its full potential. They also are available to assist adults with their computer questions.

Families benefit by keeping these marvelous technologies in perspective, thus encouraging family members to engage in physical activity, offline reading and writing, social interaction, hobbies, and spiritual growth.

Technology in its many forms is often blamed for distracting families and destroying family time, when in fact it holds significant potential as a tool to enhance or maintain this precious experience. Digital technologies are tools, marvelous servants, unless families allow them to become virtual masters of family time.

Family time is not simply what is left over at the end of the hectic day of members' schedules. Rather, it demands care and priority. Families and their members need to tell their stories, their preferred images of time together, so as to re-author their lives to better meet the need to balance the expectations, perceptions, demands, and technological tools that turn the hands of family time.

GLOSSARY

Care time	Quality time
Caregiving	Residential mobility
Connected families	Time bind
Edutainment	Time deepening
Family time	Time famine
Flow	Time-relaxed families
Lived moments	Time-urgent families
Multitasking	Weekend-families

FOR YOUR CONSIDERATION

1. In Box 4.2, Daly discusses the politics of family time. Design an example of a family with unfair gender and age politics of time. Using your example, describe how this family could modify their family-time choices so as to improve their politics of time.

2. You are working with Maria from the time-urgent family described in Box 4.3. Maria is having trouble staying awake in school. You invite Maria's parents, Pat and Chris, in for a consultation related to a situation that Maria has described as her family's "weird and pushy schedule." At this point, she can most clearly articulate that she does not like piano and wants time to play with her friends. Outline two to three issues you would want to raise with her parents or guardians.

3. You work in the human resources department of a middle-sized business. Several of the employees have complained that the required daily overtime and Saturday morning meetings are cutting too deeply into their family time. Your boss (who represents a time-urgent family) functions strictly under "clock time" and does not understand why the employees cannot get their families better organized. You are asked to represent the employees by explaining the difference between "clock time" and "care time" and outlining two strategies to better ensure care time is recognized at work.

4. You are a nurse practitioner consulting with a family referred to you by their pediatrician. Both of the children (and one of the parents) are significantly overweight, and the children's weight gain shows an upward trend. What issues, including family lifestyle options, will you raise with this family?

FOR FURTHER STUDY: WEB SITES, ORGANIZATIONS, AND PUBLICATIONS

Web Sites and Organizations

American Academy of Child and Adolescent Psychiatry (AACAP)
www.aacap.org
This organization represents over 6,900 child and adolescent psychiatrists who are physicians with at least 5 years of additional training beyond medical school in general (adult) and child and adolescent psychiatry. *AACAP* often takes vocal stands on issues relating to the media and other issues.

Center for Media Literacy
www.medialit.org
This site is "dedicated to a new vision of literacy for the 21st century." The site provides resources and educational materials in print and electronic forms and emphasizes the need to be able to "access, understand, analyze and evaluate the powerful images, words and sounds" of current mass media. They do not claim to be a "watchdog agency" but support the need for parents and children to be critical consumers of media in its many forms.

Children Now
www.childrennow.org
Children Now is a research organization focused on the welfare of children regarding the media. The site includes a link to *Media Now*, which explores cultural attitudes and diversity issues in the media.

Citizens for Independent Public Broadcasting (CIPB)
www.cipbonline.org

The CIPB web site is one of the better educational resources available on the Web. CIPB challenges public broadcasters to focus on authentic educational programming, while providing information of quality programs for the public.

Family Life First

www.familylifefirst.org

Family Life First is a grass roots movement that aspires to build communities where family life is "an honored and celebrated priority." The site provides narratives and suggestions from parents struggling to redefine family time.

Kaiser Family Foundation

www.kff.org

The *Kaiser Family Foundation* site offers a rich array of resources and research related but not limited to media, education, health, and politics as those issues impact families. This site offers solid information and extensive links to related materials and is updated frequently and easily navigated.

Media Awareness Network

www.media-awareness.ca

This network emerged from meetings focusing on children and television sponsored by the Canadian Radio-Television and Telecommunications Commission. This site offers curriculum-related materials, Web literacy teaching materials for schools, and media awareness resources for communities. This site also provides links for educators, parents, students, and community leaders.

Media Scope

www.mediascope.org

This national, nonprofit research and policy organization provides information and tools to better understand the entertainment industry. *Media Scope* covers video games, television, music, the Internet, film, and advertising and examines violence, substance abuse, and sexual explicitness, plus ratings, diversity concerns, and artists' rights and responsibilities.

National Parent Teacher Association

www.pta.org

This site offers resources for schools, families, and communities with links to child development and education organizations. National PTA is the largest volunteer child advocacy organization of parents, educators, students, and other citizens active in their schools and communities. PTA works toward raising issues such as the realities of digital divides.

Publications

Bryant, Jennings, and Alison Bryant eds. 2001. *Television and the American Family*, 2/e. Mahwah, NJ: Lawrence Erlbaum Associates.
Bryant and Bryant have arranged an extensive discussion related to the uses, attitudes toward, meanings, and effect of impacts from and policy issues of families and television. The contributing authors provide well-documented chapters with extensive resources.

Daly, Kerry. 1996. *Families and Time: Keeping Pace in a Hurried Culture*. Thousand Oaks, CA: Sage.
Daly emphasizes the need to let go of nostalgic images of family time. This book provides a solid foundation for Family Studies professionals as it studies the dynamics of family time and how to regain control over it.

Doherty, William J., and Barbara Carlson. 2002. *Putting Family First: Successful Strategies for Reclaiming Family Life in a Hurry Up World.* New York, NY: Henry Holt.
Doherty, a marriage and family therapist and former president of the *National Council of Family Relations*, and Carlson co-founded *Family Life First*, an organization committed to helping parents reclaim family

time. *Putting Family First* offers strategies for forging family connections and relationships in a proactive pursuit of family time.

Levine, Robert. 1997. *A Geography of Time: The Temporal Misadventures of a Social Psychologist*. New York, NY: Basic Books.

Levine's geography of the abstract concept of time and how this concept impacts human life is thought provoking. He offers numerous resources and diverse points of view, and his discussion on the relative speed of lived time benefits those who wish to better understand how we "spend" our time.

Papert, Seymour. 1996. *The Connected Family: Bridging the Digital Generation Gap*. Atlanta, GA: Longstreet. Papert's position on the issue of technology and families is to "get going and learn from these tools." He is highly supportive of children engaging in telecommunications, especially computing and surfing the net. His position helps to balance an often "doom and gloom" environment when families discuss children and technology.

REFERENCES FOR CITED WORKS

American Academy of Pediatrics. 2004. "Television and the Family." http://www.aap.org/family/tv1.htm (Retrieved 09/24/04).

Anderson, Virginia. 2004. "Multitasking Meltdown." *StarTribune* (January 13): E1, E9.

Baranowski, Thomas. 2002. "The Best Mealtime Ingredient: Good Conversation." www.bcm.tmc.edu/cnrc/consumer/nyc/vol1-01b.htm (Retrieved 10/08/02).

Begley, Sharon. 1997–98. "The Transitor." *Newsweek Extra: 2000 the Power of Invention*. (Winter): 25–6.

Block, Richard. 1990. "Models of Psychological Time." In *Cognitive Models of Psychological Time*, ed. R. Block. Hillsdale, NJ: Lawrence Erlbaum Associates, 1–36.

Bohannan, Paul. 1980. "Time, Rhythm, and Pace." *Science* 80, 1: 18–20.

Bryant, Jennings, and Alison Bryant. eds. 2001. *Television and the American Family*, 2/e. Mahwah, NJ: Lawrence Erlbaum Associates.

Bryant, W. Keith, and Cathleen D. Zick. 1996. "An Examination of Parent-Child Shared Time." *Journal of Marriage and the Family* 58, 1 (February): 227–37.

Cancian, Francesca, and Stacey Oliker. 2000. *Caring and Gender*. Thousand Oaks, CA: Pine Forge.

Children's Nutrition Research Center CNRC. 2002. "Time-Savvy Tips Cut Meal-Prep Stress." www.bcm.edu/cnrc/consumer/nyc/vol1-01a.htm (Retrieved 10/04/02).

Clark, Lois. 2002. "Building a Strong Marriage—Finding Time." http://ohioline.osu.edu/flm02/FS02.html (Retrieved 08-20-04).

Coontz, Stephanie. 1992. *The Way We Never Were: American Families and the Nostalgia Trap*. New York, NY: Basic Books.

Coontz, Stephanie. 1997. *The Way We Really Are: Coming to Terms with America's Changing Families*. New York, NY: Basic Books.

Crawford, Duane, Houte Renate, Ted. L. Huston, and Laura J. George. 2002. "Compatibility, Leisure, and Satisfaction in Marital Relationships." *Journal of Marriage and Family* 64 (May): 433–49.

Crouter, Ann, Melissa Head, and Susan Jenkins-Tucker. 2004. "Family Time and the Psychosocial Adjustment of Adolescent Siblings and Their Parents." *Journal of Marriage and Family* 66 (February): 147–62.

Csikszentmihalyi, Mihaly. 1990. *Flow: The Psychology of Optimal Experience*. New York: Harper Perennial.

Daly, Kerry. 1996. *Families and Time: Keeping Pace in a Hurried Culture*. Thousand Oaks, CA: Sage.

Daly, Kerry. 2001a. "Deconstructing Family Time: From Ideology to Lived Experience." www.ncfr.org/about_us/j_press (Retrieved 10/20/01).

Daly, Kerry. 2001b. "Clock Time and Care Time: Clashing Values, Competing Demands." www.uoguelph.ca/cfww/daly_time.html (Retrieved 10/26/01).

Daly, Kerry. 2002. "Time, Gender, and the Negotiation of Family Schedules." *Symbolic Interaction* 25: 323–42.

Daly, Kerry. 2003. "Family Theory Versus the Theories Families Live By." *Journal of Marriage and Family* 65 (November): 771–84.

Daly, Kerry. 2004. "The Changing Culture of Parenting." *Vanier Institute of the Family*. www.vifamily.ca/library/cft/parenting.html (Retrieved 09/23/04).

Doherty, William J., and Barbara Carlson. 2002. *Putting Family First: Successful Strategies for Reclaiming Family Life in a Hurry Up World*. New York, NY: Henry Holt.

Economic Policy Institute. 2004. "The Rise in Family Work Hours Leads Many Americans to Struggle to Balance Work and Family." www.epinet.org/content.cfm/ webfeatures_snapshots_07072004 (Retrieved 10/01/04).

Elkind, David. 1981. *The Hurried Child: Growing Up Too Soon*. Reading, MA: Addison-Wesley.

Elkind, David. 1998. *Ties That Stress: The New Family Imbalance*. Boston, MA: Harvard University Press.

Elkind, David. 2001. "2001 Childhood Lost." Presentation at the *North Carolina Medical Society* meetings *2001 Hurried Child*, Raleigh, November.

Ellis, Michael. 1973. *Why People Play*. Englewood Cliffs, NJ: Prentice Hall.

Ezzell, Carol. 2002. "Telling the Time." *Scientific American* (September): 74–5.

Faulkner, Jeanne. 2002. "Talking With Kids in Cars." *Better Homes and Gardens* (October): 162, 164.

Gober, Patricia. 1993. "Americans on the Move." *Population Bulletin* 48, 3: 1–48.

Hochschild, Arlie Russell. 1989. *The Second Shift: Working Parents and the Revolution at Home*. New York, NY: Viking.

Hochschild, Arlie Russell. 1997. *The Time Bind: When Work Becomes Home and Home Becomes Work*. New York, NY: Metropolitan Books.

Holmes, Steven A. 1998. "Children Study Longer and Play Less, A Report Says." *The New York Times* (November 11): A18.

Hunt, Diana, and Pam Hait. 1990. *The Tao of Time: Time Management for the Real World—A Right Brain Approach that Gives You the Control You Need and Freedom You Want*. New York, NY: Fireside.

Jordan, Amy. 2002. "A Family Systems Approach to Examining the Role of the Internet in the Home." In *Children in the Digital Age: Influences of Electronic Media on Development,* eds. S. L. Calvert, A. B. Jordan, and R. R. Cooking. Westport, CT: Praeger, 231–48.

Kaiser Family Foundation. 1998. "Facts and Figures About Our TV Habit." *TV Turn Off Network*. www.tvturnoff.org (Retrieved 10/01/02).

Kaiser Family Foundation. 1999. "Kids & Media @ the New Millennium: A Comprehensive National Analysis of Children's Media Use." (November). www.kff.org/content/1999/1535/ChartPack.pdf (Retrieved 10/04/02).

Kaiser Family Foundation. 2004a. "Entertainment Education and Health in the United States." Issue Brief. Spring. www.kff.org (Retrieved 8/26/04).

Kaiser Family Foundation. 2004b. "Kaiser Family Foundation Releases New Report on Role of Media in Childhood Obesity." www.kff.org/entmedia/entmedia022404nr.cfm (Retrieved 10/15/04).

Kotler, Jennifer, John Wright, and Aletha Huston. 2001. "Television Use in Families With Children." In *Television and the American Family*, 2/e, eds. J. Bryant and A. Bryant. Mahwah, NJ: Lawrence Erlbaum Associates, 33–48.

Kubey, Robert, and Mihaly Csikszentmihalyi. 2002. "Television Addiction Is No Mere Metaphor." *Scientific American* (February 23). www.sciam.com/article.cfm?articleID=0005339B-A694-1CC5-B4A8809EC588EEDF (Retrieved 1/30/02).

Lang, Susan. 1997. "Parents Put in a Full Day's Work Raising Two Children—Triple the Time Experts Had Previously Estimated." *Science News* (May). www.news.cornell.edu/releases/May97/parent.time2.SSL.html (Retrieved 1/30/02).

Levin, Doug, and Sousan, Arafeh. 2002. "The Digital Disconnect: The Widening Gap Between Internet-Savvy Students and Their Schools." PEW Internet & American Life Project (August). www.pewinternet.org/report_display.asp?r=67 (Retrieved 10/15/04).

Levine, Robert. 1997. *A Geography of Time: The Temporal Misadventures of a Social Psychologist*. New York, NY: Basic Books.

Milke, Melissa, Marybeth Mattingly, Kei Nomaguchi, Suzanne Bianchi, and John Robinson. 2004. "The Time Squeeze: Parental Status and Feelings About Time With Children." *Journal of Marriage and Family* 66, 3: 739–61.

Muller, Chandra. 1995. "Maternal Employment, Parent Involvement, and Mathematics Achievement Among Adolescents." *Journal of Marriage and the Family* 57, 1 (February): 85–100.

Myers, Scott. 1999. "Residential Mobility as a Way of Life: Evidence of Intergenerational Similarities." *Journal of Marriage and the Family* 61, 4 (November): 871–80.

National Center for Education Statistics. 2001. "Internet Access in U.S. Public Schools and Classrooms: 1994–2000." http://nces.ed.gov/pubs2001/InternetAccess (Retrieved 10/15/04).

Newburger, Eric C. 2001. "Home Computers and Internet Use in the United States: August 2000." *Current Population Reports, U.S. Census Bureau*, (September). www.census.gov/prod/2001pubs/p23-207 (Retrieved 09/30/02).

Noll, Elizabeth. 2004. "Paid Family Leave." *The Minnesota Women's Press* 20 (October 6–19): 1, 10–11.

Papert, Seymour. 1996. *The Connected Family: Bridging the Digital Generation Gap*. Atlanta, GA: Longstreet.

Rankine, Polly. 2002. "Just a Minute: Is Quality Family Time a Thing of the Past?" www.uoguelph.ca/research/publications/health/page66.html (Retrieved 02/03/02).

Robinson, John P., and Geoffrey Godbey. 1997. *Time for Life: The Surprising Way Americans Use Their Time*. University Park, PA: The Pennsylvania State University Press.

Rosenfeld, Alvin, and Nicole Wise. 2001. *Over Scheduled Child: Avoiding the Hyper-Parenting Trap*. New York, NY: St. Martin's.

Schor, Juliet B. 1991. *The Overworked American*. New York, NY: Basic Books.

Shapiro, Laura. 1997-1998. "Household Appliances." *Newsweek Extra* 130, 22 (Winter): 38–9.

Shaw, S. 1992. "Dereifying Family Leisure: An Examination of Women's and Men's Everyday Experiences and Perceptions of Family Time." *Leisure Sciences* 14: 271–86.

Silliman, Bill. 2002. "Families in the Fast Lane." *Human Develop and Family Life*. www.uwyo.edu/CES/FAMILY/FastLane.htm (Retrieved 8/1/02).

Snow, Catherine E., Patton O. Tabors, and David K. Dickinson. 2001. "Language Development in the Preschool Years. In *Beginning Literacy with Language*, eds. D. K. Dickinson and P. O. Tabor. Baltimore, MD: Paul H. Brookes, 1–25.

de Tocqueville, Alexis. (R. Heffner, ed.). 1831. *Democracy in America*. New York, NY: Penguin Putnam.

Ulmer, Diane, and Leonard Schwartzbard. 1996. "Treatment of Time Pathologies." In *Heart and Mind: The Practice of Cardiac Psychology*, eds. R. Allan and S. Scheidt. Washington, DC: American Psychological Association.

United States Census Bureau. 2000. "Census Finds the Commutes are Getting Longer as Traffic Congestion Worsens." *U.S. Census 2000 Report* www.tripnet.org/CensusDataCongestionJun2002.PDF. (Retrieved 10/02/02).

United States Department of Commerce. 2000. "Falling Through the Net: Toward Digital Inclusion." www.ntia.doc.gov/ntiahome/fttn00/Falling.htm(Retrieved 10/15/04).

Webster's II New Riverside Dictionary. 1996. New York: Houghton Mifflin.

Weitz, Amy. 1999. "New Study Finds Kids Spend Equivalent of Full Work Week Using Media." *Kaiser Family Foundation Report*. www.kff.org/content/1999/1535/pressreleasefinal.doc.html (Retrieved 10/04/02).

Williams, Treva. 2002. "Quality Family Time." www.ohioline.osu.edu/hyg-fact/5000/5285.html (Retrieved 10/1/02).

Woznicki, Katrina. 2001. "Multitasking Creates Health Problems." www.umich.edu/~bcalab/document/upi.html (Retrieved 1/12/04).

Wright, L., S. McCurdy, and G. Rogoll. 1992. *Jenkins Activity Survey: Forms*. New York, NY: Psychological Corporation.

Wright, Karen. 2002. "Time of Our Life." *Scientific American* (September): 59–65.

Yeung, Jean W., John F. Sandberg, Pamela E. Davis-Kean, and Sandra L. Hofferth. 2001. "Children's Time With Fathers in Intact Families." *Journal of Marriage and Family* 63, 1 (February): 136–54.

FAMILY WELLNESS: BEYOND ABSENCE OF ILLNESS

CHAPTER PREVIEW

Family health is more than absence of illness, whereas *family wellness* refers to an expanded idea of health that includes behaviors and processes plus action over inertia. A salutogenic view of family wellness weaves threads of physical, psychological, social, spiritual, occupational, and environmental wellness into the tapestry of family life. This view of family wellness incorporates *biocultural* approaches and recognizes mind–body–spirit interconnections (*psychoneuroimmunology*), while blending both *conventional* and *complementary medicine*. We refer to this as an *integrative medicine* approach to family wellness. As health care coverage shrinks, families often avoid necessary immunizations and other preventive care practices.

Prevention and risk reduction demand a proactive approach on the part of families and communities, beginning with better understanding of health risks, strategies to reduce these risks, and behaviors that enhance family wellness. Wise eating includes choosing foods with high *nutrient density* and increasing consumption of foods rich in *omega-3* and *monounsaturated fatty acids* along with *phytochemicals*. Likewise, increased physical activity plus adequate sleep and relaxation are important foundations for wellness and satisfying family relationships.

Psychological and emotional wellness warrants the same measure of family attention and candor as does physical wellness. *Depressive disorders* such as *anxiety* and *eating disorders* affect a significant number of families and require medical treatment and therapy. Emotional disorders impact families of all socioeconomic classes, yet families in the lowest socioeconomic levels have the least health insurance and access to appropriate health care for mental wellness. *Chronic stress response* plays a key role in the physical and mental wellness of all family members. Strategies to manage stress response include incorporating relaxation into family time.

Social and spiritual wellness serve as important threads in family well-being. Although religion is often defined as a distinct set of beliefs and practices associated with an organization, spirituality reflects a personal sense of purpose and connection to others and the universe. Social and spiritual wellness are revealed in caring and connected relationships that provide feelings of calmness and a sense of purpose and meaning.

American workers and their families experience greater strain from working more hours and enjoying fewer vacation days than do workers and their families in other developed countries. Likewise, adolescents who work more than 20 hours per week can suffer detrimental impacts to their wellness, school, and family life. Environmental wellness encompasses overpopulation, urban sprawl, limited freshwater supplies, and numerous forms of pollution (e.g., air, water, and toxic waste). All of these have significant impacts on family wellness.

The increase in the number and proportion of elderly in American society is directly linked to an increase in *life expectancy*. Although living life with minimum frailty is increasingly possible and highly desired on personal, family, and community levels, a significant percentage of elders require disproportionately more health care. As society ages, the care of family members with chronic conditions such as Alzheimer's disease is an increasing challenge. Yet, 21st-century retirees challenge not only caregiving capacities but also a demand for more meaningful experiences during retirement, which places new influences on families.

American families often avoid addressing death, yet it is part of the individual and family life cycle. *Mortality rates* continue to decline, although disparities in death rates by sex, race, and socioeconomic factors remain. Death, however, remains the concluding experience to life. Dying well can be seen as part of and not the failure of health care. *Hospice* centers that offer *palliative care* are increasingly valuable parts of comprehensive family wellness.

DEFINING WELLNESS AND APPROACHES TO HEALING

Family health and *family wellness* are often used interchangeably. We argue that they are complementary but different concepts. According to the World Health Organization (2002a: 9), "Health is a state of complete physical, mental, and social well-being and not merely the absence of disease and infirmity." Some health educators see wellness as a process and a lifestyle, while arguing that health includes concerns about morbidity and mortality (Payne and Hahn 2002). Insel and Roth (2002: 2) clarify that

> ... some aspects of your health are determined by your genes, your age, and other factors that may be beyond your control. But true wellness is largely determined by the decisions you make about how to live your life.

In this chapter we use the term **wellness**. Family wellness is determined by the wellness of its members and the family community as a whole. With accurate health information and skills, families have the potential to positively influence their wellness. This salutogenic approach places families at the core of family wellness.

Family wellness includes physical, psychological (intellectual and emotional), social, spiritual, occupational, and environmental well-being. This multidimensional concept of family wellness recognizes mind–body–spirit interconnections and is part of the field of *psychoneuroimmunology*. Such a dynamic description of wellness also appears in family studies research in identifying wellness (physical, spiritual, and emotional) as one of eight personal resources used by families as they adapt to challenges and crises (McCubbin, Thompson, and McCubbin 1996). More recently, heart rates, blood pressure, and serum cortisol levels were employed by Worthman, DeCaro, and Brown (2002) in a *biocultural* approach in mapping some of the physiological results of such factors as complicated family schedules.

Conventional and Complementary Approaches to Healing

Shifts in defining wellness can also be seen in changes in approaches to healing and medicine. Until recently, *conventional medicine* distanced itself from *complementary medicine*. (The latter are sometimes called alternative or traditional medicines). Conventional medicine adheres to a medical model which emphasizes the search for a cause to an illness by diagnosing symptoms, then administers treatments with pharmaceutical, surgery, or other interventions. Conventional medicine emphasizes an approach to wellness that is episodic and often invasive.

In 1992, the governing body of complementary medicine changed its name to the National Center of Complementary and Alternative Medicine. Complementary medicines focus on rebalancing body systems through acupuncture, acupressure, massage, chiropractic, herbal therapies, homeopathy, and other practices. In some cultural traditions, this practice is referred to as rebalancing a life force (Chi, Ki, Qi, and Prana). Disruption of the life force's energy flow is believed to cause the body to malfunction. Complementary medicine emphasizes preventive medicine[1] and less invasive treatment. Preventive medicine works from the premise that it is better and less costly in money, emotions, and health to engage in practices that prevent or at least reduce the risk of illness. Families need to be aware of what to watch for when a member is sick, but they also need to be proactive in preventing illness and staying well. Increasingly, conventional medical professionals appreciate and incorporate complementary practices.

Integrative medicine is a combination of conventional and complementary medicines. Clinics such as the *George Center for Health and Healing* in Minneapolis, MN, incorporate integrative medicine and families as keys to healing (Abbot Northwestern News Release 2002).

BOX 5.1 "A Journey Through Healing"
Penny George, Ph.D.

The Journey Begins

In late February 1996, I went for a routine mammogram, which I had scheduled between appointments with clients. I was surprised to learn that it had been 2 years since I'd had a mammogram, since I intend to be conscientious about checkups. I remember having a sense that there was a problem, because the technician added a sonogram and asked the radiologist to look at it. I watched their concerned faces with curiosity more than alarm, because I knew I was fine. After all, I had no reason to distrust my body and was in better physical shape than ever before. Besides, I had no time for cancer in my life. I had enough stress as it was. Eventually, I was told I would be called with the results, and I left. The next day, my denial was punctured when I heard a message on my answering machine telling me there was a probability of breast cancer. I was told to contact a surgeon for a biopsy, so I made an appointment.

Because the needle kept bouncing off whatever it was in my breast, that biopsy was unsuccessful. But the surgeon made it clear that the shadowy form on the x-ray was cancer, identifiable by its characteristic shape. A stereotactic biopsy was conducted the next day at the Virginia Piper Cancer Institute, where I was officially diagnosed as having an invasive tumor of 1.78 cm. The moment when all hope of this being a giant mistake collapsed was indescribably awful, as anyone diagnosed with breast cancer will tell you. To mask how scared I was and buy myself some time to absorb the reality, I adopted an optimistic cheerfulness, which alternated with a deep inner pessimism. There were moments when I was convinced I would die of this, and quickly. I experienced waves of emotion and couldn't concentrate. I knew this was normal reaction to trauma and that the shock would eventually pass, but at the time I felt out-of-control and overwhelmed.

---

[1]Some forms of complementary medicine may also treat "symptoms" and thus are not just preventive (e.g., chiropractors). At times this raises controversy with conventional practitioners.

The Road to Recovery

I began chemotherapy a month postsurgery and continued for seven months. I lost no hair and, although I was fatigued, I experienced no nausea, because of the antinausea medication I was given. I worked out and did yoga when my energy permitted, and I meditated and rested when I needed to. I continued taking vitamins and certain supplements throughout chemo, despite the lack of clear research concerning them. The decision to do so was part of my assuming responsibility for myself. I knew that although a cure couldn't be guaranteed, there was plenty I could do to ensure a longer, healthier life.

I believe that attitude of self-responsibility is an important place for patients to come to. For their part, the medical field needs to do a better job of helping patients understand they can and should be in charge of their own healing, in active partnership with their physicians and others on their healing team. In addition to conventional treatment, I also made use of acupuncture, psychotherapy, massage, energy work, Ayurvedic detoxification and more, which I'm convinced mitigated the side effects of the harsh treatments and contributed to my return to wellness. I could afford to pay for these treatments, unlike many women, but the new medicine I envision will make available to patients a wide variety of evidence-based healing modalities.

My experience led my husband and me to want to influence medicine in a systemic way, so that others could benefit from what we'd learned. Medicine currently deals mainly with the disease process. This is obviously important, but it is also incomplete. People with cancer, or other chronic illnesses, need to be seen as individuals with unique needs and to be cared for in an integrative, relationship-centered way. Our foundation's approach to creating systemic change in medicine involves harnessing the resources of a larger group of private fund providers committed to the same vision we have. Working collaboratively, we are attempting to change how health professionals are trained and educated, and we are helping identify, support, and research the best models for clinical care nationwide. Our hope is that one day what we now call Integrative Medicine will be, simply, medicine—a medicine, which helps patients, heal in body, mind, heart and spirit, whatever the outcome of the illness. We can't all be cured—life itself is a terminal condition—but we can all potentially die healed when our time comes.

Penny George, Ph.D., After 21 years as a consulting psychologist, Penny George now serves as President of the *George Family Foundation.*

Shrinking Family Health Care Coverage

Whereas definitions of wellness and even approaches to healing change to match the needs of families, the United States struggles with providing health care coverage and services to its population. With all the marvelous medical developments of the past 50 years, the tragedy of shrinking availability of health care coverage in the early 21st century plagues American families. The number of Americans without health insurance surged from 41.2 million in 2001 to 45 million in 2003 (Stoll 2004). This number includes 11 million American children who do not have health insurance (Children's Defense Fund 2004). Such statistics represent swelling numbers of families without basic health coverage.

Reasons for this increase stem from a rise in unemployment from 4.7% in 2001 to 5.8% in 2003, the rising costs of health care, and the practice of employers passing these costs on to workers. In 2004, there was a 12.3% increase in health care costs with a projected additional increase of 11.3% in 2005 (MedlinePlus 2004a).[2] These increases push experts such as Kassirer[3] to accuse medicine of being corrupted by big business and driven by greed. He challenges the American health care system to shift away from a profit-centered to a people-centered medicine (Kassirer 2004).

The impact on families is detrimental with many forgoing not only regular health care needs but also preventive physical exams and vaccinations. In September 2004, families felt additional strain when the administration allowed $1.1 billion in federal funds allocated to the State Children's Health Insurance Program (SCHIP) to be returned to the U.S. Treasury. This cutback left an additional 750,000 children uninsured (Klein and Steinberg 2004). Even before these cuts in child health care funds, American children were found to be relatively unhealthy. When compared to children in 187 other developed countries, the United States ranked 68th in immunizing against diptheria–pertussis–tetanus, 89th for polio, and 84th for measles. American adolescents did not fare any better, ranking only 18th out of 28 developed countries in a self-report survey of not feeling healthy (MedlinePlus 2004b).

Most agree that family wellness is vital not only to the family but also to the external community and to the nation as a whole. Family wellness is complex not only in the dimensions it includes but also in the many external agencies that influence it. As you read this chapter, keep in mind the roles government and business play, or choose not to play, in the wellness of families.

FAMILY WELLNESS BASICS

Healthy People 2010 (Healthy People 2004) developed a list of 10-year health objectives for American society and steps individuals and families can take to maintain and enhance their wellness. The list includes concerns regarding overweight and obesity, physical inactivity, mental health disorders, tobacco use and substance abuse, insufficient immunization, limited access to health care services, irresponsible sexual behavior, injury and violence, and diminishing environmental quality (National Center for Health Statistics 2004a). In this chapter, we address six of these challenges as they relate to families. Sexual wellness concerns are covered in chapter 6, and violence is covered in chapter 12.

Physical Wellness

Acute and chronic impacts of overweight and obesity remain a critical physical wellness problem for Americans with serious implications for their families. According to the Centers for Disease Control and Prevention (2004), 61% of American adults 20 years and older are overweight or obese.[4] Of these, one third (59 million people) are obese. Table 5.1 presents a more complete view of the overweight and obesity patterns and how these

---

[2]MedlinePlus Health is a service of the U.S. National Library of Medicine and the National Institutes of Health.

[3]Dr. Kassirer, former Editor-in-Chief of *The New England Journal of Medicine*, charges American medicine of being *On the Take* in terms of an environment of greed and serious conflicts of interest in health care.

[4]Body Mass Index [BMI = Weight (kg)/Height2 (m)]. Obesity is defined as having a BMI score of > 25. Note that controversy exists in use of BMI with children and some adults because it does not include body composition factors such as percentage of body fat.

TABLE 5.1

Disparities in Obesity by Sex and Race/Ethnicity

- In women, overweight and obesity are higher among members of racial and ethnic minority populations than in non-Hispanic White women.

- In men, Mexican Americans have a higher prevalence of overweight and obesity than non-Hispanic Whites or non-Hispanic Blacks. The prevalence of overweight and obesity in non-Hispanic White men is greater than that in non-Hispanic Black men.

- 69% of non-Hispanic Black women are overweight or obese compared to 58% of non-Hispanic Black men.

- 62% of non-Hispanic White men are overweight or obese compared to 47% of non-Hispanic White women. However, when looking at obesity alone (Body Mass Index > 30), slightly more non-Hispanic White women are obese compared to non-Hispanic White men (23%; 21%).

- For all racial and ethnic groups combined, women of lower socioeconomic status (income < 130% of poverty threshold) are approximately 50% more likely to be obese than those of higher socioeconomic status.

- Mexican-American boys tend to have a higher prevalence of overweight than non-Hispanic Black or non-Hispanic White boys.

- Non-Hispanic Black girls tend to have a higher prevalence of overweight than Mexican American or non-Hispanic White girls.

- Non-Hispanic White adolescents from lower income families experience a greater prevalence of overweight than those from higher income families.

Note: Based on national survey data collected between 1988 and 1994.
Source: Adapted from *Surgeon General's Report.* 2002: 1. www.surgeongeneral.gov/topics/obesity/calltoaction/fact_glance.htm (Retrieved 11/7/02).

patterns differ by gender and ethnicity. Obesity relates to a number of health problems such as increased risks of cardiovascular disease and Type 2 diabetes. Since 1990 health care professionals have seen a 76% increase in Type 2 diabetes in adults (30–49 years old).

In addition to adults, 15% of children aged six to 19 years of age (almost nine million) are overweight, a percentage that has tripled in just two decades as shown in Figure 5.1 (National Center for Health Statistics 2004b). Overweight and obese children and youth also experience increased risks of heart disease and stroke, Type 2 diabetes, certain types of cancer, arthritis, respiratory problems, and psychological disorders such as depression. For example, the prevalence of Type 2 diabetes in children and adolescents has surged. In newly diagnosed cases of children with diabetes, in 1990, less than 5% had Type 2, whereas in subsequent years, 30% to 50% of childhood new cases had Type 2 (National Institutes of Health 2002).

Wise Eating Habits for Families.   The causes of obesity are complex and include genetic, biological, behavioral, and cultural factors. If one parent is obese, a child has a 50% chance that he or she will also be obese, but when both parents are obese, a child has an 80% chance of being obese (Counseling Corner 2002). Yet, genetics is only part of the story; eating behaviors learned in families have a significant influence on weight patterns. Obesity in childhood and adolescence can be related to poor eating habits (overeating or binging), lack of regular exercise, medical illnesses (endocrine

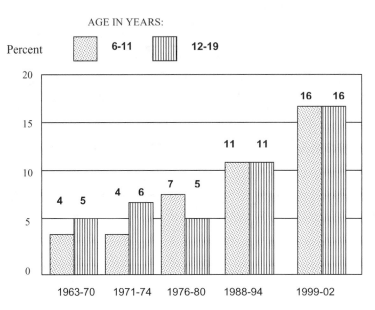

FIG. 5.1. Prevalence of Overweight Among Children and Adolescents.
Source: Adapted from *National Center for Health Statistics. 2004.* "Prevalence of Overweight Among Children and Adolescents: United States, 1999–2002." www.cdc.gov/nchs/products/ pubs/pubd/hestats/overwght99.htm (Retrieved 10/24/04).

problems), medications (steroids and some psychiatric medications), stressful life events or changes (separations, divorce, moves, deaths, and abuse), family and peer problems, low self-esteem, and depression or other emotional distress (Counseling Corner 2002).

Although certain medical disorders can cause obesity, less than 1% of all obesity is caused by physical problems. The prevailing causes for the rapid increase in the proportion of overweight and obese adults and children are excessive calorie consumption and in-adequate physical activity. Families need to be aware of and active in wise food choices. Schlosser (2001) challenges American families and especially the fast-food restaurant in-dustry to take responsibility for childhood overweight and obesity, including the spiraling rates of childhood Type 2 diabetes and cardiovascular disease.

In chapter 4, the issue of family time is couched in cultural demands to do more in less time. This attitude carries over into mealtime as families rush through meals in order to hurry up and eat fast so as to move on to the next event of the day. Along with an increased frequency in families eating fast food and convenience foods, Americans are consuming increasingly large portion sizes. Examinations of the relationship between the 2001 marketplace portion sizes and those typically offered in the 1950s reveal significant increases (Young and Nestle 2002). They (2002: 247) concluded:

> . . . that marketplace portions of foods that are major contributors of energy to US diets have increased significantly since the 1970's and exceed federal standards for dietary guidance and food labels. This trend can be attributed to multiple causes, some of them economic.

Furthermore, as noted in Table 5.1, wellness disparities among families such as overweight and obesity often fall in line with socioeconomic disparities.

Getting huge food portions for less money results in costly impacts on a family's wellness. The "Big Gulp" contest within the fast-food industry is an example of an industry aiming at families with promises of cheap large portions, but no mention of *nutrient density* (other nutrients in addition to the calories). This situation has not gone unnoticed among health agencies. The World Health Organization includes the following in its 2002 annual *World Health Report* recommendations:

> Governments may have to consider legislation to reduce the proportion of salt, sugar and other unhealthy components in manufactured foods. [They also note] in rich nations, the biggest peril was tobacco, closely followed by the entangled bevy of blood pressure, alcohol, cholesterol, overweight, low fruit and vegetable intake and inadequate exercise (World Health Organization 2002a: 1-2)

In 1993, a collaborative group from the Harvard University School of Public Health and the Oldways Preservation and Exchange Trust reviewed the epidemiological studies on diets of Mediterranean and traditional cultures that had low rates of cardiovascular disease and Type 2 diabetes. Based on their findings the "Mediterranean Food Pyramid" model was proposed in 1994 (Escobar 1997; Gilford 2002).

The significance of this and others' research into wise diets (Willett 2001, Willett and Stampfer 2003) became apparent in 2005 when the United States Department of Agriculture proposed replacing its 1995 Food Pyramid with a New Food Pyramid Guide. This new guide provides families with more complete information so they can make healthier dietary choices. Examples of healthy food choices include limiting red meat to infrequent intake of a few times per month and replacing it with nuts, legumes (e.g., beans and peas), and fish (an excellent source of essential *omega-3 fatty acids*). The new food pyramid guide emphasizes the use of plant oils, such as canola and olive (high in *monounsaturated fatty acids*), complex carbohydrates over simple (high in sugar and often highly processed) carbohydrates, and more vegetables than fruit. This guide also recommends inclusion of a daily multivitamin and mineral supplement, daily physical activity, and a moderate intake of wine or other alcoholic beverage. Beverages containing grapes, such as wine, are recognized sources of flavonoids (a *phytochemical*), which are beneficial to the body in its resistance to cancers, and small amounts of alcohol as beneficial to heart health.

Weaving Exercise and Play Into Family Time. A study of twins reveals that the increasing rates of overweight and obesity have less to do with genes and more to do with a lack of physical activity (Griffith 2000). Families realize their members need daily physical activity, but knowing does not necessarily equal doing. The National Center for Health Statistics (2002) reports that approximately seven out of 10 American adults 18 years of age and older do not meet basic Surgeon General's recommendations for basic activity. Of these, 78% of adults, 25% are completely sedentary. On closer examination studies show that among Americans 18 to 64 years of age, married adults spend less time than unmarried adults on exercise or physical activity.

Regular physical activity is defined as light to moderate exercise at least five days per week for a minimum of 30 minutes each time or vigorous physical activity at least three times a week for a minimum of 20 minutes each time. In Figure 5.2, a comparison of adult physical activity by gender and age shows men more physically active than women, but both genders are less active with age.

Parents and other adults are role models for children, shaping children's attitudes and behaviors regarding physical activity. Maintaining adequate levels of physical activity among children and adolescents (along with their parents or guardians) is made all the more difficult as families spend more time watching television, playing computer and

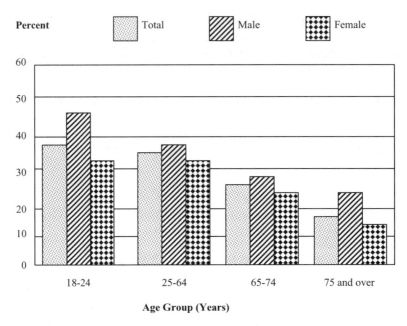

FIG. 5.2. Regular Physical Activity by Gender and Age for First Quarter 2002.
Source: Adapted from National Center for Health Statistics. www.cdc.gov/nchs/about/major/nhis/release200209/figure07_htm (Retrieved 11/1/2002).

video games, and engaging in other sedentary activities. The Surgeon General's report (2004) notes that problems with physical activity levels are particularly marked among girls as they move through adolescence. Yet, the potential wellness benefits of a Federal requirement, Title IX, on girls needs noting. The 1972 law is credited with short-term effects of weight control, stress relief, and sense of well-being for girls who participated (Smith 1998). Long-term effects for women who continue to exercise include reduced cardiovascular and respiratory diseases, reduced risk of some cancers, and decreased risk of hip fractures. In addition to benefits to physical wellness, significant evidence supports that regular physical activity enhances mood, reduces fatigue and anger, plus positively helps to manage depression with empowered levels of confidence, self-esteem, and positive distraction (Mayo Clinic 2004a).

Families need to be proactive in communicating and engaging in healthful diets and physical activity for all members. Examples of physical activity that families can experience together are nature walks, biking, outdoor play, or skating. Families can join with agencies and organizations in pressuring the food and beverage industry to become partners in reversing overweight and obesity trends among youth and adults. Families must also support school and community fitness programs.

Ahhh Sleep: An Underrated Part of a Family's Day. Every human being, regardless of age, gender, or socioeconomic standing, requires a certain amount of sleep in order to function effectively. Sleep is not merely the opposite of being awake. Sleep, as necessary to wellness as food and activity, is vital to cognitive processing, growth, and numerous bodily functions.

American families are sleep deprived. According to a recent National Sleep Foundation study, 63% of adults fail to get the recommended 8 hours of sleep per night for optimum performance. Thirty-one percent report less than seven hours on weeknights. Such sleep schedules results in one in five adults being so sleepy during the day that their performances are negatively impacted. Women suffer more from sleep deprivation (25%) than men (18%) and in experiencing chronic daytime sleepiness (National Sleep Foundation 2002a).

Sexual intimacy (discussed in chapter 6) is a vital component of a couple's relationship. Yet, sleep-deprived couples may experience reduced sexual relations due to fatigue, which can harm relationships. Weary parents do not fare any better as they struggle and may fail at being attentive to children's needs or may employ harsher responses than warranted.

Adults are not the only ones to experience sleep deprivation, however. Sixty percent of children under 18 years of age complain of being tired during the day, and 15% fall asleep at school (National Sleep Foundation 2002a). Teens require 8.5 to 9.25 hours of sleep each night, but only 15% achieve that number of hours, and 25% sleep fewer than seven hours each night (Mullin 2003). Sixty-nine percent of young adults 18 to 29 years of age report one or more symptoms of sleep deprivation a few nights each week. Furthermore, sleep problems are increasing among adults and youth (National Sleep Foundation 2002b).

Sleep deprivation is related to frustrated moods and poor cognitive and physical performance. People who sleep fewer than six hours each night report being tired during the day. When compared to rested people, sleepy people report greater dissatisfaction with life, more anger and impatience, more mistakes on the job, and increased difficulty getting along with family members and others. A common sleep problem in families is insomnia, which involves difficulty falling asleep, waking frequently during the night, waking too early and not being able to return to sleep, and waking feeling unrefreshed.

A lack of sleep is also a safety hazard. The British Medical Association cites international studies on sleep deprivation in finding that not only do sleep-deprived individuals suffer impaired motor skills, but also they experience higher levels of stress, anxiety, and depression (CNN 2000). The correlation between sleep deprivation and injuries is underscored in the National Highway Traffic Safety Administration estimates that sleepiness is a factor in at least 100,000 car crashes, 40,000 injuries, and 1,500 fatalities each year (Wylle 2001).

Individuals are most sleepy during two periods during the day. The first period is from 3:00 to 5:00 a.m. when our bodies experience the slowest breathing and heart rates, the lowest body temperature, and the least alertness. The second period is during the late afternoon, from approximately 3:00 to 5:00 p.m. (Rosekind 2002).[5] Some cultures, respect this drowsy time and encourage a period of afternoon repose. Americans encourage young children to take regular afternoon naps, but something about a napping teen or adult violates our sense of the work ethic. Some school systems begin the school day at such an early hour that children who ride buses or other common transportation to school must rise and be on the bus before 7 a.m. The National Sleep Foundation (2002a) encourages families and schools to consider modifying the start of the school day to better match the sleep and rest needs of school-age children, teens, and young adults.

Families struggle with meeting deadlines and fitting everyone's schedule into the grand plan of the family day. Weariness and overtiredness are real family wellness issues. Whether it is the couple with an infant who will not sleep through the night, families with adolescents who are too busy to sleep, or couples going through sleep disturbance episodes as seen in premenopausal women, all families must learn how to live with sleep-deprived members. They also face the challenge to modify adjustable sleep-depriving behaviors.

---

[5]Former Director of NASA's "Fatigue Countermeasures Program."

Psychological and Emotional Wellness

Psychological and emotional problems impact approximately 22% of American adults 18 years of age or older and interfere with everyday family functioning often placing families under considerable strain (Lewis 2003). They appear in families regardless of social class or background; no family is immune. Even for families fortunate enough to have health insurance, coverage often falls short regarding treatment for psychological or emotional needs.

Yet, according to the Surgeon General's report on mental health, children are at the greatest risk due to factors such as "physical problems; intellectual disabilities (retardation); low birth weight; family history of mental and addictive disorders; multigenerational poverty; and caregiver separation or abuse and neglect" (2002: 1).

Sadly, adults often doubt that children and teenagers experience anxiety or depression. "Twenty years ago, the prevailing theory was that depression in teens, like moodiness, was normal and that teenagers who weren't depressed were abnormal. Now we know that's not accurate" (Wingert and Kantrowitz 2002: 60). Depression, it appears, is an equal-opportunity family problem.

Four out of 10 causes of disability in developed countries are emotional disorders including *depressive disorders*, *anxiety disorders,* and *eating disorders* (National Institute of Mental Health 2002a). The treatment of emotional illness, especially among children, is contentious. For example, a major public health concern involves the advisability of prescribing antidepressant medication to children with depression, especially in the wake of several widely publicized cases of suicide among children. Serotonin reuptake inhibitors are effective in treating depression among children, but appear to result in a 2% increase in the risk of suicide among those under 18 years of age (National Institute of Mental Health 2004a). This controversy illustrates how families need to be active partners in health decisions including understanding the full impact of medications.

Depressive Disorders and Families.   Depression is more than just having the blues or just feeling the regular ups and downs of life. It occurs in all genders, ages, and backgrounds. Those who are depressed often present a dejected mood, loss of interest or pleasure, feelings of guilt or low self-esteem, disturbed sleep or appetite, low energy, and or an inability to concentrate (World Health Organization 2004). Although studies conclude that depression is over twice as prevalent in women as in men, male depression may be underdiagnosed because males' depressive symptoms such as headaches, sexual dysfunction, decreased work productivity, irritability, anger, substance abuse, or interrupted sleep patterns may be missed signs of depressive states (Shaw 2004). These symptomatic differences between women and men appear to result from sex-specific genes associated with depression. Zubenko and colleagues (2002) identified 16 genes specifically connected to depression in either men or women but not in both.

Although a common and treatable illness, depression is among the leading causes of disability worldwide. A family member who cannot snap "out of it" or "move on" within approximately two weeks may be suffering from depression. Depression does not just happen to individuals in isolation, for it impacts those closest to them as well. Depression challenges solid relationships and shakes the foundation of more porous ones, plus it becomes a significant barrier to building new connections. "It doesn't matter whether depression begins as a slow burn or a five alarm blaze, the result is the same" (American Association for Marriage and Family Therapy 2004: 1).[6] As families strive to understand

---

[6]"Intimacy and Depression: The Silent Epidemic" is an awareness program sponsored by the American Association for Marriage and Family Therapy and the National Depressive and Manic-Depressive Association.

and help depressed members, they must recognize the complex triggers of depressive episodes often include psychosocial events (e.g., unemployment, failure in school, money concerns, relationship troubles, and illness). Depression disconnects family members from not only themselves but also those they love. The greater the level of anxiety and or depression of either partner, the greater the dissatisfaction felt with the marriage (Whisman, Weinstock, and Uebelacker 2002).

The American College of Obstetricians states approximately 70% to 85% of women experience baby blues after childbirth with an additional 10% suffering postpartum depression, hence, a normal part of childbirth (Mayo Clinic 2004b). Postpartum depression often expresses itself with feelings of sadness, anxiety, and restlessness and can interfere with daily routines. In rare cases, this depression can become a severe form called postpartum psychosis, which can be dangerous to both the mother and the child. Recently, experts recognized that postpartum depression can extend beyond infancy into childhood. "Children of depressed mothers are at risk for developmental and behavioral problems and may be predisposed to developing depressive disorders themselves" (Bernard-Bonnin 2004: 1). As with any depressive disorder, it is not a weakness but a medical condition in need of professional care as soon as symptoms emerge.

The National Institute of Mental Health (2002a) reports that the rates of depressive disorders among American families are far greater than those previously believed. Approximately 18.8 million American adults 18 years and older suffer from a depressive disorder, and almost twice as many women (12.4 million or 12.0%) as men (6.4 million or 6.6%) live with depression. Additional disturbing findings reveal that depressive disorders are appearing earlier in life and often co-occur with anxiety disorders and substance abuse.

Almost three million adolescents (approximately 8.3%) in the United States struggle with depression. Unfortunately, depression in children and adolescents is associated with increased risks of suicide. In 1996 (the most recent year for suicide statistics), suicide was the third leading cause of death among youth 15 to 24 years of age (National Institute of Mental Health 2002a). Many depressed teens do not seek help because of ignorance and stigma associated with mental issues and or inadequate mental health resources and coverage. Adolescents face special challenges in battling depression. Older individuals who are depressed may have developed coping skills, but younger individuals may not have those skills and, furthermore, may be handicapped in developing coping skills because of their illness (Wingert and Kantrowitz 2002).

Families often find it difficult to understand what is happening when their teen is struggling with depression. Koplewicz (2002: 60) asks: "Most teens are moody. When should parents start to worry?" Family studies professionals can partner with the medical community in addressing the need for accessible and affordable care of psychiatric diseases.

When a member of a family is depressed, other members may have anger, guilt, or fear as they share a life with someone who is withdrawn, morose, or angry a great deal of the time (University of Michigan 2001). The University of Michigan's depression program has developed workshops and other programs to educate families on depression and involve them in the treatment process. These programs bring families together as they struggle to help a depressed member heal with appropriate treatments, including medication and talk-therapies. Assisting families in effective communication is vital to recovery from depression (Voelker 2001). Likewise, the National Institute of Mental Health (2004b) offers effective tips on parenting for mothers with depression including seeking medical care and support, and working to stay connected with the family.

Anxiety Disorders and Families. A certain level of anticipation heightens alertness and prepares the body for action, but anxiety that is a chronic, unpleasant mental tension can interfere with daily functioning. Approximately 19.1 million (13.3%) of American adults 18 to 54 years of age have an anxiety disorder with many experiencing more than one. Studies also confirm that almost twice as many women as men suffer from panic disorder, whereas equal numbers of women and men have obsessive–compulsive disorder and social phobia. Also, anxiety disorders frequently co-occur with depressive disorders, eating disorders, or substance abuse (National Institute of Mental Health 2002a).

Unlike daily trying events, anxiety disorders invade family members' lives with relentless, chronic fear and may become progressively worse over time. Anxiety disorders include generalized anxiety disorder (a condition of excessive worrying), obsessive-compulsive disorder (which includes repeated upsetting thoughts and images, obsessions, or compulsions), panic disorder (where one feels suddenly terrified), and posttraumatic stress disorder (being haunted by the memory of and reliving a traumatic event repeatedly). Other anxiety disorders such as social phobia (extreme worry and excess self-consciousness) along with specific phobias (intense fear of something that poses little threat, e.g., heights, water, and flying) also plague some families. Seasonal affective disorders (milder form of depression often linked to seasonal darkness) may also strike family members, but because there are many conditions that contribute to depressive states it is wise to seek professional over self diagnosis (National Institute of Mental Health 2002b, 2003).

Anxiety disorders can negatively impact the body's immune system due to chronic levels of cortisol[7] and interfere with normal daily functioning. Anxiety disorders also contribute to substance abuse behaviors. There is prevalence and co-occurrence of alcohol and drug abuse with anxiety disorders (National Institute of Health 2004).

The National Institute of Mental Health (2001) reports that four million adults suffer from generalized anxiety disorder, 3.3 million from obsessive-compulsive disorder, 2.4 million from panic disorder, 5.2 million from posttraumatic stress disorder, and 5.3 million from social phobia (National Institute of Mental Health 2002a). These numbers do not include specific phobias or children and youth who also suffer from anxiety disorders. Experts (e.g., *Anxiety Disorders Association of America*) are increasingly recognizing anxiety disorders not only in the young but also in the elderly. Success in diagnosing and treating early-life and late-life anxiety disorders requires families to serve as advocates and work in partnership with the medical community.

As noted with depressive disorders, strong evidence suggests genetic influence in anxiety disorders. Research indicates that children of parents with panic disorder and depression are at risk of developing these disorders themselves (Biederman et al 2001). Body dysmorphic disorder (a distorted, often negative view of one's appearance) may be experienced by adolescents, particularly females. It is associated with a chemical imbalance in the brain, which may be genetically based. A child from a family with a history of generalized anxiety or obsessive-compulsive disorders appears to be much more prone to body dysmorphic disorder (Robins 2000). Although often confused with eating disorders, body dysmorphic disorder is a significant cognitive distortion in belief of perceived flaws and requires appropriate treatment.

Eating Disorders and Families.   Eating disorders include clinically diagnosed conditions: anorexia nervosa, bulimia nervosa, and binge-eating disorder. These disorders lack nationally representative epidemiological data, which impede progress in identifying risk factors. Yet, society bears a significant responsibility in fueling this disorder due in part to

---

[7]Cortisol is a necessary hormone, but with prolonged exposure it negatively impacts the immune system.

a fat phobia and perfect-body mentality perpetuated in media and popular culture (Areton 2002; Laksmana 2002).

Eating disorders affect five million Americans, primarily girls between 10 and 34 years of age, each year (Support, Concern, and Resources for Eating Disorders 2003). Many more women than men develop an eating disorder; yet disorders are found in an increasing number of men, with recent estimates of 5% to 10% of those with eating disorders being males (Gordon 2004). Anorexia affects 0.5% to 3.7% of American females; bulimia affects 1.1% to 4.2% of American females; and binge-eating disorder affects 2% to 5% of American females (National Institute of Mental Health 2002a). Eating disorders are not merely a problem of "the young, rich, and white," as the number in low socioeconomic status and ethnic minority groups may be underestimated (Smolak and Striegel-Moore 2001). Eating disorders also increase the risk of other medical conditions, such as bone loss (Harvard Medical School 2002). Helping family members with eating disorders includes being an attentive listener while focusing on the concerns related to health and not on weight or appearance, plus encouraging members to seek professional help.

Depressive, anxiety, and eating disorders are as serious a threat as any other health condition requiring comprehensive medical intervention and follow-up along with proactive protective processes to help prevent and reduce the risk and severity. These disorders are complex and can have dramatic affects on the total wellness of the person and her or his family. Organizations such as *The Caring for Every Child's Mental Health Campaign*[8] encourages families to talk with their children, listen to their concerns, focus on the positive, and seek medical assistance when unsure. Families must become essential partners with the medical profession in observation, intervention, and rehabilitation.

Family Stress: A Continual State of Change and Response. Contrary to popular understanding, stress is normal and healthful to humans, for change is the essence of living. Family wellness concerns over stress occur when a member's stress response becomes a *chronic stress response* that leads to decreases in cognitive ability (memory, focusing, and decision making), increased fatigue, varying levels of depression, and decreased immune response. Increased risks of contracting infectious diseases, hypertension, and or heart disease may also result.

To the surprise of some families, children increasingly suffer from chronic stress response (Rutherford 2002). DeBord (2002: 2) identifies signs and symptoms of stress for children. Under stress, preschoolers' behaviors vary but may include irritability, anxiety, uncontrollable crying, trembling with fright, eating or sleep problems, aggression, nightmares, and increase in accident-proneness. Elementary-age children under stress may be withdrawn and express feelings of being unloved, distrust, or worry about the future. They also may not attend to school or friendships or may complain of head- or stomachaches, trouble sleeping, or loss of appetite. Signs and symptoms for preteens and adolescents under stress may include anger, disillusion, or lack of self-esteem, distrust and acts of rebellion through stealing or skipping school. Major concerns with this age group are depression and suicide.

Waslick (Center for Health and Health Care in Schools 2002: 1) of the American Psychiatric Association notes "that children and adolescents rarely seek help on their own, and families and other adults who interact regularly with youngsters usually do not request evaluation until they have noticed persistent changes in a child's mood or demeanor."

---

[8]*The Caring for Every Child's Mental Health Campaign* is part of the Comprehensive Community Mental Health Services for Children and Their Families of the Federal Center for Mental Health Services.

Stressors can overwhelm, and in so doing, drive individual family members to seek relief. Some may respond with unhealthy behaviors (e.g., aggression and violence, withdrawal, and substance abuse). The National Institute of Drug Abuse reports that although White children begin to use alcohol and other drugs at a younger age than African-, Hispanic-, or Asian-American youths, these minority groups are overrepresented in the statistics on addiction and drug-related problems (Swan 1995). Families and external communities need to recognize chronic stress response and teach family members relaxation strategies. Relaxation practices[9] lower heart rate, blood pressure, and breathing, and increase sense of calm.

In addition to effective coping and relaxation strategies, the National Institute of Drug Abuse (2002) outlines aspects for families to incorporate into family talks about substance use and abuse. These strategies include having the entire family engaged in the discussions, targeting all forms of drug abuse (e.g., tobacco, alcohol, marijuana, ecstasy, cocaine, and inhalants), practicing resistance skills, and increasing social competency (e.g., communication, peer relations, self-efficacy, and assertiveness).

Social and Spiritual Wellness

Social wellness is revealed in caring and connected relationships. Families with such relationships appear to handle stress better and tend to be healthier in that they live longer and report being happier. Caring and connections include sharing quality time, along with ample encouragement and praise for family members and acceptance and tolerance for the uniqueness of family members. Families hold significant power in the connectiveness they create among their members. Studies emphasize the positive impact of caring and connectedness on adolescents' wellness (Resnick, Harris, and Blum 1993; Rossi 2001). Connections with external communities can also contribute to the social wellness of families and their members by providing resources and outlets for energies and interests.

The importance of creating caring and connected relationships between individuals has not been lost on the medical community. The health care organization often refers to "patients as partners" and emphasizes listening to families who seek medical assistance, thus empathizing with those on the other end of the stethoscope. Thus, an important element of improved health care involves the enhancement of the relationship between patient and physician. Leonard Snellman, M.D., offers a glimpse at how some physicians aim to connect and communicate with individuals and their families in the art and science of healing.

BOX 5.2   "Are You Listening?: Patient-Doctor Communication"
Leonard Snellman, M.D., F.A.A.P.

Communication with my patients is predicated on trust. The parents and patient must have confidence that I am motivated by their best interest and am willing to listen to their concerns. I need to know that they are being honest with me and that I can glean the information necessary to address their problems. As a pediatrician, to get the confidence of my younger patients, I have to relate to them on their level. For me, that means talking with them directly, asking the child about things that are important to someone their age. In addition, I wear novelty ties and watches with characters they recognize. Finger puppets of Disney and Sesame Street characters

---

[9] Abdominal breathing, Autogenic training, Progressive relaxation, Visualization.

hide in my desk drawers to emerge at the right time to help me elicit information and generate trust. This direct communication with the child conveys to the parent that the youngster is the focus of the visit. In addition, during well child visits, I take the time to explore nonmedical family issues (e.g., family values and extended family members). Bonds are strengthened when a physician knows their patients.

Ideally, when interviewing the parents, I ask open-ended questions and try to give them time to elucidate their concerns and describe the issues as they see them. I find it difficult not to jump into the discussion as soon as a complaint has been stated, in order to pursue potential complicating and clarifying details. Although these may be important, it shifts the agenda from that of the patient (parent) to my own. Too often, when this is the scenario, questions go unanswered, concerns are not relieved, and the patient ends up requiring further care to address issues that could have been taken care of at the initial visit. When I am successful at permitting the patient's agenda to be presented and discussed, the encounter invariably is more rewarding, for all involved.

Leonard Snellman, M.D., F.A.A.P., is Assistant Chair of the Department of Pediatrics at *HealthPartners* and Assistant Clinical Professor, Department of Pediatrics at the University of Minnesota Medical School.

Spiritual wellness focuses on how families define spirituality for themselves. Although often used interchangeably, for many, spirituality and religion hold different meanings. Religion is viewed as a specific set of beliefs and practices often associated with an organized group. Spirituality reflects a more individual sense of purpose, peace, connection to others and the universe along with beliefs regarding life's meaning. Spirituality may or may not be expressed in an organized religion, for families may consider themselves spiritual and religious or spiritual but not religious. Regardless of how families define it, spirituality embraces a universal need to find balance and peace in life through designing an ethical lens through which respect and tolerance for others is possible. Recognition of the role of spirituality in family wellness is relatively recent. Although individuals have engaged in spiritual wellness practices, such as meditation and prayer throughout history, only recently have such practices received serious attention among conventional health professionals.

In 1976, Dr. Herbert Benson, a physician at Harvard Medical School, coined the term "relaxation response" to describe the healthful benefits resulting from meditation. The documented physiological benefits of calming practices include reduced heart rate and blood pressure and slowed breathing. Meditation and prayer may serve as means to focus energies and find balance, connectedness, and calm. Benson (1996) asserts that meditation and prayers hold significant healing potential and that prayer allows those who believe to better cope with their anguish. His discussion of the placebo effect of meditation—which he terms "remembered wellness"—focuses on the power of belief and faith in something other than self (20). This remembered wellness is the emotional and physiological memories of calmness and balance.

The power of meditation and prayer eclipse rigid, exclusionary practices that may be done in the name of a religion. Spirituality, however, may be a double-edged sword when families and or external communities use spirituality to blame individuals for inadequate or unacceptable beliefs or behaviors. Spirituality wellness (not rigid religiosity) can connect families and their members to meaningful external communities through shared rituals such as baptism and marriage and such rites as forgiveness and reconciliation. This is the family extension of what sociologist Durkheim called the "social glue" of religion (1961) and the social cohesion of spirituality that bind us to one another.

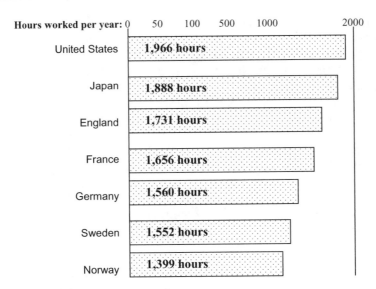

FIG. 5.3. Comparison of Seven Nations Employees' Work Hours.
Source: Adapted with permission from ABCNews.com. 2001 "Hard Work: Downturn or Not,
Americans Spend More Time on the Job Than Anyone." From the Bureau of Labor. www.abcnews.
go.com/sections/us/DailyNews/work_howmuch_dayone.html (Retrieved 10/2/2004).

Occupational and Environmental Wellness

On November 24, 2002, the headline of the Money & Business section of the Minneapolis
Star Tribune read, "Stress is Stalking America's Workplaces." Workers' unemployment
benefits were to abruptly end one month and four days from that date for 800,000 Americans. Congress's and the administration's unwillingness to intervene weighed heavily on
American workers. Those individuals who still had jobs identified the anxiety and uncertainty regarding job security as their number one concern (Cruz 2002). This event serves
as but one example of the impact of occupational wellness on families.

Occupational wellness involves the premise that healthy workers are more productive
and raise healthier families than do unhealthy workers. Occupational wellness includes
workplace safety; fair exchange of intellectual and physical talents for salary; an engaged,
caring, and connected workplace environment; reasonable health care coverage; and opportunities for advancement and growth.

American workers and their families enjoy fewer vacation days (i.e., 13 days per year)
compared to other nations' work forces (e.g., Italy at 42, France at 37, Germany at 35,
Brazil at 34, Britain at 28, Canada at 26, and Japan at 25 days per year). Figure 5.3
compares U.S. work hours and those of other developed countries. Americans also work
longer days and retire later than do other advanced societies (*ABC News* 2002). American
workers are working more and feeling increased anxiety on the job and at home (Andresky
Fraser 2001; Ciulla 2001; Milke et al. 2004; Schor 1992). Families working more hours,
along with marriage and parenthood, also decrease engagement in needed physical activity
(Nomaguchi and Bianchi 2004).

One fourth of Americans believe they work too hard just to make ends meet, as compared
to one eighth in 1965. Half of those sampled thought that working so hard and long unfairly
reduced family time and increased pressures at home over childcare and household chores
(Schabner 2001).

As described throughout this text, families come in a variety of arrangements, and the concept "working family" likewise represents different experiences. Heymann, an expert on family and work issues, states that "this country has experienced rapid changes in labor and family demographics, employment conditions, and care responsibilities of the family unit. But we as a nation have failed to respond, which has left a widening gap between working families' needs and the combination of high workplace demands, outdated social institutions, and inadequate public policies" (Benis Moloy 2002). Regardless of which family workers are asked (white collared, blue collared, pink collared, or uncollared),[10] an increasing number of individuals' occupational wellness suffers under the growing weight of work demands in a time of uncertain future.

Stress in the American workplace, therefore, can trigger heavy tolls on workers in terms of ill health, on their families in terms of decreased family time, and on organizations in terms of lost productivity. An estimated cost resulting from worker illness is over $200 billion per year in terms of sick days, hospitalization, outpatient care, and decreased productivity (Greenberg 2002). A longitudinal study followed 812 healthy employees for 25 years gathering data on blood pressure, cholesterol levels, BMI statistics, along with reported work stress factors including job strain (high work demands and low job control) and effort–reward imbalance (high demands, low job security, and limited career advancement). High occupational stress (high job strain and effort–reward imbalance) is directly linked to a doubling of the risk of cardiovascular death among initially healthy workers (*British Medical Journal* 2002).

Youth also experience high strain and effort–reward imbalance, especially high school and college students who work more than 20 hours per week while carrying a full load of courses. Approximately 85% of American adolescents have or have had part-time jobs while in high school (Lancaster 2004). Although early employment has some benefits such as increased responsibility levels (Mortimer 2003; Stern and Briggs 2001), these may be blurred in the rush of youth working too many hours at the expense of their academic and family lives. Specifically, this overextension is detrimental to many teens in terms of diminished engagement with school, decreased academic performance, increased psychological distress, higher drug and alcohol use, higher rates of delinquency, and increased distance from parental control (Kelly 1998; Steinberg, Fegley, and Dornbusch, 1993; Swinney 2004). In terms of physical injury, the *National Institute of Occupational Safety and Health* estimates that 231,000 American workers under the age of 18 are injured on the job each year (National Consumers League 2002).

In the absence of authentic school–work partnerships in which youth's wellness and academic needs supercede work demands, families need to restrict the number of hours a student works. Under federal law, students under 16 years of age cannot work more that 3 hours on a school day and 18 hours in an entire weekend. No guidelines or rules exist for youth over 16 years of age, however. Family studies researchers encourage government to institute a permit process that hinges on Grade Point Average along with greater supervision of teen workers and greater participation of families, educators, and family study professionals in identifying and demanding quality workplace experiences for youth (Kelly 1998).

How individuals and their families cope with the challenges to occupational wellness affects family wellness. Developing mutually respectful and responsible communication and interventions between workers and their occupations appears as a quest not only for

---

[10]Uncollared workers telecommute and or work from home (Grochowski 1999).

business and labor but also for families. Families need to be aware of the impacts of job strain and effort–reward imbalances on wellness and take action to modify such influences.

Compromises on the ecosystem affect family life as well. Historically, environmental wellness focused on the spread of infectious diseases through waste, food, water, insects, and rodents. Although the spread of infectious disease remains a serious concern, as the outbreak of the West Nile Virus demonstrates, environmental wellness today includes greater concern regarding environmental pollutants and their impact on infectious and chronic diseases. One such example is the probable link among pediatric asthma, lupus, and developmental problems in children and environmental pollution (*Boston Herald* 2002).

Environmental wellness reveals dynamic interrelationships between families and the earth. Although few would argue that families require clean air and safe environments, business and governmental interests may supercede environmental wellness. Classic environmental concerns such as clean water, waste disposal (including solid waste and toxic waste, e.g., mercury), food inspection, plus insect and rodent control often are under the jurisdiction of local and state sanitation and public health departments. Other environmental issues demand attention beyond local control, however. Population growth and expansion of development, which demands greater use of resources, is linked to increased pollution concerns including degradation of air, water (freshwater and seawater), wildlife habitat, land, and sound level (i.e., noise pollution) (Insel and Roth 2002).

As an example, consider impacts of air pollution on families. The Air Quality Index (i.e., measures of pollutants and particulates from burning of fossil fuels) results not only in increased rates of respiratory problems, melanomas, droughts, and floods, but also in data suggesting that human and wildlife exposure to airborne particles "may be at risk of developing germline (inheritable) mutations" (McMaster University 2002: 2). Now consider the Bush administration's environmental policy to roll back clean air quality by allowing major air polluters to avoid installing pollution-control equipment when they expand their facilities (CNN 2004).

Families and family studies professionals' efforts to heal and protect our environment locally, regionally, nationally, and globally will be an essential challenge in the 21st century. These are urgent concerns, as indicated by the relaxing of air, water, and chemical pollution regulations for economic and political reasons over family and environmental reasons. Families have a role to play in acting locally, thinking globally, and demanding protection of the environment by those who govern.

OVER THE LIFE SPAN

Family wellness stretches over the life span of each family member and the family as a whole. Resnick (Box 5.3) explains the vital element of connections in family wellness.

BOX 5.3 "Connections that Matter: Fostering Healthy Youth Development"
Michael D. Resnick, Ph.D.

As threats to adolescent health have shifted from primarily biological causes to social factors, efforts at prevention and health promotion have focused on such issues as substance use, self-directed and interpersonal violence, effects of exposure to violence, pregnancy prevention, and emotional distress, among others. Although many programs and interventions address these as discrete, individual concerns, there is growing understanding that across an array of adverse outcomes, there are recurring, cross-cutting *protective factors* that show promise for application across varied populations of youth. Protective factors refer to the events, experiences, and opportunities that young people have that protect them from harm and buffer them from involvement in risky behaviors. In contrast to narrow, categorical programs that direct interventions at targeted, specific groups of adolescents, the results of these studies suggest that across gender, racial, and ethnic groups, certain protective factors have great potential for reductions or prevention of many health-jeopardizing behaviors. Building on core concepts of *resiliency* and *resistance* to harm, some of these most commonly cited cross-cutting protective factors link back to the concept of *connectedness*—the experience of belonging and closeness to caring, competent others.

What kind of connections does this mean? Key protective factors in the adolescent health literature include a strong sense of connectedness to parents and family. This is evident whether one focuses on single or dual parent families, adoptive or foster families or the extended kin network. Adolescents' perceptions that parents and family care, respect, and understand them are associated with better emotional health and less risky behavior. Similarly, a strong sense of connection to school is highly protective, based on the perceptions that teachers care, teachers are fair, and school is a place where one feels a sense of *belonging*. The sense of mastery that comes from doing well in school academically is also protective against a variety of health-jeopardizing behaviors, but school connectedness refers to a dynamic above and beyond academic success.

A sense of connectedness can include other kinds of community institutions as well as adults outside of the family. These other adults may play a particularly important protective role when that sense of connectedness with parents and family members is not present. Similarly, there are protective effects when young people describe themselves as spiritual—having a sense of connection to a creative force outside of themselves.

In short, rather than thinking about the achievement of absolute *independence* among adolescents, a healthy developmental pathway is one that includes the emergence of meaningful *interdependence* with others, particularly adults. Opportunities to nurture a strong sense of connectedness with others within and outside of the family represent important building blocks for the healthy development of all of our young people.

Michael D. Resnick, Ph.D., is Professor and Director of Research for the Division of General Pediatrics and Adolescent Health and Director of the National Teen Pregnancy Prevention Research Center at the University of Minnesota.

Families can take an active role in preventive care.[11] To ensure that children and their families receive adequate immunizations, family health professionals can help families critically evaluate the controversy over side effects (e.g., research from the *New England Journal of Medicine* found that the rate of autism was the same in children who had received vaccinations for childhood diseases and those who had not [*Associated Press* 2002].

---

[11] *The National Initiative to Improve Adolescent Health* serves as a guide and listing of resources for families and communities to the spirit of enhancing adolescent wellness.

Families also can take greater control over their wellness by participating in regular screening examinations. Such regular attention requires adequate preventive health care coverage, especially for the newest and youngest family members. Ethnic minorities continue to suffer disparities in access to health (wellness) services and innovations (American Association for Cancer Research 2003). Children of immigrants are more than twice as likely than other American children to be in poor or only fair health (Reardon-Anderson, Capps, and Fix 2002).

Family wellness not only sweeps wide (lifewide) in terms of multiple dimensions, but also runs long (lifelong) for family members and their families.

Aging: An Individual and Family Experience

Life expectancy and age-specific (especially infant) mortality rates are often used as summary measures of a nation's wellness. Life expectancy is the average number of years of life remaining at a given age if death rates in the population remain constant. In 1997, the life expectancy at birth was 79 years for women and 74 years for men compared to a life expectancy for both genders of 70 years in 1960 and 49 years in 1900 (*Federal Interagency Forum on Aging-Related Statistics* 2002). When life expectancy increases, the ranks of elders and senior elders expand.

The *Federal Interagency Forum on Aging-Related Statistics* (2002) reports an estimated 35 million people over age 65 or older in the United States, accounting for approximately 13% of the total population. This number is a 10-fold increase over the past 100 years. This same report offers a stunning projection that by 2030, one in five individuals will be age 65 or older. Women account for about 58% of those aged 65 and older and 70% of those aged 85 or older. The most senior elders—those aged 85 or older—are projected to increase to 5% of the American population by 2050. These demographic shifts vary by race and ethnicity as revealed in Figure 5.4.

Living longer raises challenges. The rate of chronic conditions, such as arthritis, diabetes, heart disease, osteoporosis, dementia, and Alzheimer's Disease, increases with aging. Aging is all too commonly viewed as the cause of chronic illnesses, when in reality, these diseases result from the breakdown in the body's natural processes. Aging is a natural part of living, not something to be "cured."

Still, chronic illnesses demand significant amounts of time, emotional, and financial investments by families. Alzheimer's Disease results in enormous economic costs—over $61 billion in the United States in 2002 (Koppel 2002). Great also are the physical and emotional tolls on family, caregivers, and friends of the Alzheimer patient. The time demands on caregivers of those with dementia is far greater than for those caregivers of individuals with other illnesses. According to the Alzheimer's Disease Education and Referral Center (2003), women (wives, daughters, and daughters-in-law) are the primary physical, emotional, and day-to-day caregivers, whereas men (husbands and sons) often focus on the financial, legal, and business aspects of caregiving (Kramer and Thompson 2002). Siblings and grandchildren may be caregivers, but often are engaged in their own or others' care. These caregivers may experience significant costs in terms of time, finance, fatigue, and social isolation, which may heighten family conflict and decrease family time with other members. Yet, for some, along with these costs may come added meaning in life, an opportunity to give back, renewal of religious faith, and or strengthening of family relationships.

Much progress has been made in our understanding and approach to helping individuals age well. Stem cell research holds promise for an Alzheimer's vaccine. Better screening for cardiovascular disease is already possible with C-reactive protein tests, and Cyclin E

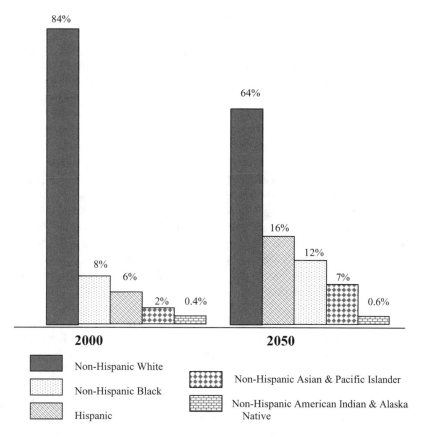

FIG. 5.4. Projected Distribution of Population Age 65 and Older.
Source: **Adapted from Federal Interagency Forum of Aging Related Statistics. 2002. "Older Americans 2000: Key Indicators of Well-Being." Indicator 2, page 2. http://www.agingstats. gov/chartbook2000/tables-population.html (Retrieved 2/25/05).**

is already being used to detect the most aggressive forms of breast cancer. We know more every day about the affects of such simple healthful living practices as eating wisely and staying physically active on aging well. Abundant evidence supports positions that vigorous exercise like running and brisk walking help to counteract some of the negative consequences of aging and even adds years to life (Friedrich 2001). Likewise, sleeping and relaxing, meeting emotional needs with caring and connectedness, (and professional intervention if needed), engaging in meaningful interpersonal relationships, striving to make work valuable, and living as part of, not ruler over this planet all contribute to wellness as we age.

Increasing longevity and vitality, as well as dependency, among elders results in major shifts in family arrangements and functions. Duka and Nicholson (2002: 3) report "more older Americans are working, volunteering, and going back to school than ever before." These increases place demands on the public health systems, medical and social services, and especially families. Yet, the challenges facing families and their elderly members are not limited to increased demands for caregiving. The baby boomers who teeter on the edge of retirement represent a growing and virtually untapped civic resource to meet social needs for both paid and unpaid work. A real demand for this new or soon-to-retire group who is better educated, healthier, and longer-lived is sufficient opportunity for meaningful engagement (Gerontological Society of America 2004). The elderly and super elderly will need families who recognize the general independence and vitality of the boomers by understanding their retired parents and grandparents will often remain active and even working. This trend also means family study professionals need to stay abreast of this demographic shift and retool 20th-century definitions of and programs for the 21st-century elders.

Dying Well: A Part of Living Well

Mortality rates are statistical measures of a death rate, the number of people in a given population who will die per 1,000 people in that population. Mortality among children and young adults (1–24 years of age) declined since 1950 by one half. A 40% decline in mortality rates was also seen among 24- to 44-year-olds from 1950 to 1999. Death rates for those 45 to 64 years of age declined by nearly 50% in the same 50-year period. The one-third mortality rate decline for elders (65 plus years of age) occurred over the past 50 years (Centers for Disease Control and Prevention 2002). Disparities remain requiring families' and family study professionals' close attention.

Disparities in Death Rates by Sex and Race. Some troubling data include mortality rates from lung cancer declining for men in the 1990s but increasing for females. Even in light of mortality rate declines, racial and ethnic disparities in death rates continue. In terms of infant mortality, non-Hispanic Black Americans had the highest rate (13.9 deaths per 1,000 births) whereas Chinese Americans had the lowest rate (3.3 per 1,000 births). HIV is more deadly among minorities. Latinos in managed care have poorer blood sugar compared to Whites in similar care settings. Some physicians are reluctant to recommend heart procedures for Black patients making data on race and ethnicity often inaccurate. Hispanics and Asians are less satisfied with health care than are Blacks or Whites (*American Journal of Public Health* 2003).

The Centers for Disease Control and Prevention offer additional examples of wellness disparities among race and ethnic and gender groups (i.e., Blacks, Hispanics, American Indians/Alaska Natives, and Asians/Pacific Islanders) in their report on mortality rates from four major forms of cancer—1990 to 1998 (Gargiullo et al. 2002). In 1998, the Centers for Disease Control and Prevention (2002) revealed that 53% of all cancer-related deaths were associated with four cancer sites (i.e., lung and bronchus, colon and rectum, prostate, and female breast).

Aid to Dying Family Members. We argue that society is responsible not only for providing accessible and affordable health care to all its citizens but also for educating family members and others in the basics of family wellness. In terms of death and dying well, families, governmental agencies, educational institutions, religious organizations, and medical communities need to acknowledge that dying and death are part of living, and all have a responsibility to make that part of life's journey one of dignity, grace, and as painless as possible. Dying well is emerging as "part of," not "failure of," the medical community's mission. In 1997, the American Medical Association's recommendation was that hospitals design a "medical futility" policy that allows limiting of aggressive lifesaving measures if physicians concur that the patient cannot be cured. Yet the battle of end-of-life decisions continues as families and the medical community struggle to find humanistic ways to resolve the realities of a dying loved one. Sadly, outside organizations often weigh in on the matter making the final stage of life's journey a struggle for death with dignity a fight to die.

Hospice organizations aid families and the medical community in preparing for the final stage of living. Hospices provide support and *palliative care* for persons in the last phase of an incurable disease so that they may live their final days as fully, comfortably, and respectfully as possible. Hospices can provide palliative care and supportive services not only to dying individuals but also to their family members and significant others 24 hours a day, seven days a week. These facilities may be based in the patient's home or in a hospital, nursing home, or other facility organized for this purpose. The hospice team is ideally a clinically directed interdisciplinary team consisting of patients and their families, professionals, and volunteers who provide physical, social, spiritual, and emotional care during the last stages of an illness, the dying process, and the bereavement period (Center for Advanced Palliative Care 2002: 1).

Palliative care assists families in recognizing that the dying process is a part of the normal process of living and focuses on enhancing the quality of remaining life and that human growth and development can be a lifelong process. This is accomplished with affirming life and neither hastening nor postponing death. Hospice support and care aims to provide dying individuals an opportunity to attain a degree of peace and growth in preparation for death. Hospices offer palliative care for all individuals and their families without regard for age, gender, race or ethnicity, religion, sexual orientation, disability, diagnosis, availability of a primary caregiver, or ability to pay (Center for Advanced Palliative Care 2002; World Health Organization 2002b).

SUMMARY THOUGHTS

What is a family to do to preserve and enhance wellness? Medical and health education professionals support several measures toward this aim. Wise food selection and reduced portion sizes lead the list along with increases in physical activity for all family members. Making adequate sleep and daily relaxation practices valued parts of family routine would contribute to family wellness. Awareness of and intervention when family members experience depressive, anxiety, and other emotional disorders also are vital. Caring and connection within and without the family and an authentic spirituality that provides purpose and meaning to life offer opportunities for enhanced family wellness as well. In addition, external communities of work, school, friends, extended family, medicine and health agencies, and government all interact with families impacting family wellness. Finally, an encompassing dimension of environment wellness truly makes preserving a fragile planet crucial to all families' wellness.

Family wellness, therefore, is multidimensional and highly interactive. When individuals and their families recognize this and their participatory roles, family wellness moves beyond the absence of illness toward a dynamic presence of families living well and in the end, dying well.

GLOSSARY

Anxiety disorders	Complementary medicine
Biocultural	Depressive disorders
Chronic stress response	Eating disorders
Conventional medicine	Family health

Family wellness	Nutrient density
Hospice	Omega-3 fatty acids
Integrative medicine	Palliative care
Life expectancy	Phytochemicals
Monounsaturated fatty acids	Psychoneuroimmunology
Mortality rates	Wellness

FOR YOUR CONSIDERATION

1. You are the health care manager working with a family living with a chronic wellness issue with one of its members. This illness might be Alzheimer's Disease, brittle bone disease, HIV/AIDS, or another chronic wellness issue. Although the family is well acquainted with conventional medicine, they are less familiar with alternative medicine. How will you explain the potential benefits of a complementary approach to wellness?

2. You are a family therapist working with a couple experiencing relationship problems. Both partners struggle with being overweight and complain that they do not sleep well or enough. Their busy work and other commitments leave little time for physical exercise and often result in fast food meals dominating their food choices. What information do they need about nutrient density, physical activity, and sleep? What can you tell them about how these factors may impact relationship quality?

3. Differentiate between "growing old" and "aging well" in terms of behaviors and attitudes?

FOR FURTHER STUDY: WEB SITES, ORGANIZATIONS, AND PUBLICATIONS

Web Sites and Organizations

American Medical Association Health Insight
www.ama.assn.org/ama/pub/category/3457.html
The *American Medical Association*'s site provides user-friendly information for health consumers plus means to search the Web for physicians and hospitals.

Bureau of Primary Health Care
http://healthdisparities.net/partners.html
The site reflects how grants are monitored to needy communities that attempt to address health and wellness disparities.

Centers for Disease Control and Prevention
www.cdc.gov
The CDC provides the public with a variety of resources, including fact sheets and summaries, advice for overseas travelers, and other information.

Center for Nutrition Policy and Promotion
www.usda.gov/cnpp
This site provides information and links regarding healthful eating.

Health A to Z
www.healthatoz.com
This family-oriented site provides user-friendly information on a variety of family wellness concerns.

Healthy People 2010

www.health.gov/healthypeople

Healthy People 2010 is a comprehensive list of 10-year health objectives for the nation. The site lists sites related to major health indicators that represent the greatest public health challenges, including:

Physical activity: www.fitness.gov and www.cdc.gov/nccdphp/dnpa
Overweight and obesity: www.nhlbi.nih.gov/about/oei/index.htm
Tobacco use: www.cdc.gov/tobacco/ and www.cis.nci.nih.gov/

Substance abuse: www.health.org/ and www.nida.nih.gov/   www.niaaa.nih.gov

Responsible sexual behavior: www.cdc.gov/hiv/hivinfo/nah/htm
www.cdc.gov/nchstp/dstd/dstdp.html   www.cdcnpin.org

Mental health: www.mentalhealth.org/cmhs/index.htm
www.mentalhealth.org
www.nimh.nih.gov/publicat/depressionmenu.cfm

Injury and violence: www.cdc.gov/ncipc/ncipchm.htm
www.ojp.usdoj.gov/home.htm   www.nhtsa.dot.gov/hotline

Environmental quality: www.epa.gov/iaq/iaqinfo.html
www.epa.gov/hatlibra/hqirc/about.htm

Immunization: www.cdc.gov/nip

Access to health care: www.insurekidsnow.gov
www.ahrq.gov/consumer.index.html#plans   www.mchb.hrsa.gov
www.Medicare.gov

Intelihealth

www.intelihealth.com

This site is managed by *Aetna Intelihealth* in association with *Harvard Medical School* and *The University Pennsylvania School of Dental Medicine. Intellihealth* offers consumer-friendly health and wellness information that is reviewed and approved by recognized medical and dental experts from over 150 health care organizations, including the National Institute of Health, nonprofit organizations, other publishers, and news media sources.

Intimacy and Depression: The Silent Epidemic

www.aamft.org/families/Intimacy_Depression/

This awareness campaign is sponsored by the American Association for Marriage and Family Therapy and the National Depressive and Manic-Depressive Association. The emphasis is on providing families a better understanding of the influence of depressive disorders on relationships and on how to assist in the recovery and healing process. It also lists resources and Web Sites.

John's Hopkins University Center for Communication Programs

www.jhuccp.org

This site offers information in English, Spanish, and French, and includes international health-related information along with online database services concerning immunization and other health conditions and treatments.

Mayo Clinic

www.mayoclinic.com

The editors of this site are Mayo Clinic physicians who offer current health and wellness information with frequent dated revision. This site includes health information on specific diseases and conditions, how to take charge of personal wellness, and guides for those traveling abroad.

MedlinePlus Health Information
www.medlineplus.gov
MedlinePlus is a service of the National Library of Medicine and the National Institute of Health. It provides current wellness and health care news on a 24-hour basis. This is a helpful site for families seeking the latest and accurate medical findings and information

National Center for Environmental Health
www.cdc.gov/nceh
This offers accurate and timely information on the wellness and quality of life of Americans, including diseases, birth defects, disabilities, and deaths that arise from unhealthy interfaces between people and their environments (e.g., home, work, and play). This federal agency provides data from applied research (i.e., epidemiological studies, laboratory and statistical analyses, behavioral interventions, plus operations and systems research), as well as guidelines and recommendations for health. The site includes information on each state's training and technical assistance resources in the area of health.

National Eating Disorders Association
www.nationaleatingdisorders.org
This consumer-friendly site provides current information, resources, and links to eating disorders sites.

National Hospice and Palliative Care Organization
www.nhpco.org
This site provides information on the role of hospice and palliative care in medicine and in the lives of families. The site also lists locations of hospice services. A related site is the *International Association for Hospice and Palliative Care* www.hospicecare.com

National Institute of Environmental Health and Science
www.niehs.nih.gov
This agency conducts basic research on environmental wellness and provides user-friendly material.

National Institute of Mental Health
www.nimh.nih.gov
The *National Institute of Mental Health* provides information related to mental wellness concerns. This site offers information and publications on a wide range of mental wellness topics and treatments.

National Sleep Foundation
www.sleepfoundation.org
The *National Sleep Foundation* is a nonprofit organization whose mission is to promote better understanding of sleep and sleep disorders and to provide support for sleep-related education, research, and advocacy.

Pre-School Stress Relief Project
www.samhsa.gov/centers/CSAP.html
The Pre-School Stress Relief Project is part of a federal substance abuse prevention and mental wellness program developed to provide training, consultation, and educational resources in stress management for Head Start, daycare centers, and public school teachers.

United States Food and Drug Administration

www.fda.gov

This organization is the "watchdog" agency for consumer wellness. Although some charge that the FDA does not always successfully meet this charge, the agency does provide valuable information and cautions related to health products.

United States Government Health Finder

www.healthfinder.org

This directory provides menu links to online articles and medical directories on a variety of topics, including minority health issues, disease prevention, and self-care.

Publications

Family Health Guides: The following are a sample for both basic and in-depth wellness information for families.

Clayman, Charles, ed. 1994. *American Medical Association Family Medical Guide.* New York, NY: Random House.

Klag, Michael, ed. 1998. *John's Hopkins Family Health Book: The Essential Home Medical Reference to Help You and Your Family Promote Good Health and Manage Illness.* New York, NY: Harper

Komaroff, Anthony, ed. 1999. *Harvard Medical School Family Health Guide.* New York, NY: Free Press.

Kotulak, Donna, Dennis Connaughton, and Edward Traisman. 1998. *American Medical Association Complete Guide to Children's Health.* New York, NY: Random House.

Waller, Robert. 1997. *Mayo Clinic Family Health Book.* New York, NY: William Morrow.

REFERENCES FOR CITED WORKS

Abbott Northwestern News Release. 2002. "Abbott Northwestern Hospital Establishes the George Center for Health and Healing." November 12. www.allina.com/ahs/news.nsf/newspage/anw_11_12_02 (Retrieved 11/17/02).

ABC News. 2002. "Hard Work: Downturn or Not, Americans Spend More Time on the Job Than Anyone." *ABC News.com* www.abcnews.go.com/sections/us/DailyNews/work_howmuch_dayone.html (Retrieved 11/24/03).

Alzheimer's Disease Education and Referral Center. 2003. "Alzheimer's Disease—Unraveling the Mystery: Improving Support for Families and Other Caregivers." www.alzheimers.org/unraveling/12.htm (Retrieved 2/2/03).

American Association for Cancer Research. 2003. "Understanding U.S. Minorities Face 'Unequal Burden of Cancer' That Must Be Corrected." www.intelihealth.com/IH/ihtPrint/EMIHC268/333/8012/362597.html (Retrieved 9/28/04).

American Association for Marriage and Family Therapy. 2004. "Intimacy and Depression: The Silent Epidemic." www.aamft.org/families/Intimacy_Depression/index.htm (Retrieved 10/26/04)

American Journal of Public Health. 2003. "October 2003 Highlights." www.ajph.org/news/archive/2003.09.29.shtml (Retrieved 9/4/04).

Andresky Fraser, Jill. 2001. *The White-Collar Sweatshop: Deterioration of Work and Its Rewards in Corporate America.* New York, NY: Norton.

Areton, Lilka Woodward. 2002. "Factors in the Sexual Satisfaction of Obese Women in Relationships." *Electronic Journal of Human Sexuality 5* (January) www.ejhs.org/volume5/Areton/03Background.htm (Retrieved 9/1/04).

Associated Press. 2002. "No Evidence Vaccine Causes Autism." *Intellihealth* (November 7). www.intelihealth.com/IH/ihtPrint/EMIHC000/333/72282.html (Retrieved 11/9/03).

Benis Moloy, Alexandria. 2002. "Labor Pains." *Harvard Public Health Review* www.hsph.harvard.edu/review/review_winter_02/featurelabor.html (Retrieved 9/24/04).

Benson, Herbert. 1996. *Timeless Healing: The Power and Biology of Belief.* New York, NY: Scribner and Sons.

Bernard-Bonnin, Anne Claude. 2004. "New Mom's Depression Affects Kids." *The Vancouver Sun* (October 23): 1.

Biederman, Joseph, Stephen Faraone, Dina Hirshfeld-Becher, Deborah Friedman, Joanna Robin, and Jerrold Rosebaum. 2001. "Patterns of Psychopathology and Dysfunction in High-Risk Children of Parents with Panic Disorder and Major Depression." *American Journal of Psychiatry* 158: 49–57.

Boston Herald. 2002. "Poison... Right In Your Backyard." *Boston Herald* (Winter) www.generationgreen.org/ Newsletter1-2002web.pdf (Retrieved 11/9/02).

British Medical Journal. 2002. "Work Stress Doubles Heart Risk." *BBC News*. (October 17). http://news. bbc.co.uk/1/hi/health/2337611.stm (Retrieved 11/25/02).

Centers for Disease Control and Prevention. 2002. "Health, United States, 2002—Highlights." *Centers for Disease Control and Prevention*. www.cdc.gov/nchs/hus.htm (Retrieved 12/10/03).

Centers for Disease Control and Prevention. 2004. "Obesity Still on the Rise, New Data Show." *Centers for Disease Control and Prevention*. www.cdc.gov/nchs/pressroom/02news/obesityonrise.htm (Retrieved 9/29/04).

Center for Advanced Palliative Care. 2002. *Center for Advanced Palliative Care*. www.nhpco.org (Retrieved 12/8/02).

Center for Health and Health Care in Schools. 2002. "Adolescent Depression and Mental Health Services." *Health In Schools*. (November 14). www.healthinschools.org/focus/2002/no5.htm (Retrieved 11/19/02).

Children's Defense Fund. 2004. "Fey Facts About American Children." (August). www.childrensdefense.org/ data/keyfacts.asp (Retrieved 10/12/04).

Ciulla, Joanne. 2001. *The Working Life: The Promise and Betrayal of Modern Work*. New York, NY: Crown.

CNN News. 2000. "Sleep Deprivation as Bad as Alcohol Impairment, Study Suggests." *CNN News* www.cnn.com/2000/HEALTH/09/20/sleep.deprivation/ (Retrieved 11/5/02).

CNN News. 2004. "Church Group Slams Bush on Clean Air Act." *CNN Science & Space* (June 4) www.cnn.com/ 2004/TECH/science/04/22/churches.bush/ (Retrieved 7/27/04).

Counseling Corner. 2002. "Childhood Obesity." *Counseling Corner* www.counselingcorner.net/disorders/ obesity.html (Retrieved 12/11/02).

Cruz, Sherri. 2002. "Stress is Stalking American's Workplaces." *Star Tribune* (November 24): D1, D9.

Debord, Karen. 2002. "Helping Children Cope With Stress." *National Network for Child Care*. www.nncc.org/ Guidance/cope.stress.html (Retrieved 11/14/02).

Duka, Walt, and Trish Nicholson. 2002. "Retirees Rocking Old Roles." *AARP Bulletin* (December): 3–6.

Durkheim, Emile. 1961. *Elementary Forms of Religious Life*. New York, NY: Collier.

Escobar, Alyson. 1997. "Are All Food Pyramids Created Equal?" *Nutrition Insights* 12 (April): 1–3.

Federal Interagency Forum on Aging-Related Statistics. 2002. "Older Americans 2000: Key Indicators of Well-Being." *Federal Interagency Forum on Aging Related Statistics*. www.agingstats.gov/chartbook2000/ population.html (Retrieved 12/10/02).

Friedrich, M.J. 2001. "Women, Exercise, and Aging: Strong Message for the "Weaker" Sex." *Journal of American Medical Association* 285, 11: 1429–31.

Gargiullo, P., P. A. Wingo, R. J. Coates, and T. D. Thompson. 2002. "Recent Trends in Mortality Rates for Four Major Cancers, by Sex and Race/Ethnicity—United States, 1990–1998." *Division of Cancer Prevention and Control, National Center for Chronic Disease Prevention and Health Promotion*. www.cdc.gov/mmwr/ preview/mmwrhtml/mm5103a1.htm (Retrieved 12/10/02).

Gerontological Society of America. 2004. "Promoting the Health of an Aging Population: Experts Present New Research on Hot Topics at GSA's Annual Meetings in Washington, DC, November." www.geron.org/press/2004meeting.htm (Retrieved 10/26/04).

Gilford, K. Dun. 2002. "The Mediterranean Diet Pyramid." www.oldwayspt.org/pyramids/med/p_med.html (Retrieved 10/4/04).

Gordon, Debra. 2004. "Eating Disorders in Men." www.intelihealth.com/IH/ihtIH/WSIHW000/9105/29709. html (Retrieved 9/20/04).

Greenberg, Jerrold. 2002. *Comprehensive Stress Management*. New York, NY: McGraw Hill.

Griffith, Robert. 2000. "Genetics, Environment, and Obesity." *Health and Age*. www.healthandage.com/PHome/ gid2=5731gm=21 (Retrieved 12/11/2002).

Grochowski, Janet. 1999. "Meeting Challenges of 21st Century Health Education: A Self-Reflective and Self-Projective Classroom Strategy that Promotes Resiliency Enhancement." Paper presented at the annual meetings of the *American Association of Health, Physical Education, Recreation, and Dance*, April, Boston, MA.

Harvard Medical School. 2002. "Young Men and Women with Anorexia Nervosa or Inflammatory Bowel Disease at Greater Risk for Osteoporosis." *Harvard Education Letter*. www.health.harvard.edu/fhg/fhgupdate/C/C3.shtml (Retrieved 11/4/03).

Healthy People. 2004. "Healthy People 2010." www.healthypeople.gov (Retrieved 10/1/04).

Insel, Paul, and Walton Roth. 2002. *Core Concepts in Health*. New York, NY: McGraw-Hill.

Kassirer, Jerome. 2004. *On the Take: How Medicine's Complicity With Big Business Can Endanger Your Health*. Oxford, UK: Oxford University Press.

Kelly, Karen. 1998. "Working Teenagers: Do After-School Jobs Hurt?: High Schoolers Who Work More than 20 Hours a Week May Be at Higher Risk For Failure." *Harvard Education Letter*, July/August. www.edletter.org/past/issues/1998-ja/working_shtml (Retrieved 12/8/02).

Klein, Rachel, and Marc Steinberg. 2004. " $1.1 Billion in Children's Health Insurance Funds to be Returned to U.S. Treasury." *Families USA Special Report*. (September 30): 1–8.

Koplewicz, Harold. 2002. "It's Hard for Parents To Understand." *Newsweek* (October 7): 60–61.

Koppel, Ross. 2002. "Alzheimer's Disease: The Cost to U.S. Businesses in 2002." *Alzheimer's Association* (June): 1–29. www.alz.org/Media/newsreleases/current/062602ADCosts.pdf (Retrieved 2/2/2003)

Kramer, Betty J., and Edward H. Thompson, Jr., eds. 2002. *Men As Caregivers: Theory, Research and Service Implications*. New York: Springer.

Laksmana, Theresia. 2002. "Eating Disorders and the Internet: The Therapeutic Possibilities." *Perspectives in Psychology* (Spring).http://bespin.stwing.upenn.edu/~upsych/Perspectives/2002/Laksmana.pdf. (Retrieved 7/10/04).

Lancaster, Antonia. 2004. "How Much is Too Much?—A Glance at Adolescent Employment." http://inside.bard.edu/academic/specialproj/darling/adwork.htm (Retrieved 10/26/04).

Lewis, Carol. 2003. "The Lowdown on Depression." *FDA Consumer* 37 (January–February) www.fda.gov/fdac/features/2003/103_dep.html (Retrieved 9/20/04).

Mayo Clinic. 2004a. "Exercises Eases Symptoms of Anxiety and Depression." www.mayoclinic.com/invoke.cfm?id=MH00043 (Retrieved 11/4/04).

Mayo Clinic. 2004b. "Postpartum Depression." www.mayoclinic.com/invoke.cfm?id=DS00546 (Retrieved 10/25/04).

McCubbin, Hamilton I., Anne I. Thompson, and Marilyn A. McCubbin. 1996. *Family Assessment: Resiliency, Coping, and Adaptation Inventories for Research and Practice*. Madison, WI: University of Wisconsin Press.

McMaster University. 2002. "Study Looks at Pollution, Gene Mutations." *McMaster University*. www.intelihealth.com/IH/ihtPrint/EMIHC000/333/7228/358914.html (Retrieved 12/12/02).

MedlinePlus. 2004a. "Health-Care Costs Continue to Escalate" (October 11): www.nlm.nih.gov/medlineplus/news/fullstory_20610.html (Retrieved 10/25/04).

MedlinePlus. 2004b. "U.S. Kids Relatively Unhealthy" (September 17): www.nlm.nih.gov/medlineplus/news/fullstory_20162.html (Retrieved 10/25/04).

Milke, Melissa, Marybeth Mattingly, Kei Nomaguchi, Suzanne Bianchi, and John Robinson. 2004. "The Time Squeeze: Parental Status and Feelings About Time With Children." *Journal of Marriage and Family* 66, 3: 739–61.

Mortimer, Jeylan. 2003. *Working and Growing Up in America: Adolescent Lives*. Boston, MA: Harvard University Press.

Mullin, Rita. 2004. "Helping Sleep-Deprived Teens." http://health.discovery.com/centers/sleepdreams/basics/teens.html (Retrieved 12/3/04)

National Center for Health Statistics. 2002. "HHS Report Shows 7 in 10 Adults Are Not Active Regularly." *Center for Disease Control and Prevention News Release* (April 7). www.cdc.gov/nchs/releases/02news/physical_activity.htm (Retrieved 11/7/02).

National Center for Health Statistics. 2004a. "Healthy People 2010 Leading Health Indicators at a Glance." www.cdc.gov/nchs/about/otheract/hpdata2010/2010indicators.htm Retrieved 10/20/04).

National Center for Health Statistics. 2004b. "Prevalence of Overweight Among Children and Adolescents: United States, 1999-2002." www.cdc.gov/nchs/products/pubs/pubd/hestats/overwght99.htm Retrieved (10/24/04).

National Consumers League. 2002. "Clocking in for Trouble: Teens and Unsafe Work." *National Consumers League*. www.nclnet.org/childlabor/jobreport.htm (Retrieved 12/8/03).

National Institute of Drug Abuse. 2002. "Prevention Programs." *National Institute of Drug Abuse*. www.nida.nih.gov/Prevention/PREVPRINC.html (Retrieved 11/14/02).

National Institute of Health. 2004. "Largest Ever Comorbidity Study Reports Prevalence and Co-Occurrence of Alcohol, Drug, Mood and Anxiety Disorders." (August 2). www.nih.gov/news/pr/aug2004/niaaa02a.htm (Retrieved 10/20/04).

National Institute of Mental Health. 2001. "The Numbers Count—Mental Disorders in America." *NIH Publication No. 01-4584* (October 20). www.nimh.nih.gov (Retrieved 10/25/04).

National Institute of Health. 2002. "Many Obese Youth Have Condition That Precedes Type 2 Diabetes." www.intelihealth.com/IH/ihtIH/WSIHW000/20722/8895/347102.html (Retrieved 12/10/03).

National Institute of Mental Health. 2002a. "Mental Disorders in America." *NIMH Report*. www.intelihealth. com/IH/ihtPrint/WSIHWOOD/ 8271/8849.html?hide=t&k=basePrint (Retrieved 1/26/03).

National Institute of Mental Health. 2002b. "Shedding Light on SAD." *National Institute of Mental Health*. www.intelihealth.com/IH/ihtPrint/WSIHWOOD/8596/22009.html (Retrieved 11/9/02)

National Institute of Mental Health. 2003. "Depression Research at the National Institute of Mental Health." *Fact Sheet*. www.nimh.nih.gov/publicat/depresfact.cm (Retrieved 1/26/2003).

National Institute of Mental Health. 2004a. "Antidepressant Medications for Children: Information for Parents and Caregivers." *National Institute of Mental Health—Statement*, (April 23). www.nimh.nih.gov/press/ stmntantidepmeds.cfm (Retrieved 9/30/04).

National Sleep Foundation. 2002a. "Increased Anger and Stress May Be Linked to Sleep Problems." *National Sleep Foundation*. http://health.discovery.com/centers/sleepdreams/basics/sleepinamerica2002.html (Retrieved 11/14/03).

National Sleep Foundation. 2002b. "Epidemic of Daytime Sleepiness Linked To Increased Feelings of Anger, Stress, and Pessimism." *2002 Sleep In America Poll*. (April 2). www.sleepfoundation.org/ nsaw/pk_pollresultsmood.html (Retrieved 1/26/03).

Nomaguchi, Kei, and Suzanne Bianchi. 2004. "Exercise Time: Gender Differences in the Effects of Marriage, Parenthood, and Employment." *Journal of Marriage and Family* 66 (May): 413–30.

Payne, Wayne, and Dale Hahn. 2002. *Understanding Your Health*. New York, NY: McGraw-Hill.

Reardon-Anderson, Jane, Randolph Capps, and Michael E. Fix. 2002. "The Health and Well-Being of Children of Immigrant Families." *New Federalism: National Survey of America's Families*, No. B-52, November 26. www.urban.org/uriprint.cfm?ID=7992 (Retrieved 12/01/03).

Resnick, Michael, L. J. Harris, and Robert Blum. 1993. "The Impact of Caring and Connectedness on Adolescent Health and Well-Being." *Journal of Pediatrics and Child Health* 29: 1–9.

Robins, Paul. 2000. "Body Dysmorphic Disorder." *KidsHealth* (June). http://kidshealth.org/parent/emotions/ feelings/body_dysmorphic.html (Retrieved 10/17/04).

Rosekind, Mark. 2002. "The Cost of Fatigue is Great—and a Short Nap May Just Help Pay the Debt." *Discoveryhealth Report* www.health.discovery.com/centers/sleepdreams/experts/rosekind.html (Retrieved 11/14/02).

Rossi, Alice S. 2001. *Caring and Doing for Others: Social Responsibility in the Domains of Family, Work, and Community*. John D. and Catherine T. Macarthur Foundation Series on Mental Health and Development Studies on Successful Midlife Development. Chicago, IL: University of Chicago Press.

Rutherford, Kim, MD. 2002. "Childhood Stress." *Kids Health Report*. www.kidshealth.org/parent/emotions/ feelings/stress_p2.html (Retrieved 12/4/2004.)

Schabner, Dean. 2001. "Hard Work: Downturn or Not, Americans Spend More Time on the Job Than Anyone." *ABC News.com*. www.abcnews.go.com/sections/us/DailyNews/work_howmuch_dayone.html (Retrieved 11/24/02).

Schor, Juliet. 1992. *The Overworked American: The Unexpected Decline in Leisure Time*. New York, NY: Basic.

Schlosser, Eric. 2001. *Fast Food Nation: The Dark Side of the All-American Meal*. New York, NY: Houghton Mifflin.

Shaw, Gina. 2004. "Men Get Angry, Not Sad." *WebMDHealth*. http://my.webmd.com/content/pages/7/1663_51924.htm (Retrieved 10/26/04).

Smith, Angela. 1998. "The Fit Woman of the 21st Century: Making Lifelong Exercise the Norm." *The Physician and Sportsmedicine* 26 (August). www.physsportsmed.com/issues/1998/08aug/smith.htm (Retrieved 1/8/04)

Smolak, L. and R. H. Striegel-Moore. 2001. "Challenging the Myth of the Golden Girl: Ethnicity and Eating Disorders. In *Eating Disorders: Innovative Directions in Research and Practice*, ed. R. H. Striegel-Moore and L. Smolak. Washington, DC: American Psychological Association.

Steinberg Laurence, Suzanne Fegley, and Sanford Dornbusch. 1993. "Negative Impact of Part-Time Work on Adolescent Adjustment: Evidence from a Longitudinal Study." *Developmental Psychology* 29, 2 (March): 171–80.

Stern, David, and D. Briggs. 2001. "Does Paid Employment Help or Hinder Performance in Secondary School? Insights from US High School Students." *Journal of Education and Work* 14, 3 (October): 355–72.

Stoll, Kathleen. 2004. "Census Bureau's Uninsured Number Indicates Third Increase in a Row." *Families USA The Voice for Health Care Consumers*. www.familiesusa.org/site/PageServer?pagename=Media_Statement_Census2003 (Retrieved 10/18/04).

Support, Concern and Resources for Eating Disorders. 2003. "Eating Disorders Statistics and Facts." *S.C.A.R.E.D. Report*. www.eatingdisorder.org/facts.html (Retrieved 1/27/04).

Surgeon General. 2002. "Disparities in Obesity by Sex and Race/Ethnicity." *Surgeon General's Report*. www.surgeongeneral.gov/topics/obesity/calltoaction/fact_glance.htm (Retrieved 11/7/02).

Surgeon General. 2002. "Mental Health: A Report of the Surgeon General." www.surgeongeneral.gov/library/mentalhealth/chapter3/conc3.html (Retrieved 11/7/2002).

Surgeon General. 2004. "The Surgeon General's Call to Action to Prevent and Decrease Overweight and Obesity." www.surgeongeneral.gov/topics/obesity/calltoaction/fact_adolescents.htm (Retrieved 10/20/04).

Swan, Neil. 1995. "Targeting Prevention Messages: Research on Drug-Use Risk and Protective Factors Is Fueling the Design of Ethnically Appropriate Prevention Programs for Children." *National Institute of Drug Abuse*. www.drugabuse.gov/NIDA_Notes/NNVol1ON1/Targeting.html (Retrieved 11/14/02).

Swinney, Jennifer. 2004. "Their Balancing Act." http://inside.bard.edu/academic/specialpro/darling/adwork.htm (Retrieved 10/27/04).

University of Michigan. 2001. "Understanding Depression: Families and Depression." *University of Michigan Medical School*. www.med.umich.edu/depression/familiesprn.htm (Retrieved 12/11/2003).

Voelker, Rebecca. 2001. "Communication Gaps Hinder Full Recovery From Depression." *Journal of American Medical Association* 285, 11: 1431–33.

Whisman, Mark, Lauren Weinstock, and Lisa Uebelacker. 2002. "Mood Reactivity to Marital Conflict: The Influence of Marital Dissatisfaction and Depression." *Behavior Therapy* 33: 299–314.

Willett, Walter C. 2001. *Eat Drink and Be Healthy*. New York, NY: Simon & Schuster.

Willett, Walter C., and Meir J. Stampfer. 2003. "Rebuilding the Food Pyramid." *Scientific American* (January): 64–69.

Wingert, Pat, and Barbara Kantrowitz. 2002. "Young and Depressed." *Newsweek* (October 7): 52–58, 60–61.

World Health Organization. 2002a. "WHO Ranks Top Health Hazards, Call For Bold Strategies." *World Health Organization* (October 30). www.intelihealth.com/IH/ihtPrint/EMIHCOOO/333/7228/357479.html (Retrieved 11/7/03).

World Health Organization. 2002b. "WHO Definition of Palliative Care." *World Health Organization*. www.who.int/dsa/justpub/cpl.htm (Retrieved 12/8/02).

World Health Organization. 2004. "What is Depression." www.who.int/mental_health/management/depression/definition/en/ (Retrieved 10/2/04).

Worthman, Carol, Jason DeCaro, and Ryan Brown. 2002. "Cultural Consensus Approaches to the Study of American Family Life." Working paper for project *Rituals of the Body: Stress and Everyday Life*. file:///PB-FY02img/Desktop%20Folder/chap%205%20Health/family%20stress (Retrieved 10/20/02).

Wylle, Leslie. 2001. "Sleep Loss Impairs Students." *The Daily Beacon* 88, 65. (November 27). www.dailybeacon.utk.edu/print.php/4488 (Retrieved 11/5/02).

Young, Lisa, and Marion Nestle. 2002. "The Contribution of Expanding Portion Sizes to the US Obesity Epidemic." *Journal of Public Health* 92, 2: (February): 246–49.

Zubenko, George, H. Hughes, J. Stiffler, W. Zubenko, and B. Kaplan. 2002. "D2S2944 Identifies a Likely Susceptibility Locus for Recurrent, Early-Onset, Major Depression in Women." *Molecular Psychiatry* 7, 5: 460–467.

INTIMATE PARTNERS AND PARTNERSHIPS

CHAPTER

6

SEXUAL INTIMACY: BIOLOGY AND PLEASURE

CHAPTER PREVIEW

Human sexual intimacy is a vital part of family quality-of-life. In this chapter, we begin with an explanation of the male and female sexual anatomy, including *menopause* and *male climacteric*. The cultural context of sexuality is illustrated by the case of *female genital mutilation* (*FGM*, also known as *female genital cutting* and including *clitoridectomy* and *genital infibulation*) as well as male *circumcision*. Media and technology also impact family sexual knowledge, requiring *sexuality media literacy*.

Research on human sexual response has yielded several theoretical models including Masters and Johnson's, Kaplan's Triphasic, Basson's, and Thayton's Spiritual and Theological models. Controlling conception remains a central issue to sexual intimacy decisions. Contraception strategies range from nonpenetrative contact (i.e., *outercourse*) to active prevention of fertilization or implantation, suppression of ovulation to permanent sterilization, all having varying levels of *theoretical effectiveness* and *actual effectiveness*.

Although rates of teen pregnancy have declined in recent years, unplanned pregnancy among American adolescents remains significantly higher than that in other developed countries. However, *unintended pregnancy* and *unexpected pregnancy* are not solely the concern of the unmarried. *Prochoice* and *prolife* movements debate the continued legality of abortion, the use of *abortifacients*, parental and male partner notification, as well as claims of various *postabortion syndrome*.

Sensuous sexual experiences are important aspects of sexual intimacy. Such expressions include *celibacy* or the more temporary *sexual abstinence*, as well as *autoeroticism* or *masturbation*. Conjugal couples face challenges in sustaining sexually active marriages (or other committed long-term coupled relationships) and the impacts of extramarital behavior.

Couples need accurate information and support regarding *sexual dysfunctions*, disabilities, and disease, including *sexual desire disorders* (e.g., *hypoactive sexual desire disorder* and *sexual aversion disorder*), *sexual arousal disorders* (e.g., *erectile dysfunction*), *orgasmic disorders*, and *sexual pain disorders* (e.g., *vaginismus* and *dyspareunia*). Sexually transmitted diseases, although an uncomfortable topic in many families, demand serious consideration and prevention strategies especially in light of their *asymptomatic* nature.

Learning healthful sexual intimacy is indeed a family responsibility requiring that families move beyond well-intended, but often inaccurate, approaches (e.g., *abstinence-only*) toward those based on research (e.g., *abstinence-plus*). Families, with or without children, need candid conversations and complete education about sexuality and sexual intimacy throughout the life course.

INTIMACY AND SEXUALITY

"There are few aspects of human relationships that are more sought after, more written about, and less understood than intimacy" (Giorgianni, Grana, and Sewell 2000: 6). *Webster's Ninth New Collegiate Dictionary* (1984: 634) defines intimacy as a state "marked by very close association, contact, or familiarity." Yet this definition only hints at the vital role that intimate relationships play through family members' lives in terms of their physical and emotional wellness. Chapter 5 discusses the profound connection between lifestyle and wellness. In the same way, research reveals an increasing awareness of the impact of intimate relationships on an individual's and a family's well-being.

Intimacy and Family Quality-of-Life

Our sexual desires, feelings, and behaviors are necessary aspects of living and have the capacity to bring great pleasure and satisfaction. They are indeed measures of our quality-of-life. Traditional measures of quality-of-life, however, may fail to include sexual wellness or sexual relations (Gill and Feinstein 1994). Humans crave closeness. Some families are huggers, whereas others are not. Although we vary in expressions of intimacy, families need affection and physical contact. Sexual intimacy and activity affect not only emotional and psychological health but also the physical body (Giorgianni, Grana, and Sewell 2000).

Regular, healthy sexual activity has positive effects on weight, heart disease, chronic pain, cancer, and anxiety and depression, as well as on immunity and longevity. Families, who realize that sexual intimacy is more than about procreation or recreation and that sexual intimacy is fundamental to total well-being, seek to understand and discuss sex and sexuality as positive aspects of living.

Many needs are satisfied within intimate relationships that support and affirm and provide a sense of belonging and love. Many of the skills for forming successful intimate relationships beyond the family of origin stem from lessons learned in families. Families play a vital part in encouraging and supporting positive self-concept, optimism, trust, and confidence in being loved, lovable, and able to love. Beyond the family, friendships with beginnings in childhood can significantly influence ability to establish, maintain, and dissolve future relationships. Attitudes and behaviors regarding intimacy arise from a network of influences. Keillor (Box 6.1) describes his view on what really is sexy in many sexually intimate relationships.

BOX 6.1 "What's Really Sexy"
Garrison Keillor

Somewhere, when I was young, I got the idea that the average American couple had sex twice a week, and I've carried this figure in my head for more than 30 years, as a benchmark, like the .300 batting average or the idea of three square meals a day. There have been times when any sex at all was a beautiful faraway ideal, like reincarnation, and there have been other periods when twice a day or hourly seemed pretty normal. But twice weekly was the norm, I thought, so it's a surprise to learn that according to the new survey (Sex in America), once a week is more like it. Only about a third of adults are keeping up the pace, and another third are plugging along at two or three times a month, and for the remainder, sex is rare or nonexistent.

Despite the low numbers, though, almost half the adult population claims to be *extremely pleased and satisfied*, which is a lot of pleasure in a country this big. The happiest ones are the monogamous couples, married or not. Despite jobs and careers that eat away at their evenings [,] . . . children who dog their footsteps and . . . the need to fix meals and pay bills, these couples still manage to encounter each other regularly in a lustful, inquisitive way . . . and do thrilling things in the dark and cry out and breathe hard and afterward lie sweaty together feeling *extreme pleasure. . . .*

. . . Despite all you may have read lately, there is an incredible amount of normality going on in America these days, and it is good to know. Our country is not obsessed with sex. To the contrary. We wear ourselves out working, we are surrounded with noise and distraction and all manner of entertainment, we indulge our children as they run roughshod over our lives, the ghosts of old aunts and beady-eyed preachers lurk in the shadows watching us. Considering what the American couple is up against, it's astounding to think that once a week or once a month or maybe just on Memorial Day and Christmas or whenever the coast is clear, they are enjoying this gorgeous moment that is, despite its secrecy and long, shuddering climax, essentially the same experience as everyone else has had. It's almost worth all the misery of dealing with real estate people, bankers, lawyers and contractors—to have a home that has a bedroom where the two of you can go sometimes and do this. It is worth growing up and becoming middle-aged to be able to enjoy it utterly.

Source: Adapted with permission from Keillor, Garrison. 1994. "It's Good Old Monogamy That's Really Sexy." *Time* (October 17): 71.

Sexual attitudes and behaviors result from a complex web of influences. Sexuality encompasses more than genitals and intercourse and is shaped by physiology, family, peers, and lived experiences, as well as culture.

FOUNDATIONS OF SEXUAL EXPERIENCE

Biology Basics

Many of our sexual urges and responses are governed by hormonal signals. This physiological process is part of evolutionary genetic makeup. Human sexual anatomy and physiology continue to mystify and confuse many adults in our society. This shared ignorance is not only unwise but also unhealthy for families. Uninformed partners and family members often make poor sexual decisions.

What We Don't Know . . . And Are Afraid to Ask. Individuals require accurate and current information regarding human sexual intimacy. Family members who fail to understand female and male genital anatomy and physiology often suffer confusion and frustration over sexual arousal, sexual response, and reproduction. Individuals who are skilled in sexual intimacy are equipped with complete and correct knowledge of physical,

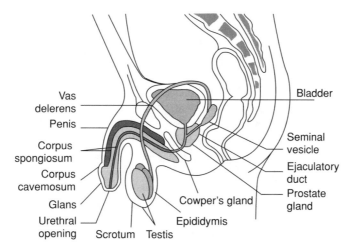

FIG. 6.1.   Male Sexual Anatomy.
Source: **Adapted with permission from EngenderHealth. 2004.** *Sexuality and Sexual Health.* **New York, NY: EngenderHealth.**

psychological, and emotional aspects of sexual intimacy. This learning begins with knowing and being able to talk about the structure and function of male and female genitalia.

Male Sexual Anatomy.   Compared to females, the male sexual arousal, response, and reproduction are less intricate physiologically. Although a complex system, the male sexual anatomy is more external than that of the female sexual anatomy, making it more accessible to exploration and visibility (see Figure 6.1). The cylindrical structure of the penis can be flaccid or erect and provides passage for both urine and semen. During sexual arousal, it is a source of pleasure and is the organ that penetrates the mouth, vagina, or anus during penetrative sex. The head of the penis, glans, is highly sensitive to stimulation and is covered by the foreskin in men who are not circumcised. Hanging immediately below the penis is the scrotum, which holds the testes. The scrotum protects the testes and maintains the temperature necessary for the production of sperm.

The oval-shaped testes are highly sensitive to touch and pressure. They produce sperm and the male sex hormone, testosterone, which is responsible for the development of male sexual characteristics and sex drive. Lying on the backside of each testes are very convoluted tubes, epididymides, which store sperm as they mature prior to ejaculation. The tubes that carry the mature sperm from the epididymides to the urethra are the vasa deferentia.

Semen consists of sperm and fluids from several structures, that is, seminal vesicles, prostate gland, and Cowper's gland that provide nourishment and an alkaline quality to neutralize the acidic environments of the male and female reproductive tracts. The prostate gland is very sensitive to stimulation and can be a source of sexual pleasure for some men.

Female Sexual Anatomy.   The female external genitalia, often referred to as the vulva, includes the labia minora, labia majora, the clitoris, the vestibule, and the mons pubis (see Figure 6.2). The labia majora are two spongy folds of skin, one on either side of the vaginal opening, covering and protecting the genital structures. The labia minora are the two erectile folds of skin between the labia majora that extend from the clitoris on both sides of the urethral and vaginal openings. The clitoris is an erectile, hooded organ at the upper joining of the labia that contains a high concentration of nerve endings and is very

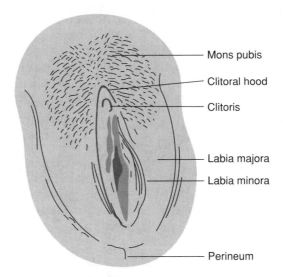

FIG. 6.2.   External Female Sexual Anatomy.
Source: Adapted with permission from EngenderHealth. 2004. *Sexuality and Sexual Health*. New York, NY: EngenderHealth.

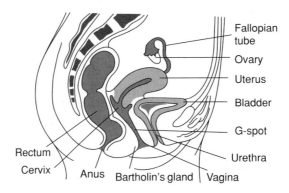

FIG. 6.3.   Internal Female Sexual Anatomy.
Source: Adapted with permission from EngenderHealth. 2004. *Sexuality and Sexual Health*. New York, NY: EngenderHealth.

sensitive to stimulation. The clitoris is the only anatomical organ whose sole function is providing sexual pleasure. Above the clitoris lies the mons pubis, a pad of fatty tissue over the pubic bone. This structure, which becomes covered with hair during puberty, protects the internal sexual and reproductive organs. The perineum is a network of muscles located between and surrounding the vagina and the anus that support the pelvic cavity and help keep pelvic organs in place.

The internal female genitals consist of the vagina, cervix, fallopian tubes, and ovaries (see Figure 6.3). The vagina is an expandable, muscular, and tubular cavity, leading from the vulva to the uterus. The vagina is the structure penetrated during vaginal intercourse, and it also serves as the path for menstrual flow. During vaginal intercourse, contact with this structure provides sexual pleasure in some women. The anterior vaginal wall highly sensitive to stimulation is the Grafenberg spot, or G-spot. This small area (about 1 to 2 cm) located on the front wall of the vagina about midway between the pelvic bone and the cervix is especially sensitive to sexual stimulation in some women and may be the source of a small amount of fluid ejaculated at orgasm. If stimulated, this area becomes engorged. The G-spot has no known function for women except as a source of sexual stimulation. Within the entrance of the vagina there also are Bartholin's glands, two small structures, that secrete a mucus-like fluid during sexual arousal, providing vaginal lubrication.

The lower part of the uterus that protrudes into the vaginal canal is the cervix with an orifice that allows passage for menstrual flow from the uterus and passage of sperm into the uterus. During vaginal intercourse, contact with this structure may provide sexual pleasure in some women.

Above the cervix is the uterus, a pear-shaped, hollowed, muscular organ. This is the site for implantation of a fertilized ovum (egg), the location for the development of a fetus during pregnancy, and the structure that sheds its lining monthly during menstruation. The upper portion of the uterus contracts during orgasm. From the upper uterus, the fallopian tubes extend out toward the ovaries (but do not touch them). Through these tubes, ova (eggs) travel from the ovaries toward the uterus in which fertilization of the ovum takes place.

Located at the end of fallopian tubes are the ovaries, two organs that produce ova (generally releasing one per month from puberty to menopause). The ovaries produce estrogen and progesterone, the hormones responsible for the development of sex characteristics, influencing ovulation, as well as maintaining the elasticity of the genitalia, integrity of the vaginal lining, and lubrication of the genitalia. Testosterone is also produced, in smaller amounts than that produced in men, and is responsible for sexual desire.

As family members age, they and their partners face the impacts of naturally occurring transitions. Two such common conditions include *menopause* (reduction of regular estrogen and progesterone levels resulting in cessation of menstruation and ovulation) and *male climacteric* (i.e., changes in male sexual responsiveness including erectile dysfunction).

The side effects of menopause are more troublesome for some women than for others. The effects include hot flashes (sudden sensations of warmth accompanied with or without chills and perspiration), headaches, dizziness, sleep disturbances, heart palpitations, and joint pain. Some women experience depression, moodiness, fatigue, irritability, and even forgetfulness during menopause. Osteoporosis (loss of bone density) and accompanying debilitating bone fractures are also greater risks as women move through menopause. Decreased estrogen levels cause vaginal wall thinning and reduced lubrication along with reduced sexual desire and arousal. These symptoms can have significant impacts on not only the individual but also her partner and family.

A common treatment for the symptoms associated with menopause was hormone replacement therapy (HRT) in which women received low doses of a combination of estrogen and progestins (laboratory-made compounds that closely relate to progesterone). In July 2002, a major study on the effectiveness of long-term use of HRT by postmenopausal women was suddenly halted because of unexpected findings. These major findings—(a) HRT should not be used for prevention of heart disease or stroke, and (b) HRT appears to slightly increase the risk of breast cancer—resulted in both a significant reduction of HRT for treating symptoms associated with menopause and in a significant decrease in the use of HRT (Working Group for the Women's Health Initiative Investigation 2002). To illustrate the individual risk:

> In a group of 10,000 women who would take the hormone combination (findings do not apply to estrogen only therapy used in women with hysterectomies) for one year would experience: seven additional heart attacks, eight more breast cancers, eight more strokes, and eight more blood clots in the lungs. (Ellis 2003: 4)

Although researchers stressed there was no need for panic, this report sent shock waves through the population of postmenopausal women and their families. What may have been missed in the aftermath of the report was the researchers' strong support for short-term treatment (usually defined as up to six months) in which the benefits far outweigh any risks. These benefits include 37% fewer colorectal cancers, over 33.3% fewer hip fractures, and 25% fewer total fractures (Ellis 2003). Menopause and treatments such as HRT offer an example of how couples and families must be fully aware of research and strategies to address unwanted symptoms and related health risks associated with this natural part of women's sexual life.

Male climacteric refers to changes in male sexual responsiveness that begins to appear in 40- to 60-year-old men. Sadly, research on male climactic—a very real transition in natural male aging—lags far behind that on menopause. Like menopause, male climacteric can also be associated with fatigue, decreased sexual desire, depression, and an inability to concentrate. Again, couples and their families benefit with awareness of natural transitions and strategies to reduce the impact of their unwanted symptoms.

Although fundamental, clear understandings of sexual anatomy and physiology are only the basics in sexual intimacy, families also need to recognize the influences of family, friends, and culture on sexual norms, attitudes, and behaviors for families.

Family, Peers, and Life Experience

Families wield tremendous influence over members' sexuality. The individual's sense of self and confidence that one is unconditionally loved, lovable, and capable of loving can originate in the family. Likewise, viewing sex and sexuality as healthy and beautiful or nasty and repulsive arises from beliefs, biases, and behaviors expressed in the family.

Families are indeed the first sexuality educators. Families need to talk with their children about sex and puberty before puberty. The approach of "one big sex talk" with a 16-year-old offers poor results and much discomfort for both teen and adult. Some family life educators find age eight to be an appropriate time to begin more formalized sex education. However, sexuality education is a "staged" protocol. Rather, sexuality education in the family is an ongoing, everyday occurrence, as every member, from the youngest child to the oldest adult explores her or his own body and the place of sexuality and intimacy in her or his life and the lives of other family members.

We know that families engaged in construction and negotiation of sexuality can significantly impact family members' sexuality and sexual behaviors (Blume and Blume 2003; Reiss 1981). Even older siblings can wield powerful influence on young siblings' sexual attitudes and behaviors (Kowal and Blinn-Pike 2004).

In Box 6.2, a parent describes the natural flow of conversation with her children as they learn about sex and sexuality. For what family members do not know and are afraid to ask about can cause harm when it comes to intimacy and sexuality.

BOX 6.2   "A Snapshot of Raising Sexually Healthy Children"
Julie Endersbe, M.S.

Before our children were born . . .

My husband and I talk about how we were raised as sexual human beings and decide to do it differently. We also choose to limit access. One television. No cable. *After the children were born . . .*

We teach the proper names for body parts. We let the children explore their bodies without judgment.

At the age of 4 ...

Our son plays dress-up with his older sister. High heels, fancy dresses, and gloves were his favorite. We let him play.

Our daughter asks how babies are born. I tell her the baby grows inside the mom and is pushed out through the vagina. She sits upside down on the couch and decides not to have children.

At the age of 7 ...

She asks questions. We answer each one honestly with an awareness to what she developmentally understands.

Our son does not ask questions. We talk in small moments—car rides and trips to the grocery store about itching, daddies, girls, and pregnancy.

Books that answer more questions are visible and accessible in the house.

During the next three years ...

We talk more in depth to each child about puberty and body changes. We dispel the rumors. We talk about the future. Would each child like to be a parent someday? How does a child practice for parenting? Both take a babysitting class.

At the age of 9 ...

The complaints begin about not having cable, video games, or not watching PG-13 movies. We chose to be the primary teachers about sexuality—not the media industry. We take the heat.

At the age of 10 ...

Classmates tease our daughter about her best friend, Josh. We talk about societal expectations of gender. Her best friends are boys. She practices ignoring the teasing and enjoys the friendship.

At the age of 11 ...

Our son receives many calls from girls. He is a cute sixth grader. He still asks few questions about sexuality. We talk about dating and relationships. We talk about communication and attractions. We ask him about the future and what's important to him.

Now he's at the age of 13 ...

Our son wears hot pink. Hot pink belts, socks, and his skateboard. He wears pink and we allow him to define his masculinity.

Now she's at the age of 15 ...

Our daughter wants to know what's the big deal about oral sex. We talk about. It leads to more intense questions talking about sexuality. We are available and we are honest. And, we hold back from asking why she wants to know.

Looking ahead ...

We think about the future. I read the research about delaying sexual intercourse. I want to define a sexually fulfilling relationship. We provide opportunities for each to develop interests and build confidence. We continue talking. In quiet moments, my husband and I smile and look forward to what the future brings.

Julie Endersbe M.S., is a middle school counselor. She has authored curriculum for the Coordinated School Health Program *Dads Make a Difference* project.

Peer pressures influence behavior, not just adolescent sexual behavior, in all age groups. The journey from childhood to adulthood includes struggles with physiological and social psychological development, struggles that may be challenging to both teens and their families as youth grapple with questions of identity and autonomy. Adults may view teenagers' peers as dangerous influences, but part of a healthy development of peer relationships during this stage of the life cycle is the extension of intimacy to intimate ties to peers. Of some comfort to parents, when teens are asked to identify major influences in their sexual attitudes and behaviors, they identify parents, peers, and media as equally influential (Brown 2001; Sexuality Information and Education Council of the United States 2001).

Relationships with peers can provide a sense of belonging and trust. Peers also serve as sources of information on a wide range of topics including sexuality. Sexually educated peers provide not only accurate information but also encouragement to make sexually healthy decisions. This is true for all age groups. When peers are armed with accurate sexuality information and effective communication skills, peers become positive influences. This is one argument for conscientious sexuality education.

An individual's lived experiences, both positive and negative, also have a dramatic influence on the development of sexuality and intimacy. For example, in chapter 10, we discuss the significance of abuse; in chapter 9 we discuss the impact of divorce on the ability to form intimate connections.

Cultural Influences on Sexuality

Traditions and rituals often determine sexual norms. What is considered sensual in one culture may be considered repulsive in another. For example, American culture deems kissing, especially deep kissing (exchange of saliva), as erotic. Yet, the Mehinaku of the Amazonian rain forest view this act as abnormal and even vulgar (Gregor 1985).

Case: Female Genital Mutilation.   Societal norms regarding sexuality are rooted in knowledge (or ignorance) as well as in cultural myths, historical traditions, and social rituals. The practice of male *circumcision*—the removal of part or all of the foreskin covering the glans of the penis—serves as an example of the power of culture and society on sexuality and even on sexual health. Many people including the ancient Egyptians and many Islamic groups have practiced circumcision of males shortly after birth, at puberty, or shortly before marriage. Circumcision is an important ritual in Judaism, symbolizing the perpetual covenant between God and the descendants of Abraham. The penalty for failure to perform the rite was deemed to be exclusion from the community of the faithful (Wigoder et al. 1986). Progress and good hygiene appears to eliminate any physical health concerns associated with uncircumcised males. The American Academy of Pediatrics (1999) reports no weight of medical evidence in favor of routine neonatal male infant circumcision and that babies being circumcised actually do feel the pain.

Female genital mutilation (FGM) or *female genital cutting*, raises much deeper concerns. This procedure occurs in approximately 28 African countries, parts of Asia, and among some immigrant communities in the United States. An estimated two million females endured some variation of genital mutilation annually (World Health Organization 1998, 2000). FGM is a cultural practice and not related to religion, yet in many cases the ritual is associated with a woman's religious identity (Moschovis 2002). The cutting may involve slitting or complete removal of the external genitalia (e.g., labia majora, labia minora) or the entire clitoris (*cliterodectomy*).

In some cases an additional procedure of *genital infibulation* occurs in which the sides of the vulva or vaginal opening may be stitched together. The lack of hygiene, or anesthetic, means the use of unclean knives, razors, or broken glass often results in excruciating pain during the procedure; and during later childbirth, infection and scarring, elimination of sexual pleasure, infertility, and death.

This procedure, rather than being a form of "female circumcision" as it is sometimes called, is in reality the female equivalent of male castration. Although the procedure is condemned as barbaric and illegal in many countries and *Amnesty International* considers the procedure to be a violation of human rights, tradition is a powerful force. In societies that practice female genital mutilation, the rite holds an important part in establishing female status. Female genital mutilation may secure cultural, gender, or religious identity, as well as control female sexuality and reproduction. In some cultures, the practice is associated with hygiene, aesthetic, and health beliefs. In societies that practice some form of female genital mutilation, women who have not undergone the procedure are regarded as unmarriageable (Karraker 2000).

Some cultures are working to outlaw FGM. In the United Kingdom, The Female Genital Mutilation Act 2003 came into force in March 2004. This act replaced the 1985 Act and makes it a crime to not only carry out FGM abroad but also aid, abet, counsel, or procure acts of FGM even in countries where it is legal (Royal College of Obstetricians and Gynaecologists 2003).

Media and Technology.   Adolescents rank media at the top, along with parents and peers, as important sources of sexual information (Brown 2001). In one study, 70% of parents of children under age 18 reported that conversations about a sexual issue emerged due to what was seen on a television program (Sexuality Information and Education Council of the United States 2001). Although television programs may stimulate conversations on sexual issues, media need to be viewed with critical thinking skills that can be taught and practiced in families. Some countries, such as Australia and Canada, require the teaching of *sexuality media literacy* across the curriculum and at all grade levels. This emphasis on media literacy may be a strategy American families want to consider.

Media pressure is not always negative. Aside from creating more critical viewers, is there hope for mass media becoming a healthy sexuality educator? Some believe that mass media has the potential for a positive impact on healthy sexuality. Organizations such as the *Henry J. Kaiser Family Foundation, Advocates for Youth*, and the *National Campaign to Prevent Teen Pregnancy* are working with media executives, screen writers, and producers along with popular magazine (e.g., *Teen People, YM*) editors to promote and encourage greater sexual responsibility including teen postponement of sexual intercourse, consistent use of effective contraceptive strategies, and assertiveness in refusing unwanted sexual activity.

"To paraphrase Charles Dickens, when it comes to the Internet and intimacy, this is the best of times and the worst of times" (Giorgianni, Grana, and Sewell 2000: 27). The Internet's role in families, as discussed in chapter 4, raises the need for responsible use and family guidelines. Ready access to ubiquitous information, instant messaging, and other just-in-time sources of information challenge families to do more than try to halt the flow of information. Families need to learn how to use media resources responsibly in this wireless world.

These technologies are a promising means to accurate, current information and services related to sexual intimacy, but they also hold duplicity, dishonesty, and even danger. Reliable organizations such as Columbia University's Web site *goaskalice* and the National

Institute of Health's *Medline* provide frequently asked questions (FAQ) options and links for accurate sexual health information sites. Movement by media and the Internet toward a healthier portrayal of sexuality is slow (Brown 2001). Families, family studies professionals, and external communities must demand more accurate sexual information from media and exercise their collective consumer muscle so that change may come.

THE SCIENCE OF SEXUAL INTIMACY

Research and Theory on Human Sexual Response

The Masters and Johnson Tradition. There are several models of human sexual response with the best known by Masters and Johnson (1966, 1976). Although previous researchers (Kinsey Institute 2003) studied self-reported human sexual behaviors, Masters and Johnson's work was seminal in that it was the first large-scale study of sexual response in a laboratory setting applying scientific rigor to this act of sexual intimacy. The Masters and Johnson's sexual response model identified four phases including excitement, plateau, orgasm, and resolution. During the first phase, excitement occurs with stimulation (cognitive and sensory) in which the genital erectile tissue becomes engorged and the body feels any overall sense of pleasurable tension. With the plateau phase, this sexual excitement and lubrication reach maximum levels. Masters and Johnson's work noted that the plateau phase is the most variable in terms of time not only between males and females (with males often achieving it more quickly than females) but also between sexually experienced and inexperienced couples. Orgasm is a dramatic release of sexual tension, and for males, ejaculation (release of semen) occurs. In the final phase, resolution, the body returns to a preexcitement level. It is a period of "recovery between orgasms." Couples may frustrate their sexual pleasure by focusing on simultaneous orgasm. Orgasm is individualistic and variable in terms of timing. Contrary to most women, men require a period of rest between orgasms, which often is influenced with age.

Kaplan's Triphasic Model. In the 1970s, researchers such as Kaplan (1974) began to disagree with the four-phase model. Kaplan's argument was that it failed to recognize the important role of sexual desire in sexual response and that the plateau and excitement phases were indistinguishable. Kaplan proposed the Kaplan Triphasic Model that included three sexual response phases: desire, excitement, and orgasm. In this model, major emphasis is placed on desire, the stimulation of the cortex and limbic systems that trigger the hormones initiating sexual response. To researchers such as Kaplan, the brain is the "sexiest organ."

Although Masters and Johnson's Model (1966, 1976) and Kaplan's (1974) expansion model are highly valued, they do have detracters. Leiblum (2000) states that the Kaplan model does not neatly match many women's sexual experiences and does not include spontaneous feelings of sexual desire. Leiblum claims that in the Triphasic Model desire and arousal may actually be in reverse order, in that for both females and males arousal comes prior to desire. For example, a male's morning erection (arousal) may then signal a desire, whereas for women an arousing touch may trigger desire. Leiblum also notes that both models (Masters and Johnson's and Kaplan's) neglect to consider the subjective nature of sexual response. Sexual intimacy is not merely physiological. Feelings of satisfaction with their partner with the sexual experience cannot be determined by whether they experienced orgasm.

Aspects of quality-of-life and emotional well-being are now recognized as essential to human sexual response. Researchers such as Leiblum (2000) and Basson (2000) stress the need to consider psychological as well as physiological variables in sexual intimacy. Additional models, such as Walen and Roth's (1987) and Zilbergeld and Ellison's (1980), also focused on the cognitive and desire factors of stimulating and maintaining sexual arousal.

Basson's Model.   A more recent model, Basson's (2000), incorporates the concept of gender-based distinctions and challenges former models to not mix female and male sexual response patterns. The Basson Model of sexual response not only recognizes the physiology (excitement, desire, and orgasm), the cognitive impacts (anger and fear vs. joy and trust) but also emphasizes emotional factors in intimacy. A significant gender-based distinction, under this model, is sexual satisfaction where females report "good" sex even without orgasm as compared to men who much more frequently equate sexual satisfaction with achieving orgasm. As the complexity surrounding sexual response unfolds, the dimension of spirituality enters the discussion.

Thayton's Spiritual and Theological Model.   Thayton (2002) proposes that sexuality research on sexual response is proof that God (however God is named in the individual's religious belief) created humans with a capacity to draw great pleasure from loving one another. Thayton notes that Jesus never taught self-denial or condemnation of sexual pleasure. According to the Thayton Model, love includes both sexual and spiritual components and that couples who combine spirituality, sex, and love enjoy the deepest form of intimacy, a loving gift of God as it were. This approach challenges more harsh and negative views toward human sexual intimacy and especially sexual response.

Controlling Conception

The right to safe and effective contraceptive strategies has a long history. Early pioneers of women's right to contraceptive health (e.g., Margaret Sanger) struggled against social and political odds just to guarantee what many today take for granted: medically safe contraception and birth control. Please read Box 6.3.

BOX 6.3   "Margaret Sanger: Pioneer in Contraceptive Rights"

Sometimes social factors slow progress toward improving health more than lack of awareness or the absence of technology. No 20th-century public health achievement demonstrates this more clearly than the struggle to provide women in the United States with safe and effective birth control. Margaret Sanger (September 14, 1879– September 6, 1966) risked scandal, danger, and imprisonment to challenge the legal and cultural obstacles that made controlling fertility difficult and illegal.

Margaret Louise Higgins was born in Corning, New York, the sixth of 11 children. Her free-thinking father's politics might have ignited her activism, but watching the process of her mother, aged 50 years, die after 18 pregnancies probably had an even deeper impact. Higgins was a nursing student in 1902 when she married architect William Sanger. Although weakened by bouts of tuberculosis, she bore three children between 1902 and 1910. The Sangers immersed themselves in the radical political and intellectual world of Greenwich Village in New York City. She worked as a visiting nurse in the city's tenements and wrote about sex education and women's health.

In 1914, Sanger's articles in *The Woman Radical* brought her a federal indictment for violating federal postal obscenity laws, prompting her to flee to England. As soon as the ship left United States' waters, she cabled a radical publisher in New Jersey to distribute 100,000 copies of her pamphlet, *Family Limitation*. Sanger remained exiled in Europe until late 1915; William Sanger had been arrested and jailed for distributing one copy of *Family Limitation*, and Margaret Sanger returned to face the charges against her. Personal tragedy intervened when the Sanger's 5-year-old daughter died suddenly from pneumonia; public sentiments resulted in dismissal of the charges against Margaret Sanger.

Rather than backing away from controversy, Sanger and her sister Ethel Byrne, also a nurse, opened the first birth control clinic in the United States, modeled after those Sanger had seen in Holland. On October 16, 1916, dozens of Jewish and Italian immigrant women from Brooklyn's crowded Brownsville section lined up to receive counseling and birth control information. Nine days later police closed the clinic and arrested Sanger, Byrne, and the clinic's interpreter. Byrne was tried and convicted first, and went on a hunger strike. Sanger was convicted and served 30 days in jail. Legal failure had brought victory, however. The publicity surrounding Sanger's activities had made birth control a matter of public debate.

After World War I, Sanger continued her United States leadership role, although during the 1920s and 1930s, she refocused her energy toward international birth control, traveling and lecturing throughout Asia and Europe. In 1952, she founded the International Planned Parenthood Federation and served as its first president until 1959. Sanger died in Tucson, Arizona, aged 87 years, a few months after the 1965 Supreme Court decision, *Griswold v. Connecticut*, that made birth control legal for married couples, the culmination of events Sanger had started 50 years earlier.

Source: Adapted from Morbidity and Mortality Weekly Reports 1999. "Margaret Sanger." *Centers for Disease Control and Prevention*. (December 3) 48, 47: 1075 www.cdc.gov/mmwr/preview/mmwrhtml/mm4847bx.htm (Retrieved 2/9/03).

Although the terms are often used interchangeably, birth control and contraception are not the same thing. Birth control encompasses a broad sweep of methods that reduces births including delayed marriage, celibacy, contraception, medications, or devices that the prevent implantation of fertilized zygote, and induced abortions. Contraception—literally "contra caption"—prevents conception.

Contraception Strategies. These strategies are generally organized into six approaches (also see Table 6.1 for more details on these strategies) including:

- Nonpenetrative Contact: *Outercourse* (kissing, hugging, rubbing, massage, masturbation, oral-genital sex)

- Preventing Fertilization—Nonsurgical: Withdrawal (removing penis prior to ejaculation); fertility awareness (combination of calendar, cervical mucus, and basal body temperature records to determine ovulation and "safe" days for intercourse)

- Preventing Sperm Meeting Egg: Mechanical barriers (e.g., male and female condoms, diaphragm, cervical cap, vaginal sponge); and chemical barriers (e.g., spermicides)

- Preventing Implantation: Intrauterine device (IUD); some forms of emergency contraception (Note: Some IUDs and emergency contraception strategies prevent fertilization instead of implantation.)

- Suppressing Ovulation: Oral contraceptives; NuvaRing; Evra patch; emergency contraception—morning-after pill; Lunelle; Depo-Provera; Implanon (replaced Norplant, which is no longer available)

TABLE 6.1
Contraceptive Strategies—Overview

Strategy	Description
Barrier strategies	
Male condom	Sheath often made of latex that fits over an erect penis. Reduces risks of unintended pregnancy, STIs & HIV. Use with spermicide highly recommended.
Female condom	Thin, loose-fitting, flexible plastic tube worn inside the vagina. A soft ring at the closed end of the condom covers the cervix. Barrier to the bodily fluids semen, blood, and saliva. Use with spermicide highly recommended.
Diaphragms, cervical caps, cervical shields	A rubber cup with flexible ring that is inserted and placed over the cervix. All required a prescription. Use with spermicide highly recommended.
Vaginal sponge	A new form of sponge available in Canada. Polyurethane shield about 2 inches infused with spermicide.
Spermicides	
Nonoxynol-9	Best when used with another strategy.
Vaginal Contraceptive Film	Paper-thin 2 inch square laced with spermicide. Folded and inserted into vagina near cervix.
Intrauterine devise IUD	
Mirena, Pregestasert, Pargard	Exactly how this strategy works is unknown. Contrary to myth, IUDs are not abortifacient. Small plastic or copper device inserted into uterus.
Sterilization	
Vasectomy	Minor surgery in which the vasa deferentia tubes are cut and tied. Vasectomies do not increase risk of prostate cancer.
Tubal ligation (laparoscopy)	Requires more invasive surgery in which the fallopian tubes are cut and tied or stapled.
Minilaparotomy Essure System	Newer procedure in which a small metallic implant is placed in each fallopian tube.
Hormonal	
Oral (Pills)	Pill with varying amounts of estrogen and progestin taken for 3 weeks followed with 1 week off. Newer schedules, see 84/7 below.
Implanon	Implanted single 4-cm-long rod. Replaces Norplant.
Injectables: Depo-Provera, Lunelle	Depo-Perva Injection every 3 months. Lunelle injection every month.
Patch: Ortho Evra	2-inch square applied to abdomen, buttocks, upper arm, or torso. Transdermal release of estrogen and projestin for 3 weeks.
Ring: NuvaRing	Thin transparent, flexible ring inserted into vagina over cervix.
84/7 Oral: Seasonale©	Similar to regular oral contraceptives but the woman takes the pill 84 days followed with 7 days off.
Emergency Contraception	"Morning-after pill" used postcoitally if sex was unprotected or method failed. Not considered a regular contraceptive strategy. Two doses of estrogen and progestin (Preven) or only progestin (Plan B) 12 hours apart with first dose taken within 72 hours (3 days) of coitus. This is not an abortifacient method.
Behavioral	
Abstinence	Complete avoidance of sexual intercourse. This includes vaginal, anal and oral sex.
Outercourse	May be considered "foreplay." Sexual activity that does not include penetration or exchange of bodily fluids (does not include anal or oral sex).
Withdrawl (coitus interruptus)	Removal of penis prior to ejaculation. High failure rate due to fact sperm found in preejaculatory fluid.
Fertility Awareness Method	Abstaining from coitus during woman's fertile period. Includes calendar, basal body temperature, and mucus methods. Note: women using no contraceptive strategy have a 60%–80% chance of not getting pregnant.

- Blocking Sperm or Egg Passage: Female sterilization (tubal ligation or miliaparaotmy—simplified form of tubal ligation); male sterilization (vasectomy and no-scalpel vasectomy).

Selecting a contraceptive method includes consideration of *theoretical effectiveness* (the lowest expected failure rate, assuming consistent and correct use) but also user or *actual effectiveness* (the failure rate associated with typical use and assuming inconsistent and incorrect use) as based on health studies conducted by medical care professionals (see Table 6.2). Generally, effectiveness increases with the use of a combination of contraceptive strategies.

Contraceptive considerations includes more than effectiveness, however. Both women's and men's attitudes toward and knowledge about contraceptives impact use and consistency

TABLE 6.2

Effectiveness Rates for Contraceptives During First Year of Use

Method	*Typical Use Rate of Pregnancy*	*Lowest Expected Rate of Pregnancy*
Sterilization		
Male Sterilization	0.15%	0.1%
Female Sterilization	0.5%	0.5%
Hormonal methods		
Implant (*Norplant and Norplant 2*)	0.05%	0.05%
Hormone Shot (*Depo-Provera*)	0.3%	0.3%
Combined Pill (*estrogen/progestin*)	5%	0.1%
Minipill (*progestin only*)	5%	0.5%
Intrauterine devices (IUDs)		
Copper T	0.8%	0.6%
Progesterone T	2%	1.5%
Barrier methods		
Male latex condom[a]	14%	3%
Diaphragm[b]	20%	6%
Vaginal sponge (*no previous births*)[c]	20%	9%
Vaginal sponge (*previous births*)[c]	40%	20%
Cervical cap (*no previous births*)[b]	20%	9%
Cervical cap (*previous births*)[b]	40%	26%
Female condom	21%	5%
Spermicide (*gel, foam, suppository, film*)	26%	6%
Natural methods		
Withdrawal	19%	4%
Natural family planning (*calendar, temperature, cervical mucus*)	25%	1%–9%
No method	85%	85%

[a]Used without spermicide.

[b]Used with spermicide.

[c]Contains spermicide.

Note: This table provides estimates of the percentage of women likely to become pregnant while using a particular contraceptive method for 1 year. These estimates are based on a variety of studies. "Typical Use" rates mean that the method either was *not always used correctly* or was *not used with every act of sexual intercourse* (e.g., sometimes forgot to take a birth control pill as directed and became pregnant), or was *used correctly* but *failed anyway.* "Lowest Expected" rates mean that the method was *always used correctly* with *every act of sexual intercourse* but *failed anyway* (e.g., always look a birth control pill as directed but still became pregnant). *Source:* Adapted from Food and Drug Administration. 1998. "Guidance for Industry—Uniform Contraceptive Labeling" (July 23). www.fda.gov/cdrh/ode/contrlab.html (Retrieved 2/5/04).

in correct use (Weill Cornell Medical College 2003). A couple's ambivalence about pregnancy or lack of male partner's support of contraceptive use appear to increase the risk of contraceptive failure and unintended pregnancy (Zabin 1999). Other concerns are cultural support (or lack of), availability, accessibility, and religious beliefs.

Families Who Plan. Approximately 60 million American women are in their childbearing years (i.e., 15–44 years of age; United States Bureau of the Census 2003) with over 64% of these 60 million women using contraceptives in hopes of avoiding unintended pregnancies (Abma et al. 1997). Sadly, over three million unintended pregnancies occur every year in the United States (Henshaw 1998). American health insurance coverage for contraceptive services falls behind coverage for obstetric care, abortion, and sterilization, which are included in many health care plans (Dailard 2003a).

For those women using reversible method of contraception, 24% receive family planning services with reimbursement by Medicaid. Such support not only makes a significant impact on family planning for these women but also, actually, is financially beneficial in that for every dollar spent on these services, an average of $3.00 is saved in Medicaid costs for pregnancy-related health care and medical care for newborns (Darroch, Forest, and Samara 1996),

Teen Pregnancy. Unprotected sexual intercourse places individuals at risk for unplanned pregnancy, as well as for exposure to human immunodeficiency virus and other sexually transmitted infections. From 1959, when the recorded rate of teen pregnancy was 96 births per 1,000 women aged 15 to 19 (and in spite of an increase in rates increased in the late 1980s), the adolescent pregnancy rate dropped to an all-time low of 49 births per 1,000 women aged 15 to 19 in 2000. Although the highest rates are found among teens living in poverty or on welfare (Hao and Cherlin 2004; Santelli et al. 2004), the downward trend is found among teens of all ages and races (Boonstra 2002).

Pregnant teens in the 21st century are less likely to enter into marriage as a result of pregnancy than were teens in the 1950s. However, the decline in teen birthrates in the past decade was not due to teens having abortions. In fact, the abortion rate among teens 15 to 19 years old dropped significantly (33%) in the decade between 1987 and 1997 (Boonstra 2002).

Why are fewer American teens getting pregnant? Are teens abstaining from sex, or are those having sex employing more effective contraceptive strategies? The answer is "both." Researchers at the Guttmacher Institute (Darroch and Singh 1999) analyzed possible causes for the decline in America's teen pregnancy rates. They concluded from the data that about one fourth of the reduction in U.S. teen pregnancy from 1988 to 1995 was due to increased abstinence. The remaining three fourths of the drop in rates was attributed to "changes in the behavior of sexually experienced teens" (Boonstra 2002: 4). This behavior change was use of more effective contraceptive strategies.

American teens continue to have pregnancy and birth rates significantly higher than those of other developed countries, almost twice as high as in Canada and Great Britain and approximately four times as high as France and Sweden (Boyle 2001). Research suggests that several factors contribute to the higher teen pregnancy rates in the United States (Alan Guttmacher Institute 2001; Singh and Darroch 1999, 2000). First, growing up in economic and socially disadvantaged environments increases the risk of engaging in sexually risky behaviors. America has a higher percentage of disadvantaged families, but also the highest per capita income of the countries included in the study. Yet, sexually active American teens at all socioeconomic levels were less likely than the teens in the other countries to use contraceptives. For example, American teens in the higher income bracket have a 14% higher birthrate than Great Britain teens in similar income levels and higher than all teens in all economic categories in France and Sweden.

Second, although American teens have more abortions than teens in the comparison countries, American teens who did become pregnant were less likely to have an abortion than teens in the other countries. The study could not determine whether this was due to antiabortion feelings, greater acceptance of teenage parenting, or limited availability and accessibility of abortion. Third, in terms of attitudes toward teen pregnancy, European and Canadian adults stress that childbearing is for adults, whereas in the United States this attitude is weaker and accompanied by greater acceptance of teen parenting.

Fourth, due to openness in discussing sexuality, the comparison countries had clearer messages about sexual behavior. Although their message stressed delay of initial sexual intercourse and especially postponement in childbearing, the comparison countries were more accepting than were American adults of teens having sex. The comparison countries also firmly expected that if teens were sexually active, they were to protect themselves and partners from infections and pregnancy. American adults held opposite views regarding teen sex: Teen sex was seen as deviant and teens were not capable of making contraceptive decisions. In addition, there was an underlying attitude in America that if a young woman becomes pregnant, the problem rests with her and not with the young man, her family, the community, or society at large.

Fifth, European and Canadian sexuality education is comprehensive, includes contraceptive information, and is taught regularly in a variety of venues. In addition, adults and parents accept their responsibility as sexuality educators. This is the opposite of what occurs in the United States where 35% of all school districts restrict sexuality education to an approach of "just say no" (i.e., no discussion of sexual issues such as communication skills, healthy behaviors, or contraception).

The final two conclusions reflect adults' attitudes toward sexuality and teens. Access to family planning services for reproductive health is more available in the comparison countries than in the United States. According to Boonstra (2002: 9), "In the United States, where attitudes about teenage sexual relationships are more conflicted, teens have a harder time obtaining contraceptive services." Also, the comparison countries all adhered to a philosophy of assistance to youth in all aspects of their health care and needs. The approach in the United States provides fewer sexual health services to youth and the number of individuals with no health insurance continues to increase.

What does this all mean for families? Rather than lament the sorry state of teen sexuality in the United States, American families and their young members would benefit if they embraced some of the lessons from comparison countries. Families can be active sexuality educators for their members, including providing them with information and access to protection against sexually transmitted infections (including HIV) and effective contraceptive strategies. Such a sexual educational philosophy would not increase the level of sexual activity among adolescents and young adults, but would minimize their risk in this important area of life.

Married and Unplanned Pregnancy.   Unplanned pregnancy, however, is not only the concern of sexually active unmarried couples. The proportion of American women using contraceptives increased from 56% in 1982 to 64% in 1995 among not only unmarried but also currently and formerly married women of reproductive age (Piccinino and Mosher 1998). Table 6.3 presents data on contraceptive use among non-Hispanic White and non-Hispanic Black American women according to marital status. Consider that almost 50% of married women using contraceptives select female or male sterilization.

TABLE 6.3

Contraceptive Method of Black (Non-Hispanic) and White (Non-Hispanic) Women Aged 15–44 Years of Age by Marital Status, 1982–1995 (Percentages)

	Marital Status											
	Currently Married				Never Married				Formerly Married			
	1982		1995		1982		1995		1982		1995	
Method	White	Black	White	Black	White	Black	White	Black	White	Black	White	Black
Female sterilization	26	37	29	54	1	13	3	23	36	55	44	66
Male sterilization	17	4	20	5	2	0	1	0	5	0	5	1
Oral (pill)	18	25	21	19	53	58	52	31	31	19	23	13
Implant	Na	Na	1	1	Na	Na	2	4	Na	Na	1	2
Injectable	Na	Na	2	2	Na	Na	4	8	Na	Na	3	2
IUD	6	10	1	1	3	8	0	1	9	12	1	0
Diaphragm	7	4	3	2	17	3	1	1	8	3	2	0
Male condom	15	7	17	12	14	8	30	28	2	2	16	12
Other	11	14	7	5	10	10	6	5	10	11	6	3

Source: Adapted with permission from Linda Piccinino & William Mosher. 1998. "Table 6 Trends in Contraceptive Use in the United States: 1982–1995." *Family Planning Perspectives* 30, 1: 4–19, 46.

One aim of the 1996 welfare reform was to reduce the frequency of out-of-wedlock births believed by some to be a primary cause of welfare dependency. Such a perspective fails to recognize the reality that marriage does not solve challenges to controlling fertility. Although married women have lower rates of *unintended pregnancy* and abortion as compared to single women, simply being married does not reduce problems in correct and consistent use of contraceptives (Dailard 2003b). Over three million married women become pregnant each year, with three out of 10 or approximately one million of these pregnancies being unintended (Henshaw 1998). Some challenge this statistic with claims that only 59% of these surprise pregnancies are unhappy and classified these as unintended or contraceptive failures (Trussell, Vaughan, and Stanford 1999). It may be valid to consider the couple's response to a surprise pregnancy. That is, if the pregnancy is received with happiness (i.e., an *unexpected pregnancy* but nonetheless a wanted pregnancy) or unhappiness (e.g., an unintended and less welcomed pregnancy, perhaps one coming at a time of severe family stress). However, pressures from family and culture may influence the couple's response to the surprise pregnancy and thus increase claims of happiness. Apparently this is an area for family studies professionals to explore.

Terminating Pregnancy. Abortion is the termination of an established pregnancy, either spontaneously or induced. Approximately one third of all abortions are spontaneous abortions, or miscarriages, resulting from a variety of causes ranging from trauma to unexplained breakdown in uterine lining. Induced abortions are surgical methods and medical approaches. Surgical abortions entail the removal of uterine contents, usually by aspiration, or a major surgical procedure, hysterotomy, in which the uterine contents are removed through an incision in the abdomen and uterus.

Medical abortions do not involve surgical intervention and instead employ medications such as RU486 (mifepistone, often marketed as Mifeprex), which can effectively be used up to eight weeks (49 days since the last period) into a pregnancy. The combination of drugs blocks the hormone required to maintain the lining of the uterus, necessary for sustaining pregnancy after conception has occurred. For some, medications such as RU486 are "human pesticide" whereas for others, RU486 represents a revolutionary advance in women's ability to make sexual health decisions safely and privately, as well as early, in the period of time when a pregnancy may have occurred.

RU486 is not the same as the "morning-after pill" (i.e., emergency contraception). RU486 prevents the uterus from maintaining a fertilized ovum. Morning-after pills prevent fertilization and in some cases implantation. This process, and for that matter intrauterine devices, are substantially different from abortion and are not *abortifacients* (Chang 2003; Hatcher et al. 1998).

The Supreme Court decision (*Roe v. Wade*) legalizing induced abortion in the United States in 1973 was one step in a long confrontational history concerning women's reproductive health and rights with most (88%) of induced abortions in the United States performed during the first trimester of the pregnancy (Alan Guttmacher Institute 2003).

Whereas six out of 10 adults state they oppose the complete overturning of *Roe v. Wade* (Pew Research Center 2003), the issue remains divisive, involving political and religious interest groups on sides that call themselves *prochoice* and *prolife*. In 2003, President Bush signed the Partial Birth Abortion Act, which attempts to ban late-term abortion (i.e., abortions during the last trimester of pregnancy). Court challenges continue over the vague language of the act along with the absence of the condition of preserving the mother's life as medical condition for the procedure. As this debate simmers and threatens to boil over, society needs to consider facts over conjectures. One of the most effective means in reducing abortions is increased sexuality education along with availability and access to effective contraceptives, such as emergency contraception (Alan Guttmacher Institute 2003).

The decision to terminate a pregnancy is complex and never made lightly. Women who suddenly find they have an unintended pregnancy often are afraid and anguish over what to do or who to ask for assistance. Women with an unintended pregnancy need support and counseling, not ridicule and lectures. Concerns for the woman's physical and emotional health need to be considered along with financial and medical constraints.

Some supporters of the right-to-life movement claim that abortions lead to serious, long-term psychological conditions, that is, *postabortion syndrome* (Levathes 1995). Contrary to this opinion and some anecdotal accounts, medically supervised abortion has not been found to be related to higher drug and alcohol use, relationship disorders, sexual dysfunction, lower self-esteem, suicide, breast cancer, infertility, or miscarriages or other complications in subsequent pregnancies. The American Psychological Association (2000) does not recognize postabortion syndrome as a disorder.

SEXUAL EXPRESSION

Toward a Sensuous Ethic

For many individuals in this culture, orgasm is the definitive meaning of sexual intimacy, for not only must orgasm be consistent, but also it must be punctual. Such preconceived performance pressures distract from sexual satisfaction. Couples who create *sensuous sexual experiences* (strong sensual appeal, and pleasure) over only reaching orgasms emphasize enjoying the entire sexual encounter (with or without orgasm). Focusing on being sexually sensuous truly is the art of loving and lovemaking. Sensuousness reveals the artistry of blending sensory stimulation, emotional bonding, and playfulness. Sexual response is undeniably sensuous and pleasurable. Recognizing, appreciating, and enjoying this pleasure is vital to sexual intimate relationships.

How individuals exercise their sexual expression varies. Yet whether celibate or coupled, people who create and honor sexual pleasure often find life more satisfying.

Celibacy and Abstinence

Celibacy is defined as being unmarried and abstaining from sexual intercourse (*Webster's Ninth New Collegiate Dictionary* 1984). This is not to say there is no sexual desire for masturbation, and fantasy may or may not be practiced. Although some religions require celibacy (e.g., Catholic priests), not all who practice celibacy do so for religious reasons. At times individuals engage in temporary celibacy in order to heal or grieve after a relationship has ended. Some may choose celibacy due to time or energy limitations such as when starting graduate school or moving to a new city. Abstinence, *sexual abstinence*, is not a chosen lifestyle, but rather a temporary or situational choice. For example, a person may abstain from sexual intercourse until they are in a committed relationship, or because of unprotected intercourse.

Autoeroticism

Autoeroticism or *masturbation* is the stimulation of the genitals by hand or other objects done either by self or partner. Childhood masturbation is a natural part of children's exploration of their bodies, originated in the child's curiosity about her or his body, rewarded by pleasurable genital sensations. However, as early as the age of four or five, many children learn that adults find their sexual interest is considered wrong and shameful (Berends and Caron 1994). Parental disapproval may instill negative feelings toward self-pleasuring and a need to conceal such activities and discussions about sexuality from adults. Families need to understand that the medical community in 1972 stated that masturbation was not only harmless but also healthy (Rowan 2000). Masturbation only becomes a health concern in the highly unlikely event that self-stimulation interferes with regular daily routines, work or social functioning, continues beyond being pleasurable, or places a person at risk of physical harm.

BOX 6.4 "Masturbation: Still A Hands-Off Subject?"
Kathy Brothen, M.A., and Grit Youngquist, M.A.

Shhhhhhh . . . Masturbation is rarely talked about or acknowledged among families or friends. It's one sexual topic teens won't likely discuss with peers. Other than joking uncomfortably, few people seem to know what to say. Today, despite increased knowledge and understanding, there's still stigma, embarrassment and shame associated with masturbation. Yet all indications suggest it is a common sexual practice by males and females throughout life.

Why talk with children and teens about masturbation? While people may hold varied views on masturbation and it can be controversial, many people view masturbation as normal, natural, and morally acceptable. Children and teens are helped when adults are honest and forthright about sex. Ignorance isn't bliss; in fact, ignorance can be dangerous. Young people's well-being, safety, and happiness depend on being informed and knowledgeable. Masturbation is no exception.

Masturbation is part of human sexuality. Parents have opportunities in early childhood to affirm sexual feelings as normal, natural, and experienced by all people throughout life. They can help their child understand masturbation is usually done alone and in a private space. Calm parent attitudes convey important, fundamental messages about self-discovery and developing a positive sense of one's body.

None of the old beliefs turn out to be true. Masturbation doesn't cause blindness, craziness, sterility, homosexuality, hairy palms, or acne. It doesn't sap one's strength or stunt sexual development. Most experts seem to agree it doesn't cause physical or mental harm except in extremely rare cases when the behavior becomes an excessive compulsive aspect of a psychological disorder.

Leaving masturbation undiscussed leaves young people vulnerable to untruths. Young people deserve (a) honest, accurate information; and (b) safe opportunities to explore attitudes and learn about social, religious, and other people's views on the topic. Masturbation is not always discussed in school health classes, even though young people often ask questions, are concerned about it, and are interested. Many boys and girls begin to masturbate at very young ages, and many young people masturbate for pleasure during puberty. It is often the first way a person experiences sexual pleasure. Masturbation is a safe alternative to sexual intercourse. There is no risk pregnancy or infection. Masturbation can help release sexual tension and lessen sexual impulses. By talking with young people, we can help break the damaging cycle of embarrassment, anxiety, and shame that can otherwise lead to sexual dysfunction later in life. Young people deserve to know it's normal to masturbate and it's normal not to masturbate.

How to talk about masturbation? A few examples to consider include: (a) parents addressing young children might say, "I know it feels good to touch your private parts and it's best to do that in a private place, like your bedroom"; and (b) parents of older children might say, "Many persons touch or rub their penis or clitoris/vagina because it feels good and helps them relax."

OK. You're anxious and uncertain about this. First parents might find it helpful to do some reading. There are many excellent books available at the library and local bookstores to help families talk about masturbation and other sexual topics. The next steps for parents include working to be:

- age and developmentally appropriate
- warm, calm, caring, nonjudging
- matter of fact
- honest
- accurate
- willing to explain related values from your spiritual beliefs and
- cultural heritage
- open to seeking help and support to prepare if you could use it
- consult with a trusted professional (health care provider, sexuality educator, therapist, et al.).

Kathy Brothen, M.A., provides programming and training on adolescent sexual health, STDs, HIV/AIDS education, sexuality education curricula and "Parents As Sex Educators" to diverse groups of adults and youth in schools and correctional and chemical treatment facilities.

Grit (Margaret) Youngquist, M.A., works as a sexual health educator and trainer in a variety of settings, including public health, community clinics, faith communities, and several local universities.

Sexual self-stimulation occurs throughout life, but remains the most common expression of adolescent sexual behavior. During adulthood, masturbation is often viewed as merely a juvenile sexual behavior. We agree with researchers (Laumann et al. 1994) who challenge this with a position that masturbation occurs because of a variety of biological and social factors. Women and men from their early adult years (18–24 years of age) through middle adult years (54–59 years of age) are more likely to masturbate than are individuals in any other age group (Michael et al. 1994). Contrary to common assumptions, individuals who have regular sex partners, live with their sex partners, or are married masturbate more than those without sexual partners or who live alone (Michael et al.). Therefore, frequency of masturbation is not related to relationship status or simply a substitute for partnered sex.

Even though masturbation is the safest sex of all, many feel guilty about engaging in such a common, healthful means to self-pleasure. Fifty percent of males and females who masturbate report feeling afraid or shamed to admit they masturbate (Halpern et al. 2000).

Masturbation provides pleasure and fulfillment regardless of age. Sexual self-pleasuring benefits peoples' physical, emotional, sexual health, and relationships. We are hopeful American culture is moving attitudes about masturbation from stigma to sign of sexual health.

Behavior Among Youth

In a relatively brief span of time, American cultural tolerance toward premarital sexual activity increased dramatically. During this period, data from the General Social Survey found the support for complete tolerance of premarital sex (i.e., "sex before marriage is not wrong") increased from 27% in 1972 to 44% in 1996. At the same time, those who expressed unqualified intolerance (i.e., "sex before marriage is always wrong") decreased from 37% in 1972 to 24% in 1996 (Wattenberg 2003: 1). A similar survey conducted in 1998 by the *Washington Post*, The Kaiser Family Foundation, and Harvard University found that 55% of Americans found premarital sex acceptable, and 43% found premarital sex unacceptable (Kaiser Family Foundation 1998).

Although American adults may be more accepting of premarital sex in general, they appear to be less tolerant of such sexual behavior among youth. Teen sex continues to be considered "deviant" in American society. Interestingly, although adults in other developed countries encourage their teens to postpone initial sexual activity, the cultural attitude in those countries is that teen sexual activity is natural but must be approached with awareness and responsibility. Although the incidence of American teen sexual intercourse has declined in the last 10 years, a troubling fact remains that the rate still lags behind all other developed countries' teen sex rates (Alan Guttmacher Institute 2001).

Social sexual desires may first be felt to stir during puberty. Although this does not mean adolescents are emotionally ready to have sexual intercourse or other sexual contact, teens need assurance that their sexual tensions and desires are normal. Adolescent sexuality often resembles a roller coaster, with each day bringing new challenges physically, emotionally, psychologically, and socially. Adults who operate under the guise of "protecting teens by keeping them innocent and ignorant" may be well intentioned, but places teens at greater risk of unhealthy outcomes, including disease and pregnancy. Families have an important part to play in preparing their youngest members for these behavioral, social, and ethical transitions.

Families and family studies professionals need to know the facts about teen nonmarital sexual activity. The Youth Risk Behavior Survey (YRBS) serves as part of the Centers for

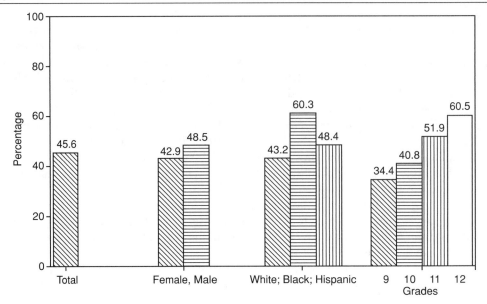

FIG. 6.4. Percentage of High School Students Who Ever Had Sexual Intercourse—United States, Youth Risk Survey, 2001.
Source: **Adapted from Grunbaum, Jo Anne, Laura Kann, Steven A. Kinchen, Barbara Williams, James G. Ross, Richard Lowry, and Lloyd Kolbe. 2001. "Youth Risk Behavior Surveillance—United States, 2001."** *Morbidity and Mortality Weekly Report* **51, (June, SS04): 1–64. www.cdc.gov/mmwr/ preview/mmwrhtml/ss5104a1.htm (Retrieved 1/23/2003).**

Disease Control and Prevention's Youth Risk Behavior Surveillance System, collecting self-reported data on health-risk behaviors among adolescents. This nationally representative survey monitors six categories of priority health-risk behaviors: tobacco use, alcohol and other drug use, unhealthy dietary behaviors, physical inactivity, behaviors contributing to unintentional injuries and violence, and sexual behaviors contributing to unintended pregnancy and or sexually transmitted diseases and infections including HIV. Experts report that these data indicate that risky teen sexual activity decreased by 16% from 1991 to 2001 (Brener et al. 2002).

Although these decreases are significant, teens continue to engage in a variety of sexual activity. Findings reveal that 60.5% of seniors, 51.9% of juniors, 40.8% of sophomores, and 34.4% of freshmen report having sexual intercourse at least once (Grunbaum et al. 2001). Please see Figure 6.4.

However, these studies only apply to youth who are attending a public or private high school. We know little about the sexual activity of the 5% of 16- to 17-year-olds who are not in school. These studies also fail to assess sexual activity, including oral sex, among middle-school-age adolescents (Grunbaum et al. 2001).

Risky sexual behaviors and corresponding risks for unintended pregnancy and contraction of sexually transmitted infections are declining (Centers for Disease Control and Prevention 2004). Politicians and other adults of every political stripe are scrambling to lay claim to this shift in teen sexual activity. The most sanguine agree that the explanation for such declines in risky teen sexual activity is multifaceted and likely includes both declines in teens having sex as well as significant increases in their use of effective contraceptives (Darroch and Singh 1999).

Although the rates of vaginal intercourse among older teens are dropping, the reported rise in middle-school- and high-school-age teens engaging in oral sex is of growing concern. Teens (and some adults) often view this noncoital sex as abstaining and believe that oral sex is considerably safer behavior than vaginal sex (Remez 2000). The increasing numbers of younger teens engaging in oral coital sex reflects ignorance or denial of the very real risks of transmitting and contracting disease through noncoital sex. Complicating an effective solution to the problem of protecting youth from risky sexual behaviors is not only teens' social construction of what exactly "having sex" means and from what exactly are adults asking teens to abstain.

Warnings about new trends in adolescent sexual behaviors are not new. Researchers began alerting parents to the new trend toward oral sex among young teens in the mid-1990s (Remez 2000). These warnings are too often drowned out by the noise over "no sex until marriage" programs that fail to discuss what is sex and how to safely meet sexual needs, desires, and urges.

Conjugal Behavior Over the Marital Life Cycle

Since the seminal Kinsey studies in the middle part of the 20th century, scholars have searched to better understand the association between marital sexuality and marital satisfaction. Certainly, sexually inactive marriages were viewed as less happy and satisfying than sexually active ones (Donnelly 1993). Other research indicates that married Americans are conservative in their sexual behaviors (Laumann et al. 1995).

- During the year proceeding the study, 80% had no or only one sexual partner
- Over a lifetime, the median number of partners were two for women and six for men
- Most (85% of women and 75% of men) claimed they have never had extramarital sex
- Cohabitating couples engaged in more sex than married couples, but the latter engaged in more sex than singles
- Married couples were more likely to orgasm during sex

The Janus Report (Janus and Janus 1993) and the *American Couples Study* (Blumstein and Schwartz 1983) indicate that couples who enjoy frequent sex report not only higher levels of sexual satisfaction but also higher levels of relationship contentment. Regarding frequency of sexual activity, Laumann and Michael (2000) found that 49% of men and 54% of women were comfortable in their monogamous relationships, even though they had sexual intercourse less than once per week.

Berry and Williams (1987) offer a developmental model of relationships over the marital life cycle. Their model reveals a drop in marital satisfaction with the arrival of children. There is a rebound of marital satisfaction as the children become adults and leave, which gives the couple time and financial freedom to rediscover each other. This marital satisfaction continues to rise into later years.

Myths taint the quality of sexual life in later life. One such belief is that elders are no longer interested in sexual activity. To the contrary, the majority of adults age 45 years and older report that a satisfactory sexual relationship is a highly important factor in their lives. Furthermore, the vast majority of these same adults found sexual activity pleasurable (American Association of Retired Persons 1999). Similarly a study of married couples aged 31 to 92 years of age reports that sexual activity remained an important part of long-term marriages and if factors interfered with sex, the participants adapted with variations (Hinchliff and Gott 2004).

Extramarital Behaviors

Unlike premarital sex, extramarital sexual activity, or infidelity, continues to be met with disapproval. During a period of widespread scandals over various forms of infidelity among public figures from clergy to a president, the General Social Survey found low tolerance for extramarital sex (sometimes referred to as adultery) over the entire 25-year period. In fact, full intolerance for extramarital sex ("sex with a person other than one's spouse is always wrong") increased from 70% in 1972 to 78% in 1996 (Wattenberg 2003: 1–2). The American Values Survey likewise revealed an 88% unacceptable level for extramarital sex.

At least in attitude, Americans are increasingly intolerant of adultery. Do their actions reflect such strong opinions? The response is "not exactly." Although men are as likely as women to say adultery is wrong, men are more likely to engage in it. Cole, Dickerson, and Smilgis (1994) found that almost one fourth (24%) of married men had engaged in adultery, whereas only one out of seven (14%) of married women had done so. The National Center for Health Statistics (segment of the Centers for Disease Control and Prevention) does not keep data on rates of infidelity, yet popular opinion polls claim an increase in infidelity among married women, thus closing the gender gap (Ali and Miller 2004). Although experts may question popular opinion, others do recognize a "new crisis in infidelity" exists (Glass 2003). Glass provides a research-based approach to understanding infidelity and why good people in loving marriages find their plutonic friendships stray into romantic relationships. Infidelity is not solely about having extramarital sex (sexual intercourse). Glass (2003) states that emotional attachments outside of committed relationships betray a relationship as much as sex. Women as well as men enter extramarital affairs for numerous reasons including needs for physical and emotional sexual intimacy.

Dysfunction, Disabilities, and Diseases

Origins of Sexual Problems. In recent years an increased understanding about the complex causes of sexual problems continues to unfold. Today experts recognize physical causes such as aging, disease, injury, or drug complications (Buvat et al. 1990; Richardson 1991), as well as psychological issues including prior learning, ignorance and avoidance, performance anxiety, and poor communication (Purcell 1985; Zilbergeld 1992) negatively impacting sexual response. Certainly, a measure of sexual dysfunction is owed to the stresses experienced from employment, parenting, and the complication of other social roles, all of which make for couples' lack of time together, as well as physical and emotional exhaustion. Morin and Rosenfeld (1998) argue that the "politics of exhaustion" take a significant toll on couples' sexual health. Granted this exhaustion appears in early-adulthood dual-career, childless couples; it becomes even more evident when children are added to the mix. This mix becomes increasingly complex when stepfamilies (formed through remarriage of those who are separated, divorced, or widowed) bring two or more families together.

Sexual Dysfunctions. The American Psychological Association (2000) describes *sexual dysfunctions* as a disturbance in desire, arousal, orgasm or resolution of human sexual response. Sexual dysfunctions (sexual performance concerns) are persistent or recurrent inabilities that interfere with reacting emotionally or physically to sexual stimulation in a manner expected of a healthy individual. Although sexual dysfunctions are complex, they appear to be more prevalent in women (43%) than in men (31%; Laumann, Paik, and Rosen 1999).

Sexual desire disorders include *hypoactive sexual desire disorder*, "a persistent or recurring deficiency or absence of sexual fantasies or thoughts, or a lack of interest in sex or being sexual frustrates couples. Often women suffering with this complaint will report they feel 'flat' sexually or sexually 'dead'" (Network for Excellence in Women's Sexual Health NEWSHE 2003: 1). Another desire disorder, *sexual aversion disorder*, includes feelings of disgust, fear, anxiety, or repulsion when thinking about or engaging in sexual intimacy.

Sexual arousal disorders in females include an inability to adequately lubricate or achieve vasoconstriction of external genitalia. In males *erectile dysfunction* (impotence) is the inability to attain or maintain erection during penetration. Recent studies (Bacon et al. 2003) state that modifiable wellness behaviors (e.g., regular physical activity, no smoking, healthful body weight, and reduced television watching) were associated with maintenance of good erectile function in men over 50 years of age. In addition to enhancing general wellness, several medications provide significant assistance to erectile function. In 1998, Viagra became one of the most popular treatments for erectile dysfunction. Whereas Viagra made significant impacts on males, it was less helpful for females suffering sexual arousal disorder. Recently two more treatments appeared, Levitra and Cialis. These block the PDE5 enzyme as does Viagra, but they offer a shorter wait time prior to sex.

Orgasmic disorders are related to dysfunctions in achieving orgasm. Females with orgasmic disorder do not experience orgasm after excitement phase or delayed orgasm. In male orgasmic disorder, erection, orgasm, and ejaculation are delayed or do not occur. Dysfunctions of this type include premature ejaculation (ejaculating before or too soon) and retarded ejaculation (failure to ejaculate after erection).

Some women suffer pain during sexual response. *Sexual pain disorders* include *vaginismus* (painful muscular spasms during intercourse), or *dyspareunia* (recurrent genital pain with sexual activity).

Disabilities and Sexual Expression. An inaccurate assumption is that those who are disabled somehow are also asexual or unable to enjoy sexually satisfying relationships (Chance 2002). The opposite of course is true. Desire, arousal, and orgasm can be achieved, but may require creative approaches. Those who are unable to execute genital orgasm can learn an alternative means to climax with (a) integration of memories and or fantasies, (b) stimulating a nongenital part of the body, and (c) enjoying mutual arousal with partner (Chance 2002). American culture will be richer when the nondisabled begin to see those who are disabled not only as capable of being sexual but also as honoring their expressions of sexual intimacy.

Sexually Transmitted Diseases. Sexually transmitted diseases and infections afflict women and men of all socioeconomic levels, racial and ethnic backgrounds, and sexual orientations. Currently, approximately two thirds of all sexually transmitted diseases occur in people under age 25. Families and their members need to be aware that many infected individuals, especially women, may be *asymptomatic* and the symptoms that do develop may be confused with those of other diseases. Left untreated, sexually transmitted diseases can cause pelvic inflammatory disease (PID), a serious infection of the fallopian tubes that if untreated can contribute to infertility. In men, untreated sexually transmitted diseases can result in epididymitis, an inflammation of the epididymis (ducts that transport sperm), and possible infertility. Please see Table 6.4 for more detail on sexually transmitted diseases.

Acquired Immunodeficiency Syndrome (AIDS) is caused by the human immunodeficiency virus (HIV). HIV infection is one of the most serious health concerns in the world today. At the close of 2003, it was estimated that 37.8 million people were living with AIDS (UNAIDS 2004). The Centers for Disease Control and Prevention estimate 850,000 to 950,000 Americans are living with AIDS, with 25% of these unaware they are infected (Fleming et al. 2002).

Women face greater risk of acquiring HIV due to considerable mucosal exposure to seminal fluids, a high rate of nonconsensual sex, and ignorance of the high-risk sexual behaviors of partners. According to the United Nations' annual report (Society for Women's Health Research 2003), 50% of new HIV cases were women with a disproportionate representation of females under 15 years old. The tripling of the rate of adolescent female infections is stunning.

Worldwide, heterosexual contact accounts for the transmission of over 90% of adolescent and adult HIV infections (National Institute of Allergy and Infectious Diseases 2004). Nonetheless, many HIV/AIDS prevention programs continue to assume that women are at a low risk. Organizations such as Women and HIV/AIDS argue that one of the primary keys to reducing the spread of HIV/AIDS lies in educating women to be assertive in sexual decision making, while providing accurate information and access to effective contraceptive and other strategies to inhibit the spread of the disease.

HIV is a formidable disease that demands that families and their members fully armed with the knowledge regarding how to prevent and recognize that this epidemic impacts all of us regardless of whether we are infected. The wisest approach for families and their members is to practice prevention by making careful choices regarding sexual activities, such as careful handling of all blood products and demanding strict new-needle use (e.g., tattooing, acupuncture, or body piecing), and providing comprehensive sexuality education to dispel myths and promote facts regarding HIV and AIDS.

The needs of individuals and their families living with HIV/AIDS include:

- medical information and treatment
- psychological and emotional support
- socioeconomic and, often, welfare assistance
- household help and, often eventually, orphan support
- human rights and legal access to care protection against violence and discrimination

Caregivers for family members, including extended family, fictive kin, and others, living with HIV/AIDS also require support, including recognition of the importance of their job, training, and incentives (Family Health International 2003). As a culture, we need to recognize and treat victims of HIV/AIDS and their families with the same dignity and empathy shown to those living with and caring for other chronic illnesses.

LEARNING SEXUAL INTIMACY

If only it was a simple matter of getting the facts. A nagging question of "who to believe" makes the task difficult as families try to decipher fact from fiction, all the while wading through a political and public policy swamp surrounding charged issues (e.g., sexuality education, including contraception and abortion). The importance of sexual wellness and

TABLE 6.4

Sexually Transmitted Diseases—Basics

Infection	Description/Treatment	Symptoms
Chlamydia	Chlamydia is a bacterial infection very commonly found in young adults and teens. About 75% of infected women and 50% of men have no symptoms of infection. If untreated, it can cause pelvic inflammatory disease and possible infertility in women. Treated with antibiotics	~25% of women with this infection do have symptoms that include unusual vaginal discharge, bleeding after intercourse, bleeding between menstrual cycles, abdominal or pelvic pain. ~50% of men with this infection do have symptoms that include discharge from penis, burning with urination, swollen or painful testicles
Gonorrhea	Gonorrhea is a bacterial infection that can lead to infection of cervix, rectum, urethra, and throat. ~80% of women and ~20% of men have no symptoms of infection. If untreated, it can cause pelvic inflammatory disease and possible infertility in women. Treated with antibiotics	~20% of women with this infection do have symptoms that include unusual vaginal discharge, burning during urination or increased frequency of urination, bleeding after intercourse, bleeding between menstrual cycles, abdominal or pelvic pain. ~80% of men with this infection do have symptoms that include discharge from penis, burning with urination, swollen or painful testicles
Syphilis	Bacterial infection with different stages. If left untreated may lead to very serious complications. Treated with antibiotics	Primary or early symptoms: small painless sore (chancre) in area of sexual contact. This disappears in 2–6 weeks. Secondary symptoms: a rash all over the body, swollen lymph nodes, fever, and tiredness. These symptoms may last a few weeks. Latent symptoms: none visible but bacteria may impact eyes, brain, heart, etc.
Hepatitis B	Serious liver disease caused by a Hepatitis B virus (HBV). Very infectious and transmitted with infected bodily fluids. ~80% of women and men have no symptoms with the infection No cure, but can prevent with a safe and effective vaccine	~20% of women and men with this infection do have symptoms that include flulike symptoms, jaundice (yellowing of the skin), fatigue, nausea or vomiting, fever and chills, dark urine, light stools, pain in the right side and back.
Hepatitis C	Hepatitis C viral (HCV) infection spread to contact with blood of infected individual. Can be transmitted through shared needles, IV drugs, sexual contact (vaginal, anal, oral) pregnancy, and birth. Treatments with interferon therapy or interferon and ribavirin therapy work in some but not all cases.	Most individuals infected with HCV have no symptoms. Those who do may experience fatigue, nausea or vomiting, fever and chills, dark urine, light stools, jaundice, and pain in right side and back.

(Continued)

TABLE 6.4

(Continued)

Infection	Description/Treatment	Symptoms
Genital herpes	A common and recurrent infection caused by the herpes simplex virus (HSV). HSV-1 also known as "cold sores." HSV-2 is called genital herpes and causes blisters on mouth, face, genitals, and around anus. An individual is infected for life. There are "latent" periods with no symptoms. ~80% of women and men have no symptoms of HSV-2 infection until initial outbreak. No cure. Some antiviral drugs and creams may reduce severity of outbreaks.	~20% of women and men infected with HSV-2 do experience flulike symptoms including fever, fatigue, headaches, muscle aches, and swollen glands. Actual outbreak of blisters last 3–7 days.
Human papillomavirus (genital warts)	Human papillomavirus (HPV) is a group of over 70 types of viruses that cause warts. Genital HPVs are sexually transmitted. Some strains of HPV are associated with cervical cancer. No cure. Once infected, individual carries virus for life. Development of a vaccine against HPV may be available soon. Treatments to remove warts include gels and creams, chemical treatments, cryotherapy, laser, electrosurgery, surgery, interferon (antiviral drug).	HPV may cause warts with many differing characteristics. They may be large or small, single or multiple, raised, or flat. At times they are very difficult to see and 50% of the time those infected with HPV do not have warts.
HIV	Human immunodeficiency virus (HIV) causes AIDS. HIV can be transmitted in infected blood, semen, vaginal secretions, and breast milk. Those infected with HIV may not know they are infected up to 10 years. No cure. Treatment of combined antiviral drugs as well as drugs to prevent opportunistic infections are used.	Individual infected with HIV may not have symptoms up to 10 years after initial contact. Once symptoms begin, they may include unexplained loss of weight, diarrhea for several weeks, white coating on tongue, enlarged or sore glands, persistent cough, fever, night sweats, and vaginal yeast infections.

(Continued)

TABLE 6.4

(Continued)

Infection	Description/Treatment	Symptoms
Other reproductive tract infections		
Trichomoniasis	Caused by microscopic organism. Can be sexually transmitted	In women symptoms include: unusual and increased vaginal discharge and odor, itching, burning or redness of vulva. In men symptoms include discharge from penis, burning with urination
Bacterial vaginosis	Bacterial vaginosis (BV) occurs when the normal balance of bacteria in the vagina changes and an overgrowth of some bacteria normally found in the vagina erupt. Studies indicate that a woman with bacterial vaginosis has an increased chance of having a variety of other reproductive tract problems. Therefore, diagnosis and treatment are important. BV occurs when some types of bacteria that are normally found in the vagina begin to grow in large numbers. It is unclear why this occurs, although some risk factors have been identified. BV is not transmitted during sex, but is associated with sexual activity. BV is treated with antibiotics and may involve the use of metronidazole tablets by mouth, or vaginal creams made from metronidazole or another antibiotic called clindamycin. This treatment can cause side effects such as mild nausea, vomiting, and metallic taste in the mouth.	Women may not have symptoms. When symptoms occur, they may include unusual vaginal discharge with an unpleasant odor, vaginal itching or irritation
Yeast infection	Vaginal yeast infection or candidiasis is caused by an overgrowth of fungal organisms normally found in the vagina in small numbers. Yeast infections are caused by an overgrowth of yeast that are often present in low numbers in the vagina. Pregnancy, antibiotics, and frequent exposure to semen over a short period of time can all lead to an overgrowth of these organisms. Treated with antifungal medications	Symptoms include vaginal itching and irritation, unusual vaginal discharge (often white and thick), vaginal pain during intercourse, burning sensation during intercourse.

Note: © 2004 Janet R. Grochowski.

related issues has not been lost on families, yet the need for families to become effective sexuality educators remains poorly met.

One area in particular, that of adolescent sexual health, demonstrates the contention over the what, when, how, and why of human sexuality education. Two approaches dominate this discussion. The *abstinence-plus* approach is comprehensive sexuality education that includes effective communications skills, encourages abstinence for teens, and presents effective contraceptive strategies for those who are sexuality active. The *abstinence-only* approach (abstinence-until marriage) limits its message to one should remain a chaste until marriage with little to no information on other sexual issues as discussed earlier. Although both sides firmly believe it is healthier for teens to postpone sexual activity until they are older, their approaches differ significantly.

According to the National Council of Juvenile and Family Court Judges report (2004), in a study of over 12,000 teenagers, 88% who pledged chastity reported having sexual intercourse before they married, plus rates of sexually transmitted diseases (chlamydia, gonorrhea, and trichomoniasis) were identical for teenagers who took the chastity pledges and for those who did not. Also, teens taking the chastity pledges were less likely to know they had an infection, and only 40% used a condom compared with 60% of those teens who had not pledged.

Increases in teen abstinence do account for one fourth of the decline in teen pregnancy, but the remaining three fourths are attributed "to changes in behaviors of sexually experienced teens" (Boonstra 2002: 4). The Society for Adolescent Medicine finds that "both delayed initiation of sexual intercourse and improved contraceptive practice contributed to declines in pregnancy rates among high-school-age teens during the 1990's" (Santelli et al. 2004: 87). In line with this recommendation, research on the effectiveness of only using "fear-based, abstinence-only-until-marriage" curriculum reveals poor results for teens (Sexuality Information and Education Council of the United States 2004).

Few would question the important roles that parents, peers, and schools play in creating sexually healthy environments. The content of the message and how that message is presented, however, burn at the heart of the debate. Families need accurate information regarding what, when, and how to discuss sexual health with their members. These discussions are not just reserved for parents and children. Sexuality and sexual intimacy are lifelong, and family members need to be able to help each other negotiate sexual transitions with accurate information, resources, and effective communication skills. The Annie E. Casey Foundation developed an effective skills-based program to assist families in learning how to talk together about sexuality and sexual intimacy (see Box 6.5).

BOX 6.5 *"Plain Talk About Teens, Sex and Communication"*
Debra Delgado

In 1994 the Annie E. Casey Foundation launched Plain Talk in five cities. The project was designed to reduce teen pregnancy; Sexually Transmitted Infections (STIs)/Sexually Transmitted Diseases (STDs), and Human Immunodeficiency Virus (HIV)/Acquired Immune Deficiency Syndrome (AIDS) by helping parents and caretakers improve their ability to talk openly and frankly with teens about the risks of unprotected sex. In the *Plain Talk* sites, residents conducted neighborhood surveys to determine the rates of teen sexual activity as well as to learn more about what young people wanted to hear from their parents. Across all sites, adults were surprised by three findings:

1. The high rates of teen sexual activity. At least 50% of the teens were sexually active by age 17.

2. Parents really matter. Teens reported that parents were important information resources for them. They wanted their parents to talk about relationships, intimacy and decision-making skills. However, teens also indicated that their parents seemed unsure about how to have the conversations and what to say.

3. Teens' access to contraceptive services was limited. The prevailing myth among adults was that teens could walk into any clinic at any time to get birth control methods. However, the surveys revealed that few if any clinical services were available to teens during evenings or weekends.

These data are consistent with other national surveys that attempt to get at the question: What can parents do to help teens reduce their risk for pregnancy, STIs/STDs and HIV/AIDS? For the *Plain Talk* sites, parents and other neighborhood stakeholders decided there was a lot they could do. They developed adult peer education courses to help parents become more comfortable in their role as sexuality educators. Recognizing that it's not enough just to "say no," the neighborhood groups also used Plain Talk survey data to form consensus about the messages that teens should hear. Finally, they worked together to ensure that young people had access to developmentally appropriate services. According to the evaluation conducted by Public/Private Ventures, a national social research firm, *Plain Talk* achieved significant outcomes.

- Adults reported an increased ability to engage children in a frank dialog about sex and teen sexual activity
- Teens reported knowing where they could go for services and information
- There was an increase in the availability and quality of reproductive health services
- Teen pregnancy and STIs/STDs were reduced by at least 50%.

Concurrent to the implementation of *Plain Talk*, the body of research about the positive outcomes associated with adolescent/adult communication has been growing. Recent literature reviews conducted by the University of California and the Joint Center for Political and Economic Studies revealed the following information. If a mother is generally responsive to her child, her teen will be:

- More likely to delay having sex.
- More likely to talk to partner about the need for contraception
- More likely to use condoms.

Furthermore, if a mother talks to her child specifically about sex and sexuality, her child (daughter) will be:

- Less likely to be sexually active
- More likely to use condoms if she does become sexually active
- Less likely to get pregnant

Talking Matters. The advice that teens give to parents includes:

- Don't act like you know it all.
- Don't preach one thing and do another.
- Don't jump to conclusions. I may just need information.
- Talk about when you grew up and what it was like for you.

Debra Delgado is a Senior Associate at the Annie E. Casey Foundation, a national philanthropic organization dedicated to improving child and youth outcomes by making neighborhoods a better, safer place for families.

Jorgensen (2001: 7), previous president of the National Council on Family Relations (NCFR), challenges family study professionals not to merely sit on the sidelines in the "a political tug-of-war between the 'conservative right' and 'liberal left'" over the question of which sexuality education approach is best.

Families, with or without children, flourish when family members engage in accurate and tactful conversations about sexual intimacy. Such discussions require not only knowledge and understanding but also skills and attitudes conducive to creating lifelong sexual intimacy. Sensuality, sexuality, and spirituality necessitate lifelong family conversations over one-big-talk about sex. These conversations flow from recognition of a sensuous, loving life.

GLOSSARY

Abstinence-only
Abstinence-plus
Abortifacients
Actual effectiveness
Asymptomatic
Autoeroticism
Celibacy
Circumcision
Clitoridectomy
Dyspareunia
Erectile dysfunction
Female genital mutilation or FGM (female genital cutting)
Genital infibulation
Hypoactive sexual desire disorder
Male climacteric
Masturbation
Menopause

Orgasmic Disorders
Outercourse
Postabortion syndrome
Prochoice
Prolife
Sensuous sexual experiences
Sexual abstinence
Sexual arousal disorders
Sexual aversion disorder
Sexual desire disorders
Sexual dysfunctions
Sexual pain disorders
Sexuality media literacy
Theoretical effectiveness
Unexpected pregnancy
Unintended pregnancy
Vaginismus

FOR YOUR CONSIDERATION

1. You are asked to be part of a community group organized to counter "unhealthy sexual messages" found in prime-time television and video games. Explain research findings regarding the impacts of media and technology that would be helpful for this group to know.

2. Based on the findings of Dailard (2003a), explain possible wellness and financial implications if Federal Medicaid services for contraception are cut to unmarried, single mothers? What do policymakers need to understand regarding information, access, and availability of contraceptive strategies for (a) single adults and (b) married adults?

3. Discuss two lessons from the comparison of European and American approaches to reducing unplanned pregnancy and birth rates.

4. Public health officials are alarmed about the increase in unprotected oral sex among middle-school-age teenagers. Why the increase? Why the alarm? What public health programs would be helpful in this area?

5. You have been asked to moderate a discussion between advocates of abstinence-only and advocates of abstinence-plus sexuality health education in your community's middle and secondary schools. What are the primary issues that both sides need to know? How would you attempt to get both sides to communicate? Would your approach change vary, depending on the type of community (rural, suburban, or urban)?

FOR FURTHER STUDY: WEB SITES, ORGANIZATIONS, PUBLICATIONS

Web Sites and Organizations

Alan Guttmacher Institute
www.guttmacher.org
The *Institute's* mission is "to protect the reproductive choices of all women and men in the United States and throughout the world" through information and services related to health, responsibility, relationships, reproduction, and family formation. This site provides information on abortion, law and public policy, pregnancy and birth, contraception, sexual behavior, and sexually transmitted disease and HIV/AIDS syndrome.

Centers for Disease Control and Prevention
www.cdc.gov
As the title implies, this site offers information on the current findings related to health, including sexual health. The site also provides reports by federal agencies and links to conferences.

Centers for Disease Control and Prevention: National AIDS Hotline
800.342.AIDS
This toll-free hotline administered by the *Centers for Disease Control and Prevention* offers accurate information 24 hours a day, seven days per week. Callers remain anonymous and can obtain referral information regarding clinics, hospitals, counseling, and testing sites.

Data Archive on Adolescent Pregnancy and Pregnancy Prevention
www.socio.com/dapcat.htm
This site provides social science data on the prevalence, antecedents, and consequences of teen sexual decision making and teen family planning.

Dr. Drew

www.drDrew.com

This popular site is aimed at youth and offers answers to frequently asked questions regarding sexual relationships and sexuality. Dr. Drew has become a media-cult figure over the past several years because of his candid, youth-friendly approach to sexual issues.

EngenderHealth

440 Ninth Avenue

New York, NY 10001

Telephone: 212-561-8000

Fax: 212-561-8067

e-mail: info@engenderhealth.org

Web Site: www.engenderhealth.com

Founded in 1943, *EngenderHealth* is an international, nonprofit organization that works to support and strengthen reproductive health services for women and men. This group provides technical assistance, training, and information to families, with a focus on practical solutions that improve services in sexuality education where resources are scarce. *EngenderHealth* states that individuals have the right to make informed decisions about their reproductive health and to receive care that meets their needs. This organization also works in partnership with governments, institutions, and health care professionals to make this right a reality.

Family Project

(130 West 42nd Street, Suite 350)

New York, NY 10036

212-819-9770

www.familiesaretalking.org

This project of the *Sexuality Information and Education Council of the United States* (SIECUS) provides materials to aid families in discussion of sexuality issues, including parent–child communication about sexuality and sexuality in media messages.

Go Ask Alice

www.goaskalice.columbia.edu

Individuals can use this site to ask professionals and peer educators questions regarding sexuality issues. This is a popular and trusted site, especially for young adults.

Kaiser Family Foundation

www.kff.org

The easy-to-navigate site provides materials related to sexual health issues from a variety of sources (e.g., entertainment media studies, information on HIV and AIDS, sexual health programs within Medicaid and Medicare, public education partnerships, and public opinion polls on reproductive health and sexual health issues).

Network for Excellence in Women's Sexual Health

www.newshe.com

This organization offers an extensive coverage of women's sexual health issues, problems, and disorders. It also links to other gender-specific sexual health resources.

Planned Parenthood Federation of America

www.plannedparenthood.org

Planned Parenthood Federation of America, Inc. is one of the world's largest and most trusted voluntary reproductive health care organizations. It was founded by Margaret Sanger in 1916 as America's first birth control clinic. The mission is to "provide comprehensive reproductive and complementary healthcare; advocate public policies [guaranteeing access to such services]; provide educational programs; promote research and the advancement of technologies in reproductive health care and encourage understanding of their inherent bioethical, behavioral, and social implications."

Population Reference Bureau

www.prb.org

The site sponsored by the *Population Reference Bureau* reviews research and policy regarding women's reproductive health. This site offers links to four focus areas including environment, HIV/AIDS, population trends, and reproductive health.

Sexuality Information and Education Council of the United States SIECUS

www.siecus.org

Established in 1964, SIECUS is a national, nonprofit organization that "affirms that sexuality is a natural and healthy part of living." This site has access to an extensive number of research findings related to sexuality.

Talking With Kids

www.talkingwithkids.org

Talking with Kids provides information on how to discuss tough topics such as sex, violence, HIV/AIDS, drugs, and alcohol with children.

The Kinsey Institute for Research in Sex, Gender, and Reproduction

The Kinsey Institute

Morrison 313

Indiana University

Bloomington, IN 47405

812-855-7686

www.indiana.edu/~kinsey

The Kinsey Institute is an established and respected institution conducting research and disseminating findings on premarital, marital, and extramarital sexual activity, homosexuality, prostitution, and most other areas of social behavior and attitudes.

REFERENCES FOR CITED WORKS

Alan Guttmacher Institute. 2000. *Fulfilling the Promise: Public Policy and U.S. Family Planning Clinics*. New York, NY: Alan Guttmacher Institute.

Alan Guttmacher Institute. 2001. "Teenage Sexual and Reproductive Behavior in Developed Countries: Can More Progress Be Made?" www.guttmacher.org/pubs/euroteens_summ.pdf (Retrieved 1/11/03).

Alan Guttmacher Institute. 2003. "Induced Abortion." *Facts In Brief*. www.agi-usa.org/pubs/fb_induced_abortion.html (Retrieved 12/17/04).

Abma, Joyce, A. Chandra, William Mosher, L. Peterson, and Linda Piccinino. 1997. "Fertility, Family Planning, and Women's Health: New Data from the 1995 National Survey of Family Growth." *Vital Health Statistics* 23, 19: 1–114.

Ali, Lorraine, and Lisa Miller. 2004. "The New Infidelity: Overworked and Underappreciated, More American Wives are Seeking Comfort in the Arms of Other Men." *Newsweek* (July 14): 46–52.

American Academy of Pediatrics. 1999. "New AAP Circumcision Policy Released." www.aap.org/advocacy/archives/marcircum.htm (Retrieved 10/10/04).

American Association of Retired Persons. 1999. "Sexual Survey." *Modern Maturity* (March). http://research.aarp.org/health/mmsexsurvey_1.html (Retrieved 1/23/04).

American Psychological Association. 2000. *Diagnostic and Statistical Manual of Mental Illness*, 4/e. Washington, DC: American Psychological Association.

Bacon, Constance, Murray Mittleman, Ichiro Kawachi, Edward Giovannucci, Dale Glasser, and Eric Rimm. 2003. "Sexual Function in Men Older Than 50 Years of Age: Results from the Health Professionals Follow-up Study." *Annals of Internal Medicine* 139 (August): 161–68.

Basson, Rosemary. 2000. "The Female Sexual Response: A Different Model." *Journal of Marital Therapy* 26: 51–65.

Berends, M. M., and S. L. Caron. 1994. "Children's Understanding and Knowledge of Conception and Birth: A Developmental Approach." *Journal of Sex Education and Therapy* 20, 1: 18–29.

Berry, R., and E. Williams. 1987. "Assessing the Relationship Between Quality of Life and Marital and Income Satisfaction: A Path Analytic Approach." *Journal of Marriage and the Family* 47: 107–16.

Blume, Libby B., and Thomas W. Blume. 2003. "Toward a Dialectical Model of Family Gender Discourse: Body, Identity, and Sexuality." *Journal of Marriage and Family* 65: 785–94.

Blumstein, Philip, and Pepper Schwartz. 1983. *American Couples*. New York, NY: Morrow.

Boonstra, Heather. 2002. "Teen Pregnancy: Trends and Lessons Learned." *Guttmacher Report on Public Policy* 2 (February). www.guttmacher.org/pubs/ib_1-02.html (Retrieved 1/4/04).

Boyle, Patrick. 2001. "Why Are Dutch Teens So Sexually Safe?" *Youth Work* (October): 1, 34, 36–37.

Brener, N., R. Lowry, L. Kann, Lloyd Kolbe, J. Lehnherr, R. Janssen, and H. Jaffe. 2002. "Trends in Sexual Risk Behaviors Among High School Students—United States, 1991–2001." *Morbidity and Mortality Weekly Report* 51, 38 (September 27): 856–59. www.cdc.gov/mmwr/preview/mmrhtml/ mm5138a2.htm (Retrieved 6/23/04).

Brown, Jane. 2001. *Sexual Teens, Sexual Media: Investigating Media's Influence on Adolescent Sexuality*. Mahwah, NJ: Lawrence Erlbaum Associates.

Buvat, J., M. Buvat-Herbaut, A. Lemaire, G. Marcolin, and R. Quittelier. 1990. "Recent Developments in the Clinical Assessment and Diagnosis of Erectile Dysfunction." *Annual Review of Sex Research* 1: 265–308.

Centers for Disease Control and Prevention. 1999. "Margaret Sanger." (December) 47: 1075. www.cdc.gov/ mmwr/preview/mmwrhtml/mm4847bx.htm (Retrieved March 9, 2003).

Centers for Disease Control and Prevention. 2004. "New Report Revises Birth and Fertility Rates for the 1990s Uses 2000 Census Population Estimates to Improve Accuracy" (August). www.cdc.gov/nchs/pressroom/ 03facts/revisesrates.htm (Retrieved 12/18/04).

Chance, R. 2002. "To Love and Be Loved: Sexuality and People With Physical Disabilities." *Journal of Psychology and Theology* 30, 3: 195–209.

Chang, Alice. 2003. "How Does This Article Relate to Me? ('Morning After Pill' [30 Years After *Roe s. Wade*])." *A Perspective from Harvard Medical School* (January 23). www.intelihealth.com/IH/ihtPrint/WSWOOD/ 23414/22002/360343.html (Retrieved 1/30/03).

Cole, Wendy, John F. Dickerson, and Martha Smilgis. 1994. "Now for the Truth About Americans and Sex: The First Comprehensive Survey Since Kinsey Smashes Some of Our Most Intimate Myths." *Time* (October 17): 62–70.

Dailard, Cynthia. 2003a. "The Cost of Contraception Insurance Coverage." *Guttmacher Report on Public Policy* 6, 1: 12–13.

Dailard, Cynthia. 2003b. "Marriage Is No Immunity From Problems With Planning Pregnancies." *The Alan Guttmacher Report on Public Policy* (May): 10–13.

Darroch Forest, Jacqueline, and Renee Samara. 1996. "Impact of Publicly Funded Contraceptive Service on Unintended Pregnancies and Implications for Medicaid Expenditures." *Family Planning Perspectives* 28 (September/October): 188–95.

Darroch, Jacqueline, and Susheela Singh. 1999. "Why Teenage Pregnancy Declining? The Roles of Abstinence, Sexual Activity and Contraceptive Use." www.agi-usa.org/pubs/or_teen_preg_decline.html (Retrieved 11/9/04).

Donnelly, Denise. 1993. "Sexually Inactive Marriages." *Journal of Sex Research* 30, 2: 171–79.

Ellis, Lisa. 2003. "Researchers: HRT Risks Outweigh Benefits." *Health Focus* (July 17). www.intelihealth. com/IH/ihtPrint/WSIHWOOD/9103/32191/352439/html (Retrieved 1/30/03).

EngenderHealth. 2004. "Sexuality and Sexual Health." New York, NY: EngenderHealth.

Family Health International. 2003. "Care and Support for HIV/AIDS: Building Capacity." *Family Health International Focus On*. www.fhi.org/en/aids/impact/briefs/caresupport.htm (Retrieved 2/2/2003).

Fleming, P. L., R. H. Byers, P. A. Sweeney, D. Daniels, J. M. Karon, and R. S. Janssen. 2002. "HIV Prevalence in the United States, 2000." Paper presented at the 9th Conference of the Retroviruses and Opportunistic Infections, Centers for Disease Control and Prevention, Atlanta, GA.

Food and Drug Administration. 1998. "Guidance for Industry-Uniform Comprehensive Labeling." (July 23). www.fda.gov/cdnh/ode/contralab.html (Retrieved February 5, 2004).

Gill, T. M., and A. R. Feinstein. 1994. "A Critical Appraisal of the Quality-of-Life Measurements." *Journal of the American Medical Association* 272, 8: 619–26.

Giorgianni, Salvatore, John Grana, and Sylvia Sewell. 2000. "Intimate Relationships: A Vital Component of Health." *The Pfizer Journal* 4, 4: 1–38.

Glass, Shirley P. 2003. *Not "Just Friends."* New York, NY: The Free Press.

Gregor, T. 1985. *Anxious Pleasures: The Sexual Lives of Amazonian People.* Chicago, IL: University of Chicago Press.

Grunbaum, Jo Anne, Laura Kann, Steven A. Kinchen, Barbara Williams, James G. Ross, Richard Lowry, and Lloyd Kolbe. 2001. "Youth Risk Behavior Surveillance—United States, 2001." *Morbidity and Mortality Weekly Report* 51, SS04): 1–64. www.cdc.gov/mmwr/preview/mmwrhtml/ss5104a1.htm (Retrieved 1/23/03).

Halpern, Carolyn Tucker, Richard J. Udry, Chirayath M. Suchindran, and Benjamin C. Campbell. 2000. "Adolescent Males' Willingness to Report Masturbation." *The Journal of Sex Research 37*, 4: 327–32.

Hao, Lingzin, and Andrew Cherlin. 2004. "Welfare Reform and Teenage Pregnancy, Childbirth, and School Dropout." *Journal of Marriage and Family* 66: 179–94.

Hatcher, R., J. Trussel, F. Stewart, W. Cates, G. K. Stewart, F. Guest, and D. Kowal. 1998. *Contraceptive Technology.* New York, NY: Ardent Media.

Henshaw, Stanley. 1998. "Unintended Pregnancy in the United States." *Family Planning Perspectives* 30, 1: 24–29, 46.

Hinchliff, Sharron, and Merryn Gott. 2004. "Intimacy, Commitment, and Adaptation: Sexual Relationships within Long-Term Marriages." *Journal of Social and Personal Relationships* 21, 5: 595–609.

Janus. S. S., and C.L. Janus. 1993. *The Janus Report on Sexual Behavior.* New York, NY: Wiley.

Jorgensen, Stephen. 2001. "Adolescent Sexual Risk-Taking and Pregnancy: NCFR and Public Policy Debate." *Report Linking Family Research, Education, and Practice* 46 (March): 1–24.

Kaiser Family Foundation. 1998. "Washington Post, Kaiser, Harvard Survey Project, American Values: 1998 National Survey of Americans on Values. www.kff.org/content/archive/1441/values.pdf (Retrieved 1/20/03).

Kaplan, Helen. 1974. *The New Sex Therapy.* New York, NY: Times Books.

Karraker, Meg Wilkes. 2000. "Making a Difference: Female Genital Mutilation." In *Social Problems for the Twenty-first Century*, ed. John J. Palen. New York, NY: McGraw-Hill 119.

Kinsey Institute. 2003. "The Kinsey Heterosexual-Homosexual Rating Scale." *The Kinsey Institute.* www.kinseyinstitute.org/resources/ak-hhscale.html (Retrieved 1/27/03).

Kowal, Amanda Kolburn, and Lynn Blinn-Pike. 2004. "Sibling Influences on Adolescents' Attitudes toward Safe Sex Practices." *Family Relations* 53 (July): 377–84.

Laumann, Edward, John Gagnon, Robert Michael, and Stuart Michaels. 1994. *The Social Organization of Sexuality: Sexual Practices in the United States.* Chicago, IL: University of Chicago Press.

Laumann, Edward O., John H. Gagnon, Robert T. Michael, and Stuart Michaels. 1995. *Sex in America: A Definitive Survey.* Boston, MA: Little, Brown.

Laumann, Edward O., and Robert R. Michael, eds. 2000. *Sex, Love, and Health in America: Private Choices and Public Policies.* Chicago, IL: University of Chicago Press.

Laumann, Edward O., Anthony Paik, and Raymond Rosen. 1999. "Sexual Dysfunction in the United States: Prevalence and Predictors." *Journal of American Medical Association* 281: 537–44.

Leiblum, Sandra. 2000. "Refining Female Sexual Response." *Contemporary Obstetrics and Gynecology 45* (November): 120–31.

Levathes, L. 1995. "Listening to RU-486." *Health* (January/February): 86–89.

Masters, William, and Virginia Johnson. 1966. *Human Sexual Response.* Boston, MA: Little, Brown.

Masters, William, and Virginia Johnson. 1976. *The Pleasure Bond.* New York, NY: Bantam.

Michael, Robert, John Gagnon, Edward Laumann, and Gina Kolata. 1994. *Sex In American: A Definitive Study*. Boston, MA: Little, Brown.

Morin, Richard, and Megan Rosenfeld. 1998. "The Politics of Fatigue." *Washington Post* (April 20): 6–7.

Moschovis, Peter. 2002. "When Cultures Are Wrong." *Medical Student Journal of the American Medical Association* 288, 9: 1131–32.

National Council of Juvenile and Family Court Judges. 2004. "Teen Pregnancy/Sexuality." http://training.ncjfcj.org/teen_pregnancy.htm (Retrieved 10/2/04).

National Institute of Allergy and Infectious Diseases. 2004. "HIV Infection in Women." Research On—National Institutes of Health (May). www.niaid.nih.gov/factsheets/womenhiv.htm (Retrieved 12/18/04).

Network for Excellence in Women's Sexual Health. 2003. "Hypoactive Sexual Desire Disorder." www.newshe.com/factsheets/Hypoactive_Sexual_Desire_Disorder.shtml (Retrieved 1/26/03).

Pew Research Center. 2003. "Most Americans Favor Abortion." *Pew Research Center for the People and the Press* (January). www.cbsnews.com/stories/2003/01/20/health/main537243.shtml (Retrieved 12/20/04).

Piccinino, Linda, and William Mosher. 1998. "Trends in Contraceptive Use in the United States: 1982–1995." *Family Planning Perspectives* 30, 1: 4–10, 46.

Purcell, S. 1985. "The Relationship between Religious Orthodoxy and Marital Sexual Functioning." Paper presented at the Second International Consultation on Erectile and Sexual Dysfunctions, Paris August.

Reiss, Ira. 1981. "Some Observations on Ideology and Sexuality in America." *Journal of Marriage and the Family* 43 (May): 271–83.

Remez, Lisa. 2000. "Oral Sex Among Adolescents: Is It Sex or Is It Abstinence?" *Family Planning Perspectives* 32 (November/December): 298–304.

Richardson, J. 1991. "Medical Causes of Sexual Dysfunction." *Medical Journal of Australia* 155: 29–33.

Rowan, Edward. 2000. *The Joy of Sex-Pleasuring*. New York: Prometheus Books.

Royal College of Obstetricians and Gynaecologists. 2003. "Female Genital Mutilation." *Royal College of Obstetricians and Gynaecologists Statement* (May): 1–6. www.rcog.org.uk/resources/Public/RCOG_Statement_No3.pdf (Retrieved 12/16/04).

Santelli, John, Joyce Abma, Stephanie Ventura, Laura Lindberg, Brian Morrow, John Anderson, Sheryl Lyss, and Brady Hamilton. 2004. "Can Changes in Sexual Behaviors among High School Students Explain the Decline in Teen Pregnancy Rates in the 1990s?" *Journal of Adolescent Health* 35: 80–90.

Sexuality Information and Education Council of the United States (SIECUS). 2001. "Teens Talk About TV, Sex, and Real Life." *Families Are Talking* 1, 2 (November): 1–4.

Sexual Information and Education Council of the United States. 2004. "SIECUS Reviews Fear-Based, Abstinence-Only-Until-Marriage Curriculum." www.siecus.org/reviews.html (Retrieved 10/3/04).

Singh, Susheela, and Jacqueline Darroch. 1999. "Trends in Sexual Activity Among Adolescent American Women: 1982–1995." *Family Planning Perspectives* 31, 5: 212–19.

Singh, Susheela, and Jaqueline E. Darroch. 2000. "Adolescent Pregnancy and Childbearing: Levels and Trends in Developed Countries." *Family Planning Perspectives* 32, 1: 14–23.

Society for Women's Health Research. 2003. "The Feminization of HIV." *Society for Women's Health Research Report* (January 24). www.intelihealth.com/IH/ihtPrint/WSIHWOOD/23414/22002/360369.html (Retrieved 1/30/03).

Trussell, James, Barbara Vaughan, and Joseph Stanford. 1999. "Are All Contraceptive Failures Unintended Pregnancies? Evidence from the 1995 National Survey of Family Growth." *Family Planning Perspectives* 31 (September/October): 246–47, 260.

Thayton, William. 2002. "A Theology of Spiritual Pleasure." *Sexuality Information and Education Council of the United States (SIECUS)* 30 (April–May): 27–30.

UNAIDS. 2004. *Report on the Global AIDS Epidemic*. New York, NY: United Nations. www.unaids.org/bangkok2004/report.html (Retrieved 12/17/04).

United States Bureau of the Census. 2003. "National Population Estimates—Characteristics." www.census.gov/popest/estimates.php (Retrieved 12/10/04).

Walen, S. R., and D. Roth. 1987. "A Cognitive Approach To Sex Therapy." In *Theories of Human Sexuality*, ed. J. H. Geer and W. T. O'Donohue. New York, NY: Plenum Press, 335–62.

Wattenberg, Ben. 2003. "Attitudes about Sex." *The First Measured Century*. Alexandria, VA: Public Broadcasting System. www.pbs.org/fmc/book/4family5.htm (Retrieved 1/23/04).

Webster's Ninth New Collegiate Dictionary. 1984. Spring Field, MA: Merriam-Webster.

Weill Cornell Medical College. 2003. "New Research May Lead to New Male Contraceptives and New Treatment Approaches to Sterility/Infertility." www.med.cornell.edu/news/press/july_28_contracept.html (Retrieved 1/24/03).

Wigoder, Geoffrey, Shalom M. Paul, Benedict T. Viviano, and Ephraim Stern. 1986. *Illustrated Dictionary & Concordance of the Bible*. Jerusalem, Israel: The Jerusalem Publishing House.

World Health Organization. 1998. *Female Genital Mutilation: An Overview*. Geneva: World Health Organization.

World Health Organization. 2000. *A Systematic Review of the Health Complications of Female Genital Mutilation Including Sequelae in Childbirth*. Geneva: World Health Organization.

Working Group for the Women's Health Initiative Investigations. 2002. "Risks and Benefits of Estrogen Plus Progestin in Healthy Postmenopausal Women." *Journal of American Medical Association* 288, 3 (July 17). http://jama.ama-assn.org/issues/V288n3/ffull/joc21036.html (Retrieved 1/30/03).

Zabin, Laurie Schwab. 1999. "Ambivalent Feelings About Parenthood May Lead to Inconsistent Contraceptive use—and Pregnancy." Family Planning Perspectives 31 (September/October): 1–3.

Zilbergeld, B., and C. R. Ellison. 1980. "Desire Discrepancies and Arousal Problems in Sex Therapy." In *Principles and Practice of Sex Therapy*. eds. S. R. Leiblum and L. A. Pervin. New York: Guilford, 65–101.

Zilbergeld, B. 1992. *The New Male Sexuality*. New York, NY: Bantam.

FORMING RELATIONSHIPS: DATING, COHABITATING, AND STAYING SINGLE

Jillian K. Berg collaborated in an early draft of this chapter. Her participation in this project was funded by a *Partnership-In-Learning Grant* from the Office of Faculty Development at the Unversity of St. Thomas.

CHAPTER PREVIEW

What are the individual, interpersonal, and social factors that draw people together for intimate, romantic relationships, including *marriage*? In this chapter, we examine what social scientists have traditionally called *courtship* in the context of *romantic attraction* and *mate selection*. Although social science has documented the importance of physical attractiveness, the *rating-dating complex*, and *propinquity*, considerable variation exists between the expectation that one's partner will be chosen by others, as in *arranged marriage*, and the possibility that one can freely choose a partner. However, even a free-choice system is constrained by social systems regarding the *pool of eligibles* and by norms of *endogamy* and *exogamy* (including *miscegenation*), resulting in more complicated, sometimes paradoxical, patterns of *homogamy* and *heterogamy*.

A system such as that which operates in the United States today—a system that constrains the selection of romantic partners—also reifies free-choice through the *romantic love ethic*. Such a system may be further reinforced through various myths about love and tensions among intimacy, passion, and commitment (i.e., the *triangle theory of love*), as well as expectations romantic partners will find in each other ways to meet *complementary needs*.

Through a recent historical overview of *dating*, we discuss the extent to which dating is shaped by gender differences, the influence of the *marriage premise* (*primariness*, *exclusivity*, and *permanence*) on the *intimacy and commitment spiral*, and various recreational dating processes. We consider what is known (but mostly unknown) about dating and mate selection among gays and lesbians as well.

Cohabitation is the focus of much recent research. This research provides us with better estimates of the frequency and variety of this option. Also we examine how cohabitation compares to marital commitment in terms of relationship dynamics and relationship outcomes.

This chapter concludes with a statistical profile of the *single option*, including race, sex, and other demographic influences (and the possibility of the previously married becoming *re-singled*). Because the population of those who are single includes *voluntary singles* and *involuntary singles* as well as *temporary singles* or *permanent singles*, we describe the pushes and pulls of being single. Finally, we discuss the social implications of being single.

ATTRACTION AND SELECTION

Bases of Romantic Attraction

Social science has yielded several generalizations that reveal the nature of the individual, interpersonal, and social factors that draw people together for intimate, romantic relationships, including *marriage*. *Romantic attraction* follows many of the same principles that guide other types of interpersonal attraction. First, although characteristics viewed as physically appealing vary widely from culture to culture, social psychological research provides compelling evidence that physical attractiveness is at the top of the list of desirable traits in a potential partner (Simpson and Gangestad 1992).

Second, interpersonal attraction of any type is more likely when the parties involved share common values and role expectations (Eshleman 2000). In sum, individuals are more likely to be attracted to and select one another as romantic partners when they have similar backgrounds, in which they learn similar values. Interaction with others like one's self promotes effective communication and less tension. Experiences resulting from such interaction are rewarding and satisfying. This in turn increases the probability that an individual will seek to continue the interaction and pursue the relationship.

Third, although any individual might desire to associate with the most attractive person in the social milieu, a *rating-dating complex* substantially shapes the probability of success in securing a match with such an attractive partner. In such a system, first described by Waller in 1937, the most desirable females are likely to be selected by the most desirable males. The least desirable males, for example, freshmen on a fraternity-dominated college campus, have little or no chance of securing a date with any female, especially if females are in scarcer supply.

Other factors, including *propinquity*, or proximity, have also been found to play a strong role in the selection of romantic partners. Although some question the significance of factors involving residential proximity in a highly mobile society (see, e.g., Eshleman 2000), proximity certainly facilitates contact with potential partners and likely represents a proxy for social characteristics such as socioeconomic status, religion, race and ethnicity, and even education.

Social Systems of Mate Selection

Considerable variation exists between the expectation one's partner will be chosen by others, as in *arranged marriage*, or the possibility that one can freely choose a partner. As described in Box 7.1, David Weinlick offers an alternative perspective on selecting a romantic partner, even a spouse. (At the time this book goes to print, David and Elizabeth will have been married for over five years and have had two children together.) However, even a free-choice system is constrained by social systems regarding the *pool of eligibles*, or those among whom one may legitimately select a romantic partner.

BOX 7.1 "Arranged Marriage, American Style—How My Friends Chose My Wife"
David Weinlick

In 1998, I was ready to make a commitment to marriage. As I said in the spot I ran on local cable television to advertise my search for a bride, I only needed a bride, so my friend Steve and I began a unique search for my potential mate. I would not choose my own bride—I would rely on the wisdom of friends and rely on them to find my partner for life. I would commit to making a relationship work and would devote my energies to making that union a joyous one, but I would rely on outside observers to decide whom I should choose.

In preparing for the big day, Steve and I contacted those who would interview candidates. On June 13, 1998, a group of about five dozen of my friends and family chose a 28-year-old pharmacy student from among 28 women who arrived that day. Shortly thereafter, with many of our friends and family members present, Elizabeth and I walked down the aisle. We had all the trappings of a traditional wedding, with a few exceptions. The "aisle" was in the *Mall of America*'s rotunda. Over

---

2,000 onlookers who were fascinated by our arrangement surrounded us. When the minister said to me "you may now kiss the bride," that kiss was our first.

Looking back, I had always found dating to be immensely enjoyable. I would go out on a few dates with someone, explore my attraction to her, and consider how to pursue our connection. More often than not we had fun together, yet it was often because we were both puffed up with anticipation and excitement . . . not necessarily because we were all that similar or grooved to the same ideas. This is what makes dating such a twisted endeavor in our society. We want the exhilaration of that first date, but much of that exhilaration comes from sublimated nervousness—we are often deliberating about how to make the best first impression. We all want the second date.

Elizabeth and I avoided the problems of those first dates because we never had to worry about whether or not we would have a second. We were already married. We had no reason to be shy about expressing ourselves, or worry about impressions, because we had already committed to exploring these surprises over the long course of our marriage. Once we made that early decision to be together, we eliminated much of the deliberation involved in dating. We didn't need to ask, "Is this the one for me?" nor "Will this relationship last?" We could focus on making the relationship magnificent.

Many relationships suffer because we expect the constant excitement found in those first dates. Eventually though, many relationships slump, when "it just doesn't have that spark it used to." Too many people confuse the giddy excitement of initial attraction with the heartfelt experience of loving another person and sharing a life together. One is "sparky," whereas the other is closer to the comfort of a warm blanket by a burning hearth—it is rich and enveloping—it comes not from hormone spikes or champagne bubbles, but from the committed wills of two individuals choosing to be happy together.

David Weinlick is a teacher and political activist in Minneapolis. He majored in psychology and religion at Moravian College and has studied anthropology and education at the University of Minnesota. He and Elizabeth have two children.

Endogamy refers to the social requirement that marital relationships be formed within specified groups. No society gives its members total freedom in selecting an intimate partner, and Americans have traditionally been endogamous with respect to race (and to a lesser extent ethnicity or national origin) and religion. On the other hand, *exogamy* refers to the social requirement that marital relationships be formed outside specified groups. Although the basis for excluding kin to whom one is related by blood or by marriage within two generations is often assumed to be based on concerns about undesirable genetic consequences for offspring, even societies that have no sense of the biological principles of genetics forbid relations among immediate kin. The likely reason for this is concern that marriage among kin removes the potential for useful economic or political alliances between families. Another factor may be the extent to which close-kin sexual relations make for more confusing status relations. (The humorous song *I'm My Own Grandma* comes to mind.)

Regardless of the reason, societies do not usually encourage and often actively discourage intermarriage. The last state law forbidding *miscegenation*—interracial marriage, that is, marriage between individuals of White-European and African-American descent—was not declared unconstitutional by the United States Supreme Court until 1967 in *Loving v. Virginia*.

Exogamy is influenced by such factors as size, diversity, and the sex ratio of the community from whom partners may be selected. A small group is likely to have a higher degree of exogamy, as in the case of Mormons living in Florida in the 20th century (Barlow 1977). Blau, Blum, and Schwartz (1982) found the more diverse a group, the more likely intermarriage or *heterogamy* is to occur. Today, interfaith marriages account for 30% of all marriages sanctioned by the Catholic Church, but interfaith marriages are highest in dioceses in which the number of Catholics is small relative to other religious groups. This explains why the rate of intermarriage in Brownsville, Texas, is 6%, whereas the rate of intermarriage in Burlington, Vermont, is 71%. (Davidson 1998).

These patterns of intermarriage also apply to immigrants to the United States. For example, Kulczycki and Lobo (2002) found the highest rates of marriage of Arab Americans to non-Arab-Americans were among Arab Americans who had only part Arab ancestry, who had been born in the United States, who had strong English-language ability, and who were highly educated.

To a great extent, marriage is an institution that functions to preserve race, as well as class, education, and other social distinctions (Rytina, Blum, and Schwartz 1988). Inequality is a force for *homogamy*, posing significant barriers for marriage across social barriers. In cases in which relationships do occur across race or other lines, the participants may need to use a variety of narrative (storytelling or account-making) strategies to affirm their racial identities while engaging in interracial relationships. Hill and Thomas (2000) found that to be the case among both Black and White women who date across race lines.

The Romantic Love Ethic

A system such as that which operates in the United States today—a system that constrains the selection of romantic partners—also reifies free-choice through the *romantic love ethic*. In 1997 greeting card publishers shipped $277 million worth of Valentine cards—more than any other type of greeting card except Christmas cards ("Love by the Numbers" 2001). According to a series of cross-cultural studies, idealistic, even impractical, passionate (in other words romantic) love may be universal, at least among college students (Hatfield and Rapson 1987; Sprecher et al. 1994).

The romantic love ethic includes at least four myths about love (Sprecher and Metts 1989). First, love is believed to occur spontaneously (i.e., "at first sight"). Second, only one "true love" exists in each lifetime for each individual. Third, love that is true is love without conflict. Finally, no barrier exists that love cannot overcome (i.e., "love conquers all").

Cobb, Larson, and Watson's (2003) analysis indicates the romantic love ethic constrains effective mate selection through nine attitudes:

1. The One and Only. There is a "one and only" right person in the world for me to marry.

2. The Perfect Partner. Until I find the perfect person to marry I should not get married.

3. The Perfect Self. Until I feel completely confident as a future spouse, I should not get married.

4. The Perfect Relationship. We must prove our relationship will work before getting married.

5. Try Harder. I can be happy with anyone I choose to marry, if I work hard enough.

6. Love is Enough. "Falling in love with someone is sufficient reason for me to marry that person."

7. Cohabitation. "If my future spouse and I live together before marriage, we will improve our chances of being happily married."

8. Opposites Complement. "I should choose someone to marry whose personal characteristics are the opposite of my own."

9. Choosing Should be Easy. Mate selection is easy and a matter of chance or accident.

Of course, how does one know when the perfect mate is present (or when the perfect mate might have been overlooked)? No one is perfect in every way and no one feels completely confident to become a spouse. Marriage success cannot be guaranteed, and a successful marriage requires two individuals that are willing to work at the relationship. Personal and interpersonal qualities, as well as love, should be prerequisites for marriage. Cohabitation neither ensures marital happiness nor protects against marital instability. Similarity in attitudes, beliefs, personality, and values is a better predictor of marital success than is difference in those areas. Mate selection requires activities, preparation, and thought to bring one closer to marriage.

The objection to the romantic love ethic is not that love is irrelevant to developing and maintaining authentic intimate relationships. Who in American society would marry someone she or he does not love? On the contrary, the objection is that the infatuation and idealization of romantic love set the stage for unhealthy dependency and mutually unrealistic expectations if that is the primary basis for selecting a partner.

Lasswell and Lobsenz (1980) have developed a typology that speaks to different varieties of love. Lasswell and Lobsenz's typology includes ludus (game-playing love in short-term recreational relationships), eros (romantic love based on powerful sexual attraction), mania (possessive love, including jealousy and an inability to think rationally), storge (love as comfortable intimacy between platonic friends), pragma (love based on practicality and rational assessment of the relationship), and agape (self-sacrifice and unconditional care for another).

Sternberg (1986) conceptualizes love as a dynamic tension among intimacy, passion, and commitment (Fig. 7.1). In this *triangle theory of love*, intimacy refers to feelings of closeness and being bonded to the other. Passion refers to a drive that leads to romance, physical attraction, and sexual involvement with another. Commitment refers to a decision that one loves and will remain with another in the long term.

A system of attraction and partner selection guided by the romantic love ethic is further reinforced through expectations that romantic partners will find in each other ways to meet *complementary needs*. Winch (1958) acknowledged couples make homogamous choices in mate selection, that is, on the basis of social characteristics. Beyond that, he hypothesized that men and women in a relatively free-choice society will choose romantic partners not on the extent to which others are psychologically similar, rather, on the extent to which they perceive the other's personality will complement their own basic needs.

Complementary needs theory is appealing to those who seek an individual explanation for why we select the partners we seek, but empirical support is slim for this theory or any theory based on biology, parental image, or other individual traits (Eshleman 2000). We are left with the conclusion that the choice of one's romantic partner is guided, to a large extent by social systems of selection, which are colored by the romantic love ethic and likely shaped by values and roles, needs, and systems of exchange (Murstein 1987).

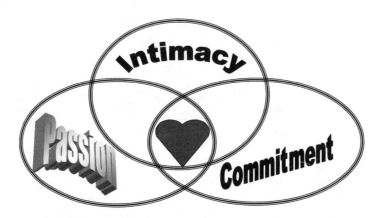

FIG. 7.1.   Interacting Components of Love.
Source: **Adapted from Sternberg, Robert. 1986. "A Triangle of Love."** *Psychology Review* **93.**

DATING

> By long practice courtship is a social term involving obligation, a kind of chain process which, once initiated, one is under social pressure to carry through to completion in marriage. (Lowrie 1951: 337)

Courtship then is the process by which the unmarried move toward creating a married life together. From personal ads to speed dating, the place of *dating* in courtship is increasingly characterized by freedom and lack of commitment or public obligation to future action (Lowrie 1951)—"dalliance and experimentation" in Waller's terminology (1937: 727).

Gender Differences in Dating

Dating nonetheless retains a highly gendered context. Before the 1900s, women held the central role in initiating and entertaining young men in whom they had a romantic interest. Men came "calling on" women, which meant the woman or her parents extended an invitation to the man. The encounter took place in the woman's sphere—the home, where the woman and her family provided refreshments and planned the entertainment.

By the mid-1910s, courtship—by then called dating—took on a new look for middle-class Americans. Courtship and the less formal, more recreational dating moved to public spaces. Men held the resources needed to pay for meals, recreation, and other activities. The man was responsible for inviting the woman, planning the activities, and funding the date. Of equal importance, men had considerably greater social freedom than did women. Respectable young ladies were not permitted to move about in public unescorted.

By the "roaring '20s" more relaxed sexual mores and the increasing availability of the personal automobile allowed couples more freedom and privacy to engage in more intimate courting activities. Still, the dating game has never been equal. Greater social freedom and economic resources gave men the opportunity to acquire control of the date, encumber obligation from the woman, and reinforce inequality within the relationship. In one way or another, one gender has had the upper hand in courting the other.

The more austere 1930s heralded an era when dating was less a thrill-seeking amusement than a clear step toward serious commitment. With the economic depression, couples were again seeking a life partner more than the sexual excitement of the previous decade. Elder found female children and adolescents growing up in the Great Depression developed role preferences consistent with "a lifestyle dependent on marriage and husband's career" (i.e., a woman's contingent life; Elder 1974: 202). The women in the Great Depression cohort preferred "companionship and affection" (286), coupled with the financial security of marriage.

For some young women, college was a place to find a possible mate and women's college attendance and degree completion increased into the 1940s. Of course, for many young Americans, college was not an option during the 1930s or even beyond.[1]

The 1950s, with a booming post-World War II economy, found adolescents freer to remain in school, rather than enter the labor force to contribute to the family income. Although dating still retained a strong element of mate selection, dating was becoming institutionalized as a more casual, recreational activity with one's same-age peers. This is reflected in dating practices among contemporary individuals, for whom dating involves spending time with multiple partners selected on the basis of personal interest at the moment. Identifying a possible future life partner is a much lower priority.

But are 21st-century dating and courtship rituals more egalitarian? Media images of changing women's roles give the illusion gender stereotypes are no longer relevant to courtship and mate selection. Today's women feel it is acceptable to ask a man out on a date and to pay for date activities (Korman 1983). Although McNamara and Grossman (1991) found college men were more likely to initiate dates than were women, men are increasingly willing to accept women doing the asking.

However, women still tend to be more traditional than men are in this aspect of dating. Research conducted primarily on college students indicates traditional gender roles still guide the process of dating (Laner and Ventrone 1998). The events that take place before, during, and after a first date are very much scripted by gender (Rose and Frieze 1989, 1993). Women spend more time preparing for the date, discussing the date before and after with friends, waiting for the man to arrive, flirting, and creating small talk. Women also report being the ones to mention the idea of a second date. Men, on the other hand, still plan the activities, clean the car, secure finances, pick up the women, open doors, pay the bill, and walk women to the door at the end of the evening (Laner and Ventrone 1998).

This gender segregation of dating roles, at least among college students at the end of the 20th century, indicates this aspect of courtship is still traditional and a long way from being egalitarian. Further, Elizabeth Marquardt (affiliated with the *Institute for American Values* and co-author of a report on the college dating scene prepared for the *Independent Women's Forum*, a conservative organization) reports some college women find the undefined nature of dating relationships, the expectation of casual sex, and the absence of the "implicit understanding that each party was shopping for a mate . . . bewildering and unfulfilling" (Fletcher 2001: E5). Dating remains a gendered experience, with men's and women's expectations differing and often poorly communicated, leaving many members of both genders feeling confused.

---

[1]By 1940, 3.7% of women 25 years of age or older had earned a bachelor's degree and women earned 41 percent of all bachelor's degrees awarded. By 1950 women earned only 24% of all bachelor's degrees awarded (United States Bureau of the Census 1976, 2001b).

The Intimacy and Commitment Spiral

Dating has become more recreational, even among the youngest, most casual couples. Dating still remains, in most forms, part of a process through which two people establish an identity as a couple to each other, to family and friends, and to society as a primary, exclusive pair with intentions for a permanent relationship. *Primariness* refers to the principle that the couple relationship takes precedence over other relationships (e.g., relationships defined by family of origin). *Exclusivity* refers to the code that a man and woman will be sexually intimate only with each other. *Permanence* refers to the commitment of the couple to work to continue their relationship.

Lamanna and Riedmann (2000) refer to these three features as the *marriage premise*. Traditionally, courtship involved a man pursuing a woman he intended to marry. Establishing regular rituals as a couple—kissing and other forms of physical intimacy, and uttering the words "I love you"—were symbolic steps leading to the engagement and marriage (Waller 1937). During this period a man and woman were considered by others to be "taken." No gentleman would court a woman while she was entertaining the attentions of another and a woman risked losing her respectability by encouraging the physical (or even emotional) attentions of multiple suitors.

Individual dating episodes in the 21st century are likely to be less oriented toward finding a life partner than in the past. However, contemporary dating continues to be guided by the *intimacy and commitment spiral*. According to this ideology, as a couple's level of psychic commitment increases from friendship to love, their level of sexual intimacy is also allowed—and may even be expected—to increase from physical restraint to sexual contact.

Contemporary Forms of Dating

On the surface, dating in the 21st century looks very different from dating in earlier eras. "Getting together," "hanging out," "hooking up," "going out," and "getting serious" may be followed by "getting dumped" or "breaking up." These new forms of dating (it is inaccurate to call them courtship because they so infrequently lead to engagement or marriage) have received remarkably little attention from family scholars, in spite of the rich symbolic content of each form.

Glenn and Marquardt (2001: 5) argue that the ambiguity in some of the vernacular surrounding dating today is part of the appeal.

> To say "we hooked up" could mean a couple kissed, or had sex, or had oral sex, but no one will know for sure. . . . Although premarital sex is much more acceptable now than in the past, women are still wary of getting a bad reputation. Saying "we hooked up" allows women to be vague about the nature of the physical encounter while stating that it happened.

Both females and males have equal rights when it comes to asking the other to join her or him and a group of people of both sexes who will be "getting together" and "hanging out." "Hanging out" allows contemplation of a more exclusive relationship, but in the company of a supportive group.

If "hanging out" allows for the initial "scoping out" of a possible future dating partner, then "hooking up" (whatever the precise meaning) may be more conducive to one-on-one exchange of more personal information. However, Glenn and Marquardt's (2001) research suggests the contrary. They studied the attitudes and values regarding sexuality, dating, courtship, and marriage through a diverse, albeit limited, sample of 62 college women on 11 campuses, supplemented by 20-minute telephone interviews with a nationally representative sample of 1,000 college women. They concluded, although practiced by a minority, such sex without commitment as "hooking up" is widespread, at least on college campuses, and may in fact preclude more intimate exploration of a possible relationship. Men still initiate this next—but still not exclusive—stage, which may or may not provide an opportunity to probe similarities and differences and test the depth of initial infatuation. Glenn and Marquardt's research also indicated "hanging out" is replacing dating, and mutual commitment is increasingly difficult to gauge.

As the couple's dating frequency increases and they find themselves "getting serious," they may introduce one another to family members and even attend family functions together as a couple. As commitment deepens, the couple may move toward engagement with the intention to marry or, increasingly, to cohabitation.

More frequently, one member of the couple finds herself or himself "getting dumped," often learning this first from others in her or his extended social circle. "Breaking up" signifies the end of the exclusive relationship and a return to availability. Remaining in or leaving a relationship represents a calculus of exchange based on rewards and costs, consideration of prior investments and future alternatives, evaluation of the match of the current relationship to an ideal relationship, and assessment of barriers to breaking up (Kurdek 1995; see chapter 2 on exchange theory).

BOX 7.2 "E-Dating"
Nadine Beth Wiernick

Dating is not fun. Actually, dating itself is lots of fun, but the steps to get there can be cumbersome to say the least. So, as singles try to simplify the process it seems tempting to have the first few dates without ever leaving the comfort of a desk chair. You order books, clothes, and groceries online, so why not order a date online as well?

A taboo still exists regarding meeting online. (I have yet to meet someone who admitted to it without cupping their mouths while whispering "we met online"), but e-dating has been gaining popularity among singles (and some marrieds) mainly because it makes the meeting process easier. You post your profile online (with or without a photo) and for a nominal sum (e.g., $25 a month) your inbox floods with e-mails from potential dates. Your first date is via e-mail or instant message and is not affected by the charming way he opens the door for you or by that repulsive noise her jaw makes when she chews. But it does not completely protect potential mates from the superficial. E-daters will break off a date for a reason like "he used too many exclamation points."

A certain leap of faith is required in e-dating, as you must take a person's word as true without using your other senses to back up your intuition. When a person is on an actual date and is told that their date graduated from Harvard with a degree in mathematics and then cannot calculate the tip, you know something is amiss. This lack of physical interaction opens the door for deception. If you cannot see the person you have no distinct way of knowing that the 26-year-old woman you have been speaking to via the Internet is not a 62-year-old male felon. E-dating can provide daytime talk shows with plenty of material. Given the risk of deception for relationships initiated over the Internet, e-dating can be dangerous and a serious measure of caution is warranted.

Those who have successfully met partners via the Internet recommend e-dating as a way to delay a face-to-face meeting until both parties have warmed to the idea and established some mutual interests. They also recommend it as a way to broaden their pool of potential partners beyond the immediate places where they live and work.

Nadine Beth Wiernick graduated from New York University with a degree in Communications. She currently lives in Philadelphia where she is the Lead Search Consultant for *On Time Professional Search*.

Dating Among Gays and Lesbians

We know remarkably little from empirical research on the dating and courtship patterns of gays and lesbians. From Savin-Williams and Diamond (2000) and Risman and Schwartz (1988), we know relationships are a main source of affection and companionship for gays and lesbians. Furthermore, steady relationships are as important to gays and lesbians as they are to heterosexual men and women. Finally, gays and lesbians report as high or higher levels of relationship satisfaction or adjustment as do heterosexual men and women.

Same-sex couples may have greater role flexibility and equality in their relationships than heterosexual couples (Risman and Schwartz 1988). However, gender influences even these relationships, as "lesbians resemble heterosexual women just as gay men are similar to heterosexual men" (Risman and Schwartz: 135). Generally, sexual activity is the more important aspect of a relationship to gay men, whereas emotional attachment is more important to lesbians. Gay men are more likely to have more one-time partners than are lesbians (Levine and Evans 1996).

COHABITATION

Trends in Cohabitation and Postponing Marriage

Living together outside the legal or religious sanctions of marriage—*cohabitation*—is not a new practice. In circumstances when civil authorities or clergy were not available, for example, on the Western frontier, men and women proceeded to set up households as husband and wife, even raising children together. They only formalized their bonds when the civil or religious opportunity presented itself.

As Waite, Goldscheider, and Witsberger (1986) argue, does cohabitation and other "nonfamily living [signal] the erosion of traditional family orientations among young adults?" Certainly, the last decades of the 20th century saw increases in American attitudes accepting cohabitation (Thornton and Young-DeMarco 2001), as well as the actual practice of living together outside of marriage. Unmarried couples make up only about 5% of American households at any given time. However, about half of couples who marry today live together first. Although these changes are dramatic—in the 1960s only 8% of first marriages were preceded by cohabitation—the most recent data indicate the rate of increase in cohabitation began to slow in the 1990s (Population Reference Bureau 2001).

Some speculate the rise in cohabitation is related to the erosion of norms regarding sexual relations outside of marriage and the wider availability of reliable birth control measures. Other signs point to increased uncertainty about the permanence of marriage.

Some pundits argue cohabitation is part of a larger symptom of increased individualism and secularism. Some research even suggests cohabitation significantly changes the perceived costs and benefits of marriage and therefore intentions and expectations to marry and even actual marriage (McGinnis 2003).

In the early part of this decade, Whitehead and Popenoe (2002: 2) of the *National Marriage Project* at Rutgers University presented findings which they believed indicated men are "'commitment phobic' and dragging their feet about marriage." They argued although young men wish eventually to marry and have children, they enjoy being single and feel little traditional pressure to marry from employers, religion, or society in general.

In Whitehead and Popenoe's (2002) study, men said they want to enjoy the single life as long as they can and they could get sex without marriage and could enjoy the benefits without the obligations of marriage. The men in their study also said they have not married because they have not yet found the perfect mate, they are not ready for the changes and compromises marriage requires, they want to wait until they are older to have children, and they want to avoid divorce.

More recently, Whitehead and Popenoe (2004) have fine-tuned their position. Based on a national sample of heterosexual men age 25 to 34, they conclude most men are "the marrying kind." The men most likely to plan to marry, seek marriage, and have favorable views of marriage, women, and children were also from traditional, religiously observant families. Still, they found two out of 10 men strongly expressed negative views of marriage, both as an option for themselves and in general.

Contrary to Whitehead and Popenoe's (2004) conclusions, the reasons men gave for not entering into marriage may signify that men are being more thoughtful today, rather than rushing into what they view as a life-changing, serious commitment. Bianchi and Casper's data, collected for the United States Bureau of the Census, indicated "young people are postponing, not rejecting matrimony" (Population Reference Bureau 2001: 2).

After all, of Americans 18 years of age and older, six out of 10 are married. That figure does not include those who are widowed or divorced and have not remarried. When those last two categories are added, over three fourths are or have been married (United States Bureau of the Census 2001). Marriage remains a popular choice for most Americans, although with the average age at first marriage around 27 for men and 25 for women, we are marrying later than at any other time in our history (Population Reference Bureau 2001).

Relationship Dynamics

Cohabiting couples are more likely than married couples to hold equalitarian ideals for relationships. Batalova and Cohen (2002), who have studied cohabitation in 22 countries, argue cohabitation may be part of greater social trends toward egalitarianism in gender roles. Still, although housework tasks are more equally shared in cohabiting relationships than in marriages, women still do more housework than men in both forms of relationships (Batalova and Cohen; South and Spitze 1994).

The persistence of these gender dynamics among otherwise nontraditional, that is, cohabiting, couples testifies to the persistence of gender as a powerful force shaping relationships. This is all the more surprising, considering that, more so than among married couples, among cohabiting couples the woman is more likely to be older than the man. Among cohabiting couples the woman is also more likely to have a higher education than the man. Finally, the earnings gap between the woman and the man is likely to be smaller among cohabiting couples (Population Reference Bureau 2001).

Relationship Outcomes

Research indicates couples cohabit for a variety of reasons. Relatively few individuals (Bianchi and Casper estimate about 10% [Population Reference Bureau 2001: 2]) view cohabitation as a substitute for marriage. Sassler (2004) interviewed 25 couples who had lived together for at least three months. Over half of the couples had moved in together within six months of their initial intimate relationship. The couples gave convenience, finances, and housing (but not trial marriage) as primary reasons to begin cohabitating. Plans to marry were abstract for these couples.

Still for couples such as Miller and Solot, founders of *The Marriage Alternative* (see Box 7.3), cohabitation represents a serious commitment and a permanent alternative to marriage. In fact, one fifth of those who cohabit do not expect to ever marry or to marry again (Bumpass, Sweet, and Cherlin 1991).

For some, cohabitation is a form of co-residential dating. Judging by the 40% for whom marriage follows within seven years, for many individuals cohabitation is a precursor to marriage—the last step in the dating and courtship process. Cohabitation and marriage have much in common: shared living space; emotional, psychological, and sexual intimacy; and economic interdependence. Nonetheless, cohabitation and marriage differ in important ways. Civil marriage is an intimate relationship in the context of values and roles that are defined and enforced formally and informally by society. Cohabitation has no such explicit normative consensus. Forste and Tanfer (1996) suggest cohabitation has more similarities to dating than to marriage in terms of sexual commitment, including sexual exclusivity. Furthermore, the regulation of economic, legal, or other social proprieties of cohabitation are highly variable.

Cohabitation is a more unstable union than marriage. A study of 11,000 women age 15 to 44 years of age revealed almost half of all cohabiting relationships end within five years. Only 20% of all marriages end within or after the first five years. After 10 years, almost two thirds of cohabiting relationships ended, compared to only one third of marriages (Centers for Disease Control and Prevention 2002a).

People who cohabit with one or more partners before marriage seem to experience more communication problems when they do marry. Cohan and Kleinbaum (2002) found couples who cohabit before marriage used more negative problem-solving and communication techniques and behaviors in their marriage relationship. Studies indicate individuals who cohabit believe in individual independence and may be therefore less committed to maintaining a commitment to a marriage. Finally, women who cohabit for long periods of time before marriage are at a higher risk of having their marriage dissolve than are women who do not cohabitate before marriage (Bennett, Blanc, and Bloom, 1988).

Some couples choose cohabitation before marriage to find out if they truly are compatible with each other. Living together before marriage is supposed to reveal each individual's undesirable habits and provide the couple the opportunity to "fix what needs fixing" or terminate the relationship altogether (Watson 1983). Cohabitation offers a couple opportunities to experience benefits of living in an intimate relationship without the commitment and difficulty in termination marriage entails. Because most studies on cohabiting couples have been done on college students—a population in the midst of multiple life-cycle transitions—final conclusions are difficult regarding the efficacy of cohabitation as a pretest for marriage.

Research does not support the validity of cohabitation as a way to ward off eventual divorce. Cohabitations, like marriages, tend to last longer under certain social structural conditions. Those conditions include a woman's older age at the time she enters the relationship. Her experience growing up in a two-parent family and the significance of religion in her life are also relevant. Finally, whether a woman lives in a community with high median family income, low male unemployment, and low poverty also affects the chances a cohabitating relationship will last over time (Centers for Disease Control and Prevention 2002a).

Popenoe and Whitehead (2002) of the *National Marriage Project* conclude from their review of research that cohabitation increases the risk of subsequent marital breakup, domestic violence for women, and the risk of physical and sexual abuse for children. However, a more cautious conclusion is those who cohabit are, as a population, more likely to be at less stable, more transitional stages of life and, therefore, are at higher risk, regardless of their living circumstances, than those who are married.

Cohabitation per se may not impact marital stability. Using data from the 1995 *National Survey of Family Growth*, Teachman (2003) asked women if they had cohabited with a man other than the man they eventually married. He found more than 82% of the women in the study had engaged in premarital sex and then cohabitation prior to marriage, suggesting this sequence has become a part of the track to a committed marriage. Teachman's research found women who engage in sexual intercourse and who cohabit before marriage only with their eventual husband have no higher rate of divorce than women who abstain prior to marriage.

BOX 7.3 "Happily Unmarried"
Dorian Solot and Marshall Miller

Have you and your significant other considered, or do you know others who are considering, cohabitation? Do you view cohabitation as an ideal method of testing or "checking out" an existing relationship? Do you view cohabitation as an ideal alternative to marriage?

Some reports indicate that more than a third of people have lived with unmarried partners by the time they are 24 and that a majority of people will live together (co-habit) before they marry. Yet unlike marriage, there's surprisingly little information available about how to cohabit successfully.

We've gathered all the advice we can find, from our own experience as an un-married couple and the conversations we've had with thousands of people in un-married relationships who contact us through our Web site and attend the lectures and workshops we give. If you're considering cohabitation, here are our top five recommendations to increase the chances your decision will be right for you.

1. *Go slow*. It's better to delay moving in together a little too long than to do it a little too soon. And it's easier to assess the relationship honestly, to make sure it's supportive and healthy, while you each have your own place to go home to. (Another bonus of taking it slow: It'll help your relationship's sexual spark last longer.)

2. *Talk about what it means*. Before you move in together, be very clear about what you each expect. Do you both definitely plan to marry? Does neither of you want to get hitched? Do you see cohabitation as a trial that will help you decide? An explicit conversation now can ensure you're on the same page, and prevent surprises and heartache later.

3. *Live together because things are going well, not to make things better*. Sharing a bedroom and kitchen will not magically transform an "I'll never get married" guy

into one who proposes on one knee. Sharing a kitchen and bedroom will not sweeten a volatile relationship. As psychologist Nancy Saunders recommends, "Don't move in together to check out [the relationship] . . . Move in together *after* you've checked it out."

4. *Put it in writing.* Consider writing and signing a "cohabitation agreement" to help clarify your expectations and define how you'll handle finances and property. The conversations you'll need to have in order to do this will strengthen your relationship—and protect you later if you decide it's best to go your separate ways. You can find samples to get you started in books and online.

5. *Celebrate the big day*! Newlycohabs (maybe someday it'll have the same ring as newlyweds) often don't get much attention, but living together is a rite of passage and a major step in a relationship. Do something special to celebrate the joys and challenges that lie ahead—even if it's just pizza by candlelight amidst the unpacked boxes.

Dorian Solot and *Marshall Miller* are the authors of *Unmarried to Each Other: The Essential Guide to Living Together as an Unmarried Couple* and co-founders of the *Alternatives to Marriage Project* (www.unmarried.org/).

THE SINGLE OPTION

The first waves of immigrants from Europe to North America were young and middle-aged men, followed by families and, only rarely, single women. Through the 19th century, men and especially women remained at home with their family until they married. Urbanization and industrialization led to more young men and women leaving their families and becoming involved in wage labor outside the home. The separation of spheres of home and work meant young adults moved to where the jobs in the factories were located, taking up residence in boarding houses which were filled with other young, single adults (DeFrain and Olson 1999).

The proportion of American households classified as families has declined sharply (from 85% in 1960 to 69% in 2000). Although not all singles live alone, the percentage of households with just one person has risen dramatically, doubling from 13% to 26% between 1960 and 2000 (Population Reference Bureau 2001).

A Statistical Profile of Singles

The *single option* includes not only those who have never been married but also those who are widowed and those who are divorced, some of which can be considered to be *re-singled*. Although the percentage of Americans who are divorced increased somewhat (and the percentages of Americans who are widowed decreased slightly) during the period, most of the increase in the percentage of those who are single is due to an increase in the percentage of those who have never married.

Statistics on the marital status of Hispanics closely parallel those for Whites. However, the changes in marital status are striking among Black Americans, for whom the percentage of those never married rose from about 30% to almost 40% during the last two decades. In particular, differences in the percentages of White women and Black women who are married are remarkable. In 2000, fewer than four out of 10 Black women were married, whereas six out of 10 White women were married (see Table 7.1).

TABLE 7.1

Marital Status of the Population by Sex, Race, and Hispanic Origin, 1980 to 2000, in Percentages

	Total		Men		Women	
	1980	*2000*	*1980*	*2000*	*1980*	*2000*
Marital status, total						
Married	65.5	59.5	68.4	61.5	63.0	57.6
Never married	20.3	23.9	23.8	27.0	17.1	21.1
Widowed	8.0	6.8	2.6	2.7	12.8	10.5
Divorced	6.2	9.8	5.2	8.8	7.1	10.8
Total	100.0	100.0	100.0	100.0	100.0	100.0
Marital status, White						
Married	67.2	62.0	70.0	63.5	64.7	60.2
Never married	18.9	21.4	22.5	24.9	15.7	18.1
Widowed	7.8	6.8	2.5	2.7	12.8	10.7
Divorced	6.0	9.8	5.0	8.8	6.8	10.7
Total	100.0	100.0	100.0	100.0	100.0	100.0
Marital status, Black						
Married	51.4	42.1	54.6	46.7	48.7	38.3
Never married	30.5	39.6	34.3	40.2	27.4	38.3
Widowed	9.8	7.1	4.2	2.8	14.3	10.5
Divorced	8.4	11.7	7.0	10.3	9.5	12.8
Total	100.0	100.0	100.0	100.0	100.0	100.0
Marital status, Hispanic						
Married	65.6	60.2	67.1	59.6	64.3	60.7
Never married	24.1	28.0	27.3	32.7	21.1	23.4
Widowed	4.4	4.2	1.6	1.9	7.1	6.5
Divorced	5.8	7.6	4.0	6.7	7.6	9.3
Total	100.0	100.0	100.0	100.0	100.0	100.0

Source: Adapted from U.S. Bureau of the Census, 2001a, *Statistical Abstracts, 2000*, Table No. 49.

Although some of these differences may reflect different attitudes among Black and White women toward living an independent lifestyle, the data also reflect the lower availability of Black men to marry.[2] Close (2003: 46–47) refers to this as "The Black Gender Gap" and writes:

> Black women are making historic strides on campuses and in the workplace. But professional progress is making them rethink old notions of race, class and romance.

Deborah Wright, who is a bank CEO and African American, acknowledges

> ... there are days when I walk out of a boardroom ... and think it would be nice to call somebody and say, "Baby, you're not going to believe what happened today. . . . [But] being single is not being alone. It would be great to be married and to find that perfect person. But I'm still a whole person one way or another." (Samuels 2003: 54, 55)

---

[2]Although the overall life expectancy for Americans is at a record high of 76.9 years, the life expectancy at birth for Black males is 68.2 years, compared to 74.8 for White males (Centers for Disease Control and Prevention 2002b). The lifetime chance of a Black man going to prison is 16.2%, compared to 9.4% for Hispanic men and just 2.5% for White men (Bureau of Justice Statistics 2002).

More men are never-married singles today than are women. The 2000 Census found 30,980,734 men have never been married, whereas 27,009,217 women have never been married (United States Bureau of the Census 2001a). This reflects the greater social pressures on women than on men to marry and have children (Shostak 1987), as well as the marriage gradient that constructs that a bride should marry a groom who is at least two years her senior.

Pushes and Pulls of Being Single

They enjoy the life of a single: change, freedom, and mobility, coupled with the opportunity to pursue education, employment, travel, and other lifestyle choices. They may be highly educated professionals with the income to support a pleasurable, independent quality of life. They may even be cohabiting, but they place a low priority on seeking a mate. These are the *voluntary singles*. Some are *stable singles* who have no plans to marry; they have chosen and are satisfied with their choice to remain single. Some are *temporary singles* who plan to marry someday, but are satisfied with their decision to remain single at the present time (Stein 1981).

However, not all singles are voluntary. *Involuntary singles* are those who would prefer to be married, are actively looking for a partner to marry, but for some reason have not found the right person (Stein, 1981). Involuntary singles may be temporary singles, as in the case of someone who would like to be married but find themselves at the moment in circumstances where marriage is not an option. Such would be the case for someone who is divorced or widowed, but wishes to be married. Involuntary singles may also be stable singles, as in the case of someone who might wish to marry but is forbidden to do so. Such is the case for clergy who wish to marry, but are required to abide by a vow of celibacy, and for those who are prohibited from marrying because of a developmental impairment.

Pushes are negative aspects of life that cause one to leave one lifestyle for another. An unhappy relationship or a feeling of being "stuck" or "trapped" in a life not wanted can push an individual from a married state into living single. Pulls are positive aspects that move one to change his or her lifestyle. The pulls or benefits of being single include privacy, independence, and freedom from responsibility; an exciting and changing lifestyle; meeting friends with different interests, varied sexual experiences (including cohabitation); and economic autonomy (Stein 1981).

Social Implications of Being Single

Single men and women may be the subject of prejudice and even discrimination. The stereotype of singles as immature and unsettled, selfish and maladjusted may impede their employment and other social opportunities. On the other hand, supervisors and fellow members of voluntary organizations may believe singles have no other commitments and can therefore devote more time than others to after-hours and overtime work tasks (Cejka 1993).

A legitimate, healthy, and happy life as a single person is possible. However, in general, being single seems to be more hazardous for men than being married. Single men have higher rates for mortality, alcoholism, suicide, and mental health problems in general (Coombs 1991; Rowe and Kahn 1997). Perhaps this is because they have more time and money to engage in riskier behaviors than do married men and are less likely to have someone who is concerned about their health. Also, single men are less likely than married men to have intimate contact with another human being on a daily basis. Single women, on the other hand, may face a harder time securing their person and their property, especially when moving about on their own. This does not, however, stop an increasing number of women from traveling alone.

The single option also tests the individual's ability to be economically independent. Because their greater combined incomes often place them in a higher tax bracket, two-earner married couples pay federal and often state taxes at a higher rate than do many singles. A proposal to eliminate most of the marriage penalty in the federal tax codes passed the United States Congress in 2000, but was vetoed by President Bill Clinton as compromising the budget surplus (Francis 2000).

However, consider the economies of scale that can be achieved by two people sharing food, housing, and other daily living costs. In the case of apartment rental—and even the feasibility of accruing sufficient funds to make a down payment on a house—and the purchase of durable consumer goods and even utilities, two can certainly live "as cheaply as one." The same judgments may also apply to recreational and more discretionary items as well. However, perhaps one of the greatest economic advantages of a dual-earning union is the safety net two incomes can provide for the inevitable, periodic downturns in the economy. When a single woman is layed off by her employer, she may have only her own savings on which to rely.

BOX 7.4   "The Growing Crop of 'Parasitic Singles' in Japan"
Meg Wilkes Karraker, Ph.D.

The number of employed young adults who continue to live in their parents' homes is on the rise in Japan. The Japanese Ministry of Health and Welfare estimated that 80% of employed women 20 to 29 years old and 70% of employed women 30 to 39 years old lived with their parents.

Although adult children remaining in or returning to the parental home is not new for Japan, the current trend seems to be linked to smaller family size. In the past, larger family size meant that second or third children would be more likely to leave the parental home. Also, postwar demands for labor drew many young workers to urban areas with high housing costs. Japanese men and women now marry at 28.6 and 26.7 years of age, respectively, and still conform to the custom of remaining in the parental home until marriage. Delayed marriage has further reduced fertility and, consequently, household size, thereby making a return to the parental home more feasible.

Yamada (1999) has written about "spoiled singles" and *parasaito shinguru no Jidai* (the age of parasite singles). Living in the parental home has clear economic advantages for the single adult. Takahashi and Voos (2000) report that most adult children do not pay rent or purchase durable consumer goods and some receive extra money from their parents. In addition, life can be more comfortable, as most of these singles rely on their parents to provide housekeeping and meal services. This arrangement enables singles to spend their money and their time on themselves.

Takahashi and Voos (2000) have analyzed the parents' motives as well. Takahashi and Voos argue that, compared to the extremely high cost of funding education, providing a household for the adult child is a relatively small expenditure. Parents may have altruistic motives, wanting to provide their children with the freedom to pursue a career without the constraints of housework. Parents may also be exchanging financial support for their adult child's companionship. (If such is the case, then as the child's income rises, so do the expectations for the amount of financial contribution of the parent.) Finally, parents may be investing in their children's ability to provide future assistance, financial and otherwise, to the parent.

The case of the "parasitic singles" is not limited to Japan. Advancing age at first marriage, plus the increasing instability of marriage, signals the end of marriage as the symbolic commencement of adulthood across cultures. The percentage of adults living in parental households is even greater in some societies (e.g., Italy). However, in those cultures, the phenomenon is unlikely to be viewed as a social problem unless the young adult is unemployed. In fact, *mammoni*—momma's boys—experience little stigma in Italy.

In the short run, the custom of adult children living with parents appears to have little effect on the consumption of durable goods. Takashi and Voos (2000) argue that downturns in the consumption of durable goods in Japan are more likely a reaction to general recessionary trends, including reductions in the demand for new hires by employers. Japanese singles who live with their parents may in fact be increasing the demand for certain other consumer goods and services. In the long run, however, the trend to live with parents is correlated with other demographic trends, such as the delay in age at first marriage and declining fertility rates, which will only reinforce the trend while changing the functions of the family and parent-child relationship.

REFERENCES

Takahashi, Hiroyuki, and Jeannette Voss. 2000. "'Parasite Singles'—A Uniquely Japanese Phenomenon?" *Japan Economic Institute Report,* No. 31A (August 11).

Yamado, Masahiro. 1999. *Parasaito Shinguru no Jidai.* Tokyo: Chikuma Shinsho.

GLOSSARY

Arranged marriage	Marriage premise
Cohabitation	Mate selection
Complementary needs	Miscegenation
Courtship	Permanence
Dating	Pool of eligibles
Endogamy	Primariness
Exclusivity	Propinquity
Exogamy	Rating-dating complex
Heterogamy	Re-singled
Homogamy	Romantic attraction
Intimacy and Commitment spiral	Romantic love ethic
Involuntary singles	Single option
Involuntary temporary singles	Stable singles
Involuntary stable singles	Temporary singles
Marriage	Triangle theory of love

Voluntary Singles   Voluntary stable singles

Voluntary temporary singles

FOR YOUR CONSIDERATION

1. Think of a couple you know who represent heterogamy, perhaps an interfaith or interracial couple or a pair who comes from a family of considerably higher socioeconomic status than the other. Can love really "conquer all" in such a relationship?

2. What changes in contemporary forms of dating—which are not only rapidly changing but are also highly variable by subculture—have your authors missed? What explains the development of these new forms?

3. Why does belief in the validity of cohabitation as a way to pretest marriage persist?

4. Under what social, economic, or cultural conditions might the proportion of never-married continue to rise? What effects do you predict this will have on economic, educational, political, religious, and other institutions?

FOR FURTHER STUDY: WEB SITES, ORGANIZATIONS, AND PUBLICATIONS

Alternatives to Marriage Project
www.unmarried.org/
This is a national nonprofit organization that advocates equality and fairness for unmarried people, including people who choose not to marry, cannot marry, or live together before marriage.

Interfaith Family
www.interfaithfamily.com/
This site provides resources on interfaith marriage between Jews and non-Jews.

Booth, Alan, and Ann C. Crouter. 2002. *Just Living Together: Implications of Cohabitation on Families, Children, and Social Policy*. Mahwah, NJ: Lawrence Erlbaum and Associates.
This chapter summarizes research on cohabitation: the historical and cross-cultural foundations, the role of cohabitation in North America, the impact cohabitation has on children, and current and future policies that affect cohabitating relationships.

Merkle, Erich R., and Rhonda A. Richardson. 2000. "Digital Dating and Virtual Relating: Conceptualizing Computer Mediated Romantic Relationships." *Family Relations* 49: 187–92.
Merkle and Richardson review Internet history and culture in the area of romantic interpersonal relationships.

Solot, Dorian, and Marshall Miller. 2002. *Unmarried to Each Other: The Essential Guide to Living Together as an Unmarried Couple*. New York, NY: Marlowe.
Solot and Miller are co-founders of the Alternatives to Marriage Project (and authors of one of the boxes in this chapter). Their guide provides legal, employment, and extended-family advice.

Steiers, Gretchen A. 2000. *From This Day Forward: Commitment, Marriage, and Family in Lesbian and Gay Relationships*. New York, NY: St. Martin's.
Steiers' book is based on interviews with 90 gay men and lesbians living in Massachusetts in the 1990s.

REFERENCES FOR CITED WORKS

Barlow, Brent A. 1977. "Notes on Mormon Interfaith Marriages." *The Family Coordinator* 26 (April): 148.

Batalova, Jeanne A., and Philip N. Cohen. 2002. "Premarital Cohabitation and Housework: Couples in Cross-National Perspective." *Journal of Marriage and the Family* 64 (August): 743–55.

Bennett, Neil G., Ann Klimas Blanc, and David E. Bloom. 1988. "Commitment and the Modern Union: Assessing the Link between Premarital Cohabitation and Subsequent Marital Stability." *American Sociological Review* 53, 1 (February): 127–38.

Blau, Peter M., Terry C. Blum, and Joseph E. Schwartz. 1982. "Heterogeneity and Intermarriage." *American Sociological Review* (February): 45–62.

Bumpass, Larry L., James A. Sweet, and Andrew Cherlin. 1991. "The Role of Cohabitation in Declining Rates of Marriage." *Journal of Marriage and Family* 53, 6 (November): 913–27.

Bureau of Justice Statistics. 2002. *Criminal Offenders Statistics.* http://www.ojp.usdoj.gov/bjs/crimoff.htm (Retrieved 9/18/02).

Cejka, M. A. 1993. "A Demon with No Name: Prejudice against Single Women." In *Single Women: Affirming Our Spiritual Journey*, eds. M. O'Briend and C. Christie. Westport, CT: Bergin and Garvey, 3–11.

Centers for Disease Control and Prevention. 2002a. *Cohabitation, Marriage, Divorce, and Remarriage in the United States: Data from the National Survey of Family Growth.* Vital and Health Statistics Series 23, No. 22 (July). Hyattsville, MD: Department of Health and Human Services, National Center for Health Statistics.

Centers for Disease Control and Prevention. 2002b. *Deaths: Final Data for 2000.* National Vital Statistics Report 50, 15 (September). Hyattsville, MD: Department of Health and Human Services, National Center for Health Statistics.

Close, Ellis. 2003. "The Black Gender Gap." *Newsweek* March 3: 46–51.

Cobb, Nathan P., Jeffry H. Larson, and Wendy L. Watson. 2003. "Development of the Attitudes About Romance and Mate Selection Scale." *Family Relations* 52, 3 (July): 222–31.

Cohan, Catherine L., and Stacey Kleinbaum. 2002. "Toward a Greater Understanding of the Cohabitation Effect: Premarital Cohabitation and Marital Communication." *Journal of Marriage and Family* 64, 1 (February): 180–92.

Coombs, R. H. 1991. "Marital Status and Personal Well-being: A Literature Review." *Family Relations* 40 (January): 97–102.

Davidson, James D. 1998. "Interfaith Marriage." Commonweal (September 11). http://www.findarticles.com/cf_dls/m1252/n15_v125/21148201/p1/article.jhtml (Retrieved 11/8/02).

DeFrain, John, and David H. Olson. 1999. "Contemporary Family Patterns and Relationships." In *Handbook of Marriage and the Family*, eds. Marvin B. Sussman, Suzanne K. Steinmetz, and Gary W. Peterson. New York, NY: Plenum, 309–26.

Elder, Glen H., Jr. 1974. *Children of the Great Depression: Social Change in Life Experience.* Chicago, IL: University of Chicago Press.

Eshleman, J. Ross. 2000. *The Family*, 9/e. Boston, MA: Allyn & Bacon.

Fletcher, Michael. 2001. "Survey: Lack of Courtship 'Rules' Confusing to Some College Women." *Star Tribune* (from the *Washington Post*) July 29: E5.

Forste, Renata, and Koray Tanfer. 1996. "Sexual Exclusivity Among Dating, Cohabitating, and Married Women." *Journal of Marriage and Family* 58: 33–47.

Francis, David R. 2000. "Will 'Marriage Penalty' Relief Be Left at the Altar?" *Christian Science Monitor* 6: 17.

Glenn, Norval, and Elizabeth Marquardt. 2001. *Hooking Up, Hanging Out, and Hoping for Mr. Right: College Women on Dating and Mating Today.* New York, NY: Institute for American Values.

Hatfield, E., and R. L. Rapson. 1987. "Passionate Love: New Directions in Research." In *Advances in Personal Relationships*, Vol. 1, eds. W. H. Jones and D. Perlman. Greenwich, CT: JAI, 109–37.

Hill, Miriam R., and Volker Thomas. 2000. "Strategies for Racial Identity Development: Narratives of Black and White Women in Interracial Partner Relationships." *Family Relations* 49, 2: 193–200.

Korman, Shelia. 1983. "Nontraditional Dating Behavior: Date-Initiation and Date-Expense-Sharing Among Feminists and Nonfeminists." *Family Relations* 32: 575–81.

Kulczycki, Andrezei, and Arun Peter Lobo. 2002. "Patterns, Determinants, and Implications of Intermarriage Among Arab Americans." *Journal of Marriage and the Family* 64, 1 (February): 202–10.

Kurdek, Lawrence A. 1995. "Assessing Multiple Determinants of Relationship Commitment in Cohabiting Gay, Cohabiting Lesbian, Dating Heterosexual, and Married Heterosexual Couples." *Family Relations* 44: 261–66.

Lamanna, Mary Ann, and Agnes Riedmann. 2000. *Marriages and Families: Making Choices in a Diverse Society*, 7/e. Belmont, CA: Wadsworth.

Laner, Mary Riege, and Nicole A. Ventrone. 1998. "Egalitarian Daters/Traditionalist Dates." *Journal of Family Issues:* 468–77.

Lasswell, M. E., and N. Lobsenz. 1980. *Stages of Loving.* Garden City, NJ: Doubleday.

Levine, Heidi, and Nancy J. Evans. 1996. "The Development of Gay, Lesbian, and Bisexual Identities." In *The Meaning of Difference*, ed. Karen E. Rosenblum and Toni-Michelle Travis. New York: McGraw Hill, 130–36.

"Love by the Numbers." 2001. *Star Tribune* (February 9): E1.

Lowrie, Samuel Harman. 1951. "Dating Theories and Student Responses." *American Sociological Review* 16, 3 (June): 334–40.

McGinnis, Sandra L. 2003. "Cohabitating, Dating, and the Perceived Costs of Marriage: A Model of Marriage Entry." *Journal of Marriage and the Family* 65, 1 (February): 106–16.

McNamara, J. R., and K. Grossman. 1991. "Initiation of Dates and Anxiety Among College Men and Women." *Psychological Reports* 69: 252–54.

Murstein, Bernard I. 1987. "A Clarification and Extension of the SVR Theory of Dyadic Pairing." *Journal of Marriage and the Family* 49 (November): 929–33.

Popenoe, David, and Barbara Dafoe Whitehead. 2002. "Should We Live Together? What Young Adults Need to Know about Cohabitation before Marriage. A Comprehensive Review of Recent Research, 2/e." National Marriage Project, http://marriage.rutgers.edu/SWLT2%20TEXT.htm (Retrieved 8/1/02).

Population Reference Bureau. 2001. "American Families." http://www.prb.org/pubs/population_bulletin/bu55-4/55_4_struct.html (Retrieved 3/4/01).

Risman, Barbara J., and Pepper Schwartz. 1988. "Sociological Research on Male and Female Homosexuality." *American Review of Sociology* 14: 125–47.

Rose, Suzanna, and Irene Hanson Frieze. 1989. "Young Singles' Scripts for a First Date." *Gender & Society* 3, 2 (June): 258–68.

Rose, S., and I. H. Frieze. 1993. "Young Singles' Contemporary Dating Scripts." *Sex Roles* 28: 499–509.

Rowe, J., and R. Kahn. 1997. *Successful Aging.* New York, NY: Pantheon.

Rytina, Steven, Terry C. Blum, and Joseph E. Schwartz. 1988. "Inequality and Intermarriage: A Paradox of Motive and Constraint." *Social Forces* 66 (March): 645–75.

Samuels, Allison. 2003. "Time to Tell It Like It Is." *Newsweek* (March 3): 52–55.

Sassler, Sharon. 2004. "The Process of Entering into Cohabiting Unions." *Journal of Marriage and the Family* 66, 2 (May): 491–505.

Savin-Williams, Rich C., and Lisa M. Diamond. 2000. "Sexual Identity Trajectories Among Sexual Minority Youths." *Archives of Sexual Behavior* 29, 6 (December): 607–27.

Shostak, Arthur B. 1987. "Singlehood." In *Handbook of Marriage and the Family*. New York, NY: Plenum, 355–67.

Simpson, J. A., and S. W. Gangestad. 1992. "Socio-sexuality and Romantic Partner Choice." *Journal of Personality* 60: 31–51.

South, Scott J., and Glenna Spitze. 1994. "Housework in Marital and Nonmarital Households." *American Sociological Review* 59, 3 (June): 327–47.

Sprecher, S., A. Aron, E. Hatfield, A. Cortese, E. Potapova, and A. Levitskaya. 1994. "Love American Style, Russian Style, and Japanese Style." *Personal Relationships* 1: 349–69.

Sprecher, S., and S. Metts. 1989. "Development of the *Romantic Beliefs Scale* and Examination of the Effects of Gender and Gender-Role Orientations." *Journal of Social and Personal Relationships* 6: 387–411.

Stein, Peter J. 1981. *Single Life: Unmarried Adults in Social Context.* New York, NY: St. Martin's.

Sternberg, R. J. 1986. "A Triangular Theory of Love." *Psychological Review* 93: 119–35.

Teachman, Jay. 2003. "Premarital Sex, Cohabitation, and Divorce: The Broken Link." *Journal of Marriage and the Family* 65, 2 (May): 444–55.

Thornton, Arland, and Linda Young-DeMarco. 2001. "Trends in Attitudes Toward Family Issues in The US: 1960s through 1990s." *Journal of Marriage and Family* 63, 4 (November): 1009–37.

United States Bureau of the Census. 1976. *Historical Statistics of the United States, Colonial Times to 1970, Part I.* Washington, DC: Government Printing Office.

United States Bureau of the Census. 2001a. "Marital Status of the Population by Sex, Race, and Hispanic Origin: 1980–2000." Table 49 in *Statistical Abstract of the United States, 2001.* Washington, DC: Government Printing Office.

United States Bureau of the Census. 2001b. "Years of School Completed by People 25 Years Old and Over, by Age and Sex: Selected Years 1940 to 2000." Table A-1. www.census.gov/population/socdemo/education/tableA-2.txt (Retrieved 7/29/02).

Waite, Linda J., Frances Kobrin Goldscheider, and Christina Witsberger. 1986. "Nonfamily Living and the Erosion of Traditional Family Orientations among Young Adults." *American Sociological Review* 51 (August): 541–54.

Waller, Willard. 1937. "The Rating and Dating Complex." *American Sociological Review* 2, 5 (October): 727–34.

Watson, Roy E. L. 1983. "Premarital Cohabitation vs. Traditional Courtship: Their Effects on Subsequent Marital Adjustment." *Family Relation* 32: 139–47.

Whitehead, Barbara Dafoe, and David Popenoe. 2002. *The State of Our Unions: The Social Health of Marriage in America, 2002.* http://marriage.rutgers.edu/Publications/SOOU/SOOU2002.pdf (Retrieved 8/01/02).

Whitehead, Barbara Dafoe, and David Popenoe. 2004. *The State of Our Unions: The Social Health of Marriage in America, 2002.* http://marriage.rutgers.edu/Publications/SOOU/SOOU2004.pdf (Retrieved 9/20/04).

Winch, Robert F. 1958. *Mate Selection.* New York, NY: Harper and Row.

CHAPTER

8

THE CONJUGAL COMMITMENT: MARRIED AND OTHER COMMITTED PARTNERSHIPS

CHAPTER PREVIEW

In modern societies, especially in American society, most weddings are preceded by an enormous amount of planning for the critical elements of the wedding day. Nonetheless, clergy and others involved in preparing couples for marriage often bemoan the fact that wedding planning takes far greater precedence than does marriage preparation. However, about four out of 10 couples who are marrying for the first time and who marry in a church, synagogue, or mosque have participated in *PREPARE* or some other form of premarital education. Such premarital education may lower the risk for later marital stress or marital dissolution and can slow a couple's progress toward the altar. Likewise, *prenuptial agreements*, which may complement the *community property* provisions of state laws, offer couples an opportunity to communicate about important issues in the marriage.

Americans are among the most marrying people on the planet, but the median age at first marriage crept steadily upward in the last half of the 20th century. Reflecting the important public functions of the family, laws about marriage have served civic, economic, and moral purposes. An exception to the tradition of reciprocity regarding state marriage laws is the *Defense of Marriage Act*. Religion—through *religious affiliation* and *religiosity*, and *spirituality* impact marriages and families in significant ways as well.

In assessing the quality of marital life, *marital satisfaction*, *marital happiness*, and *marital success* should not be confused with *marital stability* and *marital duration*. Marital quality is affected by communication patterns, which are the process through which a *sender encodes* a *message* and transmits it to a *receiver* who *decodes* the message, sometimes encountering *noise* along the way. Communication can be *nonverbal*, as well as verbal. Marital communication is effected by the different communication patterns of men, who are more likely to use *report talk*, and women, who are more likely to use *rapport talk*. In marital communication, the presence of the *four horsemen of the apocalypse—criticism, contempt, defensiveness*, and *stonewalling*—may signal the breakdown of the marital relationship. Happily married couples use a variety of tactics to avoid hostile communication, including *repair attempts* and *positive sentiment override*.

The *Marriage Encounter movement* and the *ENRICH* programs assist couples in strengthening their relationships. Recent government initiatives intended to encourage or support marriages may be well intended but may miss the point that some of the greatest stresses to marriage are not lack of commitment or personal problems but lack of tangible financial assistance.

In the final section of this chapter, we briefly address some approaches to enhancing the quality of marriage. We close with a call to replace *naïve familialism* with *critical familialism*.

BECOMING MARRIED

A Saturday in September would, ordinarily, be a very popular choice for a wedding day. However, in 2004, Saturday September 11 was avoided by couples who did not want the anniversary of their marriage to forever be associated with the date of the bombings of the World Trade Center and the Pentagon (Barbieri 2004).

Wedding and customs associated with marriage are among the most symbolically dense rituals in society associated with one of the most important rites of passage. The wedding and related events function to socialize the bride and groom into their new identities and roles as wife and husband, reducing uncertainty for the couple (and others) about the transition to marriage. For example, Kalmijn's (2004) research on couples marrying in the Netherlands found that couples who cohabit before marriage are more likely than are those who do not to forgo the church wedding, the large party, and the elaborate honeymoon.

"Extravagance is now the norm" in weddings, with the average cost of an American wedding rising to $22,360. This 47% increase since 1990 was at least in part supported by the booming economy in the 1990s. Also, the higher median age at marriage means couples can cover more of the cost of an opulent wedding themselves (Earnest 2002: E6).

Wedding practices vary considerably, even within Christian traditions. For example, Martyn (2001) has described the marriage ceremony for Eastern Rite Catholics[1] as organized around the Rite of Betrothal and the Crowning. The Rite of Betrothal occurs in the narthex of the church, before the couple approaches the altar. The priest officiates at this formal engagement of the wedding couple, shared by their parents and their attendants. In the Rite the priest references the Old Testament:

> Lord, our God, you betrothed the Church, a pure virgin called from among the nations; bless this betrothal, join together your servants, and keep them in peace and concord. (Galadza 1996: 27, as cited in Martyn 2001)

Finally, the Crowning, at which the bride and groom are actually crowned with myrtle wreaths (symbols of love, purity, and fertility) signifies the husband and wife are the king and queen of the universe created by God (Martyn).

Preparation for Marriage

Even with the enormous amount of planning and commitment of time, financial, and other resources that go into organizing a wedding, clergy and others involved in preparing couples for marriage often bemoan the fact wedding planning takes far greater precedence than does marriage preparation. Clearly, the decision to marry is no guarantee a couple will systematically consider how best to prepare for that relationship. Even cohabitation prior to marriage does not appear to offer effective preparation for marriage. In fact, as we saw in chapter 7, and contrary to popular belief, those who cohabit before marriage have higher, not lower, rates of marital dissolution than those who do not.

Today many high schools offer and some require courses in family life education. In the United States, the Catholic Church requires a couple planning to marry to complete a course of premarital study taught by trained married couples and approved by the diocese. Many Protestant denominations and other faith traditions also require or strongly recommend some sort of premarital counseling. According to Olson (2003), about four out of 10 couples who are marrying for the first time and who marry in a church, synagogue, or mosque have had some form of premarital education. The type of program varies widely, ranging from a brief meeting with clergy to small groups of couples attending retreats that may last over many weekends.

Olson (2003), who developed the widely used *PREPARE* program, believes that to be effective premarital programs need to provide couples with assessment and training in communication and problem-solving skills. Further, he believes, the program format should involve small group discussions by the couples themselves. Also, the program

---

[1] Eastern Rite Catholics share some traditions and rituals with the Eastern Orthodox Church.

should ideally begin a full year before the wedding and should last 6 to 8 weeks. Olson argues such programs should also instill in couples a long-term commitment for marital enrichment through the course of the marriage.

Scholars such as Olson (2003) argue the most effective premarital programs also involve some sort of premarital inventory. *PREPARE* is one such program currently offered by over 50,000 clergy and counselors and to date completed by over 1,500,000 engaged couples in the United States. Couples first complete a 165-item questionnaire, in which they gain insight into their areas of agreement and disagreement from six couple exercises. They also work to improve communication and conflict resolution skills.

But how effective are these programs? Participants in such programs are self-selected and therefore may be more amenable to the kind of personal and couple development offered through *PREPARE* and similar programs. However, Knutson and Olson (2002) compared *PREPARE* participants with a control group on a waiting list to participate in the program. The *PREPARE* participants reported higher couple satisfaction and also improved their communication and conflict resolution skills. The control group showed no such change. Other research (Cavedo and Guerney 1999) has found such programs can increase couples' empathy and self-disclosure skills and their positive feelings about their relationship, although these traits decline somewhat over time.

Marriage preparation programs may lower the risk for later marital stress or marital dissolution and can inform couples of options, should they find themselves in need of marital assistance at some time in the future. Furthermore, these programs can send an important institutional and societal message regarding the importance of marriage. Finally, and perhaps most importantly, these programs may slow couples' progress toward the altar, thus encouraging thoughtful deliberation of the marital commitment (Stanley 2001).

Prenuptial Agreements

Property settlements of the rich and famous whose marriages have ended in divorce provide titillating grist for the media mill. With the exception of the very wealthiest, most Americans who marry enter into marriage with no such formal agreement as to how assets are to be divided in the case of divorce. *Prenuptial agreements* run contrary to the romantic love ethic and the principle of marital permanency (see chapter 7). Furthermore, some elements of such an agreement, for example, the agreement not to have children, may be successfully challenged at a later date in court.

Most prenuptial agreements focus on the division of financial assets brought by the husband and wife into the marriage. These agreements may even supersede state inheritance laws, especially in the case of second or subsequent marriages and when there are children involved from prior unions. Most states provide that only *community property*, property acquired during a marriage, is subject to be equitably divided after a marriage ends in divorce. However, maintaining the separation between community property and property acquired by the husband or wife prior to the marriage may not be easy.

Should a couple consider entering into a prenuptial agreement? Although such agreements may not stand the test of legal challenge, communications about financial assets and debts, employment and children, residence and naming practices, and other aspects of the marital relationship are conversations best held prior to planning the wedding. Furthermore, the opportunity to periodically revisit the agreement at intervals during the marriage may help a couple to retain flexibility and openness in the face of changing circumstances along with personal and couple growth over the course of the relationship.

BOX 8.1 "Ketubah"
Judy Freeman

> *I am my beloved's and my beloved is mine . . .*
> *Two lives forever intertwined.*

Those words express the dream of every bride and groom who come to me to create their Ketubah. A Ketubah is a legitimate, signed, wedding contract in its original text and has never been updated. A 2,000-year-old tradition, the Ketubah is in fact one of the first documents created solely for the protection of the woman. In essence, the Ketubah was the prenuptial agreement of ancient times. Having made Ketubahs for over 26 years has allowed me a peek into the psyche of a man and woman before they are married.

Creating the Ketubah is very often a couple's initial experience of collaboration and cooperation with each other. Each Ketubah is a highly customized work of art that will hang in their home until "death do them part." However, both the bride and groom must work together to help make this treasure come to life. If the bride says "I like neutral colors," and the groom says, "I like a more primary palette," I know that compromise will have to happen between the two of them. I can always tell the strength of the couples upcoming commitment by watching this interaction. If, one of them is willing to back down and adapt to the others wishes, I can see that their marriage will be a success. Or on the other hand, if they cannot reach a common denominator, I envision their marriage may be a struggle.

One of my most interesting Ketubah was created for a Russian Jew who had lived in Israel and an Arab from Saudi Arabia. Watching them interact in creating their Ketubah was quite an enlightening experience, as their one common denominator was their deep love of family. They decided that as long as they both believed in this love, their religious and cultural differences would become secondary. Their Ketubah was an incredible three-dimensional collage of Russian, Arabic, Hebrew, and English. I knew this would be a marriage of compassion and love.

A couple celebrating a 60th wedding anniversary wanted a Ketubah to commemorate the occasion. She thought it should reflect only their hobbies and travels. He felt it should focus on children, grandchildren, and great-grandchildren. With compromise, their Ketubah had it all. As a beautiful work of art, it also became a symbolic family heirloom for generations to enjoy.

The beauty of give and take, of compromise and sensitivity can be found in couples creating their Ketubah. The final product is a treasured work of art that hangs in their home and reminds all that see it that this is a marriage to be coveted. For two people to be forever intertwined takes compromise. Just as the Ketubah is a beautiful reminder of tradition, family and love . . . it continues to live . . .

> *From generation to generation . . .*

Judy Freeman has been creating Ketubah for couples for over a quarter of a century. Selections of her work can be viewed at www.jewishart.org/freeman.

MARITAL QUALITY OVER THE FAMILY LIFE CYCLE

Although when, to whom, and how many times they marry has changed dramatically over the last century, Americans are among the most marrying people on earth. Of all persons 18 years of age and older,[2] slightly more than three-fourths are or have been married. According to the most recent census, 59.5% are presently married, 6.8% are widowed, and 9.8% are divorced (United States Bureau of the Census 2001b). By the time they reach 75 years of age, 95.9% of men and 96.5% of women have been married at least once (United States Bureau of the Census 2001a). In 1998, 2.3 million marriages were contracted in the United States. That averages 6,200 marriages per day.[3]

The median age of first marriage crept steadily upward in the last half of the 20th century, from 20 for women and 23 for men in 1956 to 25 for women and 27 for men in the late 1990s. Although men remain approximately two years older than the women they marry, the age gap between women and men has narrowed very slightly since the middle of the 20th century.

The later age at first marriage has several effects on young adulthood.

- Lengthening the time to settle into education, employment, and other adult roles and responsibilities
- Increasing the likelihood of cohabitation, returning to live with parents, and experimenting with other living arrangements before marriage
- Delaying entry into parenthood
- Increasing the likelihood of birth before marriage

The decision to marry is shaped by demographic, economic, and other social factors. For example, education, family, and work transitions are shaped by recessions, housing costs, and job markets, as well as by changing values about family life (Population Reference Bureau 2001).

For example, the pattern during the first part of the 20th century had been for the young to leave home at younger and younger ages, by the 1980s this trend had reversed. Fifty-seven percent of young men aged 18 to 24 were living in their parents' home in 2000 (about the same as in 1970), but the percentage of young women 18 to 24 living in their parents home increased from 39% in 1970 to 47% in 2000. This reflects the higher age at first marriage for men, but also a closing gap in differences between men and women (Population Reference Bureau 2001).

Today young adults leave home later, but are also more likely to return home again. By the 1980s, approximately 40% of young adults who had left home eventually returned to their parents' home. Those most likely to return are those who left the parental home to live with their partner outside of marriage. In the past, parents were reluctant to take young adults back into the parental home after they had left for the independence of education, employment, or the military. However, Goldscheider and Goldscheider (1998) argue, whereas leaving in the past for independence was likely a result of tension between the parent and the adult child, patterns of leaving and returning to the parental home are today less stigmatized and may be defined as part of normal transition to adulthood.

---

[2]This excludes members of the Armed Forces except those living off post or with their families on post.

[3]Of course, some couples, for example, gays and lesbians, who may wish to marry are not permitted to do so. Others seek in cohabitation or other arrangements an alternative to conventional marriage. See chapter 7 for a discussion of these issues.

Law, Religion, and Marriage

Marriage, the most private of institutions, has always served very important public functions, mediating between the state and the family. Throughout history, laws governing marriage have served civic, economic, and moral purposes. At a very primary level, marriage laws have determined those who are suitable marriage partners. Sometimes those laws institutionalized barriers between individuals who found they wanted to marry, such as forbidding interracial and same-sex unions. Laws about marriage also function to shape gender relations in roles in home and society (Cott 2000), as in the case of laws that have required women to share a domicile with their husbands or otherwise risk being sued for desertion.

With few exceptions, laws about marriage and family are state laws. Ordinarily, states extend reciprocity to couples who are legally married in another state. For example, even if a state does not permit marriage until the age of 18, that state would not prosecute a couple who had legally married in another state at a younger age. An exception to this reciprocity is the *Defense of Marriage Act*. This federal statute declares marriage is a "legal union of one man and one woman." Thus, the *Defense of Marriage Act* exempts any state from recognizing the marital status of two men, two women, or marriages of multiple partners, even if those marriages are legally accepted in another state. The *Defense of Marriage Act* was passed in 1996 when state legislators were concerned their state might have to recognize and extend legal benefits to marriages between two men or two women, as was proposed at the time by legislation pending (but later defeated) in Hawaii.

In 2000, Vermont became the first state to allow gay and lesbian couples to form civil unions that have the same rights and responsibilities as a marriage between a man and a woman. Same-sex households have certainly become more visible, accounting for nearly 600,000 households in nearly every county in the United States (Armas 2001). By the end of 2000, thirty-two states had passed legislation refusing to recognize marriages from other states by gay and lesbian couples. Hawaii did not pass the original legislation that would have legalized marriages between men and between women. However, both Hawaii and Vermont have passed domestic partnership laws, which extend some of the benefits enjoyed by married couples to same-sex couples who register with the state. These rights extend to joint property and joint tenancy, inheritance without a will, and hospital visitation and health care decisions in case one partner is seriously ill. The benefits do not, of course, extend to either federal benefits, such as the financial rights of survivors' under Social Security, or the right to American citizenship through marriage. The *Defense of Marriage Act* ensures no other state is required to recognize these benefits.

Same-sex unions have occurred throughout history and in a variety of cultural contexts (Halsall 1996). Yet, the limitation of marriage rights and benefits to heterosexual couples are contested. Those who support human rights also call for an end to discrimination on the basis of sexual orientation. The argument that the *Defense of Marriage Act* is a not so subtle veil for discrimination continues.

The opposition to the legal recognition of gay and lesbian marriages can partly be found in the implications such recognition would have for the state-funded health, pension, and other financial benefits that accrue to individuals who are legally married. However, the opposition is also deeply rooted in religious and other moral opposition to same-sex marriages.

Religion is a primary consideration in establishing an endogamous marriage. Most religions have had some sort of prohibition against members marrying outside the faith. Exceptions have often been accepted as in the case when the couple agrees to either unite in one faith or at least rear the children in the faith. However, even the Catholic church today permits marriages between Catholics and those of other faiths, although most of these unions are between Catholics and Protestants from traditional, mainline denominations.

Religion impacts marriage and families in other significant ways. A careful distinction among related terms—*religious affiliation*, *religiosity*, and *spirituality*—is necessary. Religious affiliation refers to one's nominal identification with a particular organized religion. For example, "I am a Baptist" or "I am a Muslim." Religiosity refers to the depth and breadth of one's religious devotion, faith, and practice.

Spirituality is a broader term. Spirituality may include religious identification and religiosity, but also refers to one's philosophy of life, sense of purpose, and reason for living. Spirituality may exist outside of structured religion and is considered by some to be essentially private. As discussed in chapter 5, the universal need to find balance and peace in life is at the heart of family spirituality. However, research on families recognizes the importance of spirituality in families' ability to make sense of the world and to cope with adversity. Stinnett and DeFrain (1985) identified "spirituality wellness" as one of the secrets to strong families. McCubbin, Thompson, and McCubbin (1996) identified family "spiritual health" as one of the key factors in family resiliency.

Some critics find American society to have a culture lacking substantial connection to religious values and practices. Over the last two decades, the percentage of Americans identifying themselves as members of mainstream Protestant denominations declined from 61% to 55%, whereas membership in other less mainstream sects grew. Still, only about 8% of Americans are not affiliated with any religion (United States Bureau of the Census 2000). Pointing to growing alienation from religion, these critics find the absence of religious ties in everything from the shootings at a Colorado high school to the increasing distance between the sacred meaning of certain religious observances and mass consumerism. However, dogmatic adherence to religious teachings, particularly those with an authoritarian tone, are found among some of America's most troubled families, including some in which children murder their parents and siblings in some sort of ultimate rebellion against totalitarian control in the family.

Active engagement and practices in religious organizations are also linked to certain attitudes and behaviors that may have positive outcomes in the family. Individuals with higher levels of religiosity tend to hold fewer permissive sexual attitudes (Thornton and Camburn 1989), have lower rates of cohabitation (Thornton, Axinn, and Hill 1992: 59), have lower rates of voluntary childlessness (Heaton, Jacobson, and Fu 1992), and more positive mother–child relationships (Pearce and Axinn 1998).

Individuals with higher levels of religiosity also report higher levels of marital commitment (Larson and Goltz 1989). Divorce rates are highest among those with no religious affiliation. However, divorce occurs even among those who belong to religions that forbid divorce, such as the Catholic church that considers marriage a sacrament. Still, those with religious affiliation may be more conventional in their lifestyles in general, but a religious community may also offer support for marriages.

The impact of religion on *marital stability*, the endurance of a marriage, may be found in the prevalence and strength of religion as a system of shared beliefs that can reinforce relationships and support couples during stressful times. Writing in the early 20th century, Durkheim (1915/1965) emphasized the importance of participation in rituals as a way to inculcate a sense of purpose and to cement bonds among societal members. The religious rituals surrounding baptism and marriage communicate family membership and purpose. Regular shared worship is one type of ritual that can also reinforce common values and priorities, while providing family members with reference groups that support certain choices.

At the same time, conventional religion can place demands on marriages and family, particularly in a society that emphasizes individualism, materialism, and secularism. Such is the case when conservative religious organizations expect their members to conform to traditional teachings on gender and sexual behavior when the media, peers, and others are sending contradictory messages. In some communities, immigrant groups who have religious teachings that support early marriage have run afoul of state laws regarding sexual contact between children and men. Likewise, parents whose religion teaches them that corporal punishment or female genital infibulation is consistent with religious teachings may be acting in opposition to state laws regarding child abuse and endangerment.

Marital Quality—Happiness and Satisfaction

From research conducted for the *National Marriage Project*, Whitehead and Popenoe (2001: 1) have concluded:

> Young adults today are searching for a deep emotional and spiritual connection with one person for life. At the same time, the bases for marriage as a religious, economic, or parental partnership are receding in importance.

Among "The Top Ten Myths of Marriage" (which he disputes with empirical research), Popenoe (2002) lists:

> Marriage benefits men much more than women. People can't be expected to stay in a marriage for a lifetime as they did in the past because we live so much longer today.

Marriage is correlated with a variety of beneficial effects. For example, two analysts at the Federal Reserve Bank of St. Louis found several recent studies support the conclusion that men with higher earnings potential are more likely than other men to get married and to stay married. Their review of the research did not explain why married men tend to make more money. Perhaps the need to provide for a wife and children provides men with an incentive to be more responsible and productive. They suggest attitudes associated with their earning productivity are attractive to mates, as well as to bosses (Chiodo and Owyang 2002).

For the near poor (i.e., those living below 150% of the poverty level), recent studies from the Urban Institute confirm that marriage has a positive impact on couples and their children. Married parents are materially better off than are parents who are single or who cohabit. The children of married parents are less likely to be poor, food insecure, read to infrequently, or have behavioral problems (*The Urban Institute* 2002).

The quality of marital life has been conceptualized variously as *marital satisfaction*, *marital happiness*, and more recently as *marital success*. Often measured on a Likert-type scale (e.g., "on a scale of 1 to 5, with one being the lowest and five being the highest . . . "), the concepts are used somewhat interchangeably. Marital satisfaction, marital happiness, and other indicators of marital quality are linked to such factors as duration of marriage (how long the marriage has lasted), but not always marital stability (the chance the relationship will end in divorce). Glenn's (1991) concept of marital success connotes marriages that are both stable, that is, have not ended in divorce, and are satisfactory or happy.

Marriage appears to be linked to overall happiness, more so than cohabitation, for both men and women, and in many countries. Stack and Eshleman (1998) believe this connection is due to two intervening processes: the promotion of financial satisfaction and the improvement of health. Some research has studied the connection between marital status and mental health. Generally, married people score higher on such indicators as friend and relative support, self-esteem, and mastery; but women, both married and never married, have higher distress levels than do men. (Cotton 1999; Marks and Lambert 1998).

However, sociologists have found marital satisfaction generally follows a U-shaped curve over the family life cycle. Marital happiness has been found to be highest in the earliest and latest years of marriage and lowest in the middle years (Cherlin 1996; Coltrane and Collins 2001; Gelles 1995; Glenn 1990; Spanier and Lewis 1980). However, most of this research has relied on cross-sectional samples, rather than on longitudinal studies of the same couples over a long period of time.

Recent research over a 17-year period using a five-wave panel study found no support for an upswing in marital happiness in the later years. Although that study did find a slight curvilinear relationship between marital happiness and *marital duration* (the length of time a marriage lasts), the steepest declines occurred in both the earliest and the latest years of marriage (VanLaningham, Johnson, and Amato 2001)

What then does cause changes in marital quality? Most researchers attempting to explain this decline focus on changes in family roles and structures. In early marriage, partners' roles are likely to be the most similar and undifferentiated, making sharing household labor, empathy, and negotiation easier.

The additional (and eventual departure) of children impacts the quality of conjugal interaction and increases parental stress as financial, time, and other resources are stretched (see White, Booth, and Edwards 1986.) Indeed, couples without children in the home report higher levels of marital quality than couples with children in the home (McLanahan and Adams 1989). Furthermore, marital quality has been found to increase as the children leave home (White and Edwards 1990).

The decline in marital quality over the course of a marriage is not solely linked to the presence of children. Other such changes in family roles include entry or exit from employment for wives and husbands (e.g., retirement), changes in home ownership, and changes in family income (increases as well as decreases). In general, increases in role responsibilities and demands are associated with lower marital quality.

Patterns of initial attraction generally decline after the "honeymoon" period of marriage. Declines in marital quality in the early years of marriage have been observed among couples both with and without children. These declines may be linked to social and psychological processes (Lindahl, Clements, and Markman 1998). In addition, modern marriages are encumbered with unrealistic expectations regarding married life, and couples face significant social psychological and individual challenges in the earliest years of marriage. Couples must adjust to kin, establish a division of labor, and determine the ways in which they will manage conflict. Further, individuals' attitudes and behaviors change throughout the life course, potentially contributing to a situation in which even a compatible couple find themselves less compatible over time.

Although marital quality is certainly related to intrinsic features of the marriage couple, marital quality is also susceptible to changes in the social circumstances surrounding marriages. VanLaningham, Johnson, and Amato's (2001) five-wave study also suggests a period effect, with marital happiness declining more in the 1980s than in the 1990s. Research found economic hardship, such as men's unemployment, to be linked to marital disharmony (e.g., Conger and Elder 1994; Voydanoff 1988) and the rise in the employment of mothers of young children to be associated with parental stress that may affect marital quality (Spain and Bianchi 1996).

Other period and cohort effects may be related to individualistic values in American society in general (Bellah et al. 1985; Glenn 1996) and the stresses in marriages related to changing gender roles (Amato and Booth 1995), including conflicts over women's employment roles and the division of household labor (Hochschild 1989). In fact, Amato and Booth have found wives with egalitarian attitudes may become less satisfied with their marriages, particularly if they perceive the division of labor in the household to be unfair (Lavee and Katz 2002).

Much can be made of the grim prognosis for marital quality from these studies. Still, some marriages (including your authors' and their parents') weather multiple decades of marriage. These long-lasting marriages sometimes endure in very trying circumstances, not just surviving but thriving and flourishing. Although older married couples may value the practical aspects of marriage more highly than do young married couples, Montgomery and Sorell (1997) found both companionship and passion are valued not only by the younger couples but also by the older couples. Furthermore, recent research indicates the happiness of marriages and the likelihood of divorce changed very little in the last two decades of the 20th century (Amato et al. 2003).

Three "ethics" may play a part in the stability of couples who endure through the inevitable conflicts and difficult times over the life of a marriage (Cummins 2002a).

1.   The marital endurance ethic: a fundamental commitment to outlasting any marital problems

2.   The marital work ethic: a value on marriage as valuable and worthy of care

3.   The personal happiness ethic: a willingness to find sources of happiness outside the marriage

In contrast to the widespread attention given to unmarried unions and divorce, we hasten to note that most people who form families marry, and of those who are married, the vast majority will not divorce; rather, they will see the death of one of the spouses. As the grave marker from Bath Abbey illustrates, marital bliss over the long run is not an unrealistic expectation. (One of the authors of this book has celebrated over 30 years of marriage; the other has celebrated 25.) Although marriages have always been faced with a tremendous array of stresses, conjugal commitment and satisfaction are both attainable, even over the span of decades.

The key to achieving a high level of marital quality lies in holding realistic expectations for marriage and an intimate life with another, the ability to develop resources for family resiliency, and a willingness to engage in effective, respectful communication with one's partner.

BOX 8.2   "Inscription From a Grave Marker in Bath Abbey"

Beneath this Pavement
Are deposited the Remains of
Henry, and Sarah Rosewell Archbould
Their Love was disinterested,
Their affection mutual,
and their Sensibilities equal. thus attached,
and thus bound in every tender Cord
which winds about the Heart,
their incessant Prayer was never to be separated;
most indulgent Heaven translated them
from this vale of wretcheness,
and, in kindness to their Prayer,
united them in the blissful Regions
of Eternity.

MARITAL COMMUNICATION

Communication is one of the key forces acting on marital satisfaction. When a couple is ineffective in communicating about issues and feelings, both inside and outside of their relationship, they are likely to have negative feelings about and be dissatisfied with their relationship. On the other hand, when a couple is effective in communicating about issues and feelings, even when they are faced with troubling issues inside or outside of their relationship, they are likely to have positive feelings about and be satisfied with their relationship.

Communication, whether between husbands and wives, between parents and children, between coworkers, or between friends, can be expressed in a simple model. In order to send a *message*, a person—the *sender*—must *encode* the message using words, gestures, or other symbols, and transmit the coded message through *noise* in the form of environmental and other distractions. The *receiver* must *decode* the message and consider how to respond in another message.

Principles of Intimate Communication

A blaring television, a crying child, or other noises in the physical environment may restrict a couple's ability to hear and see clearly. Situational factors, such as crowded living arrangements or prolonged absences such as those occurring during imprisonment, prolonged travel, or wartime can restrict a couple's intimate exchanges. Psychological barriers to communication include fears of embarrassment, rejection, and ridicule. Certain cultural differences can also provide noise, if the members of the couple come from different age, class, ethnic, racial, or other backgrounds from which they have learned different ways to communicate in relationships.

The bulk of a message is not verbal but *nonverbal communication* (Birdwhistell 1970). Nonverbal communication includes not only facial expressions and body language but also proxemics and touch (the uses of personal space and physical contact), paralanguage

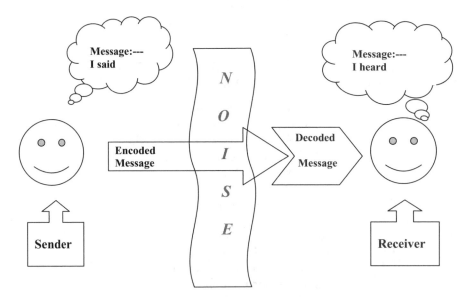

FIG. 8.1.   Model of Interpersonal Communication.

(nonverbal cues surrounding speech, such as pacing, pauses, and volume), and even artifacts (objects that communicate to others attitude, rank, and status); (Hughes, Kroehler, and Vander Zanden 2002).

Tannen (1990) has written about the different communication patterns of women and men in *You Just Don't Understand*. Tannen's observations of men's and women's conversational styles indicates men engage in *report talk*, whereas women engage in *rapport talk*. Men approach conversation as a way of collecting and sharing information, whereas women approach conversation as a way of sharing details and strengthening the relationship.

Communication Differences in Happy and Unhappy Marriages

Over three decades of research on marital communication has led to several conclusions. First, couples who are happy spend more time conversing than do unhappy couples (Kirchler 1988). Second, couples who are unhappy or distressed are more likely to miscommunicate with one another. They tend to express themselves in a hostile manner and to misinterpret affection, love, and other positive feelings (Gaelick, Bodenhausen, and Wyer 1985). Happy couples use more self-disclosure, humor, and laughter in their communications. Unhappy couples use more criticism, disagreement, and putdowns in their communication (Noller and Fitzpatrick 1990; Weiss and Heyman 1990).

Gottman (1994) has developed a technique that predicts in 90% of couples which couples will get divorced. Gottman videotapes couples interacting and watches for what he has termed the *four horsemen of the apocalypse* (because they are signs the end of the relationship is near):

1. *Criticism*: Beyond stating a complaint or expressing a dissatisfaction, this involves attacking a person's character or personality

2. *Contempt*: This involves eye rolling, hostile humor, name calling, mocking, or sarcasm to convey disgust or disrespect for the other person

3. *Defensiveness*: This involves blaming the other partner, while denying one has a role in an issue, often as a way to increase conflict and hurt the other partner

4. *Stonewalling*: By not responding and tuning out, one partner signals lack of interest and thus lack of concern for the other partner

The happily married couples in Gottman's (1994) study exhibited a variety of tactics that enabled even the most heated discussion to avoid erupting into a hostile exchange. These couples used what Gottman termed *repair attempts*, actions or other exchanges, that prevent negativity from escalating and may even deescalate tensions. These attempts may include efforts to inject humor into a stressful situation. A *positive sentiment override*, in which the favorable emotions shared by the partners far outweigh the unfavorable emotions, is critical to the success of any repair attempts. Likewise, couples who can remember happy memories from their life together, such as what attracted them to one another in the first place, are more likely to be able to weather the inevitable tensions and stresses of everyday life.

Like others who have studied marital discord, Gottman (1994) believed identifying the predictors of divorce in patterns of marital communication and interaction would enable him to "crack the code" to save marriages. He now believes the key to helping couples strengthen their marriages lies in helping them build on "the friendship that is at the heart of any marriage" (Gottman and Silver 1999: 46).

BOX 8.3 "Myrt, Forgot the Hamburger. Ern"
Sue Ann Schramm, M.A.

As newlyweds, my parents lived in Trinidad, Colorado, where my father worked as a mechanic at the Chevrolet garage. One bitterly cold night Dad was dispatched on an emergency call. He was gone for hours. A search party eventually located his truck in the river beneath a shattered guardrail.

My mother, near collapse from worry, was taken home. On the kitchen table she found a scrap of paper on which she had, early that morning, jotted a reminder to her husband to stop at the grocery. Below her note was scrawled, "Myrt, forgot the hamburger. Ern." Dad had managed to escape the truck, swim to shore, and walk home where he collapsed into bed!

That message illustrates perfectly my parents' communication style and both what does work and what does not work in contemporary marital communication. Dad said what was essential, and my mother provided the commentary. Following my mother's untimely death and with two young daughters still at home, Dad valiantly attempted to modify his communication style. He tried, but the gendered patterns of interaction were just too deeply ingrained in this loving but laconic man. He needed Mom's cheery prattle to complement his silence.

As a teenager, I was enthralled by the couples I saw on television. Those people really talked to each other. They seemed so romantic, and I was determined to create just that aura in my own home. Instead, I chose a husband who is a version of my father. Paul is a trial lawyer who speaks eloquently with clients, attorneys, and judges. However, when he enters his home his communication style closely resembles that of my father. Conversations with family members are likely to be monosyllabic responses on his part. This works very well for a teenage son (who considers parental silence a gift), but is not as satisfying for a spouse whose career and interests focus on interpersonal communication. Talk about a mismatch!

Fortunately, as a friend put it when describing her own husband, "He has other charms." For me, that seems key in determining the significance of communication in a relationship. Do actions truly speak louder than words? My parents would have answered in the affirmative. In this modern marriage, I confess to an occasional yearning for lingering discourse over a tantalizing topic, yet Paul and I have negotiated a special order.

Sue Ann Schramm earned her Master of Art degree in Communication Studies at the University of Minnesota. She is an adjunct professor at the University of Missouri-St. Louis and teaches high school English in St. Louis, Missouri. She lives with husband Paul and has a college-age son Jeremy.

ENHANCING THE QUALITY OF MARRIAGE

Unrealistic and romantic beliefs about marriage have been linked to the decline in marital happiness in the early years of marriage. Sharp and Ganong (2000) found family life education can lower adherence to romantic beliefs.

The Marriage Project conducted focus groups with couples in New Jersey and northern Virginia in order to determine how marriages "went bad" and then how the same couples turned their marriages around (Cummins 2002a). These couples reported problems similar to those of other couples reporting marital problems, including communication problems (discussed earlier). The research yielded two other interesting findings that suggest how easily marriages can face problems:

1.   Bad things happen to good spouses (clinical depression, job loss, and even ordinary stresses like wives feeling overwhelmed by caring for young children).

2.   Men behave badly (drinking, infidelity, and belittling and criticizing their wives).

The Marriage Encounter Movement

The *Marriage Encounter movement* began in the Catholic Church as a weekend experience for couples who wanted to strengthen their relationship through renewal of the marriage sacrament. Since this beginning in 1968, over one million couples from at least 10 other Christian denominations and the Jewish faith in 55 countries beyond the United States have participated in Marriage Encounter weekends.

Marriage Encounter and other marriage enrichment or enhancement programs are not therapy or intervention for couples whose marriages are in serious trouble, perhaps at risk of dissolution. Rather, these programs have been described as primary prevention or "seeking help before professional problems arise" (Shehan 2003). These programs bring married couples together, most often for a weekend away from children and distractions. In the company of other couples, and marriage professionals or other trained couples, these husbands and wives spend intense periods of time together engaging in guided discussion of key couple issues. Those who have participated in these programs report they are intense but valuable experiences.

ENRICH is one of the inventories that illuminates areas of couple strength and development. Olson has identified 15 areas of relationships, including communication and conflict resolution, that play a part in establishing a couple's satisfaction or dissatisfaction in marriage. One study (Olson 2003; Olson and Olson 2000) surveyed 21,501 American couples (some of whom were participants in a marriage-enrichment program and some of whom were participants in marriage counseling for a troubled marriage). They found, although the couples were similar in background characteristics (age, years of marriage, and number of children), the happily and unhappily married couples differed on six areas that predict marital happiness. For example, of those who were happily married, 91% had high couple agreement on the level of closeness in their marriage. Of those who were unhappily married, only 27% had couple agreement on the level of closeness in their marriage. Of those who were happily married, only 4% said they had considered divorce. Of those who were unhappily married, fully 97% said they had considered divorce.

Olson and Olson's (2000) ENRICH inventory discriminates between those who are happily married and those who are unhappily married. In general, happily married couples have good communication and conflict resolution skills, are flexible and close, and have compatible personalities.

Government Initiatives for Marriages

In 1998, the state of Florida passed *The Marriage Preparation and Preservation Act*. The following are the four key components of the *Act* (Ooms 1998):

1.   High school students are required to complete a course in marriage and family skills.

2.   Engaged couples are encouraged to take a premarital preparation course of at least 4 hours selected from a list of approved religious and secular courses.

3. Each couple applying for a marriage license is given a publication prepared by the Florida Bar Association informing them of their legal rights and responsibilities to each other and to their children, during the course of the marriage and afterwards in the event of divorce.

4. Each couple who files for divorce must complete a parent-education and family-stabilization course.

Several states have passed legislation favoring some form of premarital education. Some states, including Florida, Maryland, Minnesota, and Oklahoma, have even begun offering a discount on a marriage license to couples who complete a marriage education course. An informal survey from the Minnesota state legislature indicated almost one fourth (24%) of couples applying for a license in that state between June 2001 and July 2002 took advantage of the opportunity to receive a $50 discount on a $70 marriage license. However, in Florida, the first state to offer such an incentive has reported considerably fewer—only 3% to 5%—couples taking advantage of the discount (Cummins 2002b).

The Minnesota sample may have overrepresented those who took advantage of the discount for premarital education. (The survey was voluntary, and only about half of Minnesota's counties responded.) Counties that publicize the incentive seem to have considerably higher rates of couples taking advantage of the discount. One county in Minnesota (that of the sponsor of the legislation, Senator Steve Dille) reported 45% of couples took advantage of the discount. The appeal of such incentives may also be related to the availability of family life education; Minnesota has a long-standing tradition in that area (Cummins 2002b).

The National Marriage Project is an interdisciplinary program located at Rutgers, the State University of New Jersey, funded by that University and private foundations. The directors of the *Project*, David Popenoe and Barbara Dafoe Whitehead, have been at the forefront of a *marriage movement.* Drawing on scholars from a wide variety of fields, the mission of the *National Marriage Project* is:

> . . . to strengthen the institution of marriage by providing research and to provide analysis that informs public policy, educates the American public, and focuses attention on a problem of enormous scope and consequences. Simply stated, the problem is this: marriage is declining as an institution for childbearing and child rearing, with devastating consequences for millions of children. (The National Marriage Project 2002: 1)

Although the lower household income and higher poverty rates of families with an unmarried parent (usually the mother) is easy to document, the precise nature of the relationship between economic hardship and family structure is less sure. Indeed, a comprehensive analysis of research in the field conducted by a social historian and an economist indicates having one parent does not guarantee a child will live in poverty and having two married parents does not protect children from poverty (Coontz and Folbre 2002). Rather than being a cause of poverty, lack of marriage is more likely a symptom of poverty. That being the case, policies that artificially induce couples to marry or stay married for economic benefit may well subject the adults and their children to a host of negative consequences, including later divorce.

Funded by the Lilly Foundation through 2003, *The Religion, Culture, and Family Project* at the School of Divinity at the University of Chicago sought to approach the situation of contemporary American families from theological, legal, and cultural perspectives.

The *Religion, Culture, and Family Project* espoused an explicitly communitarian family policy,

> ...aspiring to balance the good of society with the good of families and their individual members. [The *Project* holds that] the well being of families, individual family members, and society is best guaranteed when the health of each is promoted equally. (Browning 1998: 1)

BOX 8.4 "Conjugal Love in the Bible"
Bernard V. Brady, Ph.D.

As a fundamental experience of human life, love has an important place in the Bible. Love in the Old Testament/Hebrew Scriptures has two forms: God's love and human loves. The Hebrew word often used to describe God's love is *hesed*. *Hesed* is usually translated as loving kindness or steadfast love. The book of Hosea portrays God's *hesed* in a dramatic and passionate moment as God refuses to punish his sinful, wayward people.

> I led them with cords of human kindness, with bands of love. I was to them like those who lift infants to their cheeks. I bent down to them and fed them. (Hosea 11: 4)

In this way God's *hesed* is the model for human love, as we see in Ruth's relationship to her mother-in-law Naomi.

> Where you go, I will go; Where you lodge, I will lodge; your people shall be my people, and your God my God. (Ruth 1: 16)

The Old Testament contains some moving, sensual passages about romantic, passionate love. In the Song of Solomon (a series of love poems between a man and a woman), the man says:

> You have ravished my heart, my bride; you have ravished my heart with a glance of your eyes. (Song 4: 9)

And the woman replies:

> Love is strong as death ... many waters cannot quench love, neither can floods drown it. (Song 8: 7)

Likewise, the book of Tobit tells the story of the love between Tobias and Sarah, who, we are told, were matched in heaven before the world was made.

In the New Testament love is a command, *agape*. In contrast to contemporary views of love, love in the Bible is not simply an emotion. To the contrary, love is always expressed as direct action. In the New Testament love describes the very being of God and includes love for friends and neighbors (the next person you meet), as well as enemies (people who will harm you). The life, teachings, death, and resurrection of Jesus are the expression of God's love for people. St. Paul's words are often cited as the summary statement of love. He writes:

> Love is patient; love is kind. ... it never ends. ... And now faith, hope, and love abide, these three; and the greatest of these is love. (I Corinthians 13: 4, 8, 13)

Two themes on marriage predominate in the New Testament: the prohibition against divorce (with an exception clause) and Paul's expectation of the mutual subordination between husband and wife. In words that seem archaic today, but which challenged the dominant view of his time, Paul counsels husbands to love their wives as Christ loves the Church and wives to respect their husbands as the Church is subject to Christ, see Ephesians 5: 21–33.

Bernard V. Brady, Ph.D., is a Professor of Theology at the University of St. Thomas in St. Paul, MN. He is the author of *Christian Love: How Christians through the Ages Have Understood Love* (2003), published by Georgetown University Press.

The *Religion, Culture, and Family Project* was guided by *critical familialism.* Critical familialism balances "family cohesion with equal regard" and uncovers and critiques power differentials in families. This is in contrast to what Browning calls *naïve familialism*, an ethic that places family togetherness above gender equality, children's well-being, and the development of individual family members.

Some suggest then Vice President Dan Quayle's 1992 condemnation of television character Murphy Brown (an unmarried woman who found herself pregnant and did not marry the father) signaled the first volley in the "marriage wars." Since then, debate over the state of marriage in America has been central in the debate over welfare. In fact, in 2001, President George W. Bush spearheaded a $300 million *Faith-Based and Community Initiative* aimed at promoting heterosexual marriage as a part of the solution to poverty and welfare dependency (Berkowitz 2002). The Senate ultimately approved only $100 million for programs that promote marriage (Furstenberg 2002).

Libertarians are generally opposed to such meddling in the private decisions of American citizens. Many social scientists too are at best skeptical about the feasibility of government efforts to improve the institution of marriage. Furstenberg (2002), who has studied teenage mothers and their children in Baltimore for over 3 decades, summarizes concerns over such governmental efforts:

1. Over half of the women in his study married the father of their child.

2. But four out of five of these marriages were dissolved over the next 15 years.

The marriages of women who married men who were not the fathers of their children fared even worse (Furstenberg 2002).

The problem does not seem to be that people need convincing that marriage is a good thing. Rather, they seem to need support in making unions that will be sustained over a long period of time and, in Furstenberg's (2002: 2) words,

> . . . money alone will not bring couples into marriage. . . . Family counseling and marriage workshops can help couples better understand each other and improve their chances for success. But most couples can't acquire these skills without a sustained and costly effort. . . . [C]ounseling can be helpful and even necessary, but it is hardly sufficient. If the Bush administration truly wants to promote marriage, it should start by providing tangible financial assistance to families that need it.

Organizations that train a critical eye on marriage are likely to be controversial. The *Council on Contemporary Families* was founded in 1996 in response to concerns that much of the public discourse about research and public policy has been unnecessarily oversimplified and politicized. Although the *Council* does not speak with a single voice on all issues related to families, the *Council* aims to bring more sophisticated understanding of research about families and family life to the media, policymakers, and the public through publication of discussion papers, symposia, and consultation with the media. Members of the *Council* are in agreement that diversity is a contemporary reality for families, and the goal of society should be to support the strength and quality of all families (Stacey 2002).

GLOSSARY

Community property	Message
Contempt	Naïve familialism
Critical familialism	Noise
Criticism	Nonverbal communication
Decodes	Positive sentiment override
Defense of Marriage Act	Prenuptial agreements
Defensiveness	*PREPARE*
Encodes	Rapport talk
ENRICH	Receiver
Four horsemen of the apocalypse	Religiosity
Marital duration	Religious affiliation
Marital happiness	Repair attempts
Marital satisfaction	Report talk
Marital stability	Sender
Marital success	Spirituality
Marriage Encounter movement	Stonewalling

FOR YOUR CONSIDERATION

1. Make the cases for and against prenuptial agreements. What are the primary elements you would include in such an agreement?

2. Conduct an assessment of a religious organization with which you are familiar. In what ways does that organization promote marriage? In what ways does that organization add stresses to marriage?

3. In 1991, Laura Doyle published *The Surrendered Wife*. She advocated wives should relinquish control of finances to their husbands, should never criticize their husbands (even when they are wrong), and should display only their "tender side" at home (even if they are tough at their places of employment). Analyze this type of relationship (which was foreshadowed by the publication of a similar book, *The Total Woman* in the 1970s) in terms of potential for marital quality.

4. Identify the elements of a plan to increase the chance of marital success in your community. How much would you be willing to pay (in tax dollars, in church offering, or in other costs) to strengthen marriages in your community?

FOR FURTHER STUDY: WEB SITES, ORGANIZATIONS, AND PUBLICATIONS

Web Sites and Organizations

Council on Contemporary Families
http://www.contemporaryfamilies
The *Council on Contemporary Families* is an independent group that aims to educate media, policymakers, and the public about current research on families and family life. The *Council* is responding to a concern by practitioners, researchers, and other scholars that the tenor of the discussion about families has become both oversimplified and politicized.

Human Rights Campaign
http://www.hrc.org
The Human Rights Campaign works for the rights of gay, lesbian, bisexual, and transgendered individuals. This site includes information on legislation related to same-sex marriage partners.

The National Marriage Project
Rutgers University
54 Joyce Kilmer Avenue, Lucy Stone Hall, B217
Piscataway, NJ 08901
Telephone (732) 445-7922
http://marriage.rutgers.edu
marriage@rci.rutgers.edu
The National Marriage Project aims to strengthen marriage through research and analysis directed at public policy and public education. The *Project* conceptualizes the problem as "marriage is declining as an institution for childbearing and childrearing, with devastating consequences for millions of children."

Recognition of Same-Sex Marriage: Time for Change?
http://www.murdoch.edu.au/elaw/issues/vln3/lauw2.txt
Inge Lauw's well-referenced research article "Recognition of Same-Sex Marriage: Time for Change?" presents case law on same-sex marriage, as well as policy arguments for and against legal recognition of same-sex marriages.

Task Force for Gay and Lesbian Couples
http://www.buddybuddy.com/toc.html
A wide-ranging site that includes information (e.g., on ceremonies) and links (e.g., to organizations that support same-sex marriage), the site presents the results of a survey on attitudes to legal marriage for same-sex couples.

Publications

Holmberg, Diane, Terri Orbuch, and Joseph Veroff. 2003. *Thrice Told Tales: Married Couples Tell Their Stories.* Mahwah, NJ: Lawrence Erlbaum Associates.
The authors provide a forum for a representative sample of 199 Black and 177 White married couples to tell the stories of their relationships. Using coding schemes and quantitative analysis, the authors analyze such questions as how couples' stories change over time and how stories differ by gender and by race.

Journal of Family Communication
This quarterly journal publishes empirical reports, theoretical treatises, and review essays on all aspects of family communication, including communication in family relationships and systems and intersections between family communication and education, health, law, media, and policy.

Journal of Marriage and the Family

Volume 66, No. 4 (November 2004) of this journal includes a symposium on marriage and its future. Contributors include Paul Amato, Andrew Cherlin, Stephanie Coontz, and others. Articles address cohabitation, gay and lesbian relationships, Hispanics and marriage, marriage promotion, and a range of topics related to the future of marriage.

Leeds-Hurwitz, Wendy. 2002. *Wedding as Text: Communicating Cultural Identities Through Ritual.* Mahwah, NJ: Lawrence Erlbaum Associates.

Leeds-Hurwitz has documented the weddings of 112 couples in the United States who represent marriages across cultural difference. She reports on the acceptance and management across class, ethnicity, faith, nationality, and race through the concepts of community, identity, ritual, and meaning.

Lewis, Jane. 2001. *The End of Marriage?: Individualism and Intimate Relations.* Cheltanham, UK: Northhampton, MA: Edward Elgar.

The "decline of marriage" (and the rise of cohabitation) concerns social scientists on both sides of the Altantic. Lewis, a British social policy analyst, approaches this matter from the perspective of repeated public episodes of public concern over the last century.

Pimetel, Ellen Efron. 2000. "Just How Do I Love Thee?: Marital Relations in Urban China." *Journal of Marriage and the Family* 62, 1: 32–47.

Pimetel has conducted one of the few studies on marital quality outside the United States. She drew a large, representative sample of urban couples in China and considered the importance of such traditional Chinese values as parental approval of mates, as well as feminist values such as the division of household labor and family decision making.

Segrin, Chris, and Jeanne Flora. 2005. *Family Communication.* Mahway, NJ: Lawrence Erlbaum Associates.

This is an advanced text, but one which accessibly presents the most current theory and research on family communication. The authors include major sections on communication during family stress and the associations among interaction, health, and well-being, as well as the "basics" of family communication.

Vangelisti, Anita L., ed. 2003. *Handbook of Family Communication.* Mahwah, NJ: Lawrence Erlbaum Associates.

This volume synthesizes research and theory on family communication. Contributing authors from across the social sciences present cutting-edge work on a variety of topics: communication across the life cycle, communication in diverse family forms, relational communication, communication processes, and contemporary issues in family communication.

Walker, Alexis, Margaret Manoogian-O'Dell, Lori McGraw, and Diana L. White, eds. 2001. *Families in Later Life: Connections and Transitions.* Thousand Oaks, CA: Sage.

This collection of essays is drawn from literature, as well as social science. An introductory essay begins each of five sections, covering ties with young adults, intergenerational connections in mid-life, intimacy in later midlife, work and home transitions in early old age, and challenges and possibilities in later life.

Wilson, James Q. *The Marriage Problem: How Our Culture Has Weakened Families.* New York, NY: Harper Collins.

Wilson, a sociologist, summarizes the concerns surrounding the problems facing the American family. His emphasis is on the significance of values and norms in the social context.

REFERENCES FOR CITED WORKS

Amato, Paul R., and Alan Booth. 1995. "Changes in Gender Role Attitudes and Perceived Marital Quality." *American Sociological Review* 60: 48–66.

Amato, Paul R., David R. Johnson, Alan Booth, and Stacy J. Rogers. 2003. "Continuity and Change in Marital Quality Between 1980 and 2000." *Journal of Marriage and the Family* 65, 1 (February): 1–22.

Armas, Genero C. 2001. "Gay Homes More Visible." http://detnews.com/2001/census/0110/15/a05-275269.htm (Retrieved 10/16/01).

Barbieri, Susan M. 2004 "Wedding Reservations." *Star Tribune* September 11: 1E.

Bellah, Robert N., Richard Madsen, William N. Sullivan, Ann Swidler, and Steven N. Tipton. 1985. *Habits of the Heart: Individualism and Commitment in American Life.* Berkeley, CA: University of California Press.

Berkowitz, Bill. 2002. "The Mullahs of Marriage." *The Nation*. http://thenation.com/doc.hmhtml?I+special&s-berkowitz20020514 (Retrieved 7/25/02).

Birdwhistell, Raymond L. 1970. *Kinesics and Context*. Philadelphia, PA: University of Pennsylvania Press.

Browning, Don. 1998. "The Task of Religious Institutions in Strengthening Families." Joint paper issued by the *Religion, Culture, and Family Project* of the School of Divinity of the University of Chicago and the *Communitarian Family Policy Statement*. http://divinity.uchicago.edu/family/communitarianpolicy.html (Retrieved 11/8/02).

Cavedo, C., and B. G. Guerney. 1999. "Relationship Enhancement, Enrichment and Problem Prevention. In *Preventive Approaches in Couple Therapy*, eds. R. Berger and M.T. Hannah. Philadelphia, PA: Brunner/Mazel, 73–105.

Cherlin, Andrew J. 1996. *Public and Private Families: An Introduction*. New York, NY: McGraw-Hill.

Chiodo, Abigail, and Michael T. Owyang. 2002. "For Love or Money: Why Married Men Make More." *Regional Economist* (April). www.stls.frb.org/publiations/re/2002//b/pages/marriage.html (Retrieved 8/9/02).

Coltrane, Scott, and Randall Collins. 2001. *Sociology of Marriage and the Family: Gender, Love, and Property*, 5/e. Belmont, CA: Wadsworth.

Conger, Rand D., and Glenn H. Elder, Jr. 1994. *Families in Troubled Times: Adapting to Change in Rural American*. New York: Aldine de Gruyter.

Coontz, Stephanie, and Nancy Folbre. 2002. *Marriage, Poverty and Public Policy*. http://www.contemporaryfamilies (Retrieved 1/11/03).

Cott, Nancy F. 2000. *Public Vows: A History of Marriage and the Nation*. Cambridge, MA: Harvard University Press.

Cotton, Shelia R. 1999. "Marital Status and Mental Health Revisited: Examining the Importance of Risk Factors and Resources." *Family Relations* 48, 3: 225–33.

Cummins, H. J. 2002a. "How Some Couples Turned Their Marriages Around." *Star Tribune* (July): 12.

Cummins, H. J. 2002b. "Marriage Education Discount is Popular." *Star Tribune* (October 8): E1.

Durkheim, Emile. 1915/1965. *The Elemental Forms of Religious Life*, Trans. Karen E. Feld. New York, NY: Free Press.

Earnest, Leslie. 2002. "More Saying 'We Do' to Big Wedding Expenses." *Star Tribune* November 7: E6, E7.

Furstenberg, Frank. 2002. "What a Good Marriage Can't Do." *The New York Times* (August 13). (Retrieved 8/18/02)

Gaelick, Lisa, G. Bodenhausen, and Robert S. Wyer. 1985. "Observational Biases in Spouse Interaction: Toward a Cognitive Behavioral Model of Marriages." *Journal of Personality and Social Psychology* 49: 1246–65.

Gelles, Richard J. 1995. *Contemporary Families: A Sociological View*. Thousand Oaks, CA: Sage.

Glenn, Norval D. 1990. "Quantitative Research in Marital Quality in the 1980s: A Critical Review." *Journal of Marriage and the Family* 52: 818–31.

Glenn, Norval D. 1991. "The Recent Trend in Marital Success in the United States." *Journal of Marriage and the Family* 53: 261–70.

Glenn, Norval D. 1996. "Values, Attitudes, and the State of American Marriage." In *Promises to Keep: Decline and Renewal of Marriage in America*, eds. David Popenoe, Jean Bethke Elshtain, and David Blankenhorn. Lanham, MD: Rowman & Littlefield, 15–34.

Goldscheider, Frances K., and Calvin Goldscheider. 1998. "The Effects of Childhood Family Structure on Leaving and Returning Home." *Journal of Marriage and the Family* 60: 745–56.

Gottman, John M. 1994. *What Predicts Divorce? The Relationship Between Marital Processes and Marital Outcomes*. Hillsdale, NJ: Lawrence Erlbaum Associates.

Gottman, John M., and Nan Silver. 1999. *The Seven Principles for Making Marriage Work*. New York: Crown.

Halsall, Paul. 1996. "Lesbian and Gay Marriage through History and Culture." http://condor.depaul.edu/~mwilson/extra/hislesmar.html (Retrieved 1/17/03).

Heaton, T. B., C. K. Jacobson, and X. N. Fu. 1992. "Religiosity of Married Couples and Childlessness." *Review of Religious Research* 33: 244–55.

Hochschild, Arlie Russell. 1989. *The Second Shift: Working Parents and the Revolution at Home*. New York, NY: Viking.

Hughes, Michael, Carolyn J. Kroehler, and James W. Vander Zanden. 2002. *Sociology: The Core*, 6/e. New York, NY: McGraw-Hill.

Kalmijn, Matthus. 2004. "Marriage Rituals as Reinforcers of Role Transitions: An Analysis of Weddings in The Netherlands." *Journal of Marriage and the Family* 66, 3 (August): 583–94.

Kirchler, E. 1988. "Marital Happiness and Interaction in Everyday Surroundings: A Time-Sample Diary Approach for Couples." *Journal of Social and Personal Relationships* 5: 375–82.

Knutson, L., and David H. Olson. 2002. *Effectiveness of the PREPARE Program for Marriage Preparations.* Minneapolis, MN: Life Innovations.

Larson, L. E., and J. W. Goltz. 1989. "Religious Participation and Marital Commitment." *Review of Religious Research* 30: 387–400.

Lavee, Yoav, and Ruth Katz. 2002. "Division of Labor, Perceived Fairness, and Marital Quality: The Effect of Gender Ideology." *Journal of Marriage and the Family* 64 (February): 27–39.

Lindahl, Krisstin, Mari Clements, and Howard Markman. 1998. "The Development of Marriage: A 9-Year Perspective." In *The Developmental Course of Marital Dysfunction*, ed. Thomas N. Bradbury. New York, NY: Cambridge University Press, 205–36.

Marks, Nadine F., and James David Lambert. 1998. "Marital Status Continuity and Change Among Young and Midlife Adults: Longitudinal Effects on Psychological Well-Being." *Journal of Family Issues* 19, 6 (November): 652–86.

Martyn, Joann. 2001. "Marriage and Wedding Traditions in Eastern Rite Catholicism: The Rite of Betrothal and Crowing." Unpublished paper. St. Paul, MN: University of St. Thomas.

McCubbin, Hamilton I., Anne I. Thompson, and Marilyn A. McCubbin. 1996. *Family Assessment: Resiliency, Coping, and Adaptation-Inventories for Research and Practice.* Madison, WI: University of Wisconsin Press.

McLanahan, Sara S., and J. Adams 1989. "The Effects of Children on Parents' Psychological Well-being: 1957–1976." *Social Forces* 68: 1124–46.

Montgomery, Marilyn J., and Gwendolyn T. Sorell. 1997. "Differences in Love Attitudes Across Family Life Stages." *Family Relations* 46: 55–61.

Noller, Patricia, and Mary Anne Fitzpatrick. 1990. "Marital Communication in the Eighties." *Journal of Marriage and the Family* 52: 832–43.

Olson, David H. 2003. *Marriages and Families: Intimacy, Diversity, and Strengths*, 4/e. New York, NY: McGraw-Hill.

Olson, David H., and Amy K. Olson. 2000. *Empowering Couples: Building on Your Strengths.* Minneapolis, MN: Life Innovations.

Ooms, Theodora. 1998. *Toward More Perfect Unions: Putting Marriage on the Public Agenda.* Washington, DC: Family Impact Seminar.

Pearce, L. D., and W. G. Axinn. 1998. "The Impact of Family Religious Life on the Quality of Mother-Child Relations." *American Sociological Review* 63: 810–28.

Popenoe, David. 2002. "The Top Ten Myths of Marriage." http://marriage.rutgers.edu/pubmuths%20of%20marriage.htm (Retrieved 8/1/02).

Population Reference Bureau. 2001. "American Families." http://www.prb.org/pubs/population_bulletin/bu55-4/55_4_struct.html (Retrieved 3/4/01).

Sharp, Elizabeth A., and Lawrence H. Ganong. 2000. "Raising Awareness About Marital Expectations: Are Unrealistic Beliefs Changed by Integrative Teaching." *Family Relations* 49, 1: 71–76.

Shehan, Constance L. 2003. *Marriages and Families*, 2/e. Boston, MA: Allyn & Bacon.

Spain, Daphne, and Suzanne M. Bianchi. 1996. *Balancing Act.* New York, NY: Russell Sage Foundation.

Spanier, Graham B., and Robert A. Lewis. 1980. "Marital Quality: A Review of the Seventies." *Journal of Marriage and the Family* 42: 825–39.

Stacey, Judith. 2002. "Virtual Truth with a Vengence." *Contemporary Sociology* 28, 1 (January): 18–23.

Stack, Steven, and J. Ross Eshleman. 1998. "Marital Status and Happiness: A 17-Nation Study." *Journal of Marriage and the Family* 60 (May): 527–36.

Stanley, Scott. 2001. "Making a Case for Premarital Education." *Family Relations* 50, 3: 272.

Stinnett, N., and J. DeFrain. 1985. *Secrets of Strong Families.* Boston, MA: Little, Brown.

Tannen, Deborah. 1990. *You Just Don't Understand: Women and Men in Conversations.* New York, NY: William Morrow.

The National Marriage Project. 2002. "About the Project." http://marriage.rutgers.edu/about.htm (Retrieved 8/1/02).

Thornton, Arland, W. G. Axinn, and D. H. Hill. 1992. "Reciprocal Effects of Religiosity, Cohabitation, and Marriage." *American Journal of Sociology* 98: 628–51.

Thornton, Arland, and D. Camburn. 1989. "Religious Participation and Adolescent Sexual Behavior and Attitudes." *Journal of Marriage and the Family* 51: 641–53.

The Urban Institute. 2002. "The Marital Edge." http://www.urban.org/ (Retrieved 11/8/02).

United States Bureau of the Census. 2000. *Statistical Abstract of the United States.* Washington, DC: Government Printing Office.

United States Bureau of the Census. 2001a. "Marital Status of the Population by Sex and Age: 2000." Table 51 in *Statistical Abstract of the United States.* Washington, DC: Government Printing Office.

United States Bureau of the Census. 2001b. "Marital Status of the Population by Sex, Race, and Hispanic Origin: 1980-2000." Table 49 in *Statistical Abstract of the United States.* Washington, DC: Government Printing Office.

VanLaningham, Jody, David R. Johnson, and Paul Amato. 2001. "Marital Happiness, Marital Duration, and the U-Shaped Curve: Evidence from a Five-Wave Panel Study." *Social Forces* 78, 4 (June): 1313–41.

Voydanoff, Patricia. 1988. "Work Role Characteristics: Family Structure Demands, and Work/Family Conflict." *Journal of Marriage and the Family* 50: 749–61.

Weiss, Robert L., and Richard E. Heyman. 1990. "Observations of Marital Interaction." In *The Psychology of Marriage*, eds. Frank D. Fincham & Thomas N. Bradbury. New York, NY: Guilford, 87–117.

White, Lynn K., Alan Booth, and John N. Edwards. 1986. "Children and Marital Happiness: Why the Negative Correlation?" *Journal of Family Issues* 7: 131–47.

White, Lynn K., and John Edwards. 1990. "Emptying the Nest and Parental Well-being: Evidence from National Panel Data." *American Sociological Review* 55: 235–42.

Whitehead, Barbara Dafoe, and David Popenoe. 2001. "Who Wants to Marry a Soul Mate?: New Survey Findings on Young Adults' Attitudes about Love and Marriage." *The State of Our Unions: The Social Health of Marriage in America.* http://marriage.rutgers.edu/TEXTSOOU2001.htm (Retrieved 8/1/02).

9

DECOUPLED FAMILIES: DESERTED, SEPARATED, DIVORCED, AND WIDOWED

CHAPTER PREVIEW

In this chapter we address the processes of *marriage dissolution: desertion, separation, annulment*, and *divorce*, as well as death. Divorce rates may be reported as *crude divorce rate* and *refined divorce rate* with the later serving as a more useful tool. After peaking in 1981, divorce rates leveled off. However, divorce rates remain at approximately half of all marriages, and the rate increases to about 60% for second marriages.

Contemporary divorce has moved from the *adversarial* element that was required in the early part of the 20th century. With *no-fault divorce* provisions in all 50 states, the process no longer presents insurmountable *barriers to divorce*, although the effect of no-fault divorce is a matter of some contention. Recent data challenge conventional wisdom that unhappy adults who divorce fare better. The negative impacts on most women's financial standard after they divorce are certainly significant, and children appear to feel the financial impact of divorce most deeply.

Children's adjustment to divorce is a matter of serious social concern. Girls whose parents divorce may exhibit a *sleeper effect* as they approach adolescence. Children of both genders are at higher risk for lower educational success and poorer social competence if their parents are divorced, but some scholars caution that findings linking divorce to poor adjustment by children are overdrawn. The effects of divorce seem to be shaped by the child's economic resources after the divorce, as well as by the quality of the relationship between the parents after the divorce.

Widowhood and *widowerhood* are realities of the natural life cycle of families. Improved nutrition, greater access to health care, and other factors increased life expectancy in the later half of the 20th century. Although individuals live longer, the surviving spouse or partner must deal with the complex journey of grief and bereavement. In contrast to the premise of the *grief-loss model,* the grieving process follows no prescribed timetable, and bereavement can serve as an opportunity for discovery and growth.

Finally, the number and complexity of stepfamilies increased significantly in the second half of the 20th century, leading us to term these families lumpy, not blended but folded together. *Stepfather households* and *stepmother households* differ in terms of roles, rights, responsibilities, power, and efficacy. Although same-sex couples continue to struggle for rights, gay and lesbian stepfamilies endure a triple stigmatization. Successful stepfamilies may use *family maps* to better understand who is and is not part of their family. The Supreme Courts' consideration of the *principle of family relations* suggests society is beginning to affirm the importance of stepfamily relations.

TRENDS IN MARRIAGE DISSOLUTION

Desertion, Separation, Annulment, and Divorce in a Sociohistorical Context

At the turn of the 19th century, only one out of every 10 marriages ended in divorce. However, a substantial number of marriages that did not result in divorce resulted in separation or desertion. Furthermore, a substantial number of marriages were cut short by the premature death of one of the spouses. Desertion, separation, annulment, and divorce are different terms relative to *marriage dissolution*, or the ending of a married life. *Desertion*, or abandonment, refers to one spouse leaving the other, either with or without notice. Most desertions have been men leaving their wives or their children. Traditional family law required that women reside with their husbands. Failure to do so risked a wife being sued for divorce, with the consequent cost of loss of contact with her children that entailed.

Separation refers to either an informal agreement to live apart or a formal, court-mandated condition, which may (or may not) be a precursor to divorce. In some states, a court-supervised separation is a mandatory step in the process to secure a legal divorce. Even today, marriages that result in separation may never proceed through to divorce. Race and ethnicity, reflecting socioeconomic and cultural influences, shape the chance a couple no longer wishing to live together in marriage will end that marriage through legal *divorce* proceedings. After a three-year separation, 91% of White women terminate their marriage in divorce, whereas only 77% of separated Hispanic women and 67% of separated Black women terminate their marriages in divorce. (Department of Health and Human Services 2002)

Annulment, which can either be a civil or a religious verdict, refers to a judgment that the formal requirements for the marriage were not present at the time the marriage ceremony was performed. In the Catholic Church, annulment is not simply "Catholic divorce" but a decision rendered by a marriage tribunal that evaluates evidence to determine whether the qualifications for the marriage sacrament were present at the time of the wedding.

BOX 9.1   "Annulment in the Catholic Church"
Rev. Mr. Nathan E. Allen, J.D.

Many see annulment as "divorce Catholic-style." Others wonder why, with the prevalence of divorce and remarriage, the Church doesn't just "get with it" and accept the present state of affairs of disposable relationships. But the Catholic Church cannot do that. Jesus taught that the two become one: "What God has joined together, man must not separate." The question before the Tribunal (Church court) that meets to consider each request for annulment is: Did God join these two together? The *consent* exchanged by the parties at the time of their wedding, whereby both freely give themselves to the other, creates the marriage. So the judicial question before the Tribunal is, was there something about that exchange of consent which was defective under the laws of the Catholic Church?

Consent might be defective in one of two ways. First, either one or both parties might not have been fully free to give their consent. The "shotgun wedding" or one in which one party suffers from a mental illness or chemical addiction that rendered that party unable to live out a marriage commitment are examples of cases that might fall within this category. One party's consent might be obtained under false pretenses. The totality of circumstances may be such that one of the parties was not fully free in giving consent. For example, a dysfunctional home life may lead to an overwhelming desire to escape, the parties may be very young, or the couple may feel significant pressure from family to marry in the case of a premarital pregnancy.

Second, either or both parties may not have been clear in what they actually consented *to*. When they said, "I do," did one or both of them really mean "I don't" to some essential aspect of marriage? Cases where the parties never intended marriage but something else are relatively rare. (Immigration fraud cases might fit this category.) More often, one or both of the parties carve out their own definition of marriage, reinforced by a culture of individualistic relationships. If a party promises "till death do us part" or "forsaking all others," but really means "till death do us part *as long as I'm happy*" or "forsaking all others *until a better offer comes along,*" that person has changed the object of consent. He or she is no longer consenting to marriage as defined by the Catholic Church.

A declaration of nullity is not a reward for the "good" or "innocent" person. Neither is the "bad" or "guilty" party punished by denying a declaration of nullity. The Tribunal's declaration of nullity is a judicial decision, based on the facts of the individual case, whether one or both of the parties' consent was invalid on the day of the wedding. If the answer is yes, the marriage is not binding and the parties are free to marry in the Catholic Church.

Rev. Mr. Nathan E. Allen, J.D., is a deacon of the Archdiocese of St. Paul and Minneapolis. He serves as Auditor/Assessor of the Archdiocesan Tribunal. He is also a graduate of the University of Minnesota Law School.

Divorce refers to the termination of the rights and responsibilities of a marriage by civil authorities. The *crude divorce rate* is the number of divorces per 1,000 people in the population. This statistic is flawed, however, as it is based on total population, including children and the unmarried who are not at risk of divorce. The most useful divorce statistic is the *refined divorce rate*, the number of divorces per 1,000 married women over age 15. Unfortunately, the National Center on Health Statistics discontinued recording divorce statistics in 1996, presumably as a cost-cutting measure (Broome 1995). Currently, the best available data are drawn from the United States Census Bureau's *Current Population Survey*, which relies on individuals to report their current and past experience with divorce.

The chances a first marriage would end in separation or divorce increased from the 1950s through the 1970s. Those rates were fairly stable from the early 1970s through the late 1980s, although the chance a second marriage would end in separation or divorce rose through the 1980s (Bramlett and Mosher 2001).

Of first marriages, one out of five ends in separation or divorce within five years. (One out of two cohabitations ends within five years.) The rate increases to one out of three first marriages ending in separation or divorce within 10 years. The divorce rate for second marriages is higher, with 23% ending in divorce after five years and 39% ending in divorce after 10 years (Department of Health and Human Services 2002).

Why is the marital stability of second marriages lower than that of first marriages? Perhaps those inclined to choose an unsuitable partner once are likely to choose an unsuitable partner twice. Those who are challenged in the area of marital interaction and do not learn from their first marriages are doomed to repeat their mistakes. Also, those who experience socioeconomic hardships in a first marriage may be likely to have at least some of those hardships in a second marriage.

Some wedding chapels have begun processing paperwork for divorces, sometimes for couples who came to the chapel a few days before to be married. One wedding chapel manager even reports the busiest day for requests for divorce is Tuesday. Such divorces in California take three to six months between filing and final decree and cost only $500 if the couple has no disagreement over assets, debts, or children. Alan Tanenbaum, chair of the California State Bar of California's Family Law Advisory Commission, sees these chapels and other offices that help process the paperwork for divorce as providing a useful service.

However, he recommends couples with large family estates, sizable retirement plans, or children consult with an attorney (Fernandez 2001).

The divorce rate in the United States is among the highest in the world. Family studies scholars cite several factors, not the least of which are the changing and high expectations we hold for marriage. Contemporary marriage is no longer universally viewed as a permanent arrangement that exists for practical purposes. In a reflection of American individualism over familialism, individuals today expect to derive more from marriage than economic support and an arrangement in which to bear and raise children. Instead, married Americans expect high degree of love, intimacy, and expressiveness from their marriages (VanLaningham, Johnson, and Amato 2001). Indeed, couples who have more practical expectations for their marriages are more satisfied with their relationships (White and Booth 1991). As traditional economic, gender, parenting, sexual, and other family roles have become more negotiable, marriage is a more challenging arrangement (VanLaningham, Johnson, and Amato).

DIVORCE

Legal Contexts of Contemporary Divorce

What are the affects of changes in the legal provisions for divorce? Traditionally, an individual wishing to end a marriage, or even a couple who mutually wished to do so, faced almost insurmountable legal hurdles. Formally ending a marriage in the eyes of society required the parties adopt (or at least feign) an *adversarial* or antagonistic position with regard to one another. One person would be required to demonstrate in court that the other had committed serious offense—abandonment, adultery, or physical or mental cruelty. Such proceedings incurred high economic, moral, and other social costs. Not surprisingly, those who may have preferred to dissolve a marriage may not have been inclined to do so.

No-fault divorce refers to the provision that an individual or a couple wishing to dissolve a marriage need not demonstrate that the other party committed an offense to the marriage. Today, all 50 states have some form of no-fault divorce. Some states require a formal period of separation. Other states permit divorce based on fault, as well as no-fault.

The precise effect of no-fault divorce laws on divorce rates is a matter of some contention. Glenn (1999: 802) argues no-fault divorce laws were "largely redundant in most states in terms of lowering the legal restrictions on divorce." That is, in most states, the provisions for divorce had been liberalized several years before the enactment of no-fault provisions so everyone who wanted to secure a divorce and who was willing to pay the costs was able to do so.

Correlates of Divorce

In a study of divorce in 77 counties in Oklahoma, Nakonezny and Reddick (2004) found a significant decrease following the Oklahoma City bombings in 1985. They used "terror management theory" and "attachment theory" to argue that such large-scale community disasters contribute to family and marital solidarity and, consequently, lower divorce rates.

Family scientists have devoted proportionately more effort to detecting conditions that are related to the increased probability of divorce. These conditions include social and economic, as well as personal and attitudinal, factors. Social class as indicated by family income, home ownership, male unemployment rate, and degree of poverty is negatively associated with the probability of divorce. That is, the most stable marriages are found among those with the highest levels of family income and education. White (1990) suggests that it is not only lower income but also the failure to achieve educational or economic expectations that are associated with the risk of divorce. The higher rates of divorce among Blacks and Hispanics (at 10 years of marriage, 47% and 34%, compared to 32% among Whites) likewise probably reflect the severe strains that economic hardship complicated by institutional racism places on American marriage. Interestingly, only 20% of Asians have divorced within the first 10 years of marriage (Bramlett and Mosher 2001).

Gender role attitudes and behaviors appear to have an impact on marriage dissolution. Kaufman (2000) found egalitarian men are actually less likely to divorce than traditional men. Perhaps a man who views a woman as his equal makes for a better life partner. Wife's employment has an interesting, complex relationship to marital stability. A national longitudinal survey of marriages in the late 1980s and early 1990s found, when gender ideology, marital characteristics, and other variables were controlled, wife's employment had no effect on divorce (Sayer and Bianchi 2000).

Another study found the number of hours of wife's employment and the higher a wife's income relative to her husband's, the higher the likelihood the couple will divorce (South 2001). South argues, although it does not cause divorce, a wife's employment may make it possible to choose divorce as an alternative to an unhappy marriage. Others (Heckert, Nowak, and Snyder 1998; Ono 1998) argue a wife's earnings from employment may have a stabilizing effect on lower income marriages and during periods of economic uncertainty.

A recent study by Rogers (2004) offers some insight into the nature of the association among "dollars, dependency, and divorce." Rogers examined data on 1,704 individuals from a panel study from 1980 to 1997. She found, although wife's resources (as measured in dollars) were related in a positive fashion to chance of divorce, the odds of divorce are highest when the wife contributed 50% to 60% of the total family income.

However, Rogers also found the chance of divorce was high among spouses with equal economic contributions but with only low to moderate marital happiness. As others (e.g., Nock 2001) have explained, such couples have a higher probability of divorce because they have little keeping them together, neither satisfaction nor economics.

Children who grow up in a family in which the parents have divorced or separated have a higher probability of themselves experiencing divorce (Amato and DeBoer 2001). Amato (1996) speculates this may be due to several factors. First, parents who divorce may model divorce as a strategy to solve marital problems. Second, children who have experienced their parents' divorces may exhibit behaviors that impede forming their own happy marriages. The greatest empirical support seems to be found for the former hypothesis (Amato). Wolfinger's (1999) research indicates intergenerational transmission of divorce may be declining.

As discussed in chapter 7, couples who cohabit prior to marriage have higher rates of divorce (Wu and Penning 1997). As discussed in chapter 10, premarital pregnancy and early childbearing translate into a greater probability of lower marital satisfaction and higher divorce rates (Teti and Lamb 1989). However, having young children tends to stabilize marriages.

Knoester and Booth (2000) have evaluated various attitudinal *barriers to divorce*, those factors that serve to keep marriages intact and which may delay or even prevent divorce. Drawing on a national sample of married individuals interviewed between 1980 and 1992, Knoester and Booth found concerns for the well-being of children were significant barriers to divorce for men and women, as were religious beliefs, dependence on one's spouse, fear of losing a child, and anxiety over financial security. More than men, women were

TABLE 9.1

The Marriage Project's *Ten Myths of Divorce*

1. Because people learn from their bad marriages, second marriages tend to be more successful than first marriages.

2. Living together before marriage is a good way to reduce the chances of eventually divorcing.

3. Divorce may cause problems for many of the children who are affected by it, but by and large, these problems are not long lasting and the children recover relatively quickly.

4. Having a child together will help a couple to improve their marital satisfaction and prevent a divorce.

5. Following divorce, the woman's standard of living plummets by 73%, whereas that of the man's improves by 42%.

6. When parents don't get along, children are better off if their parents divorce than if they stay together.

7. Because they are more cautious in entering marital relationships and also have a strong determination to avoid the possibility of divorce, children who grow up in a home broken by divorce tend to have as much success in their own marriages as those from intact homes.

8. Following divorce, the children involved are better off in stepfamilies than in single-parent families.

9. Being very unhappy at certain points in a marriage is a good sign that the marriage will eventually end in divorce.

10. It is usually men who initiate divorce proceedings.

Source: Adapted by the permission of David Popenoe © 2001. Each "myth" is refuted using social science research published in reputable resources. For a full list of the sources, see the footnotes accompanying http://marriage.rutgers.edu/Publications/MythsDivorce.pdf

influenced by their religious beliefs as well as by their dependence on their spouses. Men were more influenced by their fear of losing their children as well as by the influence of family and friends more than were women.

Only dependence on one's spouse and the importance of religious beliefs served to deter subsequent divorce. Although concern for the well-being of one's children is perceived to be the most important barrier to divorce, that factor was not in fact a significant deterrent to divorce. In sum, Knoester and Booth (2000) concluded factors that have traditionally been perceived to be barriers to divorce do very little to deter subsequent divorce.

Effects of Divorce

In Table 9.1, *The Top Ten Myths of Divorce*, Popenoe (2002) explores commonly held but often misleading beliefs about divorce. In contrast to some popular beliefs about divorce, Popenoe and his colleagues argue divorce has negative consequences for adults and children's happiness and economic and psychological well-being.

Using data from the *National Survey of Families and Households* (a nationally representative survey), Waite et al. (2002), working with the *Institute for American Values*, concluded divorce does not typically make adults happier than staying in an unhappy marriage. Specifically, they found unhappily married adults who divorced were no happier than unhappily married adults who stayed married. Also, those who divorced did not show reduced symptoms of depression, higher self-esteem, or an increased sense of mastery.

Furthermore, Waite and her colleagues found almost three-fourths of those who divorced reported having been happily married five years previously. The same proportion reported being married to a spouse who was happy with the marriage.

Finally, most (two out of three) unhappily married adults who avoided divorce or separation were happily married five years later, whereas just one out of five of those who divorced or separated had happily remarried five years later. In sum, the conventional wisdom, that unhappily married adults who divorce are better off in terms of a variety of social psychological indicators, is not supported by data from the *National Survey of Families and Households*.

Unquestionably, divorce has a deleterious effect on the material standard of living for women. Following a divorce, women experience a significant financial loss, whereas men experience a slight financial gain (McManus and DiPrete 2001). The impact of divorce and living in a single-parent, usually mother-only, family is deeply felt by children. Fully one third of children who live in mother-only families live in poverty. Children who live in father-only families are considerably less likely to live in poverty (17%), but these statistics contrast dramatically with the percentage of children who live in two-parent families who live in poverty (6%). The contrast between the economic well-being of children of color living with mother-only and those living with two parents is even more startling. Forty-one percent of Black and Hispanic children living in mother-only families live in poverty, compared to 6% and 17% of Black and Hispanic children living in two-parent families (United States Census Bureau 2000).

Not surprisingly, when nonresident fathers pay child support, their children fare better (Amato and Gilbreth 1999). Nonresident fathers' payment of child support is positively correlated with frequency of their visitation with their children. However, children appear to suffer in families in which mothers are unhappy with the high level of contact between their children and the noncustodial father (King and Heard 1999).

These findings suggest the stereotypes of dead-beat dads and mothers who exclude fathers from contact with their children offer inadequate explanations of the complex arrangements among visitation, economic support, and nonresidential parenting. Such innovations such as "virtual visitation," in which nonresidential parents maintain contact with their children via the Internet, while not replacing face-to-face contact, suggests we have not exhausted the options for resolving the challenges of keeping parents and their children in touch with one another.

Over half of all divorces involve children under the age of 18. Approximately four out of every 10 children will experience their parents' divorce (Amato 2000), but the impact of divorce on children depends on the circumstances preceding and following the divorce. Contentious, stressful divorces have debilitating social, psychological, economic, and other effects on children. Although divorce may bring relief to a child living in a previously conflict-habituated marriage (L'Heureax-Dube 1998), divorce may also be severe for the child whose parents had a low-conflict marriage.

Wallerstein, Lewis, and Baleslee (2000) interviewed the members of 60 families under-going counseling at the time of their parents' separation in 1971 and subsequent divorce. They followed up with interviews in subsequent years, up to 25 years following the divorce. Not surprisingly, children experienced the deepest effects of the divorce in the year immediately following the divorce. However, most households stabilized within two years, and two thirds of the children interviewed were coping well or adequately within five years. Although most families seemed to be maintaining economic and educational sufficiency within 10 years, the boys seemed to have greater problems in their educational, occupational, and marital adjustment. Girls, on the other hand, who initially appeared to be adjusting, better than were their male peers earlier in the study, seemed to exhibit a *sleeper effect* as they approached adolescence. These girls expressed hesitancy about relationships commitment, marriage, and childbearing.

Coontz (1997), Hetherington and Kelly (2002), and others argue Wallerstein's et al. (2000) conclusions about the long-term deleterious effects of divorce are overdrawn. However, Amato (2000), Cherlin (2000), and others support their conclusions that divorce has persistent impacts on children. Children whose parents divorce may still experience some stigma from their peers, although this certainly has diminished, as divorce has become a more common childhood experience. Children forced to relocate to a different home, neighborhood, and school because of the divorce and associated economic changes may experience some upheaval. Research also confirms children whose parents divorce are also more likely to have problems with educational success, psychological adjustment, and social competence (Amato 2000).

Rodgers and Rose (2002) have found the level of resiliency is much the same in divorced and blended families as in intact families. Their study of 7th-, 9th-, and 11th-grade adolescents found peer support could moderate the effect of low parental support for those living in divorced, single-parent families. Their research confirms that adolescents need support—from parents, peers or others—after their parents divorce.

In one study, King (2002) found the presumed negative relationship between parental divorce and interpersonal trust in adult offspring essentially disappeared once the quality of the past parent–teen relationship had been taken into account. Perhaps the negative effects of divorce on children will be reduced as more religious, educational, and community groups provide support for divorcing families and their children. Unfortunately, few mediation and parent education programs that provide support services to families have evaluated their success in reducing the short- and long-term risks of divorce on children (Hughes and Kirby 2000).

BOX 9.2   "Divorce Mediation"
Jacqueline Kirby Wilkins, Ph.D., C.F.L.E.

Divorce mediation is a process where a qualified neutral party acts as a facilitator to assist divorcing couples in resolving issues related to separation and divorce. Typical issues addressed during divorce mediation include property settlement and custody and postdivorce decision making regarding the children. In addition to receiving basic mediation training on how to help people resolve issues through a win/win negotiation process, most divorce mediators receive at least an additional 40 hours advanced training specific to divorce issues. Often, divorce mediators will have at least an undergraduate degree, and many have received their masters, doctorate, or juris doctorate degrees. In addition, many divorce mediators have specific content knowledge and practical experience in the area of divorce and understand its impact on families.

Experience has shown that many situations headed toward litigation can be resolved independently through mediation. Mediation encourages clients to understand each other's perspective. The goal of the mediator is to facilitate discussion, assist the couple in identifying the real issues of the dispute, and help generate their own options for settlement. The goal of divorce mediation is to help divorcing couples arrive at a mutually acceptable agreement that resolves the dispute and encourages future negotiation and cooperation between parents.

Benefits of Divorce Mediation

Research (Dillon & Emery 1996; Emery 1994; Emery, Sbarra & Grover 2005) suggests that:

- Divorcing parents who participated in mediation were 67% more likely than those who litigated to reach agreement and avoid the courtroom.

- Mediation generally takes less time and costs less than litigation.

- Mediated agreements tend to be more comprehensive than adversarial settlements.

- Mediated agreements have a higher rate of compliance than litigated agreements.

- Most mediation clients report being happier with their experience than those who litigated.

- Nonresidential parents who mediated often report having more frequent contact with their children and to be more involved in decision making related to the children than those who litigated.

- Parents who mediated reported having more frequent communication with their former spouse about their children as compared with parents who litigated.

Perhaps most important, mediation can offer divorcing couples more control over the issues that will be decided regarding their postdivorce family, can help them negotiate tough issues in order to reach a mutually satisfying agreement, and can model skills necessary for successfully resolving future co-parental challenges.

REFERENCES

Dillon, P., and R. Emery. 1996. "Divorce Mediation and Resolution of Child Custody Disputes: Long-term Effects." *American Journal of Orthopsychiatry* 66, 1: 131–140.

Emery, R. E. 1994. *Renegotiating Family Relationships: Divorce, Child Custody, and Mediation.* New York, NY: Guilford.

Emery, R. E., D. Sbarra, and T. Grover. 2005. "Divorce Mediation: Research and Reflections." *Family Court Review* 43, 1: 22–37.

Kelly, Joan B. 1996. "A Decade of Divorce Mediation Research: Some Answers and Questions." *Family & Conciliation Courts Review* 34, 3: 373–385.

Jacqueline Kirby Wilkins, Ph.D., is a Certified Family Life Educator and mediator and a former assistant professor at The Ohio State University. She is the President of *IntelliSolve, Inc.*, a consulting firm offering mediation, group facilitation, cooperative training, and evaluation services.

WIDOWHOOD AND WIDOWERHOOD

Life expectancy continues to increase, with gaps between Blacks and Whites, men and women narrowing. The average life expectancy for a baby born in 1900 was 48 years for males and 51 years for females. In 2000, life expectancy was 74.1 years for men and 76.5 years for women. Furthermore, men and women who live to age 65 can expect to reach age 81 and 84, respectively (Consumer Health Digest 2002). Life expectancy differs by race and ethnicity, but even these gaps have been reduced. For example, in 1950, Whites lived 8.3 years longer than Blacks, but this gap receded to 5.6 years in 2000 (Meckler 2002).

Such shifts translate into more individuals living longer and facing final family transitions (and likely more chronic illness) later in life.

The greater life expectancy of women and the greater remarriage rates of men results in significantly higher rates of *widowhood* than of *widowerhood*. Among those 65 to 74 years of age, rates for living with a spouse are high for both men (77%) and women (53%). However, among those aged 75 years and older, men were more likely to be living with a spouse (67%) than women (29%) (Fields and Casper 2001). Widowhood is often a longer lasting, and permanent, state for older women.

Age, Gender, and Sexual Orientation Effects

How one handles the loss of a partner often depends on one's personality, needs, and coping strategies. As discussed in chapter 3, resilient individuals reveal "inside-out protective factors (capacities and attributes)" as well as the outside-in strengths and buffers of the family and external community (see Figure 3.4). Lieberman's (1996) interviews with 700 widows and widowers reveal the pain, anger, and challenges of the early months after their partner's death. However, Lieberman confronts the belief that widows are weak and lack resourcefulness, noting instead widows and widowers alike can be resilient. Yet, age, gender, and sexual orientation do appear to be factors in recovery from the death of a spouse.

Young widows, more so than older widows, may be expected to complete the grieving process quickly. Dealing with the loss of a loved one is difficult enough, but when family, friends, and society expect a young widow or widower to get over a death too quickly, this makes the journey confusing and lonely (Feinberg 1994). Grief does not respond to a magic timetable or a one-size-fits-all pathway.

Widows and widowers exhibit differences in their grieving and recovery. Lieberman (1996) found widowers were less likely to explore existential questions than were widows. Lieberman found that many of the widowers he interviewed rush into other relationships soon after the death of their mates.

Shernoff (1997) notes that for men, heterosexual and gay alike, widowerhood is painful, often lacking role models and social direction. Widowers, regardless of sexual orientation, often define the death of a partner or spouse as dismemberment. This is especially true for the gay widower who is deprived of a legally recognized marital relationship and often a socially recognized status as mourning a deep, significant loss.

Surviving the Death of a Spouse or Partner

According to Lieberman (1996), individuals carry a virtual mind-map of expected supports. If these family and friend supports fail, the widow or widower can be devastated. Support groups can be vital for the healing process. Effective support groups:

- Offer opportunities to share painful feelings and voice concerns
- Extend occasions to see other widows and widowers as role models who have dealt with challenges
- Grant permission for each widow and widower to work through grief and challenges in her or his own way
- Present opportunities to experience hope, develop understanding, and feel loved
- Afford a setting for new friendships
- Provide a setting to help others as well as be helped

For those seeking to support the grieving individual, listening and being present and available are more important than knowing exactly what to say. This also means allowing those who grieve to heal and move on at their own pace. Lieberman's (1996) work challenges the grief-loss model which views widows merely as victims who are powerless and can only adjust to a life half empty. Bereavement needs to be viewed as an opportunity for growth, a journey to self-discovery, but Lieberman challenges families to shed myths surrounding grief and realize thriving after the loss of a beloved spouse or partner requires more than coping with bereavement.

However, social support can result in negative as well as in positive effects. Miller et al. (1998: 200) found "some types of help, such as providing housing, money, or giving advice, may involve costs in feeling beholden to others that outweigh the support offered." This may have been the effect of negative preexisting relationships between these widows and those providing the help. Widows (and divorcees) experienced reduced stress when the help was practical and when it came from individuals who were trusted and loved.

Building a Life After the Death of a Spouse or Partner

Recent research indicates that emotional and instrumental dependence on one's mate prior to the death of that partner affects older adults' adjustment to death of a spouse. In a study of 297 men and women in an ongoing study of older couples, Carr (2004) found the highest levels of self-esteem after death of a spouse among women who were the most emotionally dependent on their spouses and who, coincidentally, had the lowest levels of self-esteem while married. Carr also found the greatest personal growth was found among men who were most dependent on their wives for home maintenance and financial management. Carr (220) concludes, when widowed, the highly dependent spouse reaps the greatest "psychological rewards from the recognition that they are capable of managing on their own."

Death remains a difficult subject in American society. Americans openly discuss such taboos as pedophilia or incest, but we continue to stumble over the topics of death and its aftermath. The journey through bereavement begins with grief but includes the challenge and for some the opportunity of building a new or at least a different life. Families, friends, and family professionals need to be aware that those who grieve the loss of a loved one should not be subject to an imposed timetable. The bereavement process is different for every individual. Life after death of a loved one needs to be embraced as a time to begin a new journey of discovery and growth. Widows and widowers need to journey from widowhood to "selfhood," and in so doing, give themselves permission to "uncouple" and reconstruct their lives (Ginsburg 2000). In Box 9.3 Lieberman shares a glimpse of shifts in widowhood and widowerhood in the future.

BOX 9.3 "Widowhood in the 21st Century"
Morton A. Lieberman, Ph.D.

A widow, in the throes of sorrow, confused about the present and worried about her future, may feel alone. She may not be aware that widows are probably one of the most misunderstood groups in America. Society judges a widow "successful" when she snaps back and acts like her "old self." My research explored the lives of over 600 widows and 100 widowers aged 28 to 75, who were followed for seven years. I demonstrate how society's attitudes move between the two stark poles of proper grieving and remarriage. One of the major burdens facing widows is the net of half-truths, which I have termed "myths," that interfere with finding a pathway that yields not only recovery but also, more important, a new beginning.

Deprivation and feelings of grief are real and universal but beyond mourning there are a host of tasks and challenges that widows must face. During the first months of widowhood the paramount task is dealing with grief and loss. However, I see grief as only one of many tasks and challenges facing widows, and that the absence of protracted grief is not a sign of pathology. Because there is no "right" length of time to grieve, the successful "resolution of grief" can follow many different pathways. Recovery from bereavement is not the end point. For many, widowhood presents an opportunity for growth and meaningful life change.

Beyond the immediate problems, widows face a number of important challenges:

- Beliefs and assumptions about what is important in life.

- A self-image which is embedded in a long-term relationship that no longer exists.

- Exploring feelings toward remarriage and relationships to men.

- Confronting regrets about both their marriage and the undeveloped aspects of their lives.

- How to reconstruct a future as the death of a spouse disrupts plans, hopes, and dreams.

I found that most widows reestablish their equilibrium over time. As time passes, irrespective of professional help, most widows do recover. Within about a year most showed significant decrease in the common symptoms associated with bereavement—anxiety, depression, intensity of grief, the abuse of alcohol and drugs, and bodily complaints. Over one third showed clear evidence, after a year, of growth and expansion.

The widowhood experience is in large measure shaped and influenced by the attitudes and beliefs of those around them, including family, friends, professionals, and the media. Society's beliefs about widowhood often reflect myths that do not match the real experiences of widows. These false beliefs and half-truths often interfere with recovery and development of women confronting a loss.

The women I studied were born at a time when the role, status, and expectations for them were radically different from those of contemporary society. Women in the 21st century will enter widowhood with different life experiences and will confront a society that is different from the one faced by contemporary women. The increasing empowerment and the development of women as separate persons beyond their marriages will more and more be the norm. Many will become widows having held major positions in life and having fully realized their potential.

Women in the 21st century will not be burdened by a view of marriage characteristic of the mid- and late-life widows' stories that comprised my study. Regrets for not having developed themselves will be rare as will the total reliance of the self-image on their marriage. It is likely that the idealization of and dependency on their spouse, characteristic of many widows, will be a rarity.

Morton A. Lieberman, Ph.D., is currently Professor of Psychology at the University of California, San Francisco. Throughout his career, he has focused on two central areas: the study of adult development and the investigation of change induction groups. He joined the University of Chicago faculty in 1957 and remained a faculty member there until 1983.

YOURS, MINE, OR OURS?

Stepfamily Arrangements in the 21st Century

Leon and Angst (2005) examined images of stepfamilies in popular films. Although the majority of films depicting stepfamilies focused on problems, Leon and Agnst indicate that media were also beginning to explore some of the complexity in stepfamily life (e.g., stepparent and parent–child relations, loyalty issues, merging different lifestyles, "parentification" when children in single-parent households assume adult responsibilities and couple relations and conflicts).

Some who lose a spouse through death and many who divorce move quickly back into the world of the married. As with other statistics on marriage, the chance a woman will remarry is very much related to her race and ethnicity. Fifty-four percent of White women who divorce remarry within five years, but only 44% of Hispanic women and only 32% of Black women do so. Also, the chance a woman will remarry following divorce is evidently declining. In the 1950s, a woman who divorced had a 65% chance of remarrying. Today a woman who divorces has a 50% chance of remarrying (Department of Health and Human Services 2002).

Pinsof, a family therapist and president of *The Family Institute* at Northwestern University, argues for "normalizing" divorce and honoring and supporting all types of families.

> Divorce is seen as this terrible thing, as a sign of selfishness, immaturity, a lack of commitment, a type of moral decay. We need to accept it and to teach the young about the realities that confront them, a new way of talking about relationships. (Peterson 2002: 4D)

Using the Correct Metaphor

Stepfamilies do not blend. In fact, they are often—comfortably or uncomfortably— "lumpy." Members from each original family sometimes struggle to adjust to new living arrangements. The term *blended* is troublesome to stepfamilies and family studies professionals who work with them. To call complex stepfamily communities blended sets up unrealistic expectations and interferes with successful adaptation to the changes that gently folded families (i.e., allowing for and even celebrating unique characteristics that each family brings to the new living arrangement) require. Children and adults in stepfamilies do not lose their identities, connections, loyalties, or attachments to previous family communities. Stepfamilies are not recreated first-families nor should they be. According to *Stepfamily Association of America* (2003: 2): "Therapists have learned (and research confirms) that when stepfamilies try to 'blend,' they are typically doomed to failure." The general public and family professionals in particular need to stop using the inadequate label of blended.

BOX 9.4 "Stepfamilies Aren't Nuclear Families: The Dynamics of Stepfamily Life"
Jana Brooker, M.A.

A stepfamily has an evolution that is different in some key aspects from that of a nuclear family. Whereas pregnancy and birth create a nuclear family, a stepfamily is born out of loss. Divorce or death, not birth, precedes a stepfamily. Unlike a nuclear family, the stepfamily has no clear societal norms or role models to follow and must persevere in the midst of a societal bias toward nuclear families. Creating a stepfamily is a process that takes place over a period of years.

My stepfamily took several years to form, and it was a journey wrought with challenges. In the beginning, the family therapists that my husband and I consulted couldn't enunciate stepfamily stages of development or help us create a family vision. We asked for some guidelines and role models to follow. We asked for a picture of what a healthy stepfamily looked like. There weren't any. It wasn't until I began to study stepfamily formation in my Master's program that I unearthed research that explained my family's developmental stages. Having recorded my family's saga in my journals, I began to apply the information I was discovering, piecing together the evolution of my stepfamily. Thus my book, *Sun and Storms: Chronicles of a Stepfamily,* was born. I wanted other stepfamilies to be able to read an honest and intimate portrayal of a real stepfamily's progression.

The stories in the book illustrate the critical lessons my family learned. Forming a stepfamily is like uniting two civilizations: Each one has its own language, laws, and culture. When they begin to merge, there is lots of confusion and little order. A lack of shared family history, societal norms, and stepfamily guidelines make the task especially challenging. Step-relationships are complex and certainly not easy in the beginning. Family members can feel like veritable strangers to one another. For a long time my husband and I felt like outsiders in regard to our stepchildren's lives: There were no biological ties or legal rights that provided reasons for us to exist in their worlds. When my stepdaughter needed emergency care, the school didn't want to talk to me. They wanted my husband. Our children felt like misfits in this new world order, too. When my son's report card was mistakenly addressed to his stepfather rather than to his biological parents, it felt awkward and unnatural for him. When teachers requested a treasured photo from the family album, they didn't take into account that our children may not be at the house where the photo resides for several days and, thus, unable to get the photo.

My family learned that forming a stepfamily is a slow, arduous task that is not readily understood or supported but one with rewards. Persevering against the odds and forming bonds with new people in our lives is indeed satisfying. Our family life after 8 years of living together is solid and strong. Real relationships have been forged. Even though we aren't a nuclear family, our stepfamily isn't a step below.

Jana Brooker is a stepparent and author of *Sun and Storms: Chronicles of a Stepfamily.* She has a Master's Degree in Human Development and serves as president of *GreatStepfamilies.*

Roles, Rights, and Responsibilities

When parents remarry, stepfamilies are formed. The Bureau of the Census only collects data on the household where a child lives most of the time. Because most children are in the physical custody of their mothers, most stepfamily statistics only reflect *stepfather households* (biological mother and stepfather). *Stepmother households* (biological fathers and stepmothers) are rarely counted. The inference that stepfather households are the "real stepfamilies" is counter-productive at a time when society struggles to emphasize the need for "continued involvement (emotionally, financially, and day-to-day activities) of both biological parents in a child's life" (*Stepfamily Association of America* 2003: 2).

Studying remarriage and resulting stepfamily situations began in earnest in the 1970s. In the early 1990s, researchers began to recognize the complex nature of stepfamilies and the challenge to move beyond seeing stepfamilies as reconstituted nuclear families (Coleman and Ganong 1990).

Stepfamilies are certainly not the same as first-time families. The *Stepfamily Association of America* (2003) offers six major differences between step-families and first-families. First, stepfamilies emerge because of a loss due to divorce, death, or abandonment. This means the adults and children may need to grieve the loss of or change in other relationships. Unresolved grief can be a source of hostilities in step-relationships.

Second, the relationship between the child and biological parent is longer than that between the new couple. Stepparents and biological parents need to be sensitive to the close relationships between children and their biological parents. Stepparents need to exhibit patience and not assume the same role as parent. Almost inevitably, a feeling of being on the "outside" is common among stepparents during the early stages of a folding family. We like to emphasize the value of approaching the new family as "gently folded."

Third, the other biological parent, the former spouse, remains part of the folded family. Even if this parent has died or rarely visits, he or she is part of the stepfamily's past. This does not mean children must be forced to maintain a relationship with a biological parent they fear or dislike. Rather, it means stepfamilies cannot pretend that the first family never happened.

Fourth, children in folded families are often members of two households and two extended family systems. Family studies professionals endorse "parenting partnerships" in which all members of both households remain involved in the lives of their children, whenever possible. Such partnerships require flexibility, maturity, and openness from all the adults involved. Consider the stepfamily reality that children may have more than two sets of grandparents. (In chapter 11, we suggest the realities of kinship and fictive kin in first and gently folded families.)

Fifth, successful stepfamilies have no blueprints. Stepparents with no prior parenting experience may be thrust into parenting responsibilities with little time to prepare. Successful bonding between stepchildren and stepparents takes time, sensitivity, and encouragement from biological parents.

Unless the biological parent has died or terminated parental rights, stepparents cannot be assumed to have any legal rights or even responsibilities toward their stepchildren. Such a low status adds to the confusion of the stepparent role. This means that without written authority, stepparents cannot access school or other records, authorize emergency care, or sign important documents related to the children. This may lead to confusion over estate rights in the case of death of a biological or stepparent. According to Hans (2002: 306)

> Although much ambiguity remains, this formative period in stepfamily law has positively affirmed the importance of stepparent-child relationships in many ways, though tempered by sensitivity toward biological and adoptive parents' rights.

A recent study, published under the title "Second-Rate Health Care Blamed on Step-moms" (Cummins 2001) has determined children who live with their stepmothers suffer from second-class medical care. Stepchildren living with their fathers' wives were less likely to have had a medical check-up in the past year and less dental care. Furthermore, less money was spent on their food and they received less education. However:

> Stepmothers are on shaky legal ground when it comes to making medical [and other] decisions about their stepchildren. Also, [some] children's mothers often insist that they stay out of

medical matters—or any others, for that matter. Never mind the stepmoms. Why aren't fathers stepping up? (Cummins 2001: E1)

Clearly, the power and efficacy of stepparenting is a tenuous balance. Along with parenting responsibilities, finances are a major issue for stepfamilies. Engel (1999) suggests stepfamilies start out with separate financial accounts, yours and mine, but over time shift to a mutual "ours" account. As in most families, money matters demand trust and accountability. Stepfamilies need to be clear on how they intend to handle their funds and communicate concerns as they may arise. We discuss family economics chapter 13.

Gay and Lesbian Stepfamilies

What about gay and lesbian stepfamilies? In chapter 10, we examine the *Defense of Marriage Act*, federal legislation that limits the rights and responsibilities of marriage to heterosexual couples. Although committed gay and lesbian relationships are more visible and even more accepted in some communities, a substantial number of Americans oppose gay and lesbian marriage and parenting (Armas 2001). Johnson and O'Connor (2002) argue the lack of male role models for children of a lesbian union or of female role models for children of a gay union is an insignificant problem compared to parental concern that children may be teased by other children. The greatest challenges of having special family arrangements, whether gay or lesbian, interracial, or some other form, often emanate most from a lack of acceptance and support from communities and society.

Although stepfamilies are more accepted in society, gay and lesbian stepfamilies still reflect a small percentage of families and often are treated as "nonexistent" by family study researchers. Like other parents, gay and lesbian parents and stepparents want what is in the best interest for their children and stepchildren. Children raised in families with gay and lesbian parents fare as well as those reared in heterosexual families. In fact, the former reveal increased acceptance of their own sexuality and higher tolerance and empathy for others (Johnson & O'Connor 2002; Whiteside and Campbell 1993).

This is not to say gay and lesbian stepfamilies have an easy time negotiating family realities. For example, Lynch and Murray (2000) speak to the unique needs of gay and lesbian stepfamilies in terms of "coming out" to ex-spouses, families of origin, children, friends, employers, teachers, and others. At times, these stepparents pay severe penalties for their decision. Such honesty may aid parenting partnerships, but publicly acknowledging gay or lesbian identity may also jeopardize custody agreements, jobs, and relationships with extended family. Gay and lesbian stepparents suffer triple stigma in that they are stigmatized by society for their sexual orientation, by some in the gay community (and most heterosexuals) for being gay parents, and finally for being in a stepfamily (Berger 2001).

FROM LUMPY TO FOLDED: RESILIENCY IN STEPFAMILIES

Family studies professionals call for future remarriage and stepfamily research focus aspects that contribute to healthful functioning in stepfamilies such as "positive stepparent–stepchild bonds, stepsibling bonds, or remarried couple relationships. Knowledge of African American, Latino, and other ethnic stepfamilies...mothers in stepfamilies" (Coleman, Ganong, and Fine 2000: 1301).

The complexity of *family maps* (mental pictures of who is "in" and who is "out" of one's family community) is enormous. Children need to be part of the folding of a family and allowed to love and connect with stepparents, stepsiblings, and other stepkin. Failing to honor or severing these connections may have implications as significant as failing to honor or severing biological connections.

Consider stepparents' rights and obligations with regard to a stepchild after dissolution of the marriage. Second marriages have a divorce rate of 60%, versus 50% for first marriages (Rutter 2001). Questions related to "Do I have an obligation to support my stepchildren?" demand discussion. Step relationships have long-lasting bonds. Recent rulings by the U.S. Supreme Court recognize a new custody doctrine, the *principle of family relations* (Holtzman 2002). Previous custody decisions have been based on the primacy of parental rights as being in almost all cases in the best interests of the child. To the contrary, the principle of family relations seriously considers a child's present and past relationships with biological and stepparents along with the child's "perceived" family image (family maps). Such shifts in legal precedent are challenging the myth that stepparents have limited legal or emotional attachments, rights, and responsibilities to their stepchildren after dissolution.

How Stepfamilies Succeed

The *Stepfamily Association of America* (2003) has identified five areas key to stepfamily success. Not surprisingly, many of these areas are vital to the success of any family, not just of stepfamilies. First, the couples' relationship requires assertive communication, demonstrated affection, fair fighting, and shared time. Second, all members of the stepfamily need to learn and be encouraged to express and process emotions.

Third, stepfamilies and those who support them must resist the myth of "one big happy family," a sure setup for failure. Visher (1994) shares how fantasy expectations that children will automatically love the new spouse are not only troublesome but self-defeating. Members of successful stepfamilies need time to get to know each other and develop authentic relationships.

Fourth, these families need to develop new roles as, for example, the family enfolds noncustodial parents and new sets of grandparents. Perhaps obviously, children should not be burdened with the role of messengers between households. Beyond that, discipline is often a highly problematic issue for stepfamilies. One study reveals that parental monitoring (often sighted as a powerful predictor of children's behavior) differs between biological and stepparents, with biological parents having higher levels of monitoring (Fisher et al. 2003). The *Stepfamily Association of America* (2003) suggests neither authoritarian nor permissive discipline work as well as a democratic approach.

Fifth, establishing effective communication patterns is one of the most important, yet hardest, aspects of establishing new roles. The most successful families (first and folded) are those that are open and assertive, rather than complacent and conflict-avoiding. Learning new patterns to respond to the dynamics, challenges, and opportunities usually requires locating and using support through community groups and Web sites (several of which are listed at the end of this chapter).

Yet what is often neglected in preparing stepfamilies is the need for optimism. As discussed in chapter 3, at the heart of resiliency lies an image of what could be, a family's sense of purpose and sense of compelling futures. Along with this, stepfamilies (and, we argue, all families) need external communities that actively care, respect, and value the family regardless of its composition or arrangement. Such communities can foster success while providing reasonable expectations, encouragement, and support. In the final chapter of this book, we challenge the reader to consider how differently a community would act if it truly valued families rather than merely preached a narrow definition of family values.

External Community Supports

Families of all arrangements require support and encouragement from external communities. Parenting in stepfamilies is not the same as parenting in first-families. Education and preparation of all stepfamily members (including extended family members such as grandparents) is vital to the success of stepfamilies. Such education could help decoupled and lumpy families move beyond the trauma of annulment, desertion, death, or divorce.

BOX 9.5 "The Four Things You Need to Financially Survive Divorce and Get on with Your Life"
Nicole Middendorf, C.D.S., C.D.P.

Divorce. The word has a certain power to it. However, divorce does not have to destroy your family or your financial future.

Divorce is not a taxable event, but what you do with the assets after the divorce can impact you for the rest of your life. So educate yourself now to avoid ending up in a financial or emotional state you may not expect. Understand your assets and how they can positively or negatively affect your future and your family.

You will need four basic things to financially survive your divorce and get on with your life: a place to live, little or no debt, retirement assets, and liquid money. You should strive for a balance among these. You need a mix of each, not an abundance of one category with none of the other.

- *A Place to Live*. Depending on the divorce, one spouse taking the home may be advantageous, while in another situation such an action could be a disadvantage for the same spouse. Understand how your divorce settlement will affect you now, as well as five, ten, fifteen, and twenty years from now. A house is not a liquid asset, and if you look historically at the stock market, a house may have less appreciation potential compared with money set aside for retirement.

- *Little or No Debt*. Understand the cost of credit. Because having debt has a high cost, you need to know the difference between good debt and bad debt. Contact credit bureaus to get a copy of your credit report. If you have credit cards that have a zero balance, cancel those cards.

- *Retirement Assets*. You have many vehicles through which you can save money for retirement. Make sure that you do not forget some accounts and leave money on the table during the settlement. Know that some benefit plans cannot be divided. In that case, you want to examine other assets of the marriage and receive those instead. For example, if a pension cannot be divided, take more of the 401(k) assets as part of your settlement.

- *Liquid Money*. The divorce process has three general phases: beginning, middle, and after. In each of these stages your budget may be different, and you should make sure that you have liquid money available at all times.

Understand the differences among assets, regardless of whether you are single, married, or divorced. Gather as much information as you can about your own, and your spouse's, financial situation. Separate your emotions from your finances.

Examine each asset, and don't forget about the growth and liquidity potential of each. Educate yourself, get organized, and ask for help and you will be on your way to financially surviving a divorce and getting on with your life.

Nicole Middendorf is a Certified Divorce Planner and a Certified Divorce Specialist with Linsco/Private Ledger, a member of NASD/SIPC. She can be reached through www.lpl.com/strategicfinancial.

GLOSSARY

Adversarial divorce

Annulment

Barriers to divorce

Crude divorce rate

Desertion

Divorce

Family maps

Grief-loss model

Marriage dissolution

No-fault divorce

Principle of family relations

Refined divorce rate

Separation

Sleeper effect

Stepfather households

Stepmother households

Widowerhood

Widowhood

FOR YOUR CONSIDERATION

1. The divorce rate appears to have leveled off and perhaps even declined. What is your projection for divorce rates for the next 20 years?

2. What is your assessment of Popenoe's (2002) *The Top Ten Myths of Divorce* presented in Table 9.1?

3. The death of a spouse or partner is part of the natural cycle of living, and grieving is a journey of discovery and growth. What does this mean? What is the value of such a view of death to couples and families?

4. Family structures are becoming more complicated. A single parent who marries, then has a biological child with a spouse, then divorces, then remarries a second time is not so unusual. First diagram this more complicated set of family relationships (or a similarly complicated one with which you are familiar). Then suggest the places where these families will need to be particularly sensitive in order to retain their resiliency.

5. What resources are available in your community to support stepfamilies?

FOR FURTHER STUDY: WEB SITES, ORGANIZATIONS, AND PUBLICATIONS

Web Sites and Organizations

Divorce Central
   www.divorcecentral.com
   Four areas serve as the framework for this site: parenting, financial, legal, and lifeline (emotional support). This site offers the opportunity to post questions on a bulletin board and includes numerous links, checklists, and articles related to divorce.

Divorce Net

www.divorcenet.com

Divorce Net provides an abundance of information specifically related to divorce, including the negative and positive impacts of divorce on children (and ways to reduce the negative impacts). The site provides links to each state and national sites.

Divorce Reform

www.divorcereform.org

The intent of this site is to share opinions, articles, and legislation that support efforts to make divorce more difficult to obtain. The site does not purport to present balanced views on the issue, but is clearly focused on providing information to make divorce harder and therefore reduce divorce rates.

Stepfamily Association of America

www.saafamilies.org

The SAA Web site provides a rich, well-organized source of information for stepfamilies and those who wish to learn more about them. The site also offers support and encouragement to stepfamilies and evaluates educational materials.

Stepfamily Information

www.stepfamilyinfo.org

This site is less extensive than SAA, but provides additional information and resources for stepfamilies.

Your Stepfamily

1-800-277-2583

http://www.yourstepfamily.com

This bimonthly magazine addresses challenges of stepfamilies, including dealing with ex-partners, assisting children's transitions among homes, legal and financial issues, and objections from adult children. One regular feature is "Your Children's Eyes," in which stepchildren answer questions addressed to the editor.

Publications

Brooker, Jana M. 2002. *Sun and Storms: Chronicles of a Stepfamily.* Haverford, PA: Infinity.
  Brooker shares her personal journey through the transitions of divorce, remarriage, and stepparenthood. She candidly explains the need to say "good bye" to the past and move on—and the difficulty of doing so. This book offers a glimpse into the process of successful stepparenting.

Ginsburg, Genevieve Davis. 2000. *Widow to Widow: Thoughtful, Practical Ideas for Rebuilding Your Life.* Cambridge, MA: Perseus Books
  Ginsburg's position is that widows and widowers need to move from widowhood to "selfhood" after the death of a loved one. She writes of this as a process and a journey. Her book provides widows and widowers, their families and friends, and family studies professionals with a deeper understanding of the grief process and development of effect support networks.

Harvey, John H., and Mark A. Fine. 2004. *Children of Divorce: Stories of Loss and Growth.* Mahwah, NJ: Lawrence Erlbaum Associates.
  This book uses personal narratives from hundreds of young people reflecting on the despair and hope, chaos and resilience experienced during and in the years following their parents' divorce.

Parkman, Allen M. 2000. *Good Intentions Gone Awry.* Lanham, MA: Rowman & Littlefield.
  Parkman contends "no-fault" divorce, although well intentioned, has provided adults with an incentive to make decisions that are against their own and their family's best interest. In this book, he reviews and analyzes divorce law in the United States and offers some proposals for legal changes guiding marriage dissolution.

REFERENCES FOR CITED WORKS

Amato, Paul R. 1996. "Explaining the Intergenerational Transmission of Divorce." *Journal of Marriage and the Family* 58, 3 (August): 628–40.

Amato, Paul R. 2000. "The Consequences of Divorce for Adults and Children." *Journal of Marriage and the Family* 62, 4 (November): 1269–87.

Amato, Paul R., and Danelle B. DeBoer. 2001. "The Transmission of Marital Instability Across Generations: Relationship Skills of Commitment to Marriage?" *Journal of Marriage and the Family* 63: 1038–51.

Amato, Paul R., and Joan G. Gilbreth. 1999. "Nonresident Fathers and Children's Well-Being: A Meta-Analysis." *Journal of Marriage and the Family* 61, 3 (August): 557–73.

Armas, Genaro C. 2001. "Gay Homes More Visible." *Detroit News* (August 22). http://detnews.com/2001/census/0110/15-a05-275269.htm (Retrieved 10/16/01).

Berger, Roni. 2001. "Gay Stepfamilies: A Triple-Stigmatized Group." In *The Gay and Lesbian Marriage and Family Reader: Analyses of Problems and Prospects for the Twenty-first Century*, ed. Jennifer Lehmann. New York, NY: Richard Altschuler & Associates, 171–94.

Bramlett, Matthew D., and William D. Mosher. 2001. "First Marriage Dissolution, Divorce, and Remarriage: United States." *Advance Data from Vital and Health Statistics*, No. 323. Hyattsville, MD: National Center for Health Statistics.

Broome, Claire V. 1995. "Change in the Marriage and Divorce Data Available from the National Center for Health Statistics." *Federal Register* 60, 241 (December 15): 64437–64438.

Carr, Deborah. 2004. "Gender, Preloss Marital Dependence, and Older Adults' Adjustment to Widowhood." *Journal of Marriage and the Family* 66, 1 (February): 220–35.

Cherlin, Andrew J. 2000. "Generation Ex-." *The Nation* (December 11): www.thenation.com (Retrieved 1/20/03).

Coleman, Marilyn, and Lawrence Ganong. 1990. "Remarriage and Stepfamily Research in the 80s: New Interest in an Old Family Form." *Journal of Marriage and Family*, 52: 925–40.

Coleman, Marilyn, Lawrence Ganong, and Mark Fine. 2000. "Reinvestigating Remarriage: Another Decade of Progress." *Journal of Marriage and Family*, 62: 1288–1307.

Consumer Health Digest. 2002. "U.S. Life Expectancy Hits New High." *Consumer Health Digest* 02-42, 1. www.ncahf.org/digest02/02-42.html (Retrieved 1/19/2003).

Coontz, Stephanie. 1997. "Divorcing Reality." *The Nation* (November 17): 21–24.

Cummins, H. J. 2001. "Second-rate Health Care Blamed on Stepmoms." *Star Tribune* (July 29): E1, E6.

Department of Health and Human Services. 2002. *Cohabitation, Marriage, Divorce, and Remarriage in the United States: Data from the National Survey of Family Growth*. Vital and Health Statistics 23, 22 (July).

Engel, Margorie. 1999. "Handling Stepfamily Money." www.saafamilies.org/education/articles/$/engel-3.htm (Retrieved 1/20/03).

Feinberg, Linda Sones. 1994. *I Am Grieving As Fast as I Can: How Young Widows and Widowers Can Cope and Heal*. Far Hills, NJ: New Horizon.

Fernandez, Maria Elena. 2001. "Some Wedding Chapels Provide Returns on Their Marriage Vows." *Star Tribune* (January 26): E1, E9.

Fields, Jason, and Lynne Casper. 2001. "America's Families and Living Arrangements." *Current Population Reports—US 2000 Census* (June): 1–16. www.census.gov/population/www/socdemo/hh-fam.html (Retrieved 1/19/03).

Fisher, Philip A., Leslie D. Leve, Catherine C. O'Leary, and Craig Leve. 2003. "Parental Monitoring of Children's Behavior: Variation Across Stepmother, Stepfather, and Two-Parent Biological Families." *Family Relations* 52, 1 (January): 45–52.

Ginsburg, Genevieve Davis. 2000. *Widow to Widow: Thoughtful, Practical Ideas for Rebuilding Your Life*. Cambridge, MA: Perseus Books.

Glenn, Norval D. 1999. "Further Discussion of the Effects of No-Fault Divorce on Divorce Rates." *Journal of Marriage and the Family* 61, 3 (August): 800–802.

Hans, Jason. 2002. "Stepparenting after Divorce: Stepparent's Legal Position Regarding Custody, Access, and Support." *Family Relations* 51, 4 (October): 301–307.

Heckert, D. Alex, Thomas C. Nowak, and Kay A. Snyder. 1998. "The Impact of Husbands' and Wives' Relative Earnings on Marital Disruption." *Journal of Marriage and the Family* 60, 3 (August): 690–703.

Hetherington, Mavis E., and John Kelly. 2002. *For Better or Worse: Divorce Reconsidered.* New York, NY: Norton.

Holtzman, Melissa. 2002. "The 'Family Relations' Doctrine: Extending Supreme Court Precedent to Custody Disputes Between Biological and Nonbiological Parents." *Family Relations* 51, 4 (October): 335–43.

Hughes, Robert, Jr., and Jacqueline J. Kirby. 2000. "Strengthening Evaluation Strategies for Divorcing Family Support Services: Perspectives of Parent Educators, Mediators, Attorneys, and Judges." *Family Relations* 49, 1 (January): 53–61.

Johnson, Suzanne, and Elizabeth O'Connor. 2002. "The National Gay and Lesbian Family Study." www.mindfully.org/Reform/Gay-Lesbian-Family-Study.htm (Retrieved 1/20/03).

Kaufman, Gayle. 2000. "Do Gender Role Attitudes Matter? Family Formation and Dissolution Among Traditional and Egalitarian Men and Women." *Journal of Family Issues* 21, 1 (January): 128–44.

King, Valerie. 2002. "Parental Divorce and Interpersonal Trust in Adult Offspring." *Journal of Marriage and the Family* 64, 3 (August): 642–56.

King, Valerie, and Holly E. Heard. 1999. "Nonresident Father Visitation, Parental Conflict, and Mother's Satisfaction: What's Best for Child Well-Being?" *Journal of Marriage and the Family* 61, 2 (May): 385–96.

Knoester, Chris, and Alan Booth. 2000. "Barriers to Divorce: When are They Effective? When are They Not?" *Journal of Family Issues* 21, 1 (January): 78–99.

Leon, Kim, and Erin Angst. 2005. "Portrayals of Stepfamilies in Film: Using Media Images in Remarriage Education." *Family Relations* 54 (January): 3–23.

Lieberman, Morton A. 1996. *Doors Close, Doors Open: Widows, Grieving, and Growing.* New York, NY: Putnam.

L'Heureax-Dube, Claire. 1998. "A Response to Remarks by Dr. Judith Wallerstein on the Long-term Impact of Divorce on Children." *Family and Conciliation Courts Review* 36, 3: 384–86.

Lynch, Jean, and Kim Murray. 2000. "For the Love of the Children: The Coming Out Process for Lesbian and Gay Parents and Stepparents." *Journal of Homosexuality* 39, 1: 1–24.

McManus, Patricia A., and Thomas DiPrete. 2001. "Losers and Winners: The Financial Consequences of Separation and Divorce for Men." *American Sociological Review* 66: 246–68.

Meckler, Laura. 2002. "U.S. Life Expectancy Hits New High." *The Associated Press.* www.aegis.com/news/ap/2002/AP020909.html (Retrieved 1/19/03).

Miller, Nancy B., Virginia L. Smerglia, D. Scott Gaudet, and Fay C. Kitson. 1998. "Stressful Life Events, Social Support, and the Distress of Widowed and Divorced Women." *Journal of Family Issues* 19, 2 (March): 181–203.

Nakonezny, Paul A., and Rebecca Reddick. 2004. "Did Divorces Decline After the Oklahoma City Bombing?" *Journal of Marriage and the Family* 66, 1 (February): 90–100.

Nock, Steven L. 2001. "The Marriages of Equally Dependent Spouses." *Journal of Family Issues* 22, 6 (September): 755–75.

Ono, Hiromi. 1998. "Husbands' and Wives' Resources and Marital Dissolution." *Journal of Marriage and the Family* 60, 3 (August): 674–89.

Peterson, Karen S. 2002. "Divorce, Living Together are New Norms, Therapist Says." *USA Today* (July 29): 4D.

Popenoe, David. 2002. *The Top Ten Myths of Divorce.* Rutgers, NJ: The Marriage Project. http://marriage.rutgers.edu/pubtoptenmyths.htm (Retrieved 8/6/02).

Rodgers, Kathleen Boyce, and Hilary A. Rose. 2002. "Risk and Resiliency Factors Among Adolescents Who Experience Marital Transitions." *Journal of Marriage and the Family* 64, 4 (November): 1024–37.

Rogers, Stacy J. 2004. "Dollars, Dependency, and Divorce: Four Perspectives on the Role of Wives' Income." *Journal of Marriage and the Family* 66, 1 (February): 59–74.

Rutter, Virginia. 2001. "Lessons From Stepfamilies." In *Debating Points: Marriage and Family Issues*, ed. Henry Tischer. Upper Saddle River, NJ: Prentice Hall, 107–13.

Sayer, Liana, and Suzanne M. Bianchi. 2000. "Women's Economic Independence and the Probability of Divorce." *Journal of Family Issues* 21: 906–42.

Shernoff, Michael. 1997. "Gay Marriage and Gay Widowhood." *Harvard Gay & Lesbian Review* 4, 4. www.gaypsychotherapy.com/hglrwidower.htm (Retrieved 1/20/03).

South, Scott J. 2001. "Time-Dependent Effects of Wives' Employment on Marital Dissolution." *American Sociological Review* 66: 226–43.

Stepfamily Association of America. 2003. "Frequently Asked Questions." www.saafamilies.org/faqs/faqs. htm#1 (Retrieved 1/20/03).

Teti, Douglas M., and Michael Lamb. 1989. "Socioeconomic and Marital Outcomes of Adolescent Marriage, Adolescent Childbirth, and their Co-occurrence." *Journal of Marriage and the Family* 51: 503–12.

United States Bureau of the Census. 2000. *Statistical Abstract of the United States.* Washington, DC: Government Printing Office.

VanLaningham, Jody, David R. Johnson, and Paul R. Amato. 2001. "Marital Happiness, Marital Dissolution, and the U-Shaped Curve: Evidence from a Five-Wave Panel Study." *Social Forces* 78: 1313–41.

Visher, Emily. 1994. "Fantasy Expectations of Life as a Stepmother." *Stepfamily Association of America.* www.saafamilies.org/education/articles/sm/visher.htm (Retrieved 1/20/03).

Waite, Linda J., Don Browning, William J. Doherty, Maggie Gallagher, Ye Luo, and Scott M. Stanley. 2002. *Does Divorce Make People Happy? Findings from a Study of Unhappy Marriages.* New York, NY: Institute for American Values.

Wallerstein, Judith S., Julia M. Lewis, and Sandra Baleslee. 2000. *The Unexpected Legacy of Divorce: A 25-Year Landmark Study.* New York, NY: Hyperion.

White, Lynn K. 1990. "Determinants of Divorce: A Review of Research in the Eighties." *Journal of Marriage and the Family* 52: 904–12.

White, Lynn K., and Alan Booth. 1991. "Divorce over the Life Course: The Role of Marital Happiness." *Journal of Family Issues* 12, 1 (January): 5–21.

Whiteside, Mary, and Patricia Campbell. 1993. "Stepparenting in Gay and Lesbian Families: Integrity, Safety, and the Real World Out There." *Stepfamily Association of America* www.saafamilies. org/education/prof/whiteside-campbell.htm (Retrieved 1/20/03).

Wolfinger, Nicholas H. 1999. "Trends in the Intergenerational Transmission of Divorce." *Demography* 36: 415–20.

Wu, Zheng and Margaret J. Penning. 1997. "Marital Instability after Midlife." *Journal of Family Issues* 18, 5 (September): 459–78.

PART

IV

CHILDREN, KITH, AND KIN

PARENTS, CHILDREN, AND SOCIALIZATION: ROLES, RIGHTS, AND RESPONSIBILITIES

CHAPTER PREVIEW

The path to parenting has never been more diverse. The *fertility rate* has been declining, while some individuals and couples consider a *child-free* option. At the same time, women who find their *fecundity* has diminished face the reality of *infertility* and the possibility they will be *childless*. Many cases of infertility may be successfully resolved through a variety of techniques, including *in vitro fertilization (IVF)*, *gamete intrafallopian transfer (GIFT)*, *zygote intrafallopian transfer (ZIFT)*, *blastocyst transfer*, *intracytoplasmic sperm injection (ICSI)*, and *nonsurgical sperm aspiration (NSA)*. Egg and sperm donation as well as *cryopreservation* and *gestational surrogacy* offer additional options for childbearing, while at the same time posing serious cultural, ethical, legal, and religous dilemmas for society.

Adoption offers yet another path to parenthood, with the *adoption triangle* composed of birth parents, adoptive parents, and the adoptee. The most numerous children available for adoption are African American, Native American, and those of mixed-race backgrounds. The *Multiethnic Placement Act* makes it illegal to prohibit interracial adoption, but opposition to interracial adoption from the National Association of Black Social Workers and from legislation such as the *Indian Child Welfare Act* limit adoptions across racial or ethnic lines.

Some children are placed with *foster parents*, usually because their parents have been found to be neglectful or abusive. Teenage boys and girls might also become single fathers or mothers. Single parents may experience role overload, as well as economic problems. As discussed in chapter 9, stepparents face several hurdles in establishing rewarding relationships with their stepchildren, as do absent or part-time parents.

In many societies, the transition to the role of parent is marked by a special *rite of passage*. Socialization to the role of mother is complicated by physiological changes during and shortly after pregnancy and by cultural expectations embodied in attachment theory. The *nurturant father* is an increasingly prominent model of male parenting. *Off-time fathers* exhibit differences in their approach to their parenting role from that observed among *on-time fathers*.

Research is persuasive that children fare least well not so much in a single-parent family as in a *conflict-habituated family*. Parenting style—*authoritarian, permissive, or authoritative*—also has an effect on child outcomes, but growing up in a family with a gay or lesbian parent apparently does not. Sibling relationships have received remarkably little study, considering their place as significant others who share significant quantity and quality of time together. Child care serves as a significant agent of socialization for many children, with the quality of care dependent on availability, cost, and schedules, as well as on parental information and preferences.

This chapter concludes with a discussion of child endangerment, that is, *child abuse* and *child neglect*, including *sexual abuse* and *incest*.

DIVERSE PATHS TO PARENTHOOD

To Parent . . . or Not

The title of a book published in 1975 said it all for women of the baby boom generation: *A Baby—Maybe? A Guide to Making the Most Fateful Decision in Your Life* (Whelan 1975). The cover of that book noted:

> It used to be a reflex: if you got married, you had children; parenthood followed marriage automatically. But the Population Explosion, Women's Liberation and the Contraceptive Revolution have made parenthood an option. Today, people wonder whether to have children or not.

Or do they? The *fertility rate* (the number of live births per 1,000 women 15 to 44 years of age) dropped slightly from 68.4 to 65.9 between 1980 and 1999 (United States Bureau of the Census 2001a, Table 70). The median age at first birth (the age at which women have their first child) has increased steadily over the last three decades to 24.5 in 1999 (Centers for Disease Control and Prevention 1999). Although fertility rates for women in their teens and 20s rose between 1980 and 1990, rates for women in those age groups have fallen in the years since then. During the same period, the fertility rates for women 30 through 40 years of age rose dramatically. Fertility rates remain highest among women in their 20s in the marked direction of later childbearing. However, data from the National Survey of Families and Households confirm most people ages 19 to 39 who have not had children want to have children but are postponing childbearing (Heaton, Jacobsen and Holland 1999).

TABLE 10.1

Fertility Rate by Age of Mother, Births per 1,000 Women (All Races), 1980 to 2001

	Fertility Rates by Age of Mother, 1980 to 2001, Births per 1,000				
Ages in Years	*1980*	*1990*	*1999*	*2000*	*2001*
10 to 14	1.1	1.4	1.9	0.9	0.8
15 to 19	53.0	59.9	50.6	47.7	45.3
Teens	**54.1**	**61.3**	**52.5**	**48.6**	**46.1**
20 to 24	115.1	116.5	112.0	109.7	106.2
25 to 29	112.9	120.2	118.8	113.5	113.4
20s	**228.0**	**236.7**	**230.8**	**223.2**	**219.6**
30 to 34	61.9	80.8	90.6	91.2	91.9
35 to 39	19.8	31.7	39.3	39.7	40.6
30s	**81.7**	**112.5**	**129.9**	**130.9**	**132.5**
40 to 44	3.9	5.5	8.4	8.0	8.1
45 to 49	0.2	0.2	1.4	0.5	0.5
40s	**4.1**	**5.7**	**9.8**	**8.5**	**8.6**
30s + 40s	**85.8**	**118.2**	**139.7**	**139.4**	**141.1**

Source: Adapted from the United States Bureau of the Census. 2003. "Births and Birth Rates by Race, Sex, and Age: 1980 to 2001." *Statistical Abstracts of the United States, Table 85*. Washington, DC: Government Printing Office.

In the last quarter century, the percentage of women aged 40 to 44 who had no children rose from 10% in 1976 to 19% in 1998 (United States Bureau of the Census 2001c). The reasons for the delay in the timing and drop in the number of births have been linked to women's increased achievement in higher education, higher participation in the labor force, and later age at marriage. Although relatively few have no children, on the average, women are bearing fewer children later.

Childless or Child Free? The terms connote very different options. The decision to remain childfree, that is, to voluntary elect not to have children, can be seen as a rational choice arrived at through weighing the costs and rewards of that option against educational, employment, and lifestyle opportunities. In an application of exchange theory, those who prefer to be childfree may well appreciate and enjoy children, but prefer not to exchange rewards of being childfree for the costs of having children. Women who are child free tend to have higher education (United States Bureau of the Census 1997) and greater career attachment than women who become mothers (Veevers 1980).

Although the woman in a couple may be more likely to initiate the childfree position than her husband (Seccombe 1991), she is also more likely to be ambivalent about the decision than he is (Gerson 1993). Some couples enter into marriage with a child free "clause" clearly stated in their agreement to marry. However, for some the journey of arriving at the childless state is a set of successive postponements until the couple's "biological clock" runs out of fertile time and they pass the upper age limit at which most states will permit adoption.

Although they face negative stereotypes, research on the quality of life for childfree couples suggests childfree marriages are neither regretful nor isolated, but are in fact vital, happy, and intensely couple oriented (Cain 2002). These child-free couples seem to be more satisfied with their relationship (Somers 1993) and may perhaps be more egalitarian than other marriages (Gerson 1993; Veevers 1980).

Infertility and the New Birth Technologies

> In my examination of the relationship between infertility and resilience, I am particularly interested in the process by which couples manage the stress of infertility individually, as a family, and within their social environment consisting of family, friends, and acquaintances. (Daly 1999:7)

Reflecting on the discussion of family resiliency in chapter 3, the challenge of infertility demands couples adjust and adapt to the rigors of new medical technologies.

Women and couples may spend years trying to avoid fertility, only to find when the time comes they would like to conceive they have difficulty doing so. Perhaps they have waited to a point when a woman's *fecundity*, her biological potential to conceive, is naturally diminished. The most recent research indicates female fertility rates, that is, the chance of conceiving in a given month, begins to drop around age 27 for women and around age 35 for men (Dunson, Colombo, and Baird 2002). That study found a woman's chance of conceiving in a given month drops from 89% when a woman is 20 years old to 66% when she is 30 years old to 33% when she is 40 years old (Centers for Disease Control and Prevention 1997). Also, a couple may have had a condition that impaired fertility all along, but that condition had been masked by what they assumed was successful contraception.

Clinical *infertility* is the inability to conceive and carry a fetus to term after a year of attempting to do so. Infertility has declined as a result of improvements in general health and reductions in the rate of sexually transmitted infections. Approximately one in 10 women (Chandra and Stephen 1998) and one in six couples (American Infertility Association 2004) experience clinical infertility, although an increasing number are able to conceive with medical assistance, whereas some eventually conceive without any intervention. Couples or individuals who wish to bear a child but cannot, that is, those who find themselves childless, may experience deep personal sadness, anguish over their inability to fulfill strong cultural norms of femininity or masculinity, a sense of loss of control (Becker 1990), and even marked marital stress. Some couples report reduced frequency of sexual intercourse and sexual satisfaction as they struggle with infertility (American Infertility Association 1994; Sabatelli, Meth, and Gavazzi 1988; Ulbrich, Coyle, and Llabre 1990)

Some infertile couples can be assisted in conception and delivery through advances in fertilization and obstetrical techniques. Fertilization occurs when an oocyte (egg) is united with a sperm within a fallopian tube and is then implanted in a uterus (womb). Yet for 6.1 million women aged 15 to 44 years of age and 2.1 million couples, this process is compromised (Centers for Disease Control and Prevention 1997). In an estimated 30% to 40% of cases, infertility is due to factors associated with the female; in another 30% to 40% of cases infertility is due to factors associated with the male; and in the remaining 20%, infertility is due to a combination of factors or unknown causes.

Many cases of infertility may be successfully resolved through hormonal regulation achieved with clomiphene, menotropin, or one of the other drugs which, when taken orally or through injection, enhance the quality of the menstrual cycle. These drugs are associated with a higher incidence of multiple births (usually twins) and, less commonly, an increased risk of ovarian cysts.

In 1978, the first child, Louise Brown of England, was conceived outside of the human body using *in vitro* ("in glass") fertilization and transferring the embryos back into the uterus. Much has been learned regarding fertility assistance since then. In the United States today, the number of children born each year through artificial reproductive technology is estimated to be higher than the number of infants who are adopted (Perry 2002).

Conventional *in vitro fertilization (IVF)* includes controlled application of ovarian over-stimulation drugs, the gathering of eggs, the collection of semen, and the selection of viable sperm. The eggs and selected sperm are united and kept *in vitro* for three days, after which they are transferred to the uterus.

Multiple births are one of the main risk factors in this process. Such births carry considerable medical risks to developing fetuses and to the woman who carries them, as well as emotional, financial, and other considerations upon the birth of multiple, often at-risk, babies. Techniques to reduce the risks associated with multiple conceptions include *gamete intrafallopian transfer (GIFT)* in which one egg and sperm are placed directly into one of the fallopian tubes for fertilization. In a related process, *zygote intrafallopian transfer (ZIFT)*, eggs and sperm are first combined in a Petri dish to ensure fertilization, and then the fertilized zygote is placed directly into one of the fallopian tubes.

Blastocyst transfer technique can further reduce the risk of multiple births. At about Day 5 or 7, some of the embryos develop into blastocysts, developed embryos which "hatch" out of the "jelly coat" (zona pellucida) immediately prior to implantation. In blastocyst transfer, two to three of the more highly developed embryos are transferred to the uterus. Although this technique increases the likelihood of implantation and reduces the risks of multiple births, blastocyst transfer also allows for diagnosis of genetic disorders prior to implantation. Remaining embryos may be destroyed or preserved for future trials. However, as not all of gathered embryos may reach this stage, at least eight viable embryos are desired to secure two to three blastocysts for transfer.

Another technique used especially with male infertility or failed IVF trials is called "microinsemination" or *intracytoplasmic sperm injection (ICSI)*. In this process, eggs and sperm are collected as in IVF. Then the eggs are exposed to an enzyme that removes the outer cumulus cells surrounding the egg. While holding the egg in place under a microscope, a technician injects selected sperm through the cell membrane to the center of the egg. Sixteen to 18 hours later, the embryos are examined and the fertilized ones are transferred to the uterus. The medical risks with this procedure include potential harm to the embryo and the perforated zona, which offers protection to the egg. A related procedure, *nonsurgical sperm aspiration (NSA)*, can be used when the male lacks living sperm in the ejaculate due to vasectomy, blocked ducts, spinal injury, or other structural damage. Here sperm are removed via syringe directly from the testis. Once the sperm is removed, the ICSI process follows.

These techniques offer childless couples exciting possibilities to conceive and bear their biological offspring (Wright et al. 2004). However, IVT, GIFT, ZIFT, and the other techniques are expensive and rarely fully covered by health insurance. In addition, the treatments are stressful, consuming not only time and emotional energy, but posing a set of additional risks beyond those associated with multiple births. A woman undergoing hormonal treatments associated with some fertilization enhancement techniques may experience fluid retention, nausea, diarrhea, pelvic discomfort, breast tenderness, mood swings, headaches, and fatigue. A woman undergoing these treatments may also place herself at risk for other potentially life-threatening conditions, including "super ovulation" stimulation (excessively enlarged ovaries which may twist or even rupture) and elevated human chorionic gonadotropin (HCG) hormone which can lead to arterial thrombosis (clotting).

Cryopreservation (freezing of tissue for future use) offers the option of freezing eggs or sperm for later use or for donation to others trying to conceive. Although males have long had the option to preserve and bank their sperm for future use, females have only had the option to preserve and bank their eggs since 1995. Cryopreservation increases the options for those who wish to delay childbearing or for those requiring chemotherapy or radiation treatments that may interfere with later efforts to conceive.

In addition to the availability of sperm and egg donors, several widely published cases have drawn public attention to the option of *gestational surrogacy* (surrogate motherhood). The number of babies conceived with a surrogate mother, while difficult to estimate, remains relatively small. However, the new birth technologies, conception through sperm and egg donation, and surrogate mothers who carry a baby to term for another woman present serious cultural, ethical, legal, and religious dilemmas for society.

Adoption

Adoption: To take voluntarily a child of other parents as one's own child (*Merriam-Webster's Collegiate Dictionary 2002*). Across cultures and throughout history, adoption has been an acceptable way to form a family across generations. The federal government stopped collecting data on adoptions in 1975, so the exact number of adoptions each year in the United States is unknown.

Birth parents, adoptive parents, and the adoptee form an *adoption triangle* (Miall 1996). In Western society, adoption has historically been bound by secrecy, including laws prohibiting sharing identifying information between the birth and the adoptive parents, as well as with the adopted individual. However, an increasing number of adoptions are open, with more communication between the birth family and the adoptive family (March

1995). Although still somewhat controversial, more open adoption procedures have made it easier for adopted children to search for and establish connections with their biological family. Those who seek information about biological kin may do so out of curiosity or for a deeper need to establish a clearer sense of identity.

Although those who wish to adopt generally prefer a healthy infant of their own race or ethnicity, many are willing to adopt a child of another race or ethnicity. However, cross-racial adoptions occur in only about one in 12 adoptions (Bachrach, Stolley, and London 1992), and most of these involve international adoption. Although the *Multiethnic Placement Act* of 1994 prohibits the use of race, color, or national origin as a factor in adoption or foster homes ("A Guide to the Multiethnic Placement Act of 1994" 2002), the opposition of organizations such as the *National Association of Black Social Workers* and of legislation such as the *Indian Child Welfare Act* has been highly influential in prohibiting cross-racial adoption as a form of "cultural genocide." Policies that discourage adoption across racial lines contradict a large body of research. Simon and Alstein (2000) have studied families that have included White parents with African-American, Hispanic, and Korean children for over 30 years. Their research attests to the positive effects of transracial and intercountry adoption.

In the past, families who adopted children from different racial, national, or ethnic backgrounds were advised to sever ties to the child's birth race or nationality and to emphasize assimilation. Today those who counsel families who adopt interracially or internationally advise parents to conceptualize their family as interracial or international and to develop resources to integrate the family with the child's birth culture (Register 1991).

Using data from the *National Survey of Families and Households*, Ceballo (2004) compared the transitions of first-time parents. Their research shows parents who gained a child biologically, through adoption, or through marriage by becoming a stepparent had many similarities in the transition to parenting. All three parenting groups reported less depressed feelings, more disagreements with spouses, and more support from their own parents. In fact, across the three groups, the process of becoming a parent through adoption or marriage may even be less stressful than becoming a parent biologically.

Although adoptive parents can be overprotective, insecure, overindulgent, and weak disciplinarians (Miall 1996), some research finds adoptive parents may be more nurturing, comforting, predictable, protective, and helpful than biological families (Marquis and Detweiler 1985). Miall suggests adoptive parents who recognize and empathize with their child's separation from the birth parent may experience different parental feelings for their adopted child (Miall). Adoptive mothers may spend more time with their children and report a higher rate of family bonding than do other mothers (Lansford et al. 2001). One study found adoptive adolescents were far less likely than other adolescents to experience divorce or to live in a single-parent home (Benson, Sharma, and Roehlkepartain 1994). Some of these differences reflect the fact that adoptive parents tend to be seven to eight years older than biological parents (Marquis and Detweiler 1985). These differences may also reflect variation in who can and does adopt in American society, as well as cultural factors that move some families to consider adoption.

Overall parent–adoptive child relationships and attachments appear to be very similar to those in biological families (Benson, Sharma, and Roehlkepartain 1994). Furthermore, adopted children tend to be confident, hold a positive view of others, and see themselves as in control of their lives (Marquis and Detweiler 1985). Level of functioning and depth of commitment, rather than biology, seem to be the primary determinants of the rewards and challenges of family life (Miall 1996).

Today only about 2% of unmarried, teenage mothers place their children for adoption, a dramatic reversal from earlier decades (Bachrach, Stolley, and London 1992). That statistic, combined with the preference for the adoption of healthy infants, results in a very short supply of the children most desirable for adoption. Children with physical or developmental disabilities and those in sibling groups are among the most difficult children for whom to find adoptive homes. The hardest children for whom to find adoptive homes, and some say the most in need of adoption, are those who have been in long-term foster care. A movement toward larger scale institutionalization of these hard-to-place children has found some supporters in some states, including Minnesota. However, the consensus among child welfare professionals seems to be that such a system does not favor healthy child development, largely because those children who are hardest to adopt are also the ones who come bearing the deepest problems. These children and their families are discussed in the following section.

Foster Parenting

Cherlin (2002: 402) has called foster care "a program with few admirers and many critics." Some find the scrutiny involved in foster parenting an unjustified intrusion into private family life (Liss 1987), whereas others charge the foster system is class-biased (Berger 1986). Steiner (1981) and other critics see foster parenting in general as "social warehousing" when the foster care system should be helping parents acquire the skills to be better parents under what are often quite challenging circumstances.

Foster parents accept temporary care of children whose parents are unable or unwilling to take on the responsibility of raising children. In most cases, children have been removed from their parent's care involuntarily on court order because one or both of the parents have been found by a child protection worker to be neglectful or abusive. Foster care is intended to be a temporary situation until permanent arrangements can be made for the child to be reunited with the birth family or placed with an adoptive family.

Systematic studies of foster parenting are few. One exception is Wozniak's (2002) study of African-American and European-American foster mothers in Connecticut. She used participant observation and focus groups, as well as interviews, with foster mothers (most of whom were working class or poor), as well as foster fathers, social workers, and a few foster children over the age of 18. Wozniak learned foster mothers' perspective differs from that of the state, especially on the matter of payment. Alhough the state views payments as reimbursement for children's room, board, clothing, and other expenses, foster mothers view payments as compensation for work associated with caring for the child. Furthermore, foster mothers do not see a contradiction between loving the children for whom they care and accepting money for the care of those children.

However, foster parents have no parental rights regarding the children in their care. Individuals who become foster parents volunteer their time to care for a child in their homes. The expectations are foster parents will be caring and nurturing, yet avoid deep attachment. At any time, the legal system may remove the children and place them elsewhere, in another foster home, with the biological mother, father, or other relative who is deemed fit to parent the child and who requests custody, or in an adoptive home when one becomes available. Too often, critics charge, the foster arrangement is a long-term, perhaps even permanent one. What begins as a short-term job may become a lifelong commitment (LeMasters and DeFrain 1989).

The number of children in long-term foster placement, with no chance of being adopted, became a serious concern in the late 1970s, when about a half million children in the United

States were living in foster care. For the next few years, through 1985, the number of children in foster care declined to a little over a quarter million, as social service agencies placed renewed emphasis on helping troubled families or placing children in permanent adoption. However, by the late 1980s, the number of children in foster care had begun to rise again sharply until, by the turn of the century, the number of children in foster care had passed a half million. The crisis was greatest in large cities and among newborns and infants at risk because mothers had received little or inadequate prenatal care, their parents were drug addicted or homeless, or the infants themselves were born drug-addicted or abandoned by their mothers (Cherlin 2002).

At this point, although some communities have explored long-term care options for children structured along the lines of group homes for relatively large numbers of nonrelated children, society has no acceptable solution to the problem of abused, neglected, or abandoned children who are still legally bound to their parents.

Single Parenting

Before World War I, the image of a single mother was one of courage, pride, and respect. The single mother was seen as surviving the tragic death of her husband, bravely struggling to care for her family. However, after World War II, as the divorce rate rose and the number of never-married women who became pregnant and chose to keep their babies increased, single mothers were increasingly stigmatized as being irresponsible or even immoral. Research by Seccombe, James, and Walters (1998) indicates the categorization of single mothers (at least those who are recipients of welfare) as lazy and unmotivated, are even accepted by women who are themselves recipients of public assistance. The authors' own research indicates single mothers may struggle to maintain an identity as a responsible member of society and as an effective parent (see Box 10.1 "I Am a *Good* Mother!").

BOX 10.1   "I am a *Good* Mother!"[1]
Meg Wilkes Karraker, Ph.D., and Janet R. Grochowski, Ph.D.

We are interested in how single mothers define family and construct resilient futures for themselves and their children. In an ongoing research project we interviewed 21 single mothers. The participants were women who had not at the time of the interview married the father of their child. All except one of the mothers had frequent contact with the child's father, although the quantity and quality of the contact varied both among the women and over time for each woman. One woman even married the father of her child shortly after the interview. Another had, since becoming a single mother, identified herself as a lesbian and was at the time of the interview in a long-term relationship with a woman.

We asked each woman to complete a *StoryLine*© (Grochowski 1997), giving us a narrative in which she explained how she has faced the demands and challenges of single motherhood with resiliency, having balanced education, employment, parenting, and other demands. We asked her to tell the story as if she was telling it to a best friend, describing the actions, attitudes, and strategies she used to arrive at the place where she is today.

The women in our study revealed descriptions of "family" that called to mind deconstruction in the sense used in postmodern theory, revealing basic assumptions and contradictions of the conventional use of "family." Beyond that, reflecting most of these women's strong connection to their own mothers, two of the women expressed a sentiment common to all of the women, in almost the same words. "Society fails to see me as a good mom, but my mother did." Each of these women drew pictures of families and told stories about futures that varied from the conventional norm. Beyond that, the women in our study revealed their willingness not only to deconstruct a stigmatized identity but also to reconstruct personal identities as adaptive and resilient.

All of the women in our study described themselves as either "highly resilient" or "mostly resilient." As women pursuing higher education at the time of the interviews, this may not be so surprising. However, they not only voiced a strong sense of social competence, problem-solving skills, and sense of purpose (as one woman noted: "Hey! I made it this far."), but also emphatically told us (in every case in almost these words) "I am a *good* mother!"

REFERENCES

Grochowski, Janet R. 1997. *Impacts of a Story-Based Delphi Strategy on Adolescents' Personal Health Projections: Creating Personal Learning Futures.* Doctoral thesis. Minneapolis, MN: University of Minnesota.

Meg Wilkes Karraker and *Janet R. Grochowski* interviewed single mothers in the mid-1990s about their experiences with families and futures. They have contacted those same women again, 10 years later, and are currently analyzing how the futures they envisioned have unfolded.

---

[1] This material is excerpted from "Single Mothers De- (and Re-) Construct 'Family': Some Considerations from Postmodern Social Theory," a paper presented at the annual meetings of *Sociologists of Minnesota*, October 1998.

Single parents may be never married, separated, divorced, or widowed. By the year 2000, one in every 10 children in the United States was being raised by a parent who had never married (Moore and Jekielek 2002). Some hardships of growing up in a single-parent family can be accounted for by the lower income of those families and by a decline in income for those who had previously lived in a two-parent family. According to McLanahan and Sandefur (1994), children in single-parent families experience hardships that are not directly related to lower income. These risks include less parental supervision, less consistent parenting, and more disagreement between single parents and their children (Dornbusch et al. 1985; Hetherington and Clingempeel 1992).

Being a single parent presents challenges, beginning with the social psychological demands of parenting alone, attempting to fill the roles otherwise occupied by two adults. Beyond that, one parent means at most one income, as well as less flexibility in scheduling for children's school activities and more fatigue in managing the demands of everyday family life (LeMasters and DeFrain 1989). Single parenting is, almost by definition, characterized by role overload.

The economic and other social problems of single parents and their children are compounded when the parents are teenagers. Psychologists consider assuming the parenting role during adolescence to be ill advised, as it interferes with the exploration of other roles and with integration of self-concept, while at the same time contributing to feelings of anxiety and crisis (Young 1988). This crisis is most often complicated by economic hardship and problems arising from truncated educational achievement and limited occupational options. Not surprisingly, children born to adolescent mothers fare better, at least on intellectual tests, when the mothers are better educated, employed, live in more desirable neighborhoods, and live with a male partner (Bunting and McAuley 2004; Luster et al. 2000).

Compared to 30 years ago, never-married women today are much less likely to place their child for adoption. In fact, by the late 1980s, few—3.2%—never-married women were relinquishing their children for adoption. This is a dramatic drop from the period before 1973, when 8.7% of unmarried women relinquished their child for adoption. The percentage of never-married Black women who relinquish their children for adoption has always been small (1.5% before 1973, compared to 1.1% in the 1980s); and the percentage for Hispanic women, even smaller. However, the percentage of never-married White women who relinquish their children for adoption has dropped from 19.3% before 1973 to 3.2% between 1982 and 1988 (Bachrach, Stolley, and London 1992).

The rate of teen parenting today is higher in the United States than in any other industrialized country (Brooks-Gunn and Chase-Lansdale 1995). Most of these pregnancies are unintended (Zelnick and Kantner 1980). However, few of those unintended births to unmarried women result in a child being relinquished for adoption. Never-married mothers who do relinquish their children are more likely to be well educated, be in school at the time of the conception, have no labor force experience, and be older than those who do not relinquish their children. Daughters are also more likely than sons to be placed for adoption (Bachrach, Stolley, and London 1992).

Although single mother families outnumber single-father families four to one, the number of single-father households grew 62% to 2.2 million, or 2% of all families over the last decade (United States Bureau of the Census 2001b). When compared to single mothers, single fathers tend to have a slightly higher income, higher education level, and tend not to change residences as much as single mothers do (LeMasters and DeFrain 1989). According to the National Longitudinal Study of Adolescent Health, adolescents in father-only families are twice as likely to become involved in violence, delinquency, and substance abuse as are children growing up in mother-only families. Data from the National Educational Longitudinal Survey and from the General Social Surveys confirm at least some of the hazards faced by children growing up in father-only families are the result of the instability many of them face before arriving in their father's household. Children do not appear to fare better or worse in one type of household over the other (Downey, Ainsworth-Darnell, and Dufur 1998).

Although the status of single mother is most likely not one most women eagerly anticipate, some women and a few men choose to parent children alone. The number of births to never-married women with professional or managerial employment has risen dramatically, accounting for as many as one out of every twelve births. These women are likely to be older, well educated, and career focused. They are likely to be financially secure and well supported by their family and friends. In these cases, the women say they are willing to undergo artificial insemination or to apply for adoption, motivated by a strong desire to nurture a child of their own (Mannis 1999).

Stepparenting

We offered some discussion of the challenges and opportunities faced by stepfamilies in general in chapter 9. Approximately one third of children will live in a family with a biological parent and a stepparent for at least one year (Dainton 1993). The quality of the relationship between stepparent and stepchild appears to depend at least in part on whether only one spouse has children from a previous relationship or if both spouses have children from previous relationships (Clingempeel and Eulalee 1985).

Although remarriage usually improves the financial circumstances of children (Thomson et al. 1994), stepparents report adjusting to their stepchildren's habits and personalities, acceptance by their stepchildren, and discipline are areas of conflict (Whitsett and Land 1992). Although children may report more difficulties with stepmothers than with stepfathers, stepmothers seem to have a better chance of developing satisfying relationships with their stepchildren than do stepfathers (Clingempeel and Segal 1986).

Effective relationships between stepparents and stepchildren face several hurdles, even beyond those associated with the complications of establishing financial responsibilities with biological parents. First, stepchildren come into the new family with previously formed values and expectations. Then custody arrangements offer generous opportunities for everyone involved to experience confusing and conflicting expectations for behavior and standards for discipline. To further complicate matters, stepparents interact not only with their spouses but also with the former spouses who are the biological parents. Finally, the stepparent role is poorly understood and encumbered by nasty stereotypes (e.g., the evil stepmother in Cinderella, the abusive stepfather) and rarely acknowledged by courts and laws guiding parent–child relationships (Visher 1984).

In some circumstances, a stepparent claims a stepchild as his own. In his study of 36 stepfathers, Marsiglio (2004) found this process of identifying one man's offspring as one's own was facilitated in certain circumstances. In particular, the men in Marsiglio's study were more likely to claim stepchildren as their own when:

1. The stepfather perceived behavioral and personality similarities between himself and the stepchild.
2. The stepfather felt secure about himself and his relationship with his partner.
3. The birth mother encouraged the stepfather's identity construction as the child's father.
4. The stepchild was willing to open the borders that may let the stepfather be seen as a father figure.
5. The biological father was marginally involved in the child's life.

Absent or Part-Time Parents

A final path to parenthood is that of the absent or part-time parent. Absent parents include those who have died, those who are away from the family because of peacetime or wartime military service or other occupational demands, those who are restrained from visiting their children, as well as those who have abandoned their children. Part-time parents include those who have intermittent custody or contact. In addition, some parents have little or no contact with their children because they are incarcerated.

The voluntary or involuntary nature of the parent's absence is likely less significant than the extent to which the child had an intimate relationship prior to the parent's departure. Even children who were too young to remember their father before he left the family may develop the sense of a relationship with that parent through the efforts of other family members and friends. As Br. Patrick Sean Moffett (see Box 1.2), former president of Boys and Girls Towns of Rome in Italy, has said in his study of boys and girls who are separated from parents and family through war or immigration, one's family is "always with you." Certainly, this is true of the relationship between parent and child, regardless of the diverse paths contributing to this significant relationship.

King, Harris, and Heard (2004) are among the first to examine nonresident father involvement in the context of race and ethnicity. Their research, based on the *National Longitudinal Study of Adolescence Health,* found race and ethnicity as well as father's education and other social structural factors had an impact on qualities of the father–child relationship. However, no one racial or ethnic group was significantly higher or lower on father involvement than were other groups. Although minority men were more likely to be nonresident fathers, minority men who were nonresident fathers were just as involved (and in some cases more involved) than White men who were nonresident fathers. Interestingly, King, Harris, and Heard found White youth with less educated fathers (those with a high school education or less) suffered the most loss in social capital when living apart from their fathers. Although gender differences were limited, King, Harris, and Heard did find boys reported more of certain types of involvement (e.g., overnight visits) with their nonresident fathers than did girls. However, Black girls reported being as close to their nonresident fathers as did Asian, Hispanic, and White boys.

In conclusion, the majority (68%) of American children live with two married parents. However, 23% of American children live with only their mothers, 5% live with only their fathers, and 4% live with neither of their parents (Federal Interagency Forum on Child and Family Statistics 2004). Although each parenting pattern has unique challenges and opportunities, they all share certain aspects of the transition to parenthood in American society.

THE TRANSITION TO PARENTHOOD

Perhaps no other life-cycle change has deeper and broader consequences than the arrival of a child. In many societies, the birth or adoption of a child is marked by a special *rite of passage.* These are rituals that recognize life's changes and help to define roles and statuses, including social bonds with significant others and with the community. Every major religious faith honors the birth of a baby.

In American society, we mark the arrival of our newest member in a variety of ways. Muslims announce the birth of a baby at services and celebrate with a dinner and a slaughtered lamb. Some Jews celebrate the arrival of an infant daughter with a *brit bat* ceremony. *Brit bat is* an adaptation of the *brit milah* (also known as a *bris*) the ritual circumcision and naming ceremony in the eighth day of life. Some Christians practice infant baptism, anointing the child with sacred oil or water, or a dedication ceremony, in which the child's physical and spiritual development is entrusted to godparents or other members of the community. Hindus practice an elaborate set of *Samskaras* (rituals) related to pregnancy, birth, and naming the child.

The transition to the status of parent is celebrated in other ways in American society. Rituals to celebrate the change to role of father have traditionally been limited to slaps on the back from coworkers and perhaps the sharing of [chocolate] cigars. Mothers (and sometimes both members of the expectant couple) are often treated to a series of baby showers and other events in which she receives gifts for the baby and celebratory recognition of her new status. In some subcultures, the new father's participation in these events is increasing, signaling perhaps an increase in the salience of the father's role and symbolizing the ideal of greater shared parenting.

The actual transition to parenthood is fraught with hazards. The arrival of a child, whether through birth or adoption, brings with it a dramatic change in the parents' routine. Sleeping, eating, and leisure patterns may be radically shifted to accommodate the new family member, with the attendant consequences of sleep deprivation and a reduction in couple-time. The birth of the first child also coincides with the end of the "honeymoon" stage of the marriage. Studies indicate, although marital satisfaction declines for all couples over the first few years of a marriage, the decline is much more dramatic for couples upon the birth of a child (Bird 1997; Glenn 1990). The birth of a child may bring to the surface conflicts over division of household labor (including the care of this new family member), employment commitments (husband's as well as wife's), and new financial demands. Nonetheless, couples are less likely to divorce in the first year after birth of a child (White 1990).

Socialization to Motherhood

Parents' satisfaction with their role as parent has been found to be highest among married parents with high marital quality, for those parenting their own biological children, and for mothers (Rogers and White 1998). This is not surprising, considering the extent to which the maternal role is so central to feminine identity in American culture.

The period during pregnancy leading up to the birth of a child can be a time of great anticipation and excitement, as well as attention and support from relatives, friends, and colleagues. Immediately after the birth hormonal fluctuations may be at their widest variation. At the same time, the new mother may experience a period of tremendous fatigue from sleep deprivation, psychological stress from expectations emanating from herself and others for performance of her new role, and sometimes not so gradual withdrawal of support from significant others. If she has been employed and is remaining at home for a period of time following the baby's birth, her sense of social isolation may be tremendous. Not all, but many women experience what has been called postpartum depression or "baby blues," accompanied by anxiety, crying, insomnia, and a general sense of sadness. Although these feelings pass quickly for most new mothers, 10% to 20% experience more severe depression requiring medical treatment (Kraus and Redman 1986). Interpersonal support systems, especially marital intimacy (Stemp, Turner, and Noh 1986), play an important part in avoiding or reducing the extent of postpartum depression.

Ishii-Kuntz and Coltrane (1992) estimate, of the total parental hours spent directly caring for their children, approximately three fourths of this time is invested by mothers. Hays (1998: 782) argues attachment theory, which was introduced in chapter 3, serves to perpetuate

> ... a series of powerful yet outdated cultural assumptions regarding the "proper" relationship between mothers and children .... a series of taxing and exacting prescriptions for completely selfless, constant mother care.

According to this model, a mother, especially one engaged in paid work outside the home, will appropriately experience guilt, sadness, or worry, that is, anxiety, when she is separated from her child (Bradley et al. 1997).

To the contrary, Davidson and Moore (1996: 546), citing research by Myers-Walls (1984), write:

> ... balancing social life and mothering is positively correlated with better total adjustment to life, more freedom in life, more acceptance of changes, ... and greater freedom from parental responsibilities and restrictions.

The combination of motherhood and employment is certainly one of the most critical issues for American women today (a fact to which these authors can attest). However, combining work and family is but one of the many role adaptations faced by women and, as we shall see in the next section, by men as well.

The New Fatherhood

According to Glen Palm, a parent educator and professor of child and family studies (Miller 2002: E10)

> [M]ost dads care deeply about their kids and want a good relationship. They say they want to be there for their kids in a way that's different than their dads.

Early, deep father–child bonding seems to serve as insulation against alienation and later conflicts over paternal authority and the child's rebellion.

Father's gender ideology has an impact on father's involvement with children. As expected, Bulanda (2004) found egalitarian fathers had greater involvement with their children than did traditional fathers. Doherty and his colleagues at the University of Minnesota found fathering, even more than mothering, is affected by other contextual factors in the family and community. Such factors as race or ethnicity, resources and challenges, cultural expectations, social support, employment opportunities, and economic factors shape the ability of men to function effectively as fathers. For example, research has documented the establishment of paternity and acceptance of economic and psychological responsibility by fathers are impeded by the lack of employment and poor occupational opportunities in African-American and other economically disadvantaged communities (Doherty 1998).

Also, in a study of low-income Mexican-American families, Coltrane, Parke, and Adams (2004) found father's egalitarian gender attitudes, mother's higher educational level, mother's employment, and family emphasis on rituals are associated with greater father involvement in supervision of children. Also, contrary to the stereotype of Hispanic men as "macho" and uninvolved in hearth and home, Mexican-identified men are more likely than their more acculturated peers to supervise children.

The traditional separation of a man's work from his family roles is an obstacle to active fathering. Long hours away from home and distractions during the workweek may leave only weekends for connecting with family. However, data from the *National Surveys of Families* indicate once fathers begin taking care of young children, they establish a continuing pattern (Aldous, Mulligan, and Bjarnason 1998). Wilcox's (2002) research on fathers finds men who are college educated, who live in a nuclear family, and who have strong community ties are most likely to spend time with their children. This is especially true of the fathers of sons. Father educators recommend fathers spend time alone with their children, developing good listening skills, and sharing feelings. They also recommend reducing expectations for the number of chores and errands that can be accomplished during father–child time (Miller 2002).

Increasingly fathers reflect a cultural construction of their role that has been called the *nurturant father* (Fox, Bruce, and Combs-Orme 2000). That is, fathers expect to participate in and support the care of their infants at a high level beyond that of "helper." However, the provider role remains paramount. In a recent study, Fox, Bruce, and Combs-Orme found fathers' economic provider role (providing food, housing, safety, and economic stability)

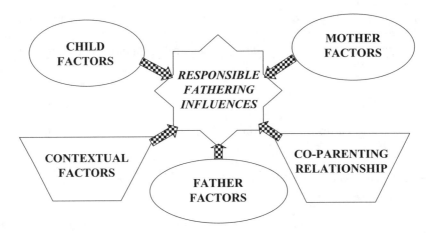

FIG. 10.1.   Responsible Fathering Influences.
Source: Adapted with permission from Doherty, William, Edward Kouneski, and Martha Erickson.
1998. "Responsible Fathering: An Overview and Conceptual Framework." *Journal of Marriage and Family* 60: 277–92.

was primary and taking care of the baby and household tasks were of less importance. These expectations for fathers were also held by mothers, although Black fathers had higher expectations of being a caregiver to the baby and helping out in the house than did other fathers.

A small but growing coterie of men is choosing to emphasize the domestic and child-care roles over employment. These men may be part of a couple who make a rational choice to forego their own employment in favor of their wives' or partners', which may be better paid or earn better benefits. They may feel better suited by temperament to the domestic sphere or spiritually called to devote themselves to caring for home and children. Networking with other stay-at-home dads seems to be a key to successful adjustment to this nontraditional role.

Off-time fathers are those who become parents after the age of 35. These fathers, compared to *on-time fathers* (those who become fathers when they are in their 20s) may exhibit more maturity when it comes to caring for their children. Off-time fathers may hold more egalitarian relationships with their wives than do other fathers, and in doing so share more of the household chores, including parenting. Off-time fathers are also likely to be more financially stable and have more freedom on the job, thus having more time to spend reading and playing with their children. These fathers also show greater amounts of affection toward their children through hugging and praising. Overall, off-time fathers put more time and effort into their role as father and exhibit more nurturing behavior toward their children than do on-time fathers (Heath 1994).

Fatherhood has received inadequate attention in family studies. However, this may be changing as the men's movement has spawned a "fatherhood movement" and as men become more vocal and assertive about engagement with their children. Nonetheless, the stereotype of the distant, uninvolved, and even toxic father persists, especially in images of African-American, Hispanic, and other minorities. Recent work by Hamer (2001) on Black fathers and by Gutmann (see Box 10.2) on Mexican fathers attempts to reveal the pleasure and pain, pride and frustration of contemporary fathers across diverse communities.

BOX 10.2 *Padres de Verdad*: Fatherhood in Working-Class Mexico City
Matthew C. Gutmann, Ph.D.

Despite advances in understanding motherhood, we have only begun to understand fatherhood. The few existing investigations of men in Mexico tend to describe fathers in homogeneous terms, as if distinctions among men by class, ethnicity, and age matter little, and as if men in Mexico exist in a timeless vacuum called "traditional society," immune to transformations of modernity. In this essay, I draw on fieldwork in a squatter settlement of Mexico City in the 1990s to provide an alternative portrait of the ideas and activities of Mexican men in real parenting situations.

Women in working class Mexico City spend far more time with children than do men. In the minds of most women and men there, children, especially young children, "belong" with their mother or other women. One morning I arrived at a corner store in the neighborhood where I lived carrying my first child, Liliana, who was then only a few months old. César, an elderly neighbor, asked me, "Doesn't she miss her mother?" I tried to explain that although her mother spent a lot of time with Liliana, so did I, and that in my mind proximity was a principal determining factor in an infant's attachment to others. To him this was beside the point: There was a natural and physically overwhelming bond involved in mother–child mutual dependency that took precedence over all others, a qualitative relation that no amount of time spent with me could unseat. In Mexico, toddlers are said to suffer from *mamitis* (mommy-itis), whereas *papitis* is to date an unknown affliction.

Though there are generational differences with respect to fathering, with younger men usually more active and involved in parenting than were their fathers and grandfathers, even some men in their 70s talk about having had a lot of responsibility for raising their children—boys in particular. These men frequently relate how they took their boys with them when they went out on errands or to visit friends during their free time, especially on weekends. Nonetheless, fathers of the older generation also say when their children were young, the men were responsible more than were the mothers for teaching their boys technical skills and a trade—things that would later be necessary in fulfilling their adult masculine responsibilities as economic providers. This was even truer when Mexico's economy was primarily agricultural and fathers would bring their small sons to the fields as soon as they could walk and not get in the way.

Overwhelmingly, the people I interviewed stated there were pronounced differences in parenting obligations for men and women. First and foremost, men should provide for a family economically and women should care for the home (meaning children, husband, and house, often in this order of importance). There was variety in the responses, with many men and women calling attention to the important role of men as fathers, but the consensus was unmistakable in terms of the ideals enunciated by both women and men.

The respondents were unambiguous about the fact that mothers were responsible for washing and feeding infants. To my surprise, a sizable number of men and women said that fathers are more, or much more, tender with their children than we mothers. The fact that many mothers spend more time with children than do the fathers may lead some men to indulge their children when they are with them.

Mothers enforce the rules far more than fathers do. Men in working-class Mexico City talk of beating their children, just as they were slapped, spanked, and whipped with belts as youngsters. But the most violent punishments inflicted on children today are often at the hands of mothers, a situation many accept as "normal."

A less gendered division of labor pertains to helping children with their homework and household chores. Often the key factor is which parent or other adult is home with the children more, though in the case of schoolwork, which adult has received more formal education is also important.

Even when both parents were concerned about emphasizing to their children the importance of ethical conduct, the mother was most often the parent involved in gathering the children to pray and to attend church and religious celebrations. The communication and organization of religious morality by women is a reflection of the greater importance of religion in the lives of many Mexican women.

Responses to my inquiries regarding parenting indicate the perils of oversimplifying fathering practices in Mexico. Although Mexican male identity is often thought of as equivalent to irresponsibility and violence, for most of the men and women interviewed, being a dependable and engaged father is as central to *ser hombre*, being a man, as any other component, including sexual potency.

I asked Toño, a single man of 27, about whether having children, especially boys, was important to him. "For me," he replied, "having a lot of kids to prove you're macho is *una chingadera* [equivalent to "a lot of bullshit"]. Those ideas are forty years old." Though not everyone would agree with Toño's assessment, he touches upon a sentiment that is more widespread than dominant images of Mexican masculinity would lead us to believe.

If fatherhood in the minds of people in Mexico City is less associated with profligate behavior than the stereotypes would indicate, then these changes should be evident in the practical, everyday experiences of men in the neighborhood. My concern here, with regard to the pragmatics of motherhood and fatherhood, is to take the uncritical acceptance of standardized routine, which is implicated in behavior and contrast it with the active shaping of human life experiences.

The point was brought home to me when I went one day to the butcher Guillermo to buy meat for Liliana. Although meat is a little more expensive there than it is in the supermarket, Guillermo always grinds the beef twice when he knows it will be fed to an infant. As I was leaving, I thanked Guillermo and said something to the effect of "OK, gotta go cook this up with some pasta and. . . ." Guillermo interrupted me and said, "No, not pasta. That's just going to make her fat. You know, the father doesn't just procreate, he's also got to make sure they eat right." Guillermo felt that because I was a new father he had the right and responsibility to give me advice when warranted. By wording his counsel of fatherly love and care in contrast to the familiar image of *Man the Procreator*, Guillermo was positioning himself in opposition to a history, or at least a story, of Mexican men.

We should revise our beliefs that all men in Mexico, today and historically, have little to do with children. Instead, more active and less active parenting by men seems to correspond more to other factors such as class, historical period, region, and generation. For numerous, though not all, men and women in Mexico City, in the 1990s, active, consistent, and long-term parenting is a central ingredient in what it means to be a man and in what men do.

Matthew C. Gutmann is Stanley J. Bernstein Assistant Professor of the Social Sciences—International Affairs in the Department of Anthropology at Brown University. He has conducted ethnographic research in Mexico since 1990.

As Americans born between 1965 and 1979—Generation X—begin to form families, polls, census data, and anecdotal evidence from parent educators suggest we might see new parenting patterns among these "Gen X" adults. This is a cohort that came of age during a period of significant social change which may feel more insecure than boomers (Rosen 2001). One third of Gen X adults had divorced parents, compared to 13% of baby boomers. Nearly half had employed mothers and experienced day care and after-school independence earlier and in larger numbers than did boomers. These generational differences translate into changes in the roles of fathers. Gen X fathers spend more time rearing children, and more of them report being stay-at-home dads (DeMarco 2004). Perhaps reflecting a general dissatisfaction with imbalance between work and family, nearly half of all parents—even older parents—report they feel they spend too little time with their children (Milke et al. 2004).

CHILD AND ADOLESCENT SOCIALIZATION IN THE FAMILY

We take for granted children will be dependent and parents will be responsible for at least 18 and perhaps more years of their children's lives. We accept as reasonable that children will defer rights and responsibilities to parents and other adults in society. In *Centuries of Childhood*, Aries (1960/1962) demonstrated childhood as we know it is a rather recent social invention. In Western Europe, until the end of the Middle Ages, the activities and artifacts, the rights and responsibilities, of people we consider children were remarkably similar to those of older members of society. A 10-year-old male would be expected to shoulder his share of the burden in a family engaged in agriculture; a 13-year-old female might be expected to marry and, shortly thereafter, bear children. The games and the clothing of adults and younger people were virtually indistinguishable. Today we consider younger people incapable of adult roles. However, such roles were routinely expected in a society where life expectancy might run only into the fourth or fifth decade. In such societies, the relative absence of social surplus inhibited many members of society from being entitled to a life devoted to such idleness as formal education or play.

Today, child development specialists speak of "play" being the "work" of childhood and fret in a bemused way over the increasingly protracted period of time occupied by American adolescence. In this section we will provide an overview of the growth and developmental needs of children and adolescents, the role of parents in guiding children, the role of siblings in childhood socialization, and the place of child care in child development.

Parents and Child Guidance

Parents and family culture are presumed to be critical in influencing adolescent acting out (Todd 2000), body image and eating disorders (Haworth-Hoeppner 2000), alcohol misuse (Barnes 2000), incarceration (Chipman et al. 2000), and an assortment of other high-risk outcomes for children.

The weight of evidence on the effect of family structure on children falls overwhelmingly on the side of children growing up with two biological parents in a low-conflict marriage (Moore and Jekielek 2002). Growing up in a two-parent family is associated with a lower probability a child will grow up in poverty. However, growing up in a *conflict-habituated family* (i.e., one in which the parents' relationship is characterized by unresolved conflict) is associated with more aggressive acting out, more shy withdrawal, and fewer academic and social skills in children (Cowan and Cowan 2002; Cummings and Davies 1994).

Hill (1999) has explicated the affects of child socialization and development in African-American families. She is critical of child-development theories that stigmatize Black parents as dysfunctional. Instead, from her surveys of Black and White parents, she found Black and other parents have similar values, discipline strategies, and perspectives on parenting. Additionally, however, Black parents were challenged with the necessity to teach their children the realities of racism and how to inculcate in their daughters and sons survival strategies. Hill finds little information on the socialization of Black sons.

More generally speaking, parenting style is related to child behavior and child development. Parenting ideals follow certain general social trends across time. Parents in some periods (e.g., the early 20th century) were advised not to "spare the rod, lest you spoil the child," whereas others a half-century later were advised to shower their children with affection and to temper physical punishment, when necessary, with love. The difficult job of parenting is not made any easier by the shifts in cultural ideals, in the lack of consensus among child development experts, or in the lack of agreement in what the "finished product," the well-adjusted, contributing adult member of society, should be.

Baumrind (1967) classified parenting styles into three types. The *authoritarian* parent exhibits a high degree of control over the child's behavior and a low level of affection. The *permissive* parent exhibits little control over the child's behavior, but may resort to manipulation to shape the child's behavior. The *authoritative* parent exhibits consistent discipline and expectations toward the child and a high level of affection.

Children raised by authoritarian parents are expected to defer and conform to parental requirements and are not encouraged to develop independence or initiative. Those raised by permissive parents face few demands by parents and are not encouraged to develop impulse control or social responsibility. Those raised by authoritative parents are encouraged to participate in open communication about decisions and to apply reason and personal responsibility in social situations. Not surprisingly, authoritative parenting is considered to have the greatest potential to facilitate development of a well-adjusted, self-actualized child.

Growing Up With Lesbian and Gay Parents

Although accurate numbers are difficult to estimate, lesbians are conceiving and bearing children through artificial insemination, substantial numbers of lesbians and gays have been in a heterosexual marriage that produced children and, increasingly, lesbians and gays are adopting children. Biases against lesbian and gay parents persist, based on the assumption that a homosexual parent may compromise a child's development (or even be a danger to a child).

Lesbian mothers appear to be very similar to heterosexual mothers in terms of maternal feelings and parenting behaviors (Kirkpatrick 1982). Children raised by mothers who are lesbians do not show any differences from other children on gender orientation and other areas of development (Green et al. 1986) or on adjustment (Patterson 1992). Research on children raised by gay fathers is virtually nonexistent. Few gay fathers are awarded custody of their children following a divorce, few gay men adopt children, and few father a child with a surrogate mother. One study of gay fathers who had custody of their children following divorce found disclosure of gay identity and providing a stable home environment for their children were priority concerns for these fathers (Bozett 1980). As discussed in chapter 9, gay and lesbian parents struggle with the need to "come out" to children, family, and friends. They may fear such disclosure could jeopardize custody and visitation rights.

Davidson and Moore (1996: 602) say at least 17 research reports have concluded "no major differences exist between children of homosexual and heterosexual parents." However, some states continue to explicitly prohibit adoption by homosexuals and the practical ease of adoption continues to be encumbered by prejudicial attitudes on the part of some social service providers and others involved in the adoption process.

Siblings and "Onlies"

The impact of siblings in socialization receives too little attention by child development and family studies scholars. Stepsibling relationships have received even less study. This gap in the research is unfortunate, given that siblings occupy a place of significant others and have the quantity and quality of time together to mutually shape outcomes for a lifetime, for better or for worse. For example, Straus and Gelles (1990) have documented that the most frequent form of intrafamilial violence occurs between siblings. Their interviews with parents revealed 40% of children had hit a sibling in the previous year.

Yet, research seems to confirm the popular belief that siblings are instrumental in helping children negotiate peer relationships outside of the family (see, e.g., Downey and Condron 2004). For children who are not in consistent contact over a long period of time with the same children from other families or children whose families frequently change residences (as in the case of children growing up in military or other families who move frequently) sibling relationships take on extra significance.

BOX 10.3   "Military Brats: Growing Up on the Move"
Morten G. Ender, Ph.D.

At any given time since World War II (WWII), roughly half a million American children lived in a military family. This number waned as U.S. men and women left military service after WWII, but rose steadily to just over 600,000 by the end of the Cold War and in July 2001 dropped to just fewer than 493,000.

My research (Ender 2002) indicates that these children range in age between birth and 22 years of age with most being younger rather than older. Boys slightly outnumber girls. They are often multilingual, having lived outside the United States for a number of years. Many are multiracial, as the military was the first institution in American society to desegregate. Many more are multiethnic. After WWII, American and other first-world countries expanded their political, military, corporate, and humanitarian responsibilities outside our national borders. As a result, ethnic mothers came to include Vietnamese, Korean, German, Italian, and British—countries where the U.S. military has stationed service members in large numbers for many years.

Some come from dual-career military families, whereas some have a single, military mother. Many follow their parents' footsteps and join the military—the largest occupational linkage pool available to military recruiters. Today, many military brats have siblings and young parents, as military members marry earlier, have more children, and have them younger than do their civilian peers of comparable age. Military brats exist in other countries around the world as well.

Military family life is demanding for children in both peace and wartime. Historically, military children watched their parents fight a revolution, followed their officer fathers and mothers out on the American Frontier, and said goodbye as they fought in a Civil War. For others, their fathers were taken as Prisoners of War or were Missing in Action during the Korean and Vietnam Wars.

The singular organizational demand of risk of death and injury is omnipresent for service members. Other demands of military family life are imposed during peace time as well. These demands intersect work and family, with each vying for the service member's commitment, and include foreign residence, frequent relocation, family separation, normative social controls, shift work and long working hours, living and working in a masculine dominated culture, and early retirement.

For military brats, and other global nomads as well, such as international business, foreign service, "MKs" (missionary kids), and "Agency Brats" (children of CIA agents), geographical mobility is the most demanding element of growing up in an organization family. They move about five to eight times before they complete high school. Military brats move the most and MKs move the least. Most moves are across state lines and national borders.

Social psychological outcomes associated with frequent moves and the military lifestyle in general include lower self-esteem, especially among girls, identity problems, enhanced personality hardiness, and feelings of rootlessness.

Yet all is not negative with military brats. As adults they are very likely to become highly educated professionals and are upwardly mobile. Many enter careers associated with the arts, teaching, and international work. Famous military brats include Senator John McCain; Dr. Patch Adams; Elvis Presley's wife, Priscilla Presley; basketball star Shaquille O'Neal; General Norman Schwarzkopf; pop singer Christina Aguilera; actor Michael J. Fox; soccer star Mia Hamm; and journalist Elizabeth Vargas.

REFERENCES

Ender, Morten G. 2002. "Introduction." In *Military Brats and Other Global Nomads,* ed. Morten G. Ender. Westport, CT: Praeger, xxv–xxxi.

Morten G. Ender, Ph.D., teaches sociology at the United States Military Academy at West Point. He earned his B.A. in sociology from Sonoma State University and Ph.D. in sociology from the University of Maryland.

Research suggests the presence of many children in a family has negative effects on child and adult achievement. In a comprehensive survey of the literature, Blake (1991) found family size is negatively correlated with educational achievement. Downey (1995) suggests that this is due to the dilution of parental resources in larger families and the concentration of resources available to children in smaller families. Parental resources include not only financial resources but also interpersonal resources. Parents with more children have not only less money to spend on each child for college savings and computers but also less time to talk with each child, to explore interests, and share experiences one-on-one.

Parental expenditures on children—financial and interpersonal—are certainly shaped by such factors as the child's gender and birth order. For example, subcultural expectations regarding the value of higher education for sons versus daughters or the expectation that the first-born will provide assistance to later-born siblings in educational and other achievements might negatively impact children in large families.

What of children who grow up in a family with no siblings? In the 1960s, approximately one out of 10 children had no siblings. By 2000, the percentage had doubled to the point where, today, approximately one out of five children is an only child (McGrath 2001). The rise in families with a single child is, in part, an artifact of later ages at marriage, as well as the increase in divorce rates in the early childbearing years of marriage. Other factors include perceptions (and rising expectations) about the high direct economic costs of raising a child, as well as the indirect costs of multiple children when their mother is employed.

Only children differ little from those who grow up with siblings when intelligence and achievement test scores or mental health or self-esteem issues are evaluated (McGrath 2001). Children without siblings have many of the same age-relevant early socialization experiences of other children, learning how to interact with others in child care and preschool, so are likely to experience loneliness less often than might be expected (McGrath). Stereotypes aside, only children are not "spoiled" any more than are children. Any parent can overindulge and fail to set appropriate expectations for their child or children. Like first-born children, only children do tend to be high achievers, perhaps because their parents have more time and other resources available for an only child.

Day-Care and Other Primary Agents of Socialization

Although one study indicated 70% of parents and child advocates believe having one parent at home with young children is ideal, such an arrangement is not feasible for many of the 80% of dual-worker families (Capizzano and Adams 2000b). Having one parent remain at home is certainly not feasible for employed single parents. The result is two thirds of children under the age of five who have employed mothers spend 15 or more hours in nonparental care each week and more than four out of 10 of those children spend 35 or more hours per week in nonparental care (Capizzano and Adams 2000a).

The child-care arrangements families use is dependent on availability, cost, and schedules, as well as parental information and preferences. The most common type of child-care arrangement for all children is before and after school care, but some families also rely on relatives. Children from lower income and poverty-level families, and African Americans more than White, and White more than Hispanic children are more likely to use child care (Capizzano, Tout, and Adams, 2000).

We know what makes a safe, nurturing environment for children away from home. The best day care programs have the following characteristics:

- Low staff-child ratio (from 1 to 3 for infants up to 1 to 12 for children over age 6)
- Low staff and family turnover rate (indicates well-compensated and respected child-care workers and satisfied family clients)
- Trained, engaged staff (express ongoing concern with upgrading the knowledge and skills of child-care workers)
- Appropriately equipped facilities (provide materials, equipment, and space for a range of activities)
- Safe, hygienic practices (establish procedures for a secure facility and adequate supervision and minimizes disease transmission)
- Responsive director (provides feedback and utilizes open community with client families)

However, many communities face a shortage of adequate child-care facilities and child-care workers are typically low-paid, receive inadequate health insurance, and often accrue little in terms of retirement and other benefits. Many other Western nations provide much more reliable, high-quality child care to their citizens. Just as France, Germany, and Italy provide free full-day public child-care programs, many European nations permit parental absence from work to care for an ill child (Kamerman 1996).

Research indicates a well-administered child-care facility has many benefits for the children it serves. Children, especially those from low-income families, may experience advances in cognitive development (National Institute of Child Health and Human Development 1999), language, interpersonal and other social skills, and better preparation for school (Rubenstein 1994). For the families served by child care, the child-care community can also become a source of friendships and other social supports, as well as a site for advice and referrals for some of the everyday challenges of parenting.

CHILD ENDANGERMENT

Although the level of violence against young people ages 12 to 17 has declined since 1993, from 44 crimes per 1,000 to 11 crimes per 1,000 (Federal Interagency Forum on Child and Family Statistics 2004), *child abuse*, *child neglect*, *sexual abuse*, and *incest* remain a pressing concern.

Child Abuse and Neglect

In September 2002 the security camera system in an Indiana department store parking lot recorded a mother beating her four-year-old child. As the scene was flashed across news programs, the national sentiment was one of profound antipathy, in much the same way we were shocked when the beating of a Black motorist by Miami policemen was caught on tape in the early 1990s. The mother acknowledged her guilt, her daughter was placed in foster care, and the case faded from the popular conscience.

Although 3.2 million cases of child abuse are reported each year (up from 2.4 million in 1989), advocates for children as well as police believe most child abuse is unreported (Crary 2002). If I observe a child being harmed or at risk of being harmed by a family member, who am I to intervene? After all, the relations between parent and child are private and, in this society (unlike in some other Western societies), the state gives parents the permission to use physical force in disciplining children. If a child reports being abused by a family member, will the child be believed?

Child abuse is usually backstage behavior in the drama of family life. Children of any socioeconomic status, children from any family structure, any child can be the victim of child abuse or child neglect. However, a stressful social structure, characterized by poverty, violence, or other risk factors, contributes to parental stress and increases the probability parents will respond with neglect or abuse of their children in an attempt to gain control over irritating, stressful events (Wolfe 1987).

Child abuse and neglect can start at the onset of pregnancy, depending how the mother cares for herself and the unborn child during this period. The use of cigarettes, alcohol, and other drugs can cause serious damage to the unborn child, and is sometimes viewed by the courts as a form of child abuse. Inadequate prenatal medical care and poor nutrition during pregnancy may also signify neglect.

The birth of a child is a major stressor event, one that can contribute to improper care, neglect or even abuse of the child. A child's temperament, perhaps a trigger for neglect and abuse, can certainly exacerbate parental neglect and abuse. Neglected children may become hungry or tired and exhibit agitation and irritability, perhaps rejecting the parent's efforts to express affection. In those circumstances, the parent may react to the child in a more frustrated or even aggressive manner, thereby perhaps causing more neglect and abuse (Wolfe 1987).

Child abuse in American society is complicated by the way violence in the form of spanking, slapping, or other forms of hitting is an acceptable, even desirable, method of disciplining children. Parents who were punished in more harsh ways during their childhood are likely to express support for the use of physical punishment in disciplining their children. Parents who were themselves hit by their own parents may not understand the connection between hitting a child and the child's own violent behavior. They may not know of other more effective techniques for disciplining a child and may fear the consequences of not subjecting their children to physical discipline. Some parents may agree with the old saying, "spare the rod, spoil the child."

Physical punishment such as spanking is widely accepted in American society, and research does not show that an occasional swat on the bottom scars a child for life. However, for some parents the line between their own frustration and anger is a fine one. Parental rage has a special danger not only because of the vulnerability of the child victims and their absence of recourse but also because the worst of such behavior likely occurs in private, behind closed doors. Furthermore, interpersonal violence of all kinds, including that directed against children, tends to become more frequent and more severe over time.

Those parents who abuse their children often live in stressful environments burdened by poverty, violence, and mental and emotional problems. Substance abuse, clinical depression, or emotional disorders may complicate the stresses of everyday life. Limited education, poor problem-solving skills, and social isolation are also common threads found in families that engage in abuse and neglect (Dore and Lee 1999).

Children who are neglected may come to school without proper hygiene, with improper clothing, hungry, or be sleep deprived. The more insidious forms of child neglect, some bordering on abuse, occur when a child lacks warm human contact, care, and love (Myers et al. 2002).

What can you do if you believe a child is at risk? If you are in a position with direct responsibility for the well-being of children (e.g., counselors and teachers, nurses and physicians) you are likely mandated by law to report suspected cases of child abuse. However, individuals and communities also can play a role in preventing child abuse. For example, violence directed against children is often impulsive behavior on the part of an angry, frustrated adult. If you come across a parent who appears on the verge of hurting a child, a sympathetic expression or supportive comment from you may help to diffuse a tense situation and divert the violence (at least temporarily). On a larger scale, groups like *Prevent Child Abuse New York* have organized community-wide campaigns to raise public consciousness about child abuse. These groups seek to effect changes that are supportive of parents, changes such as encouraging teachers to contact parents with *good* news about their child's behavior or performance or suggesting that retail merchants set up a play area in their stores.

Sexual Abuse

One fourth of crime victims in the United States are children (*Breaking the Cycle of Violence* 1999) and almost 2.8 million cases of child abuse and neglect were investigated in a recent year for which statistics are available (*Children as Victims* 2000). However, data on the extent of sexual abuse of children are harder to confirm. Of reported cases of sexual abuse, over one fourth of children were abused by a birth parent, over one fourth by a stepparent, and nearly one-half by other relatives or acquaintances. The most frequent form of sexual abuse is between fathers and daughters or between stepfathers and stepdaughters (United States Department of Health and Human Services 1996). Thornton's (1984) research indicates 17% of Americans have been involved in incest, sexual contact between blood relatives. Most of those cases go unreported.

Family members who sexually abuse children tend to have low self-esteem and low impulse control. Typically abuse begins when the child is very young, between the ages of eight and 12 (although cases of the sexual abuse of even infants are not unknown). In some families, the sexual abuse begins with one child and progresses through each of the younger siblings in turn, lasting over many childhoods (Hanson, Gizzarelli, and Scott, 1994).

Incest represents a web of problems in the family system. Some would like to place blame on the mother for not vigorously protecting her child from a sexually abusive father or stepfather. However, the wife and mother in such a family may herself lack personal or social resources to protect her children and so may deny or ignore the problem. Others may be unaware of the sexual abuse, particularly if the child fears abandonment or retribution if the situation becomes known. Finally, confronting the sexual abuse of children requires recognition by society of the existence of the problem. Addressing this tragic social problem requires a willingness to take seriously the voice of the child who alleges sexual abuse or to attend carefully to symptoms exhibited by the sexual abuse victim, symptoms that may include withdrawal or rebellion, problems in school or unusually precocious interest in sexual matters.

During the 1990s and into the early part of the 21st century, what seemed like a steady stream of adult victims came forward to testify they had suffered sexual abuse as children, adolescence, and young adults in the care of Catholic clergy. Whether in a family or in another intimate setting, children are most vulnerable to the deepest injury when in the care of someone they are required to respect and trust. As public outcry over the Catholic Church's mishandling of past charges of abuse grew, we were reminded a meaningful solution to the sexual abuse of children, as well as child abuse and neglect, will only come with concerted institutional and society effort.

BOX 10.4 "Religion and Child Abuse: Perfect Together?"
W. Bradley Wilcox, Ph.D.

The ties that bind religion and the family run deep, but these ties are controversial. In recent years, scholars have increasingly drawn attention to religious commitments to patriarchy and parental authority. This leaves some room for critical speculation that religion—especially evangelical Protestantism—exerts a baleful influence on parents and, by extension, their children. In 1991, Princeton Theological Seminary Professor Donald Capps delivered a presidential address to the Society for the Scientific Study of Religion entitled "Religion and Child Abuse: Perfect Together." He argued that the religious endorsement of corporal punishment—found, for example, in evangelical Protestant advice books like James Dobson's *Dare to Discipline* (1970)— encourages parents to adopt an abusive parenting style (Bartkowski and Wilcox 2000). Similarly, sociologists Julia McQuillan and Myra Max Ferree (1998: 213) have argued that "the religious right" is an influential force "pushing men toward authoritarian and stereotypical forms of masculinity and attempting to renew patriarchal family relations."

The social scientific research on religion and parenting, however, paints a more nuanced picture of the relationship between religion and parenting. As critics of religion would predict, parents who attend church frequently or who affiliate with evangelical Protestant churches, spank their children more often than do other parents, in large part because they place a premium on obedience from their children (Ellison, Bartkowski, and Segal 1996). But parents who are frequent churchgoers, as well as evangelical Protestant parents, also yell at their children less than other parents, and praise and hug their children more than other parents (Bartkowski and Wilcox 2000; Wilcox 1998).

Moreover, evangelical fathers are not beholden to stereotypical forms of masculinity in the way they interact with their children. Indeed, evangelical (and Catholic) fathers spend more time with their children than unaffiliated fathers. Specifically, evangelical fathers spend more time than other fathers in one-on-one activities like reading to their children do. They also have dinner with their children more often than other fathers (Wilcox 2002). Catholic fathers are more involved than are other fathers in youth-related activities like the Boy Scouts (Wilcox 2002)

Thus, religion—especially evangelical Protestantism—appears to promote a "neo-traditional approach to parenting" that combines a strict, controlled approach to discipline with a warm, involved approach to everyday parent–child interaction (Wilcox 1998). This approach flows, in part, from religious parents' belief that they should embody God's justice and love in their interactions with their children.

How does religiously informed parenting influence children? We do not know. Scholars are just beginning to investigate the effects that this neo-traditional approach to parenting has on children.

REFERENCES

Bartkowski, John P., and W. Bradford Wilcox. 2000. "Conservative Protestant Child Discipline." *Social Forces* 79: 265–90.

Ellison, Christopher G., John P. Bartkowski, and Michelle L. Segal. 1996. "Conservative Protestantism and the Parental Use of Corporal Punishment." *Social Forces* 74: 1003–29.

McQuillan, Julia, and Myra Max Ferree. 1998. "The Importance of Variation among Husbands and the Benefits of Feminism for Families." In *Men in Families*, eds. A. Booth and A. Crouter. Mahwah, NJ: Lawrence Erlbaum Associates.

Wilcox, W. Bradford. 1998. "Conservative Protestant Childrearing: Authoritarian or Authoritative?" *American Sociological Review* 63: 796–809.

Wilcox, W. Bradford. 2002. "Religion, Convention, and Paternal Involvement." *Journal of Marriage and Family* 64: 780–92.

W. Bradford Wilcox, Ph.D., is Assistant Professor of sociology at the University of Virginia. His research has appeared in the *American Sociological Review* and the *Journal of Marriage and Family*.

GLOSSARY

Adoption	Blastocyst transfer
Adoption triangle	Child abuse
Authoritarian	Child free
Authoritative	Childless

Child neglect

Conflict-habituated family

Cryopreservation

Fecundity

Fertility rate

Foster parents

Gamete intrafallopian transfer (GIFT)

Gestational surrogacy

In vitro fertilization (IVF)

Incest

Indian Child Welfare Act

Infertility

Intracytoplasmic sperm injection (ICSI)

Multiethnic Placement Act

Nonsurgical sperm aspiration (NSA)

Nurturant father

Off-time fathers

On-time fathers

Permissive

Rite of passage

Sexual abuse

Zygote intrafallopian transfer (ZIFT)

FOR YOUR CONSIDERATION

1. What supports are available in your community for families that take one of the diverse paths to parenthood discussed in this chapter? What kind of services would you like to see added in your community to serve these families?

2. What images are presented in the media regarding the competence of fathers, mothers, or parents in general in society today? Identify some images of effective parenting.

3. How did your family of origin's socioeconomic status shape your socialization experiences as a child and adolescent?

4. How would you describe the quality of media coverage of child abuse and neglect, sexual abuse, and incest in your community? To what extent does that coverage treat the problem as a personal problem versus a social problem?

FOR FURTHER STUDY: WEB SITES, ORGANIZATIONS, AND PUBLICATIONS

Web Sites and Organizations

Administration for Children and Families
    http://www.acf.dhhs.gov/programs/acyf/
    This is the official site of the United States Department of Health and Human Services.

American Coalition for Fathers and Children
    http://www.acfc.org/
    ACFC is an organization that advocates "creation of a family law system, legislative system, and a public awareness which promotes equal rights for all parties affected by divorce and the breakup of a family or establishment of paternity."

AtHomeDad.com
    This is an online newsletter for a national and regional network of stay-at-home fathers.

Child-Care Canada
    http://www.childcarecanada.org
    This organization offers online links to social scientific research on child care.

Childstats

http://childstats.gov

This site is sponsored by the Health Resources and Services Administration Information Center in association with the National Center for Health Statistics.

Civitas

1-800-TO-BEGIN

http://www.cititas.org

This not-for-profit communications group creates and distributes child development tools in English and Spanish. Recent products include *Begin with Love*, for new parents, and *Grandparenting: Enriching Lives.*

The Fatherhood Project

http://www.fatherhoodproject.org

The Fatherhood Project is a national research and education project focusing on issues of fatherhood and men's involvement in childrearing.

Mothers and More

http://www.mothersandmore.org/

This site offers information and support to women who have sequenced their careers with caring for children at home.

National Center on Fathers and Families

http://www.ncoff.gse.upenn.edu/

This organization sponsors events and offers publications related to fathers and fathering in society.

National Child Care Information Center

http://www.nccic.org

This project of the Child Care Bureau is a national resource to "complement, enhance, and promote the child-care delivery system, working to ensure all children and families have access to high-quality comprehensive services." The site also provides links to other sites on child care in states.

National Fatherhood Initiative

101 Lake Forest Boulevard, Suite 360, Gaithersburg, MD 20877

(301) 948-0599

http://www.fatherhood.org

Founded in 1994, the *National Fatherhood Initiative* was organized in 1994 to confront the problem of father absence and improve the well being of children by increasing the proportion of children growing up with involved, responsible, committed fathers. The Web site is a source of advice, resources, links to state and local organizations, and training and education opportunities.

Parents, Children, and Work

http://www.src.uchicago.edu/orgs/sloan/

This site is sponsored by the Alfred P. Sloan Foundation and the National Opinion Research Center.

Pregnancy and Infant Loss Centers

In 1974 federal legislation was enacted in response to growing interest about the causes of Sudden Infant Death Syndrome. That legislation (*SIDS Act of 1974)* and community concern for providing care for families suffering miscarriage, stillbirth, and newborn death resulted in the establishment of pregnancy and infant loss centers in several states and cities. Search the Web using "pregnancy and infant loss centers" for links to research, resources, and support.

Prevent Child Abuse America

http://www.childhelpusa.org

This nationwide group advocates a wide spectrum of community involvement to stop child abuse, including securing the involvement of businesses, churches, and schools as well as individual citizens. One of their programs is called "Promises for Parents" in which community members make individual pledges to support parents.

Resolve: The National Fertility Association

http://www.resolve.org

888-623-0744

Established in 1974, with a nationwide network of chapters, *Resolve* provides education, advocacy, and support for those facing infertility. Recent efforts have included soliciting support for federal legislation to cover infertility treatment.

SlowLane-Stay-at-Home Dads

http://www.slowlane.com

Primarily a resource for stay-at-home fathers, this site also has online searchable references and resources.

Publications

Blum, Linda M. 1999. *At the Breast: Ideologies of Breastfeeding and Motherhood in the Contemporary United States.* Boston, MA: Beacon.

Through an examination of the influence of race, gender, and class on breastfeeding, Blum compares how women's experiences with motherhood differ from the model that calls for a single-minded focus on children and their needs.

Bornstein, Marc H., ed. 2002. *Handbook of Parenting*, 2/e. Mahwah, NJ: Lawrence Erlbaum Associates.

This five-volume handbook provides deep coverage on a broad range of parenting topics, including different types of parents, basic characteristics of parenting, forces that shape parenting, problems faced by parents, and practical concerns of parenting.

Bornstein, Marc H., and Robert Bradley, eds. 2003. *Socioeconomic Status, Parenting, and Child Development.* Mahwah, NJ: Lawrence Erlbaum Associates.

The chapters in this book systematically examine the influence of socioeconomic status on parenting practices and both within and outside the home environment and the impact on child development.

Cowan, Carolyn Pape, and Philip Cowan. 2000. *When Parents Become Partners: The Big Life Change for Couples.* Mahwah, NJ: Lawrence Erlbaum Associates.

Writing for couples, as well as practitioners and researchers, Cowan and Cowan examine the stresses that accompany the transition to parenthood.

Crittenden, Ann. 2001. *The Price of Motherhood: Why the Most Important Job in the World Is Still the Least Valued.* New York, NY: Metropolitan Books.

This book is based on research (as well as interviews) with imminent scholars who have examined the status of motherhood. The author concludes with a summary of policy that could address this problem.

Daniels, Cynthia R., ed. 2000. *Lost Fathers: The Politics of Fatherlessness in America.* New York, NY: St. Martin's. Nine scholars representing diverse perspectives reflect on the concept of "fatherlessness" and the debates over welfare, poverty, sexuality, and divorce and family values and racial disorder.

Danziger, Sheldon, and Jane Waldfogel, eds. 2000. *Securing the Future: Investing in Children from Birth to College.* New York: Russell Sage Foundation.

An interdisciplinary team of scholars examine pediatric, psychological, social, and economic factors that contribute to a child's development. The authors evaluate current initiatives and offer suggestions for public and private investment in child development.

Dundas, Lauren, ed. 2002. *The Manner Born: Birth Rites in Cross-cultural Perspective.* Lanham, MA: AltaMira.

This collection of essays from distinguished contributors illustrates the wide range of attitudes, beliefs, and practices associated with birth through infancy, including birthing and placenta rituals, breast feeding, weaning, swaddling, and early infant behavior.

Federal Interagency Forum on Child and Family Statistics. 2004. *America's Children in Brief: Key National Indicators of Well-Being, 2004.* Washington, DC: Government Printing Office.

Inaugurated in 2004, *America's Children in Brief* is the product of collaboration among twelve federal Departments charged by an executive order with collecting and reporting federal data on children and families. See *Childstats*, earlier.

The Future of Children

www.futureofchildren.org

This is a publication of the David & Lucile Packard Foundation, an organization that centers on promoting marriage to improve child well being. A recent issue of the Future of Children journal issue focused on Children and Welfare Reform (Volume 12, Number 1, Winter/Spring 2002).

Garfinkel, Irwin, Sara S. McLanahan, Daniel R. Meyer, and Judith A. Seltzer, eds. 2001. *Fathers Under Fire: The Revolution in Child Support Enforcement.* New York, NY: Russell Sage Foundation.

The authors in this edition present data on nonresident fathers, including fathers education and income levels and the influence of starting a new family on likelihood of continuing to support children from an earlier relationship. The authors demonstrate the benefits and risks of stronger enforcement policies.

Glazer, Deborah F., and Jack Dreschler, eds. 2001. *Gay and Lesbian Parenting.* New York, NY: Hawthorne (co-published as the *Journal of Gay & Lesbian Psychotherapy* 4, 3/4).

The authors of this book represent legal and mental health professions and approach the "gayby boom" from a historical perspective rooted in the social movements for gay liberation and parenting as a choice rather than as an imperative.

Hewlett, Sylvia Ann, Nancy Rankin, and Cornell West, eds. 2002. *Taking Parenting Public: The Case for a New Social Movement.* Blue Ridge Summit, PA: Rowman & Littlefield.

The contributors argue parenting is undervalued in America and call for personal and public investment in child rearing. The book represents a variety of political perspectives and includes contributions from child development, economics, history, the media, political science, public health, and public policy.

O'Reilly, Andrea, ed. 2001. *Mothers and Sons: Feminism, Masculinity, and the Struggle to Raise Our Sons.* New York, NY: Routledge.

This volume examines the feminist mothering of sons, diversity in the mother–son relationship, and mother–son attachment from a variety of disciplinary perspectives.

Roberts, Dorothy. 2003. *Shattered Bonds: The Color of Child Welfare.* New York, NY: Perseus.

Roberts describes the worsening crisis of the disproportionate number of Black children in foster care in the United States and the effects on Black children and communities and on the United States.

Small, Meredith F. 2001. *Kids: How Biology and Culture Shape the Way We Raise Our Children.* New York, NY: Doubleday.

The author, an anthropologist, synthesizes research into human evolution and observations of cultures around the world to examine the lessons adults pass on to children.

Tamis-LeMonda, Catherine S., and Natasha Cabrera, eds. 2002. *The Handbook of Father Involvement: Multidisciplinary Perspectives.* Mahwah, NJ: Lawrence Erlbaum Associates.

Anthropology, demography, economics, psychology, sociology, and social policy are brought to bear on defining who are fathers, determinants of father involvement and affect on children and families, and the cultural contexts that shape father involvement.

Thornton, Arland, ed. 2001. *The Well-being of Children and Families: Research and Data Needs.* Ann Arbor, MI: University of Michigan.

Consistent with our emphasis on resiliency and salutogenesis, Thornton's paradigm shifts away from a study of negative outcomes and toward understanding of well-being. The contributors to this volume include economists, health researchers, psychologists, and sociologists, as well as a social policy analyst.

Wu, Lawrence L., and Barbara Wolfe, eds. 2001. *Out of Wedlock: Causes and Consequences of Nonmarital Fertility.* New York, NY: Russell Sage Foundation.

Scholars from a variety of disciplines examine the demographic and life chance data on unwed mothers in the United States, drawing comparisons with other industrialized societies. The contributors also examine the role of child support and the social and emotional outcomes for children of unwed mothers.

Fathering: A Journal of Theory, Research, and Practice about Men as Fathers

This multidisciplinary journal, which debuts in February 2003 and will be published three times a year, disseminates scholarship about fathers and promotes positive practices with and for fathers.

REFERENCES FOR CITED WORKS

Aldous, Joan, Gail M. Mulligan, and Thoroddur Bjarnason. 1998. "Fathering Over Time: What Makes the Difference?" *Journal of Marriage and the Family* 60 (November): 809–20.

American Infertility Association. 2004. "Infertility Facts." http://www.americaninfertility.org/faqs/aia_infertility %20facts.html (Retrieved 9/20/04).

Aries, Phillipe. 1960/1962. *Centuries of Childhood: A Social History of Family Life,* Trans. R. Baldrick. New York, NY: Vintage.

Bachrach, Christine A., Kathy Shepard Stolley, and Kathryn A. London. 1992. "Relinquishment of Premarital Births: Evidence from National Survey Data." *Family Planning Perspectives* 24, 1 (January–February): 27–32, 48.

Barnes, Grace M. 2000. "The Effects of Parenting on the Development of Adolescent Alcohol Misuse: A Six-Wave Latent Growth Model." *Journal of Marriage and the Family* 62, 1 (February): 175–86.

Baumrind, D. 1967. "Effects of Authoritative Parental Control on Child Behavior." *Genetic Psychology Monographs* 75: 43–88.

Becker, Gay. 1990. *Healing the Infertile Family*. New York, NY: Bantam.

Benson, Peter, L., Anu R. Sharma, and Eugene C. Roehlkepartain. 1994. "Growing Up Adopted: A Portrait of Adolescents and Their Families." Minneapolis, MN: *The Search Institute*.

Berger, B. 1986. "On the Limits of the Welfare State: The Case of Foster Care." In *The American Family and the State,* ed. J. R. Peden and F. R. Glahe. San Francisco, CA: Pacific Research Institute for Public Policy, 365–79

Bird, Chloe. 1997. "Gender Differences in the Social and Economic Burdens of Parenting and Psychological Distress." *Journal of Marriage and the Family* 59, 4 (November): 809–23.

Blake, Judith. 1991. "Number of Siblings and Personality." *Family Planning Perspectives* 23 (November/ December): 272–74.

Bozett, F. W. 1980. "Gay Fathers: How and Why They Disclose Their Homosexuality to Their Children." *Family Relations* 29: 173–79.

Bradley, R. H., L. Whiteside-Mansell, J. A. Brisby, and B. M. Caldwell. 1997. "Parents' Socioemotional Investment in Children." *Journal of Marriage and the Family* 59, 1 (February): 77–90.

Breaking the Cycle of Violence: Recommendations to Improve the Criminal Justice Response to Child Victims and Witnesses. 1999. Washington, DC: United States Department of Justice, Office of Justice Programs, Office for Victims of Crime.

Brooks-Gunn, Jeanne, and P. L. Chase-Lansdale. 1995. "Adolescent Parenthood." In *Handbook of Parenting: Status and Social Conditions of Parenting*, Volume 3, ed. M. H. Bornstein. Hillsdale, NJ: Lawrence Erlbaum Associates, 113–49.

Bulanda, Ronald E. 2004. "Paternal Involvement with Children: The Influence of Gender Ideologies." *Journal of Marriage and the Family* 66, 1 (February): 40–45.

Bunting, Lisa, and Colette McAuley. 2004. "Research Review: Teenage Pregnancy and Motherhood: The Contribution of Support." *Child and Family Social Work* 9 (May): 207–15.

Cain, Madelyn. 2002. *The Childless Revolution: What It Means to Be Childless Today.* New York, NY: Perseus Books Group.

Capizzano, J., and G. Adams. 2000a. *The Hours that Children Under Five Spend in Child Care: Variations Across States.* http://newfederalism.urban.org/pdf/anf_b8.pdf (Retrieved 9/20/02).

Capizzano, J., and G. Adams. 2000b. *The Number of Child Care Arrangements Used by Children Under Five: Variation Across States.* http://newfederalism.urban.org/pdf/anf-b12.pdf (Retrieved 9/20/02).

Capizzano, J., K. Tout, and G. Adams. 2000. *Child Care Patterns of School-Age Children with Employed Mothers.* Occasional Paper No. 41. Urban Institute. http://newfederalism.urban.org/pdf/occa41.pdf (Retrieved 9/20/02).

Ceballo, Rosario, Jennifer E. Lansford, Antonia Abbey, and Abigail J. Stewart. 2004. "Gaining a Child: Comparing the Experiences of Biological Parents, Adoptive Parents, and Stepparents." *Family Relations* 53, 1 (January): 38–48.

Centers for Disease Control and Prevention. 1997. "Fertility, Family Planning, and Women's Health: New Data from the 1995 National Survey of Family Growth." *Vital and Health Statistics, National Center for Health Statistics*, Series 23, No. 19 (May). www.cdc.gov/nchs/fastats/fertile.htm (Retrieved 10/23/02).

Centers for Disease Control and Prevention. 1999. "Higher Order Multiple Births Drop for First Time in Decade." *Vital and Health Statistics, National Center for Health Statistics*, Series 49, No. 1 (April). www.cdc.gov/nchs/releases/01news/multibir.htm (Retrieved 11/3/02).

Chandra, Anjani, and Elizabeth Hervey Stephen. 1998. "Impaired Fecundity in the United States, 1982–1995." *Family Planning Perspectives* 30, 1: 35–42.

Cherlin, Andrew J. 2002. *Public and Private Families: An Introduction*, 3/e. New York, NY: McGraw-Hill.

Children as Victims. 2000. Washington, DC: United States Department of Justice, Office of Justice Programs, Office of Juvenile Justice and Delinquency Prevention.

Chipman, Stacey, Susanne Frost Olsen, Shirley Klein, Craig H. Hart, and Clyde C. Robinson. 2000. "Differences in Retrospective Perceptions of Parenting of Male and Female Inmates and Non-Inmates." *Family Relations* 49, 1: 5–11.

Clingempeel, W. G., and B. Eulalee. 1985. "Quasi-Kin Relationships, Structural Complexity, and Marital Quality in Stepfamilies: A Replication, Extension, and Clinical Implications." *Family Relations* 34: 401–409.

Clingempeel, W. G., and S. Segal. 1986. "Stepparent-Stepchild Relationships and the Psychological Adjustment of Children in Stepmother and Stepfather Families." *Child Development* 57: 474–84.

Coltrane, Scott, Ross D. Parke, and Michele Adams. 2004. "Complexity of Father Involvement in Low-Income Mexican American Families." *Family Relations* 53, 2 (March): 179–89.

Cowan, Philip A., and Carolyn Pape Cowan. 2002. "Strengthening Couples to Improve Children's Well-being." *Poverty Research News* 6, 3 (May–June): 18–20.

Crary, David. 2002. "Experts Urge People to Get Involved to Stop Child Abuse." *Star Tribune* September 28: E6.

Cummings, E. M., and P. Davies. 1994. *Children and Marital Conflict: The Impact of Family Dispute and Resolution.* New York, NY: Guilford.

Dainton, M. 1993. "The Myths and Misconceptions of the Stepmother Identity: Descriptions and Prescriptions for Identity Management." *Family Relations* 42: 93–98.

Daly, Kerry. 1999. "Crisis of Genealogy: Facing the Challenges of Infertility." In *The Dynamics of Resilient Families,* eds. Hamilton I. McCubbin, E. A. Thompson, A. I. Thompson, and J. A. Futrell. Thousand Oaks, CA: Sage, 1–39.

Davidson, J. Kenneth, Sr., and Nelwyn B. Moore. 1996. *Marriage and Family: Change and Continuity.* Boston, MA: Allyn & Bacon.

DeMarco, Laura. 2004. "Gen Xers are Grown Up, Having Kids." *Star Tribune* (September 26): E1, E2.

Dore, Martha, Morrison, and Judy M. Lee. 1999. "The Role of Parent Training with Abusive and Neglectful Parents." *Family Relations* 48: 313–25.

Doherty, William J., Edward F. Kouneski, and Martha F. Erickson. 1998. "Responsible Fathering: An Overview and Conceptual Framework." *Journal of Marriage and the Family* 60, 2 (May): 277–92.

Dornbusch, S. M., J. M. Carlsmith, S. J. Bushwall, P. L. Ritter, H. Leiderman, A. H. Hastorf, and R. T. Gross. 1985. "Single Parents, Extended Households, and the Control of Adolescents." *Child Development* 56: 326–41.

Downey, Douglas B. 1995. "When Bigger is Not Better: Family Size, Parental Resources, and Children's Educational Performance." *American Sociological Review* 60 (October): 746–61.

Downey, Douglas B., James W. Ainsworth-Darnell, and Mikaela J. Dufur. 1998. "Sex of Parent and Children's Well Being in Single-Parent Households." *Journal of Marriage and the Family* 60, 4 (November): 878–93.

Downey, Douglas B., and Dennis J. Condron. 2004. "Playing Well with Others in Kindergarten: The Benefit of Siblings at Home." *Journal of Marriage and the Family* 66, 2 (May): 333–50.

Dunson, David, Bernardo Colombo, and Donna D. Baird. 2002. "Changes with Age in the Level and Duration of Fertility in the Menstrual Cycle." *Human Reproduction* 17, 5 (May): 1399–1403.

Federal Interagency Forum on Child and Family Statistics. 2004. *America's Children in Brief: Key National Indicators of Well-Being, 2004.* Washington, DC: Government Printing Office.

Fox, Greer Litton, Carol Bruce, and Terri Combs-Orme. 2000. "Parenting Expectations and Concerns of Fathers and Mothers of Newborn Infants." *Family Relations* 49, 2 (April): 123–30.

Gerson, Kathleen. 1993. *No Man's Land: Men's Changing Commitments to Family and Work.* New York, NY: Harper Collins.

Glenn, Norval D. 1990. "Quantitative Research on Marital Quality in the 1980s: A Critical Review." *Journal of Marriage and the Family* 52, 4 (November): 818–31.

Green, R., J. B. Mandel, M. E. Hotvedt, J. Gray, and L. Smith. 1986. "Lesbian Mothers and Their Children: A Comparison with Solo Parent Heterosexual Mothers and Their Children." *Archives of Sexual Behavior* 15: 167–84.

"A Guide to the Multiethnic Placement Act of 1994." 2002. http://www.acf.hhs.gov/programs/cb/publications/mepa94/mepachp1.htm.

Hamer, Jennifer. 2001. *What It Means to Be Daddy: Fatherhood for Black Men Living Away from Their Children.* New York: Columbia University Press.

Hanson, R. K., R. Gizzarelli, and H. Scott. 1994. "The Attitudes of Incest Offenders: Sexual Entitlement and Acceptance of Sex with Children." *Criminal Justice and Behavior* 21 (June): 187–202.

Haworth-Hoeppner, Susan. 2000. "The Critical Shapes of Body Image: The Role of Culture and Family in the Production of Eating Disorders." *Journal of Marriage and the Family* 62, 1 (February): 212–27.

Hays, Sharon. 1998. "The Fallacious Assumptions and Unrealistic Prescriptions of Attachment Theory: A Comment on 'Parents' Socioemotional Investment in Children'." *Journal of Marriage and the Family* 60, 3 (August): 782–95.

Heath, D. T. 1994. "The Impact of Delayed Fatherhood on the Father-Child Relationship." *The Journal of Genetic Psychology* 155, 4: 511–30.

Heaton, Tim B., Cardell K. Jacobson, and Kimberlee Holland. 1999. "Persistence and Change in Decisions to Remain Childless." *Journal of Marriage and the Family* 61, 3 (May): 531–39.

Hetherington, E. M., and W. G. Clingempeel. 1992. "Coping with Marital Transitions." *Monographs of the Society for Research in Child Development* 57, 2–3.

Hill, Shirley. 1999. *African American Children: Socialization and Development in Families.* Thousand Oaks, CA: Sage.

Ishii-Kuntz, M., and Scott Coltrane. 1992. "Predicting the Sharing of Household Labor: Are Parenting and Housework Distinct?" *Sociological Perspectives* 35: 629–47.

Kamerman, S. B. 1996. "Child and Family Policies: An International Overview." In *Children, Families, and Government: Preparing for the Twenty-First Century*, ed. E. F. Zigler, S. L. Kagan, and N. W. Hall. New York, NY: Cambridge University Press, 31–48.

King, Valerie, Kathleen Mullan Harris, and Holly E. Heard. 2004. "Racial and Ethnic Differences in Nonresident Father Involvement." *Journal of Marriage and the Family* 66, 1 (February): 1–21.

Kirkpatrick, M. 1982. "Lesbian Mother Families." *Psychiatric Annals* 12: 842–45, 848.

Kraus, M. A., and E. S. Redman. 1986. "Postpartum Depression: An Interactional View." *Journal of Marriage and Family Therapy* 12: 63–74.

Lansford, Jennifer E., Rosario Ceballo, Antoina Abbey, and Abigail J. Stewart. 2001. "Does Family Structure Matter? A Comparison of Adoptive, Two-Parent Biological, Single-Mother, Stepfather, and Stepmother Households." *Journal of Marriage and Family* 63, 4 (November): 840–51.

LeMasters, E. E., and John DeFrain. 1989. *Parents in Contemporary America: A Sympathetic View.* Belmont, CA: Wadsworth.

Liss, L. 1987. "Family and the Law." In *Handbook of Marriage and the Family*, eds. M. B. Sussman and S. K. Steinmetz. New York, NY: Plenum, 767–94.

Luster, Tom, Laura Bates, Hiram Fitzgerald, Marcia Vandenbelt, and Judith Peck Key. 2000. "Factors Related to Successful Outcomes among Preschool Children Born to Low-income Adolescent Mothers." *Journal of Marriage and the Family* 61, 2 (February): 133–46.

Mannis, Valerie, S. 1999. "Single Mothers by Choice." *Family Relations* 48: 121–28.

March, Karen. 1995. "Perception of Adoption as Social Stigma: Motivation for Search and Reunion." *Family Relations* 57 (August) 653–60.

Marquis, Kathlyn S., and Richard A. Detweiler. 1985. "Does Adopted Mean Different? An Attributional Analysis." *Journal of Personality and Social Psychology* 48, 4: 1054–66.

Marsiglio, William. 2004. "When Stepfathers Claim Stepchildren: A Conceptual Analysis." *Journal of Marriage and the Family* 66, 1 (February): 22–39.

McGrath, Ellie. 2001. "It Turns Out 'Only' Children Aren't So Only Anymore." *Star Tribune* (January 14): E1–E2.

McLanahan, Sara, and Gary Sandefur. 1994. *Growing Up with a Single Parent.* Cambridge, MA: Harvard University Press.

Merriam-Webster's Collegiate Dictionary. http://www.n-w.com (Retrieved 7/12/02).

Miall, Charlene E. 1996. "The Social Construction of Adoption: Clinical and Community Perspectives." *Family Relations* 45, 3 (July): 309–17.

Milke, Melissa A., Marybeth J. Mattingly, Kei M. Nomaguchi, Suzanne M. Bianchi, and John P. Robinson. 2004. "The Time Squeeze: Parental Statuses and Feelings about Time with Children." *Journal of Marriage and the Family* 66, 3 (August): 739–61.

Miller, Kay. 2002. "Falling Short as a Father: Father's Day Brings Alienated Relationships into Focus for Parents, Children." *Star Tribune* (June 10): E10.

Moore, Kristin Anderson, and Susan M. Jekielek. 2002. "How Family Structure and Living Arrangements Affect Children." *Poverty Research News* 6, 3 (May–June): 6–8.

Myers, John E. B., Lucy Berliner, John Briere, C. Terry Hendrix, Theresa Reid, and Carole Jenny. 2002. *The APSAC Handbook on Child Maltreatment,* 2/e. Thousand Oaks, CA: Sage.

Myers-Walls, J. A. 1984. "Balancing Multiple Role Responsibilities During the Transition to Parenthood." *Family Relations* 33: 267–71.

National Institute of Child Health and Human Development. 1999. "Child Outcomes When Child Care Center Classes Meet Recommended Standards for Quality." *American Journal of Public Health* 89 (July): 1072–77.

Patterson, C. 1992. "Children of Lesbian and Gay Parents." *Child Development* 63: 1025–42.

Perry, Yvette V. 2002. "Assisted Reproductive Technology through a Family Policy Lens: Some Lessons from Adoption Policy." *National Council on Family Relations Family Focus* (December): 1–2.

Register, Sheri. 1991. *Are Those Kids Yours? Raising Children Adopted from Other Countries.* New York, NY: Free Press.

Rogers, Stacy J., and Lynn K. White. 1998. "Satisfaction with Parenting: The Role of Marital Happiness, Family Structure, and Parents' Gender." *Journal of Marriage and the Family* 60, 2 (May): 293–308.

Rosen, Bernard Carl. 2001. *Masks and Mirrors: Generation X and the Chameleon Personality.* Westport, CT: Praeger.

Rubenstein, C. 1994. "The Confident Generation." *Working Mother* (May): 38–45.

Sabatelli, R. M., R. L. Meth, and S. M. Gavazzi. 1988. "Factors Mediating the Adjustment to Involuntary Childlessness." *Family Relations* 37: 338–43.

Seccombe, Karen. 1991. "Assessing the Costs and Benefits of Children: Gender Comparisons Among Childfree Husbands and Wives." *Journal of Marriage and the Family* 53, 1 (February): 191–202.

Seccombe, Karen, Delores James, and Kimberly Battle Walters. 1998. "'They Think You Ain't Much of Nothing': The Social Construction of the Welfare Mother." *Journal of Marriage and the Family* 60, 4 (November): 849–65.

Simon, Rita J., and Howard Alstein. 2000. *Adoption across Borders: Serving the Children in Transracial and Intercountry Adoptions.* Lanham, MA: Rowman & Littlefield.

Somers, Marsha D. 1993. "A Comparison of Voluntarily Childfree Adults and Parents." *Journal of Marriage and the Family* 55, 3 (August): 643–50.

Steiner, G. 1981. *The Futility of Family Policy.* Washington, DC: The Brookings Institution.

Stemp, P. S., R. J. Turner, and S. Noh. 1986. "Psychological Distress in the Postpartum Period: The Significance of Social Support." *Journal of Marriage and the Family* 48: 271–77.

Straus, Murray A., and Richard J. Gelles. 1990. *Physical Violence in American Families.* New Brunswick, NJ: Transaction.

Thomson, E., T. L. Hanson, and Sara S. McLanahan. 1994. "Family Structure and Child Well Being: Economic Resources vs. Parental Behaviors." *Social Forces* 73: 221–42.

Thornton, J. 1984. "Family Violence Emerges from the Shadows." *U.S. News and World Report* (January): 23, 66.

Todd, Tracy. 2000. "An Essay for Practitioners. Solution Focused Strategic Parenting of Challenging Teens: A Class for Parents." *Family Relations* 49, 2: 165–68.

Ulbrich, P. M., A. T. Coyle, and M. M. Llabre. 1990. "Involuntary Childlessness and Marital Adjustment: His and Hers." *Journal of Sex and Marital Therapy* 16: 147–58.

United States Bureau of the Census. 1997. *Statistical Abstract of the United States: 1998.* Washington, DC: Government Printing Office.

United States Bureau of the Census. 2001a. "Births and Birth Rates by Race, Sex, and Age: 1980 to 1999." Table 70. *Statistical Abstract of the United States.* Washington, DC: Government Printing Office.

United States Bureau of the Census. 2001b. "Households and Families: 2000." QT-P10. *Census 2000 Summary File 2.* Washington, DC: Government Printing Office.

United States Bureau of the Census. 2001c. "Record Share of New Mothers in Labor Force, Census Bureau Reports." http://www.census.gov/Press-\Release/www/2000/cb00-175.html (Retrieved 9/30/02).

United States Department of Health and Human Services, National Center on Child Abuse and Neglect. 1996. *Third National Incidence Study of Child Abuse and Neglect: Final Report.* Washington, DC: Government Printing Office.

Veevers, Jean. 1980. *Childless by Choice.* Toronto: Butterworth.

Visher, J. S. 1984. "Seven Myths about Stepfamilies." *Medical Aspects of Human Sexuality* 18, 1: 52, 56, 61–62, 65, 73–74, 76, 80.

Whelan, Elizabeth M. 1975. *A Baby—Maybe? A Guide to Making the Most Fateful Decision of Your Life.* Indianapolis, IN: Bobbs-Merrill.

White, Lynn K. 1990. "Determinants of Divorce: A Review of Research in the Eighties." *Journal of Marriage and the Family* 52, 4 (November): 904–12.

Whitsett, D., and H. Land. 1992. "Role Strain, Coping, and Marital Satisfaction of Stepparents." *Families in Society: The Journal of Contemporary Human Services* 73: 79–92.

Wilcox, W. Bradford. 2002. "Religion, Convention, and Paternal Involvement." *Journal of Marriage and the Family* 64: 780–92.

Wolfe, David. 1987. *Child Abuse: Implications for Child Development and Psychopathology.* Newbury Park, CA: Sage.

Wozniak, Danielle F. 2002. *They're All My Children: Foster Mothering in America.* New York, NY: New York University Press.

Wright, Victoria, Laura Schieve, Meredith Reynolds, Gary Jeng, and Dmitry Kissin. 2004. "Assisted Reproductive Technology Surveillance—United States, 2001." CDC—MMWR April 30, 53 (SS01): 1–20. www.cdc.gov/mmwr/preview/mmwrhtml/ss5301a1.htm (Retrieved 9/30/04).

Young, M. 1988. "Parenting During Mid-Adolescence: Review of Developmental Theories and Parenting Behaviors." *Maternal and Child Nursing Journal* 17, 1: 1–12.

Zelnick, M., and J. F. Kantner. 1980. "Sexual Activity, Contraceptive Use, and Pregnancy among Metropolitan-Area Teenagers." *Family Planning Perspectives* 12, 5: 230–37.

CHAPTER

11

RELATIVES, FICTIVE KIN, AND COMMUNITY: DEFAULT, DESIGN, AND SOCIAL CONTEXT

CHAPTER PREVIEW

The family exists as an institutionalized pattern of relationships in every known society. However, the precise arrangement of relatives in *kinship* patterns and the relationships and boundaries those patterns imply for descent and inheritance (*patrilineal, matrilineal,* or *bilateral*) and residence (*patrilocal, matrilocal, bilocal,* or *neolocal*) vary widely across cultures, and even over time and across subcultures in the same society.

Kinship goes beyond relationships grounded in biological connections and even beyond those established by marriage ties. In this chapter we explore those ordinary definitions of kinship (including *incest taboos*) and how expectations of kin are changing with regard to the *sandwich generation*, grandparents' role in raising children (including *co-residence*), and to adult children who return home. In the face of *family boundary ambiguity*, we also introduce the concepts of *fictive kin* and *accordion households*. We relate the experience of those who have elected a cohousing option and describe the importance of *family rituals* and *family stories*.

This chapter concludes with an examination of families within the greater social context. We focus on socioeconomic risks to children and their families and discuss arguments about family decline and family well-being. We present an overview of the association between *spirituality* and *religion*, including *religious affiliation* and the influence of *religiosity* on family life.

RELATIONSHIPS AND BOUNDARIES

The family exists as an institutionalized pattern of relationships in every known society. However, the precise arrangement of family and kinship, relationships and boundaries, rights and responsibilities varies widely across cultures, and even over time and across regions in the same society. Family boundaries are established by social and sometimes legal conventions.

The most basic unit of kinship is that formed by blood ties. To many anthropologists, the bond between biological mother and child is the essential unit of "family" and therefore kinship. In a society where the determination of genetic paternity may not be certain, in a society where a man may have more than one wife, or in a society where fathers are not likely to stick around, such a unit may make functional sense. Nonetheless, it likely represents a prejudicial view of men's role in parenting children and forming families.

Hall (1994: 26–27) believes families, and by extension kin networks over time, serve at least five basic functions:

1. Kinship enables us to experience continuities in our lives via family histories and genealogies.

2. Families (including all kinds of family substitutes or alternatives) [mean] we are not alone in the world, we have a group with which to identify closely, and we are therefore less vulnerable to the strains and stresses of everyday life.

3. Families have the capacity to persist even under conditions when close friends may abandon us. We have a right to claim lifetime membership in a family ourselves, even if our relatives choose to disown us.

4. Family history links us to our past, provides vital information about our socialization, and shows "us who we really are in the present."

5. Establishing ourselves in the context of and independent from our families sets the stage for our effective participation in the larger society.

In this chapter, we hope to expand the reader's concept of networks that can assist families beyond "kin." We encourage consideration of other than individuals to whom we relate in intimate, family ways even though they are not related to us by blood, marriage, or adoption (i.e., *fictive kin*). We hope to raise consciousness concerning the extent even broad communities serve as critical resources in nurturing and supporting families. An example of such supportive networks has surfaced recently in military communities. For example, Bowen et al. (2003) have demonstrated through a strengths-based, community practice model how both formal and informal social networks can enhance family adaptation in military communities.

Drummet, Coleman, and Cable (2003) find specific, community-based interventions to be critical in aiding military families as they traverse through relocation, separation, and reunion. The seven factors family life educators take into account when assisting military families during stressful transitions are relevant for family life professionals who seek to assist families in any community.

1. Consideration of cultural and subcultural influences on reactions to family stress and willingness to access family support systems

2. Awareness of the diversity of family structures and the need to individualize family response programs

3. Understanding of not only intrafamily communication patterns but also communication systems among the family, the military, and other social units

4. Sensitivity to the diverse employment situations of family members, both those associated with the military and those with employment outside the organization

5. Provision of information regarding living arrangements, school choice, and maintaining and renegotiating family boundaries during times of transition

6. Organizing programs directed specifically at children undergoing transitions

7. Recognizing family services may be required during periods of reunion and readjustment after the initial stressors have been resolved

Comparative Interpretations of Kinship

In the broadest sense, kinship shapes patterns of who can and cannot marry, descent and inheritance, and residence. *Incest taboos* establish patterns of exogamy, or specifying those one can or cannot marry and those with whom one cannot have sexual relations. In certain circumstances (e.g., ancient Egypt) royal brothers and sisters may have married to protect bloodlines that connected them to various deities. At earlier points in America's history and in certain regions of the country, Americans have encouraged, permitted, and tolerated marriage between first cousins. In general, however, cultural regulation, often codified into law, has ensured marriage and sexual relations will be socially sanctioned only beyond clear boundaries.

Although the popular belief is incest taboos exist to reduce the frequency of genetic abnormalities, even societies in which rudimentary genetics are not understood prohibit marriage and sexual relations among people related closely by blood. Some might also argue if interbreeding increases the probability of less desirable traits such as hemophilia appearing in the gene pool, interbreeding would also increase the probability of more desirable traits appearing in the gene pool.

However, marriage among close kin is potentially dysfunctional in at least two important ways. First, in societies in which trading marriage partners is a basis for forging alliances, keeping potential marriage partners within the group reduces the opportunity for such alliances. Second, when individuals who are already closely related intermarry, the potential for role confusion and status conflict within the family is increased. The roles and status of husband and wife, parent and child, brother and sister, and extended kin are also embedded in rights and responsibilities that could be confusing if one's cousin is also one's husband.

One such right is that of inheritance. Most African, Asian, and Indian societies are unilineal; that is, name and property are passed through one line. In a *patrilineal* system, inheritance is passed through the male line. In a *matrilineal* system, inheritance is passed through the female line. As Hammons writes in Box 11.1 on primogeniture, American inheritance patterns could at one time be characterized as patrilineal. Certainly the tradition that women will take the name of their husbands represents a vestige of patrilineage. However, today American patterns of inheritance are best described as *bilateral*; that is, property is transferred to both daughters and sons from both fathers and mothers.

BOX 11.1   "Oldest First: Primogeniture and Sibling Rivalry"
Sue Hammons, Ph.D.

Birth order, gender, and power intertwine in the cultural legacy from primogeniture, the practice of the eldest son inheriting the lion's share of a family's wealth. Biblical tales reveal that the custom was firmly entrenched early. In several cases, ancient patriarchs passed over eldest sons in favor of younger ones. As with suttee in India, the idea behind the practice was to keep widows from inheriting; sometimes they had to become prostitutes or slaves.

Although Ishmael is his eldest son, Abraham designates Issac as his heir and successor; Jacob recognizes Ephraim at the expense of a disinherited Manasseh. The two themes of primogeniture and blessing juxtapose in much of Genesis, particularly 48 and 49. Sibling rivalry today often also has elements of ageism and sexism.

After Columbus informed the old world of the new, Spain systematically looted Mexico and Peru. To secure the funds to build a castle, younger sons eagerly became conquistadors. In 1066, William the Conqueror imposed primogeniture and eldest-son succession in Saxon nations. Sometimes, however, as with Henry VIII, royals would discuss the feasibility of disinheriting the daughter in favor of a bastard son.

As with most norms, dramatic exceptions occur. A Frenchwoman, Eleanor, inherited the province of Aquitaine. Eleanor married and divorced (extremely rare at the time) the King of France. Upon her divorce she regained Aquitaine. In 1152 she married the King of England and, quarreling with him, moved back to Aquitaine to rule it independently. In her will, she chose her second and favorite son to rule England.

Upper-class families in feudal times wanted to insure later generations by having many children. Yet, if they divided estates equally, they could not retain the political and economic power that a large estate let them enjoy. Thus, many estates were intact for as much as 100 years. Younger sons did receive money to launch themselves in a career to make a living and fathers sought advantageous marriages for daughters.

Societies turned away from the principles of primogeniture at the same time as the rise of democracy and the development of capitalism. The upper middle class began to view primogeniture as thievery and unearned privilege. Thomas Jefferson abolished primogeniture in Virginia in 1776; Georgia and the other colonies followed suit. The Napoleonic Code abolished this custom in France after their revolution. However, Russia did not establish eldest-male succession until Emperor Paul I in 1797.

Interestingly, England clung to primogeniture until 1925 and applied it more harshly than other countries. By Queen Victoria's day, legal and economic customs had reduced married women to the control of husbands. Unlike most of Europe, English law did favor a daughter instead of a male relative if a property owner had no sons, but Englishwomen were more susceptible to a life of poverty.

The case Caroline Norton proved to be a force for change in England. Mrs. Norton left her home and attempted unsuccessfully to divorce her husband on the grounds of cruelty. She never saw her three sons again; her husband did not give her any money. She turned to writing as a career and used her talent to publicize her case to change the laws. A century of reform by the woman's movement resulted in further change.

Outside Europe and America, women have also been excluded as heirs. In 1999, the Zimbabwe Supreme Court upheld the right of primogeniture (although the Constitutional Court of South Africa struck down male primogeniture in October 2003). Such blatant and overt gender discrimination reinforces and speaks to the reality of unearned privileges. Perhaps primogeniture's influence today exists only as an example of culture lag. The global economy favors technological knowledge and entrepreneurs rather than power flowing from possession of huge amounts of land.

Sue Hammons, Ph.D., is Professor of Social Science at Abraham Baldwin College in Tifton, Georgia, where she teaches courses on social problems and gender studies. Her current research interests include resilience, rural women, and wiccans.

American couples who marry and begin family life together typically expect to establish *neolocal* residence that is a household apart from either parent. No expectation exists that they must set up the new household either in the household or vicinity of the husband's family (*patrilocal*) or in the household or vicinity of the wife's family (*matrilocal*). Instead, the new family may set up a household in proximity to either (*bilocal*) or in an entirely separate area.

Residence in close proximity to one's extended kin has the advantage of providing one with the opportunity for shared resources, including child care and household advice. However, residence in close proximity to one's extended kin has the disadvantage of providing one with the possibility for less privacy and autonomy, including unwanted criticism of one's child rearing and household decisions. In a society in which newly married couples are expected to reside with or in close proximity to a husband's or a wife's parents, the parents (and perhaps other family members) would have a significant vested interest in mate selection. As discussed in chapter 7, in societies that value autonomy, independence, and privacy, a free choice system of mate selection is consistent, at least in theory.

Changing Kinship in American Society

The dreaded long distance call comes in the middle of the night. Your spouse has had an accident and is in critical condition, and doctors are frantically searching for next of kin to give permission to operate. . . . You sputter into the phone yes, go ahead and perform the operation. But after a moment's hesitation, the doctor informs you that your permission is not valid. Why? Because even though you and your spouse have been legally married for many years, your marriage is not recognized in the state where the accident occurred, the state where your spouse lies dying. According to the laws of that state, you and your spouse are not married at all, and never were. (Rotello 1996)

"Next of kin" is a legal term that provides legal authority to authorize medical treatment for a family member who is deemed incapable of making those decisions. The right to authorize health care is one argument for conferring legal status on gay and lesbian unions. In the case of one partner in such a union, becoming incapable of rendering a medical decision, the other partner would be authorized to do so, just as husbands and wives are legally entitled to do for one another.

The boundaries of family and *kinship* define who is (and therefore who is not) "family." "Family" sets rights and obligations, regarding affection and caring in social contact, reciprocity, and exchange in maintaining contact and gift giving. In a highly mobile society, maintaining those affectionate and symbolic bonds presents some families with a real challenge. As we shall see in the next section, such mobility also leaves open the opportunity for families to be created by design instead of or complementary to families which occur by default.

FAMILY BONDS OVER THE LIFE CYCLE AND ACROSS GENERATIONS

Leaving Home

Perhaps no other society has had higher expectations of separate, neolocal residence than American society. Through the 19th century and into the 20th century, America was moving from a predominantly agrarian economy to a predominantly industrial and service economy. "Leaving home" often meant leaving behind the parents' farm and rural community for education or employment in the city. Remaining with parents may have been more economical, and remaining in the parental or other relative's household may have been more respectable (i.e., for single daughters) than establishing a separate household.

However, the American ideal has been children will live in the home of their parents until they complete formal education, begin full-time employment, or marry. After all, some ask, how can one really be considered an adult, if one continues to live under a parent's roof? Even if one contributes to the family economy, for example, paying rent or purchasing a portion of the groceries, living in one's parental home flies in the face of the ideal of detachment and independence, to say nothing of American ideas for privacy.

Although almost two thirds (62.8%) of young adults lived at home in 1940, the number of adult children who have left and then returned to the parental home has been increasing since the 1970s. In 1970, 9% of men and 7% of women aged 25 to 34 lived in their parents' homes. Today 15% of men and 8% of women live in their parents' homes. Today 18 million, 38% of all young adult singles 20 to 34 years old, live with their parents. Also, the transition from college to living with parents is not by accident. Over half—56%—of current college students plan to live with their parents for some period of time following graduation. According to one poll, almost one in five plans to do so for a period of time over a year. The earlier a child leaves home, the higher the probability he or she will return to the parents' home (Paul 2001).

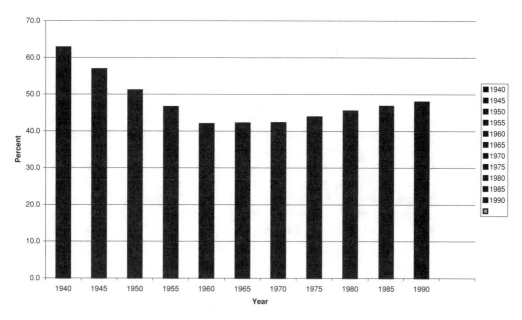

FIG. 11.1.   Percentage of Young Adults Living at Home, 1940–1990.
Source: Adapted from United States Bureau of the Census, 2001.

Stereotypes aside, living in the parental home has decided benefits, particular in the area of economics. "This new generation of post-collegiate nesters, unencumbered by room-and-board payments, is financially savvy, ready to spend, and a growing consumer force" (Paul 2001: 1). With little or none of one's own income designated for shelter and food, these young adults are a marketer's dream with large amounts of discretionary income to invest in the newest consumer electronics and automobiles.

Returning to the nest is becoming normal, reflecting a fundamental shift in attitudes from a time when returning home was a sign of failure to secure employment and when a college or professional degree that did not lead to a high status occupation was the sign of a failed slacker. Today parents are more likely to support, or even encourage, their adult children to return to the parental home. Perhaps parents are not only more supportive but also more protective. Contemporary parents want more for their children than the highest paying position; parents want their children to find fulfillment in their life. For some, this means moving back into the parents' residence for a temporary or even extended period of time while the adult child's plans become clearer.

Sharing a parent's home is part of a larger pattern of intergenerational support. The exchange of goods and services among kin who are not co-residing tends to be more frequent for whites than for African Americans or Hispanics, perhaps because the latter have fewer resources to share. Research has found minority adult children were in fact less likely to receive financial resources from their parents, but minority parents were strikingly more likely to extend financial aid if the adult child was highly educated and had a larger income. These findings contradict the assumption minority parents give support to their children primarily to ease short-term financial crises. Instead this suggests minority parents have investment and exchange motives for giving to their children (Lee and Aytac 1998).

Returning to the nest may be a distinctive reflection of postmodern life. Today's young adults face a larger range of educational, employment, and lifestyle options than ever before. Especially after leaving the clear structure of academic life, organized as it is in terms and academic years, returning to a parent's home must seem like a secure anchor in the face of economic and other uncertainties. Adult children returning home may be experiencing either a delay in securing that first job, or occasional firings, layoffs, or other unemployment during periods of economic recession or stagnation. These "adultolescents" (Newschannel2000 2000: 1) may also be among the increasing number of women who defer marriage well into their late 20s and who, therefore find themselves living across a range of household situations, some of which inevitably "fall through" leaving her occasionally without domicile or roommates.

If so, periodically returning to the parent's home seems like a reasonable part of an increasingly extended, cyclic transition from adolescence to fully independent adult status. What these returning nesters suggest is our conception of "adulthood" is changing. We can no longer determine adult status in the life cycle by the traditional markers of completion of formal education, security of full-time employment, or establishment of a family of origin through marriage.

The Sandwich Generation

The term *sandwich generation* refers to women and men at midlife who find themselves caught in the middle between responsibilities for dependent children and dependent parents. Some children leave the nest at 18 years of age, never to return except for an occasional visit. Many, probably most, parents require little or no assistance from adult children as they grow older. Still, the later age at which couples are parenting and the increased life expectancy for their parents mean many will experience a period in which their time, finances, energy, and other resources are stretched thin to breaking.

In fact, about one fourth of American families provides care for an aging member. Typically, the primary caregiver is a married woman in her 40s, working full time, with an annual household income of $35,000. She may be caring for her own mother or father, and she may also be caring for her husband's parent ("Family Caregiving in the United States" 1997). Consistent with the gendered nature of caring described in chapter 4, daughters (and daughters-in-law) outnumber sons as caregivers three to one (Cox 1993).

Grandchildren are also not exempt from responsibilities for primary caregiving of older relatives. According to one survey of caregiving families, as many as one out of every three primary caregivers for aged relatives is 40 years of age or younger (Dellman-Jenkins, Blankemeyer, and Pinkard 2000). Adult caregivers also include spouses and partners of adults who have debilitating conditions. Joyce Linquist, aged 54, cares for her partner Ron Huston, aged 61, who was diagnosed with Alzheimer's disease three years ago.

> Now she is trying to balance her studies with caring for a man who can carry on a conversation but no longer can drive, write checks, or go for a walk by himself. Huston's condition will continue to deteriorate from the progressive neurological disease that afflicts about 4 million Americans. (Wolfe 2002: E1)

Potential caregivers exhibit a range of personal styles from routine incorporation of care of the aging parent on a day-to-day basis, through backup care when other care providers are unable to meet care needs or circumscribed care in financial or other specific situations, to sporadic and unreliable care. Of course, some adult children are disassociated from care of their aging parents (Matthews and Rosner 1988); others are fully engaged and devoted in the care of their parents, taking great pleasure from this role. The strains of care giving, even for someone who finds the role very rewarding, include the disruption of daily routines, lack of training and equipment for certain care giving tasks, financial responsibilities, organizational overload, and tension among family members. These strains may be exacerbated if the aging parent's condition is sudden and unexpected and if the adjustments in the adult children's family are sudden. Such might be the case if the arrival of the aging parent requires the daughter leave the workforce, resulting in reduced family income and fewer social contacts. These challenges may be coupled with repeated negotiations of independence and dependence between adult children and their parents, as well as possible differences in commitment between a daughter and her husband regarding care of the parents.

Grandparenting Today

The extent to which American families have been multigenerational has been mythologized. Living in an extended family household with grandparents is a feature of a society in which people can be expected to live to see their children grow to adulthood and become parents, as well as of a society where families "stay put" for substantial periods of time. Neither situation has been the case among North Americans for most of known history. Even today, well before they reach adulthood, the majority of grandchildren will experience the death of at least one grandparent (Szinovacz 1998).

Most aging adults do not require living assistance from their children or grandchildren. In fact, the birth or adoption of a child creates not only parents but also grandparents, and vital grandparents at that. With increasing longevity, an American child has a greater chance than ever before of arriving in a family with three- or even four-generational relationships. Although grandparenthood is a fairly universal, midlife transitional experience for most adults (albeit one which traditionally has a "matrilineal tone," except in farm families [Longino and Earle 1996]), considerable variation exists in the availability of specific grandparents and the duration of the relationship. Also, the point at which an adult becomes a grandparent is sometimes "off-timed," as in the case of women who become grandparents in their 40s, perhaps even before they have completed their own childbearing and childrearing.

Parenting the second time around (i.e., grandparenting) can be a magical time. Grandparents who live away from their grandchildren can elect to participate in aspects of their grandchildren's lives, while avoiding (if they choose) disciplinary or other tasks related to caring for children. Grandparents may experience the joys of sharing life with children, while avoiding interpersonal, economic, and other struggles they may have experienced with their own children.

American grandparents place a high priority on building relationships with their grandchildren. Furthermore, both grandparent and grandchild seem to suffer when social structure or social circumstances impede their opportunities to form these extended relationships (Longino and Earle 1996). According to a survey commissioned by the *AARP* (2000), of grandparents who are not caregivers or who do not live in the same household as their grandchildren, 44% see a grandchild at least once a week. Another 25% see a grandchild at least once a month. Other grandparents keep in touch with their grandchildren through letter writing, e-mail, and the exchange of gifts through the mail. Only one in 10 grandparents neither sees nor talks by phone with a grandchild every few months or less. Although some grandparents may overestimate their mentoring role, Crosnoe and Elder (2002) have found the transition of grandchildren to higher education may improve the quality of the grandparent–grandchild relationship.

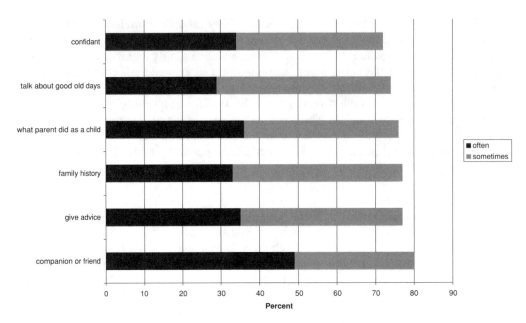

FIG. 11.2.   Staying Involved: Roles Grandparents Play in Grandkids' Lives.
Source: Adapted from AARP, 2000.

Although grandparents report spending significant amounts of money on clothes, books, toys, and other items for their grandchildren (a median of $489 in the *AARP* [2000] study), grandparents clearly perceive themselves as playing significant roles in their grandchildren's lives. Almost half of the grandparents "often" play the role of companion or friend to their grandchild. Almost three-fourths reported they "often" or "sometimes" serve as confidant to their grandchildren. Grandparents say they would most like to pass on high morals and integrity (42%), success or ambition (21%), and religion (20%) to their grandchildren (*AARP*).

Foremost among grandparents' concerns are their rights to visitation and custody. Grandparents and parents may be estranged from one another, especially when the grandparent's adult child is not the custodial parent following divorce. Grandparents may be in a position to assume care of a child when the parent has died, been incarcerated, or been found by the court to be unfit. In those situations, grandparents may still wish to maintain ties with their grandchildren. Grandparent visitation rights legislation was enacted in all 50 states between 1964 and 1987. Prior to that time, grandparents had no greater legal standing in this regard than did any nonrelative. Although these laws do not guarantee grandparents will have access to their grandchildren, these laws do give grandparents the legal standing to petition the courts for visitation (Hill 2000).

Such legislation may be part of an increasingly litigious society. Certainly the potential for disrupted connections to one's grandchildren increases when the parents' marriage ends in divorce or when the parents do not marry or cohabit. However, legislation on behalf of grandparents is also part of a general trend toward the institutionalization of the roles of grandparents (Hill 2000). Sociologists (e.g., Cherlin and Furstenberg 1992) and legal scholars (e.g., Bostock 1994; Jackson 1994) link the grandparents' rights movement to the institutionalization of the roles of grandparents (Hill).

Grandparent is an increasingly salient status as a higher percentage of adults live to be grandparents at younger ages and for longer periods of time. Similarly, lower fertility rates mean each grandparent will have fewer grandchildren, potentially increasing the grandparent's interest in maintaining contact with the smaller number of children (Cherlin and Furstenberg 1992; Jackson 1994). Family studies scholars recognize the increasing importance of multigenerational bonds. In the words of Vern Bengtson (2001), the recipient of the *National Council on Family Relations' Burgess Award* given to recognize contributions to family development:

> ... family multigenerational relations will be more important in the 21st century [because of] demographic changes in ... aging, resulting in "longer years of shared lives," between generations, the increasing importance of grandparents and other kin in fulfilling family functions, [and] the strength and resilience of intergenerational solidarity over time.

Furthermore, Bengtson notes family multigenerational relations will be increasingly diverse because of changes in family structure, particularly resulting from divorce and stepfamily relations.

BOX 11.2 "Grandparenting as a Family Commitment"
Kate O'Keefe

An African proverb reminds us that "It takes a village to raise a child." Growing up in the 1950s, members of my immediate and even extended family lived nearby. Children had the freedom to wander the neighborhood, playing and exploring, feeling safe, because we knew that adults in the neighborhood, related or not, were looking out for us and monitoring our behavior. Today many families reside in large urban areas where we are disconnected from the kind of childhood community I experienced and, because of frequent relocation due to employment, from our families as well.

When Madeline was born I became a stereotypical grandmother, seemingly overnight. All of my overachieving and striving, ever seeking the higher purpose and larger goal, dropped away. What remained was pure and simple—the joyous duty and moral imperative to love and care for the next generation. Happily, my spouse shared these values.

Our commitment was clear. However, we could not act on it unless we had the commitment of my daughter and son-in-law as well. They appreciated how much her grandparents loved their child and they experienced how wonderful it was to have support with child care and nurturing. They wanted their children—grandson Andrew was born—to have the benefit of a close grandparent relationship.

Both parents and grandparents are professionals with demanding jobs, and we all had the potential to seek positions requiring a move. However, we mutually agreed that we valued the intergenerational care the children were receiving, and that their needs were primary. Consequently, we committed to living in the same area, within 30 minutes driving time of one another.

The commitment of both parents and grandparents and open and honest communication is necessary. Once, when I was giving my daughter and her husband some input on a behavioral issue, they balked a bit, realizing later that this sort of conversation came with the territory. "We can't," my daughter acknowledged, "expect grandparents to be committed and involved, and not be open to their input as well."

When both parents are employed outside the home, it may take four adults to raise the children. In our case, we've arranged it so one of us is there to care for the children after school—no "latch-key" needed. And most recently, working out of my home as a consultant, I'm caring for little Will, the newest addition to the family, 3 days a week. The adults juggle their schedules, the children get consistent, loving care, and the adults' relationships across generations are enriched.

Kate O'Keefe is a leadership development consultant and organizational historian. She lives in the Twin Cities area in Minnesota, where she and her husband are deeply involved in caring for their three grandchildren, Madeleine, Andrew, and Will.

Grandparents Raising Children... Again

Of the 31% of Americans—about 60 million adults—who are grandparents, 11% of grandparents over 50 are caregivers for grandchildren (*AARP* 2002). Although most of these grandparents are caring for children as regular day care providers, another 3% are raising a grandchild.

The number of grandparents raising their children's children is related to the incidence of divorce and teen pregnancy, as well as AIDS, drug abuse, and other social problems which render parents unavailable to parent. Ideally, Americans express a preference for balance and independence in their family relations, so grandparent involvement in regular care of their grandchildren is counter to norms regarding intergenerational roles. Even when grandparents become involved in parenting their grandchildren, the former believe parents should be the primary caretakers of children, adult children should live on their own, and grandparents should provide help only when absolutely necessary. (Pebley and Rudkin 1999).

In most situations where a grandchild lives with a grandparent, grandparent, parent, and child share a household. In fact, *co-residence* accounts for the largest percentage (two thirds) of children living with grandparents. Co-residence lends itself to a situation in which grandmothers have a substantial role in parenting (Pebley and Rudkin 1999). Custodial care, on the other hand, may or may not involve legal custody and may or may not be relatively permanent. For some families, co-residence is a transitional stage as the single parent moves to independent living (Bengtson 2001). For teen and other single parents, sharing residence and child-care responsibilities while living in their parents' house offers substantial advantages (King and Elder 1997).

Although co-residence patterns have changed very little over the last 2 decades and the frequency of custodial grandparenting has increased only slightly overall, African-American grandchildren are more likely than children from other racial or ethnic groups to live with their grandparents (Pebley and Rudkin 1999). On the average, during the last decade, over 37% of Black children (compared to 30% of all children) were living in the custody of grandparents (without either parent). Although this reflects the higher rates of poverty and unemployment in Black communities, the higher incidence of co-residence with grandmothers also mirrors the significant role of Black grandmothers in childrearing and extended-family stability (Pebley and Rudkin).

Grandparents and great-grandparents who care for grandchildren face a variety of service needs. Contextual factors, stressors related to care giving, and lack of social support are related to the grandparents' psychological anxiety. The most susceptible to stress seem to be younger grandparents, those caring for grandchildren with physical and psychological problems, and those with low family cohesion (Sands and Goldberg-Glen 2000). Community support groups can offer advice and strategies for coping, whereas organizations such as the *AARP* have become vigorous advocates for the financial resources and legal rights of this group (see, e.g., *AARP* 2002).

FAMILIES BY DESIGN

Family Boundary Ambiguity, Fictive Kin, and Accordion Households

Family boundary ambiguity (Boss and Greenberg 1984) refers to the condition of uncertainty about who is and is not a family member. This concept is useful in understanding the fluid nature of family system boundaries and we argue the intentional potential for composing families not just by default but also by design.

"Family" can no longer be understood merely as the group composed of individuals closely related to one another through marriage, birth, or adoption. A meaningful definition of "family" easily includes relatives who constitute one's extended kin by marriage (including in-laws), birth, or adoption, although where any one of us would draw the line at extended kin obligations will vary.

For example, for years, the mother of one of your authors spoke of "Aunt Leah," a person who figured only vaguely in the author's recollections. In the absence of a face-to-face meeting, not until early adulthood did the author realize this person was the wife of her maternal grandfather's brother. Yet this distant relationship, widely separated by multiple lines of blood and marriage, is accorded a sense of importance, and even obligation by the author's mother.

The fluid nature of such family boundaries contributes to family ambiguity. However, for your authors and we suspect for many of our readers, our families have also been enriched by people to whom we are not related by marriage, birth, or adoption and yet who occupy positions of entitlement and obligation in our family. These significant others, which Stack (1974), in her classic study of strategies of survival among Black women and their families in an economically disadvantaged community, referred to as *fictive kin*, may include the older couple who befriended a young wife and her child in the absence of the serviceman husband (Karraker's Aunt Mignon and Uncle Lum). For the other author, living far away from families of origin, long-time friends became and remain her children's favorite "relatives" (Grochowski's children's Auntie Karlin and Uncle Mike). In a society in which neolocal residence is the norm and geographical mobility is a frequent fact of life, fictive kin take on special significance. For most of us, parents and siblings hold a pivotal place in anchoring the kinship system. However, in some cases close kin are geographically distant or emotionally unavailable. In those circumstances, individuals may seek out others who can provide advice, child care, financial support, or other resources, including an older, wiser ear for the strains and pleasures of everyday life.

This description of family boundary ambiguity and fictive kin still does not do full justice to the dynamic nature of "family." Drawing on Hareven's (1973) on the malleability of urban households, Stacey has used the term *accordion households* to further capture the extent to which households expand and contract as the needs of various kin change over time. For many of us, family boundaries have by necessity expanded to include former spouses (and in-laws) and stepchildren (and their extended kin), as well as long-term cohabiting couples. One of the authors' stepbrothers exemplifies this type of family structure.

George has been married three times. His first marriage ended in divorce. He remains connected to both his former wife, with whom he has two daughters, and her parents. One daughter is married, so George has acquired a son-in-law; the other daughter has a live-in boyfriend who is included in family gatherings.

His second wife died of breast cancer, leaving George with three daughters and one son. His wife's parents are involved in this family. One of these daughters is also married, so George has acquired another son-in-law; one of these daughters also has a live-in boyfriend who is included in family gatherings. This household also includes a health care worker who lives with the family full-time to care for the third daughter who is mentally disabled.

George is currently married and has acquired a stepdaughter from his wife's previous marriage. Not only his wife's parents, but also one of the parents of his wife's former husband is involved in this family. The stepdaughter's former husbands, as well as the live-in boyfriend of the stepdaughter are included, to different extents, when George considers his family.

Cohousing

The high premium Americans place on neolocal residence, as well as on individual property rights and family privacy, mitigates against preference for anything except a single-family residence and, ideally, a detached single-family residence. However, as with so many other constructions of what is normative for families, the concept of "crowding" is a relatively recent one. For example, well into the 18th century, most urban households in England, France, and Scotland had only one or two rooms. Furthermore households through the early twentieth century often included non-family members, sometimes lodgers or short-term boarders who were relative strangers (Jones, Tepperman, and Wilson 1995).

Today local regulations governing zoning restrict the places where and arrangements under which non-related individuals may live. Nonetheless, the *Fellowship for Intentional Community* (Questenberry 1996) estimates more than 8,000 people (including 2,000 children), live in 186 of the more established intentional communities in the United States and Canada. Three fourths (76.3%) of the cohousing groups included in the *Fellowship for Intentional Community* (Questenberry) data are in rural communities, or have combined rural and urban sites. Eighty percent of the rural groups reported common holdings of 34,000 acres. Forty-four urban groups listed common holdings of 98 apartments and 46 group housing units, plus additional units with 113 more bedrooms. The *Fellowship* believes these are but a small fraction of the *cohousing* movement in North America.

Cohousing is intended to blend privacy and community, offering the benefits of home ownership with the advantages of shared common facilities and connection with neighbors. Cohousing is an effort to respond to both environmental and social challenges facing society and families today. Most cohousing units offer private, fully equipped residences (i.e., bedrooms, kitchen, living and dining spaces, and bathrooms) for families and singles. Some may share some common amenities (e.g., laundry facilities and landscaped recreational areas; *The Cohousing Network* 2002)

Cohousing organizes "intentional neighborhoods" that differ from other intentional communities (e.g., "communes" or other communal living arrangements) in that the neighbors do not necessarily share political, religious, or social ideology that unites them with their cohousing peers, while setting them apart from the larger community. Cohousing may offer economies of scale in terms of certain real property, but other economic cooperation, such as the sharing of wages, wealth, or expenses is not implied. Still, cohousing offers residents

> ... an old-fashioned sense of neighborhood [in which] residents know [each other] very well and in which there is a strong sense of community often absent in cities and suburbs today. (*The Cohousing Network* 2002: 1)

Many families are not interested in communal living, cohousing, or even a community family supper like the Hebb-Pomeroy's described in Box 11.3. One of the authors participated in a meal-sharing arrangement with another family for approximately six months. The two families, who were next-door-neighbors, each had two adults and one young daughter. On a fixed day each week, one family prepared and delivered a complete dinner meal. On another fixed day each week, the other family did the same. Preparing double servings of the same meal required considerably less effort and resulted in noticeably less

---

BOX 11.3 "The New Family Supper"
Sharon Overton

"Growing up there was no real sitting down to dinner," says 26-year-old Michael Hebb, echoing the childhood memories of many latchkey kids. "Dinner more often meant a bowl of cereal in front of my *Nintendo*."

Naomi Pomeroy, 27, had the opposite experience. "My family ate together every single night," she says. Even after her parents divorced, and she was busy with after-school sports, her mom waited up so they could share a meal and their day.

How ironic then that food brought these two together. And how fitting that they've made it their mission to give others a taste of what she loved and he lacked.

Michael and Naomi run a successful catering business and coffee shop in Portland, Oregon. But their real love is getting together with 20 or 30 people several times a week for what they call the Family Suppers. Guests sit on mismatched wooden folding chairs at a long table made of hollow-core doors. They pass heaping platters of the couple's simple but sophisticated food. Their baby daughter, August, crawls from lap to lap. The wine flows, the conversation sparkles, and strangers become family over the course of an evening.

Just like supper at home, there is no wait staff; Michael and Naomi bring the food to the table themselves. And you don't get a say about what you eat (although vegetarians are gladly accommodated). Still, no one has to be reminded to clean his or her plate. And when dinner is done, someone always helps with the dishes.

Guests pitching in and being a part of something makes the family suppers more memorable than a restaurant meal. For Naomi, who learned to cook at her Southern grandmother's knee, feeding people is about more than nourishing bodies. Family suppers are about nurturing souls.

Her guests couldn't agree more. Sharing a meal in this way helps people connect with something they've lost, or maybe never had, says one young woman who attends regularly. These meals provide a sense of warmth and community that the world needs more of now."

Sharon Overton is the West Coast editor for *Better Homes and Gardens* magazine. Based in Portland, Oregon, she writes about topics relating to home, family, and community.

cleanup, leaving more time to spend together in the evening. This arrangement lasted until one of the families, and then the other, moved from the neighborhood.

Regardless, more or less formalized arrangements for sharing child care, meal preparation, and other everyday household functions suggest possibilities for intrafamily cooperation that might both lighten the workload of everyday family life, while forging instrumental and expressive bonds among families.

Rituals and Stories in Family Life

Doherty refers to rituals as "the glue that holds families together" (1999: 10). Researchers at the Myth and Ritual in American Life (2002: 1) center at Emory University describe *family rituals* as the action and talk that make up family culture. Rituals are repeatable, scripted networks of behaviors that give shape, meaning, and continuity to family life. Family rituals range from almost invisible personal rituals to public, sacred ceremonies. Rituals often reflect religious, ethnic, and cultural traditions and provide continuity with the past. The importance of rituals has less to do with what is actually done or said and more to do with how the family feels about engaging in the ritual, their sense of oneness, connection, and belonging (Wolin and Bennett 1984).

Rituals help identify and unify families regardless of what rituals are practiced. What remains important about rituals is that they continue to reflect family togetherness and connections. Friesen (1990) notes three types of rituals: (a) family celebrations such as holidays and religious or cultural observances; (b) family traditions including family vacations, birthdays, first and last days of school year, graduations, anniversaries, and wedding and funeral practices; and (c) family routines. The last may go unnoticed as family rituals, yet routines may be the most frequent type of family ritual. Ritualistic routines include family mealtime, bedtime, storytime, weekend jobs and forms of relaxation, and workout and play habits. Table 11.1 describes some of the primary purposes of family rituals.

The regular rhythm of family routines also needs to be honored. Daily family routines reduce stress responses for they provide predictability of events. Engaging in shared

TABLE 11.1
Purposes of Family Rituals

- Adapting: Adjustment to family transitions (i.e., entrances into and exits from the family), crises (e.g., war and natural disasters), or the flow of family life (e.g., beginnings and endings of school or employment)

- Believing: Affirmation of family's beliefs, values, faith, spirituality, and life experiences (e.g., regular family gatherings at which members confirm their trust and confidence in each other such as family meetings)

- Celebrating: Recognition of accomplishments (e.g., birthdays) and other special events (e.g., holiday meals)

- Communicating: Expressions of caring, concern, and support toward members (e.g., hugs when leaving or returning from work or school)

- Healing: Expressions of caring with an intent to soothe and comfort (e.g., a mother's kiss on a skinned knee and a hug from a loved family member when one is ill, exchanging words that indicate "I'm sorry" and "I forgive you")

Note: Adapted with permission from Imber-Black, Evan, and Janine Roberts. 1998. *Rituals in Our Times: Celebrating, Healing, and Changing Our Lives and Our Relationships.* Lanham, MD: Jason Aronson.

activities on a regular basis also appears to have positive impacts on members' health. Campan et al. (2002) research reveals that families living in urban Spain whose adolescents were experiencing emotional or psychological health problems reported fewer family rituals than the comparison group. Creating and practicing family rituals, celebrations, traditions or routines, appear to assist adolescents (and perhaps other family members as well) in adapting to this challenging stage of life.

Rituals provide emotional anchors that offer safety and connection among family members (Imber-Black and Roberts 1998). Hafkin Pleck (2000) explains that families often romanticize about past traditions, celebrations, and routines and visualize them as somehow being better than what exists in the present. As noted by Coontz (1997), a family's current real holiday could never live up to a nostalgic image, which may lead to frustration and diminished appreciation for the present rituals. Families need to recognize that some family rituals (traditions, celebration, and routines) will change as situations demand. They need to be proactive in designing, modifying, and valuing the rituals they choose to honor.

If rituals are the "glue" that binds, then *family stories* are the "threads" in the tapestry of family life. Not only do family stories entertain, but also they transfer traditions, process realities, and construct futures.

> Family stories... evoke pride, personal history, a sense of connectedness, and feelings of being special—even in the most ordinary family. (Myth and Ritual in American Life 2002: 2)

Some stories we tell are myths, some are based on actual facts, and some are detailed accounting of events. Yet even family myths may be "true" to members who choose to believe them, for example, one of the author's mother died when the author was 10 years old, the author believed the family myth her mother is one of the first stars that appears each night and is always near.

Like family rituals, family stories often reflect religious, ethnic, and other cultural traditions. Auslander (2002) states in his exploration of African-American family mythologies:

> For many African Americans, I suspect, genealogical narratives and family reunion provide more than just appealing zones of security and emotional validation; they appear to function as primary sites of creative self-fashioning and the social negotiation of community. (2002: 23).

Duke (2002) and Fivush and Duke (2002) are currently engaged in studying how the narratives of dual-earner families reveal the power of family storytelling to reduce negative perceptions of stressor events and to enhance coping and resilience among family members. Also, your authors' (Grochowski and Karraker 2000; Karraker and Grochowski 2003) study of single mothers demonstrates how these women proactively deconstruct and reconstruct their families as they tell stories about negotiating the challenges of everyday life and shifting family membership.

Storytelling serves as one of the oldest forms of communicating values, information, guidelines, hopes, fears, and dreams. Storytelling resides at the core of human experience for we are compelled to share events, ideas, information, and beliefs within our families, communities, and cultures. Anthropologists, historians, psychologists, and teachers recognize storytelling as a means for defining humanity in the transfer of wisdom, explanations, expectations, emotions, and entertainment. Perhaps what remains most intriguing about stories is that they are fun, magical in that they offer a rich fabric of emotional color and context.

Stories are told in many media including books and audio–video technologies (e.g., film, television, VCR, DVD, audiotape, CD). "Storytelling," however, holds a unique place as "oral tradition" or "in-person interaction." The storyteller can morph and enliven the story based on the story-listeners' responses. Think of a favorite story-teller and note how that storyteller and story-listener seem to share an engaged, shared experience.

Family stories serve as history lessons of families' lives together. Roemer (1995) argues stories affirm and deny who we are and are not and help in identifying family boundaries. Family stories also fulfill important needs. First, family stories help members to remember and to know they will be remembered. Family stories keep memories of loved ones and events alive.

Second, family stories are an important part of family communication and interaction. Family storytelling taps into emotions and allows members to share, listen, and interact with each other about events and people in their lives. Family stories offer a platform for members to share as they explain, question, and dream about their life together.

Third, family stories enable families and their members to feel unique and proud.

> [F]amily stories also help children by evoking pride, personal history, a sense of connected-ness, and feelings of being special—even in the most ordinary family. (Myth and Ritual in American Life 2002: 2)

Family pride over "who we are and what value we hold" versus "what we own and how much we earn" can be showcased in family stories.

Fourth, family stories heal. Family storytelling provides opportunities for members to describe and interpret events, plan courses of action, express powerful emotions, and make sense of things. As such, and as discussed in chapter 3, storytelling is linked to family resilience. Current research (Myth and Ritual in American Life 2002) is examining how working families tell stories and what impacts this storytelling has on family resilience.

Finally, family stories entertain. Storytelling is indeed one of human's oldest forms of amusement. Stories can provide virtual trips into times and places only limited by imagination. Stories can bring squeals of delight, tears of sadness, shivers of fears, and cries of pain, all with just the spoken word between storyteller and story-listener. Yet, family storytelling is more than this. For as much as we love entertainment, we equally desire to entertain, to tell our individual story. This aspect of storytelling—creating and sharing accounts in families and communities—is most neglected in current society. Adams laments the "lost art of family storytelling"... "crushed by the hubbub of life and drowned out by modern media" (2002: 1).

Stories are vital to the fabric of family life. Fivush is focusing on how families use storytelling in dealing with the emotion of positive and negative events. Her study asks, "[d]o they [family members] share in the telling of the story or is there one person sort of tells the story and dictates, 'no this is the way it happened'?" (Myth and Ritual in American Life 2002: 1). Storytelling is more than just listening to family stories. Rather, storytelling is the active experience in which each family member creates and shares her or his own stories. Encouraging members to engage in storytelling about their individual accomplishments, dreams, along with overcoming adversities and fears (or at least learning from the experiences) enriches a family's sense of togetherness and communication. Sharing an idea may invite thought, but sharing a story about the idea fosters understanding.

FAMILIES WITHIN THE GREATER SOCIAL CONTEXT

Socioeconomic Risk to Children and Their Families

The clear and present danger to children and their families is poverty. Socioeconomic status intersects with gender and sexism, race and racism, natality and xenophobia, and every other ascribed social characteristic related to the material quality of life of families. The federal poverty threshold for a family of four was $16,640 in 1998. This threshold is the amount the federal government estimates is necessary to provide the minimum food, clothing, and shelter needs for a family of four. According to the 2000 Census, the overall poverty rate in 2001 was 11.7%, and 6.8 million families (9.2% of all families) lived in poverty. The poverty rate for children in the United States was 16.3%, the highest rate for any other age group (United States Bureau of the Census 2002). In 18 counties in the United States, the child poverty rate exceeds 50%. At 61.8%, Buffalo County, South Dakota (a large proportion which is comprised of an Indian reservation), had the highest poverty rate (Children's Defense Fund-Minnesota 2002, "Child Poverty").

A report that tracks child and family poverty since the start of welfare reform found, in spite of a booming economy and a decline in child poverty, the number of children in working poor families increased between 1995 and 1998, the period in which the states implemented welfare reform. (A working poor family is defined as one in which two parents work at least a combined total of 35 hours per week, or in which a single parent works at least 20 hours per week.) Although 1.3 million families with children left welfare during that period (1995–1998), the percentage of poor children with working parents increased from 34% to 42%. Clearly, leaving welfare does not mean leaving poverty (*Child Trends* 2001).

The *Urban Institute* estimates states spent at least $15.6 billion on child welfare services in 1998, up 3% over 1996. The *Urban Institute* argues that although Temporary Assistance for Needy Families (TANF), Medicaid, and similar programs represent 39% of federal funds spent on child welfare, states invest little funding in services to prevent the effects of poverty on children. (Bess, Leos-Urbel, and Geen 2001) Furthermore, the effects of welfare reforms over the last decade on these at-risk children are not at all clear (Bess, Leos-Urbel, and Geen; Geen et al. 2001).

The situation is especially dire for the 1.8 million children being cared for full-time by relatives other than their parents. According to data from the *National Survey of America's Families,* almost one fourth of children cared for full time by relatives face multiple economic and other social risks, frequently not receiving benefits and services to which they are entitled (Ehrle, Geen, and Clark 2001).

The effects of poverty extend beyond the quantity and quality of basic necessities like food, clothing, and shelter. Not only are poor families more likely to live in substandard housing, but also that housing is more likely to be in neighborhoods characterized by severe unemployment and violence, as well as less adequate schools, recreational facilities, and other social services.

Poor children are less likely to receive proper medical care for common childhood illnesses (e.g., allergies, asthma, earaches, and sore throats), intervention for treatable conditions (e.g., vision problems), and are less likely to be fully immunized. Not surprisingly then, poor children are 25% more likely than are other children to be absent from school (Children's Defense Fund-Minnesota 2002: "Facts").

Family Decline and Child and Family Well-Being

Popenoe (1993) has argued changes in the American family, which he characterizes as "decline," have deleterious effects on the well-being of children. However, such assertions, although attractive to those on whom changes in the structure and diversity of American families weigh heavily, have been the subject of little empirical study.

One such study found that, although children appear to be best off in a society in which traditional family patterns are strong, changes in family structure are not necessarily associated with negative consequences across the board for children. In a comparative study of child well-being in Sweden, West Germany, Italy, and the United States, Houseknecht and Sastry (1996) found the United States was at the bottom in terms of several indicators of quality of life for children and young people. The United States was highest in percentage of children in poverty, presumed child abuse rate in infants, suicide rate of young people, and juvenile drug offense rate, and near the highest in terms of juvenile delinquency rate. Italy, on the other hand, compares most favorably of the four countries studied on each of those indicators, except percent of children in poverty.

Although child poverty rates are highest in all countries for children living in single-parent families, the gap between children living in two-parent and single-parent families is by far greatest in the United States. However, the effect of family type on family poverty varies considerably across societies. On the one hand, societies like Italy, with one of the lowest birth rates in the world, must expend disproportionately fewer resources to support children, regardless of the structure of their family. On the other hand, the United States, unlike the other countries, does not provide a public, universal, child benefit (Kamerman 1996), and so children in this society suffer disproportionately the effects of certain family structures.

Religion in Families

Much of the debate about the "decline of the family" and associated problems revolves around the place of values in American life. Have gratification and pleasure replaced sacrifice and work as guiding ethics in everyday life? Have individualism and materialism replaced family and God at the center of social life? Framing the challenges and changes facing families, as caused by the decline of the sacred element in society, is neither a recent concern nor even a particularly American concern.

Religion should be differentiated from spirituality. *Spirituality* encompasses systems of intellectualism, morality, philosophy, and theology, as well as religion. *Religion*, a part of spirituality, refers to an institutionalized system of beliefs about the meaning of life in the context of the hereafter, a supreme being, or some other divine guiding force. Seventy percent of Americans belong to a religious organization (a church, temple, or mosque), and nine out of 10 homes contain at least one Bible (Newman and Grauerholz 2002). Yet the percentage of Americans identifying themselves with mainstream Catholic, Protestant, or Jewish traditions has declined to 55% (United States Bureau of the Census 2000).

The descriptions and words families use to declare their spirituality differ vastly. For some, it means feelings of hope and optimism. For others, it is a statement of their unity with the environment and universe. Some see it in their professed religions while others find it in their children's eyes. What is common in families' spirituality is a shared belief in something beyond their individual lives (Krysan, Moore, and Zill, 1990; McCubbin, Thompson, and McCubbin 1996; Stinnett and DeFrain 1985). This belief is reflected in the feelings and values families share, which often serve as guides to how they live their lives with resiliency. Beyond that, we know little about how spirituality shapes family life or family outcomes.

Religion, or more specifically *religious affiliation* (identification with and practicing the principles of an organized religious group) and *religiosity* (degree of adherence to beliefs and practices) is associated with some adaptive family outcomes. Religion sets the stage for many of the rites of passage briefly addressed at the start of this chapter. The place of religion in guiding family life is seen in the number of religious organizations that prepare engaged couples for marriage and that provide enrichment for couples who have been married for some years.

Research has found associations between higher levels of religiosity and everything from premarital sexuality to marital stability. Higher levels of religiosity are associated with less permissive sexual attitudes (Thornton and Camburn 1989) and lower rates of co-habitation (Thornton, Axinn, and Hill 1992). Couples high on religiosity have higher levels of marital commitment (Larson and Goltz 1989), lower rates of voluntary childlessness (Heaton, Jacobson, and Fu 1992), more positive parent–child relationships (Pearce and Axinn 1998), and lower rates of divorce (Call and Heaton 1997).

Newman and Grauerholz (2002) speculate religion may strengthen family life by promoting a spiritual outlook and providing support services. However, Newman and Grauerholz posit that adherence to traditional religious organization may promote oppression of powerless groups such as women and children through patriarchal systems. As Wilcox described in chapter 10 (see Box 10.4), religious fundamentalism has been linked to abusive childrearing practices. They also note religion may lead believers to unquestioning rejection of nontraditional values and practices—even those that may be adaptive. Some religions demand strict devotion to religious beliefs, which may place their members in conflict with secular society. Finally, some religious organizations exact financial and other scarce resources from families who may not be able to afford such expenditures.

Remarkably few family texts explicitly address the place of religion in family life. This dearth of information is true of not only textbooks in family studies but also in communication studies, psychology, and sociology. This neglect is unfortunate, given the importance of the family institution for inculcating social values, for socializing family members for effective social relationships, and for transmitting social norms across generations. Religion sets forth principals and guidelines for living, encourages people to live their lives in certain ways, and defines what is good and bad or evil in social life. This neglect is surprising, given the politically inspired initiatives for recent social policies, including public funding for "faith-based initiatives" to address various social problems.

BOX 11.4   "Becoming a Member of a Royal Family: Institutionalized Forms of Lesbian and Gay Kinship"
Steven P. Schacht, Ph.D.

An all too frequent, tragic reality for lesbian, gay, bisexual, or transgendered (LGBT) individuals who "come out" is that they are often rejected by homophobic members of their family of origin. To deal with this significant loss of their original family connections, many LGBT individuals construct alternative forms of family, that over time become institutionalized and meaningful forms of kinship.

I have been involved in the Imperial Sovereign Court of Spokane (ISCS) since 1994. The ISCS is one of over 60 imperial court chapters located throughout North America (and now England) that make up the Imperial Court System (recently renamed the International Court System). The Imperial Court System (ICS) was founded by gay activist Jose Sarria in 1965 and is one of the first formally established LGBT grassroots activist groups in the world.

Although ICS chapters operate as a charitable organization for the LGBT community, the ISCS also serves as an important structural arrangement that bestows upon its members feelings of respectability, affirmation, affiliation, friendship, and even family. One of the formal ways in which this is accomplished is through elected and appointed drag titles—for example, empress and emperor, princess and prince—that confer significant group status. These titles are held by gay drag queens, gay drag kings, lesbian drag kings, and lesbian drag queens. (See Schacht 1998 for a more detailed discussion of drag performance in the ICS.)

As an honored way of conferring status, individuals are also selectively invited to join one of several families within the court. Those who become members of these families take on the family last name of their sponsors—their drag mother or father, becoming drag daughters or sons, often acquiring drag brothers and sisters. Family size ranges from a couple of members to over 100 members. Larger families often are made up of several generations of members from different regional courts (e.g., Seattle and Portland). More established court members often belong to more than one family and sometimes have kinship ties to several court chapters. In total, the ICS provides almost exclusively LGBT members an established, formal yet quite affirming venue for publicly "coming out," a place where significant friendships and families are constructed and nurtured, and ultimately a context where LGBT identities are normalized and celebrated.

REFERENCES

Schacht, Steven P. 1998. "The Multiple Genders of the Court: Issues of Identity and Performance in a Drag Setting." In *Feminism and Men: Reconstructing Gender Relations,* ed. Steven P. Schacht and Doris W. Ewing. New York University Press, 202–24.

Steven P. Schacht, Ph.D., was the author of numerous articles and books on feminism and men, drag queens and drag kings, and alliance building across difference. At the time of his death on November 21, 2003, he was serving as guest editor of a special issue of the *Journal of Homosexuality* on female impersonators and was writing a book about his experiences in the ISCS titled, *Gay and Lesbian Royalty: Inside an Imperial Sovereign Court* (Harrington Park Press). Steve co-authored *Feminism with Men: Bridging the Gender Gap* with Doris W. Ewing (Rowman and Littlefield, 2004), published a year after his death.

GLOSSARY

Accordion households	Family rituals
Bilateral	Family stories
Bilocal	Fictive kin
Cohousing	Incest taboos
Co-residence	Kinship
Family boundary ambiguity	Matrilineal

Matrilocal

Neolocal

Patrilineal

Patrilocal

Religion

Religiosity

Religious affiliation

Sandwich generation

Spirituality

FOR YOUR CONSIDERATION

1. Describe the expectations for relationships and boundaries for relatives in your extended family. Compare your expectations with those of others in your class. What accounts for the range of norms of distance, warmth, and obligation?

2. Stereotypes abound of adult children who live with their parents. To what extent do you see this as a deviant lifestyle? In what ways might this lifestyle impede individual and family development. In what ways might this lifestyle be adaptive for the individuals and families and functional for society?

3. States are wrestling with the legal rights of grandparents to have visitation and custody of their grandchildren in certain cases. Compose a *Grandparents' Bill of Rights* that addresses these legal issues, as well as other rights and responsibilities of the grandparent–grandchild relationship.

4. What is your position on family decline and child and family well-being? What is your position on faith-based initiatives, which qualify for federal funding to address social problems of families?

FOR FURTHER STUDY: WEB SITES, ORGANIZATIONS, AND PUBLICATIONS

Web Sites and Organizations

AARP Grandparent Information Center
601 E Street, NW
Washington, DC 20049
(202) 424-3410
www.aarp.org/grandparents
A service of the *AARP*, this center provides information for grandparents raising grandchildren, grandparents who are concerned about their visitation rights with their grandchildren, stepgrandparents, and "traditional" grandparents who want to have a positive role in their grandchildren's lives. The Web site includes links to advocacy, events, newsletters, research, and other information and referrals.

Children of Aging Parents
1609 Woodbourne Road, Suite 302A
Levittown, PA 19057
(800) 227-7294
http://www.caps4caregivers.org
This nonprofit, charitable organization was founded in 1977 to provide information, referrals, and support, and to raise public awareness of the importance the nation's caregivers of elderly or chronically ill.

Children's Defense Fund
   25 E Street NW
   Washington, DC 20001
   (202) 628-8787
   This nonprofit organization was founded in 1973 as a private, nonprofit organization to "provide a strong and effective voice for the children of America who can't vote, lobby, or speak for themselves." *CDF* serves as an advocate for children and their families.

Myth and Ritual in American Life (MARIAL)
   MARIAL Center
   Emory University
   Emory West Suite 413E
   1256 Briarcliff Road
   Atlanta GA 30306
   404 727-3440
   Email: marial@learnlink.emory.edu
   Fax: 404 712-9250
   Emory University's Center on Myth and Ritual in American Life is one of five Sloan Centers on Working Families, supported by the Alfred P. Sloan Foundation's Program on Dual-Career Working Middle Class Families. The MARIAL project provides a unique scholarly approach that is authentically inter- and multidisciplinary in its research and focuses. The Emory Center focuses its research on the functions and significance of ritual and myth in dual wage-earner middle-class families in the American South. The Center has four basic purposes:

- To promote scholarly studies of myth and ritual among working families in the Southeastern United States

- To train the next generation of scholars to focus attention on American middle-class families

- To publicize our findings through scholarly channels and more broadly through the media

- To find ways to use the insights gained from our research to encourage and foster positive social change

The Sandwich Generation
   www.globesyndicate.com
   This site offers a regular column on aging and elder- and parent-care issues.

Publications

Connidis, Ingrid Arnet. 2001. *Family Ties and Aging.* Thousand Oaks, CA: Sage.
   This text goes beyond the usual examination of connections between aging family members and their spouses, children, and grandchildren to include consideration of single, divorced, and childless older people, sibling relationships, live-in partnerships, and older gay and lesbian unions.
Dill, Bonnie Thornton. 1986. *Our Mothers' Grief: Racial Ethnic Women and the Maintenance of Families.* Research Paper # 4. Memphis, TN: Memphis State University, Center for Research on Women.
   This work, and other, on race and ethnicity by this prominent sociologist, documents the kinship struggles and triumphs of African American and other women of color in securing resilient families.
Johnson, Colleen L. 2000. "Perspectives on American Kinship in the 1990s." *Journal of Marriage and the Family* 62, 3 (August): 623–39.
   Johnson synthesizes what is known about American kinship through the last decade of the 20th century.

Walker, Alexis J., Margaret Manoogian-O'Dell, Lori A. McGraw, and Diana L. G. White, eds. 2001. *Families in Later Life: Connections and Transitions.* Thousand Oaks, CA: Pine Forge.

These 41 empirical and narrative pieces lead the reader through a deeper understanding of the family lives of older adults. Topics include negotiating ties with young adults, connections across the generations in midlife, the centrality of intimacy in later midlife, transitions at work and at home in early old age, and challenges and possibilities in later life.

Work and Eldercare: Facts for Caregivers and Their Employers. Washington, DC: Department of Labor, Women's Bureau Clearinghouse.

This publication describes the types of elder-care assistance available, including geriatric-care managers, home-health aides, and telephone reassurance systems. Of particular note, this document also provides suggestions for ways that employers can help their employees caught in the sandwich generation manage.

REFERENCES FOR CITED WORKS

AARP. 2000. "AARP Survey: Grandparents, Grandchildren Have Strong Bond, Visit Often." www.aarp.org/press/2000/nr010400.html (Retrieved 8/13/02).

AARP. 2002. "Financial Assistance for Grandparent Caregivers: TANF." www.aarp.org/contacts/money/tanf.html (Retrieved 8/13/02).

Adams, Brooke. 2002. "Storytelling a Lost Art for Families." www.sltrib.com/2002/Oct/10092002/Wednesda/5359.htm (Retrieved 10/16/02).

Auslander, Mark. 2002. "Something We Need to Get Back To: Mythologies of Origin and Rituals of Solidarity in African American Working Families." Working paper no. 6, April. www.emory.edu/college/MARIAL/pdfs/reunions.pdf (Retrieved 10/20/02).

Bengtson, Vern L. 2001. "Beyond the Nuclear Family: The Increasing Importance of Multigenerational Bonds." *Journal of Marriage and Family* 63, 1 (February): 1–16.

Bess, Roseanna, Jacob Leos-Urbel, and Rob Geen. 2001. "The Cost of Protecting Vulnerable Children II: What Has Changed since 1996?" http://newfederalism.urban.org/html/op46/occa46.html (Retrieved 4/9/01).

Boss, Pauline, and Jan Greenberg. 1984. "Family Boundary Ambiguity: A New Variable in Family Stress Theory." *Family Process* 23: 535–36.

Bostock, C. 1994. "Does the Expansion of Grandparent Visitation Rights Promote the Best Interests of the Child? A Survey of Grandparent Visitation Laws in the Fifty States." *Columbia Journal of Law and Social Problems* 27: 319–73.

Bowen, Gary L., Jay A. Mancini, James A. Martin, William B. Ware, and John P. Nelson. 2003. "Promoting the Adaptation of Military Families: An Empirical Test of a Community Practice Model." *Family Relations* 52, 1 (January): 33–44.

Call, V. R. A., and T. B. Heaton. 1997. "Religious Influence on Marital Stability." *Journal for the Scientific Study of Religion* 36: 382–92.

Campan, E., J. Moreno, M. T. Ruiz, and E. Pascual. 2002. "Doing Things Together: Adolescent Health and Family Rituals." www.dipalicante.es/hipokrates/noticias/archivo/articleDoingThigs.pdf (Retrieved 10/10/02).

Cherlin, Andrew J., and Frank F. Furstenberg, Jr. 1992. *The New American Grandparent: A Place in the Family, A Life Apart.* Cambridge, MA: Harvard University Press.

Child Trends. 2001. "Number of Children in Working Poor Families Increases." March 26. http://www.childtrends.org/workingpoorNews.asp (Retrieved 10/4/02).

Children's Defense Fund-Minnesota. 2002a. "Child Poverty Tops 50 Percent in 14 United States Counties." *A Child's Voice:* Newsletter of the Children's Defense Fund Minnesota (August): 3.

Children's Defense Fund-Minnesota. 2002b. "Facts About the Uninsured." *A Child's Voice:* Newsletter of the Children's Defense Fund Minnesota (August): 4.

Coontz, Stephanie. 1997. *The Way We Never Were: American Families and the Nostalgia Trap.* New York, NY: Basic Books.

Cox, C. 1993. *The Frail Elderly: Problems, Needs, and Community Responses.* Westport, CT: Auburn House.

Crosnoe, Robert, and Glen H. Elder, Jr. 2002. "Life Course Transitions, the Generational Stake, and Grandparent-Grandchild Relationships." *Journal of Marriage and the Family* 64, 4 (November): 1089–96.

Dellman-Jenkins, Mary, Maureen Blankemeyer, and Odessa Pinkard. 2000. "Young Adult Children and Grand-children in Primary Caregiver Roles to Older Relatives and Their Service Needs." *Family Relations* 49, 2: 177–86.

Doherty, William. 1999. *The Intentional Family: Simple Rituals to Strengthen Family Ties.* New York, NY: Avon.

Drummet, Amy Reinkober, Marilyn Coleman, and Susan Cable. 2003. "Military Families Under Stress: Implications for Family Life Education." *Family Relations* 52, 3 (July): 279–87.

Duke, Marshall. 2002. "Family Narratives." www.emory.edu/college/MARIAL/faculty/duke.html (Retrieved 10/20/2002).

Ehrle, Jennifer, Rob Geen, and Rebecca Clark. 2001. "Children Cared for by Relatives: Who Are They and How Are They Faring?" http://newfederalism.urban.org/html/series_b/b28/b28.html (Retrieved 4/9/01).

"Family Caregiving in the United States: Findings from a National Survey. 1997. National Alliance for Caregiving and *AARP.* www.caregiving.org/content/reports/finalreport (Retrieved 10/9/02).

Fivush, Robyn, and Marshall Duke. 2002. "Narratives and Resilience in Middle-Class, Dual-Earner Families." www.emory.edu/college/MARIAL/pdfs/wp019_02.pdf (Retrieved 10/20/02).

Friesen, John. 1990. "Rituals and Family Strength." www.directionjournal.org/article/?654 (Retrieved 11/20/02).

Geen, Rob, Lynn Fender, Jacob Leos-Urbel, and Teresa Markowitz. 2001. "Welfare Reform's Effect on Child Welfare Caseloads." http://newfederalism.urban.org/html/discussion01-04.html (Retrieved 9/20/02).

Grochowski, Janet, and Meg Wilkes Karraker. 2000. "Using Storytelling to Construct Preferred Futures and Enhance Resiliency in Families: Insights from a Participatory, Dual-Vision Methodology." Paper presented at the annual meetings of the *American Academy of Health Behavior,* Santa Fe, NM.

Hall, C. Margaret. 1994. *New Families: Reviving and Creating Meaningful Bonds.* New York: Harrington Park.

Hareven, Tamara K. 1973. "Urbanization and the Malleable Household: An Examination of Boarding and Lodging in American Families." *Journal of Marriage and the Family* 39, 3 (August): 467–78.

Hafkin Pleck, Elizabeth. 2000. *Celebrating the Family: Ethnicity, Consumer Culture, and Family Rituals.* Boston, MA: Harvard University Press.

Heaton, T. B., C. K. Jacobson, and X. N. Fu. 1992. "Religiosity of Married Couples and Childlessness." *Review of Religious Research* 33: 244–55.

Hill, Twyla J. 2000. "Legally Extending the Family: An Event History Analysis of Grandparent Visitation Rights Laws." *Journal of Family Issues* 21, 2 (March): 246–61.

Houseknecht, Sharon K., and Jaya Sastry. 1996. "Family 'Decline' and Child Well-Being: A Comparative Assessment." *Journal of Marriage and the Family* 58, 3 (August): 726–39.

Imber-Black, Evan, and Janine Roberts. 1998. *Rituals in Our Times: Celebrating, Healing, and Changing Our Lives and Our Relationships.* Lanham, MD: Jason Aronson.

Jackson, A. M. 1994. "The Coming of Age of Grandparent Visitation Rights." *American University Law Review* 43: 563-601.

Jones, Charles L., Lorne Tepperman, and Susannah J. Wilson. 1995. *The Futures of the Family.* Upper Saddle River, NJ: Prentice Hall.

Kamerman, S. B. 1996. "Child and Family Policies: An International Overview." In *Children, Families, and Government: Preparing for the Twenty-first Century*, eds. E. F. Zigler, S. L. Kagan, and N. W. Hall, New York, NY: Cambridge University Press, 31–48.

Karraker, Meg Wilkes, and Janet R. Grochowski. 2003. "'Telling Tales': Rituals and Storytelling as Methods to Bridge Contact Zones." Presented at the annual *Conference on Quality Research in Education (QUIG),* Athens, GA.

King, Valarie, and Glen H. Elder, Jr. 1997. "The Legacy of Grandparenting: Childhood Experience with Grandparents and Current Involvement with Grandchildren." *Journal of Marriage and the Family* 59, 4 (November): 848–59.

Krysan, Maria, Kristin A. Moore, and Nicholas Zill. 1990. *Identifying Successful Families: An Overview of Constructs and Selected Measures.* Washington, DC: Child Trends, Inc.

Larson, L. E., and J. W. Goltz. 1989. "Religious Participation and Marital Commitment." *Review of Religious Research* 30: 387–400.

Lee, Yean-Ju, and Isik A. Aytac. 1998. "Intergenerational Financial Support Among Whites, African Americans, and Latinos." *Journal of Marriage and the Family* 60, 2 (May): 426–41.

Longino, Charles F., Jr., and John R. Earle. 1996. "Who are the Grandparents at Century's End?" *Generations* 20, 1 (Spring): 13–16.

Matthews, S. H., and T. T. Rosner. 1988. "Shared Filial Responsibility: The Family as the Primary Caregiver." *Journal of Marriage and the Family* 50, 1 (February): 185–95.

McCubbin, Hamilton I., Anne I. Thompson, and Marilyn A. McCubbin. 1996. *Family Assessment: Resiliency, Coping and Adaptation.* Madison, WI: University of Wisconsin Press.

Myth and Ritual in American Life. 2002. "Storytelling May Be Key to Resilient Children, Healthy Working Families." www.emory.edu/college/MARIAL/newsletter/storytelling.html (Retrieved 10/16/02).

Newman, David M., and Liz Grauerholz. 2002. *Sociology of Families*, 2/e. Thousand Oaks, CA: Pine Forge.

Newschannel 2000. 2000. "'Adultolescents' Boomerang Back Home: Recent College Grads Having Tough Time on Their Own." http://www.newschannel2000.com/sh/employment/stories/employment-142680220020430- (Retrieved 10/23/02).

Paul, Pamela. 2001. "Echo Boomerang: A New Generation of College Graduates is Proving that you Can Go Home Again." *American Demographics* (June). http://www.demographics.com/publications/ad/01_ad/0106_ad/ad010601.htm (Retrieved 7/15/01).

Pearce, L. D., and W. G. Axinn. 1998. "The Impact of Family Religious Life on the Quality of Mother-Child Relations." *American Sociological Review* 63: 810–28.

Pebley, Anne R., and Laura L. Rudkin. 1999. "Grandparents Caring for Grandchildren: What Do We Know?" *Journal of Family Issues* 20, 2 (March): 218–42.

Popenoe, David. 1993. "American Family Decline, 1960–1990: A Review and Appraisal." *Journal of Marriage and the Family* 55: 527–42.

Questenberry, Dan. 1996. "Who We Area: An Exploration of What 'Intentional Community' Means." *The Fellowship for Intentional Community*. http://www.ic.org/pnp/cdir/1995/05quest.html (Retrieved 10/7/02).

Roemer, M. 1995. *Telling Stories: Postmodernism and the Invalidation of Traditional Narrative.* Lanham, MD: Rowman and Littlefield.

Rotello, Gabriel. 1996. "Anti-Marriage Laws Create Legal Swamp." Partners Task Force for Gay & Lesbian Couples. http://buddybuddy.com/rotello2.html (Retrieved 10/18/02).

Sands, Robert G., and Robin S. Goldberg-Glen. 2000. "Factors Associated with Stress Among Grandparents Raising Their Grandchildren." *Family Relations* 49, 1 (January): 97–105.

Stacey, Judith. 1990. *Brave New Families.* New York, NY: Basic Books.

Stack, Carol. 1974. *All Our Kin: Strategies for Survival in a Black Community.* New York, NY: Harper & Row.

Stinnett, Nick, and John DeFrain. 1985. *Secrets of Strong Families.* Boston, MA: Little, Brown.

Szinovacz, Maximiliane E. 1998. "Grandparents Today: A Demographic Profile." *Gerontologist* 38, 1 (February): 37–52.

The Cohousing Network. 2002. "What is Cohousing." http://www.cohousing.org/resources/faq.html (Retrieved 10/7/02).

Thornton, A., W. G. Axinn, and D. H. Hill. 1992. "Reciprocal Effects of Religiosity, Cohabitation, and Marriage." *American Journal of Sociology* 98: 628–51.

Thornton, A., and D. Camburn. 1989. "Religious Participation and Adolescent Sexual Behavior and Attitudes." *Journal of Marriage and the Family* 51: 641–53.

United States Bureau of the Census. 2000. *Statistical Abstract of the United States.* Washington, DC: Government Printing Office.

United States Bureau of the Census. 2002. "Poverty: 2001 Highlights." http://www.census.gov/hhes/poverty/poverty01/pov01hi.html (Retrieved 10/4/02).

Wolfe, Warren. 2002. "'And Thou Shalt Honor.'" *Star Tribune* October 8: E1, E8.

Wolin, Steven, and L. A. Bennett. 1984. "Family Rituals." *Family Process* 23: 401–20.

PART

V

MANAGING FAMILY RELATIONSHIPS

FAMILY POWER, CONFLICT, AND VIOLENCE

CHAPTER PREVIEW

Family power involves balancing *personal power* with *social power*. Family power is expressed as *reward, coercive, referent, informational, expert power,* as well as *legitimate power* embodied in beliefs including *conjugal power* and gender and cultural hidden impacts. Additional factors that influence family power include financial, intellectual, physical resources plus concepts of fairness and the power of love. *Family empowerment* is a process of working toward equitable and respectful interrelationships.

Conflict, that is, *family conflict*, is a natural, inevitable part of family life. Common family life includes *sibling conflict*, which can teach children how to disagree in a civilized manner. *Conflict avoidance* not only blocks opportunities for families to learn about compromise but also increases the risk of family members resorting to passive-aggressive behaviors such as *sabotage* and *displacement* to resolve their differences. Increasingly, *work–family conflict* rips at the family fabric, pulling on families as they try to meet competing work and family demands. Learning to deal with work–family conflict is important, but only part of a larger need for families to learn about fighting fairly.

Although family conflict is natural and even helpful in family life, *family violence* is not. Although welfare reform policies aim to assist, care must be taken that they do not increase the risk of family violence due to rigid policy and lack of screening for violent behavior. The effects of family violence on the family wellness of the abused and those who witness family violence include significant physical, emotional, psychological, and social harm.

Intimate partner violence may be physical or psychological and may include battering and marital rape. Females suffer greater physical harm than do males in intimate relationships. Abusers may have been victims themselves or witnessed domestic abuse. The battered partner who stays in violent relationships often does so out of fear and or *learned helplessness*. Intimate violence may take two forms: *intimate terrorism* and *situational couple violence* in which the former brings a more insidious violent experience. In *female-to-male violence* not only is the victim battered, but also often the abuser in terms of male retaliation.

Other forms of family violence include *same-sex couple violence, sibling-to-sibling abuse, child-to-parent abuse*, and *elder abuse*. Families can learn effective conflict management skills to enhance favorable outcomes of family conflict and to reduce the potential for intimate violence.

FAMILY POWER: GUIDING NOT RULING

Power is a dynamic process rather than a static characteristic. A sense of power (or powerlessness) is experienced at individual and group levels (e.g., families, cities, states, regions, nations, and world communities). Expressions of *personal power* (autonomy) include one's independence and self-sufficiency. *Social power*, when the wishes of some override the wishes of others, impacts personal power.

Family power dynamics change with time, especially during periods of stress and transitions. The perception of power—who has power and whether power is being fairly exercised—is as important as the behavioral aspects of power—how power is displayed. Olson and DeFrain (2000) offer elaboration on the complexity that is family power by questioning whether family power is actual or potential, intentional or unintentional, overt or covert, a process or an outcome, and whether there are winners and losers or win-win compromises. Family power, therefore, is as much about who decides as it is about who decides on who decides.

Conjugal Power

Three criteria (Komter 1989) help to determine balance of *conjugal power* between committed partners:

- Who has the final say in making family decisions (e.g., where to live, which car to buy, how to celebrate holidays and vacations, or who sets house rules)
- Who does what in the division of family labor (e.g., household duties)
- Who is empowered to raise issues and disagree with family behaviors or practices

Based on the earlier work of French and Raven (1959), family scholars discuss power between couples in terms of six expressions of conjugal power (Raven, Centers, and Rodrigues 1975). (1) *Reward power* is an ability to offer reward for desired behavior, such as promising a vacation at the beach in exchange for putting up with having disagreeable in-laws stay for the holidays. (2) *Coercive power* includes the use or threat of use of humiliation and or punishment (i.e., physical, emotional, psychological, or withholding affection or economic support), such as threatening to withhold sexual intimacy if the partner fails at a task. (3) *Referent power* is being trusted to make good decisions, such as when a partner trusts that the other partner will remain monogamous. (4) *Informational power* means having more knowledge about an issue, such as changing eating habits because a partner has researched the most recent dietary guidelines. (5) *Expert power* emerges when a family member has authentic experience, such as following a partner's advice on purchasing a computer because of her occupation as a computer programmer. (6) *Legitimate power* is the authority to influence another's behavior, such as women's right to use effective contraception or the assumed power of men as heads of households.

Blood and Wolfe's resource hypothesis (1960) states that the relative power between married couples depends on how many resources each partner brings to the relationship. The partner with the most resources (e.g., education, career prestige, or income) has the most power in the relationship. Although the resource hypothesis did open discussion on conjugal power as shared and not merely patriarchal, it is criticized for a methodology in which only wives were interviewed and, more importantly, for its assumption that patriarchal power is replaced by egalitarian power in committed couples (Gillespie 1971). Criticisms of the resource hypothesis focus on gender resource issues arguing, for instance, that pregnant women are at a disadvantage because they often lose not only financial power but also "sexual attractiveness" power (Blumberg and Coleman 1989).

The Hidden Power of Gender

Family power is the ability to influence members' behaviors. The French and Raven (1959) model of power recognizes that power is not solely based on status or resources, but also on a need or desire to maintain relationships. Using this model in comparing gender differences reveals that women generally hold less social power (Johnson 1976); thus, they are often given less respect in interpersonal interactions (Carli 1999). Although women have made gains in the world of work outside of the home, they still struggle for equity in power. It is not unusual that for women to be considered equal to men in terms of expert power they must be superior just to be equal (Carli). As for legitimate power, women who behave as assertively and confidently as men often are censored and receive negative responses (Wosinska et al. 1996).

The power of gender does not lie within identity or roles; rather, it is "accomplished" in social interaction (West and Zimmerman 1991). Men and women "do gender" in the workplace and in the household tasks they complete. Money can bring power in families. Women who earn more of the family income than other women often have their career valued, enjoy greater decision making, and do smaller percentages of the domestic tasks (Deutsch, Roksa, and Meeske 2003).

Contrary to a popular belief among social scientists, African-American marriages are not matriarchal. Studies reveal that more married Black women work and have greater equality in power sharing when compared to White couples with non-wage-earning wives (John, Shelton, and Luschen 1995). Similar to the myth of matriarchy in African-American families is the belief that Hispanic married couples are totally patriarchal. Although there is general agreement with the male-as-head-of-household position among Hispanic households (Wilkinson 1993), both partners increasingly report seeing their relationship as different from that of their parents in terms of flexibility and shared decision making, especially for those in dual-earner relationships (Williams 1990).

Although income remains an important factor in a balance of family power, studies of dual income, heterosexual households in which the woman earned more than the man, report that the woman's power had not increased proportionately to her income or career status (Tichenor 1999). When scholars assessed the "invisible power of men" in terms of wives agreeing with their husbands more often than not, this finding held even in relationships where wives earn more money or are more interested in the subject (e.g., politics) than their husbands (Zipp, Prohaska, and Bemiller 2004).

American marriages remain in-equalitarian. This is especially true for women who are not wage earners. Working does influence conjugal power, but even though working women enjoy greater authority and decision making, they are unequally burdened with child-rearing, household duties, and caring for extended family (Greenstein 1995; Hochschild 1989). Earning wages, although helpful in granting legitimate power to women, does not guarantee women full equal partner status in committed relationships.

Cultural Influences

Cultural influences on family power are significant. Even as equalitarian couples struggle to define shared power, the traditional legitimate power process (i.e., male as head of household) remains for the majority of the world's population. Even in developed societies, the view of men as the traditional authority continues. An example is the evangelical men's movement, Promise Keepers, whose supporters pledge to "do right by women" and also demand traditional family roles (Minkowitz 1995). Contrary to some of the myths surrounding this movement, in practice, Promise Keepers express and push at rallies and in their literature appeal to the ultraconservative wing of Christianity. Promise Keepers are a political and religious movement that openly call on women to submit responsibility to husbands who are deemed the head of household. Traditional family roles mean the removal of women's conjugal power. Contrary to such back-to-biblical-gender-roles positions, couples in equitable marriages appear to enjoy greater satisfaction and security than patriarchical couples in their relationships (Greenstein 1995; Risman and Johnson-Sumerford 1998). Homophobic, racist, and other disturbing messages from this highly political organization call on family studies professionals to be critical of groups that promise to build, but, in practice, tear the diverse fabric of families.

BOX 12.1   "Seven Promises of Promise Keepers"

1. A Promise Keeper is committed to honoring Jesus Christ through worship, prayer, and obedience to God's Word in the power of the Holy Spirit.

2. A Promise Keeper is committed to pursuing vital relationships with a few other men, understanding that he needs brothers to help him keep his promises.

3. A Promise Keeper is committed to practicing spiritual, moral, ethical, and sexual purity.

4. A Promise Keeper is committed to building strong marriages and families through love, protection, and biblical values.

5. A Promise Keeper is committed to supporting the mission of his church by honoring and praying for his pastor, and by actively giving his time and resources.

6. A Promise Keeper is committed to reaching beyond any racial and denominational barriers to demonstrate the power of biblical unity.

7. A Promise Keeper is committed to influencing his world, being obedient to the Great Commandment (Mark 12: 30–31)[1] and the Great Commission (Matthew: 19–20)[2].

Source: Promise Keepers www.promisekeepers.org/faqs/core/faqscore24.htm (Retrieved 2/2/03).

---

[1] "Love the Lord your God with all your heart and with all your soul and with all your mind and with all your strength. The second is this: Love your neighbor as yourself."

[2] "Therefore go and make disciples of all nations, baptizing them in the name of the Father and of the Son and of the Holy Spirit, and teaching them to obey everything I have commanded you. And surely I am with you always, to the very end of the age."

Fairness in Family Power

Sprecher and Schwartz (1994) acknowledge the distinction between the objective measure of power and the subjective measure of fairness. The perception of fairness (e.g., agreement on the fairness of household task responsibilities such as grocery shopping or driving children to after school events) influences conjugal power. This is particularly evident in dual-earner families where struggles over family time (see chapter 4) test couples and other family members in the dance of power. Belief regarding the fairness of family decision making and delegation of responsibilities is pivotal to how satisfied couples and other family members view the family power process (Safilios-Rothchild 1970; Wilkie, Ferree, and Ratcliff 1998). Power that is given in the spirit of fairness holds greater influence and control than power that is taken or coerced.

The Power of Love

The power of love remains at the heart of great deeds and humble daily living. For that reason, the research on the impact of earnings on family power is so disconcerting. Exchange theory offers some insights into conjugal power, through relative love and need. Each partner offers assets to and gains benefits from a relationship. How much each partner desires or needs the other often influences who has more power (i.e., the one who is valued more holds greater power). A common belief is that American women are more love dependent in marital relationships than are their male partners (Cancian 1985). Yet others argue that men are as likely as women to feel controlled by the other (Rubin 1994).

The process of family power involves all members of a family. The pushes and pulls among family members as they work together to meet individual and family needs require negotiation. As members modify their rights and responsibilities, families need to negotiate new boundaries while respecting individuals' privacy and independence.

This stretching of family boundaries begins in early childhood. Children learn about how to negotiate or not negotiate family power issues by observing their parents or guardians. These childhood lessons often endure into adolescence and adulthood. Family power struggles are natural and even healthy aspects of family living.

Too much and too little power may lead to frustration and dissatisfaction. Effective exercise of family power should not overpower but rather empower members to act in caring and responsible ways. Table 12.1 summarizes strategies for more effectively handling

TABLE 12.1

Defusing Family Power Struggles

- Guide Not Rule
  Recognize family members' natural need for autonomy. Assist them in learning effective ways to negotiate their needs instead of using authoritarian (i.e., absolute) rule. This does not mean permissiveness, but rather being respectful and just.

- Do Not Get Pulled Into Power Struggles
  Let family member know that you are not getting into a power tug-of-war. Instead, you seek to work with him or her in resolving the issue.

- Options, Not Orders
  Leaders recognize that power that is freely given is more effective than power that is taken by force. When family members feel that they are not empowered, they may react to the power imbalance in destructive ways such as engaging in unhealthy behaviors (e.g., smoking) just to spite the authority figure. Offering choices, options, respects the individual and teaches effective negotiation skills. Sims (2003) warns against the frequent use of "autocratic" choices (i.e., narrow choices that offer no real freedom of choice) and offering choices you have no intention of honoring.

- Meaningful Power
  Family members need to contribute to the family in age-appropriate ways. Families that encourage authentic member responsibilities not only actively engage members but also demonstrate respect and trust.

- Remember the Person First
  It was once said that, "one deserves a hug the least when he or she may need it the most." Remember that family members are human and bound to make mistakes. At times it may be necessary to reaffirm that the family member is valued, even though their behavior is not.

Source: Adapted with permission from Sims, Karen 2003. "Dealing With Power Struggles." *Positive Parenting.* www.positiveparenting.com/resources/feature_article_003.html (Retrieved 2/3/03).

of family power struggles. Balancing power requires communication, emotional support, tolerance for different opinions, and encouragement of independence and interdependence of family members as well as setting aside the myths of the perfect family.

Empowering Family Members

Family empowerment is a process in which family members work toward equitable and respectful relationships among themselves and with their surrounding communities. Empowerment is "power with" rather than "power over" family members, from focusing on strengths over limitations. Empowerment prevents family members from overpowering other members, as well as some members experiencing powerlessness at the hands of other members.

Building healthy family communication serves as a foundation to empowerment within families. Authentic communication is a two-way street that connects family members with feelings of being cared for, loved, safe, and valued. Family empowerment is a complex process that demands attention from within and without families. Families under distress often require assistance in providing basic needs for their members (e.g., shelter and health care). This means that for some families to be empowered, external agencies and organizations need to assist with providing basic needs. Even with such support, however, the focus needs to be on involving family members in decision making and having a voice in family discussions.

Families who are empowered recognize the uniqueness and strengths of their members and provide opportunities for meaningful, age-appropriate participation in family decision making and activities. Families who empower also provide opportunities for members to voice their views and guidance for participation (e.g., effective communication skills—see chapter 8) while offering clear messages of caring for and trust in all members (Family Empowering Committee 2000).

FAMILY CONFLICT: A NATURAL PART OF FAMILY LIFE

A conflict-free family is an oxymoron. Rather than trying to avoid conflict, families need to recognize conflict as natural and learn how to negotiate fairly when disagreements emerge. Conflict is not the same as fighting, even though the terms are used interchangeably. Although a conflict is a difference of opinion that turns into a problem over members' rights, values, plans, or responsibilities that must be resolved, a fight is a personal attack with the purpose to vent feelings and not solve problems.

Some common causes of *family conflict* include:

- Economic concerns and disagreements over money management
- Family household tasks and child-care responsibilities
- Partner's shifting career demands and opportunities
- Maturing children forming their own opinions and values, which may clash with the views held by their parents
- Children wanting more independence than parents are willing to grant
- Older children and teenagers standing their ground, not bending to discipline as easily as younger children
- Changing opinions, values, and needs of parents as they age

- Some parents feeling worried, threatened, or confused by their child's rapid emotional and physical changes during puberty
- Family changes such as separation, divorce, a new baby, moving, family member with a chronic illness or death of family member

Sibling rivalry or *sibling conflict* can teach children how to cope with disagreements and disputes in constructive ways. A key for parents or guardians is to only get involved if there is a danger of physical harm. Basically, one intervenes in sibling conflict to try to solve problems with and not for children and youth. Families can learn how to handle disputes with family meetings that incorporate guidelines (e.g., no name calling) and implement schedules (e.g., household tasks).

Although often unpleasant, family conflicts can stimulate new ideas and solutions. Experiencing conflict in the family can also assist family members in developing negotiation skills. *Conflict avoidance* robs families of a means to settle disputes and often leads to damaging passive-aggressive[1] behaviors such as hostile acts of nagging, cynicism, and sarcasm that rip at the seams of relationships. Deliberately withholding affection and using "the silent treatment" on family members inflicts emotional pain and isolation. Other passive-aggressive behaviors can cause confusion within the family and often spill over into life outside of the family. Lamanna and Riedmann (2000) identify two of these behaviors. The first is *sabotage* such as when a parent, angry with their teen, deliberately belittles the teen in front his or her peers. The other is *displacement* as illustrated when a partner, upset with their mate over her being gone so often for work, expresses this anger by degrading her career.

Families need to learn how to use disagreements and conflict as tools to strengthen rather than as weapons to wound their family communities. Just as coupled relationships can be damaged when communication includes criticism, contempt, defensiveness, and stonewalling (Gottman 1994) in place of clarity, respect, open-mindedness, and willingness to negotiate, so too can other family relationships. Stephan Kahn offers insight into parent–child conflict.

BOX 12.2 "Families in Conflict"
Stephan Kahn, Ph.D.

Normal, healthy families struggle with power and grapple in varied ways about many different things. One unifying approach to family power is to look for who owns what, or rather, who thinks they own what, or who wants to own what. An example will probably help.

Let's say a 16-year-old starts spending time with someone who isn't doing very well academically, has been in trouble with the law, and dresses unconventionally. The parents may view this with alarm and try to interfere with this friendship, viewing the new friend as a threat to their teenager's safety and well-being. The parental attempts to "break up" the friendship may seem meddlesome and overprotective to the teenager. Although this conflict has several dimensions, it is probably best viewed as a battle over family power. Who owns this? Do 16-year-olds have the power to choose their own friends, even if they make a mistake now and then? Do they have the

---

[1]Passive-aggression is a chronic response in which a person seems to acquiesce to the desires and needs of others, but actually passively resists them and becomes increasingly hostile and angry.

right to learn from experience, good and bad? Does the parent have the responsibility to step in when they grow concerned about core issues of health and safety?

Parents and teenagers clash over a variety of issues: curfews, freedoms and privileges, choice of friends, and chores; but the clash is probably best understood from this perspective of the above "who owns what" paradigm. The teenager might think of themselves as powerful, autonomous, and invulnerable and clearly the one who should have the power to make the decision over their use of time, choice of friends, freedoms and privileges. The parent might view their teenager as young, somewhat thoughtless, a poor planner, and reckless in matters of personal safety. The parent's perspective of the ownership issue is almost always very different from the teenager's. The parent might feel an urgent sense of responsibility to exert power to inhibit the teenager's impulses or to contribute to the development of important personal attributes pertaining to maturity, judgment, and safety.

The families who fight about choice of friends (as previously) or chores, academic achievement, or curfew violations and think they are only fighting about the specific battle of the moment are at a real disadvantage compared with the families who fight about something and know they are fighting about ownership. Once the venue has shifted from the symbol of ownership (friendship, chores, etc.) to the psychological issue of ownership, the parents and teenager can have a very different conversation that is more about power and less about choice of friends or chores.

It is unlikely that the teenager will be the one with the insight to reformulate this conversation, and many parents have great difficulty with this as well. Parents have to be reminded that their greatest emotion pertaining to their children usually involves fear of loss. Are my children safe? Will they grow up with the skills to be successful at whatever they confront in their lives? Have I been a good parent? The conversation that includes reference to these sensitive issues is very different from the conversation about setting rules and limits and insisting on where they can and cannot go and when they need to be home. Teenagers can tell the difference between a parent who says "I need to own this right now but soon it will be yours" and a parent who merely says: "Because I say so, that's why" I do not believe it is a reach to say that the intimate attachment between teenagers and their parents hinges on how this issues of "who owns what" is approached and resolved.

Steven Kahn, Ph.D., is a child and adolescent psychologist in Minneapolis, MN. In addition to seeing clients in an outpatient setting, he also provides consultation to private schools on the interaction between family dynamics and academic and social competence.

Work–Family Conflicts

Work–family conflict is an incompatibility with role demands stemming from work or family (Greenhaus and Beutell 1985; Kahn et al. 1964). Work–family conflict can be time based (e.g., requiring overtime, which makes it difficult to meet family demands) or strain based (e.g., an ill child in the hospital so adult can not concentrate on work) as noted in chapter 13. Yet, work–family conflict can also be behavior based (e.g., career that demands aggressiveness but when using this same behavior at home leads to conflict; (Frone, Yardley, and Markel 1997; Greenhaus and Beutell 1985). This bidirectional nature of work–family conflict is revealed as more families juggle multiple roles (e.g., employee, parent, student, caretaker of elder).

High levels of work–family conflict can contribute to negative outcomes for the family member in terms of life dissatisfaction, anxiety, depression, and lower levels of wellness. It also is related to challenges to relationships (e.g., interpersonal conflict at home) and to organizations (e.g., increased absenteeism and loss of valued workers; Hammer and Thompson 2004). These stress and strain "crossover effects" (Westman 2001) from work and family conflicts demand family friendly interventions that promote flexible scheduling and support of positive work–family culture such as family leave policies (Thompson, Beauvais, and Lyness 1999).

The recent increase in telecommuting or telework has significant impacts on work–family conflict. Telework individuals are those who work from home at least two to three days a week. These uncollared[2] workers report lower levels of work–family conflict in all three areas of conflict (time based, strain based, and behavior based). These same workers also report higher wellness levels while working more hours at home than those who did not telecommute (Madsen 2003).

Families Fighting Fairly

Teaching all family members how to fight fairly appears to be as important as most family living skills. Over 30 years ago, Bach and Wyden, in *The Intimate Enemy* (1970), challenged conflict avoidance behavior and claimed that disagreements, done fairly, were normal and necessary for couples in resolving some problems between intimate partners. More recently, Gottman (1994) claims that successful marriages are not "fight-free" and that couples who develop fair conflict (fighting) skills report more positive than negative interactions. Psychoeducational approaches created to assist couples in enhancing relationship skills, with special emphasis on constructive conflict resolution, have proven beneficial (Christensen and Heavey 1999; Cole and Cole 1999; Schneewind and Gerhard 2002; Stanley, Blumberg, and Markman 1999; Wallerstein and Blakeslee 1995). Likewise, families need to understand that even when members learn to engage in fair fighting, there may be some family conflicts that are not resolved. In those cases, the best that can be done is to agree to disagree or to seek professional help.

Seeking professional help remains difficult for many families in terms of determining when, where, and how to pay for counseling related to anger management or hostility control. Children, for example, occasionally fight and hit each other, but frequent or severe physical aggression may mean that a child is having serious emotional or behavioral problems that require professional help. Persistent fighting when a child is in day care or preschool can be a serious problem. At this age, children have much more contact with other children their own age and are expected to be able to make friends and get along.

A concern of the authors is that families seek professional support only when things are really, really bad. What may be missing in American families is some set of mechanisms to give people chances to "check in" or address issues, get ideas, and or gain skills before things blow up. Church groups offer this in the form of marriage enrichment as discussed in chapter 8. We present an option for fighting fairly by offering a synthesis of earlier work (Bach and Wyden 1970; Gottman 1994) in Table 12.2.

The acceptance and expressions of conflict are influenced by cultural traditions and expectations. In cultures with family systems that use dominance and aggression, family conflict is all too often linked to violence in families. Violence in families is an international problem that crosses racial, ethnic, and cultural groups. Social class and economics are

---

[2]Uncollared workers telecommute and or work from home (Grochowski 1999).

TABLE 12.2

Families Fighting Fairly: A Win-Win Approach

Usually the first angry impulse is to win an argument at any cost. Using a win-win approach is challenging, but it is more beneficial than a win-lose approach to all who engage and or witness the argument or conflict.

Basic rules: Keeping it safe

No violence

Avoidance of physical, emotional, and verbal abuse including belittling, name calling.

No ambush or sneak attacks

Make an appointment to talk. Specify time, place, and issue. Do not engage in the disagreement when tired or hungry.

Cool off first if necessary

If possible, take some time to cool off if you are too angry to talk calmly.

Dialog over monolog: Careful listening and sharing view points

Try to stay calm and find points of common ground.

Do not interrupt while other member is speaking.

Be sure you understand; ask questions to clarify.

State your side of the story clearly and honestly.

Stick to the issue

Disagree about no more than two related issues at a time.

Keep all comments fair

Discuss the behavior you want changed; do not attack the individual.

Do not embarrass or humiliate the family member by bringing up aspects of personality or limitations. Using manipulation such as shaming or guilt (e.g., "if you loved me you would . . . ") is unfair.

Authentic negotiation: Working toward win-win over win-lose

Don't be afraid to disagree or argue.

Remember you are trying to resolve a conflict, not win a argument.

Come up with as many possible solutions as you can.

If issue not resolved, schedule a specific time and place to return to it.

If family members can agree, decide how to carry out the decision.

Who will do what? Is there a deadline? When someone is sincere and says "I am sorry," be sure he or she also says "Please forgive me."

If you cannot agree on an issue, decide if you can both live with the reality that you "agree to disagree."

Consider seeking professional assistance such as family counseling.

Source: Adapted with permission from Gottman, John Mordechai. 1994. *What Predicts Divorce? The Relationship Between Marital Processes and Marital Outcomes.* Mahwah, NJ: Lawrence Erlbaum, Associates.

major factors in family violence (Rennison and Planty 2003), with unemployment of the abuser as the strongest predicator of domestic violence (Brock 2003). Yet the complex web of violence in families demands closer examination. A future challenge to family scholars is to recognize and study the additional impacts of racism, sexism, classism, and homophobia on violence in the home (Phillips 1998; West 2002, 2004).

FAMILY VIOLENCE: A CRUEL AND BRUTAL REALITY

A brutal irony exists that the very intimate and family relationships we often cherish may increase our risk of physical, emotional, and sexual abuse as well as violence. *Family violence*, also termed domestic violence, is a serious, widespread social concern in the United States with conservative estimates of one million women suffering nonfatal violence by an intimate (Bureau of Justice Statistics 1995). Nearly 25% of American women reported that, in their lifetime, they were raped or physically assaulted by a date, cohabiting partner, or current or former spouse (Tjaden and Thoennes 2000). This means that everyday in the United States, four women (approximately 1,400) die as a result of domestic violence, murdered by husbands and boyfriends (National Organization for Women 2004). (Note: We discussed child abuse and neglect in chapter 10.)

Violence is an "exertion of physical [psychological, emotional, or sexual] force so as to injure or abuse" (Webster 1984: 1316). Identification of the use of violence in intimate relationships as a significant social problem emerged only recently with child abuse in the 1960s, spouse abuse in the 1970s, and elder abuse in the 1980s. Family violence is the use of aggression—physical, psychological, emotional, or sexual—to gain or show control and power over other family members.

Common myths regarding family violence include the idea that family violence is not in "my" community, or it only happens to poor women and women of color. Others wrongly believe that some people deserve being victims of abuse or that family violence is not premeditated but caused by alcohol, drug abuse, stress, and mental illness. Additional myths include beliefs that family violence is a personal problem between partners, and, if it were that bad, the abused partner would leave. Hidden forms of family violence, such as marital rape or gay and lesbian violence, lurk along side these cultural myths. Sibling abuse, parent abuse, elder abuse, and abuse of the disabled may also be dismissed or not reported.

Welfare Reform and Family Violence

Government policies also influence family conflict and possible violence, especially among low-income or never-married parents. The Personal Responsibility and Work Reconciliation Act of 1996 explicitly encourages marriage and a nuclear family structure. Although the intent of this policy is to strengthen familial bonds, the reality is an increased potential for creating or exacerbating conflict between custodial and noncustodial parents (Boggess and Roulet 2004). Poverty and family violence are more important issues for families than family structure. In assessing the relative influence of household structure versus family conflict and violence on children's well-being, frequent and negative family conflict and violence are worse for children's social and personal adjustment than divorce or living in single-parent families (Amato 1993; Emery 1988).

Impacts of welfare reform on low-income, never-married mothers and fathers actually contribute to family conflict and risk of family violence. The Center for Family Policy and Practice identified six issues stemming from welfare reform that are of particular concern. Welfare reform policies contribute (a) rigid paternity laws; (b) harsher sanctions on custodial parents; (c) failure to recognize the underemployment and lack of health care; (d) failure to allow full child support to custodial parent; (e) failure to assist low-income, never-married families to find solutions to questions of visitation, custody, and access; and (f) inadequate knowledge of the impact of work requirements, cooperation requirements, and time limits (Boggess and Roulet 2004). A positive intervention to these detrimental impacts of welfare reform on family violence is the Wellstone/Murray Family Violence option that allows states to institute programs that screen for domestic violence plus provide support and services for those identified as victims of abuse.

Family conflict is often linked to ineffective parenting and children's maladjustment (Almeida, Wethington, and Chandler 1999; Buehler and Gerard 2002). The simplistic reaction of avoiding family conflict rests on a faulty belief that somehow "good" couples and families do not have disagreements. A more accurate response is to recognize the complexity of family interactions and prepare family members to effectively negotiate differences in a fair and just manner. The way parents interact with each other and how they handle disagreements and conflicts have enormous influence on children's lessons on learning how to agree to disagree and negotiate without resorting to violence.

Effects on Family Wellness

Impacts of family violence reach beyond the victim to include those who witness the violence. A growing body of literature links family violence to a range of short-term and long-term wellness effects. In addition to physical injuries, consequences of family violence include numerous adverse physical effects such as arthritis, chronic neck or back pain, and migraine and other frequent headaches. Other outcomes for those suffering or witnessing family violence are stammering, visual disorders, sexually transmitted infections, chronic pelvic pain, or stomach ulcers (Coker et al. 2000). Babies born to women who experience physical, emotional, or psychological family violence often suffer low birth weight that is linked to childhood illnesses, disabilities, and death (National Council on Welfare 1997).

Children who experience family violence are more likely to display low self-esteem, anxiety, depression, suicidal thoughts, and posttraumatic stress disorder (Briere and Elliot 1994; Mertin and Mohr 2000). Even if family violence does not result in direct injury or illness, studies show that members exposed to family violence may cope with their situation and feelings in harmful ways such as smoking, excessive drinking, or misusing drugs (Astbury et al. 2000; Caetano, Ramisetty-Mikler, and McGrath 2004; Family Violence Prevention Fund 2004; Kuo and Mayer 2000; World Health Organization 1996).

Some victims of family violence may not care for themselves and engage in disordered eating, self-cutting, and suicide (Golding 1999). These victims or witnesses to family violence may also become sexually active, using high-risk sexual practices such as unprotected sexual activity and or sex with multiple partners. As discussed in chapter 6, such behaviors may result in sexually transmitted infections, unplanned pregnancies, and or birth complications (Champion and Shain 1998; Cohen et al. 2000; Dietz et al. 1999; Hillis et al. 2001; Rosenberg 2001; Schei 1997).

Intimate Partner Violence

Intimate partner violence is "actual or threatened physical or sexual abuse or psychological and emotional abuse directed toward current or former spouse, current or former boyfriend or girlfriend, or current or former dating partner" (Centers for Disease Control and Prevention 2003: 1). Additional terms used to describe intimate partner violence include domestic abuse, domestic violence, spouse abuse, courtship violence, battering, marital rape, and date rape (Saltzman et al. 2002). The term intimate partner violence, therefore, is used to include violence within all intimate relationships including abuse toward partners, children, siblings, parents, or elders. Such violence between intimates can be expressed in several ways including physical, emotional, and sexual abuse; coercion, threats, intimidation, economic abuse, isolation, and other forms of intentional degrading of a partner. Figure 12.1 presents forms of violence against intimates.

Female Victims. Findings from the *National Violence Against Women Survey* reveal intimate partner violence is pervasive in the United States. Tjaden and Thoennes (2000)

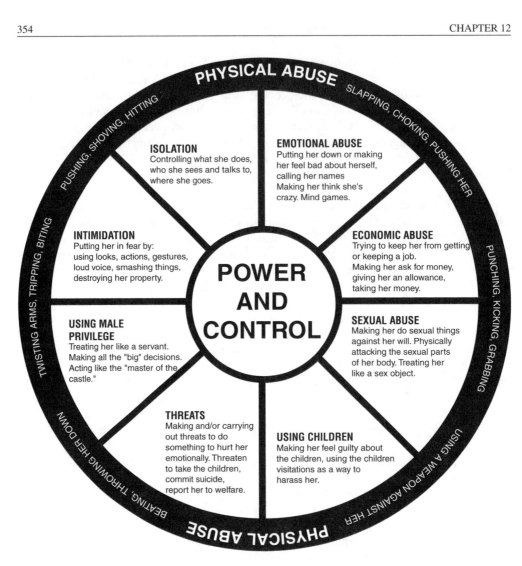

FIG. 12.1. Violence Wheel.
Source: Domestic Abuse Intervention Project www.domesticviolence.org/wheel.html (Retrieved 1/20/03).

report in their study of intimate partner violence from a nationally representative sample of 8,000 women and 8,000 men that approximately 1.5 million women (i.e., 25%) and 834,700 men (i.e., 7.5%) are raped or physically assaulted by an intimate partner at some-time in their lifetime. According to these findings, an estimated 1.5 million women and 834,732 men are raped and or physically assaulted by an intimate partner annually in the United States. Almost two thirds of women who reported being raped, physically assaulted, or stalked since age 18 were victimized by a current or former husband, cohabitating partner, boyfriend, or date. Among the women who are physically assaulted or raped by an intimate partner, one third are seriously injured.

Intimate partner violence, therefore, remains a serious concern for families. Almost one third of Black women experience intimate partner violence. American Indian/Alaskan Native women and men are more likely to report intimate partner violence, whereas Asian/Pacific Islanders women and men are least likely to report it. Other studies of violence against women state that each year 324,000 women experience intimate partner violence during pregnancy (Gazmararian et al. 2000).

Victims of abuse often do not see themselves as abused, especially when the abuse is psychological, emotional, or sexual. Even their abusers fail to accept that such behavior is abusive and damaging. Anyone can be a victim regardless of age, sex, sexual orientation, race, culture, religion, education, employment, or marital status. Although men can be victims, most victims are women.

Children who witness abuse of an intimate family member (e.g., mother abused by father or boyfriend) are at risk of long-term physical and mental health problems such as alcohol and substance abuse, being a victim of abuse, or becoming a perpetrator of intimate partner violence (Felitti et al. 1999). Children know about the violence (even though adults think they do not) and may feel helpless, scared, upset, or even responsible. Family violence in the home is dangerous to children; research reveals that child abuse occurs in these same families (Straus and Gelles 1990). The horror of intimate partner abuse stays with children exposed to it and increases the likelihood that these children will engage in youth violence as well (Cullen, Wright, and Brown 1998).

Abusers of Intimate Partners. Abusers of intimate partners are not easily identified. Although appearing as loving and friendly to the external community, behind closed doors they change. Contrary to myths noted previously, intimate partner violence is an intentional act to control another. What factors contribute to such abusive behaviors? Although complex, several conditions appear to increase the risk of abuse in intimate relationships.

Witnessing intimate partner violence as child or adolescent or experiencing violence from caregivers significantly increases the likelihood of becoming an abuser as an adult (Straus and Gelles 1990). Social context (e.g., living in disadvantaged neighborhoods, having many children, or early marriage and child bearing) also increase vulnerability to intimate partner violence (Fox et al. 2002). For some abusers, economic stress in terms of partners' perspectives on financial situation contributes to their belief that the victim needs to be punished (Szinovacz and Egley 1995). Perpetrators often have personal characteristics including a lack of social skills (e.g., poor communication, problem-solving, and resource-seeking skills), or exhibiting greater anger toward women (i.e., sexism), or displaying depression, lower self-esteem, and more aggression than nonviolent partners (Holtzworth-Monroe et al. 1997). Other social factors such as isolation and alcohol contribute to, but are not the sole causes of, intimate partner violence (Gelles 2000).

Why Victims Stay. Victims often remain in abusive relationships due to a lack of personal resources. Some argue that battered partners experience *learned helplessness* (Olson and DeFrain 2000) in which they believe they cannot be, or appear to be, competent, thus forfeiting their power. Helplessness often leads to feelings of hopelessness and powerlessness. Others factors that interfere with leaving abusive relationships include feelings of fear, actual or threatened, that the abuser will harm the abused or the children, low self-esteem (i.e., faulty beliefs that one is not deserving of a better life), and economic dependence.

Intimate Terrorism and Situational Couple Violence. Women or male partners in intimate relationships, therefore, may become victims of two forms of violence. *Intimate terrorism* aims to gain control over a partner by use of a wide range of power and control strategies including emotional abuse, economic abuse, threats, intimidation and isolation.

Situational couple violence is physical violence that is not a pattern to control or overpower but occurs when conflict escalates into violence (Johnson 1995; Leong et al. 2004). The major difference between the two is that in intimate terrorism, there is motivation and determination to control the partner in whatever means possible. Victims of intimate terrorism may have greater risk of losing economic self-sufficiency due to economic abuse or job loss because of injury sustained in the violence. This is not necessarily the case for victims of situational couple violence. Although not diminishing the seriousness of situational couple violence, we wish to point out how insidious intimate terrorism can be, especially for low-income partners.

Female to Male Violence

In nearly half of incidents of violence between intimates, both partners engaged in some type of abusive behavior (DeMaris, Pugh, and Harman 1992). Debate continues as to whether *female-to-male violence* by an intimate female partner is primarily in self-defense or retaliation. Although some contend that females inflict abuse almost as often as do men in violent relationships (Straus 1993), others hold that male abuse is done in self-defense and or retaliation (Kurtz 1993). At issue is that families and family study professionals need to face the reality that battered male partner abuse exists.

Women who use violence against their male partners often place themselves in danger.

> The danger to women of such behavior is that it sets the stage for the husband to assault her. Sometimes this is immediate and severe retaliation. But regardless of whether that occurs, the fact that she slapped him provides the precedent and justification for him to hit her when *she* is being obstinate, "bitchy," or "not listening to reason" as he sees it. (Straus and Gelles 1988: 25–26)

Gay Males and Lesbian Couple Abuse

Until recently, little attention or even recognition was given to *same-sex couple violence*. As with all intimate partner relationships, family violence occurs in gay male and lesbian couples at rates similar to straight couples. Lisa Waldner discusses the double jeopardy experienced by same-sex couples in violence relationships where they not only avoid the reality of intimate partner violence but also struggle under society's stigmatization of same-sex relationships.

BOX 12.3   "Another Burden to Bear: Domestic Violence in Lesbian and Gay Relationships"
Lisa K. Waldner, Ph.D.

Physical and sexual violence is a human problem found in all types of intimate relationships. Although references to heterosexual violence can be found in the 1950s research literature, lesbians and gay men have only recently caught the attention of social scientists. The invisibility of same-sex relationship violence is due to heterosexism, or the tendency to assume everyone is heterosexual, the reluctance of gays and lesbians to acknowledge violence as a pervasive problem, and gendered definitions of women as victims and men as perpetrators.

The ongoing battle for social and political equality prevents some activists from acknowledging any dysfunction in lesbian and gay lives. There is a perception that declaring a need for domestic violence services gives ammunition to individuals actively opposing gay rights initiatives. There is some evidence to suggest this is not mere paranoia. Right-wing policy pundits have misused my own research on same-sex domestic violence to suggest that the safest relationship for women is heterosexual marriage (Rich 1998). Finally, gendered definitions contribute to myths minimizing perceptions of both the prevalence and the severity of this problem. If women are only victims, then lesbian relationships must be violence free, and even if they are not, women cannot really hurt each other. Believing that a penis is needed to rape ignores the reality that some lesbians rape their partners.

Although not much is known regarding the dynamics of same-sex domestic violence, researchers believe that the prevalence rate is similar to that of heterosexual couples (Elliot 1996). Past studies on lesbians have found victimization rates ranging from 30% to 75% with my own research finding a prevalence rate of 48% for lesbians and 30% for gay men (Waldner-Haugrud, Gratch, and Magruder 1997). Not as much is known about gay men because few studies have examined gay male victimization. Differences in prevalence rates are due to variations in defining violence and the specificity of the time frame. In other words, using a behavioral checklist like the *Conflict Tactics Scale* and asking whether these behaviors have ever occurred yields a higher rate of reported violence when compared to studies that specify only the most recent relationship and ask a more general question such as "have you ever been physically assaulted by your lover?" Like heterosexual violence, we know that milder incidents like slapping or kicking are much more common than more severe assaults.

Although partners who are violent need to be held responsible for their behavior, it is important to recognize the contribution of a homophobic society. "Lesbian fusion" is the tendency of coupled lesbians to withdraw from the community and become socially isolated. This social isolation breeds an overdependency that increases the risk of violence (Renzetti, 1992). Homophobia is also a weapon used by perpetrators to control their partners. Like heterosexuals, gay men and lesbians can be very creative in exploiting individual and situational characteristics as a means of abusing a partner. The threat of outing a partner to the police, an employer, or family members is yet another possible means of control in a society that continues to stigmatize same-sex relationships.

REFERENCES

Elliot, Pam. 1996. "Shattering Illusions: Same-Sex Domestic Violence." *Journal of Gay and Lesbian Social Services* 4, 1–8.

Renzetti, Claire. 1992. *Violent Betrayal: Partner Abuse in Lesbian Relationships*. Newbury Park, CA: Sage.

Rich, Frank. 1998. "The Family Research Charade." *The New York Times*. December 5th.

Waldner-Haugrud, Lisa K., Linda Vaden Gratch, and Brian Magruder. 1997. "Victimization and Perpetration Rates of Violence in Gay and Lesbian Relationships: Gender Issues Explored." *Violence and Victims* 12: 173–84.

Lisa K. Waldner, Ph.D., is an Associate Professor of Sociology at the University of St. Thomas.

Sibling-to-Sibling Abuse

At this point, we draw attention to a common yet often ignored form of intimate family violence, between siblings. This is not the same as sibling rivalry or sibling conflict as discussed earlier. *Sibling-to-sibling abuse* or sibling violence involves physical, emotional, sexual abuse, coercion, threats, intimidation, and isolation. Seventy-five percent of siblings report at least one violent sibling-to-sibling incidence per year (Gelles 2000). Sibling violence is learned, often in the home from parents. Studies reveal that 76% of siblings who experience parent-to-child violence or physical punishment inflict serious abuse on a sibling, whereas only 15% of children who have not experienced parental physical punishment or violence will assault a sibling (Gelles). Parents and caregivers can prevent, or at least reduce, sibling violence by consistently exposing children and adolescents to nonviolent methods of getting along with others. Suggestions for parents and caregivers include (Olson and DeFrain 2000: 450):

- Demonstrating nonviolence toward each other
- Providing support and nurturing toward their children
- Providing children with a strong, clear message that violence is not acceptable
- Monitoring their children's behavior
- Avoiding coercive discipline

Child-to-Parent Abuse

There remains a double standard in American culture. Most of us believe that parents and guardians have the right to use physical punishment on children, but that children do not have the same right to strike a parent or guardian (or any adults for that matter). However, 10% of parents report being victims of *child-to-parent abuse*. These parents claim that they were hit, kicked, or bitten at least once in the last year, and 3% of parents report suffering more serious abuse by their children (Gelles and Straus 1988). Most of those children who use violence against parents or guardians are between 13 and 24 years of age, and many were themselves victims of parental or caregiver violence while growing up (Gelles 2000). This leads us to our last topic under violence between intimates, violence against elders.

Elder Abuse

As discussed in chapter 5, the elder population continues to increase and so do their needs for daily living assistance (e.g., dressing, bathing, mobility, medications, and eating). Caring for an elderly parent or guardian may be demanding and accompanied by a complex web of factors that increase the risk of *elder abuse* in families. Between 1986 and 1996, the incidence of reported elder abuse increased by 150% with 90% of the cases involving a family member (often a spouse or an adult child) as the abuser (National Women's Health Information Center 2003).

The types of elder abuse include passive and active neglect (e.g., not providing basic care), physical abuse, financial abuse (e.g., misuse of elder's funds, possessions, or property), psychological and emotional abuse, sexual abuse, violations of basic human rights (e.g., denying personal freedoms), and self-neglect (e.g., failure to take care of own physical, psychological, and or social needs; Fulmer, Guadagno, and Bolton 2004; Woolf 1998).

Elder abuse may be viewed from two different perspectives. A caregiver model position states that caregivers who abuse are overwhelmed with the demands of elder care. The focus is mainly on the differences among elders' physical, emotional, and social needs. Another position views elder abuse and neglect as forms of family violence. Here the focus centers on traits of the abuser and situations that contribute to incidences of elder abuse (Lamanna and Riedmann 2000).

Factors identified as contributing to elder abuse include (a) intergenerational violence (i.e., the cycle of violence in which the abused becomes the abuser), (b) caregiver overload and stress (i.e., caregivers require information, support, and resources), (c) elder dependency (i.e., as the elder's dependence increases, the caregiver may feel drained, resentful, and frustrated), (d) social isolation of caregiver and or elder, (e) external stress (e.g., financially strapped "sandwich generation" caregivers are squeezed between providing for their children and providing for their parents), and (f) personal problems of the abuser (e.g., alcoholism, drug addiction, mental illness) (Woolf 1998).

These possible causes of elder abuse are complex and often include combinations of several factors. "In many instances, both the victim and the perpetrator [are] caught in a web of interdependency and disability, which [makes] it difficult for them to seek or accept outside help or to consider separation" (Wolf 1986: 221).

Family Violence: No Longer a Private Matter

Violence within families often reflects violence within society. When a society values and honors civility, respect, and assertiveness over aggression, families within that society are more likely to respond in a similar fashion. It is also worth noting that sociocultural forces such as poverty, discrimination, and injustice negatively impact families and may increase the risk of family violence. We must remember that families are complex, adaptive communities that have the potential to live peaceful, nonviolent lifestyles. Yet, families (some more than others) require intervention with additional support, education, and resources so as to recognize and exercise nonviolence between intimates.

The Family Violence Prevention Fund (Carter 2003) offers four strategies to prevent violence in families. First, provide services for children exposed to violence in the home. This demands federal funding for intensive counseling for traumatized partners and their children plus providing supports to partners who are leaving abusive partners. Basically, the aim is to break the cycle of family violence. Second, provide supports for young and vulnerable parents. The Nurse–Family Partnership is a research-based home-visiting program for high-risk parents that not only teaches nurturing parenting skills but also supports young parents who are threatened with or have experienced battering. Third, strengthen mentoring, parenting education, and other violence prevention strategies in programs for vulnerable youth, prisoner reentry, and military personnel postwar programs. Families struggling with challenges need advocates, someone to be there for them and to serve as role models providing positive opportunities. Fourth, develop public education campaigns targeting men, teens, and children emphasizing the use of media to educate the general public on the serious nature of family violence (e.g., physical punishment is harmful and dangerous) and the prevalence of family violence in American society.

In addition to these prevention strategies, families need education on how dominance and control serve as motivators for intimate terrorism. They need skill-building activities to prevent and defuse such behavior. Learning effective communication, assertiveness, and anger management strategies serve a crucial role in combating family violence. Families also need to know they are not alone and that seeking professional help for family violence is as necessary as seeking treatment for cancer. Families also need to know how to access available resources.

Family violence should not happen to anybody, ever. Families and external communities can work toward creating a culture that is strong, vital, and able to disagree and negotiate conflicts by not modeling or tolerating family violence.

GLOSSARY

Child-to-parent abuse

Coercive power

Conflict avoidance

Conjugal power

Displacement

Elder abuse

Expert power

Family conflict

Family empowerment

Family power

Family violence

Female-to-male violence

Informational power

Intimate partner violence

Intimate terrorism

Learned helplessness

Legitimate power

Personal power

Referent power

Reward power

Sabotage

Same-sex couple violence

Sibling conflict

Sibling-to-sibling abuse

Situational couple violence

Social power

Work–family conflict

FOR YOUR CONSIDERATION

1. Create an example of how family empowerment could aid in power struggles between adolescents and parents or between husbands and wives.

2. You are working with a family with three children 8, 10, and 13 years of age. The parents or guardians complain about the unpleasant fighting (including name-calling and manipulation) the family experiences whenever there is a disagreement. The parents simply cannot understand where the children learned such behavior. Outline how you would introduce fair family fighting to them.

3. You are a member of the city council charged with reducing the rate of female partner abuse in your city. Identify two or three initiatives you believe would help reduce this abuse. Support your response.

FOR FURTHER STUDY: WEB SITES, ORGANIZATIONS, AND PUBLICATIONS

Web Sites and Organizations

Family Violence Prevention Fund
www.endabuse.org
383 Rhode Island St., Suite 304
San Francisco, CA 94103-5133
This site provides current data on prevalence and impacts of family violence. Yet the primary focus is on effective prevention strategies at family and outside community levels. Family

Violence Prevention Fund is an international organization that includes information on judicial, educational, and public policy as related to protecting children, women, and teens.

Federal Bureau of Investigation—Uniform Crime Reports

www.fbi.gov/ucr/nibrs/famvio21.pdf

This site offers empirical data and exploration of family violence in the United States. The offenses include murder, nonnegligent homicide, forcible rape, stalking, intimidation, robbery, aggravated assault, and simple assault.

Gay and Lesbian Domestic Violence

www.web.apc.org/~jharnick/violence.html

The attempts to protect heterosexuals from intimate partner violence often fail to protect individuals in same-sex couple relationships. This site offers articles, data, and resources.

Legal Momentum: Advancing Women's Rights

www.legalmomentum.org

Leading legal advocate for expanding women's and girl's rights and opportunities. This includes economic justice through litigation, policy reform, education, and training. An aim is to end gender-based violence and expand the Violence Against Women Act. The foundation of the organization is for equality under the law so as to protect and advance the constitutional and statutory rights of women.

Male Partner Abuse (Husband Battering)

www.vix.com/pub/men/battery/battery/html

This site explores the issue of male partner abuse as part of common violent couples. There are numerous articles, links, and commentary of this issue.

National Center for Victims of Crime

www.ncvc.org

One of the leading organizations that provides resources and advocacy for crime victims. They provide direct service and resources, advocacy for laws and policies that create resources and secure rights of crime victims, train and provide technical support to victim service organizations, and foster creative thinking about ways to help victims of crime.

National Center on Elder Abuse

www.elderabusecenter.org

This site provides a user-friendly search engine to locate articles, data, and resources related to elder abuse issues.

National Coalition Against Domestic Violence

www.ncadv.org

The *Coalition* works with numerous organizations to increase awareness about the prevalence and harm of domestic violence. It calls for the building of coalitions at local, state, regional, and national levels to support nonviolent alternatives, safe home and safe shelter programs.

National Institute of Justice

www.nij.gov

This site provides current data on the prevalence, incidence, and consequences of violence between intimates.

National Resources Center on Domestic Violence

www.nrcdv.org

This site is part of a national network of domestic violence resources providing information on domestic violence and related issues. Works with associations, coalitions, policy leaders, media, individuals, and communities.

Office on Violence Against Women
   www.ojp.usdoj.gov
   Provides prevalence data, resource information and explores promising practices to stop
   violence against women for criminal justice practitioners, advocates, and social service
   professionals.

United States Department of Justice: The Violence Against Women Grants Office
   www.ojp.usdoj.gov/vawgoreports.htm
   The Violence Against Women Office aims to enhance safety and ensure that offenders are
   held accountable by issuing policies, protocols, and projects that call for zero tolerance of
   violence against women.

United States Department of Justice Statistics on Intimate Violence
   www.ojp.usdoj.gov/bjs
   Statistics on crime and victims as well as related data on the justice system are available
   and easily accessible.

Publications

Barnett, Ola, Cindy Miller-Perrin, and Robin Perrin. 2004. *Family Violence Across the Lifespan: An Introduc-*
   tion. Thousand Oaks, CA: Sage.
   This expanded and updated edition assists students and family study professionals in better understanding
   of the prevalence, methodology, etiology, treatment, and prevention of family violence. With practice and
   policy perspectives, this work offers a "working text" to scholars and practitioners alike.
Booth, Alan, Ann C. Crouter, and Mari Clements, eds. 2001. *Couples in Conflict.* Mahway, NJ: Lawrence
   Erlbaum Associates.
   A central theme running through this work is that constructive conflict and effective negotiation are important
   in family relationships. Basic to this theme is an emphasis on enhancing couples' understandings and skills
   in constructively dealing with disagreements.
Brandwein, Ruth A. 1999. *Battered Women, Children, and Welfare Reform*, Thousand Oaks, CA: Sage.
   Brandwein explores the impacts of welfare reform on poor families, focusing on violence.
Gelles, Richard J., and Donileen R. Loseke, eds. 1993. *Current Controversies on Family Violence.* Newbury
   Park, CA: Sage.
   Family violence issues are debated by family study experts.
Hines, Denise, and Kathleen Malley-Morrison. 2004. *Family Violence in the United States: Defining, Under-*
   standing, and Combating Abuse. Thousand Oaks, CA: Sage.
   Hines and Malley-Morrison examine all forms of family violence by challenging the reader to consider
   assumptions and hypotheses. This work invites readers to consider effective solutions to family violence
   problems in the United States.
Loseke, Donileen, Richard Gelles, and Mary Cavanaugh. 2004. *Current Controversies on Family Violence.*
   Thousand Oaks, CA: Sage.
   Family violence research is surrounded by many controversies (e.g., is spanking violence? Is women's
   violence toward men a social problem?). This publication provides family study professionals and students
   with a wealth of insights and clear discussion of controversies without losing sight of the importance of
   family violence as a deep social problem.
Renzetti, Claire M., and Charles H. Miley. 1996. *Violence in Gay and Lesbian Domestic Partnerships.* New
   York, NY: Haworth Press.
   This work presents concepts, research findings, and applications for dealing with same-sex couple battering.
Straus, Murray A. 1994. *Beating the Devil Out of Them: Corporal Punishment in American Families.* New
   York, NY: Lexington Books.
   Straus presents a strong case against the use of physical punishment noting that corporal punishment is
   violence.

Straus, Murray A., and Richard J. Gelles. 1995. *Physical Violence in American Families* New Brunswick, NJ: Transaction Books.

   Based on Straus and Gelles' National Family Violence Survey, the authors offer conclusions and questions to ponder.

Tore, James D., and Karin Swisher. 1999. *Violence Against Women: Current Controversies.* San Diego, CA: Greenhaven Press.

   Tore and Swisher present different view points on controversial family violence issues including wife battering and husband abuse.

Wiene, Vernon. 2004. *Understanding Family Violence: Treating and Preventing Partner, Child, Sibling, and Elder Abuse.* Newbury Park, CA: Sage.

   Provides a thorough review of these major forms of family violence while including thoughtful and comprehensive discussions on intervention and prevention strategies.

REFERENCES FOR CITED WORKS

Almeida, David M., Elaine Wethington, and Amy L. Chandler. 1999. "Daily Transmission of Tensions Between Marital Dyads and Parent-Child Dyads." *Journal of Marriage and the Family* 61: 49–61.

Amato, Paul. 1993. "Children's Adjustment to Divorce: Theories, Hypotheses, and Empirical Support." *Journal of Marriage and Family* 55: 23–38.

Astbury, Jill, Judy Atkinson, Janet Duke, Patricia Easteal, Susan Kurrle, Paul Tait, and Jane Turner. 2000. "The Impacts of Domestic Violence on Individuals." *Medical Journal of Australia* 173: 427–31.

Bach, George R., and Peter Wyden. 1970. *The Intimate Enemy: How to Fair Fight in Love and Marriage.* New York, NY: Avon Books.

Blood, Robert, and Donald Wolfe. 1960. *Husbands and Wives: The Dynamics of Married Life Living.* New York, NY: Free Press.

Blumberg, Rae Lesser, and Marion Tolbert Coleman. 1989. "A Theoretical Look at The Gender Balance of Power in the American Couple." *Journal of Family Issues* 10: 225–50.

Boggess, Jacquelyn, and Marguerite Roulet. 2004. "Welfare Reform and Family Conflict Among Low-Income, Never-Married Parents." www.cffpp.org/publications/welfare_reform.html (Retrieved 11/1/04).

Briere, John, and Diana Elliot. 1994. "Immediate and Long-Term Impacts of Child Sexual Abuse." *The Future of Children* 4, 2: 55–62.

Brock, K. 2003. *When Men Murder Women: An Analysis of 2001 Homicide Data: Females Murdered by Males in Single Victim/Single Offender Incidents.* Washington, DC: Violence Policy Center. www.vpc.org/graphics/WMMW03.pdf (Retrieved 11/20/04).

Buehler, Cheryl, and Jean M. Gerard. 2002. "Marital Conflict, Ineffective Parenting, and Children's and Adolescents' Maladjustment." *Journal of Marriage and the Family* 64 (February): 78–92.

Bureau of Justice Statistics. 1995. "Violence Against Women: Estimates from the Redesigned Survey (NCJ-154348)." *Bureau of Justice Statistics Special Report* August.

Caetano, Raul, Suhasini Ramisetty-Mikler, and Christine McGrath. 2004. "Acculturation, Drinking, and Intimate Partner Violence Among Hispanic Couples in the United States: A Longitudinal Study." *Hispanic Journal of Behavioral Sciences* 26, 1: 60–78.

Carli, Linda. 1999. "Gender, Interpersonal Power, and Social Influence—Social Influence and Social Power: Using Theory for Understanding Social Issues." *Journal of Social Issues* 55: 81–99.

Carter, Janet. 2003. "Domestic Violence, Child Abuse, and Youth Violence: Strategies for Prevention and Early Intervention." www.mincava.umn.edu/link/documents/fvpf2/fvpf2.shtml (Retrieved 12/9/04).

Cancian, Francesca. 1985. "Gender Politics: Love and Power in the Private and Public Spheres." In *Gender and the Life Course*, ed. A. S. Rossi. New York, NY: Aldine, 253–64.

Centers for Disease Control and Prevention. 2003. "Intimate Partner Violence Fact Sheet." *National Center for Injury Prevention and Control.* www.cdc.gov/ncipc/factsheets/ipvfacts.htm (Retrieved 2/3/03).

Champion, Jane-Dimmit, and Rochelle Shain. 1998. "The Context of Sexually Transmitted Disease: Life Histories of Woman Abuse." *Issues in Mental Health Nursing* 19: 463–79.

Christensen, A., and C. L. Heavey. 1999. "Interventions in Couples." *Annual Review of Psychology* 50: 165–90.

Cohen, M., D. Deamant, S. Barkan, J. Richardson, M. Young, S. Holman, K. Anastos, J. Cohen, and S. Melnick. 2000. "Domestic Violence and Childhood Sexual Abuse in HIV-Infected Women and Women at Risk for HIV." *American Journal of Public Health* 90, 4: 560–65.

Coker, A., P. Smith, L. Bethea, M. King, and R. McKeown. 2000. "Physical Health Consequences of Physical and Psychological Intimate Partner Violence." *Archives of Family Medicine* 9 (May): 451–57.

Cole, Charles, and A. L. Cole. 1999. "Marriage Enrichment and Prevention Really Works: Interpersonal Competence Training to Maintain and Enhance Relationships." *Family Relations* 48: 273–75.

Cullen, Francis, John Wright, and Shayna Brown. 1998. "Public Support of Early Intervention Programs: Implications for a Progressive Policy Agenda." *Crime and Delinquency* 44, 2: 187–204.

Dietz, Patricia, Alison Spitz, Robert Anda, David Williamson, Pamela McMahon, John Santelli, Dale Nordenberg, Vincent Felitti, and Juliette Kendrick. 1999. "Unintended Pregnancy Among Adult Women Exposed to Abuse or Household Dysfunction During Their Childhood." *Journal of the American Medical Association* 282 (October): 1359–64.

DeMaris, Alfred, Meredith D. Pugh, and Erika Harman. 1992. "Sex Differences in the Accuracy of Recall of Witnesses of Portrayed Dyadic Violence." *Journal of Marriage and the Family* 54, 2: 335–45.

Deutsch, Francine, Josipa Roksa, and Cynthia Meeske. 2003. "How Gender Counts When Couples Count Their Money." *Sex Roles: A Journal of Research* 48 (April): 291–304.

Emery, Robert. 1988. *Marriage, Divorce, and Children's Adjustment*. Newbury Park, CA: Sage.

Family Empowering Committee. 2000. "Principles of Family Involvement." *Family Empowering Committee.* http://www.fed-icc.org/Family-Involvement-Principles-101100.pdf (Retrieved 2/03/03).

Family Violence Prevention Fund. 2004. "Health Consequences Over the Lifespan." 2004 National Conference on Health Care and Domestic Violence. (October). http://endabuse.org/health/conference (Retrieved 12/10/04).

Felitti, V., R. Anda, D. Nordenberg, D. Williamson, A. Spitz, V. Edwards, M. Koss, and J. Marks. 1999. "Relationships of Childhood Abuse and Household Dysfunction to Many of the Leading Causes of Death in Adults." *American Journal of Preventive Medicine* 14, 4: 245–58.

Fox, Greer Litton, Michael L. Benson, Alfred DeMaris, and Judy Van Wyk. 2002. "Economic Distress and Intimate Violence: Testing Family Stress and Resources Theories." *Journal of Marriage and the Family* 64: 793–807.

French, J. R. P., and Bertram Raven. 1959. "The Basis of Power." In *Studies in Social Power*, ed. D. Cartwright. Ann Arbor: University of Michigan Press, 150–67.

Frone, Michael, John Yardley, and Karen Markel. 1997. "Developing and Testing an Integrative Model of the Work-Family Interface." *Journal of Vocational Behavior* 50, 2: 145–67.

Fulmer, Terry, Lisa Guadagno, and Marguarette Bolton. 2004. "Elder Mistreatment in Women." *Journal of Obstetric, Gynecologic, and Neonatal Nursing* 33: 657–63.

Gazmararian, Julie, Ruth Petersen, Alison Spitz, Mary Goodwin, Linda Saltzman, and James Marks. 2000. "Violence and Reproductive Health: Current Knowledge and Future Research Directions." *Maternal and Child Health Journal* 4, 2: 79–84.

Gelles, Richard J. 2000. "Family Violence." In *The Handbook of Crime and Punishment*, ed. M. H. Tonry. New York, NY: Oxford University Press, 178–206.

Gelles, Richard J., and Murray A. Straus. 1988. *Intimate Violence*. New York, NY: Simon & Shuster.

Gillespie, Dair. 1971. "Who Has the Power? The Marital Struggle." *Journal of Marriage and the Family* 33: 445–58.

Golding, Jacqueline. 1999. "Intimate Partner Violence as a Risk Factor for Mental Disorders: A Meta-Analysis." *Journal of Family Violence* 14: 99–132.

Gottman, John Mordechai, 1994. *What Predicts Divorce? The Relationship Between Marital Processes and Marital Outcomes.* Mahwah, NJ: Lawrence Erlbaum Associates.

Greenhaus, Jeffrey, and N. Beutell. 1985. "Sources of Conflict Between Work and Family Roles." *Academy of Management Review* 10: 76–88.

Greenstein, Theodore N. 1995. "Gender Ideology, Martial Disruption and the Employment of Married Women." *Journal of Marriage and the Family* 57, 1 (February): 31–42.

Grochowski, Janet. 1999. "Meeting Challenges of 21st Century Health Education: A Self-Reflective and Self-Projective Classroom Strategy that Promotes Resiliency Enhancement." Paper presented at the annual meetings of the *American Alliance of Health, Physical Education, Recreation, and Dance*, April, Boston, MA.

Hammer, Leslie, and Cynthia Thompson. 2004. "Work-Family Role Conflict." A Sloan Work and Family Encyclopedia Entry. www.bc.edu/bc_org/avp/wfnetwork/rft/wfpedia/wfpWFRCent.html (Retrieved 11/1/04).

Hillis, Susan, Robert Anda, Vincent Felitti, and Polly Marchbanks. 2001. "Adverse Childhood Experiences and Sexual Risk Behaviors in Women: A Retrospective Cohort Study." *Family Planning Perspectives* 33 (September/October): 206–11.

Hochschild, Arlie Russell. 1989. *The Second Shift: Working Parents and the Revolution at Home*. New York, NY: Viking.

Holtzworth-Monroe, Amy, Leonard Bates, Natalie Smutzler, and Elizabeth Sandin. 1997. "A Brief Review of the Research on Husband Violence: Part I: Maritally Violent Versus Nonviolent Men." *Aggression and Violent Behavior* 2, 1: 65–99.

John, Daphne, Beth Anne Shelton, and Kristen Luschen. 1995. "Race, Ethnicity, Gender, and Perceptions of Fairness." *Journal of Family Issues* 16 (May): 357–79.

Johnson, Michael. 1995. "Patriarchal Terrorism and Common Couple Violence: Two Forms of Violence Against Women." *Journal of Marriage and the Family* 57, 2: 283–94.

Johnson, Paula. 1976. "Women and Power: Toward a Theory of Effectiveness." *Journal of Social Issues* 32: 99–110.

Kahn, R., D. Wolfe, R. Quinn, J. Snoek, and R. Rosenthal. 1964. *Organizational Stress*. New York, NY: Wiley.

Komter, Aafke. 1989. "Hidden Power in Marriage." *Gender and Society* 3: 187–216.

Kuo, Daphne, and Jonathan Mayer. 2000. "Another Factor for Smoking: Early Abuse." *Arts and Sciences Perspectives* (August). http://ascc/artsci.washington.edu/newsletter/Autumn00/Smoking.htm (Retrieved 9/1/04).

Kurtz, Demie. 1993. "Physical Assaults by Husbands: A Major Social Problem." In *Current Controversies on Family Violence*, eds. R. J. Gelles and D. R. Loseke. Newbury Park, CA: Sage, 88–103.

Lamanna, Mary Ann, and Agnes Riedmann. 2000. *Marriages and Families: Making Choices in a Diverse Society*. Belmont, CA: Wadsworth/Thomson Learning.

Leong, Janel, Michael Johnson, Catherine Cohan, and Susan Lloyd. 2004. "Consequences of male Partner Violence for Low-Income Minority Women." *Journal of Marriage and Family* 66 (May): 472–90.

Madsen, Susan. 2003. "The Effects of Home-Based Teleworking on Work-Family Conflict." *Human Resource Development Quarterly* 14, 1: 35–58.

Mertin, Peter, and Philip Mohr. 2000. "Incidence and Correlates of Post-Traumatic Stress Disorder in Australian Victims of Domestic Violence." *Journal of Family Violence* 15: 411–22.

Minkowitz, Donna. 1995. "In the Name of the Father." *MS Magazine* (November/December): 64–71.

National Council of Welfare. 1997. *Healthy Parents, Healthy Babies*. Ottawa, CA: National Council of Welfare.

National Organization for Women. 2004. "Violence Against Women in the United States." www.now.org/issues/violence/stats.html (Retrieved 10/30/04).

National Women's Health Information Center. 2003. "Elder Abuse." *Department of Health and Human Services, Office of Women's Health*. www.4woman.gov/violence/index.cfm?page=93 (Retrieved 2/10/03).

Olson, David, and John DeFrain. 2000. *Marriages and Families: Intimacy, Diversity, and Strengths*. New York, NY: McGraw-Hill.

Phillips, D. 1998. "Culture and Systems of Oppression in Abused Women's Lives." *Journal of Obstetric, Gynecologic, and Neonatal Nursing* 27: 437–61.

Raven, Bertram, Richard Centers, and Arnolds Rodrigues. 1975. "The Bases of Conjugal Power." In *Power in Families*. eds. R. Crowell and D. Olson. Newbury Park, CA: Sage, 217–32.

Rennison, C., and M. Planty. 2003. "Nonlethal Intimate Partner Violence: Examining Race, Gender, and Income Patterns." *Violence and Victims* 18: 433–43.

Risman, Barbara J., and Danette Johnson-Somerford. 1998. "Doing It Fairly: A Study of Postgender Marriages." *Journal of Marriage and the Family* 60, 1: 23–40.

Rosenberg, J. 2001. "Boyhood Abuse Increases Men's Risk of Involvement in Teenager's Pregnancy." *Family Planning Perspectives* 33: 184–85.

Rubin, Lilian. 1994. *Families on the Fault Line: America's Working Class Speaks About the Family, the Economy, Race, and Ethnicity.* New York, NY: HarperCollins.

Safilios-Rothschild, Constantina. 1970. "The Study of Family Power Structure: A Review 1960–1969." *Journal of Marriage and the Family* 29: 539–43.

Saltzman, Linda. E., Janet L. Fanslow, Pamela M. McMahon, and Gene A. Shelley. 2002. "Intimate Partner Violence Surveillance: Uniform Definitions and Recommended Data Elements." *National Center for Injury Prevention and Control.* www.cdc.gov/ncipc/pub-res/ipv_surveillance/00_Preliminary_Matter.htm (Retrieved 1/20/03).

Schei, Berit. 1997. "Reproductive Impacts: Reproductive Consequences of Violence Against Wives." *Education Wife Assault—World Congress in Obstetrics and Gynecology,* Copenhagen. www.womanabuseprevention.com/html/reproductive_consequences.html (Retrieved 8/24/04).

Schneewind, Klaus A., and Anna-Katharina Gerhard. 2002. "Relationship Personality, Conflict Resolution, and Marital Satisfaction in the First 5 Years of Marriage." *Family Relations* 51: 63–71.

Sprecher, Susan, and Pepper Schwartz. 1994. "Equity and Balance in the Exchange of Contributions in Close Relationships." In *Entitlement and the Affectional Bond: Justice in Close Relationships,* eds. M. J. Lerner and G. Mikula. New York, NY: Plenum, 89–116.

Stanley, Scott M., Susan L. Blumberg, and Howard J. Markman. 1999. "Helping Couples Fight for Their Marriages: The PREP Approach." In *Handbook of Preventive Approaches in Couple Therapy,* eds. R. Berger & M. Hannah. New York, NY: Brunner/Mazel, 297–303.

Straus, Murray A. 1993. "Physical Assaults by Wives: A Major Social Problem." In *Current Controversies on Family Violence,* eds. R. J. Gelles and D. R. Loseke. Newbury Park, CA: Sage, 67–87.

Straus, Murray A., and Richard J. Gelles. 1988. "How Violent Are American Families? Estimates From the National Family Violence Resurvey and Other Studies." In *Family Abuse and Its Consequences: New Directions in Research,* eds. G. T. Hotaling, D. Finkelhor, J. T. Kirkpatrick, and Murray A. Straus. Newbury Park, CA: Sage, 14–36.

Straus, Murray A., and Richard J. Gelles, eds. 1990. *Physical Violence in American Families: Risk Factors and Adaptations to Violence in 8,145 Families.* New Brunswick, NJ: Transaction Books.

Szinovacz, M. E., and L. C. Egley. 1995. "Comparing One-Partner and Couple Data on Sensitive Marital Behaviors: The Case of Marital Violence." *Journal of Marriage and the Family* 57: 995–1010.

Thompson, Cynthia, L. Beauvais, and K. Lyness. 1999. "When Work-Family Benefits Are Not Enough: The Influence of Work-Family Culture on Benefit Utilization, Organizational Attachment, and Work-Family Conflict." *Journal of Vocational Behavior* 54: 392–415.

Tjaden, Patricia, and Nancy Thoennes. 2000. "Extent, Nature, and Consequences of Intimate Partner Violence: Findings from the National Violence Against Women Survey." Report for Grant 93-IJ-CX-0012, funded by the National Institute of Justice and the Centers for Disease Control and Prevention. Washington, DC: National Institute of Justice.

Tichenor, Veronica. 1999. "Status and Income as Gender Resources: The Case for Marital Power." *Journal of Marriage and the Family* 61: 638–51.

Wallerstein, Judith S., and Sandra Blakeslee. 1995. *The Good Marriage: How and Why Love Lasts.* Boston, MA: Mifflin.

Webster. 1984. *Webster's Ninth New Collegiate Dictionary.* Spring Field, MA: Merriam-Webster.

West, Candace, and Don Zimmerman. 1991. "Doing Gender." In *The Social Construction of Gender,* eds. Judith Lorber and Susan Farrell. London: Sage, 13–37.

West, Carolyn. 2002. "Black Battered Women: New Directions for Research and Black Feminist Theory. In *Charting a New Course for Feminist Psychology* eds. L. H. Collins, M. R. Dunlap, and J. C. Chrisler. Westport, CT: Praeger, 216–37.

West, Carolyn. 2004. "Black Women and Intimate partner Violence: New Directions for Research." *Journal of Interpersonal Violence* 19, 12: 1487–93.

Westman, Mia. 2001. "Stress and Strain Crossover." *Human Relations* 54, 6: 717–51.

Wilkie, Jane Riblett, Mura Marx Ferree, and Kathryn Strother Ratcliff. 1998. "Gender and Fairness: Marital Satisfaction in Two-Earner Couples." *Journal of Marriage and the Family* 60, 3: 577–94.

Wilkinson, Doris. 1993. "Family Ethnicity in America." In *Family Ethnicity: Strength in Diversity,* ed. H. Pipes McAdoo. Newbury Park, CA: Sage, 15–59.

Williams, Norma. 1990. *The Mexican-American Family: Tradition and Change.* Dix Hills, NY: General Hall.

Wolf, Rosalie S. 1986. "Major Findings from Three Model Projects on Elder Abuse." In *Elder Abuse: Conflict in the Family*, ed. K. A. Pillemer and R. S. Wolf. Dover, MA: Auburn House, 218–38.

Woolf, Linda M. 1998. "Elder Abuse and Neglect." *Webster University.* www.webster.edu/~woolflm/sbuse.html (Retrieved 2/1/03).

World Health Organization. 1996. *Consultation on Violence Against Women.* Geneva, Switzerland.

Wosinska, W., A. Dabul, R. Whetstone-Dion, and R. Cialdini. 1996. "Self-Presentational Responses to Success in the Organization: The Costs and Benefits of Modesty." *Basic and Applied Social Psychology* 18: 229–42.

Zipp, John, Ariane Prohaska, and Michelle Bemiller. 2004. "Wives, Husbands, and Hidden Power in Marriage." *Journal of Family Issues.* 25, 7: 933–58.

13

MONEY MATTERS: CLASS, ECONOMICS, AND MATERIAL DYNAMICS OF FAMILY LIVING

CHAPTER PREVIEW

Although the median income for American families exceeds $50,000 per year, one out of even nine Americans lives in poverty. *Low-income working families* constitute an increasing percentage of poor families and single-mother families are the most likely to be poor. Economic hardship has detrimental consequences for families and their members. However, family resiliency around economic hardship is shaped by the family's perceptions and optimism, as well as by social supports, and even culture-specific structures, values, and behaviors. Unemployment has not only immediate but also cumulative effects on families and relationships.

Counter to the *cult of domesticity*, the percentage of women, and especially women with young children, in the labor force has increased to the point where the majority of women are now employed. Nevertheless, women continue to experience *occupational segregation*, and 4 out of every 10 women work in the *pink-collar ghetto*. The persistence of the *wage gap* as well as the *mother penalty* and the situation of women who are the *trailing spouse* are part of a larger picture of discrimination, including sexual harassment that limits women's aspirations and achievements, as well as their families' economic well-being.

Work and family linkages include the impacts of occupational characteristics and job situations, *shift work* and *commuter marriage* on families. Some organizations, such as the U.S. military with its requirement that parents in service prepare a *Family Care Plan*, recognize the value of helping couples manage the connections between work and family lives. The *two-person single-career* and *dual-earner couples* (including *dual-worker couples* and *dual-career couples*) represent types of marriages in which couples must juggle not only family with work but also, in the latter cases, family and multiple work commitments.

Innovations in work–family connections include *flexible scheduling* (*flextime, job sharing, telecommuting*), as well as the *compressed workweek* and *family leave* (e.g., *maternity leave*). Legislation such as the *Family and Medical Leave Act* mandates certain rights regarding employee's right to time off to care for their family members. The *mommy track* and the *daddy track* have been proposed as ways for employed women and men to manage their commitments to their families, albeit not without career consequences. A *life-course solution* offers ways to resolve such dilemmas, including how to organize work and family life around shifting responsibilities, including the *sandwich generation*.

We distinguish between *employment* and *household labor*, both of which are types of *work* and important aspects of the *family economy*. Research indicates women still contribute the majority of hours to unpaid labor in the family and that employed women experience a *second shift* and a *leisure gap* when compared to their husbands. We conclude this chapter with a discussion of the situation of the full-time homemaker, including a special note on the plight of *displaced homemakers*.

AN ECONOMIC PROFILE OF AMERICAN FAMILIES

The median income for families in the United States is $50,890. However, the median family income differs considerably by race, with the median family income for Black and Hispanic Americans falling at $34,192 and $35,054, respectively. Likewise, whereas fewer than 20% of White families have income levels below $25,000, more than one third of Black and Hispanic families have income levels below that amount (United States Bureau of the Census 2003a).

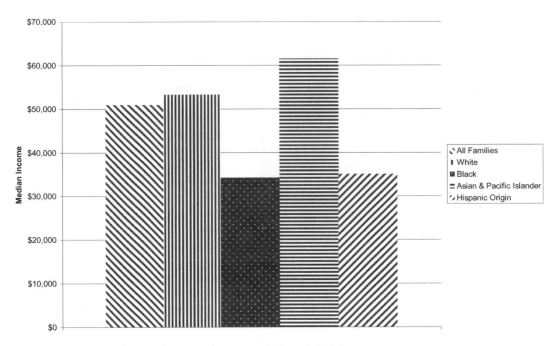

FIG. 13.1.   Median Family Income by Race and Hispanic Origin.
Source: United States Bureau of the Census. 2003a. *Statistical Abstracts of the United States, 2002.*
Table 658. Washington, DC: Government Printing Office.

Furthermore, the already enormous wealth gap between White and minority families widened during the economic downturn between 1996 and 2002. Net worth includes the value of items such as checking and savings accounts, stocks and other investments, as well as significant property such as homes and cars, minus debts such as mortgages, car loans, and credit card bills. After adjusting for inflation, between 1996 and 2002, the net worth of White households increased more than 17%, and the net worth of Hispanic households increased 14%. During the same period, the net worth of Black households decreased by about 16% (Armas 2004).

According to income guidelines from the U.S. Office of Management and Budget, one out of every nine Americans was officially poor in 2000. For a two-parent family of four, the official poverty line was $17,463. For a single-parent family of three, the official poverty line was $13,874 (Population Reference Bureau 2002).

Low-income working families are families with incomes that are more than 150% below the federal poverty line in which at least one adult is employed. For a family of three, that amount is $20,811. Between 1991 and 2000, the percentage of children in low-income working families averaged just under 22%. Part of the increase stems from the increase in the number of all children over the decade, but much of the increase in the percentage of low-income families resulted from more labor force participation among low-income parents. However, this increased participation merely shifted those families from being "low income" to being "low income working." According to the U.S. Bureau of the Census, the percentage of children in low-income families rose steadily over the last decade, to a high of 52% in 2000 (O'Hare 2003).

Family income differs considerably by family type, with single-mother families— whether the mother is employed or not—receiving much less income than all other types

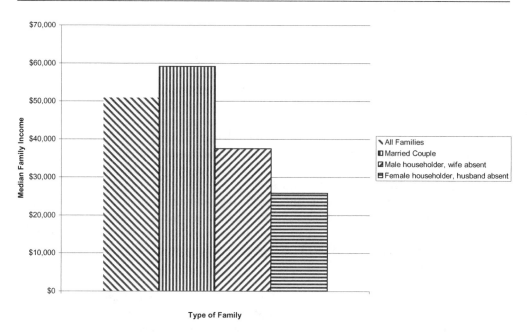

FIG. 13.2.   Median Family Income by Type of Family.
Source: United States Bureau of the Census. 2003b. *Statistical Abstracts of the United States, 2002.*
Table 660. Washington, DC: Government Printing Office.

of families (Bianchi, Casper, and Kent 2001). Figure 13.2 depicts the per capita income of four types of families: (a) single father, employed; (b) two-parent, father only employed; (c) single mother, employed; and (d) single mother, not employed. Although single father, employed families fare better than the other three types of families, all four types have lost ground relative to two-parent, dual-earner families.

Low-wage jobs often require inflexible schedules and rigid shifts or open-ended worker availability, yet these same jobs provide wages too low to cover child-care costs. Consequently, low-income households are more likely to rely on the family labor of children to manage the dual demands of employment and family life. Daughters (more than sons) are often left with responsibility for necessary, complicated, time-consuming family demands. Dodson and Dickert (2004: 318) found that these children, "detoured from childhood to do family labor," suffer not only from lost opportunities but also, later, from a higher likelihood of intergenerational transfer of poverty.

Married-couple families are more likely to have an adult member in the labor force and have more income than other family types. They are also more likely to live in the suburbs and to have college graduates than are other family types (Fields & Casper 2001). In other words, married-couple families are better able to provide their families with material resources than are other families. These resources translate into options regarding neighborhoods, education, and other choices that can enhance the health, wealth, and life chances of their members.

In this chapter, we examine the impact of economics (including the hardship of unemployment), women's employment, and work–family linkages on the quality of family life. We also consider the place of unpaid household labor in the family economy.

Economic Hardship

Before Social Security, Medicare, and Medicaid, "poor farms" provided a home and some degree of financial assistance for indigent elderly and some families. Counties often provided room, board, some clothing, and a modest monthly stipend.

The week following Christmas of 2002, individuals and families who had previously been receiving public assistance funded by the federal government faced being cut off from that source of funds. This situation resulted from the inability of President George W. Bush and Congress to agree on the terms for continuation of public assistance. In the meantime, these families faced the anxious uncertainty of the potential of weeks without their primary source of income.

Steuerle (2004), Senior Fellow at the Urban Institute and former Deputy Assistant Secretary of the U.S. Treasury, observes, over the next few years, programs for working families are scheduled to be reduced. His complaint is current law extends considerable support (a package worth $600,000) to a typical couple retiring today, but very little to children and their families.

> Consider this trade-off from a lifetime perspective. The federal government promises citizens born today very little in their early years, when an investment might have a big payoff. However, to those who grow up and enter the workforce, the government promises subsidized consumption and decades of supported retirement when they are older. Is that a trade-off anyone would choose? (Steuerle 2004: F1)

In chapter 10, we described how economic hardship has detrimental consequences for children. For children and their parents, economic hardship disrupts parenting and increases harsh and explosive parenting behaviors. Economic disadvantage is also associated with lower educational achievement, conduct problems, and depression, as well as lower self-esteem among children (Conger and Elder 1994; Conger et al. 1992; Rayman 1988; Voydanoff and Wilson 1990). For husbands and wives, economic hardship increases marital tensions and hostile marital behaviors and decreases marital satisfaction (Atkinson, Liem, and Liem 1986; Conger and Elder; Perrucci and Targ 1988; Voydanoff and Donnelly 1988).

As revealed in chapter 3, family members' perceptions of hardship and their sense of optimism regarding futures are keys to family resiliency in the face of problems. Family well-being during periods of economic hardship is shaped by family members' subjective perceptions of the extent to which daily life is disrupted. In some cases, limiting expenses, using savings and credit resources, and other financial coping efforts do not necessarily increase the sense of individual and family well-being beyond the short run. This may be due to the persistence of demoralization in the face of a readjusted lifestyle (Voydanoff and Donnelly 1988; Wilhelm and Ridley 1988). At the same time, marital happiness is higher among couples who focus on problem solving and reframe the downturn in the economic circumstances in more positive terms (Perrucci and Targ 1988).

Social supports from family, friends, community, and the broader society can ameliorate the negative effects of economic hardship on families (Atkinson, Liem, and Liem 1986; Camasso and Camasso 1986; Hashima and Amato 1994; Lorenz, Conger, and Montague 1994). However, economic hardship itself may act against the formation and maintenance of social supports (Atkinson, Liem, and Liem 1986; Lorenz, Conger, and Montague 1994). In fact, Danziger, Ananat, and Browning (2004) found, whereas child-care subsidies reduce the costs of making the transition from welfare to work, subsidies do little to reduce parenting stress or problems with child care. Clearly, the problem of providing social support to the neediest families is a complex one.

Research confirms the negative consequences of economic hardship and its resulting impact on family relations for African-American, Latino, and Euro-American families alike. However, a limited amount of research has demonstrated ethnicity and culture shapes family response and adjustment to economic hardship (Gomel et al. 1998). For example, the distinct kinship structures and bonds, communal values, strong spiritual beliefs, and frequent church attendance within African-American communities may enable families in those communities to draw on distinct strategies for coping with economic stress (Bowman 1993; Harrison et al. 1990; Thompson and Ensminger 1989).

In the words of Gomel and her colleagues (1998: 437):

> Thus, the families who are most likely to fare well in the face of economic distress are those that make effective use of the limited social supports that are available.

Family Impacts of Unemployment

The unemployment rate over the last decade has averaged 5.6%, but reached a high of 7.5% in 1992 (O'Hare 2003). Traditionally, the rule during economic downturns was "last hired, first fired" with younger, more recently hired workers the most vulnerable to losing their jobs. However, beginning with the 1990 to 1991 recession, longtime laborers, especially older and unskilled blue-collar workers have been the hardest hit by business mergers, corporate reorganization, technical change, and global competition (Meyers 2001).

In addition to the obvious financial woes presented by a layoff, individuals experience more signs of emotional and social stress during such periods. These problems include higher incidences of substance abuse, depression, anxiety disorders, sleep disorders, and suicidal thoughts. The longer the duration of unemployment, the higher the suicide rates, according to the U.S. Public Health Service. New Mexico, which recently experienced the largest jobless rate increase in the United States, saw suicides reach a record level in 2001 ("Layoffs Deliver Storm of Emotional Troubles" 2002).

Individuals who find themselves unemployed may experience deep self-doubt, lack of self-confidence, and low self-esteem. These negative consequences are not limited to men. According to Carl Greiner, professor of psychiatry at the University of Nebraska Medical Center in Omaha:

> Women have given up more for their jobs in some ways. They may have delayed child-bearing [and a layoff may leave them wondering whether] the sacrifice was worth it. ("Layoffs Deliver Storm of Emotional Troubles" 2002: 4)

Interpersonal relationships suffer during periods of unemployment as well. Individuals who are unsuccessful in securing employment may withdraw from friends and relationships. Families suffer as well. According to the Centers for Disease Control and Prevention, marital stability is highest during periods of low male unemployment ("Layoffs Deliver Storm of Emotional Troubles" 2002).

In Box 13.1, Phyllis Goudy Myers, a sociologist, describes the impacts of repeated periods of unemployment on everyday family life and what families can do to stay the course.

BOX 13.1   "The Stages of Family Unemployment"
Phyllis M. Goudy Myers, Ph.D.

When a family member—husband, wife, or other—faces unemployment, the entire family faces unemployment. As a survivor of unemployment (my husband's and my own, as well as friends' and colleagues'), I have observed that families experience a set of rather predictable stages in reaction and adjustment.

The first stage is likely to be *disbelief.* Unemployment is often a crushing blow, financial and otherwise. Unemployment catches off guard not only the individuals who lose the job but also their families. In general, financial problems are the number one marital problem cited by Americans in national polls (Olson and DeFrain 2000), and unemployment only makes these problems worse.

In addition, unemployment may stimulate fear, anger, and irrational outbursts by family members. Sometimes the results may include violence or divorce. "I've been no picnic to live with since I got canned," said Joe Phillips, an unemployed truck driver (Rubin 1999: 229). Individual worry and grief, coupled with deepening financial problems, compounded by possible denial of the problems facing the individual, the couple, and the family only increases marital and family stress. This can lead to *panic.* "The scariest part about . . . being out of a job is we don't have any medical benefits anymore . . . Do you know what it's like listening to your kid when she can't breathe and you can't send her to the hospital (Rubin 1999: 231)?"

When unemployment persists beyond a few weeks or months, there may be a *lack of motivation.* " 'Either you're overqualified or you're over the hill,' Ed Kruetsman, a forty-nine-year-old unemployed white factory worker observes in a tired voice (Rubin 1999: 235)." The case of an individual who was unemployed for 26 months during a 40-month period and who applied for 205 jobs before he was hired long term (reported in Olson and DeFrain 2000) is increasingly common. Such uncertainty can lead to overeating, alcohol abuse, excessive smoking, and other unhealthy behaviors. In addition, the conjugal relationship, especially in the most traditional marriages, can suffer, if wives lose respect for husbands who are unable to fulfill their role as primary breadwinner.

With continuing unemployment, there may be *anxiety.* "I kept thinking he should take anything, but he only wanted a job like the one he had. We fought about that a lot . . . But when you have to support a family, that should come first, shouldn't it? (Rubin 2003: 304)." For some, the anxieties associated with unemployment stem from the fear of poverty and homelessness (Hogan, Meesook, and Perrucci 1997). Even those who are not living "one paycheck away from poverty" likely experience a relative drop in material quality of living and loss of face as they lose esteem in the eyes of others.

These anxieties also occur in families suffering from underemployment due to part-time or contingent work. Families with underemployed breadwinners have lives that are less certain due to lower or unpredictable wages, no or drastically reduced benefits, little upward or even downward social mobility, and child care issues resulting from erratic work schedules (Handler 1997; Haynie and Gorman 1999).

For fortunate families, the final stage of family unemployment may be *relief* when family members become re-employed. "Fortunately, I found a good job that I enjoy. It doesn't pay all that well, but I love having it. Being without work was terrifying. Even talking about it still upsets me today, 10 years later (Olson and DeFrain 2000: 230)."

Family members who have experienced unemployment followed by reemployment never quite forget the stages of unemployment. They face each day with the knowledge that a downturn in the economy may once again place them among the ranks of the unemployed.

REFERENCES

Handler, Joel F. 1997. "The Problem of Poverty, the Problem of Work. In *Perspectives on Current Social Problems*, ed. Greg Lee Carter. Needham Heights, MA: Allyn & Bacon, 53–65.

Haynie, Dana L., and Bridget K. Gorman. 1999. "A General Context of Opportunity: Determinants of Poverty across Urban and Rural Labor Markets." *The Sociological Quarterly* 40, 2 (Spring): 177–97.

Hogan, Richard, Meesook Kim, and Carolyn C. Perrucci. 1997. "Racial Inequality in Men's Employment and Retirement Earnings." *The Sociological Quarterly* 38, 3 (Summer): 431–38.

Olson, David H., and John DeFrain. 2000. *Marriages and Families: Intimacy, Diversity, and Strengths*, 4/e. New York, NY: McGraw-Hill.

Rubin, Lillian B. 1999. "When You Get Laid Off, It's Like you Lose a Part of Yourself." In *Sociology of Families*, ed. Cheryl Albers. Thousand Oaks, CA: Pine Forge, 228–36.

Rubin, Lillian B. 2003. "Families on the Fault Line." In *Families in Transition*, ed. Arlene S. Skolnick and Jerome H. Skolnick. Boston, MA: Allyn and Bacon, 303–20.

Phyllis M. Goudy Myers, Ph.D., has been employed full time and part time. She often chose part-time employment in higher education in order to spend more time with her three children. She and her husband of 20 years have both experienced unemployment, but she is currently on the faculty of Normandale Community College, Bloomington, MN.

An employment layoff can have significant cumulative effects. In an e-mail message recently received by one of the authors:

I have just been layed-off from my "dream job." I had managed to make it into this position in spite of not having completed a college degree. [The writer was in her sophomore year, working toward a Bachelor's degree, while working full-time to support her children.] I'm in a custody fight with my children's father and I need to travel to [another state] to keep an appointment with my case worker. And I may have to quit school to move to [another state].

The sender of that e-mail did in fact have to withdraw from college in order to relocate for employment in another state.

WOMEN'S EMPLOYMENT

One of the most remarkable changes in the economic picture of families is the steady increase in women's employment over the last 50 years. The increase in women's employment is part of a larger trend related first to industrialization. Factory work created a rapid need for a large, ready pool of labor that required the hands of increasing numbers of men and also their sisters and their wives, as well as their children. By the end of the 20th century, the average number of work years of American women had grown to nearly 32 years, up from about 14 years in 1950. This puts women to within 5 years of the average number of years—37—worked by American men (Population Reference Bureau 2001a).

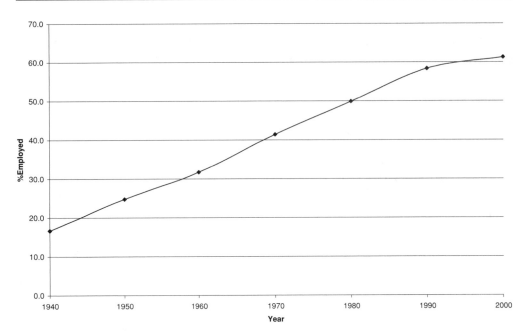

FIG. 13.3. Married Women's Labor Force, 1940–2000.
Source: [Data for 1940–1970] United States Bureau of the Census. 1975. *Historical Statistics, Colonial Times to 1970*. Washington, DC: Government Printing Office.
[Data for 1980–2000] United States Bureau of the Census. 2001. *Statistical Abstracts of the United States, 2001*. Table 576. Washington, DC: Government Printing Office.

Labor Force Participation

The number of women in the labor force increased during the 20th century through World War I, the Great Depression, and World War II. After World War II women who had filled the labor shortage created by men leaving civilian jobs for military service were encouraged to return to their homes. This fed a 20th century version of what historians and sociologists (e.g., Welter 1978) have called a *cult of domesticity*. This renewed emphasis on women's sphere being with home and family facilitated the transition from a war to a peace economy. With the GI Bill, the detached single-family home was within the grasp of many American families. What better way to stimulate the peacetime economy than to encourage the purchase of home washing machines and other new durable goods?

The percentage of women with children in the labor force remained below 50% for 25 years following World War II. However, by 1960 the number of women in the labor force began to increase rapidly, and by the beginning of the 1980s a majority of women were employed.

The number of women in the labor force tripled in the last 40 years, but the proportion of women with young children has more than quadrupled (Population Reference Bureau 2001c). Although young women, age 20 to 24, were the most likely and women with children the least likely to be employed, by the late 1990s, three fourths of women with children age 6 to 17 were in the labor force. The move of women with preschool children to the labor force came later, but by the end of the 20th century, a majority of women with preschool children were employed, and 55% of married mothers with children under 1 year of age were employed (United States Bureau of the Census 1998).

TABLE 13.1

Men's and Women's Occupational Distribution, 2000

Occupation	Percentage Men	Percentage Women
Management, professional, and related occupations	31.4	36.2
Service occupations	12.1	18.0
Sales and office occupations	17.9	36.7
Farming, fishing, and forestry occupations	1.1	0.3
Production, transportation, and material-moving occupations	20.5	8.0

Source: United States Bureau of Labor Statistics. 2002. *Current Population Survey. QT-P28.* Washington, DC: Government Printing Office

Occupations and Wages

Occupational segregation continues to characterize the world of work. Forty one percent of employed women work in the clerical or service sector (i.e., the *pink-collar ghetto*). Less than one out of every seven (only 14%) of employed women work in executive, managerial, or administrative positions (Roos and Jones 1993).

Even within occupational categories, positions are sexually segregated. For example, among professional occupations, women are concentrated in health, social work, teaching, and other traditionally female fields. Although women have made remarkable gains in medical school admissions, women are still overrepresented in lower prestige specialties such as pediatrics and psychiatry. In colleges and universities, women are still disproportionately found in the lower ranks (instructors and assistant professors) and among the part-time, untenured faculty (Roos and Jones 1993).

On the average, women who work full time outside the home earn 76 cents for every dollar earned by men. The gap between women and men's earnings is greater between White women and White men (75%) than between Black or Hispanic women and men (85% and 88%, respectively), but only because Black and Hispanic men earn considerably less than do White men (United States Bureau of Labor Statistics 2001b). Because of this discrepancy, the United States Bureau of the Census estimates employed wives contribute only about 35% to 41% of a family's income (Winkler 1998).

The continuing *wage gap* is certainly related to women's concentration in lower paying occupations and positions. The wage gap results in a substantial difference between men and women in potential lifetime earnings. For example, a woman with a Bachelor's degree can expect to earn $856,131 less than a man with the same degree during a typical 40-year employment life, from ages 25 through 64 (Minnesota Legislative Commission on the Economic Status of Women 2002).

Some women perceive barriers to nontraditional occupations or intentionally choose occupations they believe will make fewer demands on their family or other commitments. Motherhood evidently has a profoundly negative effect on women's earning potential. Budig and England (2001) speak of a *mother penalty* of 7% per child, with greater penalties accruing with second than with first children. Still, other women pay a price in their own employment ladder when they become the *trailing spouse*, relocating to accommodate their husbands' careers.

Gender discrimination aside, the United States Bureau of the Census estimates that among dual-earner households in which both the husband and wife are employed full-time, 31% of wives earn more than do their husbands (Population Reference Bureau

TABLE 13.2

Gender Segregation in Median Annual Earnings

Earnings	Percentage Men	Percentage Women
$1–9,999	2.6	4.0
$10,000–14,999	5.7	10.4
$15,999–24,999	17.3	28.5
$25,000–34,999	20.0	24.2
$35,000–49,999	22.1	18.5
$50,000–74,999	18.5	10.0
$75,000–99,999	6.4	2.5
$100,000 or more	7.4	2.0

Source: United States Bureau of the Census. 2000. *Summary File 4, Matrices PCT138, PCT139, and PCT 140*. QP-P31. Washington, DC: Government Printing Office.

2001b). Family economic well-being benefits from women's employment. However, discrimination, including sexual harassment (see Padavic 1992) and employer stereotypes of women as lacking in career commitment (see Shellenbarger 1992b) can limit women's aspirations and achievements, and therefore their families' material well-being. In a recent survey, women in senior executive positions in *Fortune 1000* corporations named "male stereotyping" along with "exclusion from informal networks" as significant obstacles to women obtaining a position as a chief executive officer of a corporation (CEOGO 2004).

A woman's employment has complex effects on the quality of her life in general. For example, Schnittker (2004) found employed mothers are healthier than are mothers who are not employed (and slightly healthier than men). However, employed mothers with children under the age of 6 pay a perceived health cost for what Schnittker calls "intensive mothering."

WORK–FAMILY LINKAGES

The linkage between work and family has been the subject of scholarly study by sociologists, psychologists, and others for several decades. Consider the following. Ellen Kirschman is a California psychologist whose clients are primarily public safety personnel. Her work indicates the very traits of a good police officer—emotional control, a skeptical nature, a constant state of vigilance, a commanding presence—can be problematic for family relationships.

> Officers have to remind themselves that not everyone in the neighborhood is a crook, that not every teenager is looking for trouble, that snap judgments so essential for survival on the street are not necessarily welcomed at home (Meier 2002: B3).

Shift work and other nonstandard work schedules—working evenings, nights, or weekends—affects marital stability. One study found, among men with children, those who worked nights had a six times greater probability of separation or divorce than did those who worked days. Among women with children, those who worked nights had a three times greater probability of separation or divorce than those who worked days (Presser 2000).

BOX 13.2   "Simon Serving Family Suppers"
Simon Foster

SimonDelivers is the leading provider of home-delivered groceries in the United States. The company began delivering in 1999 and today has over 24,000 regular ordering customers in and around the Twin Cities in Minnesota.

Families today are incredibly busy—over 70% of Minnesota spouses work full or part time. Stay-at-home spouses have interests or responsibilities that keep them equally busy. Families of all types have more choice of activities and opportunities—and a greater level of disposable income with which to pursue them—than at any time in history. The one thing we don't have enough of though is time.

Shopping for food takes 2 to 3 hours a week, and 60% of Americans say they dislike grocery shopping. Still, food is not only a basic need, a considerable amount of emotion and care that goes into people's food choices.

SimonDelivers was founded with a mission to simplify the lives of busy families by bringing the highest quality groceries and other household consumed items from growers and manufacturers direct to homes at no extra cost.

The ordering experience takes just 20 minutes or less—either on the Web or by phone—with a 100% satisfaction guaranteed policy the Company has stood by from day one. The delivery experience harkens back to the old milkman—neighborhood delivery reps that are responsible for the service and satisfaction on their regular route. The food experience brings the absolute freshest perishables, in many cases direct from growers—many days fresher than a store-based grocer. Seafood is flown in fresh several times daily. Restaurant-quality cuts of meat and deli are prepared daily to order. Fresh-baked goods are brought in several times a day from the broadest array of bakeries in the Twin Cities. Prices are better than you'd expect, because processing is done online, in a warehouse, without a store, and with a logistics system that is more efficient delivering to the home than *FedEx*. Thus, our customers pay less than the high end or neighborhood stores, and only moderately more than the price-oriented, no frills stores.

Through building *SimonDelivers* we are proud of the fact that we are making a genuine difference in the busy lives of thousands of families in the Twin Cities.

Simon Foster is the founder, president, and "head delivery boy" of *SimonDelivers.*

Although research on this family lifestyle is sparse, a *commuter marriage* in which spouses live apart, offers some couples economic and career benefits otherwise unavailable to them. Perhaps not surprising, considering commuter couples have fewer young children than other couples, commuter couples in one study reported less stress and less role overload than their single-residence counterparts. Still, the happiest commuter marriages appear to be those with frequent reunions (Bunker et al. 1992).

Perhaps the linkages between work and family are no better illustrated than in the American military family. Nancy Shea (1941: vii) wrote to Army wives in 1941:

You are wondering where you fit into the over-all picture in national and mutual defense and just what part you play on the National Security Team as an Army wife. I assure you that you are not only a significant factor in your husband's career but an important though "silent" member of the team. In the individual Service family . . . it is teamwork and loyalty between a military man and his wife that spell success.

As recent military deployments attest, Shea's version of the Service family as the husband private, noncommissioned officer, or officer with the dependent wife and their children is outmoded. Today the service members in Shea's "Service family" may be a woman, a man, or both!

The military services require single parents and two-parent couples, when both parents are serving, to complete a *Family Care Plan* ("How to Survive Double Deployment" 2003). The *Family Care Plan* specifies custody and financial arrangements in the event the parent or parents are deployed. As the military situation following the bombing of the World Trade Center on September 11, 2001, demonstrated, those deployments can come quickly, with only weeks', days', or even hours' notice. Such deployments may require parents to be separated from their children for weeks, months, or even years in the event of a longer military action.

Couples in a family business have their own set of tensions, often resulting from the blending of two social systems: family and business. Recently, Danes and Lee (2004) extended their research on family business dynamics to farm-business-owning couples. They found husbands tended to place profit as the highest priority; wives tended to place good family relationships as the highest priority. Tensions were highest in farm-owning families with preschool children and those in which family assets were transferred to the business. Decreased tension was associated with having a high level of functional integrity in the family system, having a wife who was satisfied with her role in the family business, and having the husband place family over business in importance (Danes and Lee).

Couples Linking Work and Family

Shea's (1941) model of the Service family exemplifies the *two-person single career*. The spouse, usually the wife, engages in contributions that advance their spouse's career and their spouse's employer. The religious ministry, elected and appointed political office, and executive positions in the corporate sector are professions that have traditionally been organized around the two-person single career. Testimony to the importance of the two-person single career can be found in the difficulty women experience climbing the corporate or other career ladders without someone in the role of supportive "wife."

Working- and middle-class couples are increasingly *dual-earner couples* in which both partners are employed. Some sociologists distinguish between *dual-worker couples* (those in which both partners are employed) and *dual-career couples* (those in which both partners are employed in professional or managerial positions). However, one member of the couple may be pursuing a career, whereas the other expects to enter and leave employment, especially during periods of life-course transition (e.g., saving for children's college expenses; in the years immediately prior to or following retirement).

Work, or rather stressful work roles with little support, is hazardous to family health. Voydanoff's (2004) analysis of data from the *National Study of the Changing Workforce* indicates work–family conflict has a strong association with time- and strain-based work demands. On the other hand, families with time-based family support policies and work–family organizational support is associated with lower family conflict.

Innovations in Work–Family Connections

Families have always had to accommodate family members' work outside the home. Only more recently (and most often in times of economic prosperity and full employment), employers have been called on to make modifications in the workplace to accommodate family priorities. Recent research on military families indicates the workplace can be an important source of support for families (Bowen et al. 2003). Data from the *National Survey of Midlife Development in the United States* confirms the mental health of adults suffers when work and family are in conflict (Grzywacz and Bass 2003). *Flexible scheduling options* and *family leave* can alleviate some of the pressures for working families.

According to the AFL-CIO (2003), most working adults say they have little or no control over their work schedules, more than one fourth of working women spend at least some of their nights and weekends at work, and nearly half of all women work different schedules than their partners. If true, these findings indicate the pressing need for flexible scheduling options.

Adler (1996) estimates 12% of employees have some sort of flexible schedule. These options include *flextime*, with variable starting and ending times to the day, usually around core work hours (e.g., 10 a.m. to 3 p.m.). Other options include *job sharing*, in which two people share one position, as well as working at home or *telecommuting* through the use of telephone, computer, or other technology. Some employers are implementing a *compressed workweek*, in which the workweek is concentrated in fewer days each week or, in one example, in a 9-day work cycle with every other Friday off. Such options may benefit the company in providing for more concentrated work and providing employees with designated days on which to schedule medical or other appointments and even 3-day weekends.

Employees who are offered scheduling options report higher job satisfaction (Schellenbarger 1992a). In a tight hiring market, recruiting, selecting, and training a reliable and productive workforce involves significant costs to any employer. However, the potential benefits for work-friendly practices for not only employee productivity but also organizational loyalty are considerable. In the long term, these benefits might well outweigh the costs.

Some family situations, however, cannot be planned into an employer's work schedule. The birth or adoption of a child, the prolonged illness of a child, partner, or parent, or an employee's own health concerns call for consideration on the part of employers. *Maternity leave*, in which a woman could be absent from her job for a period of time following the birth of a child, has not been a reality for the majority of employed women. In fact, American policies for leave following the birth or adoption of a child lag far behind policies in Western Europe.

With the *Family and Medical Leave Act* of 1993, employers with at least 50 employees are required by federal law to offer their employees, women and men, up to 12 weeks leave to care for a family member. The Act extends not only to mothers but also to fathers, and covers not only care of a child but also care of a spouse, parent, or other family member. However, employers are not required to pay their workers during that time. In fact, most employers do not pay their workers who take family leave or do so for only a very short period of time. During the first 3 years after passage, only 2% of workers took family leave ("Survey" 1996). Most working families need the income.

In virtually every situation, these modifications accommodate women; few men take advantage of these work-friendly policies (Adler 1996). In fact, in her study of a major corporation that offered generous accommodations for families, Hochschild (1997) found women were often reluctant to take advantage of such arrangements. She concluded both men and women preferred the less ambiguous rewards of workplace experience to the higher costs of spending more time at home.

Others may be reluctant to take advantage of family-friendly policies because of the concern, in doing so, they may jeopardize career advancement or, especially in hard economic times, even job security. Such may be the case for women in organizations that create a career-and-family track (i.e., the *mommy track*) for women (and, presumably the *daddy track* for men) who wish to devote less time and commitment to their career and the organization. Schwartz (1989) suggests such policies offer options for parents torn between work and family. Although those parents may well be willing to accept a middle-management position in their organization, will they be willing to accept the lower lifetime earnings and possibly the lower level of job autonomy and job security that come as tradeoffs for the family experience? In a syndicated article for the *Chicago Tribune*, Bonnie Miller Rubin (2003: F1) wrote:

> As the economy sputters and employers try to do more with less, the much-vaunted "Mommy Track" may be veering off course. In prosperous times, when the labor pool was smaller, employees seeking work/family balance could easily secure part-time work, job sharing and generous leaves. Now, job applicants are a dime a dozen and corporate America is asking everyone to work faster, longer, harder.

Research indicates the vast majority—83% according to a study by Belkin (1989)—of employed women feel torn between the demands of their job and wanting to spend more time with their families. *Analysis of the General Social Survey* from 1973 to 1994 indicates that in working families, women have shifted from finding work more satisfying than home to finding a refuge in home and family (Kiecolt 2003).

Research conducted by *Catalyst* ("Two Careers, One Marriage: Making it Work in the Workplace" 1998) indicates husbands and wives value dual-career arrangements. Husbands and wives both see two careers as offering increased freedom to take time off, change jobs, or start a business. Both husbands and wives want maximum flexibility at work, as well as the ability to customize their career paths over the life cycle.

The work–family practices described in this section offer a glimpse into how organizations may recognize the out-of-work lives of their employees. Innovative work–family practices may benefit not only working parents but also other employees who may wish to invest a greater proportion of their time and energy in relationships with parents, spouses, or others in education, leisure, service, or other meaningful life pursuits. Generational shifts in the meanings of work and life balance will influence individuals' desire to participate in such programs, as will the general economic outlook and concerns about financial security.

Eventually, the key may lie in what Moen (1992) has called a *life-course solution*. Moen encourages educators and regular employees, not just employers and parents, to envision a society in which life patterns are frequently reconfigured around the life course to create more options and diversity for everyone, men and women, children and elders in youth, early adulthood, midlife, and later years. Such an approach could reduce the stress, conflict, and ambivalence families experience as they find themselves, for example, caught in the *sandwich generation*, attempting to manage care of younger and older family members while maintaining employment, marriages, and other relationships.

BOX 13.3   *"Patagonia's* Family-Friendly Programs"

Meg Wilkes Karraker, Ph.D.

Most businesses assume family issues are the sole responsibility of each employee. *Patagonia* believes family issues are responsibilities shared by many groups, including employers.

Patagonia, Inc. is a midsized company based in Ventura, California, that employs approximately 1,000 people in six countries. Family-friendly programs are part of *Patagonia*'s heritage. From the earliest years of the company, parents merged their work responsibilities with family responsibilities.

Family-friendly programs at *Patagonia* include flexible work arrangements that permit colleagues to work at home, keep nontraditional hours, share jobs, or work part time. A flexible workweek gives employees the freedom to arrange their professional and personal schedules to meet individual needs.

Patagonia also operates *Great Pacific Child Development Center* onsite at the company offices in Ventura. Opened in 1984, the *Center* accommodates up to 120 children, aged 8 weeks to 9 years. Infant care, preschool, kindergarten, and after-school or summer camp programs run Monday to Friday, 7:30 a.m. to 5:30 p.m. Parents pay tuition comparable to local community rates. Tuition constitutes the majority of the *Center*'s income, supplemented by parent fundraising and company-sponsored events.

Patagonia goes far beyond most American corporations in providing company-sponsored family programs. In addition to a flexible workweek and the onsite child-care center, *Patagonia* employees can take advantage of not only plans, paid child-care leave, a family child-care provider network, and dependent care assistance plans but also adoption assistance, lactation support services, parent education programs, and elder care resources.

The company has found that work satisfaction and productivity increased while families thrived. In a typical year, *Patagonia* subsidizes work and family benefits at a rate of $532,932. The company estimates the direct and indirect quantitative savings to the company as follows:

Employee Retention $350,352
   Savings include the costs of recruitment, training, and productivity.

Federal Tax Deductions $154,666
   Approximately 35 percent of the program's subsidy is deductible as a cost of doing business.

State Tax Credits $23,918
   California gives state tax credits to employers sponsoring work/family programs.

State Tax Deductions $12,481
   The state also allows various state tax deductions.

Employment Taxes $1,764
   When applicable, employment taxes from pretax payroll programs are reduced.

Weighing the costs of the programs against the savings outlined previously, the total dollar benefit to the company in a typical year was $10,249. Although difficult to assign a dollar value, the qualitative benefits are even more valuable. Increased morale and productivity, coupled with reduction in absenteeism, makes *Patagonia* workers extremely productive and dedicated to the success of the company. The visibility of the family service programs gives *Patagonia* a recruiting advantage in periods when the labor market is very tight.

_____

Source: Adapted and quoted with permission from *Family Services* © Patagonia, Inc. 1998.

Moen and her colleagues have begun to investigate family-friendliness in communities in which dual-earner couples live. Their early research indicates living in a neighborhood with many other families with children is associated with a couple's higher ratings of a community's family-friendliness. Moen and her colleagues call this match between stage in the family life cycle and neighborhood's demographic structure the life stage neighborhood fit (Swisher, Sweet, and Moen 2004) In the same vein we argued in chapter 11 for an extension of the meaning of family and kin to a broader community, here we suggest this is only the beginning of community analyses taking into account family life-cycle, demographics, employment, leisure, spiritual, and other societal linkages.

HOUSEHOLD LABOR: HOMEMAKING AND HOUSEWORK

Work can be defined as energy expended to accomplish a task. Most of this chapter has focused on the importance of *employment*, that is, work for pay outside the home. In this final section of chapter 13, we examine the impact of *household labor*, that is, homemaking and housework, as an important part of the *family economy*.

The contribution of family members engaged in unpaid family work is not reflected in any official economic indicators of national productivity. Nonetheless, maintaining the family's residence and possessions, managing the family members' time and activities, and seeing to the psychic and emotional needs of family members and the family as a whole demand a remarkable investment of time, as well as physical, intellectual, and emotional energy. Although the type and amount of household labor have always varied widely by social class, advances in household technology over the last century have probably raised the standards for homemaking rather than reduced the time required to complete household tasks.

The Division of Household Labor

The last half of the 20th century brought revolutionary changes in women's participation in education, employment, and other public spheres. The average hours women spend on housework per week has likewise changed, from 30.0 hours in 1965 to 17.5 hours in 1995 (Bianchi and Casper 2000). The average number of hours men spend on housework has increased, from 4.9 hours in 1965 to 10.0 hours in 1996.

Women still contribute, on the average, two thirds of the hours to unpaid labor in the family. Indeed, Hochschild (1989) charges the typical, employed woman with a family essentially faces a *second shift* when she leaves her place of employment and arrives home, where another set of tasks and responsibilities await her. Hochschild argues this results in a *leisure gap* between husbands and wives. Such a gap not only reduces the time available for couples and families to spend together but also cannot help but result in anger and resentment in already time-starved families.

Gender variations in time spent in housework would seem to be effected by three factors: time to engage in domestic tasks, relative power between husband and wife, and attitudes surrounding gender roles. Indeed, husband's participation in housework bears little relationship to wife's employment (Bird, Bird, and Scruggs 1984; Blumstein and Schwartz 1991; Brayfield 1992; Coverman 1985; Ericksen, Yancey, and Ericksen 1979; Ross 1987). Fathers do not even increase their housework hours in families when mothers decrease the amount of time spent on housework due to employment (Marini and Shelton 1993).

Husband's education, a resource for marital power, appears to be more significant than wife's education in predicting time he engages in housework. The more education he has, the less likely he is to engage in housework (Coverman 1985). Findings regarding income (as another resource for marital power) are inconsistent. Research seems to suggest the more income a husband has, the less likely he is to contribute to household work (Ross 1987). Further, the more essential a wife's earnings to the family, the more the husband and children contribute to housework (Perry-Jenkins and Crouter 1990).

Arrighi and Maume's (2000) research supports the conclusion traditional masculine identity is supported by the avoidance of housework, as well as autonomy and control in the paid workforce. Their research indicates men whose masculinity is challenged in the workplace will be more likely to resist performing tasks traditionally associated with femininity, that is, housework. Retirees, both men and women, spend more time performing household tasks in both their own and their spouses' domain than do employed men and women (Szinovacz 2000).

Employed women who do not find their husbands contributing to household labor report not only emotional distress (Kessler and McCrae 1982; Kraus and Markides 1985; Pleck 1985), but also marital conflict (Barnett and Baruch 1987; Staines and Libby 1986). Children who have the opportunity to contribute to household tasks may learn responsibility and gain a sense of competence and contribution to the family, thus building self-esteem. However, research on children's contribution to housework indicates children's contribution is not regular and represents a small amount of the total household investment (Coltrane 2000). Some couples, especially upper-income, dual-earner couples hire household help. However, even there, women are likely to be the ones who arrange and coordinate these outside services (Thompson 1991).

For some women, housework remains closely identified with their identity as a good wife and mother. In other words, housework and homemaking have a symbolic meaning for women beyond that for which men are socialized. Still, Hochschild (1989) has referred to the reluctance of men to fully participate in housework a "stalled revolution." Until men engage fully in the domestic tasks necessary to maintain family life, women will continue to be profoundly disadvantaged in the paid labor force. Arrighi and Maume (2000: 465) argue:

> ... those men who are reticent to take on more of the daily household tasks inadvertently contribute to the disruption of women's labor force efforts and depress their earnings.

Full-Time Homemakers

More than one third of women with children are full-time homemakers (United States Bureau of Labor Statistics 2001a). Statistics on the number of men who take on the role of full-time homemaker are more difficult to determine. Edelman Financial Services (2002) estimate the replacement value of a homemaker's component jobs (e.g., child-care worker, housekeeper, and food and beverage service worker) would be $635,724. This is based on 17 key occupations at the median salary for each, for example, child-care worker

($18,179), housekeeper ($15,410), dietitian or nutritionist ($38,313). Nonetheless, the self esteem of the full-time homemaker is frequently challenged. In the words of one homemaker who decided to enter college: "You don't get awards for keeping house" (Hammons-Bryner 1991: 151–52).

Women with children, especially those with infants, are often of the opinion they are the best care providers for their children (Hock, Gnezda, and McBride 1984). Furthermore, in qualitative research on full-time homemakers, Karraker and Hammons-Bryner (1993) found what they described as a sense of entitlement some women feel toward the homemaker role. A significant proportion of homemakers enjoy their work (Glass 1992). Full-time homemakers who report great satisfaction from their role are those for whom remaining at home is the fulfillment of a preferred lifestyle choice and not a default due to inability to secure employment (Klein et al. 1998).

Gove and Tudor (1973) found characteristics of the traditional homemaker role contribute to the higher rate of certain types of mental illness among women. Among both working- and middle-class women, although many women like being full-time homemakers, many find housework tasks themselves lacking in satisfaction (Hochschild 1989). American society places a high value on individual achievement and extrinsic reward. Furthermore, American culture devalues unpaid labor performed by anyone. Such a society and such a culture surely contributes to the poor esteem in which homemaking is held.

Society perhaps no better reveals the disregard in which homemaking is held than when we consider the plight of *displaced homemakers*. These women, often older, due to divorce, desertion, widowhood, or disability of their spouse, find themselves without financial support.

To your authors, what Parker-Pope and Pope (2001: D6), authors of the *Wall Street Journal* column "A Balanced Life," have described as "a firestorm over stay-at-home moms" seems oddly misplaced. As Parke-Reimer, a stay-at-home mother with postgraduate education describes in Box 13.4, "the work is only half the struggle." Many, perhaps most, women are full-time homemakers at some point in the life cycle, often immediately after the birth of a child or upon their own retirement.

BOX 13.4 "The Work Is Only Half the Struggle"
Katie Parke-Reimer

People often ask me if I work. I tell them, "Yes. But nobody pays me." Usually people say, "Oh, you're a stay-at-home mom. How nice." As much as I love my work, I wouldn't call it "nice." Caring for two spirited daughters is intense social, emotional, physical, and, yes, intellectual work. I don't get pay, sick days, social security credits, or even bathroom breaks. I'm accompanied to the bathroom by a year-old who desperately wants to be held or is plotting to throw something in the toilet the second I stand up (most recently a flashlight), and a 3-year-old who has pressing questions such as: "Why don't we have tails? Why doesn't anyone live in the vacuum cleaner? What are penises for?" I tend to constant needs, 10 or more hours a day with no down time.

I'm my own boss, in a sense, and I don't cut myself a lot of slack. I evaluate how well I'm doing my work, I make changes, I make a point to keep learning about children and parenting. My husband is a teacher, and we talk about kids and kid-related things all the time, not out of duty but out of interest. Just as in any profession, you can do the bare minimum of work and be bored, but being truly engaged with kids all day long is challenging and well worth the effort. My kids and I feel very connected to each other, and I know being with them full time makes me a better parent than I would be otherwise.

But the work is only half the struggle. Many people give lip service to the value of stay-at-home mothers but don't see what we do as actual work, let alone work that requires knowledge and skill. Even those people who say, "Oh, you do such important work," show their true colors by expressing no interest in it. And I think "Don't you want to talk about language development? About the new playground equipment? Children's books? How about politics?" It's as if people think all I am capable of discussing anymore is laundry detergent and diapers. Just as my work creates a big blank in conversation, it will be a big blank on my resume. It's ironic, because I've never done more valuable work.

Katie Parke-Reimer and her family live in St. Paul, MN. Before becoming a mom, she was a video editor and writer. She earned a B.A. in anthropology from Bates College, Lewiston, ME.

GLOSSARY

Commuter marriage	Leisure gap
Compressed workweek	Life-course solution
Cult of domesticity	Low-income working families
Daddy track	Maternity leave
Displaced homemakers	Mommy track
Dual-career couples	Mother penalty
Dual-earner couples	Occupational segregation
Dual-worker couples	Pink-collar ghetto
Employment	Sandwich generation
Family Care Plan	Second shift
Family economy	Shift work
Family leave	Telecommuting
Family and Medical Leave Act	Trailing spouse
Flexible scheduling	Two-person single-career couples
Flextime	Wage gap
Household labor	Work
Job sharing	

FOR YOUR CONSIDERATION

1. Reflecting on what you have studied in previous chapters, how does social class challenge families' capacities for resiliency?

2. Employment has been viewed as an integral part of masculinity for American males. Is this changing for men? Is employment coming to be an integral part of women's identity as well? In what ways might responses to unemployment be different for men and women? In what ways might their responses to unemployment be similar?

3. In late 2002, a media source reported half of Americans now say family is more important than work. Do you believe such a statement? In practical terms, what does it mean to put family ahead of work?

4. What is at the root of the antagonism between stay-at-home moms and working moms?

FOR FURTHER STUDY: WEB SITES, ORGANIZATIONS AND PUBLICATIONS

Web Sites and Organizations

AFL-CIO's Working Families Agenda
http://www.aflcio.org/issuespolitics/worknfamily/
This site provides information on a variety of work and family issues and information on working family-friendly policies in labor contracts.

Alliance for Work/Life Professionals
http://www.awlp.org/
Academic, business, and public sector professionals who are working for a healthy balance between work and family organize this site.

Catalyst
http://www.catalystwomen.org/
Catalyst is a nonprofit organization that conducts research on women's workplace issues and develops and promotes policies on behalf of women's participation and advancement in corporations.

Cornell Employment and Family Careers Institute
BLCC MVR Hall
Cornell University
Ithaca, NY 14853
Telephone 607-255-6299
http://www.blcc.cornell.edu/cci/
The Cornell Institute is one of several institutes founded with the assistance of the Alfred P. Sloan Foundation. Established in 1997, the Institute's mission is to "conduct research, education, and outreach that promotes understanding of the dramatic changes in . . . families and work and their intersections throughout the life course.

Families and Work Institute
http://www.familiesandwork.org/
The Families and Work Institute is a nonprofit organization for research to inform decision making on workplace, family, and community. This site provides access to publications on work family issues and a link to The Fatherhood Project.

Labor Project for Working Families
Institute of Industrial Relations
University of California
2521 Channing Way # 5555
Berkeley, CA 94720
http://laborproject.berkeley.edu/
This nonprofit organization was founded in 1992 to advocate for family-friendly policies in the workplace. The Project collaborates with unions on collective bargaining, legislation, and public policy on child care, elder care, family leave, flexible work schedules, and other matters related to balancing work and family.

United States Bureau of Labor Statistics

www.bls.gov

This office of the Unites States Department of Labor provides statistical data on work and workers, including employment and income for men, women, and families. This site provides access to the *Monthly Labor Review*.

Working Mom's Internet Refuge

www.moms-refuge.com

This Web site is produced by everyday women juggling families and work and offers information as well as opportunities for participants to share information and opinions.

Publications

Blau, Francine D., and Ronald G. Ehrenberg, eds. 2000. *Gender and Family Issues in the Workplace*. New York, NY: Russell Sage Foundation.

These essays explore the extent to which motherhood remains an obstacle to women's success in the workplace.

Blossfeld, Hans-Peter, and Sonja Drobnic, eds. 2001. *Careers of Couples in Contemporary Society: From Male Breadwinner to Dual-Earner Families*. Oxford, UK: Oxford University Press.

This book enriches our understanding of the interdependence of paid employment and family processes through description of couples in twelve countries. The editors begin with an economic theory of the family, but also present alternatives, including bargaining and marital dependency models.

Community, Work, and Family

This interdisciplinary journal provides a forum for social scientists and practitioners to examine theory, research, policy, and practice concerning the interconnections among family, work, and community.

Gornick, Janet C., and Marcia K. Meyers. 2003. *Families that Work: Policies for Reconciling Parenthood and Employment*. New York: Russell Sage Foundation.

The authors present a comparison of family leave policies and labor market regulations in the United States and other countries. Their analysis leads to the conclusion that the U.S. government needs to take an expanded role to bring work–family standards up to those in many other Western societies.

Hattery, Angela Jean. 2001. *Women, Work and Families: Balancing and Weaving*. Thousand Oaks, CA: Sage.

Hattery conducted intensive interviews with 30 married, employed women with children under the age of 2. She uses structural theory, motherhood theory, and feminist theory to reveal the skills women bring to balancing their obligations to both family and employment.

Hertz, Rosanna, and Nancy L. Marshall, eds. 2001. *Working Families: The Transformation of the American Home*. Berkeley, CA: University of California Press.

This volume includes 18 chapters authored by scholars from many academic disciplines, as well as human resources, and work and family professionals. The chapters examine changing families, changes (or lack of change) in the workplace, the gendered nature of families and the workplace, and the impact of working families on children.

Himmelweit, Susan, ed. 2000. *Inside the Household: From Labour to Care*. New York, NY: St. Martin's.

Chapters in this book ranging from a 1970 "classic" analyzing domestic labor and the impact on employment patterns to studies of the effect of labor force participation on household division of labor, as well as more contemporary work on women's caring activities in the household.

REFERENCES FOR CITED WORKS

Adler, Jerry. 1996. "Building a Better Dad." *Newsweek* June 17: 58–64.

AFL-CIO. 2003. "Work and Family." http://www.aflcio.org/issuespolitics/worknfamily/ (Retrieved 2/7/03).

Armas, Genaro C. 2004. "White Families Widen Wealth Gap with Minorities." *Star Tribune* October 18: A9.

Arrighi, Barbara A., and David J. Maume, Jr. 2000. "Workplace Subordination and Men's Avoidance of Housework." *Journal of Family Issues* 21, 4 (May): 464–87.

Atkinson, T., R. Liem, and J. H. Liem. 1986. "The Social Costs of Unemployment: Implications for Social Support." *Journal of Health and Social Behavior* 27: 317–31.

Barnett, R., and G. Baruch. 1987. "Determinants of Father's Participation in Family Work." *Journal of Marriage and the Family* 49: 29–40.

Belkin, Lisa. 1989. "Bars to Equality of Women Seen as Eroding Slowly." *New York Times* August 20: 1, 26.

Bianchi, Suzanne M., and Lynne M. Casper. 2000. "American Families." *Population Bulletin* 55, 4. Washington, DC: Population Reference Bureau.

Bianchi, Suzanne M., Lynne M. Casper, and Mary Kent. 2001. "American Families Resilient After 50 Years of Change." News Release January 5. Washington, DC: Population Reference Bureau.

Bird, G. W., G. A. Bird, and M. Scruggs. 1984. "Determinants of Family Task Sharing: A Study of Husbands and Wives." *Journal of Marriage and the Family* 39: 345–55.

Blumstein, P., and Pepper Schwartz. 1991. *American Couples*. New York: William Morrow.

Bowen, Gary L., et al. 2003. "Promoting the Adaptation of Military Families: An Empirical Test of a Community Practice Model." *Family Relations* 52, 1: 33–54.

Bowman, P. J. 1993. "The Impact of Economic Marginality Among African American Husbands and Fathers." In *Family Ethnicity: Strength in Diversity*, ed. Harriet Pipes McAdoo. Newbury Park, CA: Sage, 120–37.

Brayfield, April A. 1992. "Employment Resources and Housework in Canada." *Journal of Marriage and the Family* 54: 19–30.

Budig, Michelle J., and Paula England. 2001. "The Wage Penalty for Motherhood." *American Sociological Review* 66: 204–55.

Bunker, Barbara B., et al. 1992. "Quality of Life in Dual-Career Families: Commuting Versus Single-Residence Couples." *Journal of Marriage and the Family* 54, 3 (August): 399–407.

Camasso, J. J. and A. E. Camasso. 1986. "Social Supports, Undesirable Life Events, and Psychological Distress in a Disadvantaged Population." *Social Science Review* 10: 379–94.

CEOGO. 2004. "Women CEOS: In Focus." www.ceogo.com/OTHER/WOMENCEOS/Women_CEOS_In_Focus.html (Retrieved 11/12/2004).

Coltrane, Scott. 2000. "Research on Household Labor: Modeling and Measuring the Social Embeddedness of Routine Family Work." *Journal of Marriage and the Family* 62: 1208–33.

Conger, Rand D., K. J. Conger, Glen H. Elder, Jr., F. O. Lorenz, R. L. Simons, and L. B. Witbeck. 1992. "A Family Process Model of Economic Hardship and Adjustment of Early Adolescent Boys." *Child Development* 63: 526–41.

Conger, Rand D., and Glen H. Elder, Jr. 1994. *Families in Troubled Times*. New York: Aldine de Gruyter.

Coverman, S. 1985. "Explaining Husbands' Participation in Domestic Labor." *Sociological Quarterly* 26: 81–97.

Danes, Sharon M., and Yoon G. Lee. 2004. "Tensions Generated by Business Issues in Farm Business-Owning Couples." *Family Relations* 53, 4 (July): 357–66.

Danziger, Sandra, Elizabeth Oltmans Ananat, and Kimberly G. Browning. 2004. "Childcare Subsidies and the Transition from Welfare to Work." *Family Relations* 53, 2 (March): 219–28.

Dodson, Lisa, and Jillian Dickert. 2004. "Girls' Family Labor in Low-Income Households: A Decade of Qualitative Research." *Journal of Marriage and the Family* 66, 3 (May): 318–32.

Edelman Financial Services. 2002. "How Much is Your Mother Worth this Mother's Day? Try $635,724." www.RicEdelman.com/prnews/pressrelease.asp?article=020506. (Retrieved 2/21/03).

Ericksen, J. A., W. L. Yancy, and E. P. Ericksen. 1979. "The Division of Family Roles." *Journal of Marriage and the Family* 41: 301–14.

Fields, Jason, and Lynne M. Casper. 2001. *America's Families and Living Arrangements: Population Characteristics*. Current Population Reports P20-537. Washington, DC: Government Printing Office.

Glass, Jennifer. 1992. "Housewives and Employed Wives: Demographic and Attitudinal Change, 1972–1986." *Journal of Marriage and the Family* 54: 559–69.

Gomel, Jessica N., Barbara J. Tinsley, Ross D. Parke, and Kathleen M. Clark. 1998. "The Effects of Economic Hardship on Family Relationships Among African American, Latino, and Euro-American Families." *Journal of Family Issues* 19, 4 (July): 436–67.

Gove, Walter R., and Jeannette F. Tudor. 1973. "Adult Sex Roles and Mental Illness." *American Journal of Sociology* 78, 4: 812–35.

Grzywacz, Joseph G., and Brenda L. Bass. 2003. "Work, Family, and Mental Health: Testing Different Models of Work-Family Fit." *Journal of Marriage and Family* 65, 1 (February): 248–62.

Hammons-Bryner, Sue. 1991. *"No Crystal Stair": An Ethnographic Study of the Social Construction of Achievement in Rural Females.* Doctoral dissertation. Tallahassee, FL: Florida State University.

Harrison, A. O., M. N. Wilson, C. J. Pina, S. Q. Chan, and R. Buriel. 1990. "Family Ecologies of Ethnic Minority Children." *Child Development* 61: 347–62.

Hashima, P. Y., and Paul R. Amato. 1994. "Poverty, Social Support, and Parental Behavior." *Child Development* 64: 394–403.

Hochschild, Arlie Russell (with A. Machung). 1989. *The Second Shift.* New York: Viking.

Hochschild, Arlie Russell. 1997. *Time Bind: When Work Becomes Home and Home Becomes Work.* New York, NY: Henry Holt.

Hock, Ellen, M. Therese Gnezda, and Susan L. McBride. 1984. "Mothers of Infants: Attitudes toward Employment and Motherhood following Birth of the First Child." *Journal of Marriage and the Family* 46, 2 (May): 425–31.

"How to Survive Double Deployment." 2003. *USAA Magazine* March: 20–21.

Karraker, Meg Wilkes, and Sue Hammons-Bryner. 1993. "Home Work: A Reassessment of Scholarship on Homemakers and Housework with Implications for Future Study." *West Georgia College Studies in the Social Sciences* XXXI (June): 31–50.

Kessler, R., and J. McCrae. 1982. "The Effects of Wives' Employment on the Mental Health of Married Men and Women." *American Sociological Review* 47: 216–27.

Kiecolt, K. Jill. 2003. "Satisfaction with Work and Family Life: No Evidence of a Cultural Reversal." *Journal of Marriage and Family* 65, 1 (February): 23–35.

Klein, Marjorie H., et al. 1998. "Maternity Leave, Role Quality, Work Involvement, and Mental Health One Year After Delivery." *Psychology of Women Quarterly* 22, 2: 239–66.

Kraus, N., and K. Markides. 1985. "Employment and Psychological Well-Being in Mexican-American Women." *Journal of Health and Social Behavior* 26: 15–26.

"Layoffs Deliver Storm of Emotional Troubles." 2002. *USA Today* October 29. http://www.intelihealth.com/ IH/ihtPrint/EMIHCOOO/333/7228/357406.html?hide-t&k-basePrint (Retrieved 11-9-02).

Lorenz, F. O., Rand D. Conger, and R. Montague. 1994. "Doing Worse and Feeling Worse: Psychological Consequences of Economic Hardship." In *Families in Troubled Times*, eds. Rand D. Conger and Glenn H. Elder. New York, NY: Aldine de Gruyter, 167–86.

Marini, M. M., and B. A. Shelton. 1993. "Measuring Household Work: Recent Experience in the United States." *Social Science Research* 22: 361–82.

Meier, Peg. 2002. "Good Cop, Bad Spouse? How Police Fare at Home." *Star Tribune* October 12: B3.

Meyers, Mike. 2001. "Under Pressure in the New Economy." *Star Tribune* January 22: D1, D5.

Minnesota Legislative Commission on the Economic Status of Women. 2002. Newsletter # 262 (November).

Moen, Phyllis. 1992. *Women's Two Roles: A Contemporary Dilemma.* New York, NY: Auburn.

O'Hare, William P. 2003. "Tracking the Trends in Low-Income Working Families." Washington, DC: Population Reference Bureau. www.prb.org/Template.cfm?Se. . ./ContentDisplay.cfm&ContentID=6928 (Retrieved 2/17/03).

Padavic, Irene. 1992. "White-collar Work Values and Women's Interests in Blue-Collar Jobs." *Gender & Society* 6, 2 (June): 215–30.

Parker-Pope, Tara, and Kyle Pope. 2001. "A Firestorm Over Stay-at-Home Moms." *Star Tribune* February 25: D1.

Perrucci, C. C., and D. B. Targ. 1988. "Effects of a Plant Closing on Marriage and Family Life. In *Families and Economic Distress: Coping Strategies and Social Policy,* eds. P. Voydanoff and L.C. Maijka. Newbury Park, CA: Sage, 55–72.

Perry-Jenkins, Maureen, and Ann C. Crouter. 1990. "Men's Provider Role Attitudes: Implications for Household Work and Marital Satisfaction." *Journal of Family Issues* 11, 1 (January): 136–56.

Pleck, J. H. 1985. *Working Wives/Working Husbands.* Beverly Hills, CA: Sage.

Population Reference Bureau. 2001a. "How Does the Average Number of Work Years of U.S. Women Compare with that of U.S. Men?" Quick Facts, June. Washington, DC: Population Reference Bureau. www.prb.org/template.cfm?Section=QuickFacts (Retrieved 2/17/03).

Population Reference Bureau. 2001b. "Husbands and Wives and the U.S. Workforce." Quick Facts, June. Washington, DC: Population Reference Bureau. www.prb.org/template.cfm?Section=QuickFacts (Retrieved 2/17/03).

Population Reference Bureau. 2001c. "Is It Common in the United States for Mothers of Preschoolers to be in the Work Force?" Quick Facts, August. Washington, DC: Population Reference Bureau. www.prb.org/template.cfm?Section=QuickFacts (Retrieved 2/17/03).

Population Reference Bureau. 2002. "What Percentage of the U.S. Population Lives in Poverty?" Quick Facts, July. Washington, DC: Population Reference Bureau. www.prb.org/template.cfm?Section=QuickFacts (Retrieved 2/17/03).

Presser, Harriet B. 2000. "Nonstandard Work Schedules and Marital Instability." *Journal of Marriage and the Family* 62, 1: 93–110.

Rayman, P. 1988. "Unemployment and Family Life: The Meaning for Children." In *Families and Economic Distress: Coping Strategies and Social Policy*, eds. P. Voydanoff and L. C. Maijka. Newbury Park, CA: Sage, 119–34.

Roos, Patricia A., and Catherine W. Jones. 1993. "Shifting Gender Boundaries: Women's Inroads into Academic Sociology." *Work and Occupations* 20: 395–428.

Ross, C. E. 1987. "The Division of Labor at Home." *Social Forces* 65: 816–33.

Rubin, Bonnie Miller. 2003. "More Workers Hop Off Mommy Track." *The State* January 5: F1, F3.

Schnittker, Jason. 2004. "Working More, Paid Less, and Feeling Better: Women's Health, Employment, and Family Life, 1974–2000." Paper presented at the annual meetings of the *American Sociological Association*, San Francisco, August.

Schwartz, Felice. 1989. "The 'Mommy-Track' Isn't Anti-Woman." *New York Times* March 22: A27.

Shea, Nancy. 1941. *The Army Wife*, 3/e (revised). New York, NY: Harper & Brothers.

Shellenbarger, Sue. 1992a. "Employees Take Pains to Make Flextime Work." *Wall Street Journal* August 18: B1.

Shellenbarger, Sue. 1992b. "Work & Family: Flexible Policies May Slow Women's Careers." *Wall Street Journal* April 22.

Staines, G., and P. Libby. 1986. "Men and Women in Role Relationships." In *The Social Psychology of Female-Male Relations: A critical Analysis of Central Concepts*, eds. R. D. Ashmore and F. K. DelBoca. San Diego, CA: Academic Press, 211–58.

Steuerle, C. Eugene. 2004. "The Incredible Shrinking Budget for Working Families and Children." *Family Focus On . . . Inequalities and Families*, Issue FF23 (September): Minneapolis, MN: National Council on Family Relations.

"Survey: Few Workers Use 'Emergency' Unpaid Leave." 1996. *The New York Times* May 3.

Swisher, Raymond, Stephen Sweet, and Phyllis Moen. 2004. "The Family-Friendly Community and Its Life Course Fit for Dual-Earner Couples. *Journal of Marriage and the Family* 66, 2 (May): 281–92.

Szinovacz, Maximiliane E. 2000. "Changes in Housework After Retirement: A Panel Analysis." *Journal of Marriage and the Family* 62, 1: 78–92.

Thompson, Linda. 1991. "Family Work: Women's Sense of Fairness." *Journal of Family Issues* 12, 2 (March): 181–96.

Thompson, M. S., and M. E., Ensminger. 1989. "Psychological Well-being Among Mothers with School Age Children: Evolving Family Structures." *Social Forces* 63: 715–30.

"Two Careers, One Marriage: Making it Work in the Workplace." 1998. www.catalystwomen.org/research/work.htm (Retrieved 2/18/04).

United States Bureau of the Census. 1975. *Historical Statistics, Colonial Times to 1970.* Washington, DC: Government Printing Office.

United States Bureau of the Census. 1998. *Statistical Abstract of the United States, 1998.* Washington, DC: Government Printing Office.

United States Bureau of the Census. 2000. *Summary File 4, Matrices PCT 138, PCT139, and PCT 140. QP-P31.* Washington, DC: Government Printing Office.

United States Bureau of the Census. 2001. *Statistical Abstract of the United States, 2001.* Washington, DC: Government Printing Office.

United States Bureau of the Census. 2003a. *Statistical Abstract of the United States, 2002.* Table 657. Washington, DC: Government Printing Office.

United States Bureau of the Census. 2003b. *Statistical Abstract of the United States, 2002.* Table 660. Washington, DC: Government Printing Office.

United States Bureau of Labor Statistics. 2001a. *Employment Statistics of Families in 2000.* April 19. Washington, DC: Bureau of Labor Statistics. www.bls.gov/news.release/famee (Retrieved 2/17/03).

United States Bureau of Labor Statistics. 2001b. *Highlights of Women's Earnings in 2000.* Report 952. August. Washington, DC: Government Printing Office.

United States Bureau of Labor Statistics. 2002. *Current Population Survey.* Washington, DC: Government Printing Office.

Voydanoff, Patricia. 2004. "The Effects of Work Demands and Resources on Work-to-Family Conflict and Facilitation." *Journal of Marriage and the Family* 66, 3 (May): 398–412.

Voydanoff, P., and B.W. Donnelly. 1988. "Economic Distress, Family Coping and Quality of Family Life." In *Families and Economic Distress: Coping Strategies and Social Policy*, eds. P. Voydanoff and L. C. Maijka. Newbury Park, CA: Sage, 97–116.

Voydanoff, P., and L. Wilson. 1990. "Maternal Behavior, Social Support, and Economic Conditions as Predictors of Distress in Children." In *Economic Stress: Effects on Family Life and Child Development*, eds. V. C. McLoyd and C. A. Flanagan. San Francisco, CA: Jossey-Bass, 49–69.

Welter, Barbara. 1978. "The Cult of True Womanhood, 1820–1960." In *The American Family in Social Historical Perspective*, ed. Michael Goodman. New York, NY: St. Martin's, 373–92.

Wilhelm, M. S., and C. A. Ridley. 1988. "Stress and Unemployment in Rural Nonfarm couples: A Study of Hardships and Coping Resources." *Family Relations* 37: 50–54.

Winkler, Anne E. 1998. "Earnings of Husbands and Wives in Dual-earner Families." *Monthly Labor Review* 121: 42–48.

Epilogue

CHAPTER

14

FROM "FAMILY VALUES" TO VALUING FAMILIES

CHAPTER PREVIEW

In this final chapter we address *social policy* and its relationship to *law* and *practice*. We discuss *family policy* and the standard of *family well-being*, as well as *direct effects* and *indirect effects* and *manifest consequences* and *latent consequences* of policy. We use *Aid to Families with Dependent Children (AFDC)*, the *Personal Responsibility and Work Opportunity Reconciliation Act (PRWORC),* and *Temporary Assistance for Needy Families (TANF)* as illustrations. Finally, we suggest the value of *family impact statements* as a way to gauge the impression of social policies on families.

    We also introduce you, our reader, to *family life education*. Family life educators work across the life cycle. They are employed in a variety of occupations and practice in a range of organizational settings. The *National Council of Family Relations* offers certification for individuals who wish to become family life educators. These professionals share a belief that "good families don't just happen."

Finally, we address the connections among community, culture, and families, noting so-cial attitudes, prejudices, and stereotypes often come to be translated into political agenda. While the consequences of future trends remain uncertain, families and communities can make choices as they face the future. Families thrive as Strategic Living Communities © precisely because they can creatively and proactively engage future trends. (We offer the example of *e-families*.) At times society seems not quite sure what we want with regard to families. However, in the face of changing environments, we, your authors, affirm all families are *Families with Futures*.

As we have demonstrated throughout this book, the study of families is controversial and often politicized. In this final chapter, we consider the broader social implications of the scholarship we have presented in the previous chapters. We explore the domain of family policy. We introduce you to the profession of family life education. Finally, we extend a challenge to move beyond *familiar* values using what you have learned in this book to make conscious choices, not only in your own family relationships but also in how you view and value others' families.

FAMILY POLICY

Social policy is a collection of social goals as well as legislation that is intended to achieve some measure of social well-being. *Law* refers to legislation enacted by a political body. *Practice* is the everyday execution or implementation of law and policy as put into action (or inaction) in real life. For example, a legislative body may enact laws aimed at improving the well-being of families, but unless the law is accompanied by adequate funding and qual-ified oversight, the legislation is unlikely to have any real effect on the quality of family life.

An emphasis on individual responsibility, limited government, and confidence in the marketplace to solve social problems contributes to limited spending on family benefits in the United States compared to other countries (Danziger, Danziger, and Stern 1997). The U.S. Congress has enacted legislation directed at families, including the child tax credit, dependent care tax credit, tax credit for college expenses, and unpaid family leave. Still, some scholars argue the United States lacks a comprehensive family policy (Cornia 1997).

The United States (as well as Austria and the United Kingdom) spend considerably less than do other post-industrial, Western countries (e.g., Belgium, Denmark, Finland, France, and Sweden) on programs directed at families. For example, between 1980 and 1998, the United States spent between 0.8% and 1.3% of its gross national product on family benefits. During the same period, Sweden spent between 3.3% and 5.1% of its gross national product on family benefits (Ozawa 2004).

These differences reflect different social agenda and values among societies. Beginning in the 1960s, Sweden developed comprehensive policies to address two specific policy issues (Ozawa 2004: 301–302):

1. What could the Swedish government do to facilitate the life process of women as workers and parents? What would it take for women with children to participate in the labor market as full-fledged members, regardless of their family structures?

2. How could the Swedish government provide a national minimum income for all children, regardless of the backgrounds of their parents?

In contrast to the philosophy that guides American legislators: "...the Swedish gov-ernment aspired to have greater equality between the genders and greater equity among

TABLE 14.1

Selected Family Policies Enacted by the Federal Government, 1990–1998.

Year	Legislation	Intended Family Impact
1990	Child Care and Development Block Grant	Improve child care at the state level.
1992	Child Support Recovery Act	Criminalize failure to pay child support.
1993	Family and Medical Leave Act	Provide unpaid leave to care for seriously ill member.
1993	Family Preservation and Support Act	Fund community-based family services.
1993	Intenational Parental Kidnapping Crime Act	Criminalize as a felony child abduction by parent.
1993	National Child Protection Act	Encourage criminal background checks on child-care providers.
1994	Educate American Act	Promote parental involvement in education.
1994	Full Faith and Credit for Child Support Orders Act	Enforce child support orders across state lines.
1994	Violence Against Women Act	Fund services for battered women.
1996	Defense of Marriage Act	Legally define marriage as heterosexual union.
1996	Personal Responsibility and Work Opportunity Reconciliation Act	End entitlement and set time limits on welfare to needy families.
1996	Telecommunications Reform Law	Mandate television V-chips to enable parents to screen programs.
1998	Deadbeat Parents Act	Criminalize as a felony evasion of child support across state lines.

Source: Adapted with permission from Bogenschneider, Karen. 2000. "Has Family Policy Come of Age? A Decade of Review of the State of U.S. Family Policy in the 1990s." *Journal of Marriage and the Family* 62, 4 (November): 1136–59.

children" (302). As a consequence, Swedish family policy is in intent and effect "inclusive, enabling, developmental, and nonmoralistic" (302). In other words, Swedish family policy aims to assist all children and their families, while defining no family structure as deviant.

Gallagher, columnist and affiliate scholar at the *Institute for American Values*, attributes most domestic social ills to the decline in marriage (Burris 2002). Although your authors disagree with much of the rhetoric about the decline of the family, we affirm family systems are tightly interwoven with economics, education, government, religion, and other social systems.

Zimmerman (1995: 3) defines *family policy* as "a collection of separate but interrelated policy choices that aim to address problems that families are perceived as experiencing in society." In this book we address a range of the problems families face, including establishing and maintaining resilient relationships in the face of changing social constructions of time and family health, intimate partnerships and relationships among parents, children, kin, and community. We have also examined some of the problems that beset families as places where conflict, power, and sometimes violence are exercised and where economic conditions must be negotiated.

Myrdal (1968) has opined all social policy is family policy. Zimmerman (1995: 4) argues strongly family policy can be viewed as "everything governments do that affects families." Family policy can be organized around six systems that constitute general social welfare:

- Health
- Education

- Social services
- Income maintenance
- Housing
- Employment

Using some of the same categories, Shirer (1993) encapsulates families as (a) *At Risk*, those that fail to meet their needs, with limited growth potential for family members; (b) *Safe*, those that are secure, with the potential to move forward, and (c) *Thriving*, those that are continually growing, contributing to family and community well-being.

In general, regardless of the domain, family well-being is shorthand for the strategic goal of family policy. As we have seen throughout this book, controversy rather than agreement often characterizes social intents with regard to the family. By way of illustration, one of the explicit objectives of the *Welfare Reform Act of 1996* was "to end dependence by promoting marriage" (Coontz and Folbre 2002). Likewise, the Vatican (an autonomous state which holds a seat in the United Nations) affirms the "need for an integral development of the person and of societies." The Vatican advocates family policy grounded in a particular construction of family as organized around marriage, that is,

> ...marriage and [sustaining] parents, fathers and mothers, in their mutual and responsible decisions with regard to the procreation and education of children. (Cassar 1999: 26).

Furthermore, the Vatican's insistence that a particular construction of the meaning of "respect for life and the dignity of the human person" be the foundation for population policy continues to have a dramatic influence on policies concerning not only abortion but also family planning and reproductive health across the world.

Family policy may be described as having *direct effects* or *indirect effects* and as having *manifest consequences* or *latent consequences*. Some states are currently considering repeal of the ban on first-cousin marriages—an example of direct family policy. The proposed repeal is in response to cultural customs from Hmong and other recent immigrant groups whose traditions favor such marriage patterns. (Efforts to repeal prohibitions against cousin-marriage also find support in recent evidence refuting the dire negative genetic consequences for births resulting from such unions.) As an example of indirect effects, when welfare-to-work programs increase parents' work hours and income, children's school performance improves (Meekler 2002).

We can refer to the intended effects of social policies as manifest consequences. The judicial systems in all 50 states include a juvenile court, a family court, or both. The manifest function of those courts is to enforce social standards regarding families and members' responsibilities and behaviors and to protect those who are unable to protect themselves. The courts are empowered to intervene when families cannot or will not care for, protect, or control their children. Standards of confidentiality in courts' dealings with family are intended to protect the privacy of those families and their members (McPhail 2000).

However, the *National Council of Juvenile and Family Court Judges* advocates reexamining and relaxing the long-standing ethic of strict confidentiality. McPhail (2000) argues such strict confidentiality impedes public confidence. Writing as a member of the *National Council of Juvenile and Family Court Judges*, McPhail, a county and youth court judge from Mississippi, finds:

> A community has a right to know how courts deal with its children and families. The court should be open to the media, interested professionals and students, and, when appropriate, the

public, in order to hold itself accountable, educate others and encourage greater community participation.

The *Personal Responsibility and Work Opportunity Reconciliation Act (PRWORC)* of 1996 is directly intended to shift national welfare policy from a system of entitlement to a system that would encourage independence and reduce welfare dependency for individuals and their families. Welfare reform as embodied in *PRWORC* intends to rely explicitly on three pillars: promoting self-sufficiency, protecting children, and strengthening marriage (Horn 2002). However, *PRWORC* may contribute indirect effects and latent consequences if couples form marriages or remain together under horrific circumstances, thus subjecting spouses and children to even deeper damaging effects of abuse, chemical dependency, or other serious family problems.

Shehan (2003) names three primary purposes of family policy. First, policies like the 60-year-old *Aid to Families with Dependent Children (AFDC)* which was replaced in 1996 by *Temporary Assistance for Needy Families (TANF)* are intended to assist families or family members in need. Second, legislation such as laws against fornication, prohibiting sexual intercourse between unmarried people, is intended to control families or regulate individual behavior. Third, as we describe in chapter 8 with regard to federal funding intended to encourage or support marriage, policy may be intended to change or challenge emerging trends in the family. Although of a less specific nature, the social agenda advocated by the *Call to Motherhood Movement* supports workplace and other policies that will acknowledge and support the role of women as nurturers of their children (Levine 2003).

Family policy is not just the purview of the federal government. State and regional governments, counties and cities, and even smaller units such as school boards enact legislation and organize programs that embody policies affecting families. At a more global level, the United Nations, *Family Health International*, and *Family Care International* debate and enact family policy.

Government agencies such as the *National Institute of Child Health and Development* are explicitly charged with making policy recommendations to affect children and their families. Nonprofit organizations such as the *Children's Defense Fund, Council on Contemporary Families*, the *Institute for American Values*, and the *Joint Center for Poverty Research* at the University of Chicago are in the "business" of recommending and assessing family policy (albeit on different "sides" of many questions).

Calling the gap between family research and family policy "the great divide," Bogenscheider, Friese, and Balling (2002) concede social scientists produce high quality research more effectively than they communicate this research into policy making. This occurs, they argue, because the goals, languages, needs, and values of researchers and policy makers are distinctly different.

One solution to this gap is *Family Impact Seminars*. These *Seminars* provide briefings, discussions, and newsletters around family issues of concern to legislators, other elected officials, their aides, and representatives of government agencies. While family scientists must engage in research meeting the highest scholarly standards, policy makers have less need for methodological details than for timely, comprehensive overviews of issues with an emphasis on program evaluation. Ideally, the briefing should be accompanied by rich anecdotes, descriptions, or quotations, that is, qualitative data.

When social actions are anticipated to have impact on the physical environment, we consider environmental impact statements. When social actions are anticipated to have impact on the economic environment, we consider economic impact statements. Why then, when social actions are anticipated to have impacts on families, do we not consider *family impact statements*?

BOX 14.1   Principles and Checklist for Assessing the Impact of Policies and Programs on Families[1]

Principle 1. Family Support and Responsibilities

Policies and programs should aim to support family functioning and provide substitute services only as a last resort.
   Does the program:
   —Support and supplement parents' and other family members' ability to carry out their responsibilities?
   —Provide for incentives for other persons to take over family functioning when doing so may not be necessary?
   —Strengthen adult children's ties to their elderly parents?
   —Enforce absent parents' obligations to provide financial support for their children?

Principle 2. Family Membership and Stability

Policies and programs should reinforce marital, parental, and other commitments and stability, intervening only to protect family members or at the request of the family itself.
   Does the program:
   —Provide incentives or disincentives to marry, separate, or divorce?
   —Provide incentives or disincentives to give support to, foster, or adopt children?
   —Strengthen marital commitment or parental obligations?
   —Provide resources to help keep the family together when this is appropriate?
   —Recognize that major changes in family relationships over time (e.g., adoption, divorce) have consequences that extend over time and require continuing support?

Principle 3. Family Involvement and Interdependence

Policies and programs must recognize the interdependence of family relationships, the strength and persistence of family ties and obligations, and the wealth of resources that families can mobilize to help their members.
   Does the program:
   —Recognize the reciprocal influence of the family and family members and individual needs or problems?
   —Involve immediate or extended family members in working toward a solution?
   —Acknowledge the power and persistence of family ties, especially when they are problematic?
   —Build on informal social networks (e.g., community and religious organizations) essential to families' daily lives?
   —Respect family decisions about the division of labor?
   —Address issues of power inequity in families?
   —Ensure perspectives of all family members are represented?
   —Assess and balance the competing needs, rights, and interests of various family members?
   —Protect the safety and rights of individuals in the family while respecting parents' rights and family integrity?

Principle 4. Family Partnership and Empowerment

Policies and programs must encourage individuals and their close family members to collaborate with program professionals and services. This includes collaboration in policy development, program planning, and program administration.

Does the program:

—Provide full information and a range of choices to families?

—Respect family autonomy and allow them to make their own decisions? In what circumstances are program staff allowed to intervene in family decisions?

—Encourage program professionals to collaborate with the families or with clients, patients, or students?

—Take into account the family's need to coordinate and integrate multiple services they use?

—Make services easily accessible to families in terms of location, operating hours, and applications?

—Prevent participating families from being devalued, stigmatized, or subjected to humiliating circumstances?

—Involve parents and family representatives in policy and program development, implementation, and evaluation?

Principle 5. Family Diversity

Policies and programs must acknowledge and value the diversity of family life and not discriminate against or penalize families on the basis of structure, roles, culture, or life stage.

Does the program:

—Affect various types of families differently?

—Acknowledge intergenerational relationships and responsibilities among family members?

—Provide good justification for targeting only certain family types, or does it discriminate against other types of families for insufficient reasons?

—Identify and respect the different values, attitudes, and behaviors of families from various cultural, ethnic, geographic, racial, religious, and other backgrounds that are relevant to program effectiveness?

Principle 6. Support of Vulnerable Families

Policies and programs should serve families in greatest economic and social need, as well as those most vulnerable to breakdown.

Does the program:

—Identify and publicly support services for families in the most extreme economic or social need?

—Give support to families who are most vulnerable to breakdown and who have the fewest resources?

—Target efforts and resources toward preventing family problems before they become serious crises or chronic situations?

---

[1]Reprinted with permission from The Policy Institute for Family Impact Seminars, 130 Human Ecology, 1300 Linden Drive, Madison, WI 53706. The checklist was adapted by Karen Bogenschneider from the first version published by Theodora Ooms & Stephen Preister (eds.). 1988. *A Strategy for Strengthening Families: Using Family Criteria in Policymaking and Program Evaluation.* Paper presented at the Family Impact Seminar, Washington, DC.

Organizations such as *The Urban Institute* systematically assess changing social policies, including policies related to families, through the *New Federalism* series. The fastest
growing segment of the American population under age 18 is children of immigrants. A
New Federalism report issued in late 2002 titled "The Health and Well-Being of Children
in Immigrant Families" documented:

> Children of immigrants are substantially more likely to be low-income despite the fact that
> they live in families with full-time workers. (Reardon-Anderson, Capps, and Fix 2002: 1)

The report provides a review of findings drawn from the *National Survey of America's
Families* in four areas:

Family Income and Environment:
> family income and family structure, employment and wages, parent–child involvement,
> parental community involvement, parent mental health and aggravation

Child Physical and Emotional Health:
> child physical health, child behavioral and emotional problems

Involvement in School:
> school engagement; skipping school, suspensions, and expulsions; participation in extracur-
> ricular activities

Access to Needed Benefits and Services:
> health care for children, health and mental health care for parents, housing and food assis-
> tance for families

The *Survey* is one of the few nationally representative data sets to include information
on the well being of children of immigrants. As such, the report has serious implications for
efforts to reauthorize the 1996 welfare reform law, which severely restricts non-citizens'—
including noncitizen children and their families'—access to a wide range of federal public
benefits.

A considerable number of all families have difficulty meeting basic requirements in
such areas as economics, education, health, nutrition, recreation, safety, and transportation. However, some families have greater difficulty meeting their members' needs than
do others. For example, in a study of children with chronic health conditions, Perrin,
Lewkowicz, and Young (2000) found that long-term needs for information and care may
be inadequately met, even in cases where the child and family have regular contact with
health care professionals. Who should ultimately insure that family needs are met?

The role of government in family policy is highly controversial. Chibucos (2003: F2)
sums two positions on one such policy, family promotion, as follows:

> Many proponents of the view that marriage promotion is a public responsibility believe that
> unmarried parents are poor precisely because they are unmarried and that marriage of itself is
> good for children and society as a whole. Opponents of public policies that promote marriage
> fear that such policies will discriminate against poor women and limit their right to make
> what should be private decisions about family formation and sexuality. Many feel that women
> will be coerced into marrying inappropriate partners or into staying in abusive marriages.

Your authors agree with Chibucos (2003): the role of nonpartisan organizations such as
the *National Council on Family Relations* is clear. National debates about family policy

and development of effective and fair family policy initiatives require scholarly and professional resources which can link research and policy to impacts on real families, while remaining open-minded and impartial.

Families not merely survive but thrive when they have adequate economic resources, nutrient dense nutrition, access to regular physical activity, healthful environments, good health (including mental health) care, decent housing, freedom from violence of all kinds, and family-friendly workplaces. Furthermore, every family needs a network of family, kin, and friends along with neighborhoods, community, and schools to foster a sense of respect and a connection among families and their members. In short, families thrive when the whole society has viable investments in every family.

Social policy has an important part to play in ensuring all families, whatever their structure, have supportive resources through programs that are culturally and ethnically sensitive, strength- and resiliency-focused, and tailored to the particular family needs.

FAMILY LIFE EDUCATION

We hope you share our strong belief that, resilient as they may be, the lives of families can be helped or hindered, often in dramatic ways, by the social structure around them. Still, we recognize change often occurs one family at a time. At some point while reading this book, you may have said to yourself, "I would like to make a difference in the individual lives of families experiencing these transitions or stresses." If so, you may want to explore a career in *family life education*.

Family life educators work in all the stages of the life cycle we have described in this book. Some focus on preparation of youth for the transition from family of orientation to independent living and late families. Some work in marriage preparation and marriage enrichment with couples planning to marry or hoping to enhance or improve their marriages. Some work with new parents in early childhood education. Some work with families on family living around budgeting, communication, or other relationship skills. Others assist families in adjusting to role transitions or serious family stresses.

Family life educators may be clergy, nurses, social workers, teachers, or other professionals. They may work in businesses, religious institutions, foundations, schools, or social service agencies. Box 14.2 describes the work of some family life educators with the University of Minnesota Extension Service.

BOX 14.2 "Parents Forever"
Minnell Tralle, M.E.

Fewer than half of America's children can expect to live out their childhood with both of their biological parents, whether their parents are divorced or never married. Research shows that on average, these children get sick more often, get in trouble more, get lower grades at school, and have more trouble making friends. When parents cannot work constructively through custody, child support, and other difficult divorce issues, the pain for both parents and children endures long after the divorce is final.

Families experiencing the transition of divorce can turn to *Parents Forever*, a program developed by family life educators at the University of Minnesota Extension Service. *Parents Forever* assists parents who want to minimize the trauma of this life transition for themselves and their children. The program encourages parents to work out divorce decisions without putting their children in the middle or forcing children to choose one parent over the other. Research-based, designed, and tested by University of Minnesota Extension Service family life educators, *Parents Forever* shows how to enlist a full spectrum of local community partners to help see families through divorce.

In Minnesota, legislation requires parent education for divorcing parents to meet minimum standards. *Parents Forever* uses a community collaborative approach to sustain a parent education program designed to help parents put the best interests of their child first. The curriculum teaches how divorce impacts adults and children, cooperative parenting strategies, conflict resolution, money issues, legal issues, and strategies for moving on. The course is 12 hours in length and is usually spread out over a six-week time period.

This program serves families in 64 of the 87 counties in Minnesota and is widely supported by judges, attorneys, parent educators, court administration personnel, and parents. A district court judge is quoted as saying:

> Although I sparingly cast support for programs, I enthusiastically strike the gong for *Parents Forever*. As a result of this program, I have observed more disputes settled voluntarily, less child stress, less cost in time and money to the legal system and divorcing parents and a greater likelihood of settling future disagreements.

A Parents Forever participant put it this way.

> [*Parents Forever*] changed me! It's taken the focus off of me and put it on, 'Where do my kids fall into play here?

Minnell Tralle is a Family Relations Specialist and Professor with the University of Minnesota Extension Service. She has co-authored the *Parents Forever* curriculum and has served as statewide coordinator and training coordinator for the program. She has a Masters of Education in Home Economics Education with an emphasis on family and parent education.

Some family life scholars are critical of the haphazard way individuals and couples are prepared for family life. For example, from their analysis of 10 college marriage textbooks, Larson and Hickman (2004) found only four of the 10 college textbooks presented information on two thirds or more of premarital predictors of marital quality. Morris and Ballard (2003) have found instructional techniques and even environmental considerations (e.g., lighting) impact attendance, participation, and satisfaction with programs.

Attrition from family life education programs is a significant problem, as most of these programs are voluntary. Many studies have reported higher attrition rates among minority families in comparison to White European families (e.g., Wierzbicki and Pekarick 1993). However, this may be a function of the setting of family life education. In fact, a recent study suggests African-American and Latino-American mothers may be more likely to remain as participants in home-based family support programs than White European mothers (McCurdy, Gannon, and Daro 2004).

Others are concerned with what they see as vestiges of bias against some types of families. For example, Schultz and Leslie (2004) found significantly more unfavorable attitudes about divorced mothers than about married mothers among a sample of students enrolled in five *American Association of Marriage and Family Therapy* accredited training programs. The problems indicate family life education is not effectively or universally available to all individuals and families who might benefit.

Education for marriage and parenting can make a difference in the quality of family life. However, more research is needed to assess the effectiveness of family programs. For example, Carroll and Doherty (2003) found the average person participating in a premarital prevention program was significantly better off afterwards than those who did not participate in the program. Although Carroll and Doherty concluded premarital prevention programs were effective in producing immediate and short-term benefits in interpersonal skills and relationship quality, they call for more longitudinal research to gauge the long-term effects of such programs.

One recent development at the federal level promises to expand at least the information available to couples concerned about marital quality. Beginning in 2005, the federal government is funding the *Healthy Marriage Resource Center*, a multimillion dollar Web-based information clearinghouse to help prepare couples for marriage. The *Center* is a consortium of the *National Council of Family Relations* and five universities (Smetanka 2004).

The *National Council of Family Relations* provides formal certification of family life educators, based on their academic training, professional experience, and continuing education. You can obtain more information about becoming a certified *Family Life Educator* through the *National Council of Family Relations*' Web site.

Martha Farrell Erickson is Director of the Children, Youth, and Family Consortium at the University of Minnesota and researcher on child development and maltreatment. She writes:

> Good [families don't] just happen. [They] benefit from programs that help [them] understand and meet their members' needs, sustain strong support networks and address barriers that hinder them. ... (Erickson 2000: 8)

COMMUNITIES, CULTURES, AND FAMILIES

The discourse about families is grounded in some of our most deeply held attitudes, beliefs, and values. What is the proper nature of the relationships between men and women? Between children and parents? Between youth and elders? Between kin and nonkin?

Many of our values about family are fundamentally rooted and reflected in religious institutions. Dominant paradigms about family relationships come to be institutionalized through educational and other institutions of socialization. Can our image affirm and support the diversities in families we see around us?

As some voices are honored and some voices are silenced, social beliefs about families come to be translated into political agenda. Ultimately, the institutional construction of the family translates into economic consequences for both the family unit and individual members. Debates about the family are tightly bound to not only values, but also to normative consequences. Whose needs have highest priority? Who pays?

In an article titled "The Family: What Do We Really Want?" Ruskin (2000: 19) argues in our search for formal, political solutions to family problems, we should not neglect the informal, household sector and the relations of kinship. The challenges and opportunities facing families of the future will require addressing both the public and the private spheres.

In the final analysis, why should we engage these hard questions? In his reflection on the investment of communities in families, business leader Michael Symons asks us to "change the conversation" to possibilities, relevance, values, and connectedness.

BOX 14.3 "Decide to Change the Conversation"
Michael Symons

Our families don't work the way they once did. The demands of children, marriage, work, finances, schools, neighborhoods, politics . . . the world, all grow as we have less time, energy, and money to give. How do we solve the family problem of demand exceeding supply?

One approach is to change the conversation, which means changing the language, the talk, even the people involved in the conversation. By changing the conversation about families, we have the opportunity to focus discussion on what is really important. In *Conversation: How Talk Can Change Our Lives*, Theodore Zeldin (2000) of Oxford University writes about how great events in history have occurred because someone changed the talk of their time from "What was. . . . " to "What if . . . ?"

Asking "What is important?" requires discussing today's values and their relevance. Such a conversation moves family discussion beyond rules and regulations to an authentic discussion of the needs of families and their members. Such a conversation changes the nature of the conversation and the set of possible solutions for problems.

Take public schools as an example. Today's reality is that communities need employers who pay workers. Employers can only grow when they can find workers who are able to contribute value to the enterprise and its customers. Employees need knowledge and skills to grow and keep up with a rapidly changing world. And families need income to remain viable and make positive contributions to the community.

Why not discuss how to change the conversation to what is really important? Include new resources in the dialogue, such as more senior citizens who have knowledge, talent, and time and enlarge the conversation to include business people who must find new solutions to old problems every day.

Granted, there is no guarantee of a successful outcome by simply changing the conversation. What is clear, however, is there are fewer and fewer workable solutions to problems when the conversation is limited to budgets and recitation of policies. Change the participants to include people who can enrich the landscape of possibilities. Shift the questions to:

"What do we need?" versus "What do we cut?"

"Why can't we?" instead of "Why we can't."

"What can we give?" rather than "What do we get?"

Will our *Families*—communities—*With Futures* be functional, enriched, and valuable or disturbed, depleted, and draining? The conversations we have today among families—in all their diverse forms—education, businesses, and other stakeholders will shape the directions of our neighborhoods and communities, states, nation, and world. Individually, we cannot control exactly what our futures will be, but we can influence their positive development. First, develop a sense of positive possibilities. Second, be responsible for the quality of the effort and not the outcome. Finally, build the conversation around relevance, value, and connections.

REFERENCE

Zeldin, Theodore. 2000. *Conversation: How Talk Can Change Our Lives*. Mahwah, NJ: Paulist.

Michael Symons is a consultant specializing in communication and management training.

Life is changing in ways not even imagined in the last generation. Futurist Joseph Coates (1996) has identified five key social trends that will shape the future of families:

- Stresses on family functions of socialization, expression of sexuality, companionships, and economic tasks associated with new patterns of work, leisure, and consumption

- Changes in family organization as women's employment increases and family roles shift for women, men, and children

- High rates of marriage dissolution among couples with commitment to marriage and serial marriage and other adaptations

- Proliferation of nontraditional family structures such as single-parenting, young adults returning home, cohabiting, gay, stepfamily, and other unions

- Redefinition of "family" due to increased life expectancy while older family members shape broader social trends in areas such as political participation and savings patterns

Peter Drucker (2003) identifies three key future social trends: (a) knowledge as the key resource and commodity, (b) transformation of work environments from centralized to "just in time" outsourced agencies where workers are borderless and upwardly mobile, and (c) older people becoming the dominant force in the world of work.

We offer a fourth trend that will impact families: (d) expansive information technologies including E-learning, e-commerce, e-health care, and other technology-based resources and services challenging families to learn, work, and live differently. Think about how such trends may impact families in terms of becoming lifelong learners, self-sufficient employees, and proactive partners in healthful living, if they can become wise consumers of e-living. What will these future *e-families* look like? The consequences remain unwritten, unfolded. Families need to be proactive in shaping these future shifts.

In the first chapter we invited you, our readers, to join us on a journey to examine the changing world of families. Our journey is by no means complete, for we are certain we have left some family stories—perhaps yours—untold.

Continuing the journey will require deep, scholarly thought. Let family scholarship—theories and methods—be the technical tools to reveal the economic, political, social, and other challenges facing families. Let respect for the families who inspire your study serve as the cornerstone of ethical scholarship. Be assured families and societies are inextricably interconnected.

As we conclude this book, we return to the concept of Strategic Living Communities ©, introduced in the first chapter. We invite you as a prospective family studies professional to extend your definition of family not only in terms of composition but also in perception of families as dynamic, creative, and capable. Can you see families as innovative artisans, needing to define themselves in terms of who they are, what they want, and what they are willing to do to get there? Can you see families as needing encouragement and support as they navigate changing social currents as they strive to reach their preferred futures?

As you examine where families have been, where families are today, and where they prefer to go tomorrow, our hope is you retain a sense of wonder for the ability of families to demonstrate their resiliency.

All families are families with futures.

GLOSSARY

Aid to Families with Dependent Children (AFDC)

Direct effects

E-families

Family impact statements

Family life education

Family policy

Family well-being

Indirect effects

Latent consequences

Law

Manifest consequences

Personal Responsibility and Work Opportunity Reconciliation Act (PRWORC)

Practice

Social policy

Temporary Assistance for Needy Families (TANF)

Welfare Reform Act of 1996

FOR YOUR CONSIDERATION

1. Outline a plan for educating children or youth about valuing families and family life today. Who should be involved in implementing this program? Who should pay the up-front costs for your program?

2. What do you consider to be the most pressing policy issues concerning families in your community today? In your region? In the United States? In the world?

3. What do you see as your future in family studies?

FOR FURTHER STUDY: WEB SITES, ORGANIZATIONS, AND PUBLICATIONS

Web Sites and Organizations

Childstats
http://www.childstats.gov
This site provides links to federal and state statistics and reports on children and families, including population and family characteristics and economic security.

Council on Contemporary Families
http://www.contemporaryfamilies.org
Founded in 1996 by a group of practitioners, researchers, and scholars, the *Council* aims to be an independent group focusing on educating the media, policymakers, and the public on research about families.

Children's Defense Fund
25 E Street, NW
Washington, DC 20001
www.childrensdefense.org
This organization, with offices in California, Minnesota, Mississippi, New York, Ohio, South Carolina, Tennessee, Texas, and Washington, DC, reviews national policy and legislative action in its role as advocate for children.

Center for Law and Social Policy
1616 P Street, NW
Washington, DC 20036

(202) 328-5140

www.clasp.org

Through the quarterly newsletter *Family Matters*, the Center summarizes national and state welfare and poverty-related policies.

Center on Budget and Policy Priorities

777 North Capitol Street, NE, Suite 705

Washington, DC 20002

(202) 408-1080

www.cbpp.org

The Center reports and analyzes poverty and budget issues including hunger and welfare in families.

Family Impact Seminars

1100 17th Street, NW, Suite 901

Washington, DC 20036-4601

(202) 467-5114

This organization conducts monthly seminars for federal policy staff in Washington, DC, on a wide range of family issues (e.g., child care, family poverty, family preservation, foster care, and welfare reform). The comprehensive, nonpartisan reports include the latest research, model state and local programs, and relevant references and organizations. Reports are available for purchase.

Family Research Council

700 13th Street, NW, Suite 500

Washington, DC 20005

(202) 783-HOME

www.frc.org

This advocacy group takes a "pro-family" position grounded in Judeo-Christian values in considering executive, judicial, and legislative matters.

Heritage Foundation

214 Massachusetts Avenue, NE

Washington, DC 20002

(202) 546-4400

www.heritage.org

The Foundation is a conservative think-tank addressing a wide variety of issues including those related to families.

Search Institute

122 Franklin Avenue, Suite 525

Minneapolis, MN 55404

(800) 870-4602

The *Search Institute* examines issues facing adolescents, children, and families and offers evaluative programs based on their "40 Assets" model.

Social Legislation Information Service

440 First Street, NW

Washington, DC 20001-2085

(202) 638-2952

A division of the Child Welfare League of America, Inc., this organization reports on federal legislation and agencies that affect children, the elderly, and the handicapped; and on education, employment, health, housing, and other social welfare conditions.

Youth Policy Institute
  1221 Massachusetts Avenue, NW, Suite B
  Washington, DC 20005-5333
  (202) 638-2144
  The Institute covers federal legislation and executive actions on youth-related policy on
  health, housing, and social services, as well as funding sources.

Publications

Bogenschneider, Karen. 2002. *Family Policy Matters: How Policymaking Affects Families and What Professionals Can Do.* Mahwah, NJ: Lawrence Erlbaum Associates.
  Bogenschneider's book is based on consideration of two decades of studies of family policy and its effects.
  Of particular note, Bogenschneider uses 26 case studies to illustrate the ways professionals can influence
  policy for families.
Booth, Alan, and Ann C. Crouter, eds. 2001. *Does It Take a Village? Community Effects on Children, Adolescents, and Families.* Mahwah, NJ: Lawrence Erlbaum Associates.
  The chapters in this book focus on the linkages between community characteristics (community norms,
  economic opportunities, reference groups, social support networks) and family and family member functioning.
Careers in Child and Family Policy: A Resource Guide to Policy Settings and Research Programs. 1995.
  Chicago, IL: University of Chicago.
  A listing of training opportunities organized around advocacy, foundation, government, professional, research, and policy centers.
  Available for $10 from Communications Office, Chapin Hall Center for Children, The University of Chicago,
  1155 East 60th Street, Chicago, IL 60637.
Casper, Lynne M., and Suzanne M. Bianchi. 2002. *Continuity and Change in the American Family.* Thousand
  Oaks, CA: Sage.
  Casper and Bianchi explore current issues in the family, including cohabitation, single-parenting, grandparenting, work–family issues, and economic hardship. The book draws on data from the last three decades,
  but is written in a lively, engaging style.
Duncan, Stephen F., and H. Wallace Goddard. 2005. *Family Life Education: Principles and Practices for
  Effective Outreach.* Thousand Oaks, CA: Sage.
  This book integrates theory and research with family practice. In addition to presentation of principles and
  methods of family life education, the authors explore the philosophical under foundations of family life
  education and encourage readers to develop their own philosophy.
Family Relations 53, 5 (October 2004).
  This entire issue of the interdisciplinary journal of applied family studies is devoted to marriage education
  programs and initiatives, including reviews by Doherty, Olsen, and others; discussion of new programs;
  empirical evaluations and studies; models for the future; and a commentary on the future of marriage
  education.
Henderson, Tammy L., and Pamela A. Monroe, eds. 2002. *The Intersection of Families and the Law.* Special
  Issue of Family Relations. October.
  This special issue includes articles concerning how family case law impacts families in communities,
  homes, schools, and other ecological settings and historical and contemporary contexts of family case law.
  Suggested topics include adoption, custody, divorce, euthanasia, gay and lesbian families, guardianship,
  grandparents' rights, parental rights, stepfamilies, and welfare reform.
The History of the Family: An International Quarterly
  This quarterly periodical reminds us families are grounded in historical contexts.
National Council on Family Relations. 2000. Public Policy through a Family Lens: Sustaining Families in the
  21st Century. Minneapolis, MN.
  Based on the premise "all public policies affect families," this volume considers and recommends policies
  on families and children and includes a "Checklist for Assessing the Impact of Policies and Programs on
  Families."

National Council on Family Relations. 1999. *Tools for Ethical Thinking and Practice in Family Life Education*, 2/e. Minneapolis, MN.

This booklet is a valuable resource for family life educators in three areas: ethical thinking and practice for family life educators, the levels of family involvement model, and competencies for family life educators.

Struening, Karen. 2002. *New Family Values*. Lanham, MA: AltaMira.

Struening offers a critical analysis of arguments made by those who argue law and policy should be used to foster only the intact, two-parent, heterosexual family.

Zimmerman, Shirley L. 2001. *Family Policy: Constructed Solutions to Family Problems*. Thousand Oaks, CA: Sage.

This textbook provides a comprehensive introduction to the frameworks to real life issues in family policy.

REFERENCES FOR CITED WORKS

Bogenschneider, Karen. 2000. "Has Family Policy Come of Age? A Decade Review of the State of U.S. Family Policy in the 1990s." *Journal of Marriage and the Family* 62, 4 (November): 1136–59.

Bogenschneider, Karen, Bettina Friese, and Karla Balling. 2002. "Spanning the Great Divide: Strategies for Linking Research and Policymaking from the Policy Institute for Family Impact Seminars." *National Council on Family Relations Focus* (June): F1–F3.

Burris, Roddie. 2002. "Experts at Conference Advocate Marriage." *The State* (September 13).

Carroll, Jason S., and William J. Doherty. 2003. "Evaluating the Effectiveness of Premarital Prevention Programs: A Meta-Analytic Review of Outcome Research." *Family Relations* 52: 2 (March): 105–18.

Cassar, Joseph. 1999. *The Family: Anxieties and Hopes. On the Family's Entitlement to Protection by Society and the State*. Global Research Monograph No. 012 (March). New York, NY: St. John's University Center for Global Education.

Chibucos, Thomas R. 2003. "The Role of NCFR in Family Policy Initiatives: Marriage Promotion as an Exemplar." *Family Focus on Marriage* (September): F1, F2, F3. Minneapolis: National Council on Family Relations.

Coates, Joseph F. 1996. "What's Ahead for Families: Five Major Forces of Change." *The Futurist* (September/October): 27–35.

Coontz, Stephanie, and Nancy Folbre. 2002. "Marriage, Poverty, and Public Policy: A Discussion Paper for the Council on Contemporary Families." Presented at the 5th Annual *Council on Contemporary Families* Conference, April.

Cornia, G. A. 1997. "Child Poverty and Deprivation in the Industrialized Countries from the End of World War II to the End of the Cold War." In *Child Poverty and Deprivation in the Industrialized Countries,* ed. G. A. Cornia and S. Danzier. Oxford, UK: Clarendon.

Danziger, Sheldon H., Sandra K. Danziger, and J. Stern. 1997. "The American Paradox: High Income and High Child Poverty." In *Child Poverty and Deprivation in the Industrialized Countries,* ed. Giovanni Andre Cornia and Sheldon H. Danziger. Oxford, UK: Clarendon.

Drucker, Peter. 2003. "The Great Peter Drucker Talks about the 'Next Society.'" *Bottom Line Personal* 24, 3 (February 1): 1–2.

Erickson, Martha Farrell. 2000. "What Children Need to Get a Good Start." In *Public Policy through a Family Lens: Sustaining Families in the 21st Century*. Minneapolis, MN: National Council on Family Relations, 7–8.

Horn, Wade. 2002. "Welfare Reform Reauthorization: Promoting Self-Sufficiency, Protecting Children, and Strengthening Marriage." *Poverty Research News* 6, 3 (May–June): 3–5.

Larson, Jeffry H., and Rachel Hickman. 2004. "Are College Marriage Textbooks Teaching Students the Premarital Predictors of Marital Quality?" *Family Relations* 53, 4 (July): 385–92.

Levine, Bettjane. 2003. "The Motherhood Movement." *Star Tribune* (January 6): E10.

McCurdy, Karen, Robin A. Gannon, and Deborah Daro. 2004. "Participation Patterns in Home-Based Family Support Programs: Ethnic Variations." *Family Relations* 52, 1 (January): 3–11.

McPhail, Michael W. 2000. "A Blue Print for Strengthening Family Courts." *National Council on Family Relations Family Focus* (September): F1–F3.

Meekler, Laura. 2002. "When Welfare-to-Work Boosts Family Income, Kids Improve in School." *Associated Press On-Line* (March 1) (Retrieved 1/24/03).

Morris, Michael Lane, and Sharon M. Ballard. 2003. "Instructional Techniques and Environmental Considerations in Family Life Education Programming for Midlife and Older Adults." *Family Relations* 52, 2 (March): 167–73.

Myrdal, Alva. 1968. *Nation and Family.* Cambridge: Massachusetts Institute of Technology Press.

Ozawa, Martha N. 2004. "Social Welfare Spending on Family Benefits in the United States and Sweden: A Comparative Study." *Family Relations* 53, 3 (April): 301–09.

Perrin, Ellen C., Corinne Lewkowicz, and Martin H. Young. 2000. "Shared Vision: Concordance Among Fathers, Mothers, and Pediatricians About unmet Needs of Children with Chronic Health Conditions." *Pediatrics* 105, 1 (Supplement January): 277–85.

Reardon-Anderson, Jane, Randy Capps, and Michael Fix. 2002. "The Health and Well-Being of Children in Immigrant Families." *New Federalism* Series B, No B-52 (November).

Ruskin, Michael. 2000. "The Family: What Do We Really Want?" *Dissent* (Winter): 66–71.

Schultz, M. Christine, and Leigh A. Leslie. 2004. "Family Therapy Trainees' Perceptions of Divorced Mothers: A Test of Bias in Information Recall." *Family Relations* 53, 4 (July): 405–11.

Shehan, Constance L. 2003. *Marriages and Families*, 2/e. Boston, MA: Allyn & Bacon.

Shirer, Karen. 1993. *A Measure of How Families Are Doing.* Marshalltown, IA: Mid-Iowa Community Action Agency.

Smetanka, Mary Jane. 2004. "Keeping 'I Do' from Becoming 'Who Knew?'" *Star Tribune* September 24: B3.

Wierzbicki, Michael J., and G. Pekarick. 1993. "A Meta-Analysis of Psychotherapy Dropout." *Professional Psychology Research Practice* 24: 190–95.

Zimmerman, Shirley L. 1995. *Understanding Family Policy: Theories and Applications,* 2/e. Thousand Oaks, CA: Sage.

APPENDICES

A

NATIONAL COUNCIL ON FAMILY RELATIONS

ETHICAL PRINCIPLES AND GUIDELINES

PURPOSE: These ethical principles and guidelines were developed to

- Inspire and encourage family scientists to act ethically
- Provide ethical guidance in areas that family scientists may overlook
- Provide guidance in dealing with often complex ethical issues
- Enhance the professional image and status of family scientists by increasing the level of professional consciousness

The principles that apply to family scientists in all their professional situations are included in the first section. The remaining sections relate to family scientists in specific professional arenas.

I. GENERAL PRINCIPLES FOR FAMILY SCIENTISTS

This section identifies general ethical principles that are relevant to family scientists in all professional settings.

Family scientists are respectful of all individuals, do not unethically discriminate, do not develop intimate personal relationships in their role as family scientists, are sensitive to the complications of multiple role relationships, protect the confidentiality of their students or clients, and do not engage in sexual harassment.

Source: © 1995 National Council on Family Relations, Minneapolis, Minnesota. Used with permission.

Guidelines

1.01   Family scientists are respectful of others, show sensitivity to the dignity of all humans, and avoid all forms of exploitation.

1.02   Family scientists are not unethically discriminatory on the basis of gender, sexual orientation, age, marital status, race, religion, national origin, ethnicity, disability, or socioeconomic status. We recognize that discrimination occurs in our society, and when done wisely for positive purposes it may be appropriate. For example, we may allow a student with a vision impairment to sit on the front row of the classroom.

1.03   When attempting to influence the behavior or attitudes of students or clients, family scientists should not use methods which involve undue influence, such as coercion or manipulation.

1.04   Family scientists segregate intimate personal relationships from their role as family scientists. Therefore, they do not develop inappropriate intimate personal relationships with students, clients, or research subjects.

1.05   Family scientists are sensitive to the complications in dual- or multiple-role situations and are ethical in those roles. For example, family scientists may teach classes in which a son or daughter is enrolled. Others may have professional colleagues in a workshop where some form of personal evaluation is an expected outcome.

1.06   Family scientists protect confidentiality in their professional role as family scientists whether it be in teaching, service, public speaking, writing, or consulting activities. For example, if family scientists share information with students about others, the confidentiality of those involved should be protected. This can be done by changing identifying information, creating composite cases, or summarizing information.

1.07   If information is shared with a family scientist that mandates reporting (such as child abuse or the possibility of extreme harm) such information is to be reported to the appropriate authorities. Whenever possible, individuals should be informed in advance of the family scientist's need to report.

1.08   Family scientists avoid sexually harassing all persons with whom they come in contact in a professional or personal setting. Sexual harassment involves unwelcome intimate and sexual advances, requests, or other conduct of a sexual nature which is used for grounds for providing benefits or services for terms of or conditions of employment, or for the purpose or effect of unreasonably interfering with an individual's learning or work performance or creating an intimidating, hostile, or offensive learning or working environment. Such things as inappropriate hugging, touching, or language are considered harassment.

1.09   Family scientists who belong to other professional organizations with more elaborate or role specialized guidelines should abide by them. For example, professional family therapists should use the ethical guidelines of AAMFT (American Association for Marriage and Family Therapy) and medical doctors should utilize the ethical guidelines of the AMA (American Medical Association).

PRINCIPLES II: FAMILY SCIENTISTS ARE RESPECTFUL OF STUDENTS AND CLIENTS

Family scientists are respectful of diverse family forms. They are respectful of students' sensitivity in discussing personal family issues. Family scientists do not exploit the hierarchical relationship with persons they serve and are respectful of privacy issues.

Guidelines

2.01   When family scientists teach marital and family courses, they inform students that sometimes students in classes of this nature have painful memories of personal or family experiences. They should inform students of appropriate counseling resources available to them.

2.02   Family scientists recognize the strengths and weaknesses of various family forms and do not operate from a deficit perspective in discussing various family forms.

2.03   When giving examples, family scientists utilize examples with families from diverse cultures and forms.

2.04   When subjects are discussed in a course or class, including controversial issues, family scientists encourage an open, respectful, and thoughtful atmosphere which acknowledges and respects diversity of values, beliefs, and attitudes.

2.05   Family scientists do not insist that students agree with or adopt a particular perspective. In fairness to students, teachers should, where appropriate, divulge personal values and biases.

2.06   When teaching, family scientists differentiate between knowledge or insight gained from clinical or personal experience and knowledge obtained from published theory or research.

2.07   Family scientists who are also clinicians do not pursue, or allow, clinical relationships to develop with students during the course of instruction. If students request clinical service, they should be directed to an appropriate provider of the clinical service.

2.08   Family scientists who are not clinicians do not cross into a therapeutic role while interacting with students. Family scientists make referrals for clinical services when appropriate.

2.09   Family scientists avoid any situation or the perception of any situation in which grades may be exchanged for favors of any kind.

2.10   Family scientists who ask (or allow) students in courses or classes to share personal and family experiences in class regularly remind students to treat any information received as confidential information not to be shared or discussed with anyone outside the classroom. However, the fact that confidentiality cannot be assured should be stated.

2.11   While teaching a for-credit course, family scientists do not make assignments that require students to divulge potentially painful personal or family experiences or information without providing an alternative assignment for those who do not wish to participate. An exception exists if the class is part of professional training program which requires such educational activities.

2.12   When family scientists request (or require) students to obtain potentially sensitive and painful information from family members (e.g., in a genogram assignment) or others, students are carefully instructed and cautioned about potential harm and allowed to use their own discretion about which information to seek.

2.13   Family scientists do not coerce their students to participate as subjects in research. If students enrolled in courses do not wish to participate in or assist with research projects, they should be offered alternative assignments of equal value and be assured that their decision not to participate will in no way affect their grade.

2.14   In giving assignments in which students are required to discuss their values, family scientists develop grading criteria that do not include evaluation of the students' values.

2.15   When family scientists return papers or post scores, confidentiality of the students' grades is maintained. For example, scores should not be posted nor papers returned in any hierarchical order of points earned.

2.16   Family scientists base material taught on what is appropriate for students rather than solely the instructor's personal or professional needs or interests, such as a research agenda.

PRINCIPLE III: FAMILY SCIENTISTS ABIDE BY HIGH PROFESSIONAL STANDARDS

Family scientists are responsible to uphold high professional standards. They are encouraged to be cooperative with other family scientists in gathering and sharing of scientific information. They strive to keep current material in their domain. They are ethical in representing their profession at their place of employment as well as other settings.

Guidelines

3.01   Family scientists are supportive of, and cooperative with, other family scientists and the profession at large regarding the timely sharing of new ideas, theories, research findings, and/or innovative program developments.

3.02   Whenever possible, family scientists promote the profession in such a way that members can make contributions to society for the enhancement of families and the growth and development of individuals in various family settings.

3.03   Family scientists give proper credit or acknowledgment to the works of others when formally sharing that information.

3.04   Personal information gained from or known about a colleague is treated with discretion. Sharing the information with others should be done only for the welfare of the colleague, except where appropriate disciplinary action may be involved. When questionable professional or personal conduct may have a bearing upon professional activities that concern initially should be discussed with the involved colleague(s) where feasible. If in the judgment of the family scientists that is not practical or resolution of the matter is not apparent, such behavior should be reported appropriately.

3.05   Family scientists are adequately prepared for their professional responsibilities. If there are professionally recognized standards of certification or licensing requiring experience, supervision, or additional education, family scientists seek such credentials.

3.06   Family scientists use the times under which they are under obligation to an employer for professional purposes.

PRINCIPLE IV: FAMILY SCIENTISTS CONDUCT RESEARCH ETHICALLY

Family scientists contribute to society and to the profession through research and evaluation activities. When conducting research or evaluation, family scientists recognize that their ultimate responsibility is to the participants. Family scientists honestly report the findings of their study.

Guidelines

4.01   Family scientists conduct all aspects of the research process with respect for the dignity of those who participate in the research and they ensure that those who assist in the research process do likewise.

4.02 Family scientists inform research participants of the purpose of their research, any potential risk of involvement, how confidentiality will be protected, the right to withdraw from the study at any time, the way the data will be used, and available referral resources if risks are involved.

4.03 Family scientists avoid "doing therapy" with research participants (unless therapy is a part of the research design). Researchers should provide a referral to an appropriate resource for those who request it.

4.04 Family scientists give credit to others for contributions to scholarship in proportion to the contributions made.

4.05 Family scientists do not manipulate research data for the purposes of supporting their views.

4.06 Family scientists use research money for the stated purpose described in the research proposal.

PRINCIPLE V: FAMILY SCIENTISTS ARE ETHICAL IN THEIR INTERACTIONS WITH EMPLOYING ORGANIZATIONS OR AGENCIES

Family scientists are respectful of the internal policies and procedures of current and past employers. Family scientists seek to promote the highest standards of policies and practice by their employers.

Guidelines

5.01 When family scientists and those in training have information pertaining to an organization's internal activities or planning, and the knowledge may hinder or harm the organization if known by outsiders, the information is treated as confidential unless these activities are unethical or harmful to others.

5.02 Family scientists abide by the policies and procedures of their respective employing organizations. Where such policies or procedures are believed to violate professional standards or cause unprofessional conduct by employees, attempts are made to rectify the situation. If such attempts are unsuccessful, concerns for the pertinent policies or procedures are reported to an appropriate governing or investigative body.

5.03 Family scientists cooperate with other community organizations that provide services to mutual clients. However, family scientists do not share client information with other agencies unless the client has given written permission or it is mandated by policy or law.

5.04 Family scientists are aware of other resources which may benefit their students or clients and make appropriate roles.

PRINCIPLE VI: FAMILY SCIENTISTS ARE INVOLVED IN IMPROVING SOCIETY

Family scientists are advocates for individuals and families and participate in developing policies and laws that are respectful and empowering them.

Guidelines

6.01   Family scientists are concerned for the general welfare of all individuals and families in society. Whether as professionals or private citizens, they engage in family advocacy at the local, state, and national levels.

6.02   Family scientists are encouraged to participate in developing laws and policies that are respectful of and empowering to all individuals and families and in modifying such policies and laws that are not.

PRINCIPLE VII: FAMILY SCIENTISTS UNDERSTAND AND ABIDE BY ETHICAL PRINCIPLES AND ASSIST OTHERS TO DO SO

Family scientists understand and abide by ethical principles, encourage and assist other family scientists to know and apply them, and teach ethical principles to students of family science.

Guidelines

7.01   Family scientists understand and abide by ethical principles.

7.02   Family scientists assist other family scientists to know and apply ethical principles by encouraging understanding and adherence to them and by their willingness to discuss the principles.

7.03   Family scientists teach students of family science to understand and abide by ethical principles in their professional roles.

7.04   Family scientists who are involved in an ethical dilemma consult with other family scientists about the situation. A written record of the problem, the resolution, and the justification for the resolution is given to another family scientist so that if one is accused of unethical conduct the record can be used to demonstrate that the family scientist was aware of the ethical concern and dealt with it conscientiously.

7.05   Family scientists assist the profession to further identify and articulate ethical issues. Additional ethical principles and guidelines (beyond those included herein) are to be communicated to the chair of the Family Science section of the National Council on Family Relations.

PRINCIPLE VIII: FAMILY SCIENTISTS ARE ETHICAL WHEN REVIEWING PROFESSIONAL WRITING

When a reviewer for a professional work, family scientists avoid conflicts of interest, read materials carefully in their entirety and evaluate them fairly.

Guidelines

8.01   Family scientists do not review articles where there is conflict of interest, such as when the work is that of a friend, or other where they may feel a sense of obligation to the author.

8.02   Family scientists carefully read in their entirety materials that are accepted for review and provide explicit reasons for their evaluations.

STATEMENT FROM THE NCFR REGARDING THE DEVELOPMENT OF THESE PRINCIPLES AND GUIDELINES[1]

Members of the Family Science Section of NCFR had discussed for years the need for a code of ethics. Many of the section members feel that a major component in establishing a discipline is a code of ethics. At the 1992 NCFR annual conference, Family Science Section members voted the development and adaptation of a code of ethics a top priority. Section Chairperson Kathleen Gilbert appointed Rebecca A. Adams, Ph.D., Department of Family & Consumer Sciences, Ball State University, to be the chairperson and David Dollahite, Ph.D., Department of Family Sciences, Brigham Young University, and Robert E. Keim, Ph.D., CFLE, Department of Human & Family Resources, Northern Illinois University, as committee members.

During the 1993 NCFR conference, the committee presented its draft and solicited feedback from section members. This was done again the following year, and those in attendance designated the ethical code be referred to as guidelines and principles. Additional suggestions were integrated into a document which was mailed to all section members for additional input. The preceding is the final version approved by the section membership in April 1995. The committee especially thanks Wes Buit for his significant contributions.

_____

[1]Quoted from the Original document.

B

FAMILY STUDIES RESOURCES

JAN M. ORF, M.S., M.A.
UNIVERSITY OF ST. THOMAS

Many excellent resources exist for Family Studies research. However, you must evaluate the resources you find and choose those that are authoritative, well researched, and that are relevant to your own research. In this appendix, several general resources that will be useful are listed along with information on how best to use them.

The resources will be listed by type. Both print and electronic resources are included, along with a brief annotation of the information included. The sections are:

A. Dictionaries, Encyclopedias, and Handbooks

B. Statistical Sources

C. Indexes, Abstracts, and other Databases

D. Subject World Wide Web Sites

Each section will include an introductory overview to identify what information is available from each type of resource, a bibliography of the sources, and annotations identifying the specific information available in each source.

A. DICTIONARIES, ENCYCLOPEDIAS, AND HANDBOOKS

The best places to start your research are with dictionaries, encyclopedias, and handbooks. These basic references that are specific to a field of study, like Family Studies, will identify the terms as used by those doing research in the field. Words may have a different meaning when used in a different subject area. By using the subject-specific dictionaries and encyclopedias, you will be able to identify the terms that will assist you in using other sources (books, indexes, and other databases) to identify resources on your topic.

Not only will subject-specific encyclopedias and handbooks give a good overview of a subject, but also they provide lists of resources on each topic. Most frequently they will be listed at the end of each article. In some cases, the bibliography is available at the end of the publication. These lists of sources provide a good starting point for doing research on that topic.

Below are listed several dictionaries, encyclopedias, and handbooks recommended for family studies research, listed alphabetically by author or editor.

Publications

Adamec, Christine, and William L. Pierce. 2000. *The Encyclopedia of Adoption.* New York, NY: Facts on File.
This resource provides articles on different aspects of adoption. The appendices include statistical tables and social service and adoption agencies worldwide. It includes a bibliography of additional sources, as well as a detailed subject index to the text.

Balter, Lawrence, ed. 2000. *Parenthood in America: An Encyclopedia.* Santa Barbara, CA: ABC-CLIO.
This is the first publication in the ABC-CLIO encyclopedia series *The American Family,* which covers family issues throughout the history of the United States. Each article in this two-volume publication is signed and includes references and suggestions for further reading. A lengthy general bibliography is also included along with a detailed subject index. Other titles in this series include *Adolescence in America, Girlhood in America, Boyhood in America, Infancy in America,* and *The Family in America.*

Bankston, Carl L., ed. 1999. *Encyclopedia of Family Life.* Pasadena, CA: Salem.
This five-volume encyclopedia provides an overview of family topics, laws, and biographies of those involved with family research. Articles cover relevant issues and their significance. Cross-references are included as well as a brief bibliography for each article. A list of support groups, a timeline of "Important Legislation and Court Decisions," a glossary of terms used in this field of study, and an annotated bibliography of general resources are also included.

Bengtson, Vern L., Alan C. Acock, Katherine R. Allen, Peggye Dilworth-Anderson, and David M. Klein, eds. 2005. *Sourcebook of Family Theory and Research.* Thousand Oaks, CA: Sage.
This resource concentrates on the methodology of family research and addresses topics such as emerging research, changes within the families, interactions within families, and how society affects families. Also a section addresses teaching family studies. Author and subject indexes are included.

Blieszner, Rosemary, and Victoria Hilkevitch Bedford, eds. 1995. *Handbook of Aging and the Family.* Westport, CT: Greenwood.
Each chapter in this publication is an in-depth article on some aspect of the study of families with aging members. A list of references is provided with each article, and there is a brief subject index in the book.

Borgatta, Edgar F., and Rhonda J.V. Montgomery, eds. 2000. *The Encyclopedia of Sociology.* New York, NY: Macmillan.
This is the basic encyclopedia for the field of Sociology. Many family studies topics are included in this five-volume set. The articles are written by experts in the field and include detailed bibliographies. An in-depth subject index is available to access specific terms within the articles.

Bornstein, Marc H., ed. 1995. *Handbook of Parenting.* Mahwah, NJ: Lawrence Erlbaum Associates.
Each volume in this four-volume set covers a separate aspect of parenting. Volume 1 is a general overview of "Children and Parenting." Volume 2 includes the "Biology and Ecology of Parenting." Volume 3 discusses the "Status and Social Conditions of Parenting." In addition to providing a subject index to the entire set, volume 4 covers "Applied and Practical Parenting." Individual articles include detailed lists of references.

Boss, Pauline G., William J. Doherty, Ralph LaRossa, Walter R. Schumm, and Suzanne K. Steinmetz. 1993. *Sourcebook of Family Theories and Methods: A Contextual Approach.* New York, NY: Plenum.
Each chapter in this publication is a separate article on some aspect of family research. Each article includes a detailed bibliography on the specific topic covered. A subject index provides access to topics within the articles.

Burgueire, Andre, Christiane Klapishc-Zuber, Martine Segalen, and Francoise Zonabend. 1996. *A History of the Family*. Cambridge, MA: Belknap.

This two-volume publication gives a succinct overview of the history of the family. Each volume has its own subject index and bibliography listing sources by chapter. This is an excellent overview for a historical study of the family.

Cayton, Mary Kupiec, Elliott J. Gorn, and Peter W. Williams, eds. 1993. *Encyclopedia of American Social History*. New York, NY: Charles Scribner's Sons.

Covering the history of American society from the time prior to European arrival, this three-volume set includes many articles on family life and topics related to families. Each lengthy article includes a bibliography, and volume 3 has a detailed subject index to the entire set.

Children's Defense Fund. Annual. *The State of America's Children*. Boston, MA: Beacon Press.

This is an annual review of policies, programs, and politics affecting children. Each chapter is a separate report. Statistics are also included at the end of the yearbook.

Corcoran, Kevin, and Joel Fischer. 2000. *Measures for Clinical Practice: a Sourcebook*. New York: The Free Press.

This two-volume publication includes information on the use, selection, and administration of measurement tools, as well as samples of specific tests and measurements. Not only does this include a description and publication information for tests and scales, but also it provides the actual questions that make part of these tests. You cannot duplicate the sample tests to administer, but the questions are available for evaluation. Volume 1 identifies resources for evaluating couples, families, and children, whereas volume 2 lists those for adults.

Damon, William, ed. 1998. *Handbook of Child Psychology*. New York, NY: Wiley.

This four-volume set covers a wide range of topics in child psychology. Each volume concentrates on a general topic. The articles included are extensive, and each one includes a detailed bibliography. Each volume has a separate author and subject index.

Demo, David H., Katherine R. Allen, and Mark A. Fine, eds. 2000. *Handbook of Family Diversity*. New York, NY: Oxford University Press.

This handbook includes many articles on the diversity of families and addresses such topics as gender, structure, culture, and class and how they affect families. Articles are written by experts in a variety of fields that study families, and there is a detailed subject index included.

Edwards, Richard L., ed. 1995. *Encyclopedia of Social Work*. Washington, DC: National Association of Social Workers.

This three-volume resource is the major encyclopedia for the field of social work. Articles cover family topics from the viewpoint of the social worker. The in-depth articles include references and further readings as well as information on the author. Volume 3 includes a detailed subject index to the entire set and biographical sketches on prominent social workers.

Groth-Marnat, Gary. 1997. *Handbook of Psychological Assessment*. New York, NY: Wiley.

Not only does this handbook provide information on the use and effectiveness of assessment, but also several major scales and inventories are discussed in detail, and many others are mentioned. A lengthy list of references is included, as well as a subject index to specific topics covered in the assessments.

Hawes, Joseph M., and Elizabeth I. Nybakken, eds. 1991. *American Families: A Research Guide and Historical Handbook*. New York, NY: Greenwood.

This publication provides an historical overview of American families and family research. Each article includes a list of references, and there is a detailed subject index at the end of the book.

Howarth, Glennys, and Oliver Leaman, eds. 2001. *Encyclopedia of Death and Dying*. London: Routledge.

This one-volume encyclopedia covers topics of interest to those doing research on family studies. The short articles are signed and include at least one source for "Further Reading." A detailed bibliography is included at the end of the volume, along with name and subject indexes.

Hurrelmann, Klaus, ed. 1994. *International Handbook of Adolescence*. Westport, CT: Greenwood.

This publication is a country-by-country study of adolescence. It provides an overview of adolescence in each country along with statistics and charts to clarify some topics. There is a bibliography of references at the end of each country section and a subject index to the entire volume.

Kastenbaum, Robert, ed. 1993. *Encyclopedia of Adult Development*. Phoenix, AZ: Oryx.

The editor collected articles on topics of interest to those who are researching adult development. The articles are written by experts in the field and include extensive bibliographies. A subject index provides access to specific topics included within the articles.

Kazdin, Alan E., ed. 2000. *Encyclopedia of Psychology*. Washington, DC: American Psychological Association and Oxford University.

This eight-volume encyclopedia covers all aspects of psychology that include many areas of family studies. Each article is signed and includes a bibliography. Volume 8 includes a detailed subject index to the entire set.

Kramarae, Cheris, and Dale Spender, II eds. 2000. *Routledge International Encyclopedia of Women: Global Women's Issues and Knowledge*. New York, NY: Routledge.

This excellent four-volume encyclopedia covers many women's studies issues. Each article is signed and includes a good list of "References and Further Reading." Cross-references are included with the articles, and there is a very detailed subject index in volume 4.

Kuper, Adam, and Jessica Kuper, eds. 1996. *The Social Science Encyclopedia*. London: Routledge. This is a one-volume encyclopedia of the social sciences. Articles of varying lengths include references and/or further readings on the topic.

Lerner, Richard M., Anne C. Petersen, and Jeanne Brooks-Gunn, eds. 1991. *Encyclopedia of Adolescence*. New York, NY: Garland.

This publication provides another excellent overview of the study of adolescence. Each article is signed and includes a lengthy bibliography of references and cross-references. There is a subject index to topics covered in this two-volume set.

Maddox, George L., ed. 2001. *The Encyclopedia of Aging: A Comprehensive Resource in Gerontology and Geriatrics*. New York, NY: Springer.

This two-volume encyclopedia provides a good overview of the topics that are involved in the field of geriatric research. Articles are signed and include cross-references. There is a large section that provides references to many resources on aging as well as a basic subject index.

Miermont, Jacques. 1995. *A Dictionary of Family Therapy*. Oxford: Blackwell.

This is the English translation of a French dictionary on family therapy. A bibliography is included at the end, along with a detailed index to ideas and concepts found within the articles. Because the Dictionary covers the topic from a French perspective, it gives a different viewpoint to the study of family therapy.

Miner, Jeremy T., and Lynn E. Miner. Annual. *Funding Sources for Children and Youth Programs*. Westport, CT: Oryx Press.

This includes a list of grant resources, as well as a guide to proposal planning and writing. It includes a list by subject and by geographic location.

Palya, William. 2002. *Encyclopedia of Psychology*. Jacksonville, AL: Jacksonville State University. http://www.psychology.org/ (Retrieved November 14, 2002).

This unusual encyclopedia provides links to research articles available on the Web on psychology topics. There are many resources available on family studies topics. Palya encourages users to recommend Web sites for inclusion in this resource. That means some of the articles are college student research papers.

Pendergast, Tom, and Sara Pendergast, eds. 2000. *St. James Encyclopedia of Popular Culture*. Detroit, MN: St. James.

This five-volume encyclopedia provides brief information about popular culture influences on society. Each article includes a list of references for more in-depth introductory research. Volume 5, includes several indexes: a Time-Frame Index, a Category Index, and a basic index of subject terms.

Ponzetti, James J., ed. 2003. *International Encyclopedia of Marriage and Family*. New York, NY: Macmillan. General articles for the study of marriage and the family topics are included in this four-volume encyclopedia. It is the second edition of the *Encyclopedia of Marriage and the Family* published in 1995. The new edition expands its coverage to include international information. Articles are signed and include cross-references and a bibliography of other sources. A detailed subject index provides access to topics covered in the broader articles.

Ramachandran, V. S., ed. 1994. *Encyclopedia of Human Behavior.* San Diego, CA: Academic.
    This four-volume set on human behavior includes many articles of interest to those studying the family. Each article is detailed with a bibliography at the end. The subject index found in volume 4 provides more specific access to topics within the articles in the entire set.

Roberts, Albert R., and Gilbert J. Greene, eds. 2002. *Social Workers' Desk Reference.* New York, NY: Oxford University.
    This excellent handbook includes signed articles of interest to social workers. Many articles deal with family topics and include suggestions for dealing with problems and a list of resources for further reading on the topics. The handbook includes a glossary of terms used in the resource, and a name index. A very detailed subject index is also available.

Rothman, Barbara Katz, ed. 1993. *Encyclopedia of Childbearing: Critical Perspectives.* Phoenix, AZ: Oryx.
    This encyclopedia covers the field of childbearing from many different viewpoints. Experts in a wide range of fields that study childbearing have written the articles that include resources for additional reading. An appendix of organizations and resources, as well as a subject index, are included.

Sauber, S. Richard, Luciano L'Abate, Gerald R. Weeks, and William L. Buchanan. 1993. *The Dictionary of Family Psychology and Family Therapy.* Newbury Park, CA: Sage.
    Although the definitions are fairly short in this publication, many of them include a couple of sources for further information. A list, alphabetical by author, of these sources is available at the end of the dictionary.

Smelser, Neil J., and Paul B. Baltes, eds. 2001. *The International Encyclopedia of the Social and Behavioral Sciences.* Amsterdam: Elsevier.
    This is a major encyclopedia in the field. It updates the *International Encyclopedia of the Social Sciences* (1968–1979). Each in-depth article is signed and includes cross-references and a bibliography of resources. Volume 25 is an index to names in the publication, and volume 26 is a subject index to the set. This is also available online with a subscription.

Smith, Charles A., ed. 1999. *The Encyclopedia Of Parenting Theory and Research.* Westport, CT: Greenwood.
    This publication is an excellent overview of parenting research. Articles include a list of sources and cross-references. A detailed subject index is located at the back of the volume along with a brief general bibliography and a list of contributors.

Spencer, Penny K. 1999. *The National Directory of Children, Youth & Family Service.* Longmont, CO: National Directory CYF.
    This resource identifies organizations, services, and agencies that work with children, youth, and families. It lists the agencies by state and then by county. There is also a section on national organizations.

Sussman, Marvin B., Suzanne K. Steinmetz, and Gary W. Peterson. 1999. *Handbook of Marriage and the Family.* New York, NY: Plenum.
    This handbook also provides extensive articles on topics pertaining to marriage and the family. Extensive lists of references are included with each article, and a detailed subject index is included at the end.

Touliatos, John, Barry F. Perlmutter, and Murray A. Straus, eds. 2001. *Handbook of Family Measurement Techniques.* Thousand Oaks, CA: Sage.
    This handbook is a collection of abstracts of measurement tools for family research. Each general section includes an introduction along with brief descriptions of the tests that can be used to study the section topic. The overview sections, and each abstract, include references for further information on the topic or the measurement technique. Volume three includes many surveys and questionnaires. There are also author, title, and subject indexes.

Vangelisti, Anita L. 2004. *Handbook of Family Communication.* Mahwah, NJ: Lawrence Erlbaum Associates.
    This resource provides detailed articles on communication and the family. Each chapter covers a broad category. A list of resources and a subject index are included.

Worell, Judith, ed. 2001. *Encyclopedia of Women and Gender: Sex Similarities and Differences and the Impact of Society on Gender.* San Diego: Academic.
    Covering topics of interest to studies on gender differences, this two-volume encyclopedia has lengthy articles written by experts in the field. Each article includes a detailed list of "Suggested Readings" and includes a glossary to the terms used within it. Author and subject indexes are included.

Many encyclopedias and other reference resources cover specific cultural groups. Below is a list of a few such publications that may be helpful for research on families in these specific areas:

Publications

Kanellos, Nicolas. 1993. *The Hispanic-American Almanac.* Detroit, MI: Gale.

Lehman, Jeffrey, ed. 2000. *Gale Encyclopedia of Multicultural America.* Detroit, MI: Gale.

Levinson, David, and Melvin Ember, eds. 1997. *American Immigrant Cultures: Builders of a Nation.* New York, NY: Macmillan.

Mabunda, L. Mpho, ed. 1997. *The African American Almanac.* Detroit, MI: Gale.

Manheimer, Ronald J., ed. 1994. *Older Americans Almanac.* Detroit, MI: Gale.

Nanji, Azim A., ed. 1996. *The Muslim Almanac.* Detroit, MI: Gale.

Salzman, Jack, David Lionel Smith, and Cornel West, eds. 1996. *Encyclopedia of African-American Culture and History.* New York, NY: Macmillan.

Williams, Michael W., ed. 1993. *The African American Encyclopedia.* New York, NY: Marshall Cavendish.

B. STATISTICAL SOURCES

Frequently, statistics are needed to support your research. There are many types of statistical resources available for your use. Many government sources are now available through the World Wide Web. Some publishers will also collect statistics on a specific topic and present them in a format that is easier to use than the original format.

Below are sources that provide statistics. Some are available only in print form, but many are now available in electronic format. Also included are guides to using and collecting statistics.

Publications

The American Marketplace: Demographics and Spending Patterns. 2003. 6/e. Ithaca, NY: New Strategist.
This resource contains many statistical charts and tables identifying lifestyle trends in the United States. Covering topics such as education, health, labor force, living arrangements, and spending, this publication is based on the 2000 census. A list of Web sites, agencies, and subject specialists is included, as well as a glossary of terms and a subject index.

American Men: Who They Are & How They Live. 2002. Ithaca, NY: New Strategist.
This is part of a series of publications from this publisher covering specific demographic groups and presenting statistics on topics that include education, health, and living arrangements. This volume also includes a section that provides Web sites and telephone numbers for contacts, agencies, and government organizations which can be contacted for further information. A glossary, a bibliography of other resources, and a subject index are included.

American Women: Who They Are & How They Live, 2/e. 2002. Ithaca, NY: New Strategist.
This publication describes American women and includes statistics on education, health, living arrangements, and other topics. This volume also includes a section that provides Web sites and telephone numbers for contacts, agencies, and government organizations which can be contacted for further information, as well as a glossary, a bibliography of other resources, and a subject index.

Centers for Disease Control and Prevention. October 1, 2004. *Morbidity and Mortality Weekly Reports.* http://www.cdc.gov/mmwr/ (Retrieved October 4, 2004).
This site provides access to the weekly reports published by the Centers for Disease Control and Prevention.

Centers for Disease Control and Prevention. October 1, 2004. *National Center for Health Statistics.* http://www. cdc.gov/nchs.htm (Retrieved October 4, 2004).

This Web site provides statistics on many different areas of interest to those studying families, including births, deaths, marriages, and divorces.

Crow, Diana. March 16, 2004. *Demography and Population Studies WWW Virtual Library.* http://demography.anu.edu.au/VirtualLibrary/ (Retrieved October 4, 2004). Collected by Australian National University, this Web site provides access to international demographic information.

Darnay, Arsen J. 2002. *American Cost of Living Survey: A Compilation of Price Data for Nearly 580 Goods and Services in 506 U.S. Cities from More Than 100 Sources,* 3/e. Detroit, MI: Gale.

This resource identifies the cost for numerous goods and services in the United States. The information is grouped alphabetically by city. The introduction includes a list of cities in alphabetical order, as well as by state.

Gauguin, Deirdre A., and Mark S. Littman, eds. Annual. *County and City Extra: Annual Metro, City and County Data Book.* Washington, DC: Bernan.

This is an annual publication that includes statistical data for counties and cities of over 25,000. Information is based on the United States census data. A companion volume, covering towns and townships under 25,000, is *Places, Towns and Townships* listed next.

Gauguin, Deirdre A. & Richard W. Dodge, eds. 2003. *Places, Towns and Townships.* Lanham, MD: Bernan.

Although a companion publication to the *County and City Extra: Annual Metro, City and County Data Book,* this resource is not published every year. Information is based on the U. S. census data.

Generation X: Americans Aged 18-34. 4/e. 2004. Ithaca, NY: New Strategist.

Like other resources by this publisher, this book provides statistical charts and tables on a particular age group. Topics covered include Education, Health, and Living Arrangements. It also includes a section that provides Web sites and phone numbers for contacts, agencies, and government organizations who can be contacted for further information. A glossary, a bibliography of other resources, and a subject index are included.

Minnesota Kids: A Closer Look. 2002. St. Paul, MN: Children's Defense Fund of Minnesota.

This resource, published annually, provides demographic information on children in Minnesota. Most of the information is available by county, but some more general statistics are identified. This is an excellent source for basic statistics on children in Minnesota.

The Millennials: Americans Under Age 25. 2/e. 2004. Ithaca, NY: New Strategist.

Like the other New Strategist generational group publications, this publication provides statistical information on the "under 25" age group. Topics covered include Education, Health, and Living Arrangements. It also includes a section that provides Web sites and phone numbers for contacts, agencies, and government organizations which can be contacted for further information. A glossary, a bibliography of other resources, and a subject index are included.

Mitchell, Susan, ed. 2000. *American Attitudes: Who Thinks What About the Issues That Shape Our Lives*, 3/e. Ithaca, NY: New Strategist.

The author has brought together data from surveys of the University of Chicago's National Opinion Research Center. Viewpoints on many different topics are identified and statistics are explained and made available in charts. A brief subject index is available, but the table of contents and the list of tables at the front are more helpful at finding what statistics are available.

Mitchell, Susan. 2003. *American Generations: Who They Are. How They Live. What They Think,* 4/e. Ithaca, NY: New Strategist.

This publication gives an overview of the different generational groups. It identifies the different groups, and then goes on to provide statistical information covering areas such as Attitudes and Behavior, Households, and Spending. It includes a section that provides Web sites and phone numbers for contacts, agencies and government organizations that can be contacted for further information. A glossary, a bibliography of other resources, and a subject index are included.

National Center for Education Statistics. 2003. *Education Statistics at a Glance.* http://nces.ed.gov/edstats/ (Retrieved October 4, 2004).

This Web site is the basic site for Education Statistics. It includes the *Digest of Education Statistics* as well as *Youth Indicators,* demographic information on children and families, published by the United States Department of Education.

Newton, Rae R., and Kjell Erik Rudestam. 1999. *Your Statistical Consultant: Answers to Your Data Analysis Questions*. Thousand Oaks, CA: Sage.

> This is a question and answer source on statistics. It provides answers to basic as well as more advanced topics in the field. An excellent list of resources for further study is included along with a brief subject index.

Older Americans: A Changing Market, 2004. 4/e Ithaca, NY: New Strategist.

> Like other resources by this publisher, this book provides statistical charts and tables on a particular age group. Topics covered include Education, Health, and Living Arrangements. It also includes a section that provides Web sites and phone numbers for contacts, agencies, and government organizations that can be contacted for further information. A glossary, a bibliography of other resources, and a subject index are included.

PollingReport.com: An Independent, Nonpartisan Resource on Trends in American Public Opinion. 2004. http://www.pollingreport.com/ (Retrieved October 4, 2004).

> This site provides access to current poll data on political, economic, and sociological topics. To obtain full access to all resources, you must subscribe to the service.

Population Reference Bureau. October 1, 2004. *Population Reference Bureau*. http://www.prb.org/ (Retrieved October 4, 2004).

> This site provides population demographics provided by the Population Reference Bureau and the Social Science Data Analysis Network. Although only national data is provided, this interactive source provides current information under specific topics such as "Marriage and Family."

Price, Gary. May 22, 2002. *Fast Facts: Almanacs/Factbooks/Statistical Reports & Related Reference Tools: An Acquisition Resource*. http://www.freepint.com/gary/handbook.htm (Retrieved October 4, 2004).

> This site is a detailed list of many Web resources, which provide statistical information. The site includes many international resources. The author also includes links to other sources that provide a similar service on the Web.

Russell, Cheryl. 2004. *The Baby Boom: Americans Aged 35 to 54*, 4/e. Ithaca, NY: New Strategist.

> This resource provides excellent information, charts, and tables on the baby boom age group. Topics covered include attitudes, behaviors, education, income, and spending. Like other publications by this publisher, it includes Web sites and phone numbers of people, organizations, and government departments. A glossary, a bibliography of other resources, and a subject index are included.

Statistical Handbook on . . . Phoenix, AZ: Oryx.

> This series of resources provides statistics on different topics and demographic groups. Individual titles in this series that might be of interest to those studying families include:

> > *Statistical Handbook on Adolescents in America.* 1996.

> > *Statistical Handbook on Consumption & Wealth in the U.S.* 2000.

> > *Statistical Handbook on Racial Groups in the U.S.* 2000.

> > *Statistical Handbook on the American Family.* 1999.

> > *Statistical Handbook on the World's Children.* 2002.

> > *Statistical Handbook on Women in America.* 1996.

Statistical Record of . . . New York, NY: Gale.

> This series of resources brings together detailed statistics on specific demographic groups. Individual titles in this series which might be of interest to those studying families include:

> > *Statistical Record of Asian Americans.* 1993.

> > *Statistical Record of Black America.* 1997.

> > *Statistical Record of Children.* 1994.

> > *Statistical Record of Health and Medicine.* 1998.

> > *Statistical Record of Hispanic Americans.* 1995.

> > *Statistical Record of Native North Americans.* 1995.

Statistical Record of Older Americans. 1996.

Statistical Record of Women Worldwide. 1995.

United Nations Population Division. 2001. *United Nations Population Information Network: A Guide to Population Information on UN System Web Sites.* http://www.un.org/popin/ (Retrieved October 4, 2004).
World population statistics information, called POPIN, are collected and maintained by the Population Division of the UN Secretariat and made available through this site.

United States Census Bureau. Annual. *Statistical Abstract of the United States.* Washington, DC: Government Printing Office.
This annual resource is the first place to go when trying to locate statistical information. It provides tables with statistics in many different areas, and provides the information to locate more in-depth statistics on the topic. The index refers you to the table number rather than to the page number. The electronic version, available at http://www.census.gov/prod/www/abs/statab.html, provides only some of the many tables available in the print publication.

United States Department of Commerce. 2004. *United States Census Bureau.* http://www.census.gov/ (Retrieved October 4, 2004).
This site provides information about the Bureau of the Census, and about access tools, as well as social demographic and economic information.

United States Federal Government Agencies. March 16, 2004. *FedStats.* http://www.fedstats.gov/ (Retrieved October 4, 2004).
Although this Web site has not been updated for a while, it is merely a subject guide to other Web sites published by individual U. S. government agencies. The actual statistics to which it links are separate Web sites updated by the specific agencies. The site brings together the many statistics provided by these separate agencies.

University of California, San Diego. August 29, 2004. *Data on the Net.* http://odwin.ucsd.edu/idata (Retrieved October 4, 2004).
This Web site, available from the University of California at San Diego, acts as a search system to provide access to archival social science statistical data on the World Wide Web.

University of Connecticut. 2004. *Roper Center for Public Opinion Research.* http://www.ropercenter.uconn.edu/ (Retrieved October 4, 2004).
This center collects public opinion polls worldwide. Although access is free, they do charge for datasets and will provide pricing information. Membership is also available.

University of Michigan. January 17, 2004. *Statistical Resources on the Web.* http://www.lib.umich.edu/govdocs/stats.html (Retrieved October 4, 2004).
This Web site provides access to federal government statistical files created by the Documents Center at the University of Michigan Library.

University of North Carolina at Chapel Hill. 2004. *Howard W. Odum Institute for Research in Social Science Louis Harris Data Archive.* http://www2.irss.unc.edu/irss/home.asp (Retrieved October 4, 2004).
This Web site provides access to the Louis Harris polls archive, as well as links to other data research sites.

Vogt, W. Paul. 1999. *Dictionary of Statistics and Methodology: A Nontechnical Guide for the Social Sciences.* Thousand Oaks, CA: Sage.
This is an excellent dictionary for social scientists who are doing statistical research. It covers the basic concepts and terms and attempts to stay away from statistical jargon, except to define it. There is also a short bibliography of sources for further reading on the topic.

Zill, Nicholas, and Margaret Daly, eds. 1993. *Researching the Family: A Guide to Survey and Statistical Data on U.S. Families.* Washington, DC: Child Trends, Inc. This publication provides an overview of statistical surveys pertaining to United States families. In addition, some of the results are included, along with ways to obtain the original, and a list of resources that report on the results of each survey.

C. INDEXES, ABSTRACTS AND OTHER DATABASES

The resources previously noted tend to be available in books or on Web sites. The following indexes and abstracts identify articles and book chapters, and occasionally books, on a particular topic. Because it takes longer for books to be published than journal articles, and because most research is published in journal articles, indexes are the place to start your search for resources. They will identify articles that have been published on a particular topic.

Although there are still some that are only published in print format, many of the indexes and abstracts are now available in electronic format. This makes them easier to search, because you can combine terms in a database, whereas print publications only let you search for one subject term at a time. Some index databases are also beginning to provide the full-text of some journals. Following are indexes and abstracts that will be useful when doing research in the field of family studies.

Publications

America: History and Life. 1964- . [Online database]. Santa Barbara, CA: ABC-Clio.
> This electronic index provides abstracts (summaries) of articles, reviews, and dissertations about the history and culture of the United States and Canada. A companion publication, *Historical Abstracts*, covers the remainder of the world.

Child Development Abstracts and Bibliography. 1927-2001. Chicago, IL: University of Chicago.
> This print abstracting service identifies articles covering all aspects of child development. The subject index at the back of the volume identifies the number of the record (not the page number) for each article on a specific topic. They ceased publication in 2001.

Child Development and Adolescent Studies. 1927- . [Online database]. Baltimore, MD: National Information Services Corporation.
> This online index includes all of the information provided in *Child Development Abstracts and Bibliography* as well as including resources on Adolescent research. Because *Child Development Abstract and Bibliography* discontinued publishing in 2001, this resource continues the overview of this topic area.

ERIC. 1966- . [Online database]. Washington, DC: United States Department of Education.
> This online index searches for citations and abstracts of journal articles and ERIC documents on education topics. Some versions of this database may provide links to the online full-text version of current ERIC documents.

Expanded Academic ASAP. 1980- . [Online database]. Farmington Hills, MI: Gale.
> This electronic database not only identifies articles on specific topics but also provides the full text of many of them. It covers a wide range of topics, and although it includes some general periodicals, it also searches the contents of research journals. This resource is a good introduction for topics that are interdisciplinary.

FactSearch. 1984- . [Online database]. Ann Arbor, MI: Pierian.
> This is a great place to start when looking for current facts and statistical information.

G.K. Hall Women's Studies Index. 1989- . Detroit, MI: Gale.
> This is an annual print index covering the field of women's studies. Articles are listed under combined alphabetical subject and author listings. Only a citation is provided for each article.

ISI Basic Social Sciences Index. 1990- . [Online database]. Philadelphia, PA: Institute for Scientific Information.
> This online source provides bibliographic access, along with cited references and related records, to 500 leading English-language journals in the social sciences.

PsycINFO. 1886- . [Online database]. Washington, DC: American Psychological Association.
> This is the basic index for psychology research. In the print form it is known as *Psychological Abstracts*. It includes abstracts of research articles on psychology topics. Depending on the version of the database that you are accessing, there may be some full-text articles, and even a few full-image (copies of the pages from the print journals, including all the charts, graphs, pictures, and advertisements that appear on each page) articles.

Sage Family Studies Abstracts. 1979- . Beverly Hills, CA: Sage.
> A basic print abstracting service which covers many topics within family studies research.

Social Sciences Abstracts. 1983- . [Online database]. New York, NY: H.W. Wilson.

    This source identifies articles in all fields of the social sciences. It is a good overall resource for any research on topics in any of those fields of study. Only abstracts are available for the source; however, it does frequently identify which libraries own the journal in which the article can be found.

Social Services Abstracts. 1980- . [Online database]. Bethesda, MD: Cambridge Scientific Abstracts.

    This resource identifies articles in the fields of social work, social policy, community development, and other social science areas that include family studies research.

Social Work Abstracts. 1977- . [Online database]. Washington, DC: National Association of Social Workers.

    This is a fairly small database that covers a limited number of social work periodicals. It is excellent for identifying specific topics pertaining to social work. However, it should be used in conjunction with other abstracting services that include similar subject coverage.

Sociological Abstracts. 1963- . [Online database]. Bethesda, MD: Cambridge Scientific Abstracts.

    This is probably the major database for sociological research on families. It includes citations and abstracts to articles from journals and books as well as to dissertations and research reports. Although available from several different vendors, the original version from Cambridge Scientific Abstracts also provides access to *Web Resources Related to the Social Sciences/Humanities.*

Studies on Women and Gender Abstracts. 1983- . Abingdon, Oxfordshire: Taylor & Francis.

    This print indexing service identifies resources available on women and gender studies topics. The subject index lists references to the number of the abstract. It is published bimonthly, and the final issue of each year includes cumulative subject and author indexes for the entire year.

D. SUBJECT WORLD WIDE WEB SITES

Although Web encyclopedias, statistical sources and databases are listed previously, there are also many subject Web sites that provide research information for family studies. The sites identified below are only a few of the many pages available on the World Wide Web. Once you have found a site that looks like it has good research information, be sure you evaluate the Web site to make sure it will provide the kind of information you need. Some questions to consider include:

1. Who is responsible for the work, what are their qualifications and associations, and can you verify them? Does it identify the authors, publishers, and format?

2. What is the focus of the work? Are there clear headings to indicate an outline to determine what aspects of the topic are covered? Is there a Table of Contents? Index? Abstract? Is navigation within the Web site clear?

3. How current is the information? Are dates listed? When was it created? When was it last updated?

4. Are biases clearly stated (any political or ideological agenda is not hidden to disguise its purpose by using a misleading name or by other means)? Are affiliations clear? Who is the intended audience? Is there a Preface or Introduction that explains these points?

5. How accurate is the information? Are sources of information and factual data listed and available for cross-checking? Does it include footnotes and bibliographies, and can you verify the existence of those resources?

6. How relevant is this information to your research? Does it actually cover the topic? Is it really research? Or just commentary? Does it cover the topic as well as other types of sources (books, journal articles, etc.)?

Remember that anyone can put anything on the Web. When doing research, be sure to use only those sites that meet the criteria listed previously.

Many of the following Web sites are webliographies of other sources on the World Wide Web. They provide links to other Web resources on topics of interest to those doing research in family studies.

Also, remember that Web sites come and go at an alarming rate. What you find today, may not be there tomorrow. Therefore, be forewarned that you may find that the following Web sites either no longer exist, or have moved to a different URL.

Publications

American Political Science Association, Section on Race, Ethnicity and Politics. August 29, 2004. *Race and Ethnicity Online.* http://www.apsanet.org/~rep/ (Retrieved October 4, 2004).

This is the official site of the Section on Race, Ethnicity, and Politics of the American Political Science Association. Not only does it include research resources, but also it provides directories, links to other Web sites, and other teaching resources.

American Psychological Association. 2004. *PsychCrawler.* http://www.psychcrawler.com/ (Retrieved October 4, 2004).

This search system was developed by the APA to provide a method to locate psychology research sites on the Web. Sites included are those that have been reviewed before they are made available through a subject search. There are many excellent resources in the field of family studies that are linked through this search system.

Bannister, J. 2000. *WCSU List: Sociology Internet Resources.* http://www.wcsu.edu/socialsci/socres.html (Retrieved October 4, 2004).

This is a compilation of numerous internet resources in the field of sociology. Included are links to web sites covering the topics of "Culture & Society," "Ethnicity," "Women," and "Family."

Blair, Mark. 2002. *The SocioWeb: Your Independent Guide to Sociological Resources on the Internet.* www.socioweb.com (Retrieved October 4, 2004).

Developed by an independent sociology researcher, this Web site provides links to biographical sources, organizations, journals, and research sites in sociology. It also supports a chat room and provides an electronic bookstore in association with Amazon.com.

Cuneo, Carl. 2002. *WWW Virtual Library: Sociology.* http://socserv2.mcmaster.ca/w3virtsoclib/ (Retrieved October 4, 2004).

This is another site that is part of the World Wide Web Virtual Library, "the oldest catalog of the web." See also Thursby's *Social Sciences Virtual Library* later. It identifies associations, directories, discussion lists, and Web resources on Sociology topics.

Dierkes, Julian. 2004. *The SocioLog: Julian Dierkes' comprehensive Guide to Sociology On-Line.* http://www.sociolog.com (Retrieved October 4, 2004).

This Web site provides links to research sites, academic sociology departments, research centers, and sociology publications on the Web. The author even identifies his personal favorites on the Web.

Electronic Journal of Sociology. 1994- . Alberta, Canada: Athabasca University. http://www.sociology.org/ (Retrieved October 4, 2004).

An online refereed journal that covers many topics that would be of interest to those studying Family Studies.

Eliot-Pearson Department of Child Development. 2003. *Tufts University Child and Family Webguide: Your Gateway to the Best Sites about Children.* http://www.cfw.tufts.edu/ (Retrieved October 4, 2004).

This Web site was designed and built by librarians and child development faculty at Tufts University. The Web sites included in this site have been evaluated for the quality of the research included.

Grefe, Dick. 2001. *Washington and Lee University, Department of Sociology and Anthropology: Links.* http://culture.wlu.edu/links/index.htm (Retrieved October 4, 2004).

This site provides links to sites that provide information on many areas of social sciences.

Institute for Research on Poverty. June 3, 2004. *Poverty-Related Links: Links by Category.* http://www.irp.wisc.edu/links.htm (Retrieved October 4, 2004).

Developed by the Institute for Research on Poverty (IRP) at the University of Wisconsin, Madison, this site is a collection of poverty Web sites grouped by subcategories.

Kearl, Michael C. 2004. *A Sociological Tour Through Cyberspace.* http://www.trinity.edu/~mkearl/index.html (Retrieved October 4, 2004).

Developed by a sociologist at Trinity University in San Antonio, TX, this Web site not only identifies Web sites on many sociological topics but also encourages interaction and stimulating the "sociological imagination." Some of his collected sites cover such topics as "Marriage & Family Life," "Social Gerontology," "Gender & Society," "Race & Ethnicity," and "Demography."

Office of Citizen Services and Communication. U.S General Services Administration. 2004. *FirstGov.gov.* http://www.firstgov.gov/ (Retrieved October 4, 2004).

This is your "first click" to the U. S. government, the official portal page to all federal government resources available on the Web.

Thursby, Gene R., ed. April 9, 2004. *Social Sciences Virtual Library.* http://www.clas.ufl.edu/users/gthursby/socsci/ (Retrieved October 4, 2004).

This Web site is part of the World Wide Web Virtual Library, "the oldest catalog of the web." See also Cuneo's *WWW Virtual Library: Sociology* listed previously. It is an extensive collection of Web sites relating to many different social science topics.

University of Kentucky. August 4, 2004. *World Wide Web Subject Catalog: Family Studies.* http://www.uky.edu/Subject/family.html (Retrieved October 4, 2004).

This Web site provides an excellent collection of Web sites of interest to those doing family studies research.

University of Southern Indiana. Sociology Department. 2003. *Social Psychology.net: Social Psychology Links of Interest.* http://www.usi.edu/libarts/socio/socpsy/socpsy.htm (Retrieved October 4, 2004).

Created by the University of Southern Indiana's Sociology department, this Web site includes links to information on many different social psychology topics, as well as to information on prominent researchers in the field.

Janice M. Orf, M.S., M.A., has 25 years of experience in the field of library and information science. She is currently Reference Librarian/Library Instruction Coordinator at the University of St. Thomas Libraries, St. Paul, MN.

Author Index

Note: fn indicates this author is noted in a footnote.

SUBJECT INDEX

A

ABCX model, 62, 74–75
Abortifacients, 162, 180
Absent or part-time parenting, 286–287
Abstinence, 162, 181
Abstinence-only, 163, 192
Abstinence-plus, 163, 192
Accordion households, 312, 323–324
Actual effectiveness, 162, 176
Adaptation, 62, 72
Adjustment, 62, 72
Adoption, 31–33, 35–36, 276, 280–282
    adoption triangle, 276, 280
Adversarial divorce, 250, 253
Aging well, 146–148
*Aid to Families with Dependent Children
    (AFDC),* 397, 401
*American Association of Marriage and Family
    Therapy,* 136, 406
Annulment, 250–252
Antonovsky, Aaron, 64–65
Anxiety disorders, 94, 136, 137–138
Appraisals, 62–63
Appraisals, family meanings, 75–76
Archival research, 29, 48–49
Arranged marriage, 203, 204–205
Assessing impacts of policies and programs on
    families, 402–403
Asymptomatic, 162, 187
At-risk, 62, 66
Authoritarian parenting, 276, 294
Authoritative parenting, 276, 294
Autoeroticism, 162, 181–183

B

Bilateral descent, 312, 314
Bilocal residence, 312, 315
Biocultural, 94, 127
Biology basics, 164–168
Birth control, 174
Blastocyst transfer, 276, 279

C

Care time, 94, 110–111
Caregiving, 94, 109–110
Case study, 29, 447–48
Celibacy, 162, 181
Child abuse, 276, 298–299
Child neglect, 276, 298–299
Childfree, 276, 278
Childless, 276, 278
Children leaving and returning home,
    316–318
Child-to-parent abuse, 342, 358
Chronic stress response, 94, 139–140
Circumcision, 162, 170
Client privilege, 46
Clinical cases, 47
Clitoridectomy, 162, 170
Close-ended questions, 46
Coercive power, 342, 343
Cohabitation, 203, 212–216
    relationship dynamics, 213
    relationship outcomes, 213–214
Co-housing, 324–325
Communication, 236–238

449